NINTH EDITION

THE ESSENTIAL WORLD HISTORY

VOLUME II: SINCE 1500

William J. Duiker

The Pennsylvania State University

Jackson J. Spielvogel

The Pennsylvania State University

CENGAGE

Australia • Brazil • Mexico • Singapore • United Kingdom • United States

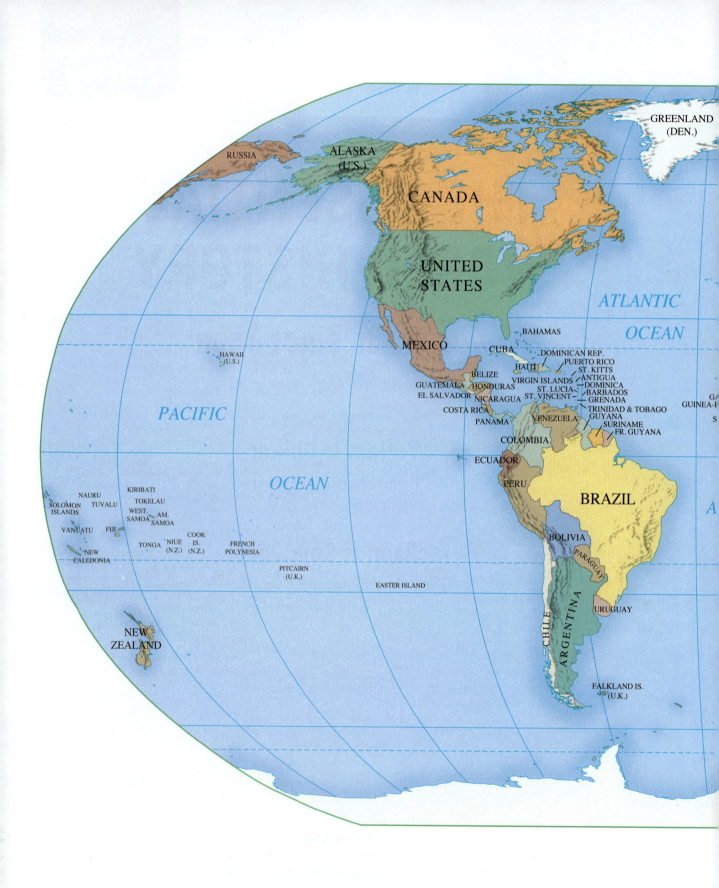

The Essential World History,
Volume II: since 1500
Ninth Edition
William J. Duiker and
Jackson J. Spielvogel

Product Manager: Joseph D. Potvin

Senior Content Manager: Philip Lanza

Learning Designer: Kate MacLean

Product Assistant: Haley Gaudreau

Marketing Manager: Valerie Hartman

Senior IP Analyst: Alexandra Ricciardi

IP Project Manager: Betsy Hathaway

Production Service/Compositor:
MPS Limited

Art Director: Sarah Cole

Text Design: Deborah Dutton/
Dutton & Sherman Design

Cover Design: Sarah Cole

Cover Image: Afghan boys in Bamiyan
play soccer in front of the empty seat of
one of two nearly 2,000-year-old Buddha
statues, destroyed by the Taliban in 2001.
The town lies in central Afghanistan, on
the former Silk Road that once linked
China with Central Asia and beyond.

Credit: SHAH MARAI/Getty Images.

For product information and technology assistance, contact us at
Cengage Customer & Sales Support, 1-800-354-9706
or **support.cengage.com.**

For permission to use material from this text
or product, submit all requests online
at **www.cengage.com/permissions.**

Library of Congress Control Number: 2018955210
Student Edition:
ISBN: 978-0-357-02687-8
Loose-leaf Edition:
ISBN: 978-0-357-02696-0

Cengage
20 Channel Center Street
Boston, MA 02210
USA

Cengage is a leading provider of customized learning solutions with
employees residing in nearly 40 different countries and sales in more
than 125 countries around the world. Find your local representative at
www.cengage.com.

Cengage products are represented in Canada by Nelson Education, Ltd.

To learn more about Cengage platforms and services, register or access
your online learning solution, or purchase materials for your course,
visit **www.cengage.com.**

Printed in the United States of America
Print Number: 01   Print Year: 2018

ABOUT THE AUTHORS

WILLIAM J. DUIKER is liberal arts professor emeritus of East Asian studies at The Pennsylvania State University. A former U.S. diplomat with service in Taiwan, South Vietnam, and Washington, D.C., he received his doctorate in Far Eastern history from Georgetown University in 1968, where his dissertation dealt with Chinese educator and reformer Cai Yuanpei. At Penn State, he has written widely on the history of Vietnam and modern China, including the widely acclaimed *The Communist Road to Power in Vietnam* (revised edition, Westview Press, 1996), which was selected for a Choice Outstanding Academic Book Award in 1982–1983 and 1996–1997. Other recent books are *China and Vietnam: The Roots of Conflict* (Berkeley, 1987); *U.S. Containment Policy and the Conflict in Indochina* (Stanford, 1995); *Sacred War: Nationalism and Revolution in a Divided Vietnam* (McGraw-Hill, 1995); and *Ho Chi Minh: A Life* (Hyperion, 2000), which was nominated for a Pulitzer Prize in 2001. While his research specialization is in the field of nationalism and Asian revolutions, his intellectual interests are considerably more diverse. He has traveled widely and has taught courses on the history of communism and non-Western civilizations at Penn State, where he was awarded a Faculty Scholar Medal for Outstanding Achievement in the spring of 1996. In 2002 the College of Liberal Arts honored him with an Emeritus Distinction Award.

TO YVONNE,
FOR ADDING SPARKLE TO THIS BOOK, AND TO MY LIFE
W.J.D.

JACKSON J. SPIELVOGEL is associate professor emeritus of history at The Pennsylvania State University. He received his Ph.D. from The Ohio State University, where he specialized in Reformation history under Harold J. Grimm. His articles and reviews have appeared in such journals as *Moreana, Journal of General Education, Catholic Historical Review, Archiv für Reformationsgeschichte,* and *American Historical Review.* He has also contributed chapters or articles to *The Social History of the Reformation, The Holy Roman Empire: A Dictionary Handbook, Simon Wiesenthal Center Annual of Holocaust Studies,* and *Utopian Studies.* His work has been supported by fellowships from the Fulbright Foundation and the Foundation for Reformation Research. At Penn State, he helped inaugurate the Western civilization courses as well as a popular course on Nazi Germany. His book *Hitler and Nazi Germany* was published in 1987 (seventh edition, 2014). He is the author of *Western Civilization,* first published in 1991 (tenth edition, 2018). Professor Spielvogel has won five major university-wide teaching awards. During the year 1988–1989, he held the Penn State Teaching Fellowship, the university's most prestigious teaching award. In 1996, he won the Dean Arthur Ray Warnock Award for Outstanding Faculty Member and in 2000 received the Schreyer Honors College Excellence in Teaching Award.

TO DIANE,
WHOSE LOVE AND SUPPORT MADE IT ALL POSSIBLE
J.J.S.

BRIEF CONTENTS

CONTENTS

PART IV

MODERN PATTERNS OF WORLD HISTORY (1800–1945) 470

19 THE BEGINNINGS OF MODERNIZATION: INDUSTRIALIZATION AND NATIONALISM IN THE NINETEENTH CENTURY 472

20 THE AMERICAS AND SOCIETY AND CULTURE IN THE WEST 498

MAPS

DOCUMENTS

FEATURES

PREFACE

FOR SEVERAL MILLION YEARS after primates first appeared on the surface of the earth, human beings lived in small communities, seeking to survive by hunting, fishing, and foraging in a frequently hostile environment. Then suddenly, in the space of a few thousand years, there was an abrupt change of direction as human beings in a few widely scattered areas of the globe began to master the art of cultivating food crops. As food production increased, the population in those areas rose correspondingly, and people began to gather in larger communities. They formed governments to provide protection and other needed services to the local population. Cities appeared and became the focal point of cultural and religious development. Historians refer to this process as the beginnings of civilization.

For generations, historians in Europe and the United States pointed to the rise of such civilizations as marking the origins of the modern world. Courses on Western civilization conventionally began with a chapter or two on the emergence of advanced societies in Egypt and Mesopotamia and then proceeded to ancient Greece and the Roman Empire. From Greece and Rome, the road led directly to the rise of modern civilization in the West.

There is nothing inherently wrong with this approach. Important aspects of our world today can indeed be traced back to these early civilizations, and all human beings the world over owe a considerable debt to their achievements. But all too often this interpretation has been used to imply that the course of civilization has been linear in nature, leading directly from the emergence of agricultural societies in ancient Mesopotamia to the rise of advanced industrial societies in Europe and North America. Until recently, most courses on world history taught in the United States routinely focused almost exclusively on the rise of the West, with only a passing glance at other parts of the world, such as Africa, India, and East Asia. The contributions made by those societies to the culture and technology of our own time were often passed over in silence.

Two major reasons have been advanced to justify this approach. Some have argued that it is more important that young minds understand the roots of their own heritage than that of peoples elsewhere in the world. In many cases, however, the motivation for this Eurocentric approach has been the belief that since the time of Socrates and Aristotle Western civilization has been the sole driving force in the evolution of human society.

Such an interpretation, however, represents a serious distortion of the process. During most of the course of human history, the most advanced civilizations have been not in the West, but in East Asia or the Middle East. A relatively brief period of European dominance culminated with the era of imperialism in the late nineteenth century, when the political, military, and economic power of the advanced nations of the West spread over the globe. During recent generations, however, that dominance has gradually eroded, partly as a result of changes taking place within Western societies and partly because new centers of development are emerging elsewhere on the globe—notably in Asia, with the growing economic strength of China and India and many of their neighbors.

World history, then, has been a complex process in which many branches of the human community have taken an active part, and the dominance of any one area of the world has been a temporary rather than a permanent phenomenon. It will be our purpose in this book to present a balanced picture of this story, with all respect for the richness and diversity of the tapestry of the human experience. Due attention must be paid to the rise of the West, of course, since that has been the most dominant aspect of world history in recent centuries. But the contributions made by other peoples must be given adequate consideration as well, not only in the period prior to 1500 when the major centers of civilization were located in Asia, but also in our own day, when a multipolar pattern of development is clearly beginning to emerge.

Anyone who wishes to teach or write about world history must decide whether to present the topic as an integrated whole or as a collection of different cultures. The world that we live in today, of course, is in many respects an interdependent one in terms of economics as well as culture and communications, a reality that is often expressed by the phrase "global village." The convergence of peoples across the surface of the earth into an integrated world system began in early times and intensified after the rise of capitalism in the early modern era. In growing recognition of this trend, historians trained in global history, as well as instructors in the growing number of world history courses, have now begun to speak and write of a "global approach" that turns attention away from the study of individual civilizations and focuses instead on the "big picture" or, as the world historian Fernand Braudel termed it, interpreting world history as a river with no banks.

On the whole, this development is to be welcomed as a means of bringing the common elements of the evolution of human society to our attention. But this approach also involves two problems. For the vast majority of their time on earth, human beings have lived in partial or virtually total isolation from each other. Differences in climate, location, and geographic features have created human societies vastly different from each other in culture and historical experience. Only in relatively recent times (the commonly accepted date has long been the beginning of the age of European exploration at the end of the fifteenth century, but some would now push it back to the era of the Mongol Empire or even further) have cultural interchanges begun to create a common "world system," in which events taking place in one part of the world are rapidly transmitted throughout the globe, often with momentous consequences. In recent generations, of course, the process of global interdependence has been proceeding even more rapidly. Nevertheless, even now the process is by no means complete, as ethnic and regional differences continue to exist and to shape the course of world history. The tenacity of these differences and sensitivities is reflected not only in the rise of internecine conflicts in such divergent areas as Africa, India, and eastern Europe, but also in the emergence in recent years of such regional organizations as the African Union, the Association for the Southeast Asian Nations, and the European Union.

The second problem is a practical one. College students today are all too often not well informed about the distinctive character of civilizations such as China and India and, without sufficient exposure to the historical evolution of such societies, will assume all too readily that the peoples in these countries have had historical experiences similar to ours and will respond to various stimuli in a similar fashion to those living in western Europe or the United States. If it is a mistake to ignore those forces that link us together, it is equally a mistake to underestimate those factors that continue to divide us and to differentiate us into a world of diverse peoples.

Our response to this challenge has been to adopt a global approach to world history while at the same time attempting to do justice to the distinctive character and development of individual civilizations and regions of the world. The presentation of individual cultures is especially important in Parts I and II, which cover a time when it is generally agreed that the process of global integration was not yet far advanced. Later chapters begin to adopt a more comparative and thematic approach, in deference to the greater number of connections that have been established among the world's peoples since the fifteenth and sixteenth centuries. Part V consists of a series of chapters that center on individual regions of the world while at the same time focusing on common problems related to the Cold War and the rise of global problems such as terrorism, climate change, and environmental pollution.

We have sought balance in another way as well. Many textbooks tend to simplify the content of history courses by emphasizing an intellectual or political perspective or, most recently, a social perspective, often at the expense of sufficient details in a chronological framework. This approach is confusing to students whose high school social studies programs have often neglected a systematic study of world history. We have attempted to write a well-balanced work in which political, economic, social, religious, intellectual, cultural, and military history have been integrated into a chronologically ordered synthesis.

FEATURES OF THE TEXT

To enliven the past and let readers see for themselves the materials that historians use to create their pictures of the past, we have included **primary sources** (boxed documents) in each chapter that are keyed to the discussion in the text. The documents, appearing in two features called **Historical Voices** and **Opposing Viewpoints**, include examples of the religious, artistic, intellectual, social, economic, and political aspects of life in different societies and reveal in a vivid fashion what civilization meant to the individual men and women who shaped it by their actions. Questions at the end of each source aid students in analyzing the documents.

Each chapter has a **lengthy introduction** to help maintain the continuity of the narrative and to provide a synthesis of important themes. Anecdotes in the chapter introductions dramatically convey the major theme or themes of each chapter. A **timeline** at the end of each chapter enables students to see the major developments of an era at a glance and within cross-cultural categories, while the more **detailed chronologies** reinforce the events discussed in the text.

Updated maps and extensive illustrations serve to deepen the reader's understanding of the text. **Detailed map captions** are designed to enrich students' awareness of the importance of geography to history, and numerous spot maps enable students to see at a glance the region or subject being discussed in the text. Map captions also include a question to guide students' reading of the map. To facilitate understanding of cultural movements, illustrations of artistic works discussed in the text are placed near the discussions. A **Chapter Outline and Focus Questions**, as well as **Critical Thinking** questions at the beginning of each chapter give students a useful overview and guide them to the main subjects of each chapter. The focus questions are then repeated at the beginning of each major section in the chapter to reinforce the main themes. A focus question entitled **Connections to Today** is intended to help students appreciate the relevance of history by asking them to draw connections between the past and present. A **glossary of important terms** (boldfaced in the text when they are introduced and defined) is provided at the back of the book to maximize reader comprehension. A **guide to pronunciation** is provided in parentheses in the text following the first mention of a complex name or term.

Comparative Essays, keyed to the seven major themes of world history (see p. xxviii), enable us to more concretely draw comparisons and contrasts across geographic, cultural, and chronological lines. Some new essays have been added to the ninth edition. **Comparative Illustrations,** also keyed to the seven major themes of world history, continue to be a feature in each chapter. Both the comparative essays and the comparative illustrations conclude with focus questions to help students develop their analytical skills. We hope that the comparative essays and the comparative illustrations will assist instructors who wish to encourage their students to adopt a comparative approach to their understanding of the human experience. The **Film & History** feature, included in many chapters, now appears in a new, brief format.

The **Opposing Viewpoints** feature presents a comparison of two or three primary sources to facilitate student analysis of historical documents. This feature has been expanded and now appears in almost every chapter. Focus questions are included to guide students in evaluating the documents.

To help students examine how and why historians differ in their interpretation of specific topics, new historiographical subsections were introduced in the eighth edition. Each of these sections is now preceded by the heading **Historians Debate** to make students more aware of the interpretive nature of history.

End-of-chapter elements, first added in the seventh edition, provide study aids for class discussion, individual review, and/or further research. The **Chapter Summary** is illustrated with thumbnail images of chapter illustrations. **Reflection Questions** and the **Chapter Timeline** aid students in reviewing the chapter.

New to This Edition

After reexamining the entire book and analyzing the comments and reviews of many colleagues who have found the book to be a useful instrument for introducing their students to world history, we have also made a number of other changes for the ninth edition.

We have continued to strengthen the global framework of the book, but not at the expense of reducing the attention assigned to individual regions of the world. New material has been added to most chapters to help students

be aware of similar developments globally, including new comparative sections. New illustrations appear in every chapter. A number of the Part I through Part V opening essays have been substantially revised, and questions relating to the issues discussed in these essays have been added in the chapters that follow. The enthusiastic response to the primary sources (boxed documents) led us to evaluate the content of each document carefully and add new documents throughout the text, including new comparative documents in the Opposing Viewpoints features.

To keep up with the ever-growing body of historical scholarship, new or revised material has been added throughout the book on the following topics:

Chapter 1 Possible discovery of new hominids in Indonesia; Neanderthals and modern humans; cave painting; new Historians Debate section "Why did Early Civilizations Develop?"; the Hebrew Bible, including the Documentary Hypothesis; new illustration and material on the Ten Commandments.

Chapter 2 A new opening vignette focusses on the Indus Valley Civilization; section on Indian religion and the Comparative Essay have been revised; new document "The Duties of a King."

Chapter 3 The comparative essay on metals has been revised; new document "The Mandate of Heaven."

Chapter 4 Minoan Crete; Mycenaean Greece; the so-called "Dark Age" in Greece; the *polis*; Greek cultural identity; Greek settlements abroad; the Persian Wars; role of Persian threat for a growing sense of Greek cultural identity; growing sense of Greek cultural identity due to athletic games; new document feature "The Character of Alexander"; Hellenistic political institutions.

Chapter 5 Aeneas and Romulus and Remus and the legendary founding of Rome; citizenship policy and the Roman army; Roman imperialism; comparison of Augustus and Julius Caesar; revolts against Roman rule during the *Pax Romana*; new Historians Debate section "What was Romanization?"; contacts with Han China; Roman women; revolts against Roman rule in Judaea.

Chapter 6 The section on stateless societies has been revised and repositioned in the chapter; comparative essay on the environment revised; added material on Inka civilization; new document "The Legend of the Feathery Serpent."

Chapter 7 Revised opening vignette on Muhammad; new Historians Debate question on reasons for Islamic expansion; new document "Ibn Khaldun: Islam's Greatest Historian."

Chapter 8 New document "Beware the Troglodytes."

Chapter 9 The section on Indian religion has been substantially revised; new Historians Debate section "The

Indian Economy: Promise Unfulfilled?"; much new material has been added on early statehood in Southeast Asia and the role of the region in the maritime trade network; new document "Education of a Brahmin."

Chapter 10 New material on Empress Wu; revised section on traditional society in China; new document "Confucianism and its Enemies"; section on Admiral Zheng He revised and expanded.

Chapter 11 Revised section on Japanese borrowing from China; added information on Korean technology; two new documents: "Seduction of the Akashi Lady" and "The First Vietnam War."

Chapter 12 Monks as missionaries, particularly St. Patrick; Charlemagne as emperor; new Historians Debate section "What was Feudalism?"; peasant women; role of agriculture in the development of trade in the High Middle Ages; Bernard of Clairvaux; the Fourth Crusade; new material in Historians Debate section "What were the Effects of the Crusades?"

Chapter 13 The Fourth Crusade; new Historians Debate section "Why did the Eastern Roman Empire (Byzantine Empire) Last a Thousand Years Longer Than the Western Roman Empire?"; the English use of the longbow; the Great Schism; new C-head section "The Artist and Social Status"; new document feature "The Genius of Michelangelo."

Chapter 14 Revised introduction; new document "For God, Gold, and Glory in the Age of Exploration." New information on maritime trade in Asia and the motives for European exploration.

Chapter 15 Luther; the Jesuits; women and witchcraft; the Thirty Years' War; new document feature "The Destruction of Magdeburg in the Thirty Year's War."

Chapter 16 New document "A Portrait of Suleyman the Magnificent;" added discussion on Ottoman technology; revised and expanded section on Safavid Persia; revised comparative essay on war; new Historians Debate section "The Ottoman Empire: A Civilization in Decline?"

Chapter 17 New Historians Debate section "The Qing Economy: Ready for Takeoff?" New Opposing Viewpoints document "The Debate over Christianity."

Chapter 18 Women and the Scientific Revolution; Rococo art; global trade; the consumer revolution; new Historians Debate section "Was There an Agricultural Revolution?"; Jamestown; the Seven Years' War; new document feature "Frederick the Great and His Father"; the Three Estates; the French clergy; the Reign of Terror.

Chapter 19 New document feature "The Steam Engine and Cotton"; early railroad transportation; the Industrial Revolution on the Continent; British policies in India.

Chapter 20 Latin America; the United States; new document feature "A Radical Critique of the Land Problem in Mexico"; new Film & History feature, *Suffragette;* Courbet; Impressionism; Mary Cassatt; Japanese influence in the arts.

Chapter 21 Revised opening vignette on Cecil Rhodes; new Film & History vignette *A Passage to India*; revised discussion on colonial policies in Africa; new Historians Debate section "Imperialism: Drawing up the Balance Sheet."

Chapter 22 Two new Historians Debate sections "Was the October Revolution a Success or a Failure?" and "The Meiji Restoration: A Revolution from Above?" New documents "An Insignificant and Detestable Race" and "The Rules of Good Citizenship in Meiji Japan."

Chapter 23 New document "The Reality of War: The Views of British Poets"; life in the trenches; the end of World War I; the Great Depression.

Chapter 24 New opening vignette on Lenin and the East; revised section on the early Nanjing Republic; new Historians Debate section "Taisho Democracy: An Aberration?"; revised section on communism in Asia.

Chapter 25 New material on socialism and the rise of fascism in Italy and Germany; the Enabling Act; economic differences between fascism and communism; the Nazi economy; the Soviet economy; naval battles, including Battle of North Atlantic and Battle of Leyte Gulf; new B-head section "The Impact of Technology"; Japan and war crimes.

Chapter 26 New opening vignette on the rise of the Iron Curtain; new information on the Soviet takeover of Eastern Europe; new Film & History vignette *Bridge of Spies;* new information on the collapse of Soviet power in Eastern Europe; new closing section on "The Revenge of History."

Chapter 27 New document feature "One Day in the Life of Ivan Denisovich"; sections on Eastern Europe moved to Chapter 26; revised section on the collapse of the USSR; substantial updating and revision of material on contemporary China.

Chapter 28 French politics and immigration; France and terrorism; Germany, Great Britain and Brexit, Poland, Czech Republic, and Russia; the European Union; Canada; Argentina and Mexico; the Women's Movement; terrorism; immigration; new document feature "The West and Islam"; the environment; technology; new C-head section on "Art in the Contemporary World."

Chapter 29 New opening vignette on terrorism in West Africa; substantial revisions and updating of contemporary situation in Africa; new document on the OAU; fully revised an updated material on politics, economics, religion, and the recent crisis in the Middle East; new material on the Syrian civil war; revised Comparative Essay "Religion and Society."

Chapter 30 Revised opening vignette; revised section on communalism in India; new document "The Golden Throat of President Sukarno"; current conditions in South Asia, Southeast Asia, Japan, and the Little Tigers substantially revised. New Historians Debate section "The East Asian Miracle: Fact or Myth?"

Epilogue New material on the global economy.

Instructor Resources

MINDTAP MindTap for *The Essential World History* 9e is a flexible, online learning platform that provides students with a relevant and engaging learning experience that builds their critical thinking skills and fosters their argumentation and analysis skills. Through a carefully designed chapter-based learning path, MindTap supports students as they develop historical understanding, improve their reading and writing skills, and practice critical thinking by making connections between ideas.

Students read sections of the ebook and take Check Your Understanding quizzes that test their reading comprehension. They put higher-level critical thinking skills into practice to complete chapter tests. They also use these skills to analyze textual and visual primary sources in each chapter through an autograded image primary source activity and a manually graded short essay in which students write comparatively about multiple primary sources.

Beyond the chapter-level content, students can increase their comfort in analyzing primary sources through thematically-organized primary source autograded activities that span the text. They also practice synthesizing their knowledge and articulating what they have learned through responding to essay prompts that span broader themes in the book.

MindTap also allows instructors to customize their content, providing tools that seamlessly integrate YouTube clips, outside websites, and personal content directly into the learning path. Instructors can assign additional primary source content through the Instructor Resource Center and Questia, primary- and secondary-source databases located on the MindTap app dock that house thousands of peer-reviewed journals, newspapers, magazines, and books.

The additional content available in MindTap mirrors and complements the authors' narrative, but also includes primary-source content and assessments not found in the printed text. To learn more, ask your Cengage sales representative to demo it for you—or go to **www.cengage.com/mindtap**.

Instructor's Companion Website The Instructor's Companion Website, accessed through the Instructor Resource Center (login.cengage.com), houses all of the supplemental materials you can use for your course. This includes a Test Bank, Instructor's Manual, and PowerPoint Lecture Presentations. The Test Bank contains essay, multiple-choice, true-or-false, and historical identification questions for each chapter. The Instructor's Resource Manual includes instructional objectives and focus questions, chapter summaries, suggested lecture topics, map exercises, discussion questions for the primary sources, topics for student research, relevant websites, suggestions for additional videos, and online resources for information on historical sites. Finally, the PowerPoint Lectures are ADA-compliant slides that collate the key takeaways from the chapter in concise visual formats perfect for in-class presentations or for student review.

Cengage.com/student Save your students time and money. Direct them to www.cengage.com/student for a choice in formats and savings and a better chance to succeed in your class. Cengage.com/student, Cengage's online store, is a single destination for more than 10,000 new textbooks, ebooks, study tools, and audio supplements. Students have the freedom to purchase à la carte exactly what they need when they need it. Students can save up to 70% off on the ebook electronic textbook.

CENGAGE UNLIMITED We now offer CENGAGE UNLIMITED, the first-of-its-kind digital subscription designed specifically to lower costs. Students get everything Cengage has to offer—in one place. For $119.99 per term (or $179.99 per year), students have access to:

- Award-winning products proven to boost outcomes and increase engagement
- Over 20,000 digital products, covering 70 disciplines and 675 courses
- A free print rental with any activated digital learning product (like MindTap)
- Dozens of study guides matched to the most common college courses
- Twelve-month free access for up to six ebooks

Currently available in selected markets. For more information, please contact your local Learning Consultant or visit **cengage.com/unlimited**

Learn more at Cengage.com about books that build skills in doing history, including:

- *Doing History: Research and Writing in the Digital Age,* 2e (ISBN: 9781133587880) Prepared by Michael J. Galgano, J. Chris Arndt, and Raymond M. Hyser of James Madison University.

- *Writing for College History,* 1e (ISBN: 9780618306039) Prepared by Robert M. Frakes of Clarion University.
- *The Modern Researcher,* 6e (ISBN: 9780495318705) Prepared by Jacques Barzun and Henry F. Graff of Columbia University.

Reader Program   Cengage publishes a number of readers. Some contain exclusively primary sources, others are devoted to essays and secondary sources, and still others provide a combination of primary and secondary sources. All of these readers are designed to guide students through the process of historical inquiry. Visit **www .cengage.com/history** for a complete list of readers.

Custom Options   Nobody knows your students like you, so why not give them a text that is tailor-fit to their needs? Cengage offers custom solutions for your course—whether it's making a small modification to *The Essential World History* 9e, to match your syllabus or combining multiple sources to create something truly unique. Contact your Cengage representative to explore custom solutions for your course.

ACKNOWLEDGMENTS

Both authors gratefully acknowledge that without the generosity of many others, this project could not have been completed.

William Duiker would like to thank Kumkum Chatterjee and On-cho Ng for their helpful comments about issues related to the history of India and premodern China. His long-time colleague Cyril Griffith, now deceased, was a cherished friend and a constant source of information about modern Africa. Art Goldschmidt has been of invaluable assistance in reading several chapters of the manuscript, as well as in unraveling many of the mysteries of Middle Eastern civilization. He would like to thank Charles Ingrao for providing information on Spanish policies in Latin America, and Tony Hopkins and Dan Baugh for their insights on British imperial policy. Finally, he remains profoundly grateful to his wife, Yvonne V. Duiker, Ph.D. She has not only given her usual measure of love and support when this appeared to be an insuperable task, but she has also contributed her own time and expertise to enrich the sections on art and literature, thereby adding life and sparkle to this edition, as well as the earlier editions of the book. To her, and to his daughters Laura and Claire, he will be forever thankful for bringing joy to his life.

Jackson Spielvogel would like to thank Art Goldschmidt, David Redles, and Christine Colin for their time and ideas. Daniel Haxall of Kutztown University provided valuable assistance with materials on postwar art, popular culture, Postmodern art and thought, and the digital age. He is especially grateful to Kathryn Spielvogel for her work as research associate. Above all, he thanks his family for their support. The gifts of love, laughter, and patience from his daughters, Jennifer and Kathryn; his sons, Eric and Christian; his daughters-in-law, Liz and Laurie; and his sons-in-law, Daniel and Eddie, were especially valuable. He also wishes to acknowledge his grandchildren, Devyn, Bryn, Drew, Elena, Sean, Emma, and Jackson, who bring great joy to his life on a daily basis. Diane, his wife and best friend, provided him with editorial assistance, wise counsel, and the loving support that made a project of this magnitude possible.

Thanks to Cengage's comprehensive review process, many historians were asked to evaluate our manuscript. We are grateful to the following for the innumerable suggestions that have greatly improved our work:

Henry Abramson
Florida Atlantic University

Eric H. Ash
Wayne State University

William Bakken
Rochester Community College

Suzanne Balch-Lindsay
Eastern New Mexico University

Michael E. Birdwell
Tennessee Technological University

Eric Bobo
Hinds Community College

Michael Bonislawski
Cambridge College

Connie Brand
Meridien Community College

Eileen Brown
Norwalk Community College

Paul Buckingham
Morrisville State College

Ted Butler
Darton State College

Kelly Cantrell
East Mississippi Community College

Thomas Cardoza
University of California, San Diego

Alistair Chapman
Westmont College

Nupur Chaudhuri
Texas Southern University

Richard Crane
Greensboro College

Wade Dudley
East Carolina University

E. J. Fabyan
Vincennes University

Kenneth Faunce
Washington State University

Jamie Garcia
Hawaii Pacific University

Steven Gosch
University of Wisconsin—Eau Claire

Donald Harreld
Brigham Young University

Janine C. Hartman
University of Connecticut

Greg Havrilcsak
University of Michigan—Flint

Thomas Hegerty
University of Tampa

Sanders Huguenin
University of Science and Arts of Oklahoma

Ahmed Ibrahim
Southwest Missouri State University

C. Barden Keeler
Gulf Coast High School

Marilynn Fox Kokoszka
Orchard Ridge Campus, Oakland Community College

James Krippner-Martinez
Haverford College

Oscar Lansen
University of North Carolina—Charlotte

David Leinweber
Oxford College, Emory University

Susie Ling
Pasadena City College

Moira Maguire
University of Arkansas at Little Rock

Jason McCollom
University of Arkansas

Andrew McGreevy
Ohio University

Daniel Miller
Calvin College

Michael Murdock
Brigham Young University

Lopita Nath
University of the Incarnate Word

Mark Norris
Grace College

Elsa A. Nystrom
Kennesaw State University

S. Mike Pavelec
Hawaii Pacific University

Matthew Phillips
Kent State University

Randall L. Pouwels
University of Central Arkansas

Margaret Power
Illinois Institute of Technology

Pamela Sayre
Henry Ford Community College

Jenny Schwartzberg
Delgado Community College

Philip Curtis Skaggs
Grand Valley State University

Laura Smoller
University of Arkansas at Little Rock

Beatrice Spade
University of Southern Colorado

Jeremy Stahl
Middle Tennessee State University

Clif Stratton
Washington State University

Kate Transchel
California State University, Chico

Justin Vance
Hawaii Pacific University

Lorna VanMeter
Ball State University

Michelle White
University of Tennessee at Chattanooga

Edna Yahil
Washington State University—Swiss Center

The following individuals contributed reviews for the ninth edition:

Connie Brand
Meridian Community College

Brett Brinegar
Copiah-Lincoln Community College

Stephen P. Budney
University of Pikeville

Kelly Cantrell
East Mississippi Community College

Shawn Dry
Oakland Community College

Steven Patterson
Mississippi College

Melissa Ryckman
Martin Methodist College

Jason Toy
Cecil College

The authors are truly grateful to the people who have helped us to produce this book. The editors at Cengage have been both helpful and congenial at all times. We especially wish to thank Kate MacLean who thoughtfully, wisely, efficiently, and pleasantly guided the overall development of this edition. We also thank Philip Lanza for his valuable managerial skills. Kayci Wyatt of MPS Limited was as cooperative and cheerful as she was competent in matters of production management. And finally, we wish to thank Clark Baxter, whose initial faith in our ability to do this project was inspiring.

THEMES FOR UNDERSTANDING WORLD HISTORY

AS THEY PURSUE THEIR CRAFT, historians often organize their material according to themes that enable them to ask and try to answer basic questions about the past. Such is our intention here. In preparing the ninth edition of this book, we have selected several major themes that we believe are especially important in understanding the course of world history. Thinking about these themes will help students to perceive the similarities and differences among cultures since the beginning of the human experience.

In the chapters that follow, we will refer to these themes frequently as we advance from the prehistoric era to the present. Where appropriate, we shall make comparisons across cultural boundaries or across different time periods. To facilitate this process, we have included a comparative essay in each chapter that focuses on a particular theme within the specific time period covered by that chapter. For example, the comparative essay in Chapter 6 deals with the human impact on the natural environment during the premodern era, while the essay in Chapter 30 discusses the same issue in the contemporary world. Each comparative essay is identified with a particular theme, although many essays touch on multiple themes.

We have sought to illustrate these themes using comparative illustrations in each chapter. These illustrations are comparative in nature and seek to encourage the reader to think about thematic issues in cross-cultural terms, while not losing sight of the unique characteristics of individual societies. Our seven themes, each divided into two subtopics, are listed below.

Politics & Government 1. Politics and Government The study of politics seeks to answer certain basic questions that historians have about the structure of a society: How were people governed? What was the relationship between the ruler and the ruled? What people or groups of people (the political elites) held political power? What actions did people take to guarantee their security or change their form of government?

Art & Ideas 2. *Art and Ideas* We cannot understand a society without looking at its culture, or the common ideas, beliefs, and patterns of behavior that are passed on from one generation to the next. Culture includes both high culture and popular culture. High culture consists of the writings of a society's thinkers and the works of its artists. A society's popular culture encompasses the ideas and experiences of ordinary people. Today, the media have embraced the term *popular culture* to describe the current trends and fashionable styles.

Religion & Philosophy 3. *Religion and Philosophy* Throughout history, people have sought to find a deeper meaning to human life. How have the world's great religions, such as Hinduism, Buddhism, Judaism, Christianity, and Islam, influenced people's lives? How have they spread to create new patterns of culture in other parts of the world?

Family & Society 4. *Family and Society* The most basic social unit in human society has always been the family. From a study of family and social patterns, we learn about the different social classes that make up a society and their relationships with one another. We also learn about the role of gender in individual societies. What different roles did men and women play in their societies? How and why were those roles different?

Science & Technology 5. *Science and Technology* For thousands of years, people around the world have made scientific discoveries and technological innovations that have changed our world. From the creation of stone tools that made farming easier to advanced computers that guide our airplanes, science and technology have altered how humans have related to their world.

Earth & Environment 6. *Earth and the Environment* Throughout history, peoples and societies have been affected by the physical world in which they live. Climatic changes alone have been an important factor in human history. Through their economic activities, peoples and societies, in turn, have also made an impact on their world. Human activities have affected the physical environment and even endangered the very existence of entire societies and species.

7. Interaction and Exchange Many world historians believe that the exchange of ideas and innovations is the driving force behind the evolution of human societies. Knowledge of agriculture, writing and printing, metalworking, and navigational techniques, for example, spread gradually from one part of the world to other regions and eventually changed the face of the entire globe. The process of cultural and technological exchange took place in various ways, including trade, conquest, and the migration of peoples.

A NOTE TO STUDENTS ABOUT LANGUAGES AND THE DATING OF TIME

One of the most difficult challenges in studying world history is coming to grips with the multitude of names, words, and phrases in unfamiliar languages. Unfortunately, this problem has no easy solution. We have tried to alleviate the difficulty, where possible, by providing an English-language translation of foreign words or phrases, a glossary, and a pronunciation guide in parentheses in the text. The issue is especially complicated in the case of Chinese because two separate systems are commonly used to transliterate the spoken Chinese language into the Roman alphabet. The Wade-Giles system, invented in the nineteenth century, was the most frequently used until recent years, when the pinyin system was adopted by the People's Republic of China as its own official form of transliteration. We have opted to use the latter, as it appears to be gaining acceptance in the United States.

In our examination of world history, we also need to be aware of the dating of time. In recording the past, historians try to determine the exact time when events occurred. World War II in Europe, for example, began on September 1, 1939, when Adolf Hitler sent German troops into Poland, and ended on May 7, 1945, when Germany surrendered. By using dates, historians can place events in order and try to determine the development of patterns over periods of time.

If someone asked you when you were born, you would reply with a number, such as 2000. In the United States, we would all accept that number without question, because it is part of the dating system followed in the Western world (Europe and the Western Hemisphere). In this system, events are dated by counting backward or forward from the birth of Christ (assumed to be the year 1). An event that took place 400 years before the birth of Christ would commonly be dated 400 B.C. (before Christ). Dates after the birth of Christ are labeled as A.D. These letters stand for the Latin words *anno domini,* which mean "in the year of the Lord" (or the year of the birth of Christ). Thus, an event that took place 250 years after the birth of Christ is written A.D. 250, or in the year of the Lord 250. It can also

be written as 250, just as you would not give your birth year as A.D. 2000, but simply as 2000.

Some historians now prefer to use the abbreviations B.C.E. ("before the common era") and C.E. ("common era") instead of B.C. and A.D. This is especially true of world historians who prefer to use symbols that are not so Western or Christian oriented. The dates, of course, remain the same. Thus, 1950 B.C.E. and 1950 B.C. are the same year, as are A.D. 40 and 40 C.E. In keeping with the current usage by many world historians, this book will use the terms B.C.E. and C.E.

Historians also make use of other terms to refer to time. A decade is 10 years; a century is 100 years; and a millennium is 1,000 years. The phrase "fourth century B.C.E." refers to the fourth period of 100 years counting backward from 1, the assumed date of the birth of Christ. Since the first century B.C.E. would be the years 100 B.C.E. to 1 B.C.E., the fourth century B.C.E. would be the years 400 B.C.E. to 301 B.C.E. We could say, then, that an event in 350 B.C.E. took place in the fourth century B.C.E.

The phrase "fourth century C.E." refers to the fourth period of 100 years after the birth of Christ. Since the first period of 100 years would be the years 1 to 100, the fourth period or fourth century would be the years 301 to 400. We could say, then, for example, that an event in 350 took place in the fourth century. Likewise, the first millennium B.C.E. refers to the years 1000 B.C.E. to 1 B.C.E.; the second millennium C.E. refers to the years 1001 to 2000.

The dating of events can also vary from people to people. Most people in the Western world use the Western calendar, also known as the Gregorian calendar after Pope Gregory XIII, who refined it in 1582. The Hebrew calendar, on the other hand, uses a different system in which the year 1 is the equivalent of the Western year 3760 B.C.E., considered by Jews to be the date of the creation of the world. Thus, the Western year 2018 is the year 5778 on the Jewish calendar. The Islamic calendar begins year 1 on the day Muhammad fled from Mecca, which is the year 622 C.E. on the Western calendar.

The peoples of Mesopotamia and Egypt, like the peoples of India and China, built the first civilizations. Blessed with an abundant environment in their fertile river valleys, beginning around 3000 B.C.E. they built technologically advanced societies, developed cities, and struggled with the problems of organized states. They developed writing to keep records and created literature. They constructed monumental architecture to please their gods, symbolize their power, and preserve their culture for all time. They

developed new political, military, social, and religious structures to deal with the basic problems of human existence and organization. These first literate civilizations left detailed records that allow us to view how they grappled with three of the fundamental problems that humans have pondered: the nature of human relationships, the nature of the universe, and the role of divine forces in that cosmos. Although other peoples would provide different answers from those of the Mesopotamians and Egyptians, they posed the questions, gave answers, and wrote them down. Human memory begins with the creation of civilizations.

By the middle of the second millennium B.C.E., much of the creative impulse of the Mesopotamian and Egyptian civilizations was beginning to wane. Around 1200 B.C.E., the decline of the Hittites and Egyptians had created a power vacuum that allowed a number of small states to emerge and flourish temporarily. All of them were eventually overshadowed by the rise of the great empires of the Assyrians and Persians. The Assyrian Empire had been the first to unite almost all of the ancient Middle East. Even larger, however, was the empire of the Great Kings of Persia. The many years of peace that the Persian Empire brought to the Middle East facilitated trade and the general well-being of its peoples. It is no wonder that many peoples expressed their gratitude for being subjects of the Great Kings of Persia. Among these peoples were the Israelites, who created no empire but nevertheless left an important spiritual legacy. The evolution of monotheism created in Judaism one of the world's greatest religions; Judaism in turn influenced the development of both Christianity and Islam.

While the peoples of North Africa and the Middle East were actively building the first civilizations, a similar process was getting under way in India. The first civilization in India arose in the Indus River Valley during the fourth millennium B.C.E. This Harappan civilization made significant political and social achievements for some two thousand years until the coming of the Aryans finally brought its end around 1500 B.C.E. The Aryans established political

control throughout all of India and created a new Indian civilization. Two of the world's great religions, Hinduism and Buddhism, began in India. With its belief in reincarnation, Hinduism provided justification for the rigid class system of India. Buddhism was the product of one man, Siddhartha Gautama, whose simple message in the sixth century B.C.E. of achieving wisdom created a new spiritual philosophy that came to rival Hinduism.

With the rise of the Mauryan dynasty in the fourth century B.C.E., the distinctive features of a great civilization began to be clearly visible. It was extensive in its scope, embracing the entire Indian subcontinent and eventually, in the form of Buddhism and Hinduism, spreading to China and Southeast Asia. But the underlying ethnic, linguistic, and cultural diversity of the Indian people posed a constant challenge to the unity of the state. After the collapse of the Mauryas, the subcontinent would not come under a single authority again for several hundred years.

In the meantime, another great experiment was taking place far to the northeast, across the Himalaya Mountains. Like many other civilizations of antiquity, the first Chinese state was concentrated on a major river system. Beginning around 1600 B.C.E., the Shang dynasty created the first flourishing Chinese civilization. Under the Shang, China developed organized government, a system of writing,

and advanced skills in the making of bronze vessels. During the Zhou dynasty, China began to adopt many of the features that characterized Chinese civilization for centuries. Especially important politically was the "mandate from Heaven," which, it was believed, gave kings a divine right to rule. The family, with its ideal of filial piety, also emerged as a powerful economic and social unit.

Once embarked on its own path toward the creation of a complex society, China achieved results that were in all respects the equal of its counterparts elsewhere. A new dynasty—the Han—then established a vast empire that lasted over four hundred years. During the glory years of the Han dynasty (202 B.C.E.–221 C.E.), China extended the boundaries of its empire far into the sands of Central Asia and southward along the coast of the South China Sea into what is modern day Vietnam. Chinese culture appeared to be unrivaled, and its scientific and technological achievements were unsurpassed.

Unlike the great centralized empires of the Persians and the Chinese, ancient Greece consisted of a larger number of small, independent city-states, most of which had populations of only a few thousand. Despite the small size of their city-states, these ancient Greeks created a civilization that was the fountainhead of Western culture. In Classical Greece

(ca. 500–338 B.C.E.), Socrates, Plato, and Aristotle established the foundations of Western philosophy. Western literary forms are largely derived from Greek poetry and drama. Greek notions of harmony, proportion, and beauty have remained the touchstones for all subsequent Western art.

A rational method of inquiry, so important to modern science, was conceived in ancient Greece. Many political terms are Greek in origin, and so too are concepts of the rights and duties of citizenship, especially as they were conceived in Athens, the first great democracy. The Greeks raised and debated the fundamental questions about the purpose of human existence, the structure of human society, and the nature of the universe that have concerned thinkers ever since.

For all of their brilliant accomplishments, however, the Greeks were unable to rise above the divisions and rivalries that caused them to fight each other and undermine their own civilization. Of course, their cultural contributions have outlived their political struggles. And the Hellenistic era, which emerged after the Greek city-states had lost their independence in 338 B.C.E. and Alexander the Great had defeated the Persian Empire and carved out a new kingdom in the Middle East, made possible the spread of Greek ideas to larger areas. New philosophical concepts captured the minds of many. Significant achievements were made in art, literature, and science. Greek culture spread throughout the Middle East and made an impact wherever it was carried. Although the Hellenistic world achieved a degree of political stability, by the late third century B.C.E. signs of decline were beginning to multiply, and

the growing power of Rome would eventually endanger the Hellenistic world.

In the eighth and seventh centuries B.C.E., the Latin-speaking community of Rome emerged as an actual city. Between 509 and 264 B.C.E., the expansion of this city brought about the union of almost all of Italy under Rome's control. Even more dramatically, between 264 and 133 B.C.E., Rome expanded to the west and east and became master of the Mediterranean Sea and its surrounding territories, creating one of the largest empires in antiquity. Rome's republican institutions proved inadequate for the task of ruling an empire, however, and after a series of bloody civil wars, Octavian created a new order that would rule the empire in an orderly fashion. His successors established a Roman imperial state.

The Roman Empire experienced a lengthy period of peace and prosperity between 14 and 180 C.E. During this era, trade flourished and the provinces were governed efficiently. In the course of the third century, however, the Roman Empire came near to collapse due to invasions, civil wars, and economic decline. Although the emperors Diocletian and Constantine brought new life to the so-called Late Empire, their efforts shored up the empire only temporarily. In its last two hundred years, as Christianity, with its new ideals of spiritual equality and respect for human life, grew, a slow transformation of the Roman world took place. The Germanic invasions greatly accelerated this process. Beginning in 395, the empire divided into Western and Eastern parts, and in 476, the Roman Empire in the west came to an end.

Although the Western Roman Empire lived on only as an idea, Roman achievements were bequeathed to the future. The Romance languages of today (French, Italian, Spanish, Portuguese, and Romanian) are based on Latin. Western practices of impartial justice and trial by jury owe much to Roman law. As great builders, the Romans left monuments to their skills throughout Europe, some of which, such as aqueducts and roads, are still in use today.

The fall of ancient empires did not mark the end of civilization. After 500 C.E., new societies eventually rose on the ashes of the ancient empires, while new civilizations were on the verge of creation across the oceans in the continents of North and South America. The Maya and Aztecs were especially successful in developing advanced and prosperous civilizations in Central America. Both cultures built elaborate cities with pyramids, temples, and palaces. Both were polytheistic and practiced human

sacrifice as a major part of their religions. Mayan civilization collapsed in the ninth century, whereas the Aztecs fell to Spanish invaders in the sixteenth century. In the fifteenth century, another remarkable civilization—that of the Inka—flourished in South America. The Inka Empire was carefully planned and regulated, which is especially evident in the extensive network of roads that connected all parts of the empire. However, the Inka, possessing none of the new weapons of the Spaniards, eventually fell to the foreign conquerors.

All of these societies in the Americas developed in apparently total isolation from their counterparts elsewhere in the world. This lack of contact with other human beings deprived them of access to developments taking place in Africa, Asia, and Europe. They did not know of the wheel, for example, and their written languages were not as sophisticated as those in other parts of the world. In other respects, however, their cultural achievements were the equal of those realized elsewhere. One development that the peoples of the Americas lacked was the knowledge of firearms. In a few short years, tiny bands of Spanish explorers were able to conquer the magnificent civilizations of the Americas and turn them into ruins.

After the collapse of Roman power in the west, the Eastern Roman Empire, centered in Constantinople, continued in the eastern Mediterranean and eventually emerged as the unique Christian civilization known as the Byzantine Empire, which flourished for hundreds of years. One of the greatest challenges to the Byzantine Empire, however, came from a new force—Islam, a new religion that arose in the Arabian Peninsula at the beginning of the seventh century C.E. and spread rapidly throughout the Middle East. It was the work of a man named Muhammad. After Muhammad's death, his successors organized the Arabs and set in motion a great expansion. Arab armies moved westward across North Africa and into Spain, as well as eastward into the Persian Empire, conquering Syria and Mesopotamia. Internal struggles, however, soon weakened the empire, although the Abbasid dynasty established an Arab empire in 750 that flourished for almost five hundred years.

Like other empires in the region, however, the Arab empire did not last. Nevertheless, Islam brought a code of law and a written language to societies that had previously not had them. By creating a flourishing trade network stretching from West Africa to East Asia, Islam also brought untold wealth to thousands and a better life to millions. By the end of the thirteenth century, the Arab

empire was no more than a memory. But it left a powerful legacy in Islam, which remains one of the great religions of the world. In succeeding centuries, Islam began to penetrate into Africa and across the Indian Ocean into the islands of Southeast Asia.

The mastery of agriculture gave rise to three early civilizations in northern Africa: Egypt, Kush, and Axum. Later, new states emerged in different parts of Africa, some of them strongly influenced by the spread of Islam. Ghana, Mali, and Songhai were three prosperous trading states that flourished in West Africa between the twelfth and fifteenth centuries. Zimbabwe, which emerged around 1300, played an important role in the southern half of Africa. Africa was also an active participant in emerging regional and global trade with the Mediterranean world and across the Indian Ocean. Although the state-building process in sub-Saharan Africa was still in its early stages compared with the ancient civilizations of India, China, and Mesopotamia, in many respects the new African states were as impressive and sophisticated as their counterparts elsewhere in the world.

In the fifteenth century, a new factor came to affect Africa. Fleets from Portugal began to probe southward along the coast of West Africa. At first, their sponsors were in search of gold and slaves, but when Portuguese ships rounded the southern coast of Africa by 1500, they began to seek to dominate the trade of the Indian Ocean as well. The new situation posed a challenge to the peoples of Africa, whose states would be severely tested by the demands of the Europeans.

The peoples of Africa were not the only ones to confront a new threat from Europe at the beginning of the sixteenth century. When the Portuguese sailed across the Indian Ocean, they sought to reach India, where a new empire capable of rivaling the great kingdom of the Mauryas was in the throes of creation. Between 500 and 1500, Indian civilization had faced a number of severe challenges. One was an ongoing threat from beyond the mountains in the northwest. This challenge, which began in the eleventh century, led to the takeover of all of northern India in the eleventh century by Turkish warriors, who were Muslims. A second challenge came from the tradition of internal rivalry that had marked Indian civilization for hundreds of years and that continued almost without interruption down to the sixteenth century. The third challenge was the religious divisions between Hindus and Buddhists, and later between Hindus and Muslims, that existed throughout much of this period.

During the same period that Indian civilization faced these challenges at home, it was having a profound impact on the emerging states of Southeast Asia. Situated at the crossroads between two oceans and two great civilizations, Southeast Asia has long served as a bridge linking peoples and cultures. When complex societies began to appear in the region, they were strongly influenced by the older civilizations of neighboring China and India. All the young states throughout the region—Vietnam, Angkor, Thailand, the Burmese kingdom of Pagan, and several states on the Malay Peninsula and Indonesian archipelago—were affected by foreign ideas and adopted them as a part of their own cultures. At the same time, the Southeast Asian peoples, like the Japanese, put their own unique stamp on the ideas that they adopted. The result was a region marked by cultural richness and diversity yet rooted in the local culture.

One of the civilizations that spread its shadow over the emerging societies of Southeast Asia was China. Between the sixth and fifteenth centuries, China was ruled by a series of strong dynasties and had advanced in many ways. The industrial and commercial sectors had grown considerably in size, complexity, and technological capacity. In the countryside, a flourishing agriculture bolstered China's economic prosperity. The civil service provided for a stable government bureaucracy and an avenue of upward mobility that was virtually unknown elsewhere in the world. China's achievements were unsurpassed throughout the world and made it a civilization that was the envy of its neighbors.

And yet some things had not changed. By 1500, China was still a predominantly agricultural society, with wealth based primarily on the ownership of land. Commercial activities flourished but remained under a high level of government regulation. China also remained a relatively centralized empire based on an official ideology that stressed the virtue of hard work, social conformity, and hierarchy. In foreign affairs, the long frontier struggle with the nomadic peoples along the northern and western frontiers continued unabated.

Along the fringes of Chinese civilization were a number of other agricultural societies that were beginning to follow a pattern of development similar to that of China, although somewhat later in time. All of these early agricultural societies were eventually influenced to some degree by their great neighbor. Vietnam remained under Chinese rule for a thousand years. Korea retained its separate existence but was long a tributary state of China and in many ways followed China's cultural example. Cut off from the mainland by 120 miles of ocean, the Japanese had little contact with the outside world during most of their early development. However, once the Japanese became acquainted with Chinese culture, they were quick to take advantage of the opportunity. In the space of a few decades, the young state adopted many features of Chinese society and culture and thereby introduced major changes into the Japanese way of life. Nevertheless, Japan was a society that was able to make use of ideas imported from beyond its borders without endangering its customs, beliefs, and institutions. Japan retained both its political independence and its cultural uniqueness.

After the collapse of the Roman Empire in the fifth century, a new European civilization slowly began to emerge in western Europe. The coronation of Charlemagne, the descendant of a Germanic tribe converted to Christianity, as Roman emperor in 800 symbolized the fusion of the three chief components of the new European civilization: the German tribes, the Roman legacy, and the Christian church. Charlemagne's Carolingian Empire fostered the idea of a distinct European identity. With the disintegration of that empire, power fell into the hands of many different lords, who came to constitute a powerful group of nobles that dominated the political, economic, and social life of Europe. But quietly and surely, within this world of castles and private power, kings gradually began to extend their public power and laid the foundations for the European kingdoms that in one form or another have dominated European politics ever since.

European civilization began to flourish in the High Middle Ages (1000–1300). The revival of trade, the expansion of towns and cities, and the development of a money economy did not mean the end of a predominantly rural European society, but they did  offer new opportunities for people to expand and enrich their lives. At the same time, the High Middle Ages also gave birth to an intellectual and spiritual revival that transformed European society. However, fourteenth-century Europe was challenged by an overwhelming number of disintegrative forces but proved remarkably resilient. Elements of recovery in the age of the Renaissance made the fifteenth century a period of significant artistic, intellectual, and political change in Europe. By the second half of the fifteenth century, the growth of strong, centralized monarchical states made possible the dramatic expansion of Europe into other parts of the world.

THE ESSENTIAL WORLD HISTORY

VOLUME II: SINCE 1500

THE EMERGENCE OF NEW WORLD PATTERNS (1500–1800)

HISTORIANS OFTEN REFER to the period from the sixteenth through eighteenth centuries as the *early modern era*. During these years, several factors were at work that created the conditions of our own time.

From a global perspective, perhaps the most noteworthy event of the period was the extension of the maritime trade network throughout the entire populated world. Traders from the Middle East had spearheaded the process with their voyages to East Asia and southern Africa in the first millennium C.E., and the Chinese had followed suit with Zheng He's groundbreaking voyages to India and East Africa, as mentioned in Chapter 10. By the end of the fifteenth century, a thriving trade network stretched from the Middle East through the Indian Ocean and all the way to China and the islands of Japan. It was at this time that a resurgent Europe suddenly exploded onto the world scene when the Portuguese discovered a maritime route to the East and Spanish adventurers opened the first European contacts with peoples of the Western Hemisphere. Although the Europeans were late to the game, they were quick learners; over the next three centuries, they gradually managed to dominate much of the shipping on international trade routes.

Some contemporary historians argue that it was this sudden burst of energy from Europe that created the first truly global economic network. Although it is true that European explorers were responsible for opening communications with the vast new world of the Americas, other historians note that it was the rise of the Arab Empire in the Middle East and the Mongol expansion a few centuries later that had played the greatest role in creating a widespread communications network by enabling goods and ideas to travel from one end of the Eurasian supercontinent to the other.

Whatever the truth of this debate, many reasons remain to consider the end of the fifteenth century a crucial date in world history. By marking the end of the long isolation of the Western Hemisphere from the rest of the inhabited world, this period led to the creation of the first truly global network of ideas and commodities that would introduce plants, ideas, and (unfortunately) many new diseases to all humanity (see Comparative Essay, "The Columbian Exchange," later in this chapter). In fact, the era gave birth to a stunning increase in trade and manufacturing that stimulated major political, economic, and social changes not only in Europe but also in other parts of the world.

But the period from 1500 to 1800 was not only an incubation period for the modern world but also the launching pad for an era of European domination that would reach fruition in the nineteenth century. To understand why the West emerged as the leading force in the world at that time, it is necessary to grasp what factors were at work in Europe that differentiated its actions from those of other major civilizations around the globe. For example, historians have identified improvements in navigation, shipbuilding, and weaponry as essential elements in promoting the European Age of Exploration. As we have seen, many of these technological advances were based on earlier discoveries that had taken place elsewhere—in China, India, and the Middle East—and had then been brought to Europe on Muslim ships or along the trade routes through Central Asia. But it was the determination of the Europeans to make practical use of the discoveries of others that was

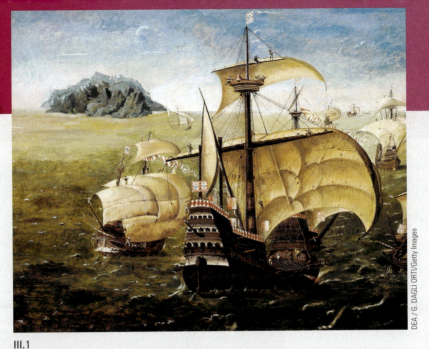

III.1

the decisive factor in the equation, thus enabling them to dominate international sea-lanes and ultimately to create vast colonial empires in the Western Hemisphere.

What explains the sudden explosion of Europe across the international scene? As with Arab expansion several hundred years previously, European expansion was not fueled solely by economic considerations but by religious motives as well. In the fifteenth century, the world of Christendom was in the midst of a major period of conflict with the forces of Islam, a rivalry that had been exacerbated by the conquest of the Byzantine Empire by the Ottoman Turks in 1453 (see Chapter 13). Although the claims of Portuguese and Spanish adventurers that their activities were motivated primarily by a desire to bring the word of God to non-Christian peoples certainly contained a considerable measure of hypocrisy, there seems no reason to doubt that religious motives played a meaningful role in the process, as King Manuel of Portugal's letter to his Spanish counterpart makes clear (see Historical Voices, "For God, Gold, and Glory in the Age of Exploration," in Chapter 14).

While Europe was on the cusp of a dynamic era of political, economic, and cultural expansion, conditions in other parts of the world were less conducive to such developments. In China, for example, the Ming Dynasty, after launching a major effort to extend its power and influence throughout the Indian Ocean in the early fifteenth century, suddenly abandoned the quest and turned inward. Smugly confident of its superiority to all potential rivals, it continued to rely on a prosperous agricultural sector as the economic foundation of the empire. In India and the Middle East, manufacturing and commerce had played a vital role in the life of societies since

the emergence of the Indian Ocean trade network in the first centuries C.E. But beginning in the eleventh century, the area had suffered through an extended period of political instability marked by invasions by nomadic peoples from Central Asia. Although the emergence of the Ottoman Empire and the rise to power of the Mughals in India signaled the revival of Islam as a major force within the region, the relative lack of interest shown by Ottoman and Mughal elites in manufacturing, technology, and commerce placed them as a significant disadvantage in their competition with Christian rivals.

In the early modern era, then, Europe was best placed to take advantage of the technological innovations that had become increasingly available as other regions were still beset by internal obstacles or had deliberately turned inward to seek their destiny. Europe now turned outward to seek a new and dominant position in the world. This does not imply, however, that significant changes were not taking place in other parts of the world as well, and many of these changes had relatively little to do with the situation in the West. As we shall see, the impact of European expansion on the rest of the world was still limited at the end of the eighteenth century. Though European political authority was firmly established in a few key areas such as the Spice Islands and Latin America, traditional societies remained relatively intact in most regions of Africa and Asia. And processes at work in these societies often operated independently of events in Europe and would later give birth to forces that acted to restrict or shape the Western impact. One of these forces was the progressive emergence of centralized states, some of them built on the concept of ethnic unity.

NEW ENCOUNTERS: THE CREATION OF A WORLD MARKET

Chapter Outline and Focus Questions

14-1 *An Age of Exploration and Expansion*

Q How did Muslim merchants expand the world trade network at the end of the fifteenth century? How did their achievements extend the era of commercial expansion that took place under the Mongols in the thirteenth and fourteenth centuries?

14-2 *The Portuguese Maritime Empire*

Q Why were the Portuguese so successful in taking over the spice trade? Why was their period of hegemony in Asia so brief?

14-3 *The Conquest of the "New World"*

Q How did Portugal and Spain acquire their empires in the Americas, and why were they so much more successful in setting down deep roots there than was the case in Asia?

14-4 *Africa in Transition*

Q What were the main features of the African slave trade, and what effects did European participation have on traditional African practices?

14-5 *Southeast Asia in the Era of the Spice Trade*

Q What were the main characteristics of Southeast Asian societies, and how were they affected by the coming of Islam and the Europeans?

William J. Duiker

14.1 The Vasco da Gama Pillar at Malindi

Critical Thinking

Q *Christopher Columbus has recently become a controversial figure in world history? Why do you think this is so, and how would you evaluate his contribution to the modern world?*

Connections to Today

Q *In hindsight, do you think that European explorers can be held accountable for transmitting Old World diseases to the peoples of the Western Hemisphere?*

IN THE SPRING OF 1498, when the Portuguese fleet arrived at the town of Calicut (KAL-ih-kuht) (now known as Kozhikode) on the western coast of India, the fleet commander Vasco da Gama (VAHSH-koh dah GAHM-uh) ordered a landing party to go ashore to contact local authorities. The first to greet them, a Muslim merchant from Tunisia, said, "May the Devil take thee! What brought thee hither?" "Christians and spices," replied the visitors. "A lucky venture, a lucky venture," replied the Muslim. "Plenty of rubies, plenty of emeralds! You owe great thanks to God, for having brought you to a country holding such riches!"[1]

Such words undoubtedly delighted the Portuguese, who explored the immediate vicinity of the town and soon convinced themselves that the local population appeared to be Christians originally converted by the apostle Thomas in the first century C.E. Although it later turned out that they were mistaken—the local faith was a form of Hinduism—their spirits were probably not seriously dampened because the conversion of the indigenous population was probably less important than gold and glory to sailors who had undergone considerable hardships to become the first Europeans since the ancient Greeks to sail across the Indian Ocean. They left two months later with a cargo of spices and the determination to return soon with a second and larger fleet.

Vasco da Gama's voyage to India inaugurated a period of European expansion into Asia that lasted several hundred years and had effects that are still felt today. His tiny fleet had rounded the Cape of Good Hope and sailed up the eastern coast of Africa, where his sailors encountered an Arab navigator in the port of Malindi who promised to take them across the Indian Ocean to seek the riches of Asia. To memorialize the occasion and mark the spot for their return voyage, the Portuguese erected a pillar of coral stone mounted by a cross that still stands on the site today (see the chapter-opening illustration).

Da Gama's voyage was a fateful one because it eventually led to a Western takeover of existing trade routes in the Indian Ocean and the establishment of colonies throughout the region, as well as in Africa and Latin America. In later years, Western historians would begin to describe the era as an "Age of Discovery" that significantly broadened the maritime trade network and set the stage for the emergence of the modern world.

As we now know, of course, the voyages of Vasco da Gama and his European successors were a discovery only in the sense that Europeans for the first time began to take part in a regional trade network that had existed for centuries and was already flourishing at a time when European maritime commerce was still essentially restricted to the Mediterranean Sea and the stormy waters of the North Atlantic Ocean. By that time, Chinese fleets had roamed the Indian Ocean and linked the Ming Empire with societies as distant as the Middle East and the coast of East Africa. Arab and Indian ships regularly passed between India, Southeast Asia, eastern Africa, and the Middle East, bringing goods from one part of the region to another. Elsewhere, Muslim caravans snaked across the Sahara Desert from the Mediterranean to the civilizations that flourished along the banks of the Niger River.

The Europeans, then, were not the trailblazers their chroniclers announced they were, but latecomers to the process. It was, after all, a Muslim from North Africa who greeted the Portuguese on their first appearance off the coast of India. In this chapter, we turn our attention to the stunning expansion in the scope and volume of commercial and cultural contacts that took place in the generations preceding and following da Gama's historic voyage to India as well as the factors that brought about this expansion.

14-1 AN AGE OF EXPLORATION AND EXPANSION

Q **Focus Questions:** How did Muslim merchants expand the world trade network at the end of the fifteenth century? How did their achievements extend the era of commercial expansion that took place under the Mongols in the thirteenth and fourteenth centuries?

Western historians have customarily regarded the voyage of Vasco da Gama as a crucial step in the opening of trade routes to the East. This view has merit in the sense that the voyage was a harbinger of future European participation in the spice trade and that a new maritime route between the Atlantic and the Indian Oceans had been discovered. In fact, however, the Indian Ocean had been a busy thoroughfare for centuries. The spice trade had been carried on by sea in the region since the days of the legendary Queen of Sheba, and Chinese junks had sailed to the area in search of cloves and nutmeg since the Tang Dynasty (see Chapter 10).

14-1a Islam and the Spice Trade

For centuries, Arabs or Indian converts to Islam had also taken part in the Indian Ocean trade, and by the thirteenth century Islam had established a presence in seaports on the islands of Sumatra and Java. In 1292, Venetian traveler Marco Polo observed that Muslims were engaging in missionary activity in Sumatra: "This kingdom is so much frequented by the Saracen merchants that they have converted the natives to the Law of Mahomet—I mean the townspeople only, for the hill people live for all the world like beasts, and eat human flesh, as well as other kinds of flesh, clean or unclean."[2]

But the major impetus for the spread of Islam in Southeast Asia came in the early fifteenth century with the foundation of a new sultanate at Malacca (muh-LAK-uh) on the strait that now bears that name. The founder was Paramesvara (pahr-uh-muss-VAHR-uh), a vassal of the Hindu state of Majapahit (mah-jah-PAH-hit) on Java. Paramesvara's previous base of operations had been at Tumasik (tuh-MAH-sik) (modern Singapore) at the tip of the Malay Peninsula, but in 1390 he moved his base to Malacca to take advantage of its strategic location (see Map 14.1). As a sixteenth-century visitor from Portugal would observe, Malacca "is a city that was made for commerce; . . . the trade and commerce between the different nations for a thousand leagues on every hand must come to Malacca."[3]

Shortly after its founding, Malacca was visited by a Chinese fleet under the command of Admiral Zheng He (see Chapter 10). To protect his patrimony from local rivals, Paramesvara accepted Chinese vassalage and cemented the new relationship by making an official visit to the Ming emperor in Beijing. Later, he converted to Islam, a move that enhanced Malacca's ability to participate in the trade that passed through the strait, much of which was dominated by Muslim merchants. Within a few years, Malacca had become the leading economic power in the region and helped promote the spread of Islam to trading ports throughout the islands of Southeast Asia.

Map 14.1 The Strait of Malacca

eventually appeared: the empire of Songhai (song-GY). Its founder was Sonni Ali, a local chieftain who seized Timbuktu from its Berber overlords in 1468 and then sought to restore the formidable empire of his predecessors. Under his rule, Songhai emerged as a major trading state (see Map 14.2).

Shortly after Sonni Ali's death in 1492, one of his military commanders seized power as king under the name Askia Mohammed (r. 1493–1528). While Sonni Ali had been criticized by Muslim scholars for supporting traditional religious practices, the new ruler, a fervent Muslim, increasingly relied on Islamic institutions and ideology to strengthen national unity and centralize authority. After his return from a pilgrimage to Mecca, Askia Mohammed tried to revive Timbuktu as a major center of Islamic learning, although many of his subjects—especially in rural areas—continued to resist conversion to Islam. During his rule, trans-Saharan trade (the exchange of gold for salt) greatly increased, providing a steady source of income to Songhai (see Historical Voices, "The Great City of Timbuktu," p. 345). After Mohammed's death, however, centrifugal forces within Songhai eventually led to its breakup. In 1591,

14-1b The Spread of Islam in West Africa

In the meantime, Muslim commercial and religious influence continued to expand south of the Sahara into the Niger River Valley in West Africa. Muslim traders—first Arabs and later African converts—crossed the desert carrying Islamic values, political culture, and legal traditions along with their goods.

The Empire of Songhai The early stage of state formation in Africa had culminated with the kingdom of Mali under the renowned Mansa Musa (see Chapter 8). With the decline of Mali in the late fifteenth century, a new power

Map 14.2 The Songhai Empire. Songhai was the last of the great states to dominate the region of the Niger River Valley before the European takeover in the nineteenth century.

Q *What were the predecessors of the Songhai Empire in the region? What explains the importance of the area in African history?*

The Great City of Timbuktu

Interaction & Exchange

AFTER ITS FOUNDING IN THE TWELFTH CENTURY, Timbuktu became a great center of Islamic learning and a fabled city of mystery and riches to Europeans. In the sixteenth century, Timbuktu was still a major commercial center on the trade route through the Sahara. This description of the city was written in 1526 by Leo Africanus, a Muslim from the Islamic state of Granada and one of the great travelers of his time.

Leo Africanus, *History and Description of Africa*

Here are many shops of artificers and merchants, and especially of such as weave linen and cotton cloth. And hither do the Barbary merchants bring cloth of Europe. All the women of this region, except the maid-servants, go with their faces covered, and sell all necessary victuals. The inhabitants, and especially strangers there residing, are exceeding rich, insomuch that the king that now is, married both his daughters to rich merchants. Here are many wells containing sweet water; and so often as the river Niger overfloweth, they convey the water thereof by certain sluices into the town. Corn, cattle, milk, and butter this region yieldeth in great abundance: but salt is very scarce here; for it is brought hither by land from Taghaza which is 500 miles distant. When I myself was here, I saw one camel's load of salt sold for 80 ducats. The rich king of Timbuktu hath many plates and scepters of gold, some whereof weigh 1,300 pounds: and he keeps a magnificent and well-furnished court. When he travelleth any whither he rideth upon a camel which is led by some of his noblemen; and so he doth likewise when he goeth forth to warfare, and all his soldiers ride upon horses. Whoever will speak unto this king must first fall down before his feet, and then taking up earth must first sprinkle it upon his own head and shoulders: which custom is ordinarily observed by . . . ambassadors from other princes. He hath always 3,000 horsemen, and a number of footmen that shoot poisoned arrows, attending upon him. They have often skirmishes with those that refuse to pay tribute, and so many as they take, they sell unto the merchants of Timbuktu. . . . Here are great store of doctors, judges, priests, and other learned men, that are bountifully maintained at the king's cost and charges, and hither are brought divers manuscripts or written books out of Barbary, which are sold for more money than any other merchandise. The coin of Timbuktu is of gold without any stamp or superscription but in matters of small value they use certain shells brought hither out of the kingdom of Persia. . . . The inhabitants are people of gentle and cheerful disposition, and spend a great part of the night singing and dancing through all the streets of the city.

Q *What role did the city of Timbuktu play in regional commerce, according to this author? What were the chief means of payment?*

Source: From *The History and Description of Africa,* by Leo Africanus (New York: Burt Franklin).

Moroccan forces armed with firearms conquered the city to gain control over the gold trade in the region. At this point, Timbuktu and the trade route that enabled its rise began a long period of decline.

14-1c A New Player: Europe

The rise of Songhai in the mid-fifteenth century coincided with the appearance of a new competitor in the region. Europeans had long been attracted to the East. Myths and legends of an exotic land of great riches were widespread in the Middle Ages, largely sparked by the dramatic account of adventurer Marco Polo. But the conquests of the Ottoman Turks in Anatolia andthe Mediterranean Sea temporarily reduced Western traffic to the East. With the closing of the overland routes, many Europeans became interested in the possibility of reaching Asia by sea.

As we saw in Chapter 13, by the mid-fifteenth century Europe was in the process of recovering from the turmoil of the recent past. A new spirit of adventure and confidence combined with political consolidation and a vigorous economic recovery stimulated Europeans' desires to look for wealth and trading opportunities beyond their frontiers. As one Spanish conquistador (kahn-KEES-tuh-dor) explained, he and his kind went to the Americas to "serve God and His Majesty, to give light to those who were in darkness, and to grow rich, as all men desire to do."[4]

The desire for economic gain was supplemented by a renewed spirit of rivalry between the worlds of Christendom and Islam. The Ottoman seizure of the great city of Constantinople in 1453 sent shock waves

14.2 The City of Timbuktu. Timbuktu sat astride one of the major trade routes that passed through the Sahara between the kingdoms of West Africa and the Mediterranean Sea. Caravans transported food and various manufactured articles southward in exchange for salt, gold, copper, skins, agricultural goods, and slaves. Salt was at such a premium in Timbuktu that a young Moroccan wrote in 1513 that one camel's load brought 500 miles by caravan sold for 80 gold ducats, while a horse sold for only 40 ducats. Timbuktu became a prosperous city and a great center of Islamic scholarship. By 1550, it had three universities connected to its principal mosques and 180 Qur'anic schools. This pen-and-ink sketch was done by French traveler Rene Caillie in 1828 when the city was long past its peak of prosperity and renown.

readings, the portolani proved of great value for voyages in European waters. Unfortunately, because they were drawn on a flat surface and did not account for Earth's curvature, they were of little use for longer overseas voyages. Only when seafarers began to venture beyond the coasts of Europe did they begin to accumulate information about the actual shape of the earth and how to measure it.

By the end of the fifteenth century, cartography had developed to the point that Europeans possessed fairly accurate knowledge of the known world. Portuguese sailors venturing into the North Atlantic opened the process by discovering that circular wind patterns enabled them to tack against the wind and eventually return to their home ports. In addition, Europeans had developed remarkably seaworthy ships as well as new navigational techniques. Shipbuilders had mastered the use of the sternpost rudder, an import from China, and learned how to combine the use of lateen sails with a square rig. With these innovations, they could construct **caravels** (KER-uh-velz),

throughout Europe and provoked a growing desire for military action to prevent the Mediterranean from becoming "a Muslim lake." A European takeover of the spice routes from Asia would not only result in massive profits to merchants and adventurers but also undercut the growing power of Islam and open the door for missionary efforts to convert the heathen masses of Asia to Christianity. Christian zealots had long dreamed of spreading the word of the Gospel beyond the bounds of Europe to Africa, the Middle East, and elsewhere. With the opening of the Age of Exploration, the opportunity beckoned (see Historical Voices, "For God, Gold, and Glory in the Age of Exploration," p. 347).

The Means If "Christians and spices" were the primary motives, as Vasco da Gama allegedly contended, what made the voyages possible? By the end of the fifteenth century European states had a level of knowledge and technology that enabled them to regularly engage in voyages beyond Europe. Although the highly schematic and symbolic maps popular in the medieval era (see Chapter 7) were of little help to sailors, detailed charts drawn by navigators and mathematicians and known as *portolani* (pohr-tuh-LAH-nee) were more useful. With detailed information on coastal contours, distances between ports, and compass

ships mobile enough to sail against the wind and engage in naval warfare and also large enough to be armed with heavy cannons and carry substantial amounts of goods (see Image 14.3). In addition, new navigational aids such as the compass (a Chinese invention) and the astrolabe (an instrument adapted by Arab sailors from Greek examples that measured the altitude of the sun and the stars above the horizon) enabled sailors to explore the high seas with confidence.

14-2 THE PORTUGUESE MARITIME EMPIRE

Q Focus Questions: Why were the Portuguese so successful in taking over the spice trade? Why was their period of hegemony in Asia so brief?

Portugal took the lead in exploration when it began exploring the coast of Africa under the sponsorship of Prince Henry the Navigator (1394–1460), who hoped to find an ally against the Muslims and acquire new trade opportunities for Portugal. In 1419, he founded a school for navigators; shortly thereafter, Portuguese fleets began probing

For God, Gold, and Glory in the Age of Exploration

 Interaction & Exchange

MUCH HAS BEEN WRITTEN BY MODERN HISTORIANS about the motives behind the European Age of Exploration. Some researchers stress the desire for fame and riches, while others point to the importance of the missionary effort to spread the message of Christianity. As this letter from King Manuel of Portugal to the king and queen of Castile suggests, the motives for European expansion were not always subject to simple interpretation. As the slogan often voiced by participants in the Spanish conquest of the Americas suggests, the motives behind the process were a complex mixture of "God, Gold, and Glory," and not necessarily in that order.

Letter from King Manuel of Portugal

Your Highnesses already know that we had ordered Vasco da Gama, a nobleman of our household, and his brother Paulo da Gama, with four vessels to make discoveries by sea, and that two years have now elapsed since their departure. And as the principal motive of this enterprise has been . . . the service of God our Lord . . . it pleased Him in His mercy to speed them on their route. From a message which has now been brought to this city by one of the captains, we learn that they did reach and discover India and other kingdoms and lordships bordering upon it; that they entered and navigated its sea, finding large cities, large edifices and rivers, and great populations, among whom is carried on all the trade in spices and precious stones, which are forwarded in ships . . . to Mecca, and thence to Cairo, whence they are dispersed throughout the world. Of these they have brought a quantity, including cinnamon, cloves, ginger, nutmeg, and pepper . . . also many fine stones of all sorts, such as rubies and others.

And they also came to a country in which there are mines of gold, of which, as of the spices and precious stones, they did not bring as much as they could have done, for they took no merchandise with them.

As we are aware that your Highnesses will hear of these things with much pleasure and satisfaction, we thought well to give this information. And your Highnesses may believe, in accordance with what we have learnt concerning the Christian people whom these explorers reached, that it will be possible, notwithstanding that they are not as yet strong in the faith or possessed of a thorough knowledge of it, to do much in the service of God and the exaltation of the Holy Faith, once they shall have been converted and fully fortified in it. And when they shall have thus been fortified in the faith there will be an opportunity for destroying the Moors of those parts. Moreover, we hope, with the help of God, that the great trade which now enriches the Moors of those parts, through whose hands it passes without the intervention of other persons or peoples, shall, in consequence of our regulations be diverted to the natives and ships of our own kingdom, so that henceforth all Christendom, in this part of Europe, shall be able , in a large measure, to provide itself with these spices and precious stones. . . . This . . . will cause our designs and intentions to be pushed with more ardour . . . the war upon the Moors of the territories conquered by us in these parts. . . .

Q *Based on what you have learned in this chapter, how would you rate the various motives for European expansion as identified in this document?*

Source: Letter from King Manuel of Portugal to their Highnesses Ferdinand and Isabella of Castile, from *A Journal of the First Voyage of Vasco da Gama, 1497–1499* (London: Hakluyt Society, 1898), tr. E.G. Ravenstein, pp. 113–114, and cited in Nigel Cliff, *The Last Crusade: The Epic Voyages of Vasco da Gama* (New York: Harper, 2011), pp. 277–278.

---

southward along the western coast of Africa in search of gold. In 1441, Portuguese ships reached the Senegal River just north of Cape Verde. They found no gold but brought home a cargo of black Africans, most of whom were sold as slaves to wealthy buyers elsewhere in Europe. Within a few years, an estimated thousand slaves were shipped annually from the area back to Lisbon.

Continuing southward, in 1471 the Portuguese discovered a new source of gold along the southern coast of the hump of West Africa, where they leased land from local rulers and built forts along what would henceforth be labeled the Gold Coast.

14-2a En Route to India

Hearing reports of a route to India around the southern tip of Africa, Portuguese sea captains continued their probing. In 1487, Bartolomeu Dias (bar-toh-loh-MAY-oo

14.3 The Caravel, Workhorse of the Age of Exploration. Before the fifteenth century, most European ships were either small craft with triangular, lateen sails used in the Mediterranean or slow, unwieldy square-rigged vessels operating in the North Atlantic. By the sixteenth century, European naval architects began to build caravels that combined the maneuverability and speed offered by lateen sails (widely used by sailors in the Indian Ocean) with the carrying capacity and seaworthiness of the square-riggers. For a century, caravels were the feared "raiders of the oceans." Eventually, as naval technology progressed, the carrack, a larger European warship with greater firepower and both lateen and square-rigged sails, became used (see the Part Opener, p. 338).

DEE-uhs) rounded the Cape of Good Hope but returned home without continuing onward because he feared his crew was about to mutiny. Ten years later, a fleet under the command of Vasco da Gama rounded the cape and stopped at several ports controlled by Muslim merchants along the coast of East Africa, including Sofala, Kilwa, and Mombasa. Then da Gama's fleet crossed the Arabian Sea and arrived at Calicut on the Indian coast on May 18, 1498. The Portuguese crown had sponsored the voyage with the clear objective of destroying the Muslim monopoly over the spice trade, which had intensified since the Ottoman conquest of Constantinople in 1453 (see Chapter 13). Calicut was a major entrepôt on the route from the Spice Islands to the Mediterranean, but the ill-informed Europeans believed it was the source of the spices themselves (see Map 14.3). Da Gama returned to Europe with a cargo of ginger and cinnamon that earned the investors a profit of several thousand percent.

14-2b The Search for the Source of Spices

Encouraged by the results of Vasco da Gama's maiden voyage, the Portuguese set out to gain control of the spice trade. In 1510, Admiral

Map 14.3 The Spice Islands

Afonso de Albuquerque (ah-FAHN-soh day AL-buh-kur-kee) established his headquarters at Goa (GOH-uh), on India's western coast. From there, the Portuguese raided Arab shippers, provoking the following comment from an Arab source: "[The Portuguese] took about seven vessels, killing those on board and making some prisoner. This was their first action, may God curse them."[5] In 1511, Albuquerque seized Malacca and put the local Muslim population to the sword. Control of Malacca not only provided the Portuguese with a way station en route to the Spice Islands, which are known today as the Moluccas (muh-LUHK-uhz), but also gave them a means to disrupt the Arab spice trade network by blocking passage through the Strait of Malacca.

From Malacca, the Portuguese sent expeditions farther east to China in 1514 and the Spice Islands. There they signed a treaty with a local sultan for the purchase of cloves for the European market. Within a few years, they had managed to seize control of the spice trade from Muslim traders and had garnered substantial profits for the Portuguese monarchy.

Why were the Portuguese so successful? Basically, their success was a matter of guns and seamanship. The Portuguese by no means possessed a monopoly on the use of firearms and explosives, but they used the maneuverability of their light ships to maintain their distance while bombarding the enemy with their powerful cannons. Such tactics gave them a military superiority over lightly armed rivals that they were able to exploit until the arrival of other European forces several decades later.

14-2c New Rivals Enter the Scene

Portugal's efforts to dominate the trade of the Indian Ocean were never entirely successful, however. The Portuguese lacked both the numbers and the wealth to overcome local resistance and colonize Asian regions. Moreover, their massive investments in ships and laborers for their empire (hundreds of ships and hundreds of thousands of workers in shipyards and overseas bases) proved extremely costly. The empire was simply too large and Portugal too small to maintain it, and by the end of the sixteenth century, the Portuguese were being severely challenged by both local rivals and new entrants on the scene.

The Spanish First on the scene was Spain. Queen Isabella had already signaled her intent to enter the competition in 1492 when she sponsored the voyage of Christopher Columbus into the Atlantic Ocean in search of a westward route to the Indies. That led to a dispute between the two Iberian nations over the rights to newly conquered territories. In 1494, the Treaty of Tordesillas (tor-day-SEE-yass) divided the newly discovered world into separate Portuguese and Spanish spheres of influence. Thereafter, the route east around the Cape of Good Hope was reserved for the Portuguese, while the route across the Atlantic (except for the eastern hump of South America) was assigned to Spain (see Map 14.4).

Eventually convinced that the lands Columbus had reached were not the Indies but an unknown land that possessed its own attractions, the Spanish continued to seek a route to the Spice Islands. In 1519, a Spanish fleet under the command of Portuguese sea captain Ferdinand Magellan sailed around the southern tip of South America, proceeded across the Pacific Ocean, and landed in the Philippine Islands. Although Magellan and some forty of his crew were killed in a skirmish with the local population, one of the two remaining ships sailed on to the Moluccas and thence around the world via the Cape of Good Hope. In the words of a contemporary historian, they arrived in Cádiz "with precious cargo and fifteen men surviving out of a fleet of five sail."[6]

As it turned out, the Spanish could not follow up on Magellan's accomplishment, and in 1529 they sold their rights in the Moluccas to the Portuguese. But Magellan's voyage was not a total loss because Spain soon managed

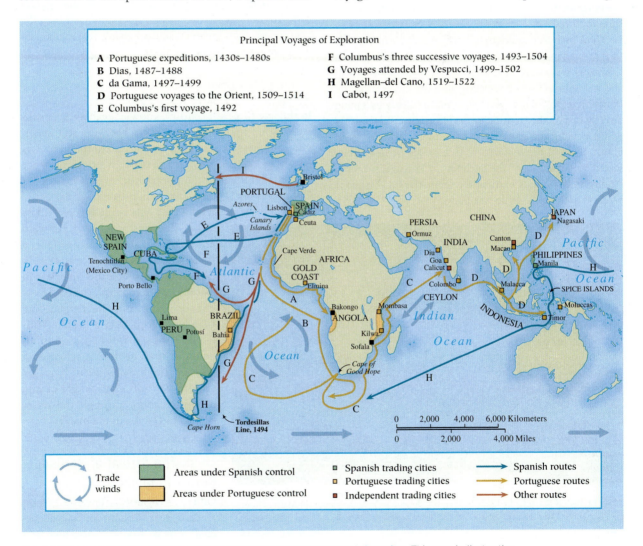

Principal Voyages of Exploration

A Portuguese expeditions, 1430s–1480s
B Dias, 1487–1488
C da Gama, 1497–1499
D Portuguese voyages to the Orient, 1509–1514
E Columbus's first voyage, 1492
F Columbus's three successive voyages, 1493–1504
G Voyages attended by Vespucci, 1499–1502
H Magellan–del Cano, 1519–1522
I Cabot, 1497

Trade winds

Areas under Spanish control
Areas under Portuguese control

Spanish trading cities
Portuguese trading cities
Independent trading cities

Spanish routes
Portuguese routes
Other routes

Map 14.4 European Voyages and Possessions in the Sixteenth and Seventeenth Centuries. This map indicates the most important voyages launched by Europeans during their momentous Age of Exploration in the sixteenth and seventeenth centuries.

Q *Why did Vasco da Gama sail so far into the South Atlantic on his voyage to Asia?*

to consolidate its control over the Philippines, which eventually became a major base in the carrying trade across the Pacific. Spanish galleons made use of the Pacific trade winds to carry silk and other luxury goods to Acapulco in exchange for silver from the mines of Mexico.

The English and the Dutch   The primary threat to the Portuguese toehold in Southeast Asia, however, came from the English and the Dutch. In 1591, the first English expedition to the Indies through the Indian Ocean returned to London with a cargo of pepper. Nine years later, a private joint stock enterprise, the East India Company, was founded to provide a stable source of capital for future voyages. In 1608, an English fleet landed at Surat (SOOR-et) on the northwestern coast of India. Trade with Southeast Asia soon followed.

The Dutch were quick to follow suit, and the first Dutch fleet arrived in India in 1595. In 1602, the Dutch East India Company was established under government sponsorship and was soon actively competing with the English and the Portuguese. In 1611, a Dutch fleet made history by sailing directly east on the "roaring forties" (the powerful westerly winds circling the globe at that southern latitude) from South Africa to the Indonesian Archipelago. In 1641, they seized Malacca, one of the linchpins of Portugal's trading empire in Asia, thus earning for themselves a dominant position in the spice trade (see Image 14.4).

14.4 The Port of Malacca in 1726. In 1641, the Dutch took over the seaport of Malacca from the Portuguese. Over the next several decades, the new owners gradually replaced their Catholic rivals in controlling the spice trade between Europe and the Indies. One of the most prominent chroniclers of this process was Dutch naturalist and author Francis Valentijn. Born in 1666, he spent many years in the Dutch East Indies and wrote a highly respected study of the Indonesian archipelago. His engraving of Malacca, shown here with European ships floating in the harbor, appeared shortly before his death in 1727. In the early nineteenth century, Malacca was ceded by treaty to Great Britain.

Photograph by William J. Duiker/Engraving of the city of Malacca by Francis Valentijn

14-3 THE CONQUEST OF THE "NEW WORLD"

Q | **Focus Question:** How did Portugal and Spain acquire their empires in the Americas, and why were they so much more successful in setting down deep roots there than was the case in Asia?

While the Portuguese were seeking access to the spice trade by sailing eastward through the Indian Ocean, the Spanish attempted to reach the same destination by sailing westward across the Atlantic. Although the Spanish came to overseas discovery and exploration later than the Portuguese, their greater resources enabled them to establish a far grander overseas empire.

14-3a The Voyages

In the late fifteenth century, knowledgeable Europeans were aware that Earth was round but were still uncertain about its size and the extent of the continent of Asia (see Map 14.5). Convinced that Earth's circumference was smaller than contemporaries believed, Christopher Columbus (1451–1506), an Italian from Genoa, maintained that Asia could be reached by sailing due west instead of eastward around Africa. He persuaded Queen Isabella of Spain to finance an expedition, which reached the Americas in October 1492 and explored the coastline of Cuba and the neighboring island of Hispaniola (his-puhn-YOH-luh or ees-pahn-YAH-luh). Columbus believed that he had reached Asia and in three subsequent voyages (1493, 1498, and 1502) sought in vain to find a route through the outer islands to the Asian mainland.

14-3b The Arrival of Hernando Cortés in Mexico

Other navigators, however, soon realized that Columbus had discovered a new frontier altogether and joined the race to benefit from the opportunity. A Venetian, John Cabot, explored the New England coastline under a license from King Henry VII of England. While en route to Asia, Portuguese captain Pedro Cabral (PAY-droh kuh-BRAHL) accidentally discovered the continent of South America in 1500. Amerigo Vespucci (ahm-ay-REE-goh vess-POO-chee), a Florentine, accompanied Cabral's voyage and wrote a series of letters describing the lands he observed. The publication of these letters led to the name *America* (after Vespucci's first name) for the new lands.

Map 14.5 Cape Horn and the Strait of Magellan

14-3c The Conquests

The territories that Europeans referred to as the "New World" actually contained flourishing civilizations populated by millions of people. But the Americas were new to the Europeans, who quickly saw opportunities for conquest and exploitation. With Portugal clearly in the lead in the race to exploit the riches of the Indies, the importance of these lands was magnified in the minds of the Spanish.

The Spanish **conquistadors** (kahn-KEES-tu-dors), as they were called, were a hardy lot of adventurous individuals motivated by a typical sixteenth-century blend of glory, greed, and religious zeal. Their superior weapons, organizational skills, and determination brought the conquistadors incredible success in their new environment. In 1519, a Spanish expedition led by Hernando Cortés landed at Veracruz on the Gulf of Mexico. Marching to Tenochtitlán (teh-nahch-teet-LAHN) with a small contingent of troops, Cortés received a friendly welcome from the Aztec monarch Moctezuma Xocoyotzin (mahk-tuh-ZOO-muh shoh-koh-YAHT-seen) (often called *Montezuma*).

But tensions soon erupted between the Spaniards and the Aztecs. When the Spanish took Moctezuma hostage and began to destroy Aztec religious shrines, the local population revolted and drove the invaders from the city. Meanwhile, the Aztecs were beginning to suffer the

first effects of the diseases brought by the Europeans, which would eventually wipe out the majority of the local residents. With assistance from the state of Tlaxcallan (tuh-lah-SKAH-lahn), Cortés finally succeeded in vanquishing the Aztecs (see Comparative Illustration, "The Spaniards Conquer a New World," p. 352). Within months, their magnificent city and its temples, believed by the conquerors to be the work of Satan, had been destroyed.

A similar fate awaited the powerful Inka Empire in South America. Between 1531 and 1536, an expedition led by Francisco Pizarro (frahn-SEES-koh puh-ZAHR-oh) (1470–1541) destroyed Inka power high in the Peruvian Andes. Here, too, the Spanish conquests were undoubtedly facilitated by the previous arrival of European diseases, which had decimated the local population.

The Portuguese in Brazil Meanwhile, the Portuguese crown had established the colony of Brazil, basing its claim on the Treaty of Tordesillas, which had allocated the eastern coast of South America to the Portuguese

14.5 The Catholic Cathedral at Cuzco. After the total destruction of the Inka Empire, the Spanish conquistadors rebuilt the Inkan capital of Cuzco in their own image. Among the many changes that they implemented, the sacred Inkan pyramid in the heart of the city was dismantled and an impressive Spanish Baroque cathedral was erected on its base. As a final humiliation, many of the materials originally used for the pyramid were later put to use in building its replacement.

Carol C. Coffin

14.6a

The Spaniards Conquer a New World

Politics & Government

THE PERSPECTIVE THAT THE SPANISH BROUGHT to their arrival in the Americas was quite different from that of the indigenous peoples. In the European painting shown in Image 14.6a, the encounter was a peaceful one, and the upturned eyes of Columbus and his fellow voyagers imply that their motives were spiritual rather than material. Image 14.6b, drawn by an Aztec artist, expresses a dramatically different point of view, as the Spanish invaders, assisted by their Indian allies, use superior weapons against the bows and arrows of their adversaries to bring about the conquest of Mexico.

14.6b

 What does the Aztec painting presented here show the viewer about the nature of the conflict between the two contending armies?

sphere of influence. Like their Spanish rivals, the Portuguese initially saw their new colony as a source of gold and silver, but they soon discovered that profits could be made in other ways as well. A formal administrative system was instituted in Brazil in 1549, and Portuguese migrants arrived to establish plantations to produce sugar, coffee, and other tropical products for export to Europe.

14-3d Governing the Empires

As Portugal came to dominate Brazil, Spain established a colonial empire that included Central America, most of South America, and parts of North America. Within the lands of Central and South America, a new civilization arose that we have come to call *Latin America* (see Map 14.6).

The State and the Church in Colonial Latin America

In administering their colonial empires in the Americas, both Portugal and Spain tried to keep the most important posts of colonial government in the hands of Europeans (known as *peninsulares*). At the head of the Portuguese and the Spanish administrative pyramid was a **viceroy**. The Spanish created viceroyalties for New Spain (Mexico) in 1535 and for Peru in 1543. Viceroyalties were in turn subdivided into smaller units. All of the major government positions were held by Spaniards. For **creoles**—American-born descendants of Europeans—the chief opportunity to hold a government post was in city councils.

From the beginning, the Spanish and Portuguese rulers were determined to convert the indigenous peoples of the Americas to Christianity (see Film & History, *The Mission*, p. 354). Consequently, the Catholic Church played an important role in the colonies, building hospitals, orphanages, and schools to instruct the Indians in the rudiments of reading, writing, and arithmetic. To facilitate their efforts, missionaries often brought Indians to live in mission villages where they could be converted, taught trades, and encouraged to grow crops, all under the control of the church.

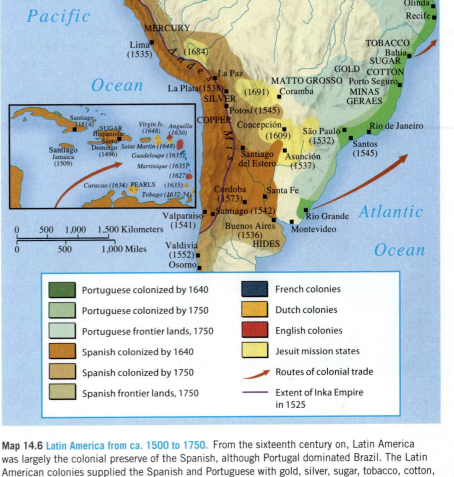

Map 14.6 Latin America from ca. 1500 to 1750. From the sixteenth century on, Latin America was largely the colonial preserve of the Spanish, although Portugal dominated Brazil. The Latin American colonies supplied the Spanish and Portuguese with gold, silver, sugar, tobacco, cotton, and animal hides.

Q *How do you explain the ability of Europeans to dominate such large areas of Latin America?*

For women in the colonies, Catholic nunneries provided outlets other than marriage. Women in religious orders, many of them of aristocratic background, often operated outside their establishments by running schools and hospitals. The nun Sor Juana Inés de la Cruz (SAWR HWAH-nuh ee-NAYSS day lah KROOZ) (1651–1695), who became one of seventeenth-century Latin America's best-known literary figures, wrote poetry and prose and urged that women be educated.

Exploiting the Riches of the Americas   Economic exploitation was the prime purpose of Spanish and Portuguese rule in the Americas. One source of wealth came from the gold and silver the Europeans sought so avidly. One Aztec observer commented that the Spanish conquerors "longed and lusted for gold. Their bodies swelled with greed, and their hunger was ravenous; they hungered like pigs for that gold."[7] Rich silver deposits were exploited in Mexico and southern Peru (modern Bolivia). Between 1503 and 1650, an estimated 16 million kilograms (17,500 tons) of silver and 185,000 kilograms (200 tons) of gold entered the port of Seville in Spain.

In the long run, however, agriculture proved to be more rewarding. The American colonies became sources of raw materials for Spain and Portugal as sugar, tobacco, chocolate, precious woods, animal hides, and other natural products made their way to Europe. In turn, the mother countries supplied their colonists with manufactured goods. Both Spain and Portugal closely regulated the trade of their American colonies to keep others out, but the English and the French eventually became too powerful to be excluded from this lucrative market (see Map 14.7).

To produce these goods, colonial authorities initially tried to rely on local sources of human labor. Spanish policy toward the Indians was a combination of misguided paternalism and cruel exploitation. Queen Isabella declared the Indians to be subjects of Castile and instituted the **encomienda system**, under which European settlers received grants of land and could collect tribute from the indigenous peoples and use them as laborers. In return, the holders of an *encomienda* (en-koh-MYEN-duh) were supposed to protect the Indians and supervise their spiritual and material needs. In practice, this meant that the settlers were free to implement the system as they pleased. Spanish settlers largely ignored their distant government and brutally used the Indians to pursue their own economic interests. Indians were put to work on sugar plantations and in gold and silver mines.

Forced labor, starvation, and especially disease took a fearful toll on Indian lives. With little or no natural resistance to European diseases, the Indians were ravaged by smallpox, measles, and typhus brought by the Europeans. Although estimates vary, in some areas at least half of the local population probably died of European diseases. In 1542, largely in response to the publications of Bartolomé de Las Casas (bahr-toh-loh-MAY day lahs KAH-sahs), the government abolished the encomienda system and provided more protection for the Indians (see Opposing Viewpoints, "The March of Civilization," p. 355). By then, however, the indigenous population had been decimated by disease, causing the Spanish and eventually the Portuguese to import African slaves to replace Indians in the sugar fields.

14-3e The Competition Intensifies

The success of the Spanish and the Portuguese in exploiting the riches of the Americas soon attracted competition from other European states. In 1607, the English established their first permanent colony at Jamestown near the mouth of the Chesapeake Bay, and other settlements appeared shortly afterward. Within a few years other European states had followed suit and soon occupied much of the eastern seaboard of North America.

The March of Civilization

Interaction & Exchange

AS EUROPEANS BEGAN TO EXPLORE new parts of the world in the fifteenth century, they were convinced that it was their duty to introduce civilized ways to the heathen peoples they encountered. This attitude is reflected in the first selection, which describes the Spanish captain Vasco Núñez de Balboa (BAHS-koh NOON-yez day bal-BOH-uh) in 1513, when from a hill on the Isthmus of Panama he first laid eyes on the Pacific Ocean.

Bartolomé de Las Casas (1474–1566) was a Dominican monk who participated in the conquest of Cuba and received land and Indians in return for his efforts. But in 1514, he underwent a radical transformation that led him to believe that the Indians had been cruelly mistreated by his fellow Spaniards. He spent the remaining years of his life fighting for the Indians. The second selection is taken from his most influential work, *Brevísima Relación de la Destrucción de las Indias,* known to English readers as *The Tears of the Indians.* This work was largely responsible for the reputation of the Spanish conquistadors as cruel and murderous fanatics.

Gonzalo Fernández de Ovieda, *Historia General y Natural de las Indias*

On Tuesday, the twenty-fifth of September of the year 1513, at ten o'clock in the morning, Captain Vasco Núñez, having gone ahead of his company, climbed a hill with a bare summit, and from the top of this hill saw the South Sea. Of all the Christians in his company, he was the first to see it. He turned back toward his people, full of joy, lifting his hands and his eyes to Heaven, praising Jesus Christ and his glorious Mother the Virgin, Our Lady. Then he fell upon his knees on the ground and gave great thanks to God for the mercy He had shown him, in allowing him to discover that sea, and thereby to render so great a service to God and to the most serene Catholic Kings of Castile, our sovereigns . . . .

And he told all the people with him to kneel also, to give the same thanks to God, and to beg Him fervently to allow them to see and discover the secrets and great riches of that sea and coast, for the greater glory and increase of the Christian faith, for the conversion of the Indians, natives of those southern regions, and for the fame and prosperity of the royal throne of Castile and of its sovereigns present and to come. All the people cheerfully and willingly did as they were bidden; and the Captain made them fell a big tree and make from it a tall cross, which they erected in that same place, at the top of the hill from which the South Sea had first been seen.

Bartolomé de Las Casas, *The Tears of the Indians*

There is nothing more detestable or more cruel than the tyranny which the Spaniards use toward the Indians for the getting of pearl. Surely the infernal torments cannot much exceed the anguish that they endure, by reason of that way of cruelty; for they put them under water some four or five ells deep, where they are forced without any liberty of respiration, to gather up the shells wherein the Pearls are; sometimes they come up again with nets full of shells to take breath, but if they stay any while to rest themselves, immediately comes a hangman row'd in a little boat, who as soon as he hath well beaten them, drags them again to their labor. Their food is nothing but filth, and the very same that contains the Pearl, with small portion of that bread which that Country affords; in the first whereof there is little nourishment; and as for the latter, it is made with great difficulty, besides that they have not enough of that neither for sustenance; they lie upon the ground in fetters, lest they should run away; and many times they are drown'd in this labor, and are never seen again till they swim upon the top of the waves; oftentimes they also are devoured by certain sea monsters, that are frequent in those seas. Consider whether this hard usage of the poor creatures be consistent with the precepts which God commands concerning charity to our neighbor. . . .

Q *Can the sentiments expressed by Vasco Núñez be reconciled with the treatment accorded to the Indians as described by Las Casas? Which selection do you think better describes the behavior of the Spaniards in the Americas?*

Source: From *The Age of Reconnaissance* by J. H. Parry (International Thomson Publishing, 1969), pp. 233–234. From *The Tears of the Indians,* Bartolomé de Las Casas. Copyright © 1970 by The John Lilburne Company Publishers.

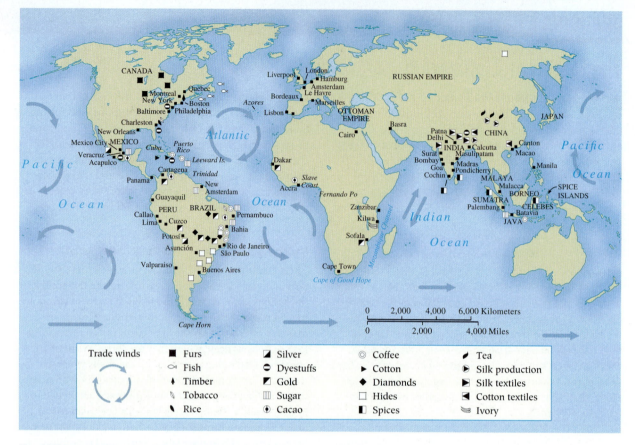

Map 14.7 Patterns of World Trade Between 1500 and 1800. This map shows the major products that were traded by European merchants throughout the world during the era of European exploration.

Q *What were the primary sources of gold and silver so sought after by Columbus and his successors?*

But the main arena of competition was farther to the south, where the lure of profits from the sugar trade was difficult to resist. By the end of the seventeenth century, several European nations competed actively for control of the islands of the Caribbean Sea, where sugar plantations were producing fabulous profits for their owners. Several islands shifted control several times during the course of the seventeenth and eighteenth centuries (see Chronology, "Spanish and Portuguese Activities in the Americas").

CHRONOLOGY	Spanish and Portuguese Activities in the Americas
Christopher Columbus's first voyage to the Americas	1492
Portuguese fleet arrives in Brazil	1500
Columbus's last voyages	1502–1504
Spanish conquest of Mexico	1519–1522
Francisco Pizarro's conquest of the Inkas	1531–1536
Viceroyalty of New Spain established	1535
Formal colonial administrative system established in Brazil	1549

HISTORIANS DEBATE 14-3f **Christopher Columbus: Hero or Villain?**

For centuries, explorer Christopher Columbus has generally been viewed in a positive light. By discovering the Western Hemisphere, he opened up the world and laid the foundations for the modern global economy. Recently, however, some historians have challenged the prevailing image of Columbus as a heroic figure and view him as a symbol of European colonial repression and a prime mover in the virtual extinction of the peoples and cultures of the Americas (see Comparative Essay, "The Columbian Exchange," p. 357).

The Columbian Exchange

Interaction & Exchange In the Western world, the discovery of the Americas has traditionally been viewed as a positive development, the first step in a process that expanded the global trade network and eventually led to increased economic well-being and the spread of civilization throughout the world. In recent years, however, that view has been sharply attacked by observers who point out that the primary legacy of the European conquest for the peoples of the Americas was not improved living standards but harsh colonial exploitation and the spread of pestilential diseases that devastated local populations.

Certainly, the record of European conquistadors leaves much to be desired, and the voyages of Columbus did not universally benefit his contemporaries or later generations. They not only destroyed vibrant civilizations in the Americas but also led to the enslavement of millions of Africans, who were separated from their families and shipped to a far-off world in deplorable, inhumane conditions.

But to focus solely on the evils committed in the name of exploration and civilization misses a larger point and obscures the long-term ramifications of the events taking place. The age of European expansion that began in the fifteenth century was only the latest in a series of population movements that included the spread of nomadic peoples across Central Asia and the expansion of Islam out of the Middle East after the death of the prophet Muhammad. In fact, the migration of peoples in search of a better livelihood has been a central theme in the evolution of the human race since the dawn of prehistory. Virtually all of the migrations involved acts of unimaginable cruelty and the forcible displacement of peoples and societies.

In retrospect, the consequences of such broad population movements are too complex to be summed up in moral or ideological simplifications. The Mongol invasions and the expansion of Islam are two examples of movements that brought benefits as well as costs for the peoples who were affected. By the same token, the European conquest of the Americas not only brought the destruction of cultures and dangerous new diseases but also initiated the exchange of plant and animal species that have ultimately fed millions and been of widespread benefit to peoples throughout the globe. The introduction of the horse, the cow, and various grain crops vastly increased food production in the Americas. The cultivation of corn, manioc, and potato, all products of the Western Hemisphere, has had the same effect in Asia, Africa, and Europe. The **Columbian Exchange**, as it is sometimes labeled, has had far-reaching consequences that transcend facile moral judgments.

The opening of the Americas had other long-term ramifications as well. The importation of vast amounts of gold and silver into Europe was a crucial factor in the growth of commercial capitalism that helped finance the Industrial Revolution and set the stage for the modern global economy (see Chapter 19).

Viewed in that context, the Columbian Exchange, whatever its moral failings, ultimately brought tangible benefits to peoples throughout the world. For some, the costs were high, and it can be argued that the indigenous peoples of the Americas might have better managed the transformation on their own. But the "iron law" of history operates at its own speed and does not wait for laggards. For good or ill, the Columbian Exchange marked a major stage in the transition between the traditional and the modern world.

14.7 **A Sugar Plantation.** For African slaves brought to the Americas, few occupations were as murderous and dehumanizing as the work on the sugar plantations. Shown here, slaves on the island of Hispaniola are cutting the cane to prepare it for transformation into cane sugar.

The Granger Collection, NYC

Q *How can the costs and benefits of the Columbian Exchange be measured? What standards would you apply in attempting to measure them?*

As we have seen, the immediate consequences of Columbus's voyages were tragic for many of the indigenous peoples. Columbus himself viewed those whom he encountered with condescension, describing them as naíve innocents who could be exploited to increase the wealth and power of Spain. As a consequence, his men frequently treated the local population brutally.

But is it fair to blame Columbus for possessing many of the character traits and prejudices common to his era? To do so is to demand that an individual transcend the limitations of his time and adopt the values of a future generation. Perhaps it is better to note simply that Columbus and his contemporaries showed relatively little understanding and sympathy for the cultural values of peoples who lived beyond the borders of their own civilization, a limitation that would probably apply to one degree or another to all generations, including our own. Whether Columbus was a hero or a villain will remain a matter of debate. That he and his contemporaries played a key role in the emergence of the modern world is a matter on which there can be no doubt.

14-4 AFRICA IN TRANSITION

Q **Focus Question:** What were the main features of the African slave trade, and what effects did European participation have on traditional African practices?

Although the primary objective of the Portuguese in rounding the Cape of Good Hope was to find a sea route to the Spice Islands, they soon discovered that profits were to be made en route along the eastern coast of Africa.

14-4a Europeans in Africa

In the early sixteenth century, a Portuguese fleet seized several East African port cities, including Kilwa, Sofala, and Mombasa, and built forts along the coast in an effort to control the trade in the area (see Map 14.5). Above all, the Portuguese wanted to monopolize the trade in gold, which was mined by Bantu workers in the hills and then shipped to Sofala on the coast (see Chapter 8). For centuries, the gold trade had been monopolized by local Bantu-speaking Shona peoples at Zimbabwe. In the fifteenth century, it had come under the control of a Shona Dynasty known as the Mwene Mutapa (MWAY-nay moo-TAH-puh). At first, the Mwene Mutapa found the Europeans useful as an ally against local rivals, but by the end of the sixteenth century the Portuguese had forced the local ruler to grant them

large tracts of land. The Portuguese lacked the personnel, the capital, and the expertise to dominate the local trade, however, and a vassal of the Mwene Mutapa succeeded in driving them from the plateau in the late seventeenth century.

The first Europeans to settle in southern Africa were the Dutch. In 1652, they set up a way station at the Cape of Good Hope to serve as a base for their fleets en route to the East Indies. Eventually, the settlement developed into a permanent colony as Dutch farmers known as **Boers** (BOORS or BORS), who spoke a Dutch dialect that evolved into Afrikaans, began to settle outside the city of Cape Town. With its temperate climate and absence of tropical diseases, the territory was practically the only land south of the Sahara that the Europeans had found suitable for habitation.

14-4b The Slave Trade

The European exploration of the African coastline had little apparent significance for most peoples living in the interior of the continent, except for a few who engaged in direct or indirect trade with the foreigners. But for peoples living on or near the coast, the impact was often great indeed. As the trade in slaves increased during the sixteenth through the eighteenth centuries, thousands and then millions of Africans were removed from their homes and forcibly exported to plantations in the Western Hemisphere.

The Arrival of the Europeans As we saw in Chapter 8, slavery existed in various forms in Africa before the arrival of the Europeans. Some slaves were used as agricultural laborers, others as household servants. After the expansion of Islam south of the Sahara in the eighth century, a vigorous traffic in slaves developed as Arab merchants traded for slaves to be transported to the Middle East. A few were sent to Europe, where, along with Slavic-speaking peoples captured in war in the regions near the Black Sea (the English word *slave* derives from "Slav"), they were used for domestic purposes or as agricultural workers.

With the arrival of the Europeans in the fifteenth century, the African slave trade changed dramatically. At first, the Portuguese simply replaced European slaves with African slaves. But the discovery of the Americas changed the situation. The cause was sugar. Cane sugar had been introduced to Europeans from the Middle East during the crusades, but when the Ottoman Empire seized much of the eastern Mediterranean (see Chapter 13), the Europeans needed to seek out new areas suitable for cultivation. In 1490, the Portuguese established sugar plantations on São Tomé, an island off the central coast of Africa.

It soon became clear that the climate and soil of West Africa were not especially conducive to the cultivation of sugar, so during the sixteenth century plantations were established along the eastern coast of Brazil and on several Caribbean islands. Because the cultivation of cane sugar is an arduous process demanding large quantities of labor, the new plantations required more workers than could be provided by the local Indian population, many of whom (as described earlier) had died of diseases, so African slaves began to be shipped to Brazil and the Caribbean to work on the plantations. The first were sent from Portugal, but in 1518 a Spanish ship carried the first boatload of African slaves directly from Africa to the Americas.

The Middle Passage   Over the next two centuries, the trade in slaves saw massive increases. An estimated 275,000 enslaved Africans were exported to other countries during the sixteenth century, more than two-thirds of them to the

Americas. The total climbed to more than 1 million during the next century and jumped to 6 million in the eighteenth century when the trade spread from West and Central Africa to East Africa. As many as 10 million African slaves are estimated to have been transported to the Americas between the early sixteenth and the late nineteenth centuries (see Map 14.8). As many as 2 million were exported to other areas during the same period.

One reason for these astonishing numbers was the tragically high death rate. In what is often called the **Middle Passage**, the arduous voyage from Africa to the Americas, losses were frequently appalling. Although figures on the number of slaves who died on the journey are almost entirely speculative, during the first shipments as many as one-third may have died of disease or malnourishment. Even among crew members, mortality rates were sometimes as high as one in four. Later merchants became more efficient and reduced losses to around 10 percent. Still, the future slaves were treated inhumanely, chained together in the holds of ships

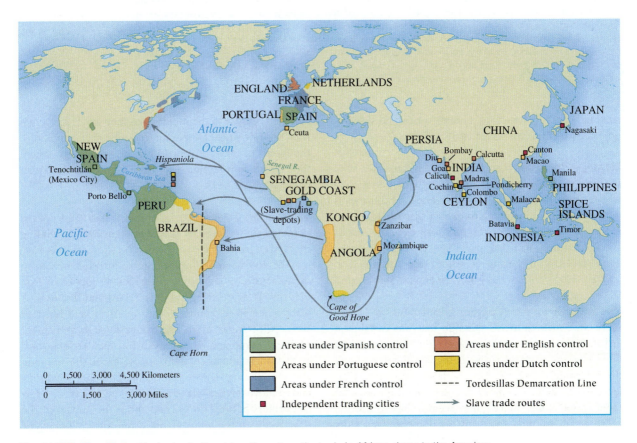

Map 14.8 The Slave Trade. Beginning in the sixteenth century, the trade in African slaves to the Americas became a major source of profit for European merchants. This map traces the routes taken by slave-trading ships, as well as the territories and ports of call of European powers in the seventeenth century.

Q *What were the major destinations for the slave trade?*

14.8 **Gateway to Slavery.** Of the 12 million slaves shipped from Africa to other parts of the world, some passed through Gorée (GOR-ay) prison on a small island just off the coast of Senegal near Cape Verde. Beginning in the sixteenth century, European traders began to ship African captives from the region of West Africa to the Americas to be used as slave labor on sugar plantations. Although the number of individuals shipped from Gorée was relatively small, the prison has been promoted as a poignant symbol of the cruelty afflicted by the slave trade on millions of innocent Africans. As a sign on a doorway in the prison reads, "From this door, they would embark on a voyage with no return, eyes fixed on an infinity of suffering." The modern African city of Dakar looms in the distance.

reeking with the stench of human waste and diseases carried by vermin (see Image 14.8).

Slavery in the Americas Ironically, African slaves who survived the brutal voyage fared somewhat better than whites after their arrival. Mortality rates for Europeans in the West Indies were ten to twenty times higher than in Europe, and death rates for new arrivals in the islands averaged more than 125 per 1,000 annually. But the figure for Africans, many of whom had developed at least a partial immunity to yellow fever, was only around 30 per 1,000.

The reason for these staggering death rates was clearly more than maltreatment, although that was certainly a factor. As we have seen, the transmission of diseases from one continent to another brought high death rates among those lacking immunity. African slaves were somewhat less susceptible to European diseases than the American Indian populations. Indeed, they seem to have possessed a degree of immunity, perhaps because their ancestors had developed antibodies to diseases common to the Old World from centuries of contact via the trans-Saharan trade. Still, working conditions for slaves were onerous, especially on sugar plantations, where laborers were forced to cut the sugarcane in the heat of the tropical sun

and then bring it to the mill for crushing and transformation into raw sugar. Desperate to escape such conditions, thousands of slaves escaped into the wilderness, where they set up communities safe from control of European colonial authorities.

Sources of Slaves For the most part, Europeans obtained their slaves by traditional means, purchasing them from local African merchants at the infamous slave markets in exchange for gold, guns, or other European manufactured goods such as textiles or copper or iron utensils. The "third leg" of this **Triangular Trade** took place when slave owners in the Americas paid for their slaves with sugar or its by-products (such as rum or molasses) exported to buyers in Europe. At first, local slave traders obtained their supply from the immediate surrounding regions, but as demand increased they had to move farther inland to locate their victims. A few local rulers became concerned about the impact of the slave trade on the political and economic well-being of their societies (see Historical Voices, "A Plea Between Friends," p. 361). More frequently, however, local monarchs viewed the slave trade as a source of income, and many launched forays against defenseless villages in search of victims.

A Plea Between Friends

Interaction & Exchange

KING AFONSO I OF THE STATE OF KONGO was one of Portugal's chief African allies during the early sixteenth century. A convert to Christianity, he used his relationship with the Portuguese to extend the territory of his kingdom at the expense of neighboring states in the region. Captives obtained during his military campaigns were sold to merchants and then exported abroad as slaves. As the demand for slaves increased, however, traders began to trap and enslave Afonso's own subjects while flooding the country with goods from abroad that undermined his royal authority.

In this letter, written in 1526, Afonso appealed to his "brother" sovereign, Dom João III, king of Portugal, to prevent such unscrupulous merchants from seizing his subjects and selling them as slaves to European sea captains. The letter is vivid testimony to how the slave trade destabilized African societies on or near the coast during the sixteenth and seventeenth centuries.

A Letter to King João

[1526] Sir, your Highness [of Portugal] should know how our Kingdom is being lost in so many ways that it is convenient to provide for the necessary remedy, since this is caused by the excessive freedom given by your factors and officials to the men and merchants who are allowed to come to this Kingdom to set up shops with goods and many things which have been prohibited by us, and which they spread throughout our Kingdoms and Domains in such an abundance that many of our vassals, whom we had in obedience, do not comply because they have the things in greater abundance than we ourselves; and it was with these things that we had them content and subjected under our vassalage and jurisdiction, so it is doing a great harm not only to the service of God, but the security and peace of our Kingdoms and State as well.

And we cannot reckon how great the damage is, since the mentioned merchants are taking every day our natives, sons of the land and the sons of our noblemen and vassals and our relatives, because the thieves and men of bad conscience grab them wishing to have the things and wares of this Kingdom which they are ambitious of; they grab them and get them to be sold; and so great, Sir, is the corruption and licentiousness that our country is being completely depopulated, and Your Highness should not agree with this nor accept it as in your service. And to avoid it we need from those [your] Kingdoms no more than some priests and a few people to teach in schools, and no other goods except wine and flour for the holy sacrament. That is why we beg of Your Highness to help and assist us in this matter, commanding your factors that they should not send here either merchants or wares, because it is our will that in these Kingdoms there should not be any trade of slaves nor outlet for them. Concerning what is referred above, again we beg of Your Highness to agree with it, since otherwise we cannot remedy such an obvious damage. Pray Our Lord in His mercy to have Your Highness under His guard and let you do for ever the things of His service. I kiss your hand many times.

At our town of Congo, written on the sixth day of July.
João Teixeira did it in 1526.
The King, Dom Afonso.

[On the back of this letter the following can be read: To the most powerful and excellent prince Dom João, King our Brother.]

Q *In what ways were the European merchants destabilizing the kingdom of Kongo? What remedy did Afonso propose?*

Source: From *The African Past: Chronicles from Antiquity to Modern Times* by Basil Davidson (Boston: Little, Brown and Company, 1964), pp. 191–192.

The Effects of the Slave Trade The effects of the slave trade varied from area to area. One assumes the practice would have led to the depopulation of vast areas of the continent, and this did occur in some areas, notably in modern Angola, south of the mouth of the Congo River, and in thinly populated areas in East Africa. It was less true, however, in West Africa. High birthrates there were often able to counterbalance the loss of able-bodied adults, and the introduction of new crops from the Western Hemisphere such as maize, peanuts, and manioc led to an increase in food production that made it possible to support a larger population. One of the many cruel ironies of history is that while the institution of slavery was a tragedy for many, it benefited others.

Still, there is no denying that from a moral point of view, the slave trade represented a tragic loss for millions of Africans, for families as well as individuals. As many as 20 percent of those sold to European slavers were children, a statistic that may be partly explained by the fact that many European countries had enacted regulations that permitted more children than adults to be transported aboard the ships.

How did Europeans justify cruelty of such epidemic proportions? Some rationalized that slave traders were only carrying on a tradition that had existed for centuries throughout the Mediterranean and African world. In fact, African intermediaries were active in the process and were often able to dictate the price, volume, and availability of slaves to European purchasers. Other Europeans eased their consciences by noting that slaves would now be exposed to the Christian faith.

14-4c Political and Social Structures in a Changing Continent

Of course, the Western economic penetration of Africa had other dislocating effects. The importation of manufactured goods from Europe undermined the foundations of the local cottage industry and impoverished countless families. The introduction of firearms intensified political instability and civil strife. As the European demand for slaves increased, African slave traders began to use their newly purchased guns to raid neighboring villages in search of captives, initiating a chain of violence that created a climate of fear and insecurity. Old polities were undermined, and new regimes ruled by rapacious "merchant princes" began to proliferate on the coast.

At the same time, the impact of the Europeans on the African continent as a whole should not be exaggerated. Only in a few isolated areas, such as South Africa and Mozambique, were permanent European settlements established. Elsewhere, at the insistence of African rulers and merchants, European influence generally did not penetrate beyond the coastal regions. Nevertheless, inland areas were often affected by events taking place elsewhere. In the western Sahara, for example, the diversion of trade routes toward the coast led to the weakening of the old Songhai trading empire and its eventual conquest by a vigorous new Moroccan dynasty in the late sixteenth century.

European influence had a more direct impact along the coast of West Africa, but no European colonies were established there before 1800. Most of the numerous African states in the area from Cape Verde to the delta of the Niger River were sufficiently strong to resist Western encroachments. Some, like the powerful Ashanti kingdom, established in 1680 on the Gold Coast, profited substantially from the rise in seaborne commerce. Some states, particularly along the so-called Slave Coast in what are now Benin and Togo or in the densely populated Niger River Delta

CHRONOLOGY	The Penetration of Africa
Life of Prince Henry the Navigator	1394–1460
Portuguese ships reach the Senegal River	1441
Bartolomeu Dias sails around the tip of Africa	1487
First boatload of slaves to the Americas	1518
Dutch way station established at Cape of Good Hope	1652
Ashanti kingdom established in West Africa	1680
Portuguese expelled from Mombasa	1728

took an active part in the slave trade. The demands of slavery and the temptations to profit, however, also contributed to the increase in conflict among the states in the area.

This was especially true in the region of the Congo River, where Portuguese activities eventually led to the splintering of the Kongo Empire and two centuries of strife among its successor states. Similarly, in East Africa, Portuguese activities led to the decline and eventual collapse of the Mwene Mutapa. Northward along the coast in present-day Kenya and Tanzania, African rulers were assisted by Arab forces from the Arabian Peninsula and expelled the Portuguese from Mombasa in 1728. Swahili culture now regained some of its earlier dynamism, but with much shipping now diverted to the route around the Cape of Good Hope the area never completely recovered and was increasingly dependent on the export of slaves and ivory obtained through contacts with African states in the interior. (See Chronology, "The Penetration of Africa," above.)

14-5 SOUTHEAST ASIA IN THE ERA OF THE SPICE TRADE

> **Focus Question:** What were the main characteristics of Southeast Asian societies, and how were they affected by the coming of Islam and the Europeans?

As noted earlier, Southeast Asia was affected in various ways by the expansion of the global trade network that began to accelerate in the fifteenth century. Not only did the Muslim faith begin to make inroads in the region, but the seizure of Malacca by the Portuguese in 1511 inaugurated a period of conflict among various European competitors for control of the spice trade. At first, the rulers of most of the local states were able to fend off these challenges and maintain their independence. As we shall see in a later chapter, however, the reprieve was only temporary.

14-5a The Arrival of the West

Where the Portuguese had trod, others soon followed. By the seventeenth century, the Dutch, the English, and the French had begun to join the scramble for rights to the lucrative spice trade. Within a short time, the Dutch appeared to seize the advantage. Formed in 1602, the aggressive and well-financed East India Company (Vereenigde Oost-Indische Compagnie or VOC) soon succeeded in elbowing rivals out of the spice trade and the Dutch began to consolidate their control over the area. On the island of Java, where they established a fort at Batavia (buh-TAY-vee-uh) (today's Jakarta) in 1619, the Dutch found it necessary to bring the inland regions under their control to protect their position. Rather than establishing a formal colony, however, they tried to rule through the local aristocracy. On Java and Sumatra, the VOC established pepper plantations, which became the source of massive profits for Dutch merchants in Amsterdam. Elsewhere they attempted to monopolize the clove trade by limiting cultivation of the crop to one island. By the end of the eighteenth century, the Dutch had succeeded in bringing much of the Indonesian Archipelago under their control. (See Chronology, "The Spice Trade.")

The arrival of the Europeans initially had somewhat less impact on the states of mainland Southeast Asia, where cohesive monarchies in Burma, Thailand (then known as Ayuthaya) (see Image 14.9), and Vietnam (then Dai Viet) vigorously resisted foreign encroachment. Local ruling elites were interested in exploiting trade opportunities, however, and by the seventeenth century several European nations began to compete actively commercial and missionary privileges within the region. As was the case elsewhere, the European powers characteristically began to intervene in local politics, supporting different sides in civil wars in Burma (now Myanmar) and Vietnam as a means of obtaining political and commercial advantage. By the end of the seventeenth century, however, when it became clear that economic opportunities were limited, most European states abandoned

CHRONOLOGY	The Spice Trade
Vasco da Gama lands at Calicut in southwestern India	1498
Albuquerque establishes base at Goa	1510
Portuguese seize Malacca	1511
Portuguese ships land in southern China	1514
Magellan's voyage around the world	1519–1522
English East India Company established	1600
Dutch East India Company established	1602
English arrive at Surat in northwestern India	1608
Dutch fort established at Batavia	1619

their factories (trading stations) in the area, although some missionaries sought to persevere in their efforts to convert locals to the Christian faith.

14-5b State and Society in Precolonial Southeast Asia

Between 1500 and 1800, Southeast Asia experienced the last flowering of traditional culture before the advent of European rule in the nineteenth century. Although the arrival of the Europeans had an immediate and direct impact in some areas, notably in the Philippines and parts of the Malay world, in most areas Western influence was

14.9 The Thai Capital at Ayuthaya. The longest-lasting Thai capital was at Ayuthaya, which was one of the finest cities in Asia from the fourteenth to eighteenth centuries. After the Burmese invasion in 1767, most of Ayuthaya's inhabitants were killed, and all official Thai records were destroyed. Here the remains of some Buddhist stupas, erected in a ceremonial precinct in the center of the city, remind us of the greatness of Thai civilization.

still relatively limited. Europeans occasionally dabbled in local politics and commerce, but they generally were not a decisive factor in the evolution of local political or social systems.

Nevertheless, Southeast Asian societies were changing in subtle ways—in their trade patterns, their means of livelihood, and their religious beliefs. In some ways, these changes accentuated the differences between individual states in the region. Yet beneath these differences was an underlying commonality of life for most people. Despite the diversity of cultures and religious beliefs, Southeast Asians were in most respects closer to each other than to peoples outside the region. For the most part, the states and peoples of Southeast Asia were still in control of their own destiny.

Religion and Kingship   During the early modern era, Buddhism and Islam continued to earn the allegiance of most of the population of the states in Southeast Asia, although Christianity began to make some inroads, especially in port cities directly occupied by Europeans and the Philippines. Buddhism was dominant in lowland areas on the mainland from Burma to Vietnam. Muslim influence was prevalent mainly on the Malay Peninsula and along the northern coast of Java and Sumatra, where local traders regularly encountered Muslim merchants from foreign lands. Elsewhere, traditional religious beliefs continued to survive, especially in inland areas, where the local populations either ignored the new doctrines and or integrated them into their habitual forms of spirit worship.

Buddhism and Islam also helped shape Southeast Asian political institutions. The Buddhist style of kingship took shape between the eleventh and the fifteenth centuries as Theravada teachings spread throughout the area. It became the predominant political system in the Buddhist states of mainland Southeast Asia—Burma, Ayuthaya, Laos, and Cambodia. Perhaps the most dominant feature of the Buddhist model was the godlike character of the monarch, who was considered by virtue of his karma to be innately superior to other human beings and served as a link between humans and the cosmos.

On the island of Java, kingship often took the form of a blend of Buddhist and Islamic political traditions. Like their Buddhist counterparts, Javanese monarchs originally possessed a sacred quality and maintained the balance between the sacred and the material world, but as Islam penetrated the Indonesian islands in the fifteenth and sixteenth centuries the monarchs began to lose their semidivine status. On the Malay Peninsula and along the coast of the Indonesian Archipelago, a more purely Islamic model prevailed. In this pattern, the head of state

was a sultan, who was viewed as a mortal although he still possessed some magical qualities. The sultan served as a defender of the faith and staffed his bureaucracy mainly with aristocrats, but he also frequently relied on the Muslim community of scholars—the *ulama*—and was expected to rule according to the Shari'a (see Chapter 7). A display in the restored Sultan's Palace in Malacca shows the local sultan sitting on a raised dais before his advisers and assembled guests.

The Economy   During the early period of European penetration, the economy of most Southeast Asian societies was based primarily on agriculture—as it had been for thousands of years. Still, manufacturing and commercial activities were on the rise as the region increasingly served as a focal point in a widespread trading network between East Asia and the Indian Ocean. Agriculture itself was becoming more commercialized as cash crops like sugar and spices replaced subsistence farming in rice or other cereals in some areas. Spices, of course, were the mainstay of the interregional trade, but other products were exchanged as well. Tin (which had been mined in Malaya since the tenth century), copper, gold, tropical fruits and other agricultural products, cloth, gems, and luxury goods were exported in exchange for manufactured goods, ceramics, and high-quality textiles such as silk from China.

Society   In general, Southeast Asians probably enjoyed a higher living standard than most of their contemporaries elsewhere in Asia. Although most of the population was poor by modern Western standards, hunger was not widespread. Several factors help explain this relative prosperity. First, most of Southeast Asia has been blessed by a salubrious climate. Uniformly high temperatures and abundant rainfall led to the proliferation of tropical fruits and enabled farmers to grow as many as two and even three crops of rice each year. Second, although the soil in some areas is poor, the alluvial deltas on the mainland are fertile, and the volcanoes of Indonesia periodically spew forth rich volcanic ash that renews the soil of Sumatra and Java. Finally, with some exceptions, most of Southeast Asia was relatively thinly populated. Only in a few areas such as the Red River Delta in northern Vietnam was overpopulation a serious problem.

Social institutions tended to be fairly homogeneous throughout Southeast Asia. Compared with China and India, there was little social stratification, and the nuclear family predominated. In general, women fared better in the region than elsewhere in Asia. Daughters often had the same inheritance rights as sons, and family property

William J. Duiker/Palace of the Malay Sultanate of Melaka

14.10 The Sultan of Malacca and his Court. Before the conquest of Malacca by the Portuguese in 1511, the city and its surroundings were ruled by a Muslim sultan, who ruled from a spacious palace that has now been restored as a museum. In the display in this illustration, the sultan is seated on a raised dais and attending to official business in the Royal Audience Hall; his advisers and other officials are seated at his feet. It was also in this hall that he greeted visiting merchants as well as emissaries from other countries in the region.

was held jointly between husband and wife. Wives were often permitted to divorce their husbands, and monogamy was the rule rather than the exception. Although women were usually restricted to specialized work such as making ceramics, weaving, and transplanting rice seedlings into the main paddy fields, and they rarely possessed legal rights equal to those of men, they still enjoyed a comparatively high degree of freedom and status in most societies in the region and were sometimes involved in commerce.

CHAPTER SUMMARY

Beginning in the fifteenth century, the pace of international commerce throughout the world increased dramatically. Chinese fleets embarked on several visits to the Indian Ocean while Muslim traders extended their activities into the Spice Islands and sub-Saharan West Africa. Then the Europeans burst onto the world scene. Beginning with the seemingly modest ventures of the Portuguese ships that sailed southward along the West African coast, the process accelerated with the epoch-making voyages of Christopher Columbus to the Americas and Vasco da Gama to the Indian Ocean in the 1490s. Soon several other European states had entered the fray helping to create a global trade network that distributed foodstuffs, textile goods, spices, and precious minerals from one end of the globe to the other.

In less than 300 years, the expansion of the global trade network changed the face of the world. In some areas such as the Americas and the Spice Islands, it led to the destruction of indigenous civilizations and the establishment of European colonies. In others—Africa, South Asia, and mainland Southeast Asia—it left local regimes intact but had a strong impact on local societies and regional trade patterns. In some areas, it led to an irreversible decline in traditional institutions and values, setting in motion a corrosive process that has not been reversed to this day.

At the time, most European observers probably viewed the process in a favorable light. It not only led to an expansion of world trade and foster the exchange of new crops and discoveries between the Old and New Worlds but also introduced Christianity to peoples around the globe. Some modern historians have been much more critical of the process, concluding that European activities during the sixteenth and seventeenth centuries created a "tributary mode of production" based on European profits from unequal terms of trade that foreshadowed the exploitative relationship characteristic of the later colonial period. Other scholars have questioned that contention, however, and argue that although Western commercial operations had a significant impact on global trade patterns, they did not—at least not before the nineteenth century—usher in an era of

dominance over the rest of the world. Muslim merchants were long able to evade European efforts to eliminate them from the spice trade, while local traders, some of them migrants from China and South Asia, dominated commercial activities in many of the port cities within the region. In Africa, the trans-Saharan caravan trade was relatively unaffected by European merchant shipping along the western coast of the continent.

In the meantime, traditional empires continued to hold sway over many of the lands washed by the Muslim faith. Beyond the Himalayas, Chinese emperors in their northern capital of Beijing retained proud dominion over all the vast territory of continental East Asia. In Chapters 16 and 17, we shall deal with these regions and how they confronted the challenges of a changing world.

REFLECTION QUESTIONS

Q What were some of the key features of the Columbian Exchange, and what effects did they have on the world trade network?

Q How did the expansion of European power during the Age of Exploration compare with the expansion of the Islamic empires in the Middle East a few centuries earlier?

Q Why were the Spanish conquistadors able to complete their conquest of Latin America so quickly when their contemporaries failed to do so in Africa and Southeast Asia?

CHAPTER TIMELINE

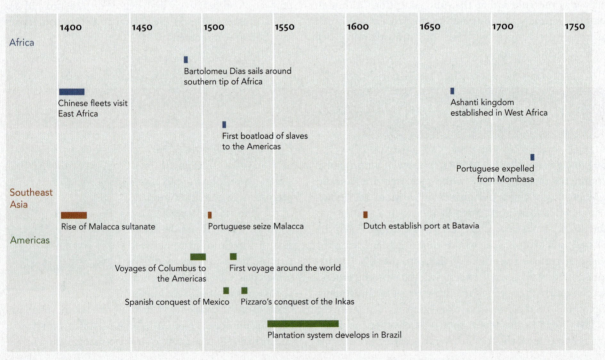

	1400	1450	1500	1550	1600	1650	1700	1750

Africa
- Chinese fleets visit East Africa
- Bartolomeu Dias sails around southern tip of Africa
- First boatload of slaves to the Americas
- Ashanti kingdom established in West Africa
- Portuguese expelled from Mombasa

Southeast Asia
- Rise of Malacca sultanate
- Portuguese seize Malacca
- Dutch establish port at Batavia

Americas
- Voyages of Columbus to the Americas
- First voyage around the world
- Spanish conquest of Mexico
- Pizzaro's conquest of the Inkas
- Plantation system develops in Brazil

CHAPTER NOTES

1. From *A Journal of the First Voyage of Vasco da Gama* (London, 1898), cited in J. H. Parry, *The European Reconnaissance: Selected Documents* (New York, 1968), p. 82.

2. H. J. Benda and J. A. Larkin, eds., *The World of Southeast Asia: Selected Historical Readings* (New York, 1967), p. 13.

3. Parry, *European Reconnaissance,* quoting from A. Cortesão, *The Summa Oriental of Tomé Pires,* vol. 2 (London, 1944), pp. 283, 287.

4. Quoted in J. H. Parry, *The Age of Reconnaissance: Discovery, Exploration, and Settlement, 1450 to 1650* (New York, 1963), p. 33.

5. K. N. Chaudhuri, *Trade and Civilization in the Indian Ocean: An Economic History from the Rise of Islam to 1750* (Cambridge, 1985), p. 65.

6. Quoted in Parry, *Age of Reconnaissance,* pp. 176–177.

7. Quoted in M. Leon-Portilla, ed., *The Broken Spears: The Aztec Account of the Conquest of Mexico* (Boston, 1969), p. 51.

CHAPTER 15

EUROPE TRANSFORMED: REFORM AND STATE BUILDING

Chapter Outline and Focus Questions

Critical Thinking

Q *What was the relationship between European overseas expansion (as traced in Chapter 14) and political, economic, and social developments in Europe?*

Connections to Today

Q *How does the exercise of state power in the seventeenth century compare with the exercise of state power in the twenty-first century? What, if anything, has changed?*

15.1 A Nineteenth-Century Engraving Showing Luther before the Diet of Worms

Art Resource, NY

ON APRIL 18, 1521, A LOWLY MONK stood before the emperor and princes of Germany in the city of Worms (VAWRMZ). He had been called before this august gathering to answer charges of heresy, charges that could threaten his very life. The monk was confronted with a pile of his books and asked if he wished to defend them all or reject a part. Courageously, Martin Luther defended them all and asked to be shown where any part was in error on the basis of "Scripture and plain reason." The emperor was outraged by Luther's response and made his own position clear the next day: "Not only I, but you of this noble German nation, would be forever disgraced if by our negligence not only heresy but the very suspicion of heresy were to survive. After having heard yesterday the obstinate defense of Luther, I regret that I have so long delayed in proceeding against him and his false teaching. I will have no more to do with him." Luther's appearance at Worms set the stage for a serious challenge to the authority of the Catholic Church. This was by no means the first crisis in the church's 1,500-year history, but its consequences were more far-reaching than any one at Worms in 1521 could have imagined.

After the disintegrative patterns of the fourteenth century, Europe began a remarkable recovery that encompassed a revival of arts and letters in the fifteenth century, a period known as the Renaissance, and a religious renaissance in the sixteenth century known as the Reformation. The resulting religious division of Europe (Catholics versus Protestants) was instrumental in beginning a series of wars that dominated much of European history from 1560 to 1650 and exacerbated the economic and social crises besetting the region.

One response to the crises of the seventeenth century was a search for order. The most general trend was an extension of monarchical power as a stabilizing force. This development, which historians have called **absolutism** or *absolute monarchy,* was most evident in France during the flamboyant reign of Louis XIV, regarded by some as the perfect embodiment of an absolute monarch.

But absolutism was not the only response to the search for order in the seventeenth century. Other states such as England reacted quite differently to domestic crises, and another system emerged in which monarchs were limited by the power of their representative assemblies. Absolute and limited monarchy were the two poles of seventeenth-century state building.

15-1 THE REFORMATION OF THE SIXTEENTH CENTURY

Q **Focus Question:** What were the main tenets of Lutheranism, Zwinglianism, and Calvinism, and how did they differ from each other and from Catholicism?

The **Protestant Reformation** is the name given to the religious reform movement that divided the western Christian church into Catholic and Protestant groups. Although the Reformation began with Martin Luther in the early sixteenth century, several earlier developments had set the stage for religious change.

15-1a Background to the Reformation

Changes in the fifteenth century—the age of the Renaissance—helped prepare the way for the dramatic upheavals in sixteenth-century Europe.

The Growth of State Power In the second half of the fifteenth century, attempts had been made to reestablish the centralized power of monarchical governments. To

characterize the results, some historians have used the label "Renaissance states"; others have spoken of the "**new monarchies**"—especially those of France, England, and Spain—at the end of the fifteenth century (see Chapter 13).

What was new about these Renaissance monarchs was their concentration of royal authority, their attempts to suppress the nobility, their efforts to control the church in their lands, and their desire to obtain new sources of revenue to increase royal power and enhance the military forces at their disposal. Like the rulers of fifteenth-century Italian states, the Renaissance monarchs were often crafty men obsessed with the acquisition and expansion of political power.

No one gave better expression to the Renaissance preoccupation with political power than Niccolò Machiavelli (nee-koh-LOH mahk-ee-uh-VEL-ee) (1469–1527), an Italian who wrote *The Prince* (1513), one of the most influential works on political power in the Western world. Machiavelli's major concerns in *The Prince* were the acquisition, maintenance, and expansion of political power as the means to restore and maintain order. In the Middle Ages, many political theorists stressed the ethical side of a prince's activity—how a ruler ought to behave based on Christian moral principles. Machiavelli bluntly contradicted this approach: "For the gap between how people actually behave and how they ought to behave is so great that anyone who ignores everyday reality in order to live up to an ideal will soon discover he had been taught how to destroy himself, not how to preserve himself."[1] Machiavelli was among the first Western thinkers to abandon morality as the basis for the analysis of political activity, thus emphasizing the ends justifying the means, or on achieving results regardless of the methods employed.

Social Changes in the Renaissance Social changes in the fifteenth century also helped create an environment in which the Reformation of the sixteenth century could occur. After the severe economic reversals and social upheavals of the fourteenth century, the European economy gradually recovered as manufacturing and trade increased in volume.

As noted in Chapter 12, society in the Middle Ages was divided into three estates: the clergy, or First Estate, whose preeminence was grounded in the belief that people should be guided to spiritual ends; the nobility, or Second Estate, whose privileges rested on the principle that nobles provided security and justice for society; and the peasants and inhabitants of the towns and cities, the Third Estate. Although this social order continued into the Renaissance, some changes also became evident.

Throughout much of Europe, the landholding nobles faced declining real incomes during most of the fourteenth and fifteenth centuries. Many members of the old nobility survived, however, and new blood also infused their ranks. By 1500, the nobles, old and new, who constituted between 2 percent and 3 percent of the population in most countries, still dominated society, as they had done in the Middle Ages, holding important political posts and serving as advisers to the king.

Except in the heavily urban areas of northern Italy and Flanders, peasants made up the overwhelming mass of the Third Estate, constituting 85 percent to 90 percent of the total European population. Serfdom had decreased as the labor dues owed by peasants to their lord were increasingly converted into rents paid in money. By 1500, especially in western Europe, more and more peasants were becoming legally free. At the same time, peasants in many areas resented their social superiors and sought a greater share of the benefits coming from their labor. In the sixteenth century, the grievances of the peasants, especially in Germany, led many of them to support religious reform movements.

Inhabitants of towns and cities, originally merchants and artisans, constituted the remainder of the Third Estate. But by the fifteenth century, the Renaissance town or city had become more complex. At the top of urban society were the patricians, whose wealth from capitalistic enterprises in trade, industry, and banking enabled them to dominate their urban communities economically, socially, and politically. Below them were the petty burghers—the shopkeepers, artisans, guild masters, and guildsmen—who were largely concerned with providing goods and services for local consumption. Below these two groups were the propertyless workers earning pitiful wages and the unemployed, living squalid and miserable lives. These poor city dwellers made up 30 to 40 percent of the urban population. The pitiful conditions of the lower groups in urban society often led them to support calls for radical religious reform in the sixteenth century.

The Impact of Printing

The Renaissance witnessed the development of printing, which made an immediate impact on European intellectual life and thought. Printing from hand-carved wooden blocks had been done in the West since the twelfth century and in China even before that. What was new in the fifteenth century in Europe was multiple printing with movable metal type. The development of printing from movable type was a gradual process that culminated sometime between 1445 and 1450; Johannes Gutenberg (yoh-HAH-nuss GOO-ten-bayrk) of Mainz (MYNTS) played an important role in bringing the process to completion. Gutenberg's Bible, completed in 1455 or 1456, was the first true book produced from movable type.

By 1500, there were more than 1,000 printers in Europe, who collectively had published almost 40,000 titles (between 8 million and 10 million copies).

The printing of books encouraged scholarly research but also stimulated the development of an ever-expanding lay reading public, a development that had an enormous impact on European society. Indeed, the printing press enabled the new religious ideas of the Reformation to spread as rapidly as they did in the sixteenth century. Moreover, printing allowed European civilization to compete for the first time with the civilization of China.

Prelude to Reformation

During the second half of the fifteenth century, the new classical learning of the Italian Renaissance spread to the European countries north of the Alps and spawned a movement called **Christian humanism** or **northern Renaissance humanism**, whose major goal was the reform of Christendom. The Christian humanists believed in the ability of human beings to reason and improve themselves and thought that through education in the sources of classical, and especially Christian, antiquity, they could instill an inner piety or an inward religious feeling that would bring about a reform of the church and society. To change society, then, they believed they must first change the human beings who composed it.

The most influential of all the Christian humanists was Desiderius Erasmus (dez-i-DEER-ee-us i-RAZZ-mus) (1466–1536), who formulated and popularized the reform program of Christian humanism. He called his conception of religion "the philosophy of Christ," by which he meant that Christianity should be a guiding philosophy for the direction of daily life rather than the system of dogmatic beliefs and practices that the medieval church seemed to stress. No doubt his work helped prepare the way for the Reformation; as contemporaries proclaimed, "Erasmus laid the egg that Luther hatched."

Church and Religion on the Eve of the Reformation

Considerable corruption in the Catholic Church was another factor that encouraged people to want reform. Between 1450 and 1520, a series of popes known as the *Renaissance popes* largely failed to meet the church's spiritual needs. The popes were supposed to be the spiritual leaders of the Catholic Church, but as rulers of the Papal States, they were all too often involved in worldly concerns. Julius II (1503–1513), the fiery "warrior pope," personally led armies against his enemies, much to the disgust of pious Christians, who viewed the pope as a spiritual leader. As one intellectual wrote, "How, O bishop standing in the room of the Apostles, dare you teach the people the things that pertain to war?" Many high church officials regarded their church offices mainly as opportunities to advance their careers and wealth, and many ordinary parish priests seemed ignorant of their spiritual duties.

While many leaders of the church were failing to meet their responsibilities, many ordinary people were clamoring for meaningful religious expression and certainty of salvation. As a result, for some the process of salvation became almost mechanical. As more and more people sought certainty of salvation through veneration of **relics** (bones or other objects intimately association with the saints), collections of relics grew. Frederick the Wise, elector of Saxony and Martin Luther's prince, had amassed nearly 19,000 relics to which were attached **indulgences** that could reduce one's time in purgatory by 1,443 years. (An indulgence is a remission, after death, of all or part of the punishment resulting from sin.)

15-1b Martin Luther and the Reformation in Germany

Martin Luther (1483–1546) was a monk and a professor at the University of Wittenberg (VIT-ten-bayrk), where he lectured on the Bible. Probably sometime between 1513 and 1516, through his study of the Bible, he arrived at an answer to a problem—the assurance of salvation—that had disturbed him since his entry into the monastery.

Catholic doctrine had emphasized that both faith and good works were required for a Christian to achieve personal salvation. In Luther's eyes, human beings, weak and powerless in the sight of an almighty God, could never do enough good works to merit salvation. Through his study of the Bible, Luther came to believe that humans are saved not through their good works but through faith in the promises of God, which was made possible by the sacrifice of Jesus on the cross. This doctrine of salvation, or justification by grace through faith alone, became the primary doctrine of the Protestant Reformation (**justification by faith** is the act by which a person is made deserving of salvation). Because Luther had arrived at this doctrine from his study of the Bible, the Bible became for Luther, as for all other Protestants, the chief guide to religious truth.

Luther did not see himself as a revolutionary innovator or a heretic, but he was greatly upset by the widespread selling of indulgences. Especially offensive in his eyes was the monk Johann Tetzel, who hawked indulgences with the slogan: "As soon as the coin in the coffer [money box] rings, the soul from purgatory springs." Greatly angered, in 1517 Luther issued a stunning indictment of the abuses in the sale of indulgences known as the Ninety-Five Theses. Thousands of copies were printed and quickly spread to all parts of Germany.

Unable to accept Luther's ideas, the church excommunicated him in January 1521. He was also summoned to appear before the imperial diet or Reichstag (RYKHSS-tahk) of the Holy Roman Empire convened by the newly elected Emperor Charles V (1519–1556). Ordered to recant the heresies he had espoused, Luther refused and made the famous reply that became the battle cry of the Reformation:

> Unless I am convicted by Scripture and plain reason—I do not accept the authority of popes and councils, for they have contradicted each other—my conscience is captive to the Word of God. I cannot and I will not recant anything, for to go against conscience is neither right nor safe. Here I stand, I cannot do otherwise. God help me. Amen.[2]

Members of the Reichstag were outraged and demanded that Luther be arrested and delivered to the emperor. But Luther's ruler, Elector Frederick of Saxony, stepped in and protected him.

During the next few years, Luther's movement began to grow and spread. As it made an impact on the common people, it also created new challenges. This was especially true when the Peasants' War erupted in 1524. Social discontent created by their pitiful conditions became entangled with religious revolt as the German peasants looked to Martin Luther for support. But when the peasants took up arms and revolted against their landlords, Luther proved to be a conservative on economic and social issues. He turned against the peasants and called on the German princes, who in Luther's eyes were ordained by God to maintain peace and order, to crush the rebels. By May 1525, the German princes had ruthlessly suppressed the peasant hordes. By this time, Luther found himself dependent on the state authorities for the growth of his reformed church.

Luther now succeeded in gaining the support of many of the rulers of the 300 or so German states that made up the Holy Roman Empire. These rulers quickly took control of the churches in their territories. The Lutheran churches in Germany (and later in Scandinavia) became territorial or state churches in which the state supervised the affairs of the church. As part of the development of these state-dominated churches, Luther also instituted new religious services to replace the Catholic Mass. These focused on Bible reading, preaching the word of God, and singing hymns. Following his own denunciation of clerical celibacy, Luther married a former nun, Katherina von Bora, in 1525. Their union provided a model of married and family life for the new Protestant minister.

Politics and Religion in the German Reformation From its very beginning, the fate of Luther's movement was closely tied to political affairs. In 1519, Charles I, king

15.2 A Reformation Woodcut. In the 1520s, after Luther's return to Wittenberg, his teachings began to spread rapidly, ending ultimately in a reform movement supported by state authorities. Pamphlets containing picturesque woodcuts were important in the spread of Luther's ideas. In the woodcut shown here, the crucified Jesus attends Luther's service on the left, while on the right the pope is at a table selling indulgences.

of Spain and the grandson of Emperor Maximilian, was elected Holy Roman emperor as Charles V. As Charles V, he ruled over an immense empire consisting of Spain and its overseas possessions, the traditional Austrian Habsburg lands, Bohemia, Hungary, the Low Countries, and the kingdom of Naples in southern Italy. Politically, Charles wanted to maintain his enormous empire; religiously, he hoped to preserve the unity of his empire in the Catholic faith.

The internal political situation in the Holy Roman Empire was not in Charles's favor, however. Although all the German states owed loyalty to the emperor, in the Middle Ages these states had become quite independent of imperial authority. By the time Charles V was able to bring military forces to Germany in 1546, Lutheranism had become well established, and the Lutheran princes were well organized. Unable to defeat them, Charles was forced to negotiate a truce. In 1555, the Peace of Augsburg (OUKS-boork) formally acknowledged the division of Christianity; Lutheran states were to have the same legal rights as Catholic states. Although the German states were now free to choose between Catholicism and Lutheranism, the peace settlement did not recognize the principle of religious toleration for individuals. The right of each German ruler to determine the religion of his subjects was accepted, but not the right of the subjects to choose their own religion. With the Peace of Augsburg, what had at first been merely feared was now certain: the ideal of Christian unity was forever lost. The rapid spread of new Protestant groups made this a certainty for all of Europe.

15-1c The Spread of the Protestant Reformation

Switzerland was home to two major Reformation movements: Zwinglianism and Calvinism. Ulrich Zwingli (OOL-rikh TSFING-lee) (1484–1531) was ordained a priest in 1506 and accepted an appointment as a cathedral priest in the Great Minster of Zürich (ZOOR-ik or TSIH-rikh) in 1518. Zwingli's preaching of the Gospel caused such unrest that in 1523 the city council decided to institute evangelical reforms. Relics and images were abolished. All paintings and decorations were removed from the churches and replaced by whitewashed walls. A new liturgy consisting of scripture reading, prayer, and sermons replaced the Mass. Monasticism, pilgrimages, the veneration of saints,

A Reformation Debate: Conflict at Marburg

 Religion & Philosophy

DEBATES PLAYED A CRUCIAL ROLE IN THE REFORMATION PERIOD. They were a primary instrument for introducing the Reformation in innumerable cities as well as a means of resolving differences among like-minded Protestant groups. This selection contains an excerpt from the vivacious and often brutal debate between Luther and Zwingli over the sacrament of the Lord's Supper at Marburg in 1529. The two protagonists failed to reach agreement.

The Marburg Colloquy, 1529

The Hessian Chancellor Feige: My gracious prince and lord [Landgrave Philip of Hesse] has summoned you for the express and urgent purpose of settling the dispute over the sacrament of the Lord's Supper. . . . Let everyone on both sides present his arguments in a spirit of moderation. . . . Now then, Doctor Luther, you may proceed.

Luther: Noble prince, gracious lord! Undoubtedly the colloquy is well intentioned. . . . Although I have no intention of changing my mind, which is firmly made up, I will nevertheless present the grounds of my belief and show where the others are in error. . . . Your basic contentions are these: In the last analysis you wish to prove that a body cannot be in two places at once, and you produce arguments about the unlimited body which are based on natural reason. I do not question how Christ can be God and man and how the two natures can be joined. For God is more powerful than all our ideas, and we must submit to his word. Prove that Christ's body is not there where the Scripture says, "This is my body!" Rational proofs I will not listen to. . . . It is God who commands, "Take, eat, this is my body." I request, therefore, valid scriptural proof to the contrary.

Zwingli: I insist that the words of the Lord's Supper must be figurative. This is ever apparent, and even required by the article of faith: "taken up into heaven, seated at the right hand of the Father."

Otherwise, it would be absurd to look for him in the Lord's Supper at the same time that Christ is telling us that he is in heaven. One and the same body cannot possibly be in different places. . . .

Luther: I call upon you as before: your basic contentions are shaky. Give way, and give glory to God!

Zwingli: And we call upon you to give glory to God and to quit begging the question! The issue at stake is this: Where is the proof of your position? I am willing to consider your words carefully—no harm meant! You're trying to outwit me. . . . You'll have to sing another tune.

Luther: You're being obnoxious.

Zwingli: (excitedly) Don't you believe that Christ was attempting in John 6 to help those who did not understand?

Luther: You're trying to dominate things! You insist on passing judgment! Leave that to someone else! . . . It is your point that must be proved, not mine. But let us stop this sort of thing. It serves no purpose.

Zwingli: It certainly does! It is for you to prove that the passage in John 6 speaks of a physical repast.

Luther: You express yourself poorly and make about as much progress as a cane standing in a corner. You're going nowhere.

Zwingli: No, no, no! This is the passage that will break your neck!

Luther: Don't be so sure of yourself. Necks don't break this way. You're in Hesse, not Switzerland.

Q *How did the positions of Zwingli and Luther on the sacrament of the Lord's Supper differ? What was the purpose of this debate? How does this example show why many Reformation debates led to further hostility rather than compromise and unity between religious and sectarian opponents? What implication did this have for the future of the Protestant Reformation?*

Source: "The Marburg Colloquy," edited by Donald Ziegler, from *Great Debates of the Reformation*, edited by Donald Ziegler, copyright © 1969 by Donald Ziegler.

clerical celibacy, and the pope's authority were all abolished as remnants of papal Christianity.

As his movement began to spread to other cities in Switzerland, Zwingli sought an alliance with Martin Luther and the German reformers. Although both the German and the Swiss reformers realized the need for unity to defend against the opposition of the Catholic authorities, they were unable to agree on the interpretation of the Lord's Supper, the sacrament of Communion (see Opposing Viewpoints, "A Reformation Debate," above). Zwingli believed that the scriptural words "This is my body, this is my blood" should be taken figuratively, not literally, and refused to accept Luther's insistence on the real presence of the body and blood of Christ "in, with, and under the bread and wine." In October 1531, war erupted between the Swiss Protestant and Catholic states. Zürich's army was routed, and Zwingli was found wounded on the battlefield. His enemies killed him, cut up his body, burned the pieces, and scattered the ashes. The leadership of Swiss Protestantism now passed to John Calvin, the systematic theologian and organizer of the Protestant movement.

Calvin and Calvinism John Calvin (1509–1564) was educated in his native France, but after converting to Protestantism he was forced to flee to the safety of Switzerland. In 1536, he published the first edition of the *Institutes of the Christian Religion*, a masterful synthesis of Protestant thought that immediately secured his reputation as one of the new leaders of Protestantism.

On most important doctrines, Calvin stood close to Luther. He adhered to the doctrine of justification by faith alone to explain how humans achieved salvation. But Calvin also placed much emphasis on the absolute sovereignty of God or the all-powerful nature of God— what Calvin called the "power, grace, and glory of God." One idea derived from his emphasis on the absolute sovereignty of God—**predestination**—gave a unique cast to Calvin's teachings. This "eternal decree," as Calvin called it, meant that God had predestined some people to be saved (the elect) and others to be damned (the reprobate). According to Calvin, "He has once for all determined, both whom He would admit to salvation, and whom He would condemn to destruction."[3] Although Calvin stressed that there could be no absolute certainty of salvation, his followers did not always make this distinction, and later Calvinists had an unshakable conviction that they were doing God's work on earth, making Calvinism a dynamic and activist faith.

In 1536, Calvin began working to reform the city of Geneva. He was able to fashion a tightly organized church order that employed both clergy and laymen in the service of the church. The Consistory, a special body for enforcing moral discipline, functioned as a court to oversee the moral life, daily behavior, and doctrinal orthodoxy of Genevans and to admonish and correct deviants. Citizens of Geneva were punished for such varied "crimes" as dancing, singing obscene songs, being drunk, swearing, and playing cards.

Calvin's success in Geneva enabled the city to become a vibrant center of Protestantism. Following Calvin's lead, missionaries trained in Geneva were sent to all parts of Europe. Calvinism became established in France, the Netherlands, Scotland, and central and eastern Europe.

15.3 John Calvin. After a conversion experience, John Calvin abandoned his life as a humanist and became a reformer. In 1536, Calvin began working to reform the city of Geneva, where he remained until his death in 1564. This is a seventeenth-century portrait of Calvin done by a member of the Swiss school.

By the mid-sixteenth century, Calvin's Geneva stood as the fortress of the Reformation.

The English Reformation The English Reformation was rooted in politics, not religion. King Henry VIII (1509–1547) had a strong desire to divorce his first wife, Catherine of Aragon, with whom he had a daughter, Mary, but no male heir. The king wanted to marry Anne Boleyn (BUH-lin or buh-LIN), with whom he had fallen in love. Impatient with the pope's unwillingness to grant him an annulment of his marriage, Henry turned to England's own church courts. As archbishop of Canterbury and head of the highest church court in England, Thomas Cranmer ruled in May 1533 that the king's marriage to Catherine was "absolutely void." At the beginning of June, Anne was crowned queen, and three months later, a child was born; much to the king's disappointment, the baby was a girl (the future Queen Elizabeth I).

In 1534, at Henry's request, Parliament moved to finalize the break of the Church of England with Rome. The Act of Supremacy of 1534 declared that the king was "the only supreme head on earth of the Church of England," a position that gave him control of doctrine, clerical appointments, and discipline. Although Henry VIII had broken with the papacy, little change occurred in matters of doctrine, theology, and ceremony. Some of his supporters, including Archbishop Cranmer, sought a religious reformation as well as an administrative one, but Henry was unyielding. When he died in 1547, he was succeeded by his son, the underage and sickly Edward VI (1547–1553). During Edward's reign, Cranmer and others inclined toward Protestant doctrines were able to move the Church of England (or Anglican Church) in a more Protestant direction. New acts of Parliament gave the clergy the right to marry and created a new Protestant church service.

Edward VI was succeeded by Mary (1553–1558), a Catholic who attempted to return England to Catholicism. Her actions aroused much anger, however, especially when "bloody Mary" burned more than 300 Protestant heretics. By the end of Mary's reign, England was more Protestant than it had been at the beginning.

15-1d The Social Impact of the Protestant Reformation

The Protestants were especially important in developing a new view of the family. Because Protestantism had eliminated any idea of special holiness for celibacy and had abolished both monasticism and a celibate clergy, the family could be placed at the center of human life, and a new stress on "mutual love between man and wife" could be extolled (see the Comparative Essay, "Marriage in the Early Modern World," p. 376).

But were doctrine and reality the same? Most often, reality reflected the traditional roles of husband as the ruler and wife as the obedient servant whose chief duty was to please her husband. Luther stated it clearly: "The rule remains with the husband, and the wife is compelled to obey him by God's command. He rules the home and the state, wages war, defends his possessions, tills the soil, builds, plants, etc. The woman on the other hand . . . [looks] after the affairs of the household."[4]

Obedience to her husband was not a wife's only role; her other important duty was to bear children. To Calvin and Luther, this function of women was part of the divine plan; for most Protestant women, family life was their only destiny. Overall, the Protestant Reformation did not noticeably alter women's subordinate place in society.

15-1e The Catholic Reformation

By the mid-sixteenth century, Lutheranism had become established in Germany and Scandinavia and Calvinism in Scotland, Switzerland, France, the Netherlands, and eastern Europe. In England, the split from Rome had resulted in the creation of a national church. The situation in Europe did not look particularly favorable for the Roman Catholic Church. Nevertheless, the Catholic Church underwent a revitalization in the sixteenth century that gave it new strength.

HISTORIANS DEBATE ## 15-1f Catholic Reformation or Counter-Reformation?

But was this revitalization a **Catholic Reformation** or a counter-reformation? Some historians prefer the term *counter-reformation* to focus on the aspects that were a direct reaction against the Protestant movement. Historians who prefer the term *Catholic Reformation* point out that elements of reform were already present in the Catholic Church at the end of the fifteenth century and the beginning of the sixteenth century. Especially noticeable were the calls for reform from the religious orders of the Franciscans, Dominicans, and Augustinians. Members of these groups put particular emphasis on preaching to laypeople. Another example was the Oratory of Divine Love. First organized in Italy in 1497, the Oratory was an informal group of clergy and laymen who worked to foster reform by emphasizing personal spiritual development and outward acts of charity.

No doubt, both positions on the nature of the reformation of the Catholic Church contain elements of truth. The Catholic Reformation revived the best features of medieval Catholicism and then adjusted them to meet new conditions, as is most apparent in the emergence of a new mysticism, closely tied to the traditions of Catholic piety, and the revival of monasticism by the regeneration of older religious orders and the founding of new orders.

The Society of Jesus Of all the new religious orders, the most important was the Society of Jesus, known as the Jesuits, founded by a Spanish nobleman, Ignatius of Loyola (ig-NAY-shuss of loi-OH-luh) (1491–1556). Loyola brought together a small group of individuals who were recognized as a religious order by the pope in 1540. The new order was grounded on the principles of absolute obedience to the papacy, a strict hierarchical order for the society, the use of education to achieve its goals, and a dedication to engage in "conflict for God." A special vow of absolute obedience to the pope made the Jesuits an important instrument for papal policy. Jesuit missionaries proved

Marriage in the Early Modern World

Family & Society

Marriage is an ancient institution. In China, myths about the beginnings of Chinese civilization maintained that the rites of marriage began with the primordial couple Fuxi and Nugun and that these rites actually preceded such discoveries as fire, farming, and medicine. In the early modern world, family and marriage were inseparable and at the center of all civilizations.

During this period, the family was still at the heart of Europe's social organization. For the most part, people viewed the family in traditional terms as a patriarchal institution in which the husband dominated his wife and children. The upper classes in particular thought of the family as a "house," an association whose collective interests were more important than those of its individual members. Parents (especially fathers) generally selected marriage partners for their children based on the interests of the family. When the son of a French noble asked about his upcoming marriage, the father responded, "Mind your own business." Details were worked out well in advance, sometimes when children were only two or three years old, and were set out in a legally binding contract. An important negotiating point was the size of the dowry, money presented by the wife's family to the groom upon marriage. The dowry could be a large sum, and all families were expected to provide dowries for their daughters.

Arranged marriages were not unique to Europe but were common throughout the world. In China, marriages were normally arranged for the benefit of the family, and the groom and bride were usually not consulted. Frequently, they did not meet until the marriage ceremony. Love was obviously not a reason for marriage and in fact was often viewed as a detriment because it could distract the married couple from their responsibility to the larger family unit. In Japan, too, marriages were arranged, often by the heads of dominant families in rural areas, and the new wife moved in with the family of her husband. In India, marriages were not only arranged but also not uncommon for women before age ten. In colonial Latin America, parents selected marriage partners for their children. In many areas, before members of the lower classes could marry, they had to offer gifts to the powerful noble landlords in the region and obtain their permission. These nobles often refused to allow women to marry in order to keep them as servants.

The Granger Collection, NYC

Iberfoto/Iberfoto/Superstock

15.4a

15.4b

15.4 Marriage Ceremonies. Image 15.4a is a detail of a marriage ceremony in Italy from a fresco painted by Dominico di Bartolo in 1443. Image 15.4b is a seventeenth-century Mughal painting showing Shah Jahan, the Mughal emperor (with halo). He is riding to the wedding celebration of his son, who rides before him.

Arranged marriages were the logical result of a social system in which men dominated and women's primary role was to bear children, manage the household, and work in the fields. Not until the nineteenth century did a feminist movement emerge in Europe to improve the rights of women. By the beginning of the twentieth century, that movement had spread to other parts of the world. The New Culture Movement in China, for example, advocated the free choice of spouses. Although the trend throughout the world is toward allowing people to choose their mates, in some places, especially in rural communities, families continue to play an active role in selecting marriage partners.

Q *In what ways were marriage practices similar in the West and East during the early modern period? Were there any significant differences?*

singularly successful in restoring Catholicism to parts of Germany and eastern Europe.

Another prominent Jesuit activity was the propagation of the Catholic faith among non-Christians. Francis Xavier (ZAY-vee-ur) (1506–1552), one of the original members of the Society of Jesus, carried the message of Catholic Christianity to the East. After attracting tens of thousands of converts in India, he traveled to Japan in 1549. He spoke highly of the Japanese: "They are a people of excellent morals—good in general and not malicious."[5] Thousands of Japanese, especially in the southernmost islands, became Christians. Although conversion efforts in Japan proved short lived, Jesuit activity in China was longer lasting. The Jesuits attempted to draw parallels between Christian and Confucian concepts and to show the similarities between Christian morality and Confucian ethics. For their part, the missionaries were much impressed with many aspects of Chinese civilization, and reports of their experiences heightened European curiosity about this great society on the other side of the world.

The Jesuits were also determined to carry the Catholic banner and fight Protestantism. Jesuit missionaries succeeded in restoring Catholicism to parts of Germany and eastern Europe. Poland was largely won back for the Catholic Church through Jesuit efforts.

A Reformed Papacy A reformed papacy was another important factor in the development of the Catholic Reformation. The involvement of Renaissance popes in dubious finances and Italian political and military affairs had created numerous sources of corruption. It took the jolt of the Protestant Reformation to bring about serious reform. Pope Paul III (1534–1549) perceived the need for change and took the audacious step of appointing a reform commission to ascertain the church's ills. The commission's report in 1537 blamed the church's problems on the corrupt policies of popes and cardinals. Paul III also formally recognized the Jesuits and summoned the Council of Trent.

The Council of Trent In March 1545, a group of high church officials met in the city of Trent on the border between Germany and Italy and initiated the Council of Trent, which met intermittently from 1545 to 1563 in three major sessions. The final decrees of the council reaffirmed traditional Catholic teachings in opposition to Protestant beliefs. Scripture and tradition were affirmed as equal authorities in religious matters; only the church could interpret scripture. Both faith and good works were declared necessary for salvation. Belief in purgatory and in the use of indulgences was strengthened, although the selling of indulgences was prohibited.

After the Council of Trent, the Roman Catholic Church possessed a clear body of doctrine and a unified structure under the acknowledged supremacy of the popes. Although it had become one Christian denomination among many, the church entered a new phase of its history with a spirit of confidence.

15-2 EUROPE IN CRISIS, 1560–1650

Q **Focus Question:** Why is the period between 1560 and 1650 in Europe considered an age of crisis?

Between 1560 and 1650, Europe experienced religious wars, revolutions and constitutional crises, economic and social disintegration, and a witchcraft craze. It was truly an age of crisis.

15-2a Politics and the Wars of Religion in the Sixteenth Century

By 1560, Calvinism and Catholicism had become activist religions dedicated to spreading the word of God as they interpreted it. Although their struggle for the minds and hearts of Europeans was at the center of the religious wars of the sixteenth century, economic, social, and political forces also played important roles in these conflicts.

The French Wars of Religion (1562–1598) Religion was central to the French civil wars of the sixteenth century. The growth of Calvinism had led to persecution by the French kings, but the latter did little to stop the spread of Calvinism. Huguenots (HYOO-guh-nots) (as the French Calvinists were called) constituted only some 7 percent of the population, but 40 percent to 50 percent of the French nobility became Huguenots, including the house of Bourbon (boor-BOHN), which stood next to the Valois (val-WAH) in the royal line of succession. The conversion of so many nobles made the Huguenots a potentially dangerous political threat to monarchical power. Still, the Calvinist minority was greatly outnumbered by the Catholic majority, and the Valois monarchy was staunchly Catholic.

For thirty years, battles raged in France between Catholic and Calvinist parties. Finally, in 1589, Henry of Navarre, the political leader of the Huguenots and a member of the Bourbon Dynasty, succeeded to the throne as Henry IV (1589–1610). Realizing, however, that he would never be accepted by Catholic France, Henry converted to Catholicism. With his coronation in 1594, the wars of religion had finally come to an end. The Edict of Nantes (NAHNT) in 1598 solved the religious problem by acknowledging Catholicism as the official religion of France while guaranteeing the Huguenots the right to worship and to enjoy all political privileges, including the holding of public offices.

Philip II and Militant Catholicism The greatest advocate of militant Catholicism in the second half of the sixteenth century was King Philip II of Spain (1556–1598), the son and heir of Charles V. Philip's reign ushered in an age of Spanish greatness, both politically and culturally. Philip II had inherited from his father Spain, the Netherlands, and possessions in Italy and the Americas. To strengthen his control, Philip insisted on strict conformity to Catholicism and strong monarchical authority. Achieving the latter was not an easy task, because each of the lands of his empire had its own structure of government.

Philip's attempt to strengthen his control over the Spanish Netherlands, which consisted of seventeen provinces (modern-day Netherlands and Belgium), soon led to a revolt. The nobles, who stood to lose the most politically, strongly opposed Philip's efforts. Religion also became a major catalyst for rebellion when Philip attempted to crush Calvinism. Violence erupted in 1566, and the revolt became organized, especially in the northern provinces, where the Dutch, under the leadership of William of Nassau, the prince of Orange, offered growing resistance. The struggle dragged on for decades until 1609, when the war ended with a twelve-year truce that virtually recognized the independence of the northern provinces. These seven northern provinces, which called

themselves the United Provinces of the Netherlands, became the core of the modern Dutch state. Spain continued to play the role of a great power, but much power had shifted to England.

The England of Elizabeth When Elizabeth Tudor, the daughter of Henry VIII and Anne Boleyn, ascended the throne in 1558, England was home to fewer than 4 million people. Yet during her reign (1558–1603), the small island kingdom became the leader of the Protestant nations of Europe and laid the foundations for a world empire.

Intelligent, cautious, and self-confident, Elizabeth moved quickly to solve the difficult religious problem she inherited from her half-sister, Queen Mary. She repealed the Catholic laws of Mary's reign, and a new Act of Supremacy designated Elizabeth as "the only supreme governor" of both church and state. The Church of England under Elizabeth was basically Protestant, but it was of a moderate bent that kept most people satisfied.

Elizabeth proved as adept in government and foreign policy as in religious affairs. Assisted by competent officials, she handled Parliament with considerable skill. Caution and moderation also dictated Elizabeth's foreign policy. Nevertheless, Elizabeth was gradually drawn into conflict with Spain. Having resisted for years the idea of invading England as too impractical, Philip II of Spain was finally persuaded to do so by advisers who assured him that the people of England would rise against their queen when the Spaniards arrived. A successful invasion of England would mean the overthrow of heresy and the return of England to Catholicism. Philip ordered preparations for a fleet of warships, the *armada*, to spearhead the invasion of England.

The armada was a disaster. The Spanish fleet that finally set sail had neither the ships nor the manpower that Philip had planned to send. Battered by several encounters with British ships in the English Channel, the Spanish fleet sailed back to Spain by a northward route around Scotland and Ireland, where it was further pounded by storms.

15-2b Economic and Social Crises

The period of European history from 1560 to 1650 witnessed severe economic and social crises as well as political upheaval. Economic contraction began to be evident in some parts of Europe by the 1620s. In the 1630s and 1640s, as imports of silver from the Americas declined, economic recession intensified, especially in the Mediterranean area. Once the industrial and financial center of Europe in the age of the Renaissance, Italy was now facing economic difficulties.

Population Decline Population trends of the sixteenth and seventeenth centuries also reveal Europe's worsening

15.5 **Procession of Queen Elizabeth I.** Intelligent and learned, Elizabeth Tudor was familiar with Latin and Greek and spoke several European languages. Served by able administrators, Elizabeth ruled for nearly forty-five years and generally avoided open military action against any major power. This painting done near the end of her reign shows the queen in a ceremonial procession.

conditions. The population of Europe increased from 60 million in 1500 to 85 million by 1600, the first major recovery of the European population since the devastation of the Black Death in the mid-fourteenth century. By 1650, however, records indicate a decline in the population, especially in central and southern Europe. Europe's longtime adversaries—war, famine, and plague—continued to affect population levels. These problems created social tensions, some of which were manifested in an obsession with witches.

Witchcraft Mania Hysteria over witchcraft affected the lives of many Europeans in the sixteenth and seventeenth centuries. Perhaps more than 100,000 people were prosecuted throughout Europe on charges of witchcraft. As more and more people were brought to trial, the fear of witches, as well as the fear of being accused of witchcraft, escalated to frightening levels (see Historical Voices, "A Witchcraft Trial in France," p. 380).

Common people—usually those who were poor and without property—were more likely to be accused of witchcraft. Indeed, where lists are given, those mentioned most often are milkmaids, peasant women, and servant girls. In the witchcraft trials of the sixteenth and seventeenth centuries, more than 75 percent of the accused were women, most of them single or widowed and many fifty years of age and older.

That women were most often the victims of the witch hunt has led some scholars to argue that the witch hunt was really a woman hunt or "genderized mass murder," arguing that men hunted witches because they caused disorder and were sexual beings in a patriarchal society. Other scholars have rejected this approach and argue first that men were also accused of witchcraft and second that women accused other women of witchcraft. These scholars believe that people in the sixteenth and seventeenth century believed in witchcraft as a constant threat in their society.

Despite scholarly differences about the nature of the witch hunts, there is no doubt that women were the primary victims. Current estimates are that there were 100,000 to 110,000 witch trials between 1450 and 1750

A Witchcraft Trial in France

Art & Ideas

PERSECUTIONS FOR WITCHCRAFT reached their high point in the sixteenth and seventeenth centuries, when tens of thousands of people were brought to trial. In this excerpt from the minutes of a trial in France in 1652, we can see why the accused witch stood little chance of exonerating herself.

The Trial of Suzanne Gaudry

28 May, 1652. . . . Interrogation of Suzanne Gaudry, prisoner at the court of Rieux. . . . [During interrogations on May 28 and May 29, the prisoner confessed to a number of activities involving the devil.]

Deliberation of the Court—June 3, 1652

The undersigned advocates of the Court have seen these interrogations and answers. They say that the aforementioned Suzanne Gaudry confesses that she is a witch, that she had given herself to the devil, that she had renounced God, Lent, and baptism, that she has been marked on the shoulder, that she has cohabited with the devil and that she has been to the dances, . . .

Third Interrogation, June 27

This prisoner being led into the chamber, she was examined to know if things were not as she had said and confessed at the beginning of her imprisonment.

—Answers no, and that what she has said was done so by force.

Pressed to say the truth, that otherwise she would be subjected to torture . . .

—Answers that she is not a witch. . . .

She was placed in the hands of the officer in charge of torture . . .

The Torture

On this same day, being at the place of torture.

This prisoner, before being strapped down, was admonished to maintain herself in her first confessions . . . .

—Says that she denies everything she has said, ... Feeling herself being strapped down, says that she is not a witch, . . . and being a little stretched [on the rack] screams ceaselessly that she is not a witch.

Asked if she did not confess that she had been a witch for twenty-six years.

—Says that she said it, that she retracts it, crying that she is not a witch . . . .

The mark having been probed by the officer, . . . it was adjudged by the aforesaid doctor and officer truly to be the mark of the devil.

Being more tightly stretched upon the torture rack, urged to maintain her confessions.

—Said that it was true that she is a witch. . . . Asked how long she has been in subjugation to the devil.

—Answers that it was twenty years ago that the devil appeared to her, being in her lodgings in the form of a man dressed in a little cowhide and black breeches. . . .

Verdict

July 9, 1652. In the light of the interrogations, answers, and investigations made into the charge against Suzanne Gaudry, . . . seeing by her own confessions that she is said to have made a pact with the devil, received the mark from him, . . . and that following this, she . . . had let herself be known carnally by him, in which she received satisfaction. Also, seeing that she is said to have been a part of nocturnal carols and dances.

For expiation of which the advice of the undersigned is that the office of Rieux can legitimately condemn the aforesaid Suzanne Gaudry to death, tying her to a gallows, and strangling her to death, then burning her body and burying it here in the environs of the woods.

Q *Why were women, particularly older women, especially vulnerable to accusations of witchcraft? What "proofs" are offered here that Suzanne Gaudry had consorted with the devil? What does this account tell us about the spread of witchcraft persecutions in the seventeenth century?*

Source: A. Kors and E. Peters, eds., *Witchcraft in Europe, 1100–1700: A Documentary History* (Philadelphia: The University of Pennsylvania Press, 1972).

with about 50 percent of the trials leading to executions. Of those executed, 75 percent to 80 percent were women, many of them older women.

That women should be the chief victims of witchcraft trials was hardly accidental. To one witchcraft judge in France it came as no surprise that witches would confess to sexual experiences with Satan: "The Devil uses them so, because he knows that women love carnal pleasures, and he means to bind them to his allegiance by such agreeable provocations."[6]

By the mid-seventeenth century the witchcraft hysteria had begun to subside. As governments grew stronger, fewer magistrates were willing to accept the unsettling and divisive conditions generated by the trials of witches. Moreover, by the beginning of the eighteenth century, more and more people were questioning altogether their old attitudes toward religion and found it especially contrary to reason to believe in the old view of a world haunted by evil spirits.

Economic Trends in the Seventeenth Century In the course of the seventeenth century, new economic trends also emerged. Historians refer to the economic practices of the seventeenth century as **mercantilism**. According to the mercantilists, the prosperity of a nation depended on a plentiful supply of bullion (gold and silver). For this reason, it was desirable to achieve a favorable balance of trade in which goods exported were of greater value than those imported, promoting an influx of gold and silver payments that would increase the quantity of bullion. Furthermore, to encourage exports, governments should stimulate and protect export industries and trade by granting trade monopolies, encouraging investment in new industries through subsidies, and improving transportation systems by building roads, bridges, and canals. By placing high tariffs on foreign goods, a government could reduce imports and prevent them from competing with domestic industries. Colonies were also deemed valuable as sources of raw materials and markets for finished goods.

Mercantilist theory on the role of colonies was matched in practice by Europe's overseas expansion. With the development of colonies and trading posts in the Americas and the East, Europeans embarked on an adventure in international commerce in the seventeenth century. Although some historians speak of a nascent world economy, we should remember that local, regional, and intra-European trade still predominated. What made the transoceanic trade rewarding, however, was not the volume of goods but their value. Dutch, English, and French merchants were bringing back products that were still consumed largely by the wealthy but were beginning to make their way into the lives of artisans and merchants. Pepper and spices from the Indies, West Indian and Brazilian sugar, and Asian coffee and tea were becoming more readily available to European consumers.

Despite the growth of capitalism, most of the European economy still depended on an agricultural system that had experienced few changes since the thirteenth century. At least 80 percent of Europeans still worked on the land. Almost all of the peasants of western Europe were free of serfdom, although many saw little or no improvement in their lot as they faced increased rents and fees and higher taxes imposed by the state.

15-2c Seventeenth-Century Crises: Revolution and War

During the first half of the seventeenth century, a series of rebellions and civil wars rocked the domestic stability of many European governments. A devastating war that affected much of Europe also added to the sense of crisis.

The Thirty Years' War (1618–1648) The Thirty Years' War began in 1618 in the Germanic lands of the Holy Roman Empire as a struggle between Catholic forces, led by the Habsburg Holy Roman emperors, and Protestant—primarily Calvinist—nobles in Bohemia who rebelled against Habsburg authority (see Map 15.1). What began as a struggle over religious issues soon became a wider conflict perpetuated by political motivations as both minor and major European powers—Denmark, Sweden, France, and Spain—entered the war. The competition for European leadership between the Bourbon Dynasty of France and the Habsburg Dynasties of Spain and the Holy Roman Empire was an especially important factor. Nevertheless, most of the battles were fought on German soil, with considerable damage. The Thirty Years' War was undoubtedly the most destructive conflict Europe had yet experienced (see Historical Voices, "The Destruction of Magdeburg in the Thirty Years' War," p. 383).

The war in Germany was officially ended in 1648 by the Peace of Westphalia, which proclaimed that all German states, including the Calvinist ones, were free to determine their own religion. The major contenders gained new territories, and France emerged as the dominant nation in Europe. The more than 300 entities that made up the Holy Roman Empire were recognized as independent states, and each was given the power to conduct its own foreign policy; this brought an end to the Holy Roman Empire and ensured German disunity for another 200 years. The Peace of Westphalia made it clear that political motives, not religious convictions, had become the guiding force in public affairs.

Map 15.1 Europe in the Seventeenth Century. This map shows Europe at the time of the Thirty Years' War (1618–1648). Although the struggle began in Bohemia and much of the fighting took place in the Germanic lands of the Holy Roman Empire, the conflict became a continent-wide struggle.

Q *Which countries engaged in the war were predominantly Protestant, which were Catholic, and which were mixed?*

HISTORIANS DEBATE **15-2d Was There a Military Revolution?**

By the seventeenth century, war was playing an increasingly important role in European affairs. Military power was considered essential to a ruler's reputation and power, so the pressure to build an effective military machine was intense. Some historians believe that the changes that occurred in the science of warfare between 1560 and 1650 constituted a military revolution. Other historians have questioned the use of the phrase "military revolution" to describe the military changes from 1560 to 1660, arguing instead that military developments were gradual. In any

case, for the rest of the seventeenth century, warfare continued to change.

These changes included increased use of firearms and cannons, greater flexibility and mobility in tactics, and better-disciplined and better-trained armies. These innovations necessitated standing armies, based partly on conscription, which grew ever larger and more expensive as the seventeenth century progressed. Such armies could be maintained only by levying heavier taxes, making war an economic burden and an ever more important part of the early modern European state. The creation of large bureaucracies to supervise the military resources of the state contributed to the growth in the power of governments.

The Destruction of Magdeburg in the Thirty Years' War

Politics & Government AFTER KING GUSTAVUS ADOLPHUS OF SWEDEN entered the war, he was finally joined by German Protestant forces after the fall of the Protestant city of Magdeburg to the imperial forces. In the excerpt below, a writer of this period gives a vivid description of what happened to Magdeburg and its inhabitant.

An Account of the Destruction of Magdeburg

Thus it came about that the city and all its inhabitants fell into the hands of the enemy, whose violence and cruelty were due in part to their common hatred of the adherents of the Augsburg Confession [Lutherans], and in part to their being embittered by the chain shot which had been fired at them and by the derision and insults that the Magdeburgers had heaped upon them from the ramparts.

Then was there naught but beating and burning, plundering, torture, and murder. Most especially was every one of the enemy bent on securing much booty. When a marauding party entered a house, if its master had anything to give he might thereby purchase respite and protection for himself and his family till the next man, who also wanted something should come along. It was only when everything had been brought forth and there was nothing left to give that the real trouble commenced. Then, what with blows and threats of shooting, stabbing, and hanging, the poor people were so terrified that if they had had anything left they would have brought it forth if it had been buried in the earth or hidden away in a thousand castles. In this frenzied rage, the great and splendid city that had stood like a fair princess in the land was now, in its hour of direct need and unutterable distress and woe, given over to the flames, and thousands of innocent men, women, and children, in the midst of a horrible din of heartrending shrieks and cries, were tortured and put to death in so cruel and shameful a manner that no words would suffice to describe, nor no tears to bewail it. . . .

Thus, in a single day this noble and famous city, the pride of the whole country, went up in fire and smoke; and the remnant of its citizens, with their wives and children, were taken prisoner and driven away by the enemy with a noise of weeping and wailing that could be heard from afar, while the cinders and ashes from the town were carried by the wind to . . . distant places. . . .

In addition to all this, quantities of sumptuous and irreplaceable house furnishings and movable property of all kinds, such as books, manuscripts, paintings, memorials of all sorts . . . which money could not buy, were either burned or carried away by the soldiers as booty. The most magnificent garments, hangings, silk stuffs, gold and silver lace, linen of all sorts, and other household goods were bought by the army sutlers for a mere song and peddled about the by cart load all throughout the archbishopric of Magdeburg. . . . Gold chains and rings, jewels, and every kind of gold and silver utensils were to be bought from the common soldiers for a tenth of their real value. . . .

Q *What does this document reveal about the effect of war on ordinary Europeans? Compare this description with the descriptions of the treatment of civilians in other wars. Does this author exaggerate, or is this description similar to the others?*

Source: James Harvey Robinson, *Readings in European History*, Vol. 2 (Boston: Ginn and Company, 1906), pp. 211–212.

15-3 RESPONSE TO CRISIS: THE PRACTICE OF ABSOLUTISM

Q **Focus Question:** What was absolutism, and what were the main characteristics of the absolute monarchies that emerged in France, Prussia, Austria, and Russia?

Many people responded to the crises of the seventeenth century by searching for order. An increase in monarchical power became an obvious means for achieving stability. The result was what historians have called *absolutism* or *absolute monarchy* in which the sovereign power or ultimate authority in the state rested in the hands of a king who claimed to rule by divine right—the idea that kings received their power from God and were responsible to no one but God. Late-sixteenth-century political theorists believed that sovereign power consisted of the authority to make laws, levy taxes, administer justice, control the state's administrative system, and determine foreign policy.

15-3a France Under Louis XIV

France during the reign of Louis XIV (1643–1715) has traditionally been regarded as the best example of the

Experience an interactive version of this period in ❖ MINDTAP

COMPARATIVE ILLUSTRATION

Sun Kings, West and East

Politics & Government

AT THE END OF THE SEVENTEENTH CENTURY, two powerful rulers held sway in kingdoms that dominated the affairs of the regions around them. Both rulers saw themselves as favored by divine authority—Louis XIV of France as a divine-right monarch and Kangxi (GANG-zhee) of China as possessing the Mandate of Heaven. Thus, both rulers saw themselves not as divine beings but as divinely ordained beings whose job was to govern organized societies. In Image 15.6a, Louis, who ruled France from 1643 to 1715, is seen in a portrait by Hyacinthe Rigaud (ee-ah-SANT ree-GOH) that captures the king's sense of royal dignity and grandeur. One person at court said of the king: "Louis XIV's vanity was without limit or restraint." In Image 15.6b, Kangxi, who ruled China from 1661 to 1722, is seen in a portrait that shows him seated in majesty on his imperial throne. A dedicated ruler, Kangxi once wrote, "One act of negligence may cause sorrow all through the country, and one moment of negligence may result in trouble for hundreds and thousands of generations."

Q *Although these rulers practiced profoundly different religions, are there any differences or similarities in the way they justify their power?*

15.6a

15.6b

practice of absolute or **divine-right monarchy** in the seventeenth century (see the Comparative Illustration, "Sun Kings, West and East," above). French culture, language, and manners reached into all levels of European society. French diplomacy and wars overwhelmed the political affairs of western and central Europe. The court of Louis XIV seemed to be imitated everywhere in Europe.

Political Institutions One key to Louis's power was his ability to control the central policy-making machinery of government because it was part of his own court and household. The royal court, located in the magnificent palace at Versailles (vayr-SY), served three purposes simultaneously: it was the personal household of the king, the location of central governmental machinery, and the place where powerful subjects came to find favors and offices for themselves and their clients. The greatest danger to Louis's personal rule came from the highest nobles and princes of the blood (the royal princes), who considered it natural to assert the policy-making role of royal ministers. Louis eliminated this threat by removing them from the royal council, the chief administrative body of the king, and enticing them to his court at Versailles, where he could keep them preoccupied with court life and out of politics. Instead of the high nobility and royal princes, Louis relied for his ministers on nobles who came from relatively new aristocratic families. His ministers were expected to be subservient: "I had no intention of sharing my authority with them," Louis said.

Louis's domination of his ministers and secretaries gave him control of the central policy-making machinery of government and thus authority over the traditional areas of monarchical power: the formulation of foreign policy, the making of war and peace, the assertion of the secular power of the crown against any religious authority, and the ability to levy taxes to fulfill these functions. Louis had considerably less success with the internal administration of the kingdom, however.

The Economy and the Military   The cost of building palaces, maintaining his court, and pursuing his wars made finances a crucial issue for Louis XIV. He was most fortunate in having the services of Jean-Baptiste Colbert (ZHAHN-bap-TEEST kohl-BAYR) (1619–1683) as controller general of finances. Colbert sought to increase the wealth and power of France by generally adhering to mercantilism. To decrease imports and increase exports, Colbert granted subsidies to individuals who established new industries. To improve communications and the transportation of goods internally, he built roads and canals. To decrease imports directly, Colbert raised tariffs on foreign goods.

The increase in royal power that Louis pursued led the king to develop a professional army numbering 100,000 men in peacetime and 400,000 in time of war. To achieve the prestige and military glory befitting an absolute monarch as well as to ensure the domination of his Bourbon Dynasty over European affairs, Louis waged four wars between 1667 and 1713. His ambitions roused much of Europe to form coalitions that were determined to prevent the certain destruction of the European balance of power by Bourbon hegemony. Although Louis added some

territory to France's northeastern frontier and established a member of his own Bourbon Dynasty on the throne of Spain, he also left France impoverished and surrounded by enemies.

15-3b Absolutism in Central and Eastern Europe

During the seventeenth century, a development of great importance for the modern Western world took place with the appearance in central and eastern Europe of three new powers: Prussia, Austria, and Russia.

Prussia   Frederick William the Great Elector (1640–1688) laid the foundation for the Prussian state. Realizing that the land he had inherited— Brandenburg-Prussia— was a small, open territory with no natural frontiers for defense, Frederick William built an army of 40,000 men, the fourth largest in Europe. To sustain this force, he established the General War Commissariat to levy taxes for the army and oversee its growth. The commissariat soon evolved into an agency for civil government as well. The new bureaucratic machine became the elector's chief instrument for governing the state. Many of its officials were members of the Prussian landed aristocracy, the Junkers (YOONG-kers), who also served as officers in the all-important army.

In 1701, Frederick William's son Frederick (1688–1713) officially gained the title of king. Elector Frederick III became King Frederick I, and Brandenburg-Prussia simply Prussia. In the eighteenth century, Prussia emerged as a great power in Europe.

Austria   The Austrian Habsburgs had long played a significant role in European politics as Holy Roman emperors, but their hopes of creating an empire in Germany had been dashed by the end of the Thirty Years' War. In the seventeenth century, the house of Austria created a new empire in eastern and southeastern Europe.

The nucleus of the new Austrian Empire remained the traditional Austrian hereditary possessions: Lower and Upper Austria, Carinthia, Carniola, Styria, and Tyrol. To these had been added the kingdom of Bohemia and parts of northwestern Hungary. After the defeat of the Turks in 1687 (see Chapter 16), Austria took control of all of Hungary, Transylvania, Croatia, and Slovenia, thus establishing the Austrian Empire in southeastern Europe. By the beginning of the eighteenth century, the house of Austria had assembled an empire of considerable size.

The Austrian monarchy, however, never became a highly centralized, absolutist state, primarily because it contained so many different national groups. The Austrian Empire remained a collection of territories held together by the Habsburg emperor, who was archduke of Austria, king of Bohemia, and king of Hungary. Each of these regions had its own laws and political life.

From Muscovy to Russia A new Russian state had emerged in the fifteenth century under the leadership of the Principality of Muscovy and its grand dukes. In the sixteenth century, Ivan IV (1533–1584) became the first ruler to take the title of *tsar* (the Russian word for *Caesar*). When Ivan's dynasty came to an end in 1598, it was followed by a period of anarchy that did not end until the Zemsky Sobor (ZEM-skee suh-BOR), or national assembly, chose Michael Romanov (ROH-muh-nahf) as the new tsar, establishing a dynasty that lasted more than 300 years. One of its most prominent members was Peter the Great.

Peter the Great (1689–1725) was an unusual character. A towering, strong man at six feet nine inches tall, he enjoyed a low kind of humor—belching contests and crude jokes—and vicious punishments, including floggings, impalings, and roastings. Peter got a firsthand view of the West when he made a trip there in 1697–1698, and he returned to Russia with a firm determination to westernize or Europeanize Russia. He was especially eager to borrow European technology to create the army and navy he needed to make Russia a great power.

As could be expected, one of Peter's first priorities was the reorganization of the army and the creation of a navy. Employing both Russians and Europeans as officers, he conscripted peasants for 25-year stints of service to build a standing army of 210,000 men and at the same time formed the first-ever Russian navy.

To impose the rule of the central government more effectively throughout the land, Peter divided Russia into provinces. Although he hoped to create a well-ordered community governed in accordance with law, few of his bureaucrats shared his concept of loyalty to the state. Peter hoped to evoke a sense of civic duty among his people, but his own forceful personality created an atmosphere of fear that prevented any such sentiment.

The object of Peter's domestic reforms was to make Russia into a great state and military power. His primary goal was to "open a window to the west," meaning an ice-free port easily accessible to Europe. This could only be achieved on the Baltic, but at that time, the Baltic coast was controlled by Sweden, the most important power in northern Europe. A long and hard-fought war with Sweden won Peter the lands he sought. In 1703, Peter began the construction of a new city, St. Petersburg, his window to the west and a symbol that Russia was looking

westward to Europe. Under Peter, Russia became a great military power and an important European state by his death in 1725.

15-4 ENGLAND AND LIMITED MONARCHY

Q **Focus Question:** How and why did England avoid the path of absolutism?

Not all states were absolutist in the seventeenth century. One prominent example of resistance to absolute monarchy came in England, where king and Parliament struggled to determine the roles each should play in governing England.

15-4a Conflict Between King and Parliament

With the death of Queen Elizabeth I in 1603, the Tudor Dynasty became extinct, and the Stuart line of rulers was inaugurated with the accession to the throne of Elizabeth's cousin, King James VI of Scotland, who became James I (1603–1625) of England. James espoused the divine right of kings, a viewpoint that alienated Parliament, which had grown accustomed under the Tudors to act on the premise that monarch and Parliament together ruled England as a "balanced polity." Then, too, the Puritans—Protestants within the Anglican Church who, inspired by Calvinist theology, wished to eliminate every trace of Roman Catholicism from the Church of England—were alienated by the king's strong defense of the Anglican Church. Many of England's gentry, mostly well-to-do landowners, had become Puritans, and they formed an important and substantial part of the House of Commons, the lower house of Parliament. It was not wise to alienate these men.

The conflict that had begun during the reign of James came to a head during the reign of his son Charles I (1625–1649). Like his father, Charles believed in divine-right monarchy, and religious differences also added to the hostility between Charles I and Parliament. The king's attempt to impose more ritual on the Anglican Church struck the Puritans as a return to Catholic practices. When Charles tried to force the Puritans to accept his religious policies, thousands of them went off to the "howling wildernesses" of America.

15-4b Civil War and Commonwealth

Grievances mounted until England finally slipped into a civil war (1642–1648), which was won by the parliamentary forces largely because of Oliver Cromwell's New

Model Army. This army was composed primarily of more extreme Puritans known as the Independents, who, in typical Calvinist fashion, believed they were doing battle for God. As Cromwell wrote in one of his military reports, "Sir, this is none other but the hand of God; and to Him alone belongs the glory." We might give some credit to Cromwell; his soldiers were well trained in the new military tactics of the seventeenth century.

After the execution of Charles I on January 30, 1649, Parliament abolished the monarchy and the House of Lords and proclaimed England a republic or commonwealth. But Cromwell and his army, unable to work effectively with Parliament, dispersed it by force and established a military dictatorship. After Cromwell's death in 1658, the army decided that military rule was no longer feasible and restored the monarchy in the person of Charles II (1660–1685), the son of Charles I.

15-4c Restoration and a Glorious Revolution

Charles II was sympathetic to Catholicism, and Parliament's suspicions were aroused in 1672 when he took the audacious step of issuing the Declaration of Indulgence, which suspended the laws that Parliament had passed against Catholics and Puritans after the restoration of the monarchy. Parliament forced the king to suspend the declaration.

The accession of James II (1685–1688) to the crown virtually guaranteed a new constitutional crisis for England. An open and devout Catholic, his attempt to further Catholic interests made religion once more a primary cause of conflict between king and Parliament. James named Catholics to high positions in the government, army, navy, and universities. Parliamentary outcries against James's policies stopped short of rebellion because the members knew that he was an old man and that his successors were his Protestant daughters Mary and Anne, born to his first wife. But on June 10, 1688, a son was born to James II's second wife, also a Catholic. Suddenly, the specter of a Catholic hereditary monarchy loomed large. A group of prominent English noblemen invited the Dutch chief executive, William of Orange, husband of James's daughter Mary, to invade England. William and Mary raised an army and invaded England while James, his wife, and their infant son fled to France. With little bloodshed, England had undergone its "Glorious Revolution."

In January 1689, Parliament offered the throne to William and Mary, who accepted it along with the provisions of the Bill of Rights (see Historical Voices, "The Bill of Rights," p. 388). The Bill of Rights affirmed Parliament's right to make laws and levy taxes. The rights of citizens to keep arms and have a jury trial were also confirmed. By deposing one king and establishing another, Parliament had destroyed the divine-right theory of kingship

CHRONOLOGY	Absolute and Limited Monarchy
France	
Louis XIV	1643–1715
Brandenburg-Prussia	
Frederick William the Great Elector	1640–1688
Elector Frederick III (King Frederick I)	1688–1713
Russia	
Ivan IV the Terrible	1533–1584
Peter the Great	1689–1725
First trip to the West	1697–1698
Construction of St. Petersburg begins	1703
England	
Civil wars	1642–1648
Commonwealth	1649–1653
Charles II	1660–1685
Declaration of Indulgence	1672
James II	1685–1688
Glorious Revolution	1688
Bill of Rights	1689

(William was, after all, king by grace of Parliament, not God) and asserted its right to participate in the government. Parliament did not have complete control of the government, but it now had the right to participate in affairs of state. Over the next century, it would gradually prove to be the real authority in the English system of **limited (constitutional) monarchy**.

15-5 THE FLOURISHING OF EUROPEAN CULTURE

Q **Focus Question:** How did the artistic and literary achievements of this era reflect the political and economic developments of the period?

Despite religious wars and the growth of absolutism, European culture continued to flourish. The era was blessed with many prominent artists and writers.

15-5a Art: The Baroque

The artistic movement known as the **Baroque** (buh-ROHK) dominated the Western artistic world for a century and a half. The Baroque began in Italy in the last quarter of the

The Bill of Rights

Politics & Government **IN 1688, THE ENGLISH EXPERIENCED** a bloodless revolution in which the Stuart king James II was replaced by Mary, James's daughter, and her husband, William of Orange. After William and Mary had assumed power, Parliament passed a Bill of Rights that specified the rights of Parliament and laid the foundation for a constitutional monarchy.

The Bill of Rights

Whereas the said late King James II having abdicated the government, and the throne being thereby vacant, his Highness the prince of Orange (whom it hath pleased Almighty God to make the glorious instrument of delivering this kingdom from popery and arbitrary power) did (by the device of the lords spiritual and temporal, and diverse principal persons of the Commons) cause letters to be written to the lords spiritual and temporal, being Protestants, and other letters to the several counties, cities, universities, boroughs, and Cinque Ports, for the choosing of such persons to represent them, as were of right to be sent to parliament, to meet and sit at Westminster upon the two and twentieth day of January, in this year 1689, in order to such an establishment as that their religion, laws, and liberties might not again be in danger of being subverted; upon which letters elections have been accordingly made.

And thereupon the said lords spiritual and temporal and Commons, pursuant to their respective letters and elections, being now assembled in a full and free representation of this nation, taking into their most serious consideration the best means for attaining the ends aforesaid, do in the first place (as their ancestors in like case have usually done), for the vindication and assertion of their ancient rights and liberties, declare:

1. That the pretended power of suspending laws, or the execution of laws, by regal authority, without consent of parliament is illegal.
2. That the pretended power of dispensing with the laws, or the execution of law by regal authority,

as it hath been assumed and exercised of late, is illegal.
3. That the commission for erecting the late court of commissioners for ecclesiastical causes, and all other commissions and courts of like nature, are illegal and pernicious.
4. That levying money for or to the use of the crown by pretense of prerogative, without grant of parliament, for longer time or in other manner than the same is or shall be granted, is illegal.
5. That it is the right of the subjects to petition the king, and all commitments and prosecutions for such petitioning are illegal.
6. That the raising or keeping a standing army within the kingdom in time of peace, unless it be with consent of parliament, is against law.
7. That the subjects which are Protestants may have arms for their defense suitable to their conditions, and as allowed by law.
8. That election of members of parliament ought to be free.
9. That the freedom of speech, and debates or proceedings in parliament, ought not to be impeached or questioned in any court or place out of parliament.
10. That excessive bail ought not to be required, nor excessive fines imposed, nor cruel and unusual punishments inflicted.
11. That jurors ought to be duly impaneled and returned, and jurors which pass upon men in trials for high treason ought to be freeholders.
12. That all grants and promises of fines and forfeitures of particular persons before conviction are illegal and void.
13. And that for redress of all grievances, and for the amending, strengthening, and preserving of the laws, parliament ought to be held frequently.

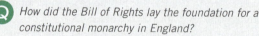 *How did the Bill of Rights lay the foundation for a constitutional monarchy in England?*

Source: *The Statutes: Revised Edition* (London: Eyre & Spottiswoode, 1871), Vol. 2, pp. 10–12.

sixteenth century and spread to the rest of Europe and Latin America. Baroque artists sought to harmonize the classical ideals of Renaissance art with the spiritual feelings of the sixteenth-century religious revival. In large part, Baroque art and architecture reflected the search for power that was characteristic of much of the seventeenth century. Baroque churches and palaces featured richly ornamented facades, sweeping staircases, and an overall splendor meant to impress people. Kings and princes wanted not only their subjects but also other kings and princes to be in awe of their power.

Baroque painting was known for its use of dramatic effects to arouse the emotions. Perhaps the greatest figure of the Baroque was Italian architect and sculptor Gian Lorenzo Bernini (ZHAHN loh-RENT-zoh bur-NEE-nee) (1598–1680), who completed Saint Peter's Basilica at the Vatican and designed the vast colonnade enclosing the piazza in front of it. In his most striking sculptural work, the *Ecstasy of Saint Theresa*, Bernini depicts a moment of mystical experience in the life of the sixteenth-century Spanish saint. The elegant draperies and the expression on her face create a sensuously real portrayal of physical ecstasy

15-5b Art: Dutch Realism

A brilliant flowering of Dutch painting paralleled the supremacy of Dutch commerce in the seventeenth century. Wealthy patricians and burghers of Dutch urban society commissioned works of art for their guildhalls, town halls, and private dwellings. The interests of this burgher society were reflected in the subject matter of many Dutch paintings: portraits of themselves, landscapes, seascapes, genre scenes, still lifes, and the interiors of their residences. Neither classical nor Baroque, Dutch painters were primarily interested in the realistic portrayal of secular everyday life.

This interest in painting scenes of everyday life is evident in the work of Judith Leyster (LESS-tur) (ca. 1609–1660), who established her own independent painting career, a remarkable achievement for a woman in seventeenth-century Europe. Musicians playing their instruments, women sewing, children laughing while playing games, and actors performing all form the subject matter of Leyster's portrayals of everyday Dutch life.

15.7 Gian Lorenzo Bernini, *Ecstasy of Saint Theresa*. The *Ecstasy of Saint Theresa*, created for the Cornaro Chapel in the Church of Santa Maria della Vittoria in Rome, was one of Bernini's most famous sculptures. Bernini sought to convey visually Theresa's mystical experience when, according to her description, an angel pierced her heart repeatedly with a golden arrow.

15.8 Judith Leyster, *Self-Portrait*. Although Judith Leyster was a well-known artist to her Dutch contemporaries, her fame diminished soon after her death. In the late nineteenth century, a Dutch art historian rediscovered her work. In her *Self-Portrait,* painted in 1635, she is seen pausing in her work in front of one the scenes of daily life that made her such a popular artist in her own day.

Experience an interactive version of this period in ⚡ MINDTAP

15-5c A Golden Age of Literature in England

In England, writing for the stage reached new heights between 1580 and 1640. The golden age of English literature is often called the *Elizabethan Era* because much of the English cultural flowering occurred during Elizabeth's reign. Elizabethan literature exhibits the exuberance and pride associated with English exploits at the time. Of all the forms of Elizabethan literature, none expressed the energy and intellectual versatility of the era better than drama. And no dramatist is more famous or more accomplished than William Shakespeare (1564–1614).

Shakespeare was a "complete man of the theater." Although best known for writing plays, he was also an actor and a shareholder in the chief acting company of the time, the Lord Chamberlain's Company, which played in various London theaters. Shakespeare is to this day hailed as a genius. A master of the English language, he imbued its words with power and majesty. And his technical proficiency was matched by incredible insight into human psychology. Whether writing tragedies or comedies, Shakespeare exhibited a remarkable understanding of the human condition.

CHAPTER SUMMARY

In Chapter 14, we observed how the movement of Europeans beyond Europe began to change the shape of world history. But what had made this development possible? After all, the Reformation of the sixteenth century, initially begun by Martin Luther, had brought about the religious division of Europe into Protestant  and Catholic camps. By the middle of the sixteenth century, it was apparent that the religious passions of the Reformation era had brought an end to the religious unity of medieval Europe. The religious division (Catholics versus Protestants) was instrumental in beginning a series of religious wars that were complicated by economic, social, and political forces.

The crises of the sixteenth and seventeenth centuries soon led to a search for a stable, secular order of politics and made possible the emergence of a system of nation-states in which power politics took on increasing significance. Within those states, there slowly emerged some of the machinery that made possible a growing centralization of power. In states called *absolutist*, strong monarchs with the assistance of their aristocracies took the lead in providing the leadership for greater centralization. In this so-called age of absolutism, Louis XIV, the Sun King of France, was the model for other rulers. Strong monarchy also prevailed in central and eastern Europe, where three new powers made their appearance: Prussia, Austria, and Russia.

But not all European states followed the pattern of absolute monarchy. Especially important were developments in England, where a series of struggles between king and Parliament took place in the seventeenth century. In the long run, the landed aristocracy gained power at the expense of the monarchs, thus laying the foundations for a constitutional government in which Parliament provided the focus for the institutions of centralized power.

In every major European state, a growing concern for power and dynamic expansion led to larger armies and greater conflict, stronger economies, and more powerful governments. From a global point of view, Europeans—with their strong governments, prosperous economies, and strengthened military forces—were beginning to dominate other parts of the world, leading to a growing belief in the superiority of their civilization.

Yet despite Europeans' increasing domination of global trade markets, they had not achieved their goal of diminishing the power of Islam, a goal first pursued during the crusades. In fact, as we shall see in the next chapter, in the midst of European expansion and exploration, three new and powerful Muslim empires were taking shape in the Middle East and South Asia.

REFLECTION QUESTIONS

Q What role did politics play in the success of the Protestant Reformation?

Q What did Louis XIV hope to accomplish in his domestic and foreign policies? To what extent did he succeed?

Q Compare and contrast the development of states in Europe and the world of Islam (see Chapter 16). What are the similarities and differences in these developments? How do you explain the similarities and differences?

CHAPTER TIMELINE

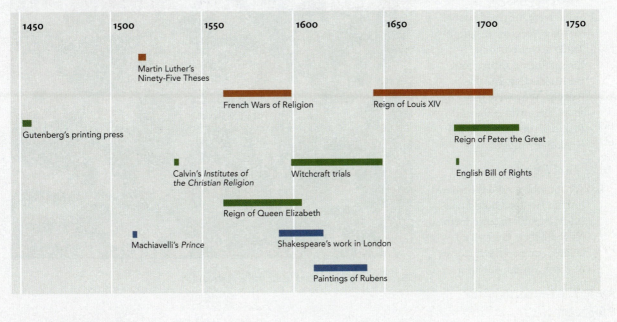

| 1450 | 1500 | 1550 | 1600 | 1650 | 1700 | 1750 |

Martin Luther's Ninety-Five Theses

French Wars of Religion

Reign of Louis XIV

Gutenberg's printing press

Reign of Peter the Great

Calvin's *Institutes of the Christian Religion*

Witchcraft trials

English Bill of Rights

Reign of Queen Elizabeth

Machiavelli's *Prince*

Shakespeare's work in London

Paintings of Rubens

CHAPTER NOTES

1. N. Machiavelli, *The Prince,* trans. D. Wootton (Indianapolis, Ind., 1995), p. 48.
2. Quoted in R. Bainton, *Here I Stand: A Life of Martin Luther* (New York, 1950), p. 144.
3. J. Calvin, *Institutes of the Christian Religion,* trans. J. Allen (Philadelphia, 1936), vol. 1, p. 228; vol. 2, p. 181.
4. Quoted in B. S. Anderson and J. P. Zinsser, *A History of Their Own: Women in Europe from Prehistory to the Present,* vol. 1 (New York, 1988), p. 259.
5. Quoted in J. O'Malley, *The First Jesuits* (Cambridge, Mass., 1993), p. 76.
6. Quoted in J. Klaits, *Servants of Satan: The Age of Witch Hunts* (Bloomington, Ind., 1985), p. 68.

MINDTAP
From Cengage

MindTap® is a fully online, highly personalized learning experience built upon Cengage Learning content. MindTap combines student learning tools—readings, multimedia, activities, and assessments—into a singular Learning Path that guides students through the course and helps students develop the critical thinking, analysis, and communication skills that are essential to academic and professional success.

Chapter Outline and Focus Questions

16-1 *The Ottoman Empire*

Q What were the chief reasons for the success of the Ottoman Turks in consolidating their influence throughout the Middle East and the Balkans. Why were they more successful at the effort than their predecessors, the Byzantine Empire?

16-2 *The Safavids*

Q What problems did the Safavid Empire face, and how did its rulers attempt to solve them? How did their success and failures compared with those of other Muslim empires?

16-3 *The Grandeur of the Mughals*

Q What role did Islam play in the Mughal Empire, and how did the Mughals' approach to religion compare with that of the Ottomans and the Safavids? What might explain the differences?

Universal Images Group / Art Resource, NY

16.1 Turks Fight Christians at the Battle of Mohács

Critical Thinking

Q *What were the main characteristics of each Muslim empire, and in what ways did they resemble each other? How were they distinct from their European counterparts?*

Connections to Today

Q *How would you compare the position of Islam in the world today with its position in the era described in this chapter?*

THE OTTOMAN ARMY, led by Sultan Suleyman the Magnificent, arrived at Mohács, on the plains of Hungary, on an August morning in 1526. The Turkish force numbered about 100,000 men, and its weapons included 300 new long-range cannons. Facing them was a somewhat larger European force clothed in heavy armor but armed with only 100 older cannons.

The battle began at noon and was over in two hours. The flower of the Hungarian cavalry had been destroyed, and 20,000 foot soldiers had drowned in a nearby swamp. The Ottomans had lost fewer than 200 men. Two weeks later, they seized the Hungarian capital at Buda and prepared to lay siege to the nearby Austrian city of Vienna. Europe was in a panic, but Mohács would end up being the high point of Turkish expansion in Europe.

In launching their Age of Exploration, European rulers had hoped that they could cripple the power of Islam and reduce its threat to the security of Europe by controlling global markets. But their strategy had not been entirely successful because the Muslim world, which appeared to have entered a period of decline with the collapse of the

Abbasid caliphate, managed to revive itself with the rise of three great Muslim empires. These powerful Muslim states—the Ottomans, the Safavids, and the Mughals—dominated the Middle East and the South Asian subcontinent and brought a measure of stability to a region that had been in turmoil for centuries.

16-1 THE OTTOMAN EMPIRE

Focus Questions: What were the chief reasons for the success of the Ottoman Turks in consolidating their influence throughout the Middle East and the Balkans? Why were they more successful at the effort than their predecessors, the Byzantine Empire?

The Ottoman Turks were among the many Turkic-speaking nomadic peoples who had spread westward from Central Asia in the ninth through the eleventh centuries. The first to appear in the Middle East were the Seljuk Turks, who initially attempted to revive the declining Abbasid caliphate in Baghdad. Later they established themselves in the Anatolian Peninsula at the expense of the Byzantine Empire. Turks served as warriors or administrators, whereas the peasants who tilled the farmland were mainly Greek.

16-1a The Rise of the Ottoman Turks

In the late thirteenth century, a new group of Turks under the tribal leader Osman (os-MAHN) (r. 1280–1326) began to consolidate their power in the northwestern corner of the Anatolian Peninsula. At first, the Osman Turks were relatively peaceful and engaged in pastoral pursuits, but as the Seljuk Empire began to disintegrate in the early fourteenth century, they began to expand and founded the Osmanli (os-MAHN-lee) Dynasty, with its capital at Bursa (BURR-suh). The Osmanlis later came to be known as the Ottomans.

The Byzantine Empire, of course, had controlled the area for centuries, but it had been severely weakened by the 1204 sacking of Constantinople in the Fourth Crusade and the Western occupation of much of the empire for the next half-century. In 1345, Ottoman forces under their leader Orkhan (or-KHAHN) I (r. 1326–1360) crossed the Bosporus for the first time to support a usurper against the Byzantine emperor in Constantinople. Setting up their first European base at Gallipoli (gah-LIP-poh-lee) at the Mediterranean entrance to the Dardanelles, Turkish troops expanded gradually into the Balkans and allied with fractious Serbian and Bulgar forces against the Byzantines. In these unstable conditions, the Ottomans established permanent settlements throughout the area, where Turkish provincial governors, called **beys** (BAYS) (from the Turkish *beg*, "knight"), drove out the previous landlords and collected taxes from the local Slavic peasants. The Ottoman leader now began to claim the title of **sultan** (SUL-tun) or sovereign of his domain.

In 1360, Orkhan was succeeded by his son Murad (moo-RAHD) I (r. 1360–1389), who consolidated Ottoman power in the Balkans and steadily reduced the Byzantine emperor to a vassal. Murad now began to build up a strong military administration based on the creation of a new elite guard. Called **janissaries** (JAN-nih-say-reez) (from the Turkish *yeni cheri*, "new troops"), they were recruited from the local Christian population in the Balkans and then converted to Islam and trained as foot soldiers or administrators. One major advantage of the janissaries was that they were directly subordinated to the sultanate and therefore owed their loyalty to the person of the sultan. Other military forces were organized by the beys and were thus loyal to their local tribal leaders.

The janissary corps also represented a response to changes in warfare. As the knowledge of firearms spread in the late fourteenth century, the Turks began to master the new technology, including siege cannons and muskets (see Comparative Essay, "The Changing Face of War," p. 394). The traditional nomadic cavalry charge was now outmoded and was superseded by infantry forces armed with muskets. Thus, the janissaries provided a well-armed infantry who served both as an elite guard to protect the palace and as a means of extending Turkish control in the Balkans. With his new forces, Murad defeated the Serbs at the famous Battle of Kosovo (KAWSS-suh-voh) in 1389 and ended Serbian hegemony in the area.

16-1b Expansion of the Empire

Under Murad's successor, Bayazid (by-uh-ZEED) I (r. 1389–1402), the Ottomans annexed Bulgaria. When Mehmet (meh-MET) II (r. 1451–1481) succeeded to the throne, he was determined to capture Constantinople. Already in control of the Dardanelles, he ordered the construction of a major fortress on the Bosporus just north of the city, which put the Turks in a position to strangle the Byzantines.

The Fall of Constantinople   In desperation, the last Byzantine emperor called for help from the Europeans, but only the Genoese came to his defense.

With massive cannons (see Chapter 13) and 80,000 troops ranged against only 7,000 defenders, Mehmet laid siege to Constantinople in 1453. The defenders stretched heavy chains across the Golden Horn, the inlet that forms the city's harbor, to prevent a naval attack from the north

The Changing Face of War

"War," as renowned French historian Fernand Braudel once observed, "has always been a matter of arms and techniques. Improved techniques can radically alter the course of events." Braudel's remark was directed to the situation in the Mediterranean region during the sixteenth century when the adoption of artillery changed the face of warfare and gave enormous advantages to those countries that stood at the head of the new technological revolution. But it could as easily have been applied to the present day when potential adversaries possess weapons capable of reaching across oceans and continents.

One crucial aspect of military superiority, of course, lies in the nature of weaponry. From the invention of the bow and arrow to the advent of the atomic era, the possession of superior instruments of war has provided a distinct advantage against a poorly armed enemy. It was at least partly the possession of bronze weapons, for example, that enabled the invading Hyksos to conquer Egypt during the second millennium B.C.E.

Mobility is another factor of vital importance. During the second millennium B.C.E., horse-drawn chariots revolutionized the art of war from the Mediterranean Sea to the Yellow River Valley in northern China. Later, the invention of the stirrup enabled mounted warriors to shoot bows and arrows from horseback, a technique applied with great effect by the Mongols as they devastated civilizations across the Eurasian supercontinent.

To protect themselves from marauding warriors, settled societies began to erect massive walls around their cities and fortresses. That, in turn, led to the invention of siege weapons such as the catapult and the battering ram. The Mongols allegedly even came up with an early form of chemical warfare, hurling human bodies infected with the plague into the bastions of their enemies.

The invention of explosives launched the next great revolution in warfare. First used as a weapon of war by the Tang Dynasty in China, explosives were brought to the West by the Turks, who used them with great effectiveness in the fifteenth century against the

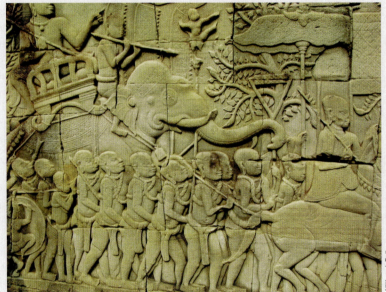

William J. Duiker

16.2 Angkor Troops Advance Against their Enemies in Champa

Byzantine Empire. But the Europeans quickly mastered the new technology and took it to new heights, inventing handheld firearms and mounting iron cannons on their warships. The latter represented a significant advantage to European fleets as they began to compete with rivals for control of the Indian and Pacific Oceans.

The twentieth century saw revolutionary new developments in the art of warfare from armored vehicles to airplanes to nuclear arms. But as weapons grow ever more fearsome, they are more risky to use, resulting in the paradox of the Vietnam War—lightly armed Viet Cong guerrilla units were able to fight the world's mightiest army to a virtual standstill. The lessons of Vietnam have been effectively absorbed in our own day as lightly armed insurgents rely on terror and assassination to promote their goals against more powerful enemies. As Chinese military strategist Sun Tzu had long ago observed, victory in war often goes to the smartest, not the strongest.

Q *Why were the Europeans rather than other peoples able to make effective use of firearms to expand their influence throughout the rest of the world?*

and prepared to make their final stand behind the thirteen-mile-long wall along the western edge of the city. But Mehmet's forces seized the tip of the peninsula north of the Golden Horn and then dragged their ships overland across the peninsula from the Bosporus and put them into the water behind the chains. Finally, the walls were breached; the Byzantine emperor died in the final battle.

The Advance into Western Asia and Africa   With their new capital at Constantinople, eventually renamed Istanbul, the Ottoman Turks became a dominant force in the Balkans and the Anatolian Peninsula. They now began to advance to the east against the Shi'ite kingdom of the Safavids (sah-FAH-weeds) in Persia (see Section 16-2, "The Safavids," p. 401),

which had been promoting rebellion among the Anatolian tribal population and disrupting Turkish trade through the Middle East. After defeating the Safavids at a major battle in 1514, Emperor Selim (seh-LEEM) I (1512–1520) consolidated Turkish control over the territory that had been ancient Mesopotamia and then turned his attention to the Mamluks (MAM-looks) in Egypt, who had failed to support the Ottomans in their struggle against the Safavids. Cairo fell in 1517, and Selim declared himself to be the new caliph or successor to Muhammad. During the next few years, Turkish armies and fleets advanced westward along the African coast, occupying Tripoli, Tunis, and Algeria, and eventually penetrating almost to the Strait of Gibraltar (see Map 16.1).

Map 16.1 The Ottoman Empire. This map shows the territorial growth of the Ottoman Empire from the eve of the conquest of Constantinople in 1453 to the end of the seventeenth century when a defeat at the hands of Austria led to the loss of a substantial portion of central Europe.

Q *Where did the Ottomans come from?*

The impact of Turkish rule on the peoples of North Africa was relatively light. Like their predecessors, the Turks were Muslims, and they preferred where possible to administer their conquered regions through local rulers known as **pashas** (PAH-shuz), who collected taxes (with a fixed percentage sent to the central government), maintained law and order, and were directly responsible to Istanbul. The Turks ruled from coastal cities such as Algiers, Tunis, and Tripoli and made no attempt to control the interior beyond maintaining the trade routes through the Sahara to the trading centers along the Niger River. Meanwhile, local pirates along the Barbary Coast—the northern coast of Africa from Egypt to the Atlantic Ocean—competed with their Christian rivals in raiding shipping in the Mediterranean.

By the seventeenth century, the links between the imperial court in Istanbul and its appointed representatives in North Africa had begun to deteriorate. Some pashas were dethroned by local elites, while others such as the bey of Tunis became hereditary rulers. Even Egypt, whose agricultural wealth and control over the route to the Red Sea made it the most important country in the area to the Turks, gradually became autonomous under a new official class of janissaries.

Turkish Expansion in Europe After their conquest of Constantinople in 1453, the Turks turned their attention back to Europe. Under the leadership of Suleyman (SOO-lay-mahn) I the Magnificent (r. 1520–1566), Turkish forces advanced up the Danube, seizing Belgrade in 1521 and winning a major victory over the Hungarians at the Battle of Mohács (MOH-hach) on the Danube in 1526. Subsequently, the Turks overran most of Hungary, moved into Austria, and advanced as far as Vienna, where they were finally repelled in 1529. At the same time, they extended their power into the western Mediterranean and threatened to turn it into a Turkish lake until the Spanish destroyed a large Turkish fleet at Lepanto (LEH-pahn-toh or LIH-pan-toh) in 1571.

A century later, the Ottomans resumed their offensive, advancing through the Hungarian plain to the gates of Vienna. Repulsed by a coalition of European forces, the Turks retreated once again. Although they retained the core of their empire, the Ottoman Turks would never again be a threat to Europe. The Turkish Empire held together for the rest of the seventeenth and the eighteenth centuries, but it faced new challenges from the ever-growing Austrian Empire in southeastern Europe and the new Russian giant to the north.

16-1c The Nature of Turkish Rule

Like other Muslim empires in Persia and India, the Ottoman political system was the result of the evolution of tribal institutions into a sedentary empire. At the apex of the Ottoman system was the sultan, who was the supreme authority both politically and militarily. The origins of this system can be traced back to the bey, who, as tribal leader, was a first among equals, and could claim loyalty from his chiefs only as long as he could provide them with booty and grazing lands. Disputes were settled by tribal law, and Muslim laws were secondary. Tribal leaders collected taxes—or booty—from areas under their control and sent one-fifth on to the bey. Both administrative and military powers were centralized under the bey, and the capital was wherever the bey and his administration happened to be.

In a manner reminiscent of the Abbasids, however, the rise of empire brought the adoption of Byzantine traditions of rule. The status and prestige of the sultan now increased relative to the subordinate tribal leaders and, with Suleyman the Magnificent—perhaps the empire's greatest ruler—the position took on the trappings of imperial rule (see Historical Voices, "A Portrait of Suleyman the Magnificent," p. 397). Court rituals inherited from the Byzantines and Persians were adopted, as was a centralized administrative system that increasingly isolated the sultan in his palace. The position of the sultan was hereditary, with a son always succeeding the father, although not necessarily the eldest. This practice led to chronic succession struggles on the death of individual sultans, and the losers were often executed (strangled with a silk bowstring) or imprisoned. Heirs to the throne were assigned as provincial governors to provide them with experience.

The Harem The heart of the sultan's power was in the Topkapi (tahp-KAH-pee) Palace in the center of Istanbul. Topkapi (meaning "cannon gate") was constructed in 1459 and served as an administrative center (known as the **Sublime Porte**) as well as the private residence of the sultan and his family. Eventually, it had a staff of 20,000 employees. The sultan's private domain was called the **harem** ("sacred place"). Here he resided with his concubines. Normally, a sultan did not marry but chose several concubines as his favorites; they were accorded this status after they gave birth to sons. When a son became a sultan, his mother became known as the queen mother and administered the royal household. This tradition, initiated by the influential wife of Suleyman the Magnificent, often resulted in considerable authority for the queen mother in affairs of state. Queen mothers also controlled the marital alliances of their daughters with senior officials or with members of other royal families to cement alliances with other states.

A Portrait of Suleyman the Magnificent

Politics & Government **SULEYMAN I WAS PERHAPS THE GREATEST** of all Ottoman sultans. Like King Louis XIV of France and Emperor Kangxi of China, he presided over his domain at the peak of its military and cultural achievement. This description of him was written by Ghislain de Busbecq (GEE-lan duh booz-BEK), the Habsburg ambassador to Constantinople. Busbecq observed Suleyman firsthand and was highly impressed by the Turkish ruler, as this selection indicates.

Ghislain de Busbecq, *The Turkish Letters*

The Sultan was seated on a rather low sofa, no more than a foot from the ground and spread with many costly coverlets and cushions embroidered with exquisite work. Near him were his bow and arrows. His expression, as I have said, is anything but smiling, and has a sternness which, though sad, is full of majesty. On our arrival we were introduced into his presence by his chamberlains, who held our arms—a practice which has always been observed since a Croatian sought an interview and murdered the Sultan Amurath in a revenge for the slaughter of his master, Marcus the Despot of Serbia. After going through the pretense of kissing his hand, we were led to the wall facing him backwards, so as not to turn our backs or any part of them toward him. He then listened to the recital of my message, but, as it did not correspond [to] his expectations (for the demands of my imperial master [the Habsburg emperor Ferdinand I] were full of dignity and independence, and, therefore, far from acceptable to one who thought that his slightest wishes ought to be obeyed), he assumed an expression of disdain, and merely answered "*Giusel, giusel,*" that is, Well, well." We were then dismissed to our lodging. . . .

You will probably wish me to describe the impression which Suleyman made upon me. He is beginning to feel the weight of years, but his dignity of demeanor and his general physical appearance are worthy of the ruler of so vast an empire. He has always been frugal and temperate, and was so even in his youth, when he might have erred without incurring blame in the eyes of the Turks. Even in his earlier years he did not indulge in wine or in those unnatural vices to which the Turks are often addicted. Even his bitterest critics can find nothing more serious to allege against him than his undue submission to his wife and its result in his somewhat precipitate action in putting Mustapha [his firstborn son, by another wife] to death, which is generally imputed to her employment of love potions and incantations. It is generally agreed that ever since he promoted her to the rank of his lawful wife, he has possessed no concubines, although there is no law to prevent his doing so. He is a strict guardian of his religion and its ceremonies, being not less desirous of upholding his faith than of extending his dominions. For his age—he has almost reached his sixtieth year—he enjoys quite good health, though his bad complexion may be due to some hidden malady; and indeed it is generally believed that he has an incurable ulcer or gangrene on his leg. This defect of complexion he remedies by painting his face with a coating of red powder, when he wishes departing ambassadors to take with them a strong impression of his good health; for he fancies that it contributes to inspire greater fear in foreign potentates if they think that he is well and strong.

Q *What were the main achievements of Suleyman that caused him to be called "the Magnificent"? Is this description the work of an admirer or a critic? Why do you think so?*

Members of the harem, like the janissaries, were often of slave origin and formed an elite element in Ottoman society. Because the enslavement of Muslims was forbidden, slaves were taken among non-Islamic peoples. Some concubines were prisoners selected for the position, while others were purchased or offered to the sultan as a gift. They were then trained and educated like the janissaries in a system called *devshirme* (dev-SHEER-may) ("collection"). Devshirme had originated in the practice of requiring local clan leaders to provide prisoners to the sultan as part of their tax obligation. Talented males were given special training for eventual placement in military or administrative positions, while their female counterparts were trained for service in the harem, with instruction in reading and the Qur'an, sewing and embroidery, and musical performance. They were ranked according to their status, and some were permitted to leave the harem to marry officials.

Unique to the Ottoman Empire from the fifteenth century onward was the exclusive use of slaves to produce its royal heirs. Contrary to myth, few of the women of the imperial harem were used for sexual purposes, as the majority were members of the sultan's extended family—sisters,

Claire L. Duiker

16.3a

Yvonne V. Duiker

16.3b

16.3 **The Sultan's Chambers in Topkapi Palace.** After his conquest of Constantinople in 1453, Mehmet II constructed the extensive palace compound known as *Topkapi* as his royal residence and the seat of the new government. Set on a high promontory overlooking the Bosporus and the Sea of Marmara, this self-contained city housed more than 4,000 people and included a royal harem, dormitories, libraries, schools, mosques, a hospital, and gardens with fountains. Shown here (Image 16.3a) is the sultan's imperial throne room. The walls of the harem are covered with magnificent tile work designs, including this design of colorful flowers in vases (Image 16.3b). Ottoman artists were renowned for the high quality of their glazed tile art, which was produced in many colors including their own secret "tomato red," which adorned palaces as well as mosques.

daughters, widowed mothers, and in-laws, with their own personal slaves and entourage. Contemporary European observers compared the atmosphere in the Topkapi harem to a Christian nunnery, with its hierarchical organization, enforced chastity, and rule of silence.

Administration of the Government The sultan ruled through an imperial council that met four days a week and was chaired by the chief minister known as the **grand vizier** (veh-ZEER) (Turkish *vezir*). The sultan often attended behind a screen, whence he could privately indicate his desires to the grand vizier. The latter presided over the imperial bureaucracy. Like the palace guard, the bureaucrats were not an exclusive group but were chosen at least partly by merit from a palace school for training officials. Most officials were Muslims by birth, but some talented janissaries became senior members of the bureaucracy, and almost all the later grand viziers came from the devshirme system.

Local administration during the imperial period was a product of Turkish tribal tradition and was similar in some respects to fief holding in Europe. The empire was divided into provinces and districts governed by officials who, like their tribal predecessors, combined civil and military functions. Senior officials were assigned land in fief by the sultan and were then responsible for collecting taxes and supplying armies to the empire. These lands were then farmed out to the local cavalry elite called the ***sipahis*** (suh-pah-heez), who obtained their salaries by exacting taxes from all peasants in their fiefdoms.

16-1d Religion and Society in the Ottoman World

The Ottoman ruling elites were Sunni Muslims. Having assumed the title of *caliph* ("defender of the faith"), Ottoman sultans were theoretically responsible for guiding the flock and maintaining Islamic law, the shari'a. In practice, the sultan assigned these duties to a supreme religious authority who administered the law and maintained schools for educating Muslims. Islamic law and customs were applied to all Muslims in the empire. Like their rulers, most Turkic-speaking people were Sunni Muslims, but some communities were attracted to Sufism (see Chapter 7) or other heterodox doctrines. The government tolerated such activities as long as their practitioners remained loyal to the state, but unrest among these groups—some of whom converted to the Shi'ite version of Islam—outraged the conservative ulama and eventually led to war against the Safavids (see Section 16-2 "The Safavids" later in this chapter).

The Treatment of Minorities Non-Muslims—mostly Orthodox Christians (Greeks and Slavs), Jews, and Armenian Christians—formed a significant minority

A janissary officer recruiting devsirme for Sultan Suleyman I (1495–1566); from the "Suleymanname" (Mss Hazine. 1517 f.31v), 1558 (ink & gold leaf on vellum), Ali Amir Beg (fl. 1558) / Topkapi Palace Museum, Istanbul, Turkey / The Bridgeman Art Library

16.4 Recruitment of the Children. The Ottoman Empire, like its Chinese counterpart, sought to recruit its officials on the basis of merit. Through the system called *devshirme* ("collection"), youthful candidates were selected from the non-Muslim population in villages throughout the empire. In this painting, an imperial officer is counting coins to pay for the children's travel expenses to Istanbul, where they will undergo extensive academic and military training. Note the concern of two of the mothers and a priest as they question the official, who undoubtedly underwent the process himself as a child. As they leave their family and friends, the children carry their worldly possessions in bags slung over their shoulders.

within the empire, which treated them with relative tolerance. Each religious group was organized as a separate administrative unit called a **millet** (mi-LETT) that governed the community according to its own laws. Non-Muslims were compelled to pay a head tax, but they were permitted to practice their religion or convert to Islam. Most of the population in European areas of the empire remained Christian, but some converted to Islam, most notably in parts of the Balkans.

Social Classes The subjects of the Ottoman Empire were also divided by occupation and place of residence. In addition to the ruling class, there were four main occupational groups: peasants, artisans, merchants, and

pastoral peoples. The first three were classified as "urban" residents. Peasants tilled land that was leased to them by the state (ultimate ownership of all land resided with the sultan), but the land was deeded to them, so they were able to pass it to their heirs. They were not allowed to sell the land and thus in practice were forced to remain on the soil. Taxes were based on the amount of land the peasants possessed and were paid to the local sipahis, who held the district in fief.

Artisans were organized according to craft guilds. Each guild was headed by a council of elders and was responsible not only for dealing with the governmental authorities but also for providing financial services, social security, and training for its members. Outside the ruling elite, merchants were the most privileged class in Ottoman society. They were largely exempt from government regulations and taxes and were therefore able in many cases to amass large fortunes. Charging interest was technically illegal under Islamic law, but the rules were often ignored in practice. In the absence of regulations, merchants often established monopolies and charged high prices, which caused bitter resentment by other subjects of the empire.

Nomadic peoples were placed in a separate millet and were subject to their own regulations and laws. They were divided into the traditional nomadic classifications of tribes, clans, and "tents" (individual families) and were governed by their hereditary chiefs, the beys. As we have seen, the beys were responsible for administration and for collecting taxes for the state.

CHRONOLOGY	The Ottoman Empire
Reign of Osman I	1280–1326
Ottoman Turks cross the Bosporus	1345
Murad I consolidates Turkish power in the Balkans	1360
Ottomans defeat the Serbian army at Kosovo	1389
Reign of Mehmet II the Conqueror	1451–1481
Turkish conquest of Constantinople	1453
Turks defeat the Mamluks in Syria and seize Cairo	1516–1517
Reign of Suleyman I the Magnificent	1520–1566
Turks defeat the Hungarians at Battle of Mohács	1526
Defeat of the Turks at Vienna	1529
Battle of Lepanto	1571
Second siege of Vienna	1683

Experience an interactive version of this period in ❖ MINDTAP

The Position of Women   Women in the Ottoman Empire were subject to the same restrictions that afflicted their counterparts in other Muslim societies, but their position was ameliorated to some degree by various factors. First, non-Muslims were subject to the laws and customs of their own religions; thus, Orthodox Christian, Jewish, and Armenian Christian women were spared some of the restrictions applied to their Muslim sisters (although they were then subject to restrictions imposed by their own faith). Second, Islamic laws as applied in the Ottoman Empire defined the legal position of women comparatively tolerantly, perhaps because Turkish tribal tradition had adopted a more egalitarian view of gender roles than was the case in the sedentary societies around them. Women were permitted to own and inherit property, including their dowries. They could not be forced into marriage and in certain cases were permitted to seek a divorce. As we have seen, women often exercised considerable influence in the palace and in a few instances even served in such senior official positions as governors of provinces.

HISTORIANS DEBATE   **16-1e The Ottoman Empire: A Civilization in Decline?**

By the late seventeenth century, the expansionist tendencies of earlier eras had largely disappeared, and the empire began to lose many of its territorial gains in the region. Many observers have interpreted these conditions as symptoms of a civilization in decline. Recently, however, some historians have taken issue with this paradigm, maintaining that in many respects the empire remained relatively healthy up to the early twentieth century when the final collapse occurred.

The issue is partly a matter of the interpretation of facts. In many respects, the dynamic forces that had predominated during the early stages of growth were no longer present. First, the quality of leadership had begun to decline. Talented early leaders such as Mehmet II and Suleyman the Magnificent gave way to incompetent sultans who lacked interest in the affairs of state and turned responsibility for governing over to administrators or members of the harem. Palace intrigue was the result.

Second, the administrative system began to break down as talented officials selected through the meritocratic devshirme system were gradually transformed into a privileged and often degenerate hereditary caste. Local administrators were corrupted, and taxes rose as the central bureaucracy lost its links with rural areas. Constant wars depleted the treasury, and transport and communications were neglected. In addition, the empire was beset by economic difficulties caused by the diversion of trade routes away from the eastern Mediterranean and the price inflation brought about by the influx of cheap American silver.

Most important, perhaps, was the failure of the Ottomans to take an interest in the technological advances that were being introduced from the scientific revolution in Europe. The adoption of printed books produced from movable type, for example, was resisted vigorously by conservative Muslim clerics, who argued that they were objectionable on religious and aesthetic grounds. Similarly, the use of mechanical clocks to keep accurate time was opposed in favor of the traditional use of the water clock and the sundial. Imports of military technology lagged as well, and the vaunted Ottoman superiority in cannonry gradually disappeared. At root, the Ottomans lacked an interest in events taking place elsewhere in the world and adopted instead an attitude of smug complacency based on the alleged superiority of traditional Islamic civilization.

Ottoman society was by no means totally isolated from the outside world. As familiarity with European civilization gradually increased, cosmopolitan officials and merchants began to mimic the habits and lifestyles of their European counterparts, dressing in the European fashion, purchasing Western furniture and art objects, and ignoring Muslim strictures against the consumption of alcohol and sexual activities outside marriage. Coffee and tobacco had been introduced into polite Ottoman society by the sixteenth century, and cafés for their consumption began to appear in the major cities (see Historical Voices, "A Turkish Discourse on Coffee," p. 401). One sultan in the early seventeenth century issued a decree prohibiting the consumption of both coffee and tobacco, arguing (correctly, no doubt) that many cafés were nests of antigovernment intrigue. He even began to wander incognito through the streets of Istanbul at night. Any of his subjects detected in immoral or illegal acts were summarily executed and their bodies left on the streets as examples to others.

16-1f Ottoman Art

The Ottoman sultans were enthusiastic patrons of the arts. In the period from Mehmet II in the fifteenth century to the early eighteenth century, pottery, rugs, silk and other textiles, jewelry, arms and armor, and calligraphy all flourished. They adorned the palaces of the rulers, testifying to their opulence and exquisite taste. The artists came from all parts of the realm and beyond.

Architecture   The greatest contribution of the Ottoman Empire to world art was probably its architecture,

A Turkish Discourse on Coffee

Interaction & Exchange

COFFEE WAS FIRST INTRODUCED to Turkey from the Arabian Peninsula in the mid-sixteenth century and supposedly came to Europe during the Turkish siege of Vienna in 1529. The following account was written by Katib Chelebi (kah-TEEB CHEL-uh-bee), a seventeenth-century Turkish author who compiled an extensive encyclopedia and bibliography. In *The Balance of Truth,* he describes how coffee entered the empire and the problems it caused for public morality. In the Muslim world, as in Europe and later in colonial America, rebellious elements often met in coffeehouses to promote antigovernment activities. Chelebi died in Istanbul in 1657, reportedly while drinking a cup of coffee.

Katib Chelebi, The *Balance of Truth*

[Coffee] originated in Yemen and has spread, like tobacco, over the world. Certain sheikhs, who lived with their dervishes in the mountains of Yemen, used to crush and eat the berries . . . of a certain tree. Some would roast them and drink their water. Coffee is a cold dry food, suited to the ascetic life and sedative of lust. . . .

It came to Asia Minor by sea, about 1543, and met with a hostile reception, *fetwas* [decrees] being delivered against it. For they said, Apart from its being roasted, the fact that it is drunk in gatherings, passed from hand to hand, is suggestive of loose living. It is related of

Abul-Suud Efendi that he had holes bored in the ships that brought it, plunging their cargoes of coffee into the sea. But these strictures and prohibitions availed nothing. One coffeehouse was opened after another, and men would gather together, with great eagerness and enthusiasm, to drink. Drug addicts in particular, finding it a life-giving thing, which increased their pleasure, were willing to die for a cup.

Storytellers and musicians diverted the people from their employments, and working for one's living fell into disfavor. Moreover the people, from prince to beggar, amused themselves with knifing one another. Toward the end of 1633, the late Ghazi Gultan Murad, becoming aware of the situation, promulgated an edict, out of regard and compassion for the people, to this effect: Coffeehouses throughout the Guarded Domains shall be dismantled and not opened hereafter. Since then, the coffeehouses of the capital have been as desolate as the heart of the ignorant. . . . But in cities and towns outside Istanbul, they are opened just as before. As has been said above, such things do not admit of a perpetual ban.

Q *Why did coffee come to be regarded as a dangerous substance in the Ottoman Empire? Were the authorities successful in suppressing its consumption?*

Source: From The *Balance of Truth* by Katib Chelebi, translated by G. L. Lewis, copyright 1927.

---

especially the magnificent mosques erected throughout the empire. Traditionally, prayer halls in mosques were divided by numerous pillars that supported small individual domes to create a private, forestlike atmosphere. The Turks, however, modeled their new mosques on the open floor plan of the Byzantine church of Hagia Sophia, which had been turned into a mosque by Mehmet II, and they began to push the pillars toward the outer wall to create a prayer hall with an uninterrupted central area under one large dome. With this plan, large numbers of believers could worship in unison in accordance with Muslim preference. By the mid-sixteenth century, the great Ottoman architect Mimar Sinan (si-NAHN) began erecting the first of his eighty-one mosques with an uncluttered prayer area topped by an imposing dome and framed with towering narrow minarets. The interiors were characterized by delicate plasterwork and tile decoration that transformed the

mosque into a monumental oasis of spirituality, opulence, and power (see Comparative Illustration, "Hagia Sophia and the Suleymaniye Mosque," p. 402).

16-2 THE SAFAVIDS

Q **Focus Questions:** What problems did the Safavid Empire face, and how did its rulers attempted to solve them? How did their successes and failures compare with those in the other Muslim empires?

After the collapse of the empire of Tamerlane in the early fifteenth century, the area extending from Persia into Central Asia lapsed into anarchy. The Uzbeks (ooz-BEKS),

Hagia Sophia and the Suleymaniye Mosque

Art & Ideas

THE MAGNIFICENT MOSQUES built under the patronage of Suleyman the Magnificent are a great legacy of the Ottoman Empire and a fitting supplement to Hagia Sophia, the cathedral built by Byzantine emperor Justinian in the sixth century C.E. Towering under a central dome, these mosques seem to defy gravity and, like Gothic cathedrals throughout Europe, convey a sense of weightlessness. The Suleymaniye Mosque (Image 16.5a), constructed in the mid-sixteenth century on a design by great architect Sinan, borrowed many elements from its great predecessor (Image 16.5b) and today is one of the most impressive and most graceful in Istanbul. A far cry from the seventh-century desert mosques constructed of palm trunks, the Ottoman mosques stand among the architectural wonders of the world.

Q *How would you compare the mosques built by the architect Sinan and his successors with the Gothic cathedrals that were being built at the same time in Europe? What do you think accounts for the differences?*

16.5a

Fergus O'Brien/The Image Bank/Getty Images

16.5b

William J. Duiker

Turkic-speaking peoples from Central Asia, were the chief political and military force in the area. From their capital at Bukhara (boh-KAHR-uh or boo-KAH-ruh), east of the Caspian Sea, they sought to control the highly fluid tribal alignments until the emergence of the Safavid Dynasty in Persia at the beginning of the sixteenth century.

The Safavid Dynasty was founded by Shah Ismail (IS-mah-eel) (r. 1487–1524), the descendant of Sheikh Safi al-Din (SAH-fee ul-DIN) (hence the name *Safavid*) (1252-1334), who traced his origins to Ali, the fourth imam of the Muslim faith. In the early fourteenth century, Safi had been the leader of one of the many mystical Sufi communities of Turkic-speaking nomadic people in Azerbaijan west of the Caspian Sea. Safi's community was only one of many Sufi mystical religious groups throughout the area. In time, the doctrine spread throughout the region and was gradually transformed into the more activist Shi'ite version of Islam. Its adherents were known as "red heads" because they wore a distinctive red cap with twelve folds that symbolized allegiance to the twelve imams of the Shi'ite faith.

In 1501, Ismail seized much of the old Abbasid Empire and proclaimed himself the shah of a new Persian state that was to be called *Iran* in deference to the ancient term derived from the ethnic word *Aryan*. Baghdad was subdued in 1508, as were the Uzbeks in Bukhara. Ismail now promoted the Shi'ite faith among the primarily Sunni local population and sent Shi'ite preachers into Anatolia to proselytize among Turkish peoples in the Ottoman Empire. In retaliation, the Ottoman sultan Selim I invaded Safavid territory and won a major battle near Tabriz (tah-BREEZ) in 1514. But Selim could not maintain control of the area, and Ismail regained the city a few years later.

The Ottomans returned to the attack in the 1580s and forced the new Safavid shah, Abbas (uh-BAHS) I the Great (r. 1587–1629), to sign a punitive peace acceding to the loss of much territory. The Safavid capital was subsequently moved for defensive reasons from Tabriz in the northwest to Isfahan (is-fah-HAHN) in the south, where the Safavids attained the zenith of their glory. Shah Abbas established a system similar to the janissaries in Turkey to train administrators to replace the traditional warrior elite. He also used the interval to build up his army, now armed with modern weapons, and attempted to regain the lost territories. War resumed in the 1620s, and a lasting peace was not achieved until 1638 (see Map 16.2).

By centralizing power in his hands and broadening the nation's economy, Abbas the Great managed to consolidate his power base, and Iran was stable and vigorous at his death in 1629. But succession conflicts plagued the dynasty, contributing to an increase in the influence of militant Shi'ites within the court and in Safavid society at large. The intellectual freedom that had characterized the empire at its height was increasingly curtailed under the pressure of religious orthodoxy; Iranian women, who had enjoyed considerable freedom and influence during the early period, were forced to withdraw into seclusion behind the veil. Meanwhile, attempts to suppress the religious beliefs of minorities led to increased popular unrest. In the early eighteenth century, rebellious Afghan warriors seized the capital of Isfahan, forcing the Safavid ruling family to retreat to Azerbaijan, their original homeland. Order was briefly restored by military adventurer Nadir

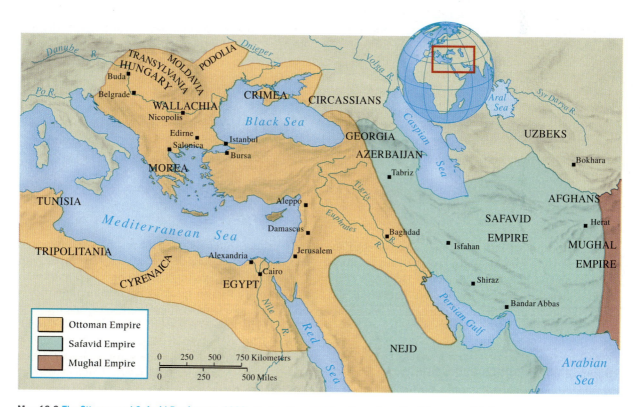

Map 16.2 **The Ottoman and Safavid Empires ca. 1683.** During the seventeenth century, the Ottoman and Safavid Empires contested vigorously for hegemony in the eastern Mediterranean and the Middle East. This map shows the territories controlled by each state in the late seventeenth century.

 Which states shared control over the ancient lands in the Tigris and Euphrates Valleys? In which modern-day countries are those lands?

Experience an interactive version of this period in MINDTAP

The Religious Zeal of Shah Abbas the Great

Religion & Philosophy

SHAH ABBAS I, probably the greatest of the Safavid rulers, expanded the borders of his empire into areas of the southern Caucasus inhabited by Christians and other non-Muslim peoples. After Persian control was ensured, he instructed that local populations be urged to convert to Islam for their own protection and the glory of God. In this passage, his biographer, Persian historian Eskander Beg Monshi (es-KAHN-der bayg MAHN-shee), recounts the story of that effort.

Eskander Beg Monshi, "The Conversion of a Number of Christians to Islam"

This year the Shah decreed that those Armenians and other Christians who had been settled in [the southern Caucasus] and had been given agricultural land there should be invited to become Muslims. Life in this world is fraught with vicissitudes, and the Shah was concerned lest, in a period when the authority of the central government was weak, these Christians . . . might be subjected to attack by the neighboring Lor tribes (who are naturally given to causing injury and mischief), and their women and children carried off into captivity. In the areas in which these Christian groups resided, it was the Shah's purpose that the places of worship which they had built should become mosques, and the muezzin's call should be heard in them, so that these Christians might assume the guise of Muslims, and their future status accordingly be assured. . . .

Some of the Christians, guided by God's grace, embraced Islam voluntarily; others found it difficult to abandon their Christian faith and felt revulsion at the idea. They were encouraged by their monks and priests to remain steadfast in their faith. After a little pressure had been applied to the monks and priests, however, they desisted, and these Christians saw no alternative but to embrace Islam, though they did so with reluctance. The women and children embraced Islam with great enthusiasm, vying with one another in their eagerness to abandon their Christian faith and declare their belief in the unity of God. Some five thousand people embraced Islam. As each group made the Muslim declaration of faith, it received instruction in the Koran and the principles of the religious law of Islam, and all bibles and other Christian devotional material were collected and taken away from the priests.

In the same way, all the Armenian Christians who had been moved to [the area] were also forcibly converted to Islam . . . . Most people embraced Islam with sincerity, but some felt an aversion to making the Muslim profession of faith. True knowledge lies with God! May God reward the Shah for his action with long life and prosperity!

Q *How do Shah Abbas's efforts to convert nonbelievers to Islam compare with similar programs by Muslim rulers in India, as described in Chapter 9? What did the author of this selection think about the conversions?*

Source: From Eskander Beg Monshi in *History of Shah Abbas the Great*, Vol. II by Roger M. Savory by Westview Press, 1978.

Shah Afshar (NAH-der shah ahf-SHAR), who launched an extended series of campaigns that recovered lost territory and even occupied the Mughal capital of Delhi (see "The Shadows Lengthen" later in this chapter). After his death, the Zand Dynasty took over and ruled until the end of the eighteenth century.

16-2a Safavid Politics and Society

Like the Ottoman Empire, Iran under the Safavids was a mixed society The dynasty had come to power with the support of Turkic-speaking pastoral peoples, and leading elements from those groups retained considerable influence. The majority of the population, however, was Persian—most were farmers or townspeople—and their attitudes often reflected the relatively sophisticated and urbanized culture of pre-Safavid Iran. Faced with the problem of integrating unruly nomadic peoples with the sedentary Persian-speaking population, the Safavids used the Shi'ite faith as a unifying force (see Historical Voices, "The Religious Zeal of Shah Abbas the Great," above). The shah himself acquired an almost divine quality and claimed to be the spiritual leader of all Islam. Shi'ism was declared the state religion.

Although there was a landed aristocracy, power and influence gravitated toward strong-minded shahs who confiscated aristocratic estates and brought them under the control of the crown. Appointment to senior positions in the bureaucracy was now by merit rather than by birth.

The Safavid shahs took a direct interest in the local economy and actively engaged in commercial and manufacturing activities, although there was also a large and affluent urban bourgeoisie, many of them of Armenian or Indian extraction. The currency was reformed, and exports such as silk products, horses, and almonds were promoted. Like the Ottoman sultan, one shah regularly traveled the city streets incognito to check on the honesty of his subjects. When he discovered that a baker and butcher were overcharging for their products, he had the baker cooked in his own oven and the butcher roasted on a spit.

At its height, Safavid Iran was a worthy successor to the great Persian empires of the past, although it was undoubtedly not as wealthy as its Mughal and Ottoman neighbors. Hemmed in by the sea power of the Europeans to the south and the land power of the Ottomans to the west, the early Safavids had no navy and were forced to divert overland trade with Europe through southern Russia to avoid an Ottoman blockade. The situation improved when Persian forces working with the English seized the island of Hormuz (hawr-MOOZ) from Portugal and established a new seaport on the southern coast at Bandar Abbas (BUHN-der uh-BAHS). As a consequence, commercial ties with Europe began to increase.

16-2b Safavid Art and Literature

Persia witnessed an extraordinary flowering of the arts under the Safavids. Abbas the Great's new capital of Isfahan was a grandiose planned city with wide visual perspectives and a sense of order almost unique in the region. Shah Abbas ordered his architects to position his palaces, mosques, and bazaars around a massive rectangular polo ground. The immense mosques are richly decorated with imaginative metalwork and elaborate blue tiles.

16.6 The Royal Academy of Isfahan. Along with institutions such as libraries and hospitals, theological schools were often included in the mosque compound. One of the most sumptuous was the Royal Academy of Isfahan, which was built by the shah of Persia in the early eighteenth century. This view shows the large courtyard surrounded by arcades of student rooms, which are reminiscent of the arrangement of monks' cells in European cloisters.

George Holton/Science Source

The palaces are delicate structures with unusual slender wooden columns. These architectural wonders of Isfahan epitomize the grandeur, delicacy, and color that defined the Safavid golden age.

Textiles and painting were also areas of great achievement. Silk weaving based on new techniques became a national industry. Carpet weaving flourished, stimulated by the great demand for Persian carpets in Europe. The long tradition of Persian painting also continued, although with some changes. Taking advantage of the official toleration of portraiture, painters began to highlight the inner character of their subjects. Artists also sought to attract an audience beyond the royal court by producing individual paintings that promoted their own distinctive styles and proudly bore their own signatures.

16-3 THE GRANDEUR OF THE MUGHALS

Focus Questions: What role did Islam play in the Mughal Empire, and how did the Mughals' approach to religion compare with that of the Ottomans and the Safavids? What might explain the differences?

The Mughal (MOO-gul) Dynasty, which seized power in northern India in the early sixteenth century, has often been viewed as a high point of traditional culture in India. Unifying the bulk of the subcontinent for the first time in

CHRONOLOGY	The Safavids
Ismail seizes Persia and Iraq and becomes shah of Persia	1501
Ismail conquers Baghdad and defeats Uzbeks	1508
Reign of Shah Abbas I	1587–1629
Truce achieved between Ottomans and Safavids	1638
Collapse of the Safavid Empire	1723

more than a millennium, the Mughals created a common culture that inspired admiration and envy throughout the entire region.

16-3a The Founding of the Empire

When the Portuguese fleet led by Vasco da Gama arrived at the port of Calicut in 1498, the Indian subcontinent was still divided into many Hindu and Muslim kingdoms. But it was on the verge of a new era of unity that would be brought about by a foreign dynasty—the Mughals. Like so many of their predecessors, the founders of the Mughal Empire were not natives of India but came from the mountainous region north of the Ganges River. The founder of the dynasty, known to history as Babur (BAH-burr) (1483–1530), had an illustrious pedigree. His father was descended from the great Asian conqueror Tamerlane, his mother from the Mongol conqueror Genghis Khan.

Babur had inherited a fragment of Tamerlane's empire in a valley of the Syr Darya (SEER DAHR-yuh) River. Driven south by the rising power of the Uzbeks and then the Safavid Dynasty in Persia, Babur and his warriors seized Kabul in 1504 and crossed the Khyber Pass to India thirteen years later.

Following a pattern we have seen before, Babur began his rise to power by offering to help an ailing dynasty against its opponents. Although his own forces were far smaller than those of his adversaries, he possessed advanced weapons, including artillery, and used them to great effect. His use of mobile cavalry, supplemented by mounted elephants, was particularly successful against the massed forces of his enemy. In 1526, with only 12,000 troops against an enemy force nearly ten times that size, Babur captured Delhi (DEL-ee). Over the next years, he continued his conquests in northern India until his early death in 1530 at age forty-seven.

Babur's success was partly the result of his vigor and his charismatic personality, which earned him the undying loyalty of his followers. His son and successor Humayun (hoo-MY-yoon) (r. 1530–1556) was, in the words of one British historian, "intelligent but lazy." In 1540, he was forced to flee to Persia, where he lived in exile for sixteen years. Finally, with the aid of the Safavid shah of Persia, he returned to India and reconquered Delhi in 1555 but died the following year, reportedly from injuries suffered in a fall after smoking opium.

Humayun was succeeded by his son Akbar (r. 1556–1605). Born while his father was in exile, Akbar was only fourteen when he mounted the throne. Highly intelligent and industrious, Akbar set out to extend his domain, then limited to the Punjab (puhn-JAHB) and the upper Ganges River Valley. "A monarch," he remarked, should be ever intent on conquest; otherwise his neighbors rise in arms against him. The army "should be exercised in warfare, lest from want of training they become self-indulgent."[1] By the end of his life, he had brought Mughal rule to most of the subcontinent—from the Himalaya Mountains to central India and from Kashmir to the mouths of the Brahmaputra (brah-muh-POO-truh) and Ganges Rivers. In so doing, Akbar had created the greatest Indian empire since the Mauryan Dynasty nearly 2,000 years earlier (see Map 16.3). Though it appeared highly centralized from the outside, the empire was actually a collection of semiautonomous principalities ruled by provincial elites and linked together by the overarching majesty of the Mughal emperor.

16-3b Akbar and Indo-Muslim Civilization

Although Akbar was probably the greatest of the conquering Mughal monarchs, he was like his famous predecessor Ashoka and best known for the humane character of his rule. Above all, he accepted the diversity of Indian society and took steps to reconcile his Muslim and Hindu subjects.

Religion and the State Though raised an orthodox Muslim, Akbar had been exposed to other beliefs during his childhood and had little patience with the pedantic views of Muslim scholars at court. As emperor, he displayed a keen interest in other religions, not only tolerating Hindu practices and taking a Hindu princess as one of his wives but also welcoming the expression of Christian views by his Jesuit advisers (the Jesuits first sent a mission to Agra in 1580). He patronized classical Indian arts and architecture and abolished many of the restrictions faced by Hindus in a Muslim-dominated society.

During his later years, Akbar became steadily more hostile to Islam. To the dismay of many Muslims at court, he sponsored a new form of worship called the Divine Faith (*Din-i-ilahi*), which combined characteristics of several religions with a central belief in the infallibility of all decisions reached by the emperor. The new faith aroused deep hostility in Muslim circles and rapidly vanished after his death.

Administrative Reforms Akbar also extended his innovations to the imperial administration. Although the upper ranks of the government continued to be dominated by nonnative Muslims, a substantial proportion of lower-ranking officials were Hindus, and a few were appointed to positions of importance. The same element of religious tolerance extended to the legal system. Although Muslims were subject to the Islamic codes (the shari'a), Hindu law was applied in areas settled by Hindus, who after 1579 were no longer required to pay the unpopular jizya (JIZ-yuh), or

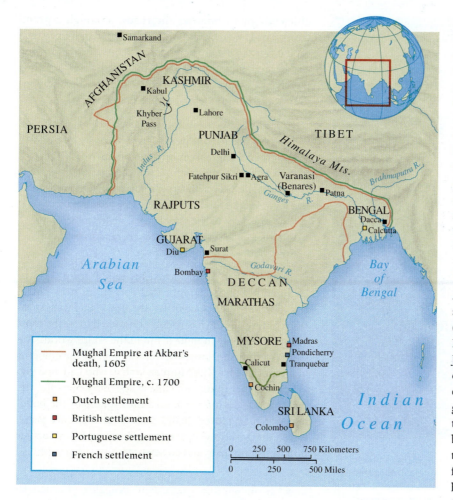

and manufacturing flourished. Foreign trade in particular thrived as Indian goods—notably textiles, tropical food products, spices, and precious stones—were exported in exchange for gold and silver. Tariffs on imports were low. Much of the foreign commerce was handled by Arab traders because the Indians, like their Mughal rulers, did not care for travel by sea. Internal trade, however, was dominated by large merchant castes, who also were active in banking and handicrafts.

16-3c Akbar's Successors

Akbar died in 1605 and was succeeded by his son Jahangir (juh-HAHN-geer) (r. 1605–1628). During the early years of his reign, Jahangir continued to strengthen central control over the vast empire. Eventually, however, his grip began to weaken (according to his memoirs, he "only wanted a bottle of wine and a piece of meat to make merry"), and the court fell under the influence of one of his wives, Persian-born Nur Jahan (NOOR juh-HAHN). The empress took advantage of her position to enrich her own family and arranged for her niece Mumtaz Mahal (MOOM-tahz muh-HAHL) to marry her husband's third son and ultimate successor, Shah Jahan (r. 1628–1657). When Shah Jahan succeeded to the throne, he quickly demonstrated the single-minded quality of his grandfather (albeit in a much more brutal manner), ordering the assassination of all of his rivals to secure his position.

Map 16.3 The Mughal Empire. This map shows the expansion of the Mughal Empire from the death of Akbar in 1605 to the rule of Aurangzeb at the end of the seventeenth century.

Q *In which cities on the map were European settlements located? When did each group of Europeans arrive, and how did the settlements spread?*

poll tax on non-Muslims. Punishments for crime were mild by the standards of the day, and justice was administered in a relatively impartial and efficient manner.

To cover the costs of administration, Akbar assigned plots of farmland to local civilian and military officials for their temporary use. These officials, known as *zamindars* (zuh-meen-DAHRZ), were expected to collect taxes from peasants tilling the lands under their control and forward them to the central government at its capital in Agra. They often accumulated considerable power in their localities. Although all Indian peasants were required to pay around one-third of their annual harvest to the state through the zamindars, in general the system was applied fairly; when drought struck in the 1590s, the taxes were reduced or even suspended altogether. Thanks to a long period of relative peace and political stability, commerce

The Reign of Shah Jahan During a reign of three decades, Shah Jahan maintained the system established by his predecessors while expanding the boundaries of the empire by successful campaigns in the Deccan Plateau and against Samarkand, north of the Hindu Kush. But Shah Jahan's rule was marred by his failure to deal with the growing domestic problems. He had inherited a nearly empty treasury because of Empress Nur Jahan's penchant for luxury and ambitious charity projects. Though the majority of his subjects lived in

Experience an interactive version of this period in MINDTAP

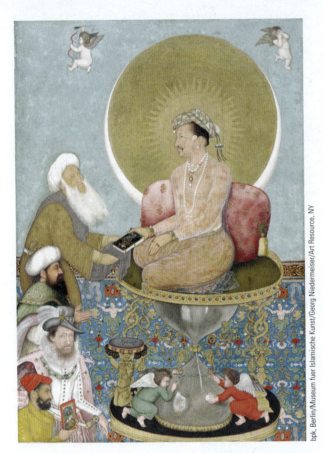

efficiency or to improve the roads, although a grand trunk road was eventually constructed between the capital Agra (AH-gruh) and Lahore (luh-HOHR), a growing city several hundred miles to the northwest. A Dutch merchant in Gujarat (goo-juh-RAHT) described conditions during a famine in the mid-seventeenth century:

> As the famine increased, men abandoned towns and villages and wandered helplessly. It was easy to recognize their condition: eyes sunk deep in head, lips pale and covered with slime, the skin hard, with the bones showing through, the belly nothing but a pouch hanging down empty, knuckles and kneecaps showing prominently. One would cry and howl for hunger, while another lay stretched on the ground dying in misery; wherever you went, you saw nothing but corpses.[2]

In 1648, Shah Jahan moved his capital from Agra to Delhi and built the famous Red Fort in his new capital city. But he is best known for the Taj Mahal (tahj muh-HAHL) in Agra, which is widely considered to be the most beautiful building in India if not in the entire world. The story is a romantic one—the Taj was built by the emperor in memory of his wife Mumtaz Mahal, who had died giving birth to her thirteenth child at age thirty-nine. But the reality has a less attractive side: the expense of the building, which employed 20,000 masons over twenty years, forced the government to raise agricultural taxes, further impoverishing many Indian peasants.

Rule of Aurangzeb Succession struggles returned to haunt the dynasty in the mid-1650s when Shah Jahan's illness led to a struggle for power between his sons Dara Shikoh (DA-ruh SHIH-koh) and Aurangzeb (ow-rang-ZEB). Dara Shikoh was described by his contemporaries as progressive and humane, but he apparently lacked political acumen and was outmaneuvered by Aurangzeb (r. 1658–1707), who had Dara Shikoh put to death and then imprisoned his father in the fort at Agra.

Aurangzeb is one of the most controversial individuals in the history of India. A man of high principle, he attempted to eliminate many of what he considered to be India's social evils, prohibiting the immolation of widows on their husband's funeral pyre (a practice known as *sati*), the castration of eunuchs, and the exaction of illegal taxes. With less success, he tried to forbid gambling, drinking, and prostitution. But Aurangzeb, a devout and somewhat doctrinaire Muslim, also adopted several measures that reversed the policies of religious tolerance established by his predecessors. The building of new Hindu temples was prohibited, and the Hindu poll tax was restored. Forced conversions to Islam were

16.7 **Jahangir the Magnificent.** In 1615, the English ambassador to the Mughal court presented an official portrait of King James I to Shah Jahangir, who returned the favor with a portrait of himself. Thus was established a long tradition of exchanging paintings between the two empires. As it turned out, the practice altered the style of Mughal portraiture, which had previously shown the emperor in action—hunting, participating at official functions, or engaging in battle. Henceforth, portraits of the ruler followed European practice by focusing on the opulence and spiritual power of the empire. In this painting, Jahangir has chosen spiritual over earthly power by offering a book to a sheikh while ignoring the Ottoman sultan, King James I, and the Hindu artist who painted the picture. Even the cherubs, a European artifice, are dazzled by the shah's divine character, which is further demonstrated by an enormous halo.

grinding poverty, Shah Jahan's frequent military campaigns and expensive building projects put a heavy strain on the imperial finances and compelled him to raise taxes. At the same time, the government did little to improve rural conditions. In a country where transport was primitive (it often took three months to travel the 600 miles between Patna, in the middle of the Ganges River Valley, and Delhi) and drought conditions frequent, the dynasty made few efforts to increase agricultural

16.8 The Taj Mahal: symbol of the exotic East. Completed in 1653, the Taj Mahal was built by Mughal Emperor Shah Jahan as a tomb to commemorate his beloved wife, Mumtaz Mahal. Raised on a marble platform above the Yamuna River, the Taj is dramatically framed by contrasting twin red sandstone mosques, magnificent gardens, and a long reflecting pool that mirrors and magnifies its beauty. The effect is one of monumental size, near blinding brilliance, and delicate lightness, a startling contrast to the heavier and more masculine Baroque style then popular in Europe. The entire exterior and interior surface of the Taj is decorated with cut-stone geometric patterns, delicate black stone tracery, or intricate inlay of colored precious stones in floral and Qur'anic arabesques.

resumed, and non-Muslims were driven from the court. Aurangzeb's heavy-handed religious policies led to a revival of Hindu fervor. The last years of his reign saw considerable domestic unrest and several revolts against imperial authority.

The Shadows Lengthen During the eighteenth century, Mughal power was threatened from both within and without. Fueled by the growing power and autonomy of the local gentry and merchants, rebellious groups throughout the empire—from the Deccan to the Punjab—began to reassert local authority and reduce the power of the Mughal emperor to that of a "tinsel sovereign." Increasingly divided, India was vulnerable to attack from abroad. In 1739, Delhi was sacked by the Persians, who left it in ashes.

We can identify several obvious reasons for the virtual collapse of the Mughal Empire, including a drain on the imperial treasury and the decline in competence of the Mughal rulers. But also note that even at its height under Akbar, the empire was a loosely knit collection of heterogeneous principalities held together by the authority of the throne, which tried to combine Persian concepts of kingship with the Indian tradition of decentralized power. Decline set in when centrifugal forces gradually began to predominate over centripetal ones.

16-3d The Impact of European Power in India

As we have seen, the first Europeans to arrive were the Portuguese. Although they established a virtual monopoly over regional trade in the Indian Ocean, they did not seek to penetrate the interior of the subcontinent but focused on establishing way stations en route to China and the Spice Islands. The situation changed at the end of the sixteenth century when the English and the Dutch appeared on the scene. Soon both powers were in active competition with Portugal and with each other for trading privileges in the region (see Opposing Viewpoints, "The Capture of Port Hoogly," p. 410).

Penetration of the new market was not easy. When the first English fleet arrived at Surat (SOOR-et), a thriving port on India's northwestern coast, in 1608, their request for trading privileges was rejected by Emperor Jahangir. Needing lightweight Indian cloth to trade for spices in the East Indies, the English persisted, and they were finally permitted to install their own ambassador at the imperial court in Agra in 1616. Three years later, the first English factory (trading station) was established at Surat.

During the next several decades, the English presence in India steadily increased while Mughal power gradually waned. By midcentury, additional English factories had been established at Fort William (now the city of Kolkata,

The Capture of Port Hoogly

 Interaction & Exchange **IN 1632, THE MUGHAL RULER, SHAH JAHAN, ORDERED AN ATTACK** on the city of Hoogly (HOOG-lee), a fortified Portuguese trading post on the northeastern coast of India. For the Portuguese, who had profited from half a century of triangular trade between India, China, and various countries in the Middle East and Southeast Asia, the loss of Hoogly at the hands of the Mughals hastened the decline of their influence in the region. Presented here are two contemporary versions of the battle. The first is from the *Padshahnama* (pad-shah-NAHM-uh) (*Book of Kings*) and relates the course of events from the Mughal point of view. The second account is by John Cabral, a Jesuit missionary who was resident in Hoogly at the time.

The *Padshahnama*

During the reign of the Bengalis, a group of Frankish [European] merchants . . . settled in a place one *kos* from Satgaon . . . and, on the pretext that they needed a place for trading, they received permission from the Bengalis to construct a few edifices. Over time, due to the indifference of the governors of Bengal, many Franks gathered there and built dwellings of the utmost splendor and strength, fortified with cannons, guns, and other instruments of war. It was not long before it became a large settlement and was named Hoogly. . . . The Franks' ships trafficked at this port, and commerce was established, causing the market at the port of Satgaon to slump. . . . Of the peasants of those places, they converted some to Christianity by force and others through greed and sent them off to Europe in their ships. . . .

Since the improper actions of the Christians of Hoogly Port toward the Muslims were accurately reflected in the mirror of the mind of the Emperor before his accession to the throne, when the imperial banners cast their shadows over Bengal, and inasmuch as he was always inclined to propagate the true religion and eliminate infidelity, it was decided that when he gained control over this region he would eradicate the corruption of these abominators from the realm.

John Cabral, *Travels of Sebastian Manrique, 1629–1649*

Hugli continued at peace all the time of the great King Jahangir. For, as this Prince, by what he showed, was more attached to Christ than to Mohammad and was a Moor in name and dress only. . . . Sultan Khurram [Shah Jahan] was in everything unlike his father, especially as regards the latter's leaning towards Christianity. . . . He declared himself the mortal enemy of the Christian name and the restorer of the law of Mohammad. . . . He sent a *firman* [order] to the Viceroy of Bengal, commanding him without reply or delay, to march upon the Bandel of Hugli and put it to fire and the sword. He added that, in doing so, he would render a signal service to God, to Mohammad, and to him. . . .

Consequently, on a Friday, September 24, 1632, . . . all the people [the Portuguese] embarked with the utmost secrecy. . . . Learning what was going on, and wishing to be able to boast that they had taken Hugli by storm, they [the imperialists] made a general attack on the Bandel by Saturday noon. They began by setting fire to a mine, but lost in it more men than we. Finally, however, they were masters of the Bandel.

Q *How do these two accounts of the Battle of Hoogly differ? Is there any way to reconcile the two accounts into a single narrative?*

Source: From *King of the World: A Mughal Manuscript from the Royal Library, Windsor Castle*, trans. by Wheeler Thackston, text by Milo Cleveland Beach and Ebba Koch (London: Thames and Hudson, 1997), p. 59.

formerly Calcutta) on the Hoogly River near the Bay of Bengal and in 1639 at Madras (muh-DRAS or muh-DRAHS) (Chennai) on the southeastern coast. From there, English ships carried Indian-made cotton goods to the East Indies, where they were bartered for spices that were shipped back to England.

English success in India attracted rivals, including the Dutch and the French. The Dutch eventually abandoned their interests in India to concentrate on the spice trade, but the French were more persistent and established factories of their own. For a brief period, under the ambitious empire builder Joseph François Dupleix (zho-ZEF frahn-SWAH doo-PLAY), the French competed successfully with the British, even capturing Madras from a British garrison in 1746. But the French government was reluctant to support Dupleix's ambitious plans, and eventually the British, under the leadership of Sir Robert Clive (CLYV), an aggressive administrator and empire builder with the East India Company, drove the French out of South India, leaving them only their fort at Pondicherry (pon-duh-CHEH-ree) and a handful of small territories on the southeastern coast.

Clive's victory over the French marked the opening stage in an intensive effort to consolidate British influence in other parts of the Mughal Empire. When a local potentate attacked the British settlement at Fort William and imprisoned the local British population in the infamous Black Hole of Calcutta (an underground prison for holding prisoners, many of whom died in captivity), the British retaliated by defeating a Mughal-led army more than ten times its size in the Battle of Plassey (PLASS-ee). As part of the spoils of victory, the British East India Company exacted from the now-decrepit Mughal court the authority to collect taxes from extensive lands in the area surrounding Calcutta (Kolkata). Less than a decade later, British forces seized the reigning Mughal emperor in a skirmish at Buxar (buk-SAHR), and the British began to consolidate their economic and administrative control over Indian territory through the surrogate power of the now powerless Mughal court (see Map 16.4).

Map 16.4 India in 1805. By the early nineteenth century, much of the Indian subcontinent had fallen under British domination.

Q *Where was the capital of the Mughal Empire located?*

Economic Difficulties The Company's takeover of vast landholdings, notably in the eastern Indian states of Orissa (uh-RIH-suh) and Bengal (ben-GAHL), may have been a windfall for enterprising British officials, but it was a disaster for the Indian economy. First, it transferred capital from the local Indian aristocracy to company officials, most of whom sent their profits back to Britain. Second, it hastened the destruction of once healthy local industries because British goods such as machine-made textiles were imported duty-free into India to compete against local products. Finally, British expansion hurt the peasants. As the British took over the administration of the land tax, they also applied British law, which allowed the lands of those unable to pay the tax to be confiscated. In the 1770s, a series of massive famines led to the death of an estimated one-third of the population in the areas under company administration. The British government attempted to resolve the problem by assigning tax lands to the local revenue collectors (zamindars) in the hope of transforming them into English-style rural gentry, but many collectors themselves fell into bankruptcy and sold their lands to absentee bankers while the now landless peasants remained in abject poverty. It was hardly an auspicious beginning to "civilized" British rule.

16.9 A Pepper Plantation. During the Age of Exploration, pepper was one of the spices most sought by European adventurers. Unlike cloves and nutmeg, it was found in other areas of Asia besides the Indonesian archipelago. Shown here is a medieval European portrayal of a pepper plantation in southern India. The illustration appeared in a fifteenth-century edition of *The Travels of Marco Polo*.

Unfortunately for India, most Indian commanders could not effectively fight the British. In the last years of the eighteenth century, the stage was set for the final consolidation of British rule over the subcontinent.

HISTORIANS DEBATE **16-3e The Mughal Dynasty: A "Gunpowder Empire"?**

To some recent historians, the success of the Mughals, like that of the Ottomans and the Safavids, was the result of their mastery of modern warfare techniques, especially the use of firearms. In this view, firearms played a central role in the rise of all three empires to regional hegemony. Accordingly, some scholars have labeled them "gunpowder empires." Although technical prowess in the art of warfare was undoubtedly a key element in their success, we should not forget that other factors such as dynamic leadership, political acumen, and ardent followers motivated by religious zeal were at least equally important. Even today, many Indians regard Akbar as the country's greatest ruler, a tribute not only to his military success but also to the humane policies adopted during his reign.

Unlike the Ottoman Turks, however, the Mughals were inconsistent in applying a policy of tolerance for the non-Muslim peoples within their borders. Aurangzeb's policy of actively converting peoples of other faiths to

the reigning ideology of Islam was undoubtedly a factor in the rise of Hindu insurgent groups seeking to break away from Mughal rule during his reign. In other respects, the Mughals suffered from the same limitations that afflicted their counterparts in Isfahan and Istanbul. Smugly confident in the superiority of their culture to that of potential rivals, they expressed little interest in the dramatic changes taking place in the fields of science and technology. Eventually, even their vaunted superiority in the art of war abandoned them as they failed to realize the importance of adopting modern naval technology and tactics, a tragic mistake that placed them as a disadvantage in an era when naval warfare was becoming the key to national survival.

16-3f Society Under the Mughals: A Synthesis of Cultures

The Mughals were the last of the great traditional Indian dynasties. Like so many of their predecessors since the fall of the Guptas nearly a thousand years before, the Mughals were Muslims. But like the Ottoman Turks, the best Mughal rulers did not simply impose Islamic institutions and beliefs on the predominantly Hindu population; they combined Muslim with Hindu and even Persian concepts and cultural values in a unique social and cultural synthesis. The new faith of Sikhism, founded in the early sixteenth

that the mystical and devotional qualities promoted by Sufi missionaries corresponded to local traditions. This was especially true in Bengal, on the eastern edge of the Indian subcontinent, where Hindu practices were not as well established and where forms of religious devotionalism had long been popular.

The Economy Although much of the local population in the subcontinent lived in poverty punctuated by occasional periods of widespread famine, the first centuries of Mughal rule were in some respects a period of relative prosperity for the region. India was a leading participant in the growing foreign trade that crisscrossed the Indian Ocean from the Red Sea and the Persian Gulf to the Strait of Malacca and the Indonesian Archipelago. High-quality cloth from India was especially prized, and the country's textile industry made it, in the words of one historian, "the industrial workshop of the world."

Long-term stability led to increasing commercialization and the spread of wealth to new groups within Indian society. The Mughal era saw the emergence of an affluent landed

16.10 The Astronomical Observatory of Jai Singh. Although Mughal elites generally expressed little interest in science and technology, one Indian ruler who broke the mold was the Hindu ruler of Jaipur, Jai Singh. In the 1720s, he ordered the construction of an astronomical observatory in his palace to study the movement of the heavenly bodies. Unfortunately, much of the equipment—some of which is shown here—consisted of outdated instruments and lacked the capacity to compete with the accurate telescopic observations then being carried out in Europe. The observatory was closed a few years later and is now merely a curiosity.

century in an effort to blend both faiths (see Chapter 9), undoubtedly benefited from the mood of syncretism promoted by the Mughal court.

To be sure, Hindus sometimes attempted to defend themselves and their religious practices against the efforts of some Mughal monarchs to impose the Islamic religion and Islamic mores on the indigenous population. In some cases, despite official prohibitions, Hindu men forcibly married Muslim women and then converted them to the native faith, while converts to Islam normally lost all of their inheritance rights within the Indian family. Government orders to destroy Hindu temples were often ignored by local officials, sometimes as the result of bribery or intimidation. Although the founding emperor Babur expressed little admiration for the country he had subjected to his rule, ultimately Indian practices had an influence on the Mughal elites as many Mughal chieftains married Indian women and adopted Indian forms of dress.

In some areas, Emperor Akbar's tireless effort to bring about a blend of Middle Eastern and South Asian religious and cultural values paid rich dividends as substantial numbers of Indians converted to Islam during the centuries of Mughal rule. Some were undoubtedly attracted to the religion's egalitarian characteristics, but others found

CHRONOLOGY	The Mughal Era
Arrival of Vasco da Gama at Calicut	1498
Babur seizes Delhi	1526
Death of Babur	1530
Humayun recovers throne in Delhi	1555
Death of Humayun and accession of Akbar	1556
First Jesuit mission to Agra	1580
Death of Akbar and accession of Jahangir	1605
Arrival of English at Surat	1608
English embassy to Agra	1616
Reign of Emperor Shah Jahan	1628–1657
Foundation of English factory at Madras	1639
Aurangzeb succeeds to the throne	1658
Death of Aurangzeb	1707
Sack of Delhi by the Persians	1739
French capture Madras	1746
Battle of Plassey	1757

gentry and a prosperous merchant class. Members of prestigious castes from the pre-Mughal period reaped many of the benefits of the increasing wealth, but some of these changes transcended caste boundaries and led to the emergence of new groups who achieved status and wealth on the basis of economic achievement rather than traditional kinship ties. During the late eighteenth century, this economic prosperity was shaken by the decline of the Mughal Empire and the increasing European presence. But many prominent Indians reacted by establishing commercial relationships with the foreigners. For a time, such relationships often worked to the Indians' benefit. As we shall see, they would later have cause to regret the arrangement.

The Position of Women   Whether Mughal rule had much effect on the lives of ordinary Indians seems somewhat problematic. The treatment of women is a good example. Women had traditionally played an active role in Mongol tribal society—many actually fought on the battlefield alongside men—and Babur and his successors often relied on the women in their families for political advice. Women from aristocratic families were often awarded honorific titles, received salaries, and were permitted to own land and engage in business. Women at court sometimes received an education, and aristocratic women often expressed their creative talents by writing poetry, painting, or playing music. Women of all classes were adept at spinning thread, either for their own use or to sell to weavers to augment the family income. They sold simple cloth to local villages and fine cottons, silks, and wool to the Mughal court.

To a certain degree, these Mughal attitudes toward women may have affected Indian society. Women were allowed to inherit land, and some even possessed zamindar rights. Women from mercantile castes sometimes took an active role in business activities. At the same time, however, as Muslims, the Mughals subjected women to certain restrictions under Islamic law. On the whole, these Mughal practices coincided with and even accentuated existing tendencies in Indian society. The Muslim practice of isolating women and preventing them from associating with men outside the home (*purdah*) was adopted by many upper-class Hindus as a means of enhancing their status or protecting their women from unwelcome advances by Muslims in positions of authority. In other ways, Hindu practices were unaffected. The custom of sati continued to be practiced despite efforts by the Mughals to abolish it, and child marriage (most women were betrothed before age ten) remained common. Women were still instructed to obey their husbands without question and to remain chaste.

16-3g Mughal Culture

The era of the Mughals was one of synthesis in culture, politics, and religion. The Mughals combined Islamic themes with Persian and indigenous motifs to produce a unique style that enriched and embellished Indian art and culture. The Mughal emperors were zealous patrons of the arts and enticed painters, poets, and artisans from as far away as the Mediterranean. Apparently, the generosity of the Mughals made it difficult to refuse a trip to India. It was said that they would reward a poet with his weight in gold.

Architecture   Undoubtedly, the Mughals' most visible achievement was in architecture. Here they integrated Persian and Indian styles in a new and sometimes breathtakingly beautiful form best symbolized by the Taj Mahal, which was built by the emperor Shah Jahan in the mid-seventeenth century. Although the human and economic cost of the Taj tarnishes the romantic legend of its construction, there is no denying the beauty of the building. Ironically, after Shah Jahan was deposed by his son Aurangzeb, he spent his last years imprisoned in a room in the adjacent Red Fort at Agra; from his windows, he could see the beautiful memorial to his beloved wife.

The Taj was not the only magnificent building erected during the Mughal era. Akbar, who, in the words of a contemporary, "[dressed] the work of his mind and heart in the garment of stone and clay," was the first of the great Mughal builders. His first palace at Agra, the Red Fort, was begun in 1565. A few years later, he ordered the construction of a new palace at Fatehpur Sikri (fah-tay-POOR SIK-ree), twenty-six miles west of Agra. The new palace was built in honor of a Sufi mystic who had correctly forecast the birth of a son to the emperor. In gratitude, Akbar decided to build a new capital city and palace on the site of the mystic's home in the village of Sikri. Over fifteen years, from 1571 to 1586, a magnificent new city in red sandstone was constructed. Although the city was abandoned before completion and now stands almost untouched, it is a popular destination for tourists and pilgrims.

Painting   The other major artistic achievement of the Mughal period was painting. Like so many other aspects of Mughal India, painting blended two cultures. While living in exile, Emperor Humayun had learned to admire Persian miniatures. On his return to India in 1555, he invited two Persian masters to live in his palace and introduce the technique to his adopted land. His successor Akbar appreciated the new style and popularized it with his patronage. He established a state workshop at Fatehpur Sikri for 200 artists, mostly Hindus, who worked under the guidance of the Persian masters to create the Mughal school of painting.

Literature The development of Indian literature was held back by the absence of printing, which was not introduced until the end of the Mughal era. Literary works were inscribed by calligraphers, and one historian has estimated that the library of Agra contained more than 24,000 volumes. Poetry, in particular, flourished under the Mughals, who established poet laureates at court. Poems were written in the Persian style and in the Persian language. In fact, Persian became the official language of the court until the sack of Delhi in 1739.

Another aspect of the long Mughal reign was a revival of Hindu devotional literature, much of it dedicated to Krishna and Rama. The retelling of the *Ramayana* in the vernacular culminated in the sixteenth-century Hindi version by the great poet Tulsidas (tool-see-DAHSS) (1532–1623). His *Ramcaritmanas* (RAM-kah-rit-MAH-nuz) presents the devotional story with a deified Rama and Sita. Tulsidas's genius was in combining the conflicting cults of Vishnu and Shiva into a unified and overwhelming love for the divine, which he expressed in some of the most moving of all Indian poetry. The *Ramcaritmanas* has eclipsed its 2,000-year-old Sanskrit ancestor in popularity and even became the basis of an Indian television series in the late 1980s.

CHAPTER SUMMARY

The three empires discussed in this chapter exhibited several striking similarities. First, they were Muslim in their religious affiliation, although the Safavids were Shi'ite rather than Sunni, a distinction that often led to mutual tensions and conflict. More important, perhaps, they were all nomadic in origin, and the political and social institutions they adopted carried the imprint of their preimperial past. Once they achieved imperial power, however, all three ruling dynasties displayed an impressive capacity to administer large empires and brought a degree of stability to peoples who had all too often lived in conditions of internal division and war.

The rise of these powerful Muslim states coincided with the opening period of European expansion at the end of the fifteenth century and the beginning of the sixteenth. The military and political talents of these empires helped protect much of the Muslim world from the resurgent forces of Christianity. In fact, the Ottoman Turks carried their empire into the heart of Christian Europe and briefly reached the gates of the great city of Vienna. By the end of the eighteenth century, however, the Safavid Dynasty had imploded, and the powerful Mughal Empire was in a state of virtual collapse. Only the Ottoman Empire was still functioning. Yet it too had lost much of its early expansionistic vigor and was showing signs of internal decay.

Why these empires declined has inspired considerable debate among historians. One factor was undoubtedly the expansion of European power into the Indian Ocean and the Middle East. But internal causes were probably more important in the long run. All three empires experienced growing factionalism within the ruling elite, incompetent leadership, and the emergence of divisive forces in the empire at large—factors that have marked the passing of traditional empires since early times. Climate change (the region was reportedly hotter and drier after the beginning of the seventeenth century) may have been a contributing factor. Paradoxically, one of the greatest strengths of these empires—their mastery of gunpowder—may have simultaneously been a serious weakness because it allowed them to develop a complacent sense of security. With little incentive to turn their attention to new developments in science and technology, they were increasingly vulnerable to attack by the advanced nations of the West.

The Muslim empires, however, were not the only states in the Old World that were able to resist the first outward thrust of European expansion. Farther to the east, the mature civilizations in China and Japan faced down a similar challenge from Western merchants and missionaries. Unlike their counterparts in South Asia and the Middle East, as the nineteenth century dawned, they continued to thrive.

REFLECTION QUESTIONS

Q How did the social policies adopted by the Ottomans compare with those of the Mughals and the Safavids? What similarities and differences do you detect, and what might account for them?

Q What is meant by the phrase "gunpowder empires," and to what degree did the Muslim states discussed here conform to this description? Can the concept be applied to other parts of the world as well?

Q What role did women play in the Ottoman, Safavid, and Mughal Empires? What might explain the similarities and differences? How did the treatment of women in these states compare with their treatment in other parts of the world?

CHAPTER TIMELINE

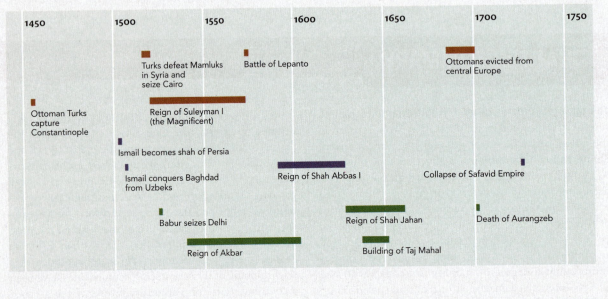

CHAPTER NOTES

1. V. A. Smith, *The Oxford History of India* (Oxford, 1967), p. 341.

2. Quoted in M. Edwardes, *A History of India: From the Earliest Times to the Present Day* (London, 1961), p. 188.

MINDTAP
From Cengage

MindTap® is a fully online, highly personalized learning experience built upon Cengage Learning content. MindTap combines student learning tools—readings, multimedia, activities, and assessments—into a singular Learning Path that guides students through the course and helps students develop the critical thinking, analysis, and communication skills that are essential to academic and professional success.

Chapter Outline and Focus Questions

17-1 *China at Its Apex*

Q Why were the Manchus so successful establishing a foreign dynasty in China, and what were the main characteristics of Manchu rule?

17-2 *Changing China*

Q How did the economy and society of China change during the Ming and Qing eras, and to what degree did these changes seem to be leading toward an industrial revolution on the European model?

17-3 *Tokugawa Japan*

Q How did the society and economy of Japan change during the Tokugawa era, and how did Japanese culture reflect those changes?

17-4 *Korea and Vietnam*

Q To what degree did developments in Korea during this period reflect conditions in China and Japan? What were the unique aspects of Vietnamese civilization?

Hu Weibiao/Panorama/The Image Works

17.1 **Emperor Kangxi**

Critical Thinking

Q *How did China and Japan respond to the coming of the Europeans, and what explains the differences in their approach? What impact did European contacts have on these two East Asian civilizations through the end of the eighteenth century?*

Connections to Today

Q *The world population was increasing dramatically in parts of the world during the eighteenth century, just as it is today. What were the main reasons for this expansion, and what lessons does it suggest for dealing with the issue in our own day?*

Experience an interactive version of this period in ❖ MINDTAP

IN DECEMBER 1717, Emperor Kangxi (KANG-shee) returned from a hunting trip north of the Great Wall and began to suffer from dizzy spells. Conscious of his approaching date with mortality—he was now nearly seventy years old—the emperor called together his sons and leading government officials in the imperial palace and issued an edict summing up his ideas on the art of statecraft. Rulers, he declared, should sincerely revere heaven's laws as their fundamental strategy for governing the country. Among other things, those laws required that the ruler show concern for the welfare of the people, practice diligence, protect the state from its enemies, choose able advisers, and strike a careful balance between leniency and strictness, principle and expedience. That, he concluded, was all there was to it.[1]

Any potential successor to the throne would have been well advised to attend to the emperor's advice. Kangxi was not only one of the longest reigning of all Chinese rulers but also one of the wisest. His era was one of peace and prosperity, and the empire was now at the zenith of its power and influence after a half-century of his rule. As his life approached its end, heaven must indeed have been pleased at the quality of his stewardship.

Kangxi reigned during one of the most glorious eras in the long history of China. Under the Ming (MING) and the early Qing (CHING) Dynasties, the empire expanded its borders to a degree not seen since the Han and the Tang. Chinese culture was the envy of its neighbors and earned the admiration of many European visitors, including Jesuit priests and Enlightenment philosophes.

On the surface, China appeared to be an unchanging society patterned after the Confucian vision of a "golden age" in the remote past. This indeed was the image presented by China's rulers, who referred constantly to tradition as a model for imperial institutions and cultural values. Although few observers could have been aware of it at the time, however, China was changing—and rather rapidly.

A similar process was under way in neighboring Japan. A vigorous new shogunate (SHOH-gun-ut or SHOH-gun-ayt) called the Tokugawa (toh-goo-GAH-wah) rose to power in the early seventeenth century and managed to revitalize the traditional system in a somewhat more centralized form that enabled it to survive for another 250 years. But major structural changes were taking place in Japanese society, and tensions were growing as the gap between theory and reality widened by the nineteenth century. As always, Korea and Vietnam sought to reconcile their own indigenous traditions with the powerful influence of Chinese culture.

17-1 CHINA AT ITS APEX

Q Focus Question: Why were the Manchus so successful establishing a foreign dynasty in China, and what were the main characteristics of Manchu rule?

In 1514, a Portuguese fleet dropped anchor off the coast of China, just south of the Pearl River estuary and present-day Hong Kong. It was the first direct contact between the Chinese Empire and the West since the arrival of Venetian adventurer Marco Polo two centuries earlier, and it opened an era that would eventually change the face of China and, indeed, all the world.

17-1a The Later Ming

Marco Polo had reported on the magnificence of China after visiting Beijing (bay-ZHING) during the reign of Khubilai Khan, the great Mongol ruler. By the time the Portuguese fleet arrived off the coast of China, of course, the Yuan Dynasty had long since disintegrated. It had gradually weakened after the death of Khubilai Khan and was finally overthrown in 1368 by a massive peasant rebellion

under the leadership of Zhu Yuanzhang (JOO yoo-wen-JAHNG), who had declared himself the founding emperor of a new Ming (Bright) Dynasty (1369–1644).

As we have seen, the Ming inaugurated a period of territorial expansion westward into Central Asia and southward into Vietnam while consolidating control over China's vast heartland. At the same time, between 1405 and 1433 the dynasty sponsored a series of voyages that spread Chinese influence far into the Indian Ocean. Then suddenly the voyages were discontinued, and the dynasty turned its attention to domestic concerns (see Chapter 10). To underline the new policy, Emperor Yongle (YOONG-luh) transplanted his capital to Beijing, where he ordered the construction of a new home—known as the Imperial City—on the grounds of Khubilai's old palace under the Yuan dynasty (see Image 17.2).

First Contacts with the West Despite the Ming's retreat from active participation in maritime trade, China was in command of a vast empire that stretched from the steppes of Central Asia to the China Sea, from the Gobi Desert to the tropical rain forests of Southeast Asia when the Portuguese arrived in 1514. From the lofty perspective of the imperial throne in Beijing, the Europeans could only have seemed like an unusually exotic form of barbarian to be inserted within the familiar framework of the tributary system, the hierarchical arrangement in which rulers of all other countries were regarded as "younger brothers" of the Son of Heaven. Indeed, the bellicose and uncultured behavior of the Portuguese so outraged Chinese officials that they initially expelled the Europeans. After further negotiations, however, the Portuguese were permitted to occupy the tiny territory of Macao (muh-KOW) on the coast of southern China, a foothold they would retain until the end of the twentieth century.

At first, the arrival of the Europeans had little effect on Chinese society. Chinese interest in European goods was limited, so Portuguese ships became involved in the regional trade network, carrying silk from China to Japan in return for Japanese silver. Eventually, the Spanish also began to participate, using the Philippines as an anchor in the galleon trade between China and the great silver mines in the Americas.

More influential than trade, perhaps, were the ideas introduced by Christian missionaries, who received permission to reside in China beginning in the last quarter of the sixteenth century. Among the most active and the most effective were highly educated Jesuits, who were familiar with European philosophical and scientific developments. Court officials were particularly impressed by the visitors' ability to predict the exact time of a solar eclipse, an event the Chinese viewed with extreme reverence.

William J. Duiker

17.2 The Imperial City in Beijing. During the fifteenth century, the Ming Dynasty erected an immense imperial city on the remnants of the palace of Khubilai Khan in Beijing. Surrounded by 6.5 miles of walls, the enclosed compound is divided into a maze of private apartments and offices; it also includes an imposing ceremonial quadrangle with stately halls for imperial audiences and banquets. Because it was off-limits to commoners, the compound was known as the Forbidden City.

The Ming Brought to Earth During the late sixteenth century, the Ming Dynasty began to decline as a series of weak rulers led to an era of corruption, concentration of land-ownership, and ultimately peasant rebellions and tribal unrest along the northern frontier. The inflow of vast amounts of foreign silver to pay for Chinese goods resulted in an alarming increase in inflation. Then the arrival of the English and the Dutch, whose ships preyed on the Spanish galleon trade between Asia and the Americas, disrupted the silver trade; silver imports plummeted, severely straining the Chinese economy by raising the value of the metal relative to that of copper. Crop yields declined because of harsh weather, and the resulting scarcity made it difficult for the government to provide food in times of imminent starvation.

Recognizing the Chinese pride in their own culture, the Jesuits sought to draw parallels between Christian and Confucian concepts (for example, they identified the Western concept of God with the Chinese character for heaven) and to show the similarities between Christian morality and Confucian ethics. European inventions such as the clock, the prism, and various astronomical and musical instruments impressed Chinese officials, who had hitherto been deeply imbued with a sense of the superiority of Chinese civilization, and that helped Western ideas win acceptance at court. An elderly Chinese scholar expressed his wonder at the miracle of eyeglasses:

> White glass from across the Western Seas
> Is imported through Macao:
> Fashioned into lenses big as coins,
> They encompass the eyes in a double frame.
> I put them on—it suddenly becomes clear;
> I can see the very tips of things!
> And read fine print by the dim-lit window
> Just like in my youth.[2]

For their part, the missionaries were much impressed with many aspects of Chinese civilization, and their reports home heightened European curiosity about this great society on the other side of the world. By the late seventeenth century, European philosophers and political thinkers had begun to praise Chinese civilization and to hold up Confucian institutions and values as a mirror to criticize their counterparts in the West.

High taxes, necessitated in part because corrupt officials siphoned off revenues, led to rural unrest and violent protests among urban workers.

As always, internal problems were accompanied by unrest along the northern frontier. Following long precedent, the Ming had attempted to pacify the frontier tribes by forging alliances with them and granting trade privileges. One alliance was with the Manchus (man-CHOOZ)—also known as the Jurchen (roor-ZHEN)—the descendants of peoples who had briefly established a kingdom in northern China during the early thirteenth century. The Manchus, a mixed agricultural and hunting people, lived northeast of the Great Wall in the area known today as Manchuria (man-CHUR-ee-uh).

At first, the Manchus were satisfied with consolidating their territory and made little effort to extend their rule south of the Great Wall. But during the first decades of the seventeenth century, a major epidemic devastated the population in many areas of the country. The suffering brought on by the epidemic, combined with widespread drought conditions, helped spark a vast peasant uprising led by the former postal worker Li Zicheng (lee zuh-CHENG) (1604–1651). By the 1630s, the revolt had spread throughout the country, and Li's forces finally occupied the capital of Beijing in 1644. The last Ming emperor committed suicide by hanging himself from a tree in the palace gardens.

Emboldened by the overthrow of the Ming Dynasty, the Manchus attacked Beijing on their own (see Map 17.1). Li Zicheng's army disintegrated, and the Manchus declared

Map 17.1 China and its Enemies During the Late Ming Era. During the seventeenth century, the Ming Dynasty faced challenges on two fronts: from China's traditional adversaries, nomadic groups north of the Great Wall, and from new arrivals, European merchants who had begun to press for trading privileges along the southern coast.

Q *How did these threats differ from those faced by previous dynasties in China?*

the creation of a new dynasty: the Qing (or Pure), which lasted from 1644 until 1911. Once again, China was under foreign rule.

17-1b The Greatness of the Qing

The accession of the Manchus to power in Beijing was not universally applauded. Some Ming loyalists fled to Southeast Asia, but others continued their resistance to the new rulers from inside the country. To make it easier to identify the rebels, the government ordered all Chinese to adopt Manchu dress and hairstyles. All Chinese males were to shave their foreheads and braid their hair into a queue (KYOO); those who refused were to be executed. As a popular saying put it, "Lose your hair or lose your head."[3]

Like all of China's great dynasties, however, the Qing was blessed with a series of strong early rulers who pacified the country, rectified many of the most obvious social and economic inequities, and restored peace and prosperity. For the Ming Dynasty, these strong emperors had been Zhu Yuanzhang and Yongle; under the Qing, they would be Kangxi and Qianlong (CHAN-loong).

The two Qing monarchs ruled China for well over a century and were responsible for much of the success achieved by the Qing Empire.

The Reign of Kangxi Kangxi (r. 1661–1722) was arguably the greatest ruler in Chinese history. Ascending to the throne at age seven, he was blessed with diligence, political astuteness, and a strong character and began to take charge of Qing administration while he was still an adolescent. During the six decades of his reign, Kangxi not only stabilized imperial rule by pacifying the restive peoples along the northern and western frontiers but also managed to make the dynasty acceptable to the general population. As an active patron of arts and letters, he cultivated the support of scholars through many major projects.

During Kangxi's reign, the activities of the Western missionaries—Dominicans and Franciscans as well as Jesuits—reached their height. The emperor was quite tolerant of the Christian presence, and several Jesuit missionaries became influential at court. Several hundred officials converted to Christianity, as did an estimated 300,000 ordinary Chinese. But the Christian effort was ultimately undermined by resentment from Confucian officials at court as well as by squabbling among the Western religious orders over the Jesuit policy of accommodating local beliefs and practices to facilitate conversion (see Opposing Viewpoints, "The Debate over Christianity," p. 421). Jealous Dominicans and Franciscans complained to the pope, who issued an edict ordering all missionaries and converts to conform to the official orthodoxy set forth in Europe. At first, Kangxi attempted to resolve the problem by appealing directly to the Vatican, but the pope was uncompromising. After Kangxi's death, his successor began to suppress Christian activities throughout China.

The Reign of Qianlong Kangxi's achievements were carried on by his successors, Yongzheng (YOONG-jehng) (r. 1722–1736) and Qianlong (r. 1736–1795). Like Kangxi, Qianlong was known for his diligence, tolerance, and intellectual curiosity, and he too combined vigorous military action against

The Debate over Christianity

Religion & Philosophy THE ARRIVAL OF CHRISTIAN MISSIONARIES at the Ming imperial court in Beijing caused a major tumult among Chinese officials there. Although some were attracted to the new faith, others expressed alarm that these strange new ideas could corrupt traditional neo-Confucian doctrine. As the following passages indicate, both supporters and opponents had only a rudimentary understanding of Christian teachings and the Western culture from which they had sprung.

Xu Guangqi: A Memorial in Defense of the [Western] Teaching (1616)

Because the teaching of the men from afar [i.e., Christian missionaries from Europe] is most correct, and because your humble servant knows from experience that it is right, he earnestly begs to memorialize the throne, to the end that blessings may last forever and peace may be handed on to all generations. . . .

[Y]our servant . . . has studied with and learned from these [Western] tributary officials, and I know that they are most honest and solid. There is nothing whatsoever about them that is dubious. Truly, they are all disciples of the sages. Their way is very correct, their discipline strict, their learning very broad, their knowledge superior, their affections true, and their views very stable. . . .

Now in their countries, men of the church all cultivate personal virtue in order to serve the Lord of Heaven. . . .This teaching has as its basic tenet serving the Lord on High; to save the body and soul is the most essential principle, while one's practice should consist in loyalty, filial piety, love, and compassion. The way to begin is to choose good and repent, and the way to advance and improve is to confess and reform. True blessing in Heaven is the glorious reward of doing good, while eternal retribution in hell is the bitter recompense of doing evil. . . .

Now there are more than thirty countries in the West, and they have accepted and practiced this teaching for a thousand and several hundred years, right up to the present time, great and small living together in harmony, superior and inferior at peace with each other. The borders are not guarded, and the rulers of the states are all of the same family. . . .As for revolt and rebellion, not even once has there been such a thing or such people. . . .

Yang Guangxian: I Cannot Do Otherwise (1665)

According to a book by [the Christian scholar] Li Zubo, the Qing dynasty is nothing but an offshoot of Judea; our ancient Chinese rulers, sages, and teachers were but the off-shoots of a heterodox sect; and our classics and the teachings of the sages propounded generation after generation are no more than the remnants of a heterodox teaching. How can we abide these calumnies! They really aim to inveigle the people of the Qing into rebelling against the Qing and following this heterodox sect, which would lead all-under-Heaven to abandon respect for rulers and fathers. . . .

Our Confucian teaching is based on the Five Relationships (between parent and child, ruler and minister, husband and wife, older and younger brothers, and friends), whilst the Lord of Heaven Jesus was crucified because he plotted against his own country, showing that he did not recognize the relationship between ruler and subject. Mary, the mother of Jesus had a husband named Joseph, but she said Jesus was not conceived by him.

Those who follow this teaching [Christianity] are not allowed to worship their ancestors and ancestral tablets. They do not recognize the relationship of parent and child. Their teachers oppose the Buddhists and Daoists, who do recognize the relationship between ruler and subject and father and son. Jesus did not recognize the relationship between ruler and subject and parent and child. . . . What arrant nonsense! . . .

Q *To what degree do you feel that the authors of these two passages misrepresent Christian teachings and the influence that such ideas have had in European society?*

Source: W. T. de Bary and R. Lufrano, *Sources of Chinese Tradition: From 1600 Through the Twentieth Century*, Vol. II (New York: Columbia University Press, 2000), pp. 148–151.

the unruly tribes along the frontier with active efforts to promote economic prosperity, administrative efficiency, and scholarship and artistic excellence. The result was continued growth for the Qing Empire throughout much of the eighteenth century.

But it was also under Qianlong that the first signs of the internal decay of the Qing Dynasty began to appear. The clues were familiar. Qing military campaigns along the frontier were expensive and placed heavy demands on the imperial treasury. As the emperor aged, he became less astute in selecting his subordinates and fell under the influence of corrupt elements at court. Corruption at the center led inevitably to unrest in rural areas, where higher taxes, bureaucratic venality, and rising pressure on the land because of the growing population had produced economic hardship. The heart of the unrest was in central China, where discontented peasants who had recently been settled on infertile land launched a revolt known as the White Lotus Rebellion (1796–1804). The revolt was eventually suppressed but at great expense.

Qing Political Institutions   One reason for the success of the Manchus was their ability to adapt to their new environment. They retained the Ming political system with relatively few changes. They also tried to establish their legitimacy as China's rightful rulers by stressing their devotion to the principles of Confucianism. Emperor Kangxi ostentatiously studied the sacred Confucian classics and issued a "sacred edict" that proclaimed to the entire empire the importance of the moral values established by the master (see Opposing Viewpoints, "Some Confucian Commandments," later in this chapter, and Image 17.3).

Still, like the Mongols, the Manchus were ethnically, linguistically, and culturally different from their subject population. The Qing attempted to cope with this reality by adopting a two-pronged strategy. As one part of this strategy, the Manchus—representing less than 2 percent of the entire population—were legally defined as distinct from everyone else in China. The Manchu nobles retained their aristocratic privileges, and their economic base was protected by extensive landholdings and revenues provided from the state treasury. Other Manchus were assigned farmland and organized into military units called **banners**, which were stationed as separate units in various strategic positions throughout China. These "bannermen" were the primary fighting force of the empire. Ethnic Chinese were prohibited from settling in Manchuria and were still compelled to wear their hair in a queue as a sign of submission to the ruling dynasty.

Although the Manchus attempted to protect their distinct identity within an alien society, they also recognized the need to bring ethnic Chinese into the top ranks of imperial administration. Their solution was to create a **dyarchy**, a system in which all important administrative positions were shared equally by Chinese and Manchus. Meanwhile, the Manchus themselves, despite official efforts to preserve their separate language and culture, were increasingly assimilated into Chinese civilization.

China on the Eve of the Western Onslaught   Unfortunately for China, the first signs of the Qing Dynasty's decline

17.3 The Temple of Heaven. Located in the capital city of Beijing, this temple is one of the most significant historical structures in China. Built in 1420 at the order of the Ming emperor Yongle, it was the site of the emperor's annual appeal to heaven for a good harvest. In this important ceremony, the emperor demonstrated to his subjects that he was their protector and would ward off the evil forces in nature. Yongle's temple burned to the ground in 1889 but was immediately rebuilt following the original design.

CHRONOLOGY	China During the Early Modern Era
Rise of Ming Dynasty	1369
Voyages of Zheng He	1405–1433
Portuguese arrive in southern China	1514
Matteo Ricci arrives in China	1601
Li Zicheng occupies Beijing	1644
Manchus seize China	1644
Reign of Kangxi	1661–1722
Treaty of Nerchinsk	1689
First English trading post at Canton	1699
Reign of Qianlong	1736–1795
Lord Macartney's mission to China	1793
White Lotus Rebellion	1796–1804

occurred just as China's modest relationship with the West was about to give way to a new era of military confrontation and increased pressure for trade. The initial challenges came in the north, where Russian traders seeking skins and furs began to penetrate the region between Siberian Russia and Manchuria. Earlier the Ming Dynasty had attempted to deal with the Russians by the traditional method of placing them in a tributary relationship. But the tsar refused to play by Chinese rules. His envoys to Beijing ignored the tribute system and refused to perform the **kowtow** (the ritual of prostration and touching the forehead to the ground before the emperor), the classic symbol of fealty demanded of all foreign ambassadors to the Chinese court. Formal diplomatic relations were finally established in 1689 when the Treaty of Nerchinsk (ner-CHINSK) settled the boundary dispute and provided for regular trade between the two countries. Through such arrangements,

the Qing were able to not only pacify the northern frontier but also extend their rule over Xinjiang (SHIN-jyahng) and Tibet to the west and southwest (see Map 17.2).

Dealing with foreigners who arrived by sea was more difficult. By the end of the seventeenth century, the English had replaced the Portuguese as the dominant force in European trade. Operating through the East India Company, which served as both a trading unit and administrator of English territories in Asia, the English established their first trading post at Canton (KAN-tun) in 1699. Over the next decades, trade with China increased rapidly, notably the export of tea and silk to Great Britain. Chinese imports of European goods was much smaller. To limit contact between Chinese and Europeans, the Qing licensed Chinese trading firms at Canton to be the exclusive conduit for trade with the West, and the Qing confined the Europeans to a small island just outside the city

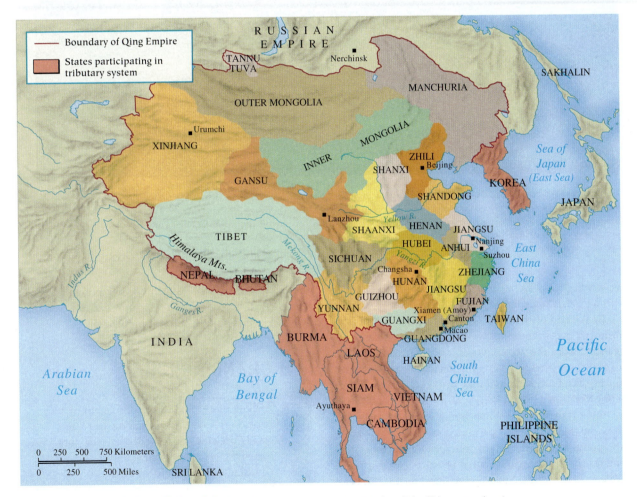

Map 17.2 The Qing Empire in the Eighteenth Century. This map shows the boundaries of the Chinese empire at the height of the Qing Dynasty in the eighteenth century.

Q *What areas were linked in tributary status to the Chinese empire, and how did they benefit the empire?*

17.4 European Warehouses at Canton. Aggravated by the growing presence of foreigners in the eighteenth century, the Chinese court severely restricted the movement of European traders in China. They were permitted to live only in a compound near Canton during the six months of the trading season and could go into the city only three times a month. In this painting, foreign flags (including, from the left, those of the United States, Sweden, Great Britain, and Holland) fly over the warehouses and residences of the foreign community while Chinese sampans and junks sit anchored in the river.

wall, where they were permitted to reside from October through March (see Image 17.4).

By the end of the eighteenth century, the British government had become restive at the uneven balance of trade between the two countries, which forced the British to ship vast amounts of silver bullion to China in exchange for its silks, porcelains, and teas. In 1793, a mission under Lord Macartney visited Beijing to press for liberalization of trade restrictions. A compromise was reached on the kowtow (Macartney was permitted to bend on one knee, the prevailing British custom), but Qianlong expressed no interest in British manufactured products (see Historical Voices, "The Tribute System in Action," p. 425). An exasperated Macartney compared the Chinese empire to "an old, crazy, first-rate man-of-war" that had once awed its neighbors "merely by her bulk and appearance" but was now destined under incompetent leadership to be "dashed to pieces on the shore."[4] With his contemptuous dismissal of the British request, the emperor had inadvertently sowed the seeds for a century of humiliation.

17-2 CHANGING CHINA

Focus Question: How did the economy and society of China change during the Ming and Qing eras, and to what degree did these changes seem to be leading toward an industrial revolution on the European model?

During the Ming and Qing Dynasties, China remained a predominantly agricultural society; nearly 85 percent of its people were farmers. Even though most Chinese

The Tribute System in Action

Interaction & Exchange

IN 1793, THE BRITISH EMISSARY Lord Macartney visited the Qing Empire to request the opening of formal diplomatic and trading relations between his country and China. Emperor Qianlong's reply to King George III of Britain illustrates how the imperial court in Beijing viewed the world. King George could not have been pleased. The document provides a good example of the complacent view the Celestial Empire had of the world beyond its borders.

A Decree of Emperor Qianlong

An Imperial Edict to the King of England: You, O King, are so inclined toward our civilization that you have sent a special envoy across the seas to bring to our Court your memorial of congratulations on the occasion of my birthday and to present your native products as an expression of your thoughtfulness. On perusing your memorial, so simply worded and sincerely conceived, I am impressed by your genuine respectfulness and friendliness and greatly pleased.

As to the request made in your memorial, O King, to send one of your nationals to stay at the Celestial Court to take care of your country's trade with China, this is not in harmony with the state system of our dynasty and will definitely not be permitted. Traditionally people of the European nations who wished to render some service under the Celestial Court have been permitted to come to the capital. But after their arrival they are obliged to wear Chinese court costumes, are placed in a certain residence, and are never allowed to return to their own countries. This is the established rule of the Celestial Dynasty with which presumably you, O King, are familiar. Now you, O King, wish to send one of your nationals to live in the capital, but he is not like the Europeans who come to Peking [Beijing] as Chinese employees, live there, and never return home again, nor can he be allowed to go and come and maintain any correspondence. This is indeed a useless undertaking.

Moreover the territory under the control of the Celestial Court is very large and wide. There are well-established regulations governing tributary envoys from the outer states to Peking, giving them provisions (of food and traveling expenses) by our post-houses and limiting their going and coming. There has never been a precedent for letting them do whatever they like. Now if you, O King, wish to have a representative in Peking, his language will be unintelligible and his dress different from the regulations; there is no place to accommodate him. . . .

The Celestial Court has pacified and possessed the territory within the four seas. Its sole aim is to do its utmost to achieve good government and to manage political affairs, attaching no value to strange jewels and precious objects. The various articles presented by you, O King, this time are accepted by my special order to the office in charge of such functions in consideration of the offerings having come from a long distance with sincere good wishes. As a matter of fact, the virtue and prestige of the Celestial Dynasty having spread far and wide, the kings of the myriad nations come by land and sea with all sorts of precious things. Consequently there is nothing we lack, as your principal envoy and others have themselves observed. We have never set much store on strange or ingenious objects, nor do we need any more of your country's manufactures.

Q *What reasons did the emperor give for refusing Macartney's request to have a permanent British ambassador in Beijing? How did the tribute system differ from the principles of international relations as practiced in the West?*

Source: Reprinted by permission of the publisher from *China's Response to the West: A Documentary Survey, 1839–1923*, by Ssu-yu Teng and John King Fairbank, pp. 24–27, Cambridge, Mass.: Harvard University Press, Copyright © 1954, 1979 by the President and Fellows of Harvard College, copyright renewed 1982 by Ssu-yu Teng and John King Fairbank.

still lived in rural villages, the economy was undergoing many changes.

17-2a The Population Explosion

In the first place, the center of gravity was continuing to shift steadily from the north to the south. In the early centuries of Chinese civilization, the administrative and economic center of gravity was clearly in the north. By the early Qing Dynasty, the economic breadbasket of China was located along the Yangzi River and regions to the south. One concrete indication of this shift occurred during the Ming Dynasty when Emperor Yongle ordered the

Experience an interactive version of this period in MINDTAP

The Population Explosion

Earth & Environment Between 1700 and 1800, Europe, China, and, to a lesser degree, India and the Ottoman Empire experienced a dramatic growth in population. In Europe, the population grew from 120 million people to almost 200 million by 1800; the Chinese population grew from less than 200 million to 300 million during the same period.

Four developments in particular contributed to this population explosion. First, better growing conditions—made possible by an improvement in climate—affected wide areas of the world and enabled people to produce more food. Both China and Europe experienced warmer summers beginning in the early eighteenth century. Second, by the eighteenth century, people had begun to develop immunities to the epidemic diseases that had caused such widespread loss of life between 1500 and 1700. The increase in travel by ship after 1500 had led to devastating epidemics. For example, the arrival of Europeans in Mexico introduced smallpox, measles, and chicken pox to a native population that had no immunities to European diseases. In 1500, between 11 million and 20 million people lived in the area of Mexico; by 1650, only 1.5 million remained. Gradually, however, people developed resistance to these diseases.

A third factor in the population increase was the introduction of new foods. As a result of the Columbian Exchange (see Comparative Essay, "The Columbian Exchange," p. 355 in Chapter 14), American food crops such as corn, potatoes, and sweet potatoes were transported to other parts of the world, where they became important food sources. China imported a new species of rice from Southeast Asia that had a shorter harvest cycle than existing varieties. These new foods provided additional sources of nutrition that enabled more people to live longer. At the same time, land development and canal building in the eighteenth century enabled government authorities to move food supplies to areas threatened with crop failure and famine.

Finally, the use of new weapons based on gunpowder allowed states to control larger territories and ensure a new degree of order. The early rulers of the Qing

Dynasty, for example, pacified the Chinese empire and ensured a long period of peace and stability. Absolute monarchs achieved similar goals in several European states. Less violence resulted in fewer deaths at the same time that an increase in food supplies and a decrease in deaths from diseases were occurring, thus making possible in the eighteenth century the beginning of the world population explosion that persists to this day.

Q *What were the main reasons for the dramatic expansion in the world's population during the early modern era?*

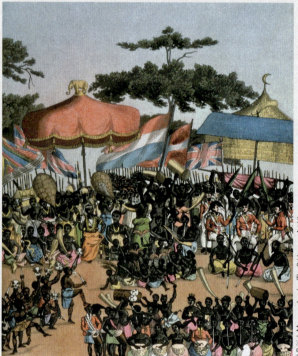

17.5 Festival of the Yam. With the spread of a few major food crops, new sources of nutrition became available to feed more people. The importance of the yam to the Ashanti people of West Africa is evident in this celebration of a yam festival at harvest time in 1817.

© British Museum, London/The Bridgeman Art Library

renovation of the Grand Canal to facilitate the shipment of rice from the Yangzi Delta to the food-starved north.

Moreover, the population was beginning to increase rapidly (see Comparative Essay, "The Population Explosion," above). For centuries, China's population had remained within a range of 50 million to 100 million, rising in times of peace and prosperity and falling in periods of foreign

invasion and internal anarchy. By 1800, however, the population had increased from an estimated 70 million to 80 million in 1390 to more than 300 million. There were probably several reasons for this population increase: the relatively long period of peace and stability under the early Qing; the introduction of new crops from the Americas, including peanuts, sweet potatoes, and maize;

and the planting of a new species of faster-growing rice from Southeast Asia.

Of course, this population increase meant much greater population pressure on the land, smaller farms, and a razor-thin margin of safety in case of climatic disaster. The imperial court attempted to deal with the problem through various means, most notably by preventing the concentration of land in the hands of wealthy landowners. Nevertheless, by the eighteenth century, almost all the land that could be irrigated was already under cultivation, and the problems of rural hunger and landlessness became increasingly serious.

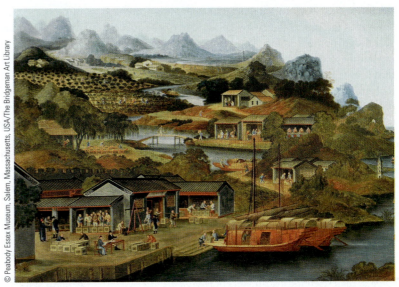

17-2b Seeds of Industrialization

The steady growth of manufacturing and commerce was another change that took place during the early Qing era. Taking advantage of the long era of peace and prosperity, merchants and manufacturers began to expand their operations beyond their immediate provinces. Commercial networks began to operate on a regional and sometimes even a national basis as trade in silk, metal and wood products, porcelain, cotton goods, and cash crops like cotton and tobacco developed rapidly. Foreign trade also expanded after the Ming court in 1567 suspended its prohibition of such activities. Chinese merchants began to establish extensive contacts with countries in Southeast Asia. As Chinese tea, silk, and porcelain became ever more popular in other parts of the world, the trade surplus grew as the country's exports greatly outnumbered its imports (see Image 17.6).

17.6 Haggling Over the Price of Tea. An important item in the China trade of the eighteenth and early nineteenth centuries was tea, which had become extremely popular in Great Britain. The painting depicts the various stages of growing, processing, and marketing tea leaves. In the background, workers are removing tender young leaves from the bushes. In the foreground, British and Chinese merchants bargain over the price. After being dried, the leaves are packed into chests and loaded on vessels for shipment abroad.

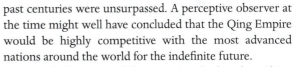

The Qing Economy: Ready for Takeoff? For many years, Western historians commonly believed that conditions in early modern China were not conducive to the onset of an industrial revolution along the Western model. In recent years, however, some have suggested that because of the impressive advances achieved during the early Qing Dynasty, China was poised to make the transition from an agricultural to a predominantly manufacturing and commercial economy by the end of the eighteenth century. The same transition began to take place in western Europe with the onset of the Industrial Revolution in the late eighteenth century (see Chapter 19).

Certainly, in most respects the Chinese economy in 1800 was as advanced as any of its counterparts around the world. China's achievements in technology over the past centuries were unsurpassed. A perceptive observer at the time might well have concluded that the Qing Empire would be highly competitive with the most advanced nations around the world for the indefinite future.

Nevertheless, several factors raise doubts that China was ready to advance rapidly into the industrial age. The mercantile class was not as independent in China as in some European societies. Trade and manufacturing remained under the firm control of the state, and political and social prejudices against commercial activity remained strong. Reflecting an ancient preference for agriculture over manufacturing and trade, the state levied heavy taxes on manufacturing and commerce while attempting to keep agricultural taxes low.

At the root of such attitudes was the lingering influence of Neo-Confucianism, which remained the official state doctrine in China down to the end of the Qing Dynasty. Although the founding fathers of Neo-Confucianism had originally focused on the "investigation of things," as time passed its practitioners tended to emphasize the elucidation of moral principles rather than the expansion of scientific knowledge. As historian Toby Huff has noted, the civil service examination during the early Qing contained no questions on science or technology, and Chinese interest in European scientific advances in areas like astronomy was limited to a few officials at court. Though the Chinese economy was gradually being transformed from an agricultural to a commercial and industrial giant, scholars

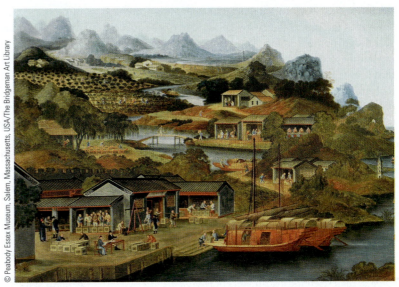 © Peabody Essex Museum, Salem, Massachusetts, USA/The Bridgeman Art Library

tended to look back to antiquity rather than to empirical science as the prime source for knowledge of the natural world and human events. The result was an intellectual environment that valued continuity over change and tradition over innovation. In effect, although the conditions for a transition to a modern industrial economy were present in early Qing China, the motivation to do so was lacking.

The Chinese reaction to European clock-making techniques provides an example. In the early seventeenth century, Matteo Ricci, a Jesuit priest, introduced advanced European clocks driven by weights or springs. The emperor was fascinated and found the clocks more reliable than Chinese timekeepers. Over the next decades, European timepieces became a popular novelty at court, but the Chinese expressed little curiosity about the technology involved, provoking one European observer to remark that playthings like cuckoo clocks "will be received here with much greater interest than scientific instruments or *objets d'art.*"[5]

17-2c Daily Life in Qing China

Daily life under the Ming and early Qing Dynasties continued to follow traditional patterns with families and the roles of women.

The Family Traditionally, Chinese society was organized around the family. The ideal social unit was the joint family in which as many as three or four generations lived under the same roof. When sons married, they brought their wives to live with them in the family homestead. Aging parents and grandparents, as well as unmarried daughters, remained under the same roof and were cared for by younger members of the household until they died. This ideal did not always correspond to reality, however, because many families did not possess sufficient land to support a large household.

The family retained its importance under the Qing for many of the same reasons as in earlier times. As a labor-intensive society based primarily on the cultivation of rice, China needed large families to help with the harvest and to provide security for parents too old to work in the fields. Sons were particularly prized, not only because they had strong backs but also because they would raise their own families under the parental roof. With few opportunities for employment outside the family, sons had little choice but to remain with their parents and help on the land. Within the family, the oldest male was king, and his wishes theoretically had to be obeyed by all family members. Arranged marriages were the norm, and the primary consideration in selecting a spouse was whether the union would benefit the family as a whole. The couple themselves usually had no say in the matter and might not even meet until the marriage ceremony. Romantic feelings were not considered unimportant

in marriage but were often viewed as undesirable because they would draw the attention of the husband and wife away from their primary responsibility to the larger family unit.

In theory, the obligations were not all on the side of the children. The father was expected to provide support for his wife and children and, like the ruler, was supposed to treat those in his care with respect and compassion. All too often, however, the male head of the family was able to exact his privileges without performing his responsibilities in return.

Beyond the joint family was the clan, which was an extended kinship unit consisting of dozens or even hundreds of joint and nuclear families linked together by a clan council of elders and a variety of other common social and religious functions. The clan served many useful purposes. Some clans possessed lands that could be rented out to poorer families, or richer families within the clan might provide land for the poor. Because there was no general state-supported educational system, sons of poor families might be invited to study in a school established in the home of a more prosperous relative. If the young man succeeded in becoming an official, he would be expected to provide favors and prestige for the clan as a whole.

The Role of Women In traditional China, the role of women had always been inferior to that of men. A sixteenth-century Spanish visitor to South China observed that Chinese women were "very secluded and virtuous, and it was a very rare thing for us to see a woman in the cities and large towns, unless it was an old crone."[6] Women were more visible, he said, in rural areas, where they frequently could be seen working in the fields.

The concept of female inferiority had deep roots in Chinese history. This view was embodied in the belief that only a male would carry on sacred family rituals and that men alone had the talent to govern others. Only males could aspire to a career in government or scholarship. Within the family system, the wife was clearly subordinated to the husband. Legally, she could not divorce her husband or inherit property. The husband, however, could divorce his wife if she did not produce male heirs, and he could take a second wife as well as a concubine for his pleasure. A widow suffered especially because she had to either raise her children on a single income or fight off her former husband's greedy relatives, who would coerce her to remarry because they could legally inherit all of her previous property and her original dowry.

Female children were less desirable because of their limited physical strength and because a girl's parents would have to pay a dowry to the parents of her future husband. Female children normally did not receive an education, and daughters might even be put to death in times of scarcity when food was in short supply.

HISTORICAL VOICES

The Art of Printing

 Art & Ideas

EUROPEANS OBTAINED MUCH OF THEIR EARLY INFORMATION ABOUT CHINA from the Jesuits who served at the Ming court in the sixteenth and seventeenth centuries. Clerics such as the Italian Matteo Ricci (ma-TAY-oh REE-chee) (1552–1610), who arrived in China in 1601, found much to admire in Chinese civilization. Here Ricci expresses a keen interest in Chinese printing methods, which at that time were well in advance of the techniques used in the West. Later Christian missionaries expressed strong interest in Confucian philosophy and Chinese ideas of statecraft.

Matteo Ricci, *The Diary of Matthew Ricci*

The art of printing was practiced in China at a date somewhat earlier than that assigned to the beginning of printing in Europe, which was about 1405. It is quite certain that the Chinese knew the art of printing at least five centuries ago, and some of them assert that printing was known to their people before the beginning of the Christian era, about 50 B.C.E. Their method of printing differs widely from that employed in Europe, and our method would be quite impracticable for them because of the exceedingly large number of Chinese characters and symbols. . . .

Their method of making printed books is quite ingenious. The text is written in ink, with a brush made of very fine hair, on a sheet of paper which is inverted and pasted on a wooden tablet. When the paper has become thoroughly dry, its surface is scraped off quickly and with great skill, until nothing but a fine tissue bearing the characters remains on the wooden tablet. Then, with a steel graver, the workman cuts away the surface following the outlines of the characters until these alone stand out in low relief. From such a block a skilled printer can make copies with incredible speed, turning out as many as fifteen hundred copies in a single day. . . . This scheme of engraving wooden blocks is well adapted for the large and complex nature of the Chinese characters, but I do not think it would lend itself very aptly to our European type, which could hardly be engraved upon wood because of its small dimensions.

Their method of printing has one decided advantage, namely, that once these tablets are made, they can be preserved and used for making changes in the text as often as one wishes. Additions and subtractions can also be made as the tablets can be readily patched. . . . We have derived great benefit from this method of Chinese printing, as we employ the domestic help in our homes to strike off copies of the books on religious and scientific subjects which we translate into Chinese from the languages in which they were written originally. In truth, the whole method is so simple that one is tempted to try it for himself after once having watched the process. The simplicity of Chinese printing is what accounts for the exceedingly large numbers of books in circulation here and the ridiculously low prices at which they are sold.

Q *How did the Chinese method of printing differ from that used in Europe at that time? What were its advantages?*

Source: From *China in the Sixteenth Century*, by Matthew Ricci, translated by Louis J. Gallagher. Copyright © 1942 and renewed 1970 by Louis J. Gallagher, S.J.

Though women were clearly inferior to men in theory, this was not always the case in practice. Capable women often compensated for their legal inferiority by playing a strong role within the family. Women were often in charge of educating the children and handling the family budget. Some privileged women also received training in the Confucian classics, although their schooling was generally for a shorter time and was less rigorous than that of their male counterparts. A few produced significant works of art and poetry.

17-2d Cultural Developments

During the late Ming and the early Qing Dynasties, traditional culture in China reached new heights of achievement. With the rise of a wealthy urban class, the demand for art, porcelain, textiles, and literature grew significantly.

The Rise of the Chinese Novel During the Ming Dynasty, a new form of literature first appeared that would eventually evolve into the modern Chinese novel. Although considered less respectable than poetry and nonfiction prose, these groundbreaking works (often written anonymously or under pseudonyms) were enormously popular, especially among well-to-do urban dwellers. Rapid advances in printing were a major factor in spreading the availability of books to the general population (see Historical Voices, "The Art of Printing," above).

Written in a colloquial style, the new fiction was characterized by a realism that resulted in vivid portraits of

Chinese society. Many of the stories sympathized with society's downtrodden—often helpless maidens—and dealt with such crucial issues as love, money, marriage, and power. Adding to the realism were sexually explicit passages that depicted the private side of Chinese life. Readers delighted in sensuous tales that, no matter how pornographic, always professed a moral lesson; the villains were punished and the virtuous were rewarded.

Dream of the Red Chamber is generally considered China's most distinguished popular novel. Published in 1791, it tells of the tragic love between two young people caught in the financial and moral disintegration of a powerful Chinese clan. The hero and the heroine, both sensitive and spoiled, represent the inevitable decline of the Chia family and come to an equally inevitable tragic end, she in death and he in an unhappy marriage to another.

The Art of the Ming and the Qing   During the Ming and the early Qing Dynasties, traditional China produced its last outpouring of artistic brilliance. Although most of the creative work was modeled on past examples, the art of this period is impressive for its technical perfection and breathtaking quantity.

In architecture, the most outstanding example is the Imperial City in Beijing. Building on the remnants of the palace of the Yuan Dynasty, the Ming emperor Yongle ordered renovations when he returned the capital to Beijing in 1421. Succeeding emperors continued to add to the palace, but the basic design has not changed since the Ming era. Surrounded by high walls, the immense compound is divided into a maze of private apartments and offices and an imposing ceremonial quadrangle with a series of stately halls for imperial audiences and banquets. The grandiose scale, richly carved marble, spacious gardens, and graceful upturned roofs all contribute to the splendor of the "Forbidden City" (see Image 17.2, p. 419).

Decorative arts flourished in this period, especially the intricately carved lacquerware and boldly shaped and colored cloisonné (kloi-zuh-NAY or KLWAH-zuh-nay), a type of enamel work in which thin metal bands separate the areas of colored enamel. Silk production reached its zenith, and the best-quality silks were highly prized in Europe, where chinoiserie (sheen-wah-zuh-REE or shee-nwahz-REE), as Chinese art of all kinds was called, was in vogue. Perhaps the most famous of all the achievements of the Ming era was its blue-and-white porcelain, which is still prized by collectors throughout the world. During the Qing Dynasty, artists produced great quantities of paintings, mostly for home consumption. Inside the Forbidden City in Beijing, court painters worked alongside Jesuit artists and experimented with Western techniques. Most scholarly painters and the literati, however, totally rejected

William J. Duiker

17.7 **A Japanese Castle.** Imitating European castle architecture, the Japanese perfected a new type of fortress palace in the early seventeenth century. Strategically placed high on a hilltop, these strongholds were constructed of heavy stone with tiny windows and were fortified by numerous watchtowers and massive walls, making them impregnable to arrows and catapults. They served as a residence for the local daimyo, and castle compounds also housed his army and contained the seat of local government. Osaka Castle was built by Toyotomi Hideyoshi essentially as a massive stage set to proclaim his power and grandeur. In 1615, the powerful warlord Tokugawa Ieyasu seized the castle, and it remained in his family's control for nearly 250 years.

foreign techniques and became obsessed with traditional Chinese styles. As a result, Qing painting became progressively more repetitive and stale.

17-3 TOKUGAWA JAPAN

Focus Question: How did the society and economy of Japan change during the Tokugawa era, and how did Japanese culture reflect those changes?

At the end of the fifteenth century, the traditional Japanese system was at a point of near anarchy. With the decline in the authority of the Ashikaga (ah-shee-KAH-guh) Shogunate at

Kyoto (KYOH-toh), clan rivalries had exploded into an era of warring states. Even at the local level, power was frequently diffuse. The typical daimyo (DYM-yoh) (great lord) domain had often become little more than a coalition of fief holders held together by a loose allegiance to the manor lord. Nevertheless, Japan was on the verge of an extended era of national unification and peace under the rule of its greatest shogunate—the Tokugawa.

17-3a The Three Great Unifiers

The process began in the mid-sixteenth century with the emergence of three extremely powerful political figures: Oda Nobunaga (1568–1582), Toyotomi Hideyoshi (1582–1598), and Tokugawa Ieyasu (1598–1616). In 1568, Oda Nobunaga (OH-dah noh-buh-NAH-guh), the son of a samurai (SAM-uh-ry) and a military commander under the Ashikaga Shogunate, seized the imperial capital of Kyoto and placed the reigning shogun (SHOH-gun) under his domination. During the next few years, the brutal and ambitious Nobunaga consolidated his rule throughout the central plains by defeating his rivals and suppressing the power of the Buddhist estates, but he was killed by one of his generals in 1582 before the process was complete. He was succeeded by Toyotomi Hideyoshi (toh-yoh-TOH-mee hee-day-YOH-shee), a farmer's son who had worked his way up through the ranks to become a military commander. Hideyoshi built a castle at Osaka (oh-SAH-kuh) (see Image 17.7) to accommodate his headquarters and gradually extended his power outward to the southern islands of Shikoku (shee-KOH-koo) and Kyushu (KYOO-shoo) (see Map 17.3). By 1590, he had persuaded most of the daimyo on the Japanese islands to accept his authority and created a national currency. Then he invaded Korea in an abortive effort to export his rule to the Asian mainland (see section 17-4a, "Korea: In a Dangerous Neighborhood" later in this chapter).

Despite their efforts, however, neither Nobunaga nor Hideyoshi was able to eliminate the power of the local daimyo. Both were compelled to form alliances with some daimyo so they could destroy other more powerful rivals. By 1590, Toyotomi Hideyoshi could claim to be the supreme proprietor of all registered lands in areas under his authority. He then reassigned those lands as fiefs to the local daimyo, who declared their allegiance to him. The daimyo in turn began to pacify the countryside, carrying out extensive "sword hunts" to disarm the population and attracting samurai to their service. The

Map 17.3 Tokugawa Japan. This map shows the Japanese islands and its key cities, including the shogun's capital of Edo (Tokyo), during the long era of the Tokugawa Shogunate.

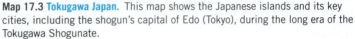

Where was the imperial court located?

Japanese tradition of decentralized rule had not yet been overcome.

After Hideyoshi's death in 1598, Tokugawa Ieyasu (toh-koo-GAH-wah ee-yeh-YAH-soo), the powerful daimyo of Edo (EH-doh) (modern Tokyo), moved to fill the vacuum. In 1603, Ieyasu named himself shogun, initiating the most powerful and long lasting of all Japanese shogunates; it remained in power until 1868, when a war dismantled the entire system. As a contemporary phrased it, "Oda pounds the national rice cake, Hideyoshi kneads it, and in the end Ieyasu sits down and eats it."[7]

17-3b Opening to the West

The unification of Japan took place almost simultaneously with the coming of the Europeans. Portuguese traders sailing in a Chinese junk that may have been blown off course by a typhoon had landed on the islands in 1543. Within a few years, Portuguese ships were stopping at Japanese ports on a regular basis to take part in the regional trade between Japan, China, and Southeast Asia. The first Jesuit missionary, Francis Xavier (ZAY-vee-ur), arrived in 1549.

Initially, the visitors were welcomed. Although Japanese leaders were somewhat ambivalent about establishing relations with the outside world, Japanese merchants were active in the regional trade network, and some ventured as far as Southeast Asia, where they quickly earned the reputation as ferocious competitors. The arrival of the Europeans added a new dimension to the equation. The curious Japanese were fascinated by tobacco, clocks, spectacles, and other European goods, and local daimyo were interested in purchasing all types of European weapons and armaments. Oda Nobunaga and Toyotomi Hideyoshi found the new firearms helpful in defeating their enemies and unifying the islands. The effect on Japanese military architecture was particularly striking, as local lords began to erect castles on the European model, many of which still exist today.

The missionaries also had some success in converting many local daimyo to the Christian faith, some of whom may have been partly motivated by the desire for commercial profits. By the end of the sixteenth century, thousands of Japanese in the southernmost islands of Kyushu and Shikoku had become Christians. But papal claims to the loyalty of all Japanese Christians and the European habit of intervening in local politics soon began to arouse suspicion in official circles. Missionaries added to the problem by deliberately destroying local idols and shrines and turning some temples into Christian schools or churches.

The Expulsion of the Christians   Inevitably, local authorities reacted. In 1587, Toyotomi Hideyoshi issued an edict prohibiting further Christian activities within his domains. Japan, he declared, was "the land of the Gods," and the destruction of shrines by the foreigners was "something unheard of in previous ages."[8] The Jesuits were ordered to leave the country within twenty days. Hideyoshi was careful to distinguish missionary from trading activities, however, and merchants were permitted to continue their operations.

The Jesuits protested the expulsion, and eventually Hideyoshi relented, permitting them to continue proselytizing as long as they were discreet. But he refused to repeal the edicts, and when the aggressive activities of newly arrived Spanish Franciscans aroused his ire, he ordered the execution of nine missionaries and several of their Japanese converts. When the missionaries continued to interfere in local politics, Tokugawa Ieyasu ordered the eviction of all missionaries in 1612.

At first, Japanese authorities hoped to maintain commercial relations with European countries even while suppressing the Western religion, but eventually they decided to regulate foreign trade more closely, restricting European access to the small island of Deshima (deh-SHEE-muh *or* deh-JEE-muh) in Nagasaki harbor, where a small Dutch community was given permission to engage in limited trade with Japan (the Dutch, unlike the Portuguese and the Spanish, had not allowed missionary activities to interfere with their commercial interests) (see Image 17.7, p. 430).

Réunion des Musées Nationaux/Art Resource, NY

17.8 Arrival of the Portuguese at Nagasaki. Portuguese traders, dressed in billowing pantaloons and broad-brimmed hats, landed in Japan by accident in 1543. In a few years, they were arriving regularly, taking part in a regional trade network involving Japan, China, and Southeast Asia. In these panels done in black lacquer and gold leaf, we see a late-sixteenth-century Japanese interpretation of Portuguese merchants at Nagasaki. Normally, Japanese screens are read from right to left, but this one is read left to right. Having arrived by ship, the Portuguese proceed in splendor to the Jesuit priests waiting in a church on the right.

Dutch ships were permitted to dock at Nagasaki harbor only once a year and were allowed to remain for two or three months after close inspection. Nor were the Japanese free to engage in foreign trade, as the *bakufu* (buh-KOO foo or bah KOO fuh)—the central government—now sought to restrict the ability of local authorities to carry out commercial transactions with foreign merchants. Skittish about maintaining official contacts with European nations because of their tendency to interfere in Japanese domestic affairs, shogunate officials resisted efforts to lure them into the establishment of formal diplomatic relations with European governments. A small amount of commerce took place with China and other parts of Asia, but Japanese were forbidden to leave the country on penalty of death.

17-3c The Tokugawa "Great Peace"

Once in power, the Tokugawa attempted to strengthen the system that had governed Japan for more than 300 years. They followed precedent in ruling through the bakufu, which was now composed of a coalition of daimyo and a council of elders. But the system was more centralized than it had been previously. Now the shogunate government played a dual role. It set national policy on behalf of the emperor in Kyoto while simultaneously governing the shogun's own domain, which included about one-quarter of the national territory as well as the three great cities of Edo, Kyoto, and Osaka. As before, the state was divided into separate territories called *domains* that were ruled by some 250 individual daimyo.

Daimyo and Samurai

In theory, the daimyo were essentially autonomous in that they were able to support themselves from taxes on their lands. In actuality, the shogunate was able to guarantee their loyalty by compelling the daimyo to maintain two residences, one in their own domains and the other at Edo, and to leave their families in Edo as hostages for the daimyo's good behavior. Keeping up two residences also put the Japanese nobility in a difficult economic position. Some were able to defray the high costs by concentrating on cash crops such as sugar, fish, and forestry products; but most were rice producers, and their revenues remained roughly the same throughout the period. The daimyo were also able to protect their economic interests by depriving their samurai retainers of their proprietary rights over the land and transforming them into salaried officials. The fief became a stipend, and the personal relationship between the daimyo and his retainers gradually gave way to a bureaucratic authority.

Thus the samurai gradually ceased to be a warrior class and were required to live in the castle towns. As a gesture to their glorious past, samurai were still permitted to wear their two swords, and a rigid separation was maintained

First phonetic alphabet in Korea	Fifteenth century
Portuguese merchants arrive in Japan	1543
Francis Xavier arrives in Japan	1549
Rule of Oda Nobunaga	1568–1582
Seizure of Kyoto	1568
Rule of Toyotomi Hideyoshi	1582–1598
Edict prohibiting Christianity in Japan	1587
Japan invades Korea	1592
Death of Hideyoshi and withdrawal of the Japanese army from Korea	1598
Rule of Tokugawa Ieyasu	1598–1616
Creation of Tokugawa Shogunate	1603
Dutch granted permission to trade at Nagasaki	1609
Order evicting Christian missionaries	1612
Choson Dynasty of Korea declares fealty to China	1630s

between persons of samurai status and the nonaristocratic segment of the population.

Seeds of Capitalism   The long period of peace under the Tokugawa Shogunate made possible a dramatic rise in commerce and manufacturing, especially in the growing cities of Edo, Kyoto, and Osaka. The growth of trade and industry was stimulated by a rising standard of living—driven in part by technological advances in agriculture and an expansion of arable land—and the voracious appetites of the aristocrats for new products.

Most of this commercial expansion took place in the major cities and castle towns where the merchants and artisans lived along with the samurai, who were clustered in neighborhoods surrounding the daimyo's castle. Banking flourished, and paper money became the normal medium of exchange in commercial transactions. Merchants formed guilds not only to control market conditions but also to facilitate government control and the collection of taxes. Under the benign if somewhat contemptuous supervision of Japan's noble rulers, a Japanese merchant class gradually began to emerge from the shadows to play a significant role in the life of the Japanese nation.

Eventually, the increased pace of industrial activity spread from the cities into rural areas. As in Great Britain, cotton was a major factor. Cotton had been introduced to China during the Song Dynasty and was introduced to Korea and Japan shortly thereafter. Traditionally, cotton cloth had been too expensive for the common people, who instead wore clothing made of hemp, but technological advances reduced the cost and specialized communities for producing cotton cloth began to appear in the countryside and in small towns. By the eighteenth century, cotton had firmly replaced hemp as the cloth of choice for most Japanese.

The expansion of trade was facilitated by the construction of a new and expanded system of roads and bridges ordered by Tokugawa Ieyasu himself. The main trunk road—known as the Tokaido, or "Eastern Coastal Highway"—connected the imperial city in Kyoto with the administrative capital of Edo, and fifty-three post stations were established along the route to provide travelers with food stalls and rest facilities to ease their journey to their destinations.

Not everyone benefited from the economic changes of the seventeenth and eighteenth centuries, however; most notable were the samurai, who were barred by tradition and prejudice from commercial activities. Most samurai still relied on their revenues from rice lands, which were often insufficient to cover their rising expenses; consequently, they fell heavily into debt. Others were released from servitude to their lord and became "masterless samurai." Occasionally, these unemployed warriors—known as **ronin** (ROH-nihn), or "wave men"—revolted or plotted against local authorities.

Land Problems The effects of economic developments on the rural population during the Tokugawa era are harder to estimate. Some farm families benefited by exploiting the growing demand for cash crops. But not all prospered. Most peasants continued to rely on rice cultivation and were whipsawed between declining profits and rising costs and taxes (as daimyo expenses increased, land taxes often took as much as 50 percent of the annual harvest). Many were forced to become tenants or to work as wage laborers on the farms of wealthy neighbors or in village industries. When rural conditions in some areas became desperate, peasant revolts erupted. According to one estimate, nearly 7,000 disturbances took place during the Tokugawa era.

Some Japanese historians, influenced by a Marxist view of history, have interpreted such evidence as an indication that the Tokugawa economic system was highly exploitative, with feudal aristocrats oppressing powerless peasants. Recent scholars, however, have tended to adopt a more balanced view, maintaining that in addition to agriculture, manufacturing and commerce experienced extensive growth, with benefits that extended to the rural population. Some point out that although the population of the country doubled in the seventeenth century, a

relatively low rate for the time period, so did the amount of cultivable land, with agricultural technology making significant advances.

17-3d Life in the Village

The changes that took place during the Tokugawa era had a major impact on the lives of ordinary Japanese. In some respects, the result was an increase in the power of the central government at the village level. The shogunate increasingly relied on Confucian maxims advocating obedience and hierarchy to enhance its authority with the general population. Decrees from the bakufu instructed the peasants on all aspects of their lives, including their eating habits and their behavior (see Opposing Viewpoints, "Some Confucian Commandments," p. 435). At the same time, the increased power of the government gave peasants more autonomy from the local daimyo. Villages now had more control over their local affairs.

At the same time, the Tokugawa era saw the emergence of the nuclear family—the *ie*—as the basic unit in Japanese society. In previous times, Japanese peasants had few legal rights. Most were too poor to keep their conjugal family unit intact or to pass property to their children. Many lived at the manorial residence or worked as servants in the households of more affluent villagers. Now, with farm income on the rise, the nuclear family took on the same form as in China, although without the joint family concept. The Japanese system of inheritance was based on primogeniture (pry-moh-JEN-ih-chur). Family property was passed to the eldest son, although younger sons often received land from their parents to set up their own families after marriage.

The Role of Women Another result of the changes under the Tokugawa was that women were somewhat more restricted than they had been previously. The rights of females were especially restricted in the samurai class, where Confucian values were highly influential. Male heads of households had broad authority over property, marriage, and divorce; wives were expected to obey their husbands on pain of death. Males often took concubines or homosexual partners, but females were expected to remain chaste. The male offspring of samurai parents studied the Confucian classics in schools established by the daimyo; females were reared at home, where only the fortunate might receive a rudimentary training in reading and writing Chinese characters. Nevertheless, some women were able to become accomplished poets and painters because, in aristocratic circles, female literacy was prized for its ability toenhance the refinement, social graces, and moral virtue of the home.

Women were similarly at a disadvantage among the common people. Marriages were arranged, and as in

Some Confucian Commandments

Family & Society
ALTHOUGH THE QING DYNASTY WAS OF FOREIGN ORIGIN, its rulers found Confucian maxims convenient for maintaining the social order. In 1670, the great emperor Kangxi issued the Sacred Edict to popularize Confucian values among the common people. The edict was read publicly at periodic intervals in every village in China and set the standard for behavior throughout the empire. Like the Qing Dynasty in China, the Tokugawa shoguns attempted to keep their subjects in line with decrees that carefully prescribed all kinds of behavior. Yet a subtle difference in tone can be detected between these two documents. While Kangxi's edict tended to encourage positive behavior, the decree of the Tokugawa Shogunate focused more on actions that were prohibited or discouraged.

Kangxi's Sacred Edict

1. Esteem most highly filial piety and brotherly submission, in order to give due importance to the social relations.
2. Behave with generosity toward your kindred, in order to illustrate harmony and benignity.
3. Show that you prize moderation and economy, in order to prevent the lavish waste of your means.
4. Extirpate strange principles, in order to exalt the correct doctrine.
5. Lecture on the laws, in order to warn the ignorant and obstinate.
6. Labor diligently at your proper callings, in order to stabilize the will of the people.
7. Instruct sons and younger brothers, in order to prevent them from doing what is wrong.
8. Put a stop to false accusations, in order to preserve the honest and good.
9. Fully remit your taxes, in order to avoid being pressed for payment.
10. Remove enmity and anger, in order to show the importance due to the person and life.

Maxims for Peasant Behavior in Tokugawa Japan

1. Young people are forbidden to congregate in great numbers.
2. Entertainments unsuited to peasants, such as playing the samisen or reciting ballad dramas, are forbidden.
3. Staging sumo matches is forbidden for the next five years.
4. Frugality . . . must be observed.
5. If a person has to leave the village for business or pleasure, that person must return by ten at night.
6. Father and son are forbidden to stay overnight at another person's house. An exception is to be made if it is to nurse a sick person.
7. Corvée [obligatory labor] assigned by the [local officials] must be performed faithfully.
8. Children who practice filial piety must be rewarded.
9. One must never get drunk and cause trouble for others.
10. Peasants who neglect farm work and cultivate their paddies and upland fields in a slovenly and careless fashion must be punished.
11. Fights and quarrels are forbidden in the village.
12. The deteriorating customs and morals of the village must be rectified.
13. Peasants who are suffering from poverty must be identified and helped.
14. This village has a proud history compared to other villages, but in recent years bad times have come upon us. Everyone must rise at six in the morning, cut grass, and work hard to revitalize the village.
15. The punishments to be meted out to violators of the village code and gifts to be awarded the deserving are to be decided during the last assembly meeting of the year.

Q *In what ways did Kangxi's set of commandments conform to the principles of State Confucianism? How do Kangxi's standards compare with those applied in Japan?*

Source: From *Popular Culture In Late Imperial China* by David Johnson et al. Copyright © 1985 The Regents of the University of California. From Chi Nakane and Oishi Shinsabura, *Tokugawa Japan: The Social and Economic Antecedents of Modern Japan* (Japan, University of Tokyo, 1990), pp. 51–52. Translated by Conrad Totman. Copyright 1992 by Columbia University Press.

China, the new wife moved in with the family of her husband. A wife who did not meet the expectations of her spouse or his family was likely to be divorced. Still, gender relations were more egalitarian than among the nobility. Women were generally valued as childbearers and homemakers, and both men and women worked in the fields. Poor families, however, often put infant daughters to death or sold them into prostitution.

Such attitudes toward women operated within the context of the increasingly rigid stratification of Japanese society. Deeply conservative in their social policies, the Tokugawa rulers established strict legal distinctions between the four main classes in Japan (warriors, artisans, peasants, and merchants). Intermarriage between classes was forbidden in theory, although sometimes the prohibitions were ignored in practice. Below these classes were Japan's outcasts, the **eta** (AY-tuh). Formerly, they were permitted to escape their status, at least in theory. The Tokugawa made their status hereditary and enacted severe discriminatory laws against them, regulating their place of residence, dress, and even hairstyles.

17-3e Tokugawa Culture

Under the Tokugawa, a vital new set of cultural values began to appear, especially in the cities. This innovative era witnessed the rise of popular literature written by and for the townspeople. With the development of woodblock printing in the early seventeenth century, literature became available to the common people, literacy levels rose, and lending libraries increased the accessibility of the printed word.

The Literature of the New Middle Class

The best examples of this new urban fiction are the works of Saikaku (SY-kah-koo) (1642–1693), considered one of Japan's finest novelists. Saikaku's greatest novel, *Five Women Who Loved Love,* relates the amorous exploits of five women of the merchant class. Based partly on real-life experiences, it broke from the Confucian ethic of wifely fidelity to her husband and portrayed women who were willing to die for love—and all but one eventually did. Despite the tragic circumstances, the tone of the novel is upbeat and sometimes comic, and the author's wry comments prevent the reader from becoming emotionally involved with the heroines' misfortunes.

In the theater, the rise of Kabuki (kuh-BOO-kee) threatened the long dominance of the No (NOH) play, replacing the somewhat restrained and elegant thematic and stylistic approach of the classical drama with a new emphasis on violence, music, and dramatic gestures. Significantly, the new drama emerged not from the rarefied world of the court but from the new world of entertainment and amusement (see Comparative Illustration, "Popular Culture: East and West," p. 437). Its commercial success, however, led to difficulties with the government, which periodically attempted to restrict or even suppress it. Early Kabuki was often performed by prostitutes, and shogunate officials—fearing that such activities could have a corrupting effect on the nation's morals—prohibited women from appearing on the stage. As a result, a new professional class of male actors emerged to impersonate female characters on stage.

In contrast to the popular literature of the Tokugawa period, poetry persevered in its more serious tradition. The most exquisite poetry was produced in the seventeenth century by the greatest of all Japanese poets, Basho (BAH-shoh) (1644–1694). He was concerned with the search for the meaning of existence and the poetic expression of his experience. With his love of Daoism and Zen Buddhism, Basho found answers to his quest for the meaning of life in nature, and his poems are grounded in seasonal imagery. The following is among his most famous poems:

> *The ancient pond*
> *A frog leaps in*
> *The sound of the water.*
> *On the withered branch*
> *A crow has alighted—*
> *The end of autumn.*

Tokugawa Art

Art also reflected the dynamism and changes in Japanese culture under the Tokugawa regime. The shogun's order that all daimyo and their families live every other year in Edo set off a burst of building as provincial rulers competed to erect the most magnificent mansion. And the prosperity of the newly rising merchant class added fuel to the fire. Japanese paintings, architecture, textiles, and ceramics all flourished during this affluent era.

Although Japan was isolated from the Western world during much of the Tokugawa era, Japanese art was enriched by ideas from other cultures. Japanese pottery makers borrowed both techniques and designs from Korea to produce handsome ceramics. The passion for "Dutch learning" inspired Japanese to study Western medicine, astronomy, and languages and led to experimentation with oil painting and Western ideas of perspective and the interplay of light and dark. Europeans desired Japanese lacquerware and metalwork inlaid with ivory and mother-of-pearl and especially the ceramics, which were now as highly prized as those of the Chinese.

Perhaps the most famous of all Japanese art of the Tokugawa era is the woodblock print. With a new literate mercantile class eager for illustrated texts that presented a visual documentation of the times, artists began to mass-produce woodblock prints to satisfy their needs. Some portrayed the "floating world" of the entertainment quarter with scenes of carefree revelers enjoying the pleasures of

Popular Culture, East and West

Family & Society

BY THE SEVENTEENTH CENTURY, a popular culture distinct from the elite culture of the nobility was beginning to emerge in the urban worlds of both the East and the West. Image 17.9a shows a festival scene from the pleasure district of Kyoto known as the Gion. Spectators on a balcony are enjoying a colorful parade of floats and costumed performers. The festival originated as a celebration of the passing of a deadly epidemic in medieval Japan. Image 17.9b shows a scene from the celebration of Carnival on the Piazza Sante Croce in Florence, Italy. Carnival was a period of festivities before Lent, celebrated primarily in Roman Catholic countries. It became an occasion for indulgence in food, drink, games, and practical jokes as a prelude to the austerity of the forty-day Lenten season from Ash Wednesday to Easter.

Q *Do festivals such as these still exist in our own day? What purpose might they serve?*

17.9a

Newark Museum/Art Resource, NY

17.9b

Scala/Art Resource, NY

17.10 Hokusai: from *Thirty-Six Views of Mount Fuji*. Along with Ando Hiroshige, Matsushika Hokusai became enormously popular in nineteenth-century Japan because of his colorful block prints portraying the people and the geography of the country. His series titled *Thirty-Six Views of Mount Fuji* were among his admired works, not least because of the symbolic importance of that symmetrical mount in Japanese culture. Long considered to be the home of the gods, Fuji became the focus of a sect of Shintoism, and even today thousands of Japanese make a pilgrimage to the peak of the mountain to view the sunrise over the eastern sea. The print shown here is entitled *Tama River in Musashi Province*.

life. Others such as Utamaro (OO-tah-mah-roh) (1754–1806) painted erotic and sardonic women in everyday poses—walking down the street, cooking, or drying their bodies after a bath. Two of the most popular, Hokusai (HOH-kuh-sy) (1760–1849) and Ando Hiroshige (AHN-doh hee-roh-SHEE-gay) (1797–1858), became famous for their bold interpretation of the Japanese landscape (see Image 17.10).

17-4 KOREA AND VIETNAM

Q **Focus Questions:** To what degree did developments in Korea during this period reflect conditions in China and Japan? What were the unique aspects of Vietnamese civilization?

On the fringes of the East Asian mainland, two of China's close neighbors sought to preserve their fragile independence from the expansionistic tendencies of the powerful Ming and Qing Dynasties.

17-4a Korea: In a Dangerous Neighborhood

As Japan under the Tokugawa Shogunate moved steadily out from the shadows of the Chinese empire by creating a unique society with its own special characteristics, the Choson Dynasty in Korea continued to pattern itself after the Chinese model— at least on the surface. The dynasty had been founded by military commander Yi Song Gye (YEE song yee) in the late fourteenth century and immediately set out to establish close political and cultural relations with the Ming Dynasty. From their new capital at Seoul (SOHL) on the Han (HAHN) River in the center of the peninsula, the Choson rulers accepted a tributary relationship with their powerful neighbor and engaged in the wholesale adoption of Chinese institutions and values. As in China, the civil service examinations tested candidates on their knowledge of the Confucian classics, and success was viewed as an essential step toward upward mobility.

There were differences, however. As in Japan, the dynasty continued to restrict entry into the bureaucracy to members of the aristocratic class, which were known in

Korea as the *yangban* (YAHNG-ban) (or "two groups," civil servants and military). At the same time, the peasantry remained locked in serflike conditions, working on government estates or on the manor holdings of the landed elite. A class of slaves called *chonmin* (CHAWN-min) labored on government plantations or served in certain occupations such as butchers and entertainers, which were considered beneath the dignity of other groups in the population.

Eventually, Korean society began to show signs of independence from Chinese orthodoxy. In the fifteenth century, a phonetic alphabet for writing the Korean spoken language (*hangul*) was devised. Although it was initially held in contempt by the elites and used primarily as a teaching device, eventually it became the medium for private correspondence and the published fiction intended for a popular audience. At the same time, changes were taking place in the economy, where rising agricultural production contributed to a population increase and the appearance of a small urban industrial and commercial sector, and in society, where the long domination of the Yangban class began to weaken. As their numbers increased and their power and influence declined, some Yangban became merchants or even moved into the ranks of the peasantry, further blurring the distinction between the aristocratic class and the common people.

Meanwhile, the Choson Dynasty faced continual challenges to its independence from its neighbors. Throughout much of the sixteenth century, the main threat came from the north, where Manchu forces harassed Korean lands just south of the Yalu (YAH-loo) River (refer back to Map 17.3). By the 1580s, however, the larger threat came from the east in the form of a newly united Japan. During much of the sixteenth century, leading Japanese daimyo had been involved in a protracted civil war as Oda Nobunaga, Toyotomi Hideyoshi, and Tokugawa Ieyasu strove to solidify their control over the islands. Of the three, only Hideyoshi lusted for an empire beyond the seas. Although born to a commoner family, he harbored visions of grandeur and in the late 1580s announced plans to attack the Ming Empire. When the Korean king Sonjo (SOHN-joe) (1567–1608) refused Hideyoshi's offer of an alliance, in 1592 the latter launched an invasion of the Korean Peninsula.

At first the campaign went well, and Japanese forces, wreaking death and devastation throughout the countryside, advanced as far as the Korean capital at Seoul. But eventually the Koreans under the inspired leadership of military commander Yi Sunshin (YEE soon-SHIN) (1545–1598), who designed fast but heavily armed ships that could destroy the more cumbersome landing craft of the invading forces, managed to repel the attack and safeguard their independence. The respite was brief, however. By the 1630s, a new threat from the Manchus had emerged from across the northern border. A Manchu force invaded northern Korea and eventually compelled the Choson Dynasty to promise allegiance to the new imperial government in Beijing.

Korea was relatively untouched by the arrival of European merchants and missionaries, although information about Christianity was brought to the peninsula by Koreans returning from tribute missions to China, and a small Catholic community was established there in the late eighteenth century.

17-4b Vietnam: The Perils of Empire

Vietnam—or Dai Viet (dy VEE-et), as it was known at the time—had managed to avoid the fate of many of its neighbors during the seventeenth and eighteenth centuries. Less directly located on the major maritime routes that passed through the region, the country was only peripherally involved in the spice trade with the West and had not suffered the humiliation of losing territory to European colonial powers. In fact, Dai Viet followed an imperialist path of its own, defeating the trading state of Champa to the south and imposing its suzerainty over the rump of the old Angkor Empire—today known as Cambodia. The state of Dai Viet now extended from the Chinese border to the shores of the Gulf of Siam.

But expansion undermined the cultural integrity of traditional Vietnamese society as migrants from the north who settled in the marshy Mekong River Delta developed a "frontier spirit" far removed from the communal values long practiced in the old national heartland of the Red River Valley. At the same time, thousands of non-Vietnamese subjects were now placed under the suzerainty of the dynasty in the north. By the seventeenth century, a civil war had split Dai Viet into two squabbling territories in the north and south, providing European powers with the opportunity to meddle in the country's internal affairs to their own benefit. In 1802, with the assistance of a French adventurer long active in the region, a member of the southern royal family managed to reunite the country under the new Nguyen (NGWEN) Dynasty, which lasted until 1945.

To placate China, the country was renamed Vietnam (South Viet), and the new imperial capital was established in the city of Hué (HWAY), a small river port roughly equidistant from the two rich river valleys that provided the country with its chief sustenance, wet rice. The founder of the new dynasty, who took the reign title of Gia Long, fended off French efforts to promote Christianity among his subjects and sought to promote traditional Confucian values among an increasingly diverse population.

CHAPTER SUMMARY

When the first European ships began to appear off the coast of China and Japan, the new arrivals were welcomed—even if only as curiosities. Eventually, several European nations established trade relations with China and Japan, and Christian missionaries of various religious orders were active in both countries and in Korea and Vietnam as well. But their welcome was short lived. Europeans eventually began to be perceived as detrimental to law and order, and the majority of the foreign merchants and missionaries were evicted from all four countries during the seventeenth century. From then until the middle of the nineteenth century, the East Asian states were minimally affected by events taking place beyond their borders.

That fact led many observers to assume that the traditional societies in the region were essentially stagnant, characterized by agrarian institutions and values reminiscent of those of the feudal era in Europe. As we have seen, however, that picture is misleading because all four countries were evolving and by the early nineteenth century were quite different from what they had been three centuries earlier.

Ironically, these changes were especially marked in Tokugawa Japan, a seemingly "closed" country, but one

where traditional classes and institutions were under increasing strain, not only from the emergence of a new merchant class but also from the centralizing tendencies of the powerful Tokugawa Shogunate. On the mainland as well, the popular image in the West of a "changeless China" was increasingly divorced from reality as social and economic conditions were marked by a growing complexity that gave birth to tensions that would strain the Qing Dynasty to its very core by the middle of the nineteenth century.

By the beginning of the nineteenth century, then, powerful tensions, reflecting a growing gap between ideal and reality, were at work in all the societies on the eastern fringe of the Eurasian supercontinent. Under these conditions, all four countries were soon forced to face a new challenge from the aggressive power of an industrializing Europe.

REFLECTION QUESTIONS

Q What factors at the end of the eighteenth century might have served to promote or impede China's transition to an advanced industrial and market economy? Which factors do you think were the most important? Why?

Q Some historians have declared that during the Tokugawa era the Japanese government essentially sought to close the country to all forms of outside influence. Is that claim justified? Why or why not?

Q What was the nature of Sino–Korean relations during the early modern era? How did they compare with Chinese policies toward Vietnam?

CHAPTER TIMELINE

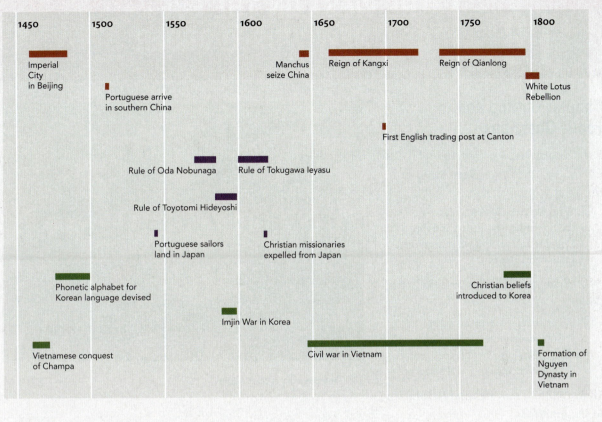

| | 1450 | 1500 | 1550 | 1600 | 1650 | 1700 | 1750 | 1800 |

Imperial City in Beijing

Portuguese arrive in southern China

Manchus seize China

Reign of Kangxi

Reign of Qianlong

White Lotus Rebellion

First English trading post at Canton

Rule of Oda Nobunaga

Rule of Tokugawa Ieyasu

Rule of Toyotomi Hideyoshi

Portuguese sailors land in Japan

Christian missionaries expelled from Japan

Phonetic alphabet for Korean language devised

Christian beliefs introduced to Korea

Imjin War in Korea

Vietnamese conquest of Champa

Civil war in Vietnam

Formation of Nguyen Dynasty in Vietnam

CHAPTER NOTES

1. From J. D. Spence, *Emperor of China: Self-Portrait of K'ang Hsi* (New York, 1974), pp. 143–144.
2. R. Strassberg, *The World of K'ang Shang-jen: A Man of Letters in Early Ch'ing China* (New York, 1983), p. 275.
3. L. Struve, *The Southern Ming, 1644–1662* (New Haven, Conn., 1984), p. 61.
4. J. L. Cranmer-Byng, *An Embassy to China: Lord Macartney's Journal, 1793–1794* (London, 1912), p. 340.
5. Quoted in D. J. Boorstin, *The Discoverers: A History of Man's Search to Know His World and Himself* (New York, 1983), p. 63.
6. C. R. Boxer, ed., *South China in the Sixteenth Century* (London, 1953), p. 265.
7. C. Nakane and S. Oishi, eds., *Tokugawa Japan* (Tokyo, 1990), p. 14.
8. Quoted in J. Elisonas, "Christianity and the Daimyo," in J. W. Hall, ed., *The Cambridge History of Japan*, vol. 4 (Cambridge, 1991), p. 360.

MINDTAP
From Cengage

MindTap® is a fully online, highly personalized learning experience built upon Cengage Learning content. MindTap combines student learning tools—readings, multimedia, activities, and assessments—into a singular Learning Path that guides students through the course and helps students develop the critical thinking, analysis, and communication skills that are essential to academic and professional success.

Chapter Outline and Focus Questions

CCI/The Art Archive at Art Resource, NY

18.1 The Storming of the Bastille

Critical Thinking

Q *In what ways were the American Revolution, the French Revolution, and the seventeenth-century English revolutions alike? In what ways were they different?*

Connections to Today

Q *What are the similarities and differences between the French Revolution and contemporary revolutions?*

IN PARIS ON THE MORNING OF JULY 14, 1789, a mob of 8,000 men and women in search of weapons streamed toward the Bastille (bass-STEEL), a royal armory filled with arms and ammunition. The Bastille was also a state prison, and although it held only seven prisoners at the time, it was a glaring symbol of the government's despotic policies in the eyes of these angry Parisians. The building was defended by the Marquis de Launay (mar-KEE duh loh-NAY) and a small garrison of 114 men. The attack on the Bastille began in earnest in the early afternoon, and de Launay and the garrison surrendered after three hours of fighting. Angered by the loss of ninety-eight protesters, the victors beat de Launay to death, cut off his head, and carried it aloft in triumph through the streets of Paris. When King Louis XVI was told the news of the fall of the Bastille by the duc de La Rochefoucauld-Liancourt (dook duh lah-RUSH-foo-koh-lee-ahn-KOOR), he exclaimed, "Why, this is a revolt." "No, Sire," replied the duc. "It is a revolution."

The French Revolution was a key factor in the emergence of a new world order. Historians have often portrayed the eighteenth century as the final phase of an old Europe that would be forever changed by the violent upheaval and reordering of society associated with the French Revolution. Before the Revolution, the old order—still largely agrarian, dominated by kings and landed aristocrats, and grounded in privileges for nobles, clergy, towns, and provinces—seemed to continue a basic pattern that had prevailed in Europe since medieval times. As the century drew to a close, however, a new intellectual order based on rationalism and secularism emerged, and demographic, economic, social, and political patterns were beginning to change in ways that proclaimed the arrival of a new and more modern order.

The French Revolution demolished the institutions of the old regime and established a new order based on individual rights, representative institutions, and a concept of loyalty to the nation rather than to the monarch. The revolutionary upheavals of the era, especially in France, created new liberal and national political ideals that were summarized in the French revolutionary slogan "Liberté, Egalité, Fraternité" ("Liberty, Equality, Fraternity") that transformed France and then spread to other European countries and the rest of the world.

18-1 TOWARD A NEW HEAVEN AND A NEW EARTH: AN INTELLECTUAL REVOLUTION IN THE WEST

Focus Question: Who were the leading figures of the Scientific Revolution and the Enlightenment, and what were their main contributions?

In the seventeenth century, a group of scientists set the Western world on a new path known as the **Scientific Revolution**, which gave Europeans a new way of viewing the universe and their place in it. The Scientific Revolution affected only a small number of Europe's educated elite.

But in the eighteenth century, this changed dramatically as a group of intellectuals popularized the ideas of the Scientific Revolution and used them to undertake a dramatic re-examination of all aspects of life. The widespread impact of these ideas on their society has caused historians ever since to call the eighteenth century in Europe the Age of Enlightenment.

18-1a The Scientific Revolution

The Scientific Revolution ultimately challenged conceptions and beliefs about the nature of the external world that had become dominant by the late Middle Ages.

Toward a New Heaven: A Revolution in Astronomy Medieval philosophers had used the ideas of Aristotle, Ptolemy (the greatest astronomer of antiquity, who lived in the second century C.E.), and Christianity to form the Ptolemaic (tahl-uh-MAY-ik) or **geocentric theory** of the universe. In this conception, the universe was seen as a series of concentric spheres with a fixed or motionless Earth at its center. Composed of material substance, Earth was imperfect and constantly changing. The spheres surrounding Earth were made of a crystalline, transparent substance and moved in circular orbits around Earth. The heavenly bodies, believed to number ten in 1500, were pure orbs of light that were embedded in the moving, concentric spheres. Working outward from Earth, the first eight spheres contained the moon, Mercury, Venus, the sun, Mars, Jupiter, Saturn, and the fixed stars. The ninth sphere imparted to the eighth sphere of the fixed stars its daily motion, while the tenth sphere was frequently described as the prime mover that moved itself and imparted motion to the other spheres. Beyond the tenth sphere was the Empyrean Heaven—the location of God and all the saved souls. Thus, God and the saved souls were at one end of the universe and humans were at the center.

Polish mathematician Nicolaus Copernicus (NEE-koh-lowss kuh-PURR-nuh-kuss) (1473–1543) felt that Ptolemy's geocentric system of the heavenly bodies was wrong and offered his iwn **heliocentric** (sun-centered) **theory** as a more accurate explanation. Copernicus argued that the sun was motionless at the center of the universe. The planets revolved around the sun in the order of Mercury, Venus, Earth, Mars, Jupiter, and Saturn. The moon, however, revolved around Earth. Moreover, what appeared to be the movement of the sun around Earth was really explained by Earth's daily rotation on its axis and its journey around the sun each year. But Copernicus did not reject the idea that the heavenly spheres moved in circular orbits.

Johannes Kepler (yoh-HAHN-us KEP-lur) (1571–1630) took the next step in destroying the Ptolemaic system. A brilliant German mathematician and astronomer, Kepler

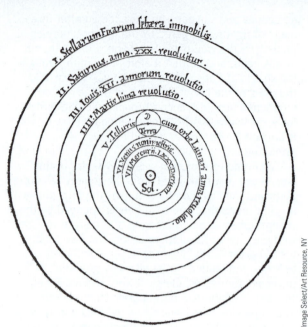

18.2 Medieval Conception of the Universe. As this sixteenth-century illustration shows, the medieval cosmological view placed Earth at the center of the universe surrounded by a series of concentric spheres. Earth was imperfect and constantly changing, whereas the heavenly bodies that surrounded it were perfect and incorruptible. Beyond the tenth and final sphere was heaven, where God and all the saved souls were located. [From the center outward, the circles read: (1) moon, (2) Mercury, (3) Venus, (4) sun, (5) Mars, (6) Jupiter, (7) Saturn, (8) firmament of the stars, (9) crystalline sphere, (10) prime mover, and at the end Empyrean Heaven—Home of God and All the Elect—that is, saved souls.]

18.3 The Copernican System. The Copernican system was presented in *On the Revolutions of the Heavenly Spheres*, which was published shortly before Copernicus's death. As shown in this illustration from the first edition, Copernicus maintained that the sun was the center of the universe while the planets, including Earth, revolved around it. Moreover, Earth rotated daily on its axis. [From the center outward, the circles read: sun: (VII) Mercury, orbit of eighty days; (VI) Venus; (V) Earth, with the moon, orbit of one year; (IIII) Mars, orbit of two years; (III) Jupiter, orbit of twelve years; (II) Saturn, orbit of thirty years; and (I) Immobile Sphere of the Fixed Stars.]

arrived at laws of planetary motion that confirmed Copernicus's heliocentric theory. In his first law, however, he revised Copernicus by showing that the orbits of the planets around the sun were not circular but elliptical, with the sun at one focus of the ellipse rather than at the center.

Kepler's work destroyed the basic structure of the Ptolemaic system. People could now think in new terms of the actual paths of planets revolving around the sun in elliptical orbits. But important questions remained; for example, what were the planets made of? An Italian scientist achieved the next important breakthrough to a new cosmology by answering that question.

Galileo Galilei (gal-li-LAY-oh GAL-li-lay) (1564–1642) taught mathematics and was the first European to make systematic observations of the heavens by means of a telescope, inaugurating a new age in astronomy. Galileo turned his telescope to the skies and made a remarkable series of discoveries: mountains on the moon, four moons revolving around Jupiter, and sunspots. Galileo's observations seemed to destroy yet another aspect of the traditional cosmology in that the universe seemed to be composed of material similar to that of Earth rather than a perfect, unchanging substance.

Galileo's revelations, published in *The Starry Messenger* in 1610, made Europeans aware of a new picture of the universe. But the Catholic church condemned Copernicanism and ordered Galileo to abandon the Copernican thesis. The church attacked the Copernican system because it threatened not only Scripture but also an entire conception of the universe. The heavens were no longer a spiritual world but a world of matter.

By the 1630s and 1640s, most astronomers had come to accept the new conception of the universe. Nevertheless, the problem of explaining motion in the universe and tying together the ideas of Copernicus, Galileo, and Kepler had not yet been done. This would be the work of an Englishman who has long been considered the greatest genius of the Scientific Revolution.

Isaac Newton (1642–1727) taught at Cambridge University, where he wrote his major work, *Mathematical Principles of Natural Philosophy*, known simply as the *Principia* (prin-SIP-ee-uh) by the first word of its Latin title. In the *Principia*, Newton defined the three laws of motion that govern the planetary bodies as well as objects on Earth. Crucial to his argument was the universal law of gravitation, which explained why planetary bodies did not travel in straight lines but continued in elliptical orbits around the sun. In mathematical terms, Newton explained that every object in the universe is attracted to every other object by a force called *gravity*.

Newton had demonstrated that one mathematically proven universal law could explain all motion in the universe. At the same time, the Newtonian synthesis created a new cosmology in which the universe was seen as one huge, regulated machine that operated according to natural laws in absolute time, space, and motion. Newton's **world-machine** concept dominated the modern worldview until the twentieth century when Albert Einstein's concept of relativity created a new picture of the universe.

Europe, China, and Scientific Revolutions   A question that arises is why the Scientific Revolution occurred in Europe and not in China. In the Middle Ages, China had been the most technologically advanced civilization in the world. After 1500, that distinction passed to the West (see Comparative Essay, "The Scientific Revolution," p. 446). Historians are not sure why. Some have contrasted the sense of order in Chinese society with the competitive spirit existing in Europe. Others have emphasized China's ideological viewpoint that favored living in harmony with nature rather than trying to dominate it. One historian has even suggested that China's civil service system drew the "best and the brightest" into government service to the detriment of other occupations.

18-1b Background to the Enlightenment

The impetus for political and social change in the eighteenth century stemmed in part from the **Enlightenment**, a movement of intellectuals who were greatly impressed with the accomplishments of the Scientific Revolution. When they used the word *reason*—one of their favorite words—they were advocating the application of the **scientific method** to the understanding of all life. All institutions and all systems of thought were subject to the rational, scientific way of thinking if people would only free themselves from the shackles of outmoded traditions, especially religious ones. If Isaac Newton could discover the natural laws regulating the world of nature, by using reason they also could find the laws that governed human society. This belief in turn led them to hope that they could create a better society than the one they had inherited. *Reason, natural law, hope, progress*—these were the buzzwords in the heady atmosphere of eighteenth-century Europe.

Major sources of inspiration for the Enlightenment were Isaac Newton and his fellow Englishman John Locke (1632–1704). Newton had contended that the world and everything in it worked like a giant machine. Enchanted by the grand design of this world-machine, the intellectuals of the Enlightenment were convinced that by following Newton's rules of reasoning, they could discover the natural laws that governed politics, economics, justice, and religion.

John Locke's theory of knowledge also made a great impact. In his *Essay Concerning Human Understanding* (1690), Locke denied the existence of innate ideas and argued that every person was born with a *tabula rasa* (TAB-yuh-luh RAH-suh), a blank mind. By denying innate ideas, Locke implied that people were molded by their environment, by whatever they perceived through their senses from their surrounding world. If the environment were changed and people were subjected to proper influences, they could be changed and a new society created. And how should the environment be changed? Newton had paved the way: reason enabled enlightened people to discover the natural laws to which all institutions should conform.

18-1c The Philosophes and Their Ideas

The intellectuals of the Enlightenment were known by the French term *philosophes* (fee-loh-ZAHFS), although they were not all French and few were philosophers in the strict sense of the term. The **philosophes** were literary people, professors, journalists, economists, political scientists, and, above all, social reformers. Although it was a truly international and cosmopolitan movement, the Enlightenment also enhanced the dominant role being played by French culture; Paris was its recognized capital, and most of the leaders of the Enlightenment were French. The French philosophes, in turn, affected intellectuals elsewhere and created a movement that touched the entire Western world, including the British and Spanish colonies in the Americas. (The terms *British* and *Great Britain* began to be used after 1707 when the Act of Union united England and Scotland.)

To the philosophes, the role of philosophy was not just to discuss the world but also to change it. A spirit of rational criticism was to be applied to everything, including religion and politics. Spanning almost a century, the Enlightenment evolved with each succeeding generation, becoming more radical as new thinkers built on the contributions of their predecessors. A few individuals, however, dominated the landscape so completely that we can gain insight into the core ideas of the philosophes by focusing on the three French giants—Montesquieu, Voltaire, and Diderot.

Montesquieu   Charles de Secondat (SHARL duh suh-KAHN-da), the baron de Montesquieu (MOHN-tess-kyoo) (1689–1755), came from the French nobility. In his most

The Scientific Revolution

Science & Technology When Catholic missionaries began to arrive in China during the sixteenth century, they marveled at the many accomplishments of Chinese civilization, including woodblock printing and the civil service examination system. In turn, their hosts were impressed with European inventions such as the spring-driven clock and eyeglasses.

It is not surprising that the Western visitors were impressed with what they saw in China, for that country had long been at the forefront of human achievement. After the sixteenth century, however, Europe would take the lead in science and technology, a phenomenon that would ultimately bring about the Industrial Revolution and begin a transformation of human society that would lay the foundations of the modern world.

18.4 The Telescope, a European Invention

Iberfoto/The Image Works

Why did Europe suddenly become the engine for rapid change in the seventeenth and eighteenth centuries? One factor was the shift in the European worldview from a metaphysical to a materialist perspective and the growing inclination among European intellectuals to question first principles. In contrast to China, empirical scientists in early modern Europe rejected received religious ideas, developed a new conception of the universe, and sought ways to improve material conditions around them.

Why were European thinkers more interested in practical applications of their discoveries than their counterparts elsewhere? No doubt the literate mercantile and propertied elites of Europe were attracted to the new science because it offered new ways to exploit resources for profit. Some early scientists made it easier for these groups to accept the new ideas by showing how they could be applied to specific industrial and technological needs. Galileo, for example, consciously appealed to the material interests of the educated elite when he explained that the science of mechanics would be quite useful "when it becomes necessary to build bridges or other structures over water, something occurring mainly in affairs of great importance."

Finally, the political changes taking place in Europe may also have contributed. Many European states enlarged their bureaucratic machinery and consolidated their governments to collect revenues and amass the armies needed to compete militarily with rivals. Political leaders desperately sought ways to enhance their wealth and power and grasped eagerly at new tools that might guarantee their survival and prosperity.

Q *Why did the Scientific Revolution emerge in Europe and not in China?*

---

famous work, *The Spirit of the Laws* (1748), Montesquieu attempted to apply the scientific method to the comparative study of governments to ascertain the "natural laws" governing the social and political relationships of human beings. Montesquieu distinguished three basic kinds of governments: republic, monarchy, and despotism.

Montesquieu used England as an example of monarchy, and his analysis of England's constitution led to his most lasting contribution to political thought—the importance of checks and balances achieved by means of a **separation**

of powers. He believed that England's system, with its separate executive, legislative, and judicial powers that served to limit and control each other, provided the greatest freedom and security for a state. American political leaders incorporated his separation of powers into the U.S. Constitution.

Voltaire The greatest figure of the Enlightenment was François-Marie Arouet (frahn-SWAH-ma-REE ahr-WEH), known simply as Voltaire (vohl-TAYR) (1694–1778). Son of a prosperous middle-class family from Paris, he studied law but achieved his first success as a playwright. Voltaire wrote an almost endless stream of pamphlets, novels, plays, letters, philosophical essays, and histories.

Voltaire was especially well known for his criticism of traditional religion and his strong attachment to the ideal of religious toleration. "Crush the infamous thing," he thundered—the infamous thing being religious fanaticism, intolerance, and superstition.

Throughout his life, Voltaire championed not only religious tolerance but also **deism**, a religious outlook shared by most other philosophes. Deism was built on the Newtonian world-machine, which implied the existence of a mechanic (God) who had created the universe. To Voltaire, the universe was like a clock, and God was the clockmaker who had created it, set it in motion, and allowed it to run according to its own natural laws.

Diderot

Denis Diderot (duh-NEE dee-DROH) (1713–1784), the son of a skilled craftsman, became a writer so that he could be free to study many subjects and languages. One of Diderot's favorite topics was Christianity, which he condemned as fanatical and unreasonable.

Diderot's most famous contribution was the *Encyclopedia*, or *Classified Dictionary of the Sciences, Arts, and Trades*, a twenty-eight-volume compendium of knowledge that he edited and referred to as the "great work of his life." Its purpose, according to Diderot, was to "change the general way of thinking." It did precisely that, becoming a major weapon of the philosophes' crusade against the old French society. The contributors included many philosophes who attacked religious intolerance and advocated social, legal, and political improvements that would lead to a society that was more cosmopolitan, more tolerant, more humane, and more reasonable. The *Encyclopedia* was sold to doctors, clergymen, teachers, lawyers, and even military officers, thus spreading the ideas of the Enlightenment.

Toward a New "Science of Man"

The Enlightenment belief that Newton's scientific methods could be used to discover the natural laws underlying all areas of human life led to the emergence of what the philosophes called a "science of man," or what we would call the social sciences. In many areas—especially economics, politics, and education—the philosophes arrived at natural laws that they believed governed human actions.

Adam Smith (1723–1790), often viewed as one of the founders of the discipline of economics, believed that individuals should be free to pursue their own economic self-interest. Through their actions, all society would ultimately benefit. Consequently, the state should in no way interrupt the free play of natural economic forces by imposing government regulations on the economy but should leave it alone, a doctrine that subsequently became known as **laissez-faire** (less-ay-FAYR) (French for "leave it alone"). In Smith's view, government had only three basic functions: to protect society from invasion (army), to defend its citizens from injustice (police), and to keep up certain public works such as roads and canals that private individuals could not afford.

The Later Enlightenment

By the late 1760s, a new generation of philosophes began to move beyond their predecessors' beliefs. Most famous was Jean-Jacques Rousseau (ZHAHNH-ZHAHK roo-SOH) (1712–1778), whose political beliefs were presented in two major works. In his *Discourse on the Origins of the Inequality of Mankind*, Rousseau argued that people had adopted laws and governors to preserve their private property. In the process, government enslaved them. What, then, should people do to regain their freedom? In his celebrated treatise *The Social Contract* (1762), Rousseau found an answer in the concept of the social contract whereby an entire society agreed to be governed by its general will. Each individual might have a particular will contrary to the general will, but if the individual put his particular will (self-interest) above the general will, he should be forced to abide by the general will. "This means nothing less than that he will be forced to be free," said Rousseau, because the general will, being ethical and not just political, represented what the entire community ought to do.

Another influential treatise by Rousseau was his novel *Émile*, one of the Enlightenment's most important works on education. Rousseau's fundamental concern was that education should foster rather than restrict children's natural instincts. But Rousseau did not necessarily practice what he preached. His own children were sent to orphanages, where many children died at a young age. Rousseau also viewed women as "naturally" different from men. In *Émile*, Sophie, Émile's intended wife, was educated for her role as wife and mother by learning obedience and nurturing skills that would enable her to provide loving care for her husband and children. Not everyone in the eighteenth century, however, agreed with Rousseau.

The "Woman Question" in the Enlightenment

For centuries, many male intellectuals had argued that the nature of women made them inferior to men and made male domination of women necessary and right. These biases restricted women's access to education. Despite these educational limitations, many women made notable contributions to the Scientific Revolution. Maria Winkelmann (VINK-ul-mahn) in Germany, for example, was an outstanding

The Rights of Women

Art & Ideas — **MARY WOLLSTONECRAFT RESPONDED TO AN UNHAPPY CHILDHOOD** in a large family by seeking to lead an independent life. Few occupations were available for middle-class women in her day, but she survived by working as a governess to aristocratic children. All the while, she wrote and developed her ideas on the rights of women. This excerpt is taken from her *Vindication of the Rights of Woman,* written in 1792, which established her reputation as the foremost British feminist thinker of the eighteenth century.

Mary Wollstonecraft, *Vindication of the Rights of Woman*

It is a melancholy truth [that] the most respectable women are the most oppressed; and, unless they have understandings far superior to the common run of understandings, taking in both sexes, they must, from being treated like contemptible beings, become contemptible. How many women thus waste life away the prey of discontent, who might have practiced as physicians, regulated a farm, managed a shop, and stood erect, supported by their own industry, instead of hanging their heads surcharged with the dew of sensibility, that consumes the beauty to which it at first gave luster. . . .

Proud of their weakness, however, [women] must always be protected, guarded from care, and all the rough toils that dignify the mind. If this be the fiat of fate, if they will make themselves insignificant and contemptible, sweetly to waste "life away," let them not expect to be valued when their beauty fades, for it is the fate of the fairest flowers to be admired and pulled to pieces by the careless hand that plucked them. In how many ways do I wish, from the purest benevolence, to impress this truth on my sex; yet I fear that they will not listen to a truth that dear-bought experience has brought home to many an agitated bosom, nor willingly resign the privileges of rank and sex for the privileges of humanity, to which those have no claim who do not discharge its duties. . . .

Would men but generously snap our chains, and be content with rational fellowship instead of slavish obedience, they would find us more observant daughters, more affectionate sisters, more faithful wives, and more reasonable mothers—in a word, better citizens. We should then love them with true affection, because we should learn to respect ourselves; and the peace of mind of a worthy man would not be interrupted by the idle vanity of his wife.

Q *What picture did Wollstonecraft paint of the women of her day? Why were they in such a deplorable state? Why did Wollstonecraft suggest that both women and men were at fault for the "slavish" situation of females?*

Source: From *First Feminists: British Women, 1578–1799* by Moira Ferguson. Copyright © 1985 Indiana University Press.

practicing astronomer. Nevertheless, when she applied for a position as assistant astronomer at the Berlin Academy, for which she was highly qualified, she was denied the post by the academy's members, who feared that hiring her would establish a precedent ("mouths would gape").

Female thinkers in the eighteenth century disagreed with this attitude and offered suggestions for improving conditions for women. The strongest statement of the rights of women was advanced by English writer Mary Wollstonecraft (WULL-stun-kraft) (1759–1797), who is viewed by many historians as the founder of modern European **feminism**.

In her *Vindication of the Rights of Woman* (1792), Wollstonecraft pointed out two contradictions in the views of women held by such Enlightenment thinkers as Rousseau. To argue that women must obey men, she said, was contrary to the beliefs of those same individuals that a system based on the arbitrary power of monarchs over their subjects or slave owners over their slaves was wrong. The subjection of women to men was equally wrong. Furthermore, the Enlightenment was based on an ideal of reason innate in all human beings. If women have reason, then they should have the same rights as men to obtain an education and engage in economic and political life (see Historical Voices, "The Rights of Women,").

18-1d Culture in an Enlightened Age

Although the Baroque style that had dominated the seventeenth century continued to be popular, by the 1730s a

18.5 Antoine Watteau, *Return from Cythera*. Antoine Watteau was one of the most gifted painters in eighteenth-century France. His portrayal of aristocratic life reveals a world of elegance, wealth, and pleasure. In this painting, Watteau depicts a group of aristocratic lovers about to depart from the island of Cythera, where they have paid homage to Venus, the goddess of love.

new style of decoration and architecture known as **Rococo** (ruh-KOH-koh) had spread throughout Europe. Unlike the Baroque, which stressed power, grandeur, and movement, Rococo emphasized grace, charm, and gentle action. Rococo rejected strict geometrical patterns and had a fondness for curves; it liked to follow the wandering lines of natural objects such as seashells and flowers. Highly secular, its lightness and charm spoke of the pursuit of pleasure, happiness, and love.

Some of Rococo's appeal is evident in the work of Antoine Watteau (AHN-twahn wah-TOH) (1684–1721), who created a specific type of Rococo art (see Image 18.5). His paintings portrayed a lyrical view of aristocratic life, refined, sensual, and civilized, with gentlemen and ladies in elegant dress—reflecting a world of upper-class pleasure and joy. Underneath that exterior, however, was an element of sadness as the artist revealed the fragility and transitory nature of pleasure, love, and life. Watteau relied on the use of color rather than representational form to highlight his subjects. Later artists such as Jean-Honoré Fragonard (FRA-go-NARD) (1732–1806) continued Watteau's use of color and subject matter (see Image 18.6).

High Culture Historians have grown accustomed to distinguishing between a civilization's high culture and its popular culture. **High culture** is the literary and artistic culture of the educated and wealthy ruling classes; **popular culture** is the written and unwritten culture of the masses, most of which has traditionally been passed down orally. By the eighteenth century, the two forms were beginning to blend, owing to the expansion of both the reading public and publishing. While French publishers issued 300 titles in 1750, about 1,600 were being published yearly in the 1780s. Although many of these books were still aimed at small groups of the educated elite, many were also directed to the new reading public of the middle classes, which included women and even urban artisans.

Popular Culture The distinguishing characteristic of popular culture is its collective nature. Group activity was especially common in the *festival*, a broad name used to cover a variety of celebrations: community festivals, annual festivals such as Christmas and Easter, and the ultimate festival, Carnival, which was celebrated in the Mediterranean world of Spain, Italy, and France as well as in Germany and Austria.

18.6 **Jean-Honoré Fragonard,** *The Swing.* In this painting, Fragonard portrays a young lady being pushed on a swing as her suitor sits below her, capturing the frivolity and decadence of French aristocracy. The lush environs and curvilinear landscape epitomize Rococo's love of nature; the delicate light and color of the lady's dress highlight the playful moment of her kicking off her shoe.

Carnival began after Christmas and lasted until the start of Lent, the forty-day period of fasting and purification leading up to Easter. Because people were expected to abstain from meat, sex, and most recreations during Lent, Carnival was a time of great indulgence when heavy consumption of food and drink was the norm. It was a time of intense sexual activity as well.

18-2 ECONOMIC CHANGES AND THE SOCIAL ORDER

Q **Focus Question:** What changes occurred in the European economy in the eighteenth century, and to what degree were these changes reflected in social patterns?

The eighteenth century in Europe witnessed the beginning of economic changes that ultimately had a strong impact on the rest of the world.

18-2a New Economic Patterns

Europe's population began to grow around 1750 and continued to increase steadily. The total European population was probably around 120 million in 1700, 140 million in 1750, and 190 million in 1790. A falling death rate was perhaps the most important reason for this population growth. Of great significance in lowering death rates was the disappearance of bubonic plague, diet was also significant. More plentiful food and better transportation of food supplies led to improved nutrition and relief from devastating famines (see section 18-2b, "Was There an Agricultural Revolution?" p. 451).

In European industry in the eighteenth century, textiles were the most important product and were still mostly produced by master artisans in guild workshops. But in many areas textile production was shifting to the countryside through the "putting-out" or "domestic" system. A merchant–capitalist entrepreneur bought the raw materials, mostly wool and flax, and "put them out" to rural workers who spun them into yarn and then wove the yarn into cloth on simple looms. The entrepreneurs sold the finished product, made a profit, and used it to purchase more raw materials. This system also became known as the **cottage industry** because the spinners and weavers did their work in their own cottages.

Overseas trade boomed in the eighteenth century. Some historians speak of the emergence of a true global economy with patterns of trade that interlocked Europe, Africa, the East, and the Americas (see Map 18.1). One important pattern involved the influx of gold and silver into Spain from its colonial American empire. Much of this gold and silver made its way to Britain, France, and the Netherlands in return for manufactured goods. British, Dutch, and French merchants in turn used their profits to buy tea, spices, silk, and cotton goods from China and India to sell in Europe.

As a result of the growth in trade, historians have argued that during the eighteenth century, England and parts of northern Europe experienced a "consumer revolution" in which ordinary people greatly increased their consumption of consumer goods. Expensive porcelain had been imported from China for centuries; however, by the eighteenth century, factories on the Continent and in England had surpassed Chinese production. Large showrooms opened in London; the most notable was that of Josiah Wedgewood. By the late eighteenth century, Wedgewood exported nearly 80 percent of its wares. In addition to porcelain, imports of inexpensive Indian fabric increased the sale of clothing. By the end of the eighteenth century, most ordinary families could consume tea, sugar, tobacco, furniture, cutlery, and clothing, goods that were once considered luxuries.

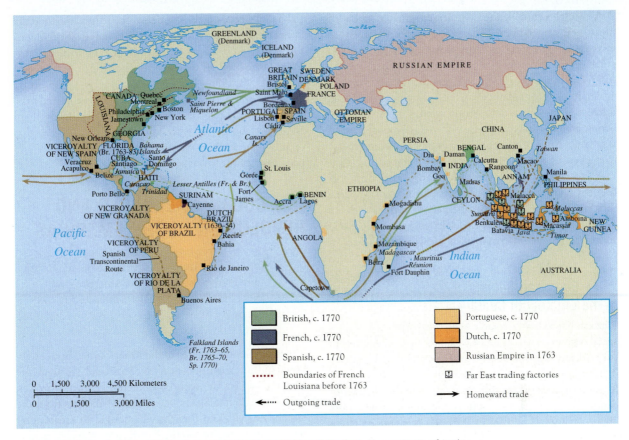

Map 18.1 Global Trade Patterns of the European States in the Eighteenth Century. New patterns of trade interlocked Europe, Africa, the East, and the Americas. Dutch, English, French, Spanish, and Portuguese colonies had been established in North and South America, and the ships of these nations followed the trade routes across the Atlantic, Pacific, and Indian Oceans.

Q *With what regions did Britain conduct most of its trade?*

Capitalism created enormous prosperity for some European countries. By 1700, Spain, Portugal, and the Dutch Republic, which had earlier monopolized overseas trade, found themselves increasingly overshadowed by France and England, which built enormously profitable colonial empires during the eighteenth century. After the French lost the Seven Years' War in 1763, Britain emerged as the world's strongest overseas trading nation, and London became the world's greatest port.

HISTORIANS DEBATE

18-2b Was There an Agricultural Revolution?

Did improvements in agricultural practices and methods in the eighteenth-century lead to an **agricultural revolution**? The topic is much debated. Some historians have noted the beginning of agrarian changes already in the seventeenth century, especially in the Low Countries. Others, however, have questioned the use of the term, arguing that significant changes occurred only in England and that even there

the upward trend in agricultural production was not maintained after 1750. Traditional interpretations of the agricultural revolution are characterized by four interrelated factors: more farmland, increased crop yields per acre, healthier and more abundant livestock, and an improved climate.

Historians dispute the increase of the amount of land under cultivation and the rate at which more land entered cultivation. One argument for greater land availability was the abandoning of the old open-field system in which part of the land was allowed to lie fallow (unplanted) to renew the soil. The formerly empty fields were now planted with new crops such as alfalfa, turnips, and clover that stored nitrogen in their roots and thereby restored the soil's fertility, allowing for a greater yield of crops. This shift in choice of plant crops certainly contributed to the higher yield of food. The increase of the new crops served another purpose: they provided winter fodder for livestock, enabling landlords to maintain ever-larger numbers of animals.

The eighteenth century witnessed greater yields of meat and vegetables. The more numerous livestock increased the amount of meat in the European diet and enhanced food production by producing animal manure. Animal manure is a prime fertilizer, and its use increased agricultural production. Landed aristocrats with an interest in the scientific experimentation of the age also adopted innovations that increased yields. Importation of vegetables from America, especially the potato and maize (Indian corn), increased food yields.

Historians also debate the role of climate in food production during the eighteenth century. Climatologists believe that the "little ice age" of the seventeenth century declined in the eighteenth, which is especially evident in moderate summers that provided more ideal growing conditions.

18-2c European Society in the Eighteenth Century

First established in the Middle Ages, the pattern of Europe's social organization continued well into the eighteenth century. Society was still divided into the traditional "orders" or "estates" determined by heredity.

Because society was still mostly rural in the eighteenth century, the peasantry constituted the largest social group, approximately 85 percent of Europe's population. There were rather wide differences within this group, however, especially between free peasants and serfs. In eastern Germany, eastern Europe, and Russia, serfs remained tied to the lands of their noble landlords. In contrast, peasants in Britain, northern Italy, the Low Countries, Spain, most of France, and some areas of western Germany were largely free.

The nobles, who constituted only 2 percent to 3 percent of the European population, played a dominating role in society. Being born a noble automatically guaranteed a place at the top of the social order with all of its attendant privileges and rights. Nobles, for example, were exempt from many forms of taxation. Since medieval times, landed aristocrats had functioned as military officers, and eighteenth-century nobles held most of the important offices in the administrative machinery of state and controlled much of the life of their local districts.

Townspeople were still a distinct minority of the total population except in the Dutch Republic, Britain, and parts of Italy. At the end of the eighteenth century, approximately one-sixth of the French population lived in towns of 2,000 people or more. The biggest city in Europe was London with 1 million inhabitants; Paris was a little more than half that size.

Many cities in western and even central Europe had a long tradition of **patrician** oligarchies that dominated town and city councils. Just below the patricians stood the upper crust of the middle classes: non-noble officeholders, financiers and bankers, merchants, wealthy **rentiers** (rahn-TYAYS) who lived off their investments, and important professionals, including lawyers. Another large urban group consisted of the lower middle class, which comprised master artisans, shopkeepers, and small traders. Below them were the laborers or working classes and a large group of unskilled workers who served as servants, maids, and cooks at pitifully low wages.

18-3 COLONIAL EMPIRES AND REVOLUTION IN THE AMERICAS

Q **Focus Question:** What colonies did the British and French establish in the Americas, and how did their methods of administering their colonies differ?

The first colonial empires in the Americas had been established in the sixteenth century by Spain and Portugal (see Chapter 14). By the early seventeenth century, however, both Portugal and Spain were facing challenges from the Dutch, English, and French, who sought to create their own colonial empires on the North American continent.

18-3a British North America

Although Spain had claimed all of North America as part of its empire, other nations largely ignored its claims. In 1606 the Virginia Company of London sponsored the first permanent English settlement in America. A ship carrying 105 passengers departed England in December 1606, landing in Jamestown in what is now Virginia in 1607. The settlers barely survived, making it clear that colonizing American lands would not necessarily mean quick profits. The Massachusetts colony fared much better; its initial 4,000 settlers had increased to 40,000 by 1660. By the eighteenth century, British North America consisted of thirteen colonies. They were thickly populated, containing some 1.5 million people by 1750, and were also prosperous.

18-3b French North America

The French also established a colonial empire in North America. In 1534, French explorer Jacques Cartier (ZHAHK kar-TYAY) had discovered the Saint Lawrence River and laid claim to Canada as a French possession. Not until Samuel de Champlain (sa-my-ELL duh shahm-PLAN or SHAM-playn) established a settlement at Quebec in 1608, however, did the French begin to take a serious interest in Canada as a colony. In 1663, Canada was made property of the French crown and administered by a French governor like any other French province.

French North America was run autocratically as a vast trading area, where valuable furs, leather, fish, and timber were acquired. The inability of the French state to persuade its people to emigrate to its Canadian possessions, however, left the territory thinly populated. Already in 1713, the French began to cede some of their American possessions to their British rival. As a result of the Seven Years' War, they surrendered the rest of their Canadian lands to Britain in 1763 (see section 18-4e, "Changing Patterns of War: Global Confrontation," p. 456).

18-3c The American Revolution

By the mid-eighteenth century, increasing trade and industry had led to a growing middle class in Britain that favored expansion of trade and world empire. These people found a spokesman in William Pitt the Elder (1708–1778), who became prime minister in 1757 and began to expand the British Empire. In North America, after the end of the Seven Years' War, Great Britain controlled Canada and the lands east of the Mississippi.

The Americans and the British had different conceptions of how the empire should be governed, however. In eighteenth-century Britain, the king or queen and Parliament shared power, with Parliament gradually gaining the upper hand. The monarch chose ministers who were responsible to the crown and who set policy and guided Parliament. Parliament had the power to make laws, levy taxes, pass budgets, and indirectly influence the ministers. The British envisioned Parliament as the supreme authority throughout the empire, but the Americans had their own representative assemblies. They believed that neither king nor Parliament should interfere in their internal affairs and that no tax could be levied without the consent of their own assemblies. After the Seven Years' War, the British tried to obtain new revenues from the colonies to pay for the cost of defending them, but the colonists resisted.

Crisis followed crisis until 1776, when the colonists declared their independence from Great Britain. On July 4, 1776, the Second Continental Congress approved a declaration of independence drafted by Thomas Jefferson. A stirring political document, the Declaration of Independence affirmed the Enlightenment's natural rights of "life, liberty, and the pursuit of happiness" and declared the colonies to be "free and independent states absolved from all allegiance to the British crown." The war for American independence had formally begun.

Of great importance to the colonies' cause was support from foreign countries eager to gain revenge for earlier defeats at the hands of the British. French officers and soldiers served in the American Continental Army under George Washington as commander in chief. When the army of British General Cornwallis was forced to surrender to a combined American and French army and French fleet under Washington at Yorktown in 1781, the British decided to call it quits. The Treaty of Paris, signed in 1783, recognized the independence of the American colonies and granted the Americans control of the territory from the Appalachians to the Mississippi River.

Birth of a New Nation   The thirteen American colonies had gained their independence, but fear of concentrated power meant they had little enthusiasm for a strong central government, and so the Articles of Confederation, ratified in 1781, did not create one. A movement for a different form of national government soon arose. In the summer of 1787, fifty-five delegates—wealthy, politically experienced, and well educated—convened in Philadelphia to revise the Articles of Confederation but decided instead to devise a new constitution.

The proposed U.S. Constitution established a central government distinct from and superior to governments of the individual states. The central or federal government was divided into three branches, each with some power to check the others. A president would serve as the chief executive with the power to execute laws, veto the legislature's acts, supervise foreign affairs, and direct military forces. Legislative power was vested in the second branch of government, a bicameral legislature composed of the Senate, with its members elected by the state legislatures, and the House of Representatives, whose members would be elected directly by the people. A supreme court and other courts "as deemed necessary" by Congress provided the third branch of government. They would enforce the Constitution as the "supreme law of the land."

The Constitution was approved by the states—by a slim margin. Important to its success was a promise to add a bill of rights as the new government's first piece of business. Accordingly, in March 1789, the new Congress enacted the first ten amendments to the Constitution. Known as the Bill of Rights, they guaranteed freedom of religion, speech, press, petition, and assembly, as well as the right to bear arms, protection against unreasonable searches and arrests, trial by jury, due process of law, and protection of property rights. Many of these rights were derived from the **natural rights** philosophy of the eighteenth-century philosophes. Is it any wonder that many European intellectuals saw the American Revolution as the embodiment of the Enlightenment's political dreams?

18-4 TOWARD A NEW POLITICAL ORDER AND GLOBAL CONFLICT

> **Q** **Focus Question:** What do historians mean by the term *enlightened absolutism*, and to what degree did eighteenth-century Prussia, Austria, and Russia exhibit its characteristics?

Enlightenment thought undoubtedly had some impact on the political development of European states in the eighteenth century. The philosophes believed there were certain natural rights that should not be withheld from any person. These rights included equality before the law, freedom of religious worship, freedom of speech and press, and the rights to assemble, hold property, and pursue happiness. But how were these natural rights to be established and preserved? Most philosophes believed that people needed to be ruled by an enlightened ruler, by which they meant a ruler who would allow religious toleration, freedom of speech and press, and the rights of private property; foster the arts, sciences, and education; and, above all, obey the laws and enforce them fairly. Only strong monarchs seemed capable of overcoming vested interests and effecting the needed reforms. Therefore, reforms should come from above (from absolute rulers) rather than from below (from the people).

Many historians once assumed that a new type of monarchy emerged in the later eighteenth century, which they called *enlightened despotism* or **enlightened absolutism**. Monarchs such as Frederick II of Prussia, Catherine the Great of Russia, and Joseph II of Austria supposedly followed the philosophes' advice and ruled by enlightened principles. Recently, however, scholars have questioned the usefulness of the concept of enlightened absolutism. We can determine the extent to which it can be applied by examining the major "enlightened absolutists" of the late eighteenth century.

18-4a Prussia

Frederick II, known as Frederick the Great (1740–1786), was well versed in Enlightenment thought and even invited Voltaire to live at his court for several years (see Historical Voices, "Frederick the Great and His Father," p. 455). A believer in the king as the "first servant of the state," Frederick was a conscientious ruler who enlarged the Prussian army (to 200,000 men) and kept a strict watch over the bureaucracy.

For a time, Frederick seemed quite willing to make enlightened reforms. He abolished the use of torture except in treason and murder cases and also granted limited freedom of speech and press, as well as complete religious toleration. He did exclude Jews, levying special taxes on Jewish subjects and barring them from civil service. Frederick attempted to improve the lives of peasants by increasing agricultural productivity; he imported clover and potatoes from Western Europe and the iron plow to help drain swamps in the lower Oder Valley. His efforts were limited, however, because he kept Prussia's rigid social structure and serfdom intact and avoided any additional reforms.

18-4b The Austrian Empire of the Habsburgs

The Austrian Empire had become one of the great European states by the beginning of the eighteenth century. Because it was a sprawling conglomerate of nationalities, languages, religions, and cultures, however, it was difficult to rule (see Map 18.2).

Joseph II (1780–1790) believed in the need to sweep away anything standing in the path of reason. As he said, "I have made Philosophy the lawmaker of my empire; her logical applications are going to transform Austria." Joseph's reform program was far-reaching. He abolished serfdom, abrogated the death penalty, and established the principle of equality of all before the law. Joseph instituted drastic religious reforms as well, including complete religious toleration.

Joseph's program proved overwhelming for Austria, however. He alienated the nobility by freeing the serfs and alienated the church by his attacks on the monastic establishment. Joseph realized his failure when he wrote the epitaph for his own gravestone: "Here lies Joseph II, who was unfortunate in everything that he undertook." His successors undid many of his reforms.

18-4c Russia Under Catherine the Great

Catherine II the Great (1762–1796) was an intelligent woman who was familiar with the works of the philosophes and seemed to favor enlightened reforms. But she was skeptical about impractical theories. She considered the idea of a new law code that would recognize the principle of the equality of all people in the eyes of the law, but in the end she did nothing because she knew her success depended on the support of the Russian nobility. In 1785, she gave the nobles a charter that exempted them from taxes. Catherine's policy of favoring the landed nobility led to even worse conditions for the Russian peasants and sparked a rebellion that soon faltered and collapsed.

Above all, Catherine proved a worthy successor to Peter the Great in her policies of territorial expansion westward into Poland and southward to the Black Sea. Russia spread southward by defeating the Turks. Russian expansion

Frederick the Great and His Father

Politics & Government

AS A YOUNG MAN, the future Frederick the Great was quite different from his strict and austere father, Frederick William I. Possessing a high regard for French culture, poetry, and flute playing, Frederick resisted his father's wishes that he study governmental and military affairs. Eventually, Frederick capitulated to his father's will and accepted the need to master affairs of state. These letters, written when Frederick was sixteen, illustrate the difficulties in their relationship.

Frederick to His Father, Frederick William I (September 11, 1728)

I have not ventured for a long time to present myself before my dear papa, partly because I was advised against it, but chiefly because I anticipated an even worse reception than usual and feared to vex my dear papa still further by the favor I have now to ask; so I have preferred to put it in writing.

I beg my dear papa that he will be kindly disposed toward me. I do assure him that after long examination of my conscience I do not find the slightest thing with which to reproach myself; but if, against my wish and will, I have vexed my dear papa, I hereby beg most humbly for forgiveness, and hope that my dear papa will give over the fearful hate which has appeared so plainly in his whole behavior and to which I cannot accustom myself. I have always thought hitherto that I had a kind father, but now I see the contrary. However, I will take courage and hope that my dear papa will think this all over and take me again into his favor. Meantime I assure him that I will never, my life long, willingly fail him, and in spite of his disfavor I am still, with most dutiful and childlike respect, my dear papa's

Most obedient and faithful servant and son,

Frederick

Frederick William I to His Son Frederick

A bad, obstinate boy, who does not love his father; for when one does one's best, and especially when one loves one's father, one does what he wishes not only when he is standing by but when he is not there to see. Moreover you know very well that I cannot stand an effeminate fellow who has no manly tastes, who cannot ride or shoot (to his shame be it said!), is untidy about his person, and wears his hair curled like a fool instead of cutting it; and that I have condemned all these things a thousand times, and yet there is no sign of improvement. For the rest, haughty, offish as a country lout, conversing with none but a favored few instead of being affable and popular, grimacing like a fool, and never following my wishes out of love for me but only when forced into it, caring for nothing but to have his own way, and thinking nothing else is of any importance. This is my answer.

Frederick William

Q *Based on these documents, why was the relationship between Frederick II and his father so difficult? What does this troubled relationship tell you about the effects of ruling on the great monarchs of Europe and their families? What new duties and concerns of rulers (such as Frederick William) may have reshaped relations between kings and sons?*

Source: From *Readings in European History*, vol. 2, by James Harvey Robinson (Lexington, Mass.: Ginn and Co., 1906).

---

westward occurred at the expense of neighboring Poland. In three partitions of Poland, Russia gained some 50 percent of Polish territory.

18-4d Enlightened Absolutism Reconsidered

Of the rulers discussed thus far, only Joseph II sought truly radical changes based on Enlightenment ideas. Both Frederick II and Catherine II liked to talk about enlightened reforms and even attempted some, but neither ruler's policies seemed seriously affected by Enlightenment thought. Necessities of state and maintenance of the existing system took precedence over reform. Indeed, many historians maintain that Joseph, Frederick, and Catherine were all primarily concerned for the power and well-being of their states. In the final analysis, heightened state power was used to create armies and wage wars to gain more power.

At the same time, the ability of enlightened rulers to make reforms was limited by political and social realities. Everywhere in Europe, the hereditary aristocracy was still the most powerful class. As the chief beneficiaries of a system based on traditional rights and privileges, the nobles were not willing to support a political ideology that trumpeted the principle of equal rights for all. The first serious

Map 18.2 Europe in 1763. By the mid-eighteenth century, five major powers dominated Europe: Prussia, Austria, Russia, Britain, and France. Each sought to enhance its domestic powers through a bureaucracy that collected taxes and ran the military as well as internationally by capturing territory or preventing other powers from doing so.

 Given the distribution of Prussian and Habsburg holdings, in what areas of Europe were they most likely to compete for land and power?

challenge to their supremacy would come with the French Revolution, an event that blew open the door to the world of modern politics.

18-4e Changing Patterns of War: Global Confrontation

The philosophes condemned war as a foolish waste of life and resources. Despite their words, the rivalries and costly struggles among the European states continued unabated in the eighteenth century. Europe consisted of many self-governing states that were chiefly guided by the self-interests of their rulers. As Frederick the Great of Prussia said, "The fundamental rule of governments is the principle of extending their territories."

By far the most dramatic confrontation was the Seven Years' War. Although it began in Europe, it soon turned into a global conflict fought in Europe, India, and North America. In Europe, the British and Prussians fought the Austrians, Russians, and French. With his superb army and military skill, Frederick the Great of Prussia was able for some time to defeat the Austrian, French, and Russian armies. Gradually, however, his forces were worn down and faced utter defeat until a new Russian tsar withdrew Russia's troops from the conflict. A stalemate ensued, ending the European conflict in 1763.

The struggle between Britain and France in the rest of the world had more decisive results. In India, local rulers allied with British and French troops fought several battles. Ultimately, the British under Robert Clive won out, not because they had better forces but because they were more persistent (see Image 18.7). By the Treaty of Paris in 1763, the French withdrew and left India to the British.

The greatest conflicts of the Seven Years' War took place in North America, where it was known as the French and Indian War. Despite initial French successes, the British went on to seize Montreal, the Great Lakes area, and the Ohio River Valley. The French were forced to make peace. By the

18.7 Robert Clive in India. Robert Clive was the leader of the army of the British East India Company. He had been commanded to fight the rule of Bengal in order to gain trading privileges. After the Battle of Plassey in 1757, Clive and the East India Company took control of Bengal. In this painting by Edward Penny, Clive is shown receiving a grant of money for his injured soldiers from the local nabob or governor of Bengal.

Treaty of Paris, they ceded Canada and the lands east of the Mississippi to Britain. Their ally Spain transferred Spanish Florida to British control; in return, the French gave their Louisiana territory to the Spanish. By 1763, Great Britain had become the world's greatest colonial power. British victories cost Great Britain substantially; the national debt of Great Britain rose from 75 million pounds in 1756 to 133 million pounds by 1763. Great Britain's attempts to raise revenue by taxing the American colonies led to the American Revolution. For France, the loss of its empire was soon followed by an even greater internal upheaval.

18-5 **THE FRENCH REVOLUTION**

> **Q** **Focus Question:** What were the causes, the main events, and the results of the French Revolution?

The year 1789 witnessed two far-reaching events: the beginning of a new United States of America under its revamped constitution and the eruption of the French Revolution. Compared with the American Revolution a decade earlier, the French Revolution was more complex, more violent, and far more radical in its attempt to construct new political and social orders.

18-5a **Background to the French Revolution**

The root causes of the French Revolution must be sought in the condition of French society. Before the revolution, France was a society grounded in privilege and inequality. During the eighteenth century, the population had increased by 44 percent from 18 million to 26 million. It was a young country, with 36 percent of citizens under age twenty and 40 percent between twenty and forty. It was divided, as it had been since the Middle Ages, into three orders or estates.

Social Structure of the Old Regime   The First Estate consisted of the clergy and numbered some 130,000 people who owned approximately 10 percent of the land. Clergy were exempt from the *taille* (TY), France's chief tax. The church was extremely wealthy; income from church property and other investments produced almost 300 million *livres* (Leev-RUH) annually—half the income of the royal crown. Clergy were also radically divided: the higher-ranking clergy came from aristocratic families and shared the interests of the nobility and lived in palaces and townhouses, while the parish priests were often poor commoners.

The Second Estate consisted of the nobility, composed of some 350,000 people who owned between 25 percent and 30 percent of the land. The nobility continued to play an important role in French society, holding many of the leading positions in the government, the military, the law courts, and the higher church offices. The nobles sought to expand their power at the expense of the monarchy and to maintain their positions in the military, church, and government. Common to all nobles were tax exemptions, especially from the taille.

The Third Estate—the commoners—constituted the overwhelming majority of the French population. They were divided by vast differences in occupation, level of education, and wealth. The peasants constituted 75 percent to 80 percent of the total population and were by far the largest segment of the Third Estate. They owned some 35 percent to 40 percent of the land, although more than half had little or no land on which to survive. The landless peasants were day laborers who increasingly migrated to Paris in search of work; they were the first to suffer in difficult times. Serfdom no longer existed on any large scale in France, but French peasants still had obligations to their local landlords whom they deeply resented. These "relics of feudalism," or aristocratic privileges, had survived from an earlier age and included the payment of fees for the use of village facilities such as the flour mill, community oven, and winepress.

Another part of the Third Estate consisted of skilled craftspeople, shopkeepers, and other urban wage earners. In the eighteenth century, these groups suffered a decline in purchasing power as consumer prices rose faster than wages. Their daily struggle for survival led many of these people to play an important role in the revolution, especially in Paris.

Some 8 percent of the population, or 2.3 million people, constituted the bourgeoisie or middle class, who owned 20 percent to 25 percent of the land. This group included merchants, industrialists, and bankers who had benefited from the economic prosperity after 1730. The bourgeoisie also included professional people—lawyers, holders of public offices, doctors, and writers. Many members of the bourgeoisie had their own grievances because they were often excluded from the social and political privileges monopolized by nobles.

Moreover, the new political ideas of the Enlightenment proved attractive to both the aristocracy and the bourgeoisie. Both elites, long accustomed to a new socioeconomic reality based on wealth and economic achievement, were increasingly frustrated by a monarchical system resting on privileges and on an old and rigid social order based on the concept of estates. The opposition of these elites to the **old order** led them ultimately to drastic action against the monarchical **old regime**. In a real sense, the revolution had its origins in political grievances.

Other Problems Facing the French Monarchy Although France had enjoyed fifty years of economic expansion, bad harvests in 1787 and 1788 and the beginnings of a manufacturing depression had resulted in food shortages, rising prices for food and other goods, and unemployment in the cities. The number of poor, estimated at almost one-third of the population, reached crisis proportions on the eve of the revolution.

The French monarchy seemed incapable of dealing with the new social realities. Louis XVI (1774–1792) had become king in 1774 at age twenty; he knew little about the operations of the French government and lacked the energy to deal decisively with state affairs. His wife, Marie Antoinette (ma-REE ahn-twahn-NET), was a spoiled Austrian princess who devoted much of her time to court intrigues (see Film & History, *"Marie Antoinette,"*). As France's crises worsened, neither Louis nor his queen seemed able to fathom the depths of despair and discontent that soon led to violent revolution.

The immediate cause of the French Revolution was the near collapse of government finances. France experienced a depression from 1778 to 1787 as a result of a loss of overseas markets and overproduction. Peasants faced increasing uncertainty as rent prices remained high because of a

rapidly growing population, while poor harvests in 1788 and 1789 sent prices of wheat and rye soaring—leaving many people desperate. Costly wars and royal extravagance drove French governmental expenditures ever higher. The government responded by borrowing. Poor taxation policy contributed to the high debt, with most of the monarchy's funds coming from the peasantry. Unlike Britain, where the Bank of England financed the borrowing of money at low interest rates, France had no central bank and instead relied on private loans. By 1788, the interest on the debt alone constituted half of all government spending.

On the verge of a complete financial collapse, the government of Louis XVI was finally forced to call a meeting of the Estates-General, the French parliamentary body that had not met since 1614. The Estates-General consisted of representatives from the three orders of French society. In the elections for the Estates-General, the government had ruled that the Third Estate should get double representation (it did—after all, it constituted 97 percent of the population). Consequently, while both the First Estate (the clergy) and the Second Estate (the nobility) had some 300 delegates each, the Third Estate had almost 600 representatives, most of whom were lawyers from French towns.

18-5b From Estates-General to National Assembly

The Estates-General opened at Versailles on May 5, 1789. The first issue was whether voting should be by order or by head (each delegate having one vote). Traditionally, each order would vote as a group and have one vote. That meant that the First and Second Estates could outvote the Third Estate two to one. The Third Estate demanded that each deputy have one vote. With the assistance of liberal nobles and clerics, that would give the Third Estate a majority. When the First Estate declared in favor of voting by order, the Third Estate responded dramatically. On June 17, 1789, the Third Estate declared itself the "National Assembly" and prepared to draw up a constitution. This was the first step in the French Revolution because the Third Estate had no legal right to act as the National Assembly. Louis XVI sided with the First Estate and prepared to use force to dissolve the Estates-General.

The common people, however, saved the Third Estate from the king's forces. On July 14, a mob of Parisians stormed the Bastille, a royal armory, and proceeded to dismantle it brick by brick. Soon informed that the royal troops were unreliable, Louis XIV accepted this reality, signaling the collapse of royal authority. The king could no longer enforce his will.

At the same time, popular revolts broke out throughout France in both cities and countryside (see Comparative Illustration, "Revolution and Revolt in France and China," p. 460). Behind the popular uprising was a growing resentment of the entire landholding system with its fees and obligations. The fall of the Bastille and the king's apparent capitulation to the demands of the Third Estate now led peasants to take matters into their own hands. The peasant rebellions that occurred throughout France had a great impact on the National Assembly meeting at Versailles.

18-5c Destruction of the Old Regime

One of the National Assembly's first acts abolished the rights of landlords and the fiscal exemptions of nobles, clergy, towns, and provinces. Three weeks later, the National Assembly adopted the Declaration of the Rights of Man and the Citizen. This charter of basic liberties proclaimed freedom and equal rights for all men and access to public office based on talent. All citizens were to have the right to take part in the legislative process. Freedom of speech and the press was coupled with the outlawing of arbitrary arrests.

But did the declaration's ideal of equal rights for "all men" also include women? Many deputies insisted that it did, provided that, as one said, "women do not hope to exercise political rights and functions." Olympe de Gouges (oh-LAMP duh GOOZH), a playwright, rejected this exclusion of women from political rights. Echoing the words of the official declaration, she penned the Declaration of the Rights of Woman and the Female Citizen, in which she insisted that women should have all the same rights as men (see Opposing Viewpoints, "The Natural Rights of the French People: Two Views," p. 461). The National Assembly ignored her demands.

Because the Catholic church was seen as an important pillar of the old order, it too was reformed. Most of the church's lands were seized. Under the Civil Constitution of the Clergy, which was adopted on July 12, 1790, bishops and priests were to be elected by the people and paid by the state. The Catholic church, still an important institution in the life of the French people, now became an enemy of the revolution.

By 1791, the National Assembly had completed a new constitution that established a limited constitutional monarchy. There was still a monarch—now called "king of the French"—but sovereign power was vested in the new Legislative Assembly, which would make the laws. The Legislative Assembly was to sit for two years and consisted of 745 representatives elected by an indirect system that preserved power in the hands of the more affluent members of society. A small group of 50,000 electors chose the deputies.

Thus, the old order had been destroyed, but the new order had many opponents—Catholic priests, nobles, lower classes hurt by the rising cost of living, peasants opposed to dues that had still not been eliminated, and political clubs like the Jacobins (JAK-uh-binz) that offered more radical solutions. The king also made things difficult for the new government when he sought to flee France in June 1791 and almost succeeded before being recognized, captured, and brought back to Paris. The flight to Varennes shattered the illusion of a loyal king. In this unsettled situation, under a discredited and seemingly disloyal monarch, the new Legislative Assembly held its first session in October 1791. France's relations with the rest of Europe soon led to Louis' downfall.

On August 27, 1791, the monarchs of Austria and Prussia, fearing that revolution would spread to their countries, invited other European monarchs to use force to reestablish monarchical authority in France. The French fared badly in the fighting in the spring of 1792, and a frantic search for scapegoats began. As one observer noted,

Revolution and Revolt in France and China

Politics & Government

BOTH FRANCE AND CHINA EXPERIENCED REVOLUTIONARY UPHEAVAL in the late eighteenth and nineteenth centuries. In both countries, common people often played an important role. Image 18.8b shows a scene from the storming of the Bastille in 1789. This early action by the people of Paris ultimately led to the overthrow of the French monarchy. Image 18.8a is an episode during the Taiping

Rebellion, a major peasant revolt in the mid-nineteenth century in China. An imperial Chinese army is shown recapturing the city of Nanjing from Taiping rebels in 1864.

Q *What role did common people play in revolutionary upheavals in France and China in the eighteenth and nineteenth centuries?*

The Art Archive/School of Oriental & African Studies/Eileen Tweedy

18.8a

Chateau de Versailles, France/Giraudon/The Bridgeman Art Library

18.8b

"Everywhere you hear the cry that the king is betraying us, the generals are betraying us, that nobody is to be trusted; . . . that Paris will be taken in six weeks by the Austrians. . . . We are on a volcano ready to spout flames."[1] Defeats in war coupled with economic shortages led to renewed political demonstrations, especially against the king. In August 1792, radical political groups in Paris took the king captive and forced the Legislative Assembly to suspend the monarchy and call for a national convention, chosen on the basis of universal male suffrage, to decide on the future form of government. The French Revolution was about to enter a more radical stage.

The Natural Rights of the French People: Two Views

 Politics & Government **ONE OF THE IMPORTANT DOCUMENTS OF THE FRENCH REVOLUTION,** the Declaration of the Rights of Man and the Citizen was adopted on August 26, 1789, by the National Assembly. Olympe de Gouges was a butcher's daughter who wrote plays and pamphlets. She argued that the Declaration of the Rights of Man and the Citizen did not apply to women and composed her own Declaration of the Rights of Woman and the Female Citizen in 1791.

Declaration of the Rights of Man and the Citizen

1. Men are born and remain free and equal in rights. Social distinctions can only be founded upon the general good.
2. The aim of all political association is the preservation of the natural and imprescriptible rights of man. These rights are liberty, property, security, and resistance to oppression.
3. The principle of all sovereignty resides essentially in the nation. No body or individual may exercise any authority which does not proceed directly from the nation.
4. Liberty consists in being able to do everything which injures no one else. . . .
6. Law is the expression of the general will. Every citizen has a right to participate personally or through his representative in its formation. It must be the same for all, whether it protects or punishes. All citizens being equal in the eyes of the law are equally eligible to all dignities and to all public positions and occupations according to their abilities and without distinction except that of their virtues and talents.
7. No person shall be accused, arrested, or imprisoned except in the cases and according to the forms prescribed by law. . . .
10. No one shall be disturbed on account of his opinions, including his religious views, provided their manifestation does not disturb the public order established by law.
11. The free communication of ideas and opinions is one of the most precious of the rights of man. Every citizen may, accordingly, speak, write and print with freedom, being responsible, however, for such abuses of this freedom as shall be defined by law. . . .
16. A society in which the observance of the law is not assured nor the separation of powers defined has no constitution at all.

17. Property being an inviolable and sacred right, no one shall be deprived thereof except where public necessity, legally determined, shall clearly demand it, and then only on condition that the owner shall have been previously and equitably indemnified.

Declaration of the Rights of Woman and the Female Citizen

Mothers, daughters, sisters and representatives of the nation demand to be constituted into a national assembly. Believing that ignorance, omission, or scorn for the rights of woman are the only causes of public misfortunes and of the corruption of governments, the women have resolved to set forth in a solemn declaration the natural, inalienable, and sacred rights of woman in order that this declaration, constantly exposed before all the members of the society, will ceaselessly remind them of their rights and duties. . . .

Consequently, the sex that is as superior in beauty as it is in courage during the sufferings of maternity recognizes and declares in the presence and under the auspices of the Supreme Being, the following.

Rights of Woman and of Female Citizens

1. Woman is born free and lives equal to man in her rights. Social distinctions can be based only on the common utility.
2. The purpose of any political association is the conservation of the natural and imprescriptible rights of woman and man; these rights are liberty, property, security, and especially resistance to oppression.
3. The principle of all sovereignty rests essentially with the nation, which is nothing but the union of woman and man; no body and no individual can exercise any authority which does not come expressly from [the nation].
4. Liberty and justice consist of restoring all that belongs to others; thus, the only limits on the exercise of the natural rights of woman are perpetual male tyranny; these limits are to be reformed by the laws of nature and reason. . . .
6. The law must be the expression of the general will; all female and male citizens must contribute either personally or through representatives to its formation; it must be the same for all: male and female citizens, being equal in the eyes of the law, must be equally

(continued)

(*continued*)

admitted to all honors, positions, and public employment according to their capacity and without other distinctions besides those of their virtues and talents.

7. No woman is an exception; she is accused, arrested, and detained in cases determined by law. Women, like men, obey this rigorous law. . . .

10. No one is to be disquieted for his very basic opinions; woman has the right to mount the scaffold; she must equally have the right to mount the rostrum, provided that her demonstrations do not disturb the legally established public order.

11. The free communication of thought and opinions is one of the most precious rights of woman, since that liberty assured the recognition of children by their fathers. . . .

16. No society has a constitution without the guarantee of rights and the separation of powers; the constitution is null if the majority of individuals comprising the nation have not cooperated in drafting it.

17. Property belongs to both sexes whether united or separate; for each it is an inviolable and sacred right; no one can be deprived of it, since it is the true patrimony of nature, unless the legally determined public need obviously dictates it, and then only with a just and prior indemnity.

Q *What "natural rights" does the first document proclaim? To what extent was this document influenced by the writings of the philosophes? What rights for women does the second document enunciate? Given the nature and scope of the arguments in favor of natural rights and women's rights in these two documents, what key effects on European society would you attribute to the French Revolution?*

Sources: Excerpt from Thomas Carlyle, *The French Revolution: A History, Vol. I* (George Bell and Sons, London, 1902), pp. 346–348. From *Women in Revolutionary Paris, 1789–1795: Selected Documents Translated with Notes and Commentary*. Translated with notes and commentary by Darline Gay Levy, Harriet Branson Applewhite, and Mary Durham Johnson. Copyright © 1979 by the Board of Trustees of the University of Illinois. Used with permission of the editors and the University of Illinois Press.

18-5d The Radical Revolution

In September 1792, the newly elected National Convention began its sessions. Dominated by lawyers and other professionals, two-thirds of its deputies were under age forty-five, and almost all had gained political experience as a result of the revolution. Almost all distrusted the king. As a result, the convention's first step on September 21 was to abolish the monarchy and establish a republic. On January 21, 1793, the king was executed, and the destruction of the old regime was complete. But the execution of the king created new enemies for the revolution both at home and abroad.

In Paris, the local government, known as the Commune, whose leaders came from the working classes, favored radical change and put constant pressure on the convention, pushing it to ever more radical positions. Meanwhile, peasants in the west and inhabitants of the major provincial cities refused to accept the authority of the convention.

A foreign crisis also loomed. By the beginning of 1793, after the king had been executed, most of Europe—an informal coalition of Austria, Prussia, Spain, Portugal, Britain, the Dutch Republic, and even Russia—aligned militarily against France. Grossly overextended, the French armies began to experience reverses; by late spring, France was threatened with invasion.

A Nation in Arms To meet these crises, the convention gave broad powers to an executive committee of twelve known as the Committee of Public Safety, which came to be dominated by Maximilien Robespierre (mak-see-meel-YENH ROHBZ-pyayr). For a twelve-month period—from 1793 to 1794—the Committee of Public Safety took control of France. To save the republic from its foreign foes, on August 23, 1793, the committee decreed a levy-in-mass, or universal mobilization of the nation:

> Young men will fight, young men are called to conquer. Married men will forge arms, transport military baggage and guns and will prepare food supplies. Women, who at long last are to take their rightful place in the revolution and follow their true destiny, will forget their futile tasks: their delicate hands will work at making clothes for soldiers; they will make tents and they will [help the wounded]. Children will make lint of old cloth. It is for them that we are fighting: children, those beings destined to gather all the fruits of the revolution, will raise their pure hands toward the skies. And old men, performing their missions again, as of yore, will be guided to the public squares of the cities where they will kindle the courage of young warriors and preach the doctrines of hate for kings and the unity of the Republic.[2]

In less than a year, the French revolutionary government had raised an army of 650,000 and had pushed the allies back across the Rhine and even conquered the Austrian Netherlands by 1795.

The French revolutionary army was an important step in the creation of modern **nationalism**. Previously, wars had been fought between governments or ruling dynasties by relatively small armies of professional soldiers. The new French army was the creation of a "people's" government; its wars were now "people's" wars that involved the entire nation. But when dynastic wars became people's wars, warfare increased in ferocity while being less restrained. The wars of the French revolutionary era opened the door to the total war of the modern world.

Reign of Terror   To meet the domestic crisis, the National Convention and the Committee of Public Safety launched a period of bloodshed that came to be called the Reign of Terror. Revolutionary courts were instituted to protect the republic from its internal enemies. Robespierre passed a law that denied suspects sent before the Revolutionary Tribunal all rights to defend themselves. This law increased the pace of executions. In the course of nine months, 16,000 people were officially killed under the blade of the guillotine—a revolutionary device designed for the quick and efficient separation of heads from bodies.

Revolutionary armies were set up to bring recalcitrant cities and districts back under the control of the National Convention. The Committee of Public Safety decided to make an example of Lyons (LYOHNH), which had defied the authority of the National Convention. By April 1794, some 1,880 citizens of Lyons had been executed. When the guillotine proved too slow, cannon fire was used to blow condemned men into open graves. As one German observed,

> Whole ranges of houses, always the most handsome, burnt. The churches, convents, and all the dwellings of the former patricians were in ruins. When I came to the guillotine, the blood of those who had been executed a few hours beforehand was still running in the street. . . . I said to a group of [radicals] that it would be decent to clear away all this human blood. Why should it be cleared? one of them said to me. It's the blood of aristocrats and rebels. The dogs should lick it up.[3]

Equality and Slavery: Revolution in Haiti   Early in the French Revolution, the desire for equality led to a discussion of what to do about slavery. A club called Friends of the Blacks advocated the abolition of slavery, which was achieved in France in September 1791. But French planters in the West Indies, who profited greatly from the use of slaves on their sugar plantations, opposed the abolition of slavery in colonial French territories. On February 4, 1794, however, the National Convention, guided by ideas of equality, abolished slavery in the colonies.

18-5e Reaction and the Directory

By the summer of 1794, the French had been successful on the battlefield against their foreign foes, making the Terror less necessary. But the Terror continued because Robespierre, who had come to dominate the Committee of Public Safety, became obsessed with purifying the body politic of all the corrupt. Many deputies in the National Convention began to fear they were not safe while Robespierre was free to act and gathered enough votes to condemn him. Robespierre was guillotined on July 28, 1794.

After Robespierre's death, a reaction set in as more moderate middle-class leaders took control. The Reign of Terror came to a halt, and the National Convention reduced the power of the Committee of Public Safety. In August, a new constitution was drafted that reflected the desire for a stability that did not sacrifice the ideals of 1789. Five directors—the Directory—acted as the executive authority.

The period of the Revolution under the Directory (1795–1799) was an era of stagnation and corruption. At the same time, the Directory faced political enemies from both the left and the right of the political spectrum. On the right, royalists continued their efforts to restore the monarchy. On the left, radical hopes of power were revived by continuing economic problems. Battered from both sides, unable to solve the country's economic problems, and still carrying on the wars inherited from the Committee of Public Safety, the Directory increasingly relied on the military to maintain its power. This led to a coup d'état in 1799 in which the popular military general Napoleon Bonaparte seized power.

CHRONOLOGY	The French Revolution
Meeting of Estates-General	May 5, 1789
Formation of National Assembly	June 17, 1789
Fall of the Bastille	July 14, 1789
Declaration of the Rights of Man and the Citizen	August 26, 1789
Civil Constitution of the Clergy	July 12, 1790
Flight of the king	June 20–21, 1791
Attack on the royal palace	August 10, 1792
Abolition of the monarchy	September 21, 1792
Execution of the king	January 21, 1793
Levy-in-mass	August 23, 1793
Execution of Robespierre	July 28, 1794
Adoption of Constitution of 1795 and the Directory	August 22, 1795

Napoleon and Psychological Warfare

Politics & Government IN 1796, AT AGE TWENTY-SEVEN, Napoleon Bonaparte was given command of the French army in Italy, where he won a series of stunning victories. His use of speed, deception, and surprise to overwhelm his opponents is well known. In this selection from a proclamation to his troops in Italy, Napoleon also appears as a master of psychological warfare.

Napoleon Bonaparte, Proclamation to French Troops in Italy (April 26, 1796)

Soldiers:

In a fortnight you have won six victories, taken twenty-one standards [flags of military units], fifty-five pieces of artillery, several strong positions, and conquered the richest part of Piedmont [in northern Italy]; you have captured 15,000 prisoners and killed or wounded more than 10,000 men You have won battles without cannon, crossed rivers without bridges, made forced marches without shoes, camped without brandy and often without bread. Soldiers of liberty, only republican troops could have endured what you have endured. Soldiers, you have our thanks! The grateful *Patrie* [nation] will owe its prosperity to you.

The two armies which but recently attacked you with audacity are fleeing before you in terror; the wicked men who laughed at your misery and rejoiced at the thought of the triumphs of your enemies are confounded and trembling.

But, soldiers, as yet you have done nothing compared with what remains to be done. . . . Undoubtedly the greatest obstacles have been overcome; but you still have battles to fight, cities to capture, rivers to cross. Is there one among you whose courage is abating? No. . . . All of you are consumed with a desire to extend the glory of the French people; all of you long to humiliate those arrogant kings who dare to contemplate placing us in fetters; all of you desire to dictate a glorious peace, one which will indemnify the *Patrie* for the immense sacrifices it has made; all of you wish to be able to say with pride as you return to your villages, "I was with the victorious army of Italy!"

Q *What themes did Napoleon use to play on the emotions of his troops and inspire them to greater efforts? Do you think Napoleon believed these words? Why or why not?*

Source: From James Harvey Robinson, *Readings in European History* (Lexington, Mass.: Ginn and Co., 1906), p. 471.

18-6 THE AGE OF NAPOLEON

Q Focus Question: Which aspects of the French Revolution did Napoleon preserve, and which did he destroy?

Napoleon dominated both French and European history from 1799 to 1815. He had been born in Corsica in 1769 shortly after France had annexed the island. The young Napoleone Buonaparte (his birth name) was sent to France to study in one of the new military schools and was a lieutenant when the revolution broke out in 1789. The revolution and the European war that followed gave him new opportunities, and Napoleon rose quickly through the ranks. In 1794, at age twenty-five, he was made a brigadier general. Two years later, he commanded the French armies in Italy, where he won a series of victories and returned to France as a conquering hero (see Historical Voices, "Napoleon and Psychological Warfare,"). After a disastrous expedition to Egypt, Napoleon returned to Paris, where he participated in the coup that gave him control of France. He was only thirty years old.

After the coup of 1799, a new form of the republic called the Consulate was proclaimed in which Napoleon, as first consul, controlled the entire executive authority of government. He had overwhelming influence over the legislature, appointed members of the administrative bureaucracy, commanded the army, and conducted foreign affairs. In 1802, Napoleon was made consul for life, and in 1804, he returned France to monarchy when he became Emperor Napoleon I.

18-6a Domestic Policies

One of Napoleon's first domestic policies was to establish peace with the oldest and most implacable enemy of the revolution: the Catholic Church. In 1801, Napoleon arranged a concordat with the pope that recognized Catholicism as the religion of a majority of the French people. In return, the pope agreed not to challenge the confiscation of church lands during the revolution.

Napoleon's most enduring domestic achievement was his codification of the laws. Before the Revolution, France had some 300 local legal systems. During the revolution, efforts were made to prepare a single code of laws for the nation, but it remained for Napoleon to bring the work to completion in the famous Civil Code. It preserved most of the revolutionary gains by recognizing the equality of all citizens before the law, abolishing serfdom and feudalism, and promoting religious toleration. Property rights were also protected.

Napoleon also developed a powerful, centralized administration and worked hard to develop a bureaucracy of capable officials. Early on, the regime showed that it cared little whether officials had acquired their expertise in royal or revolutionary bureaucracies. Promotion, whether in civil or military offices, was based not on rank or birth but on ability only. This principle of a government career open to talent was, of course, what many bourgeois had wanted before the revolution.

In his domestic policies, then, Napoleon both destroyed and preserved aspects of the Revolution. Although equality was preserved in the law code and the opening of careers to talent, the creation of a new aristocracy, the strong protection accorded to property rights, and the use of conscription for the military made it clear that much equality

had been lost. Liberty was replaced by an initially benevolent despotism that grew increasingly arbitrary. Napoleon shut down sixty of France's seventy-three newspapers.

18-6b Napoleon's Empire

When Napoleon became consul in 1799, France was at war with a second European coalition of Russia, Great Britain, and Austria. Napoleon realized the need for a pause and made a peace treaty in 1802. But in 1803 war was renewed with Britain, which was soon joined by Austria, Russia, and Prussia in the Third Coalition. In a series of battles from 1805 to 1807, Napoleon's Grand Army defeated the Austrian, Prussian, and Russian armies, giving Napoleon the opportunity to create a new European order.

The Grand Empire   From 1807 to 1812, Napoleon was the master of Europe. His Grand Empire was composed of three major parts: the French Empire, dependent states, and allied states (see Map 18.3). Dependent states were ruled by Napoleon's relatives; these came to include Spain, the Netherlands, the kingdom of Italy, the Swiss Republic, the Grand Duchy of Warsaw, and the Confederation of the

18.9 The Coronation of Napoleon. In 1804, Napoleon restored monarchy to France when he became Emperor Napoleon I. In the coronation scene painted by Jacques-Louis David, Napoleon is shown crowning his wife, Empress Josephine, while the pope looks on. The painting shows Napoleon's mother seated in the box in the background, even though she was not at the ceremony.

Reunion des Musees Nationaux/Art Resource, NY

Map 18.3 Napoleon's Grand Empire. Napoleon's Grand Army won a series of victories against Austria, Prussia, and Russia that gave the French emperor full or partial control over much of Europe by 1807.

Q *On the European continent, what was the overall relationship between distance from France and degree of French control, and how can you account for this?*

Rhine (a union of every German state except Austria and Prussia). Allied states were those defeated by Napoleon and included Prussia, Austria, Russia, and Sweden. They were forced to join his struggle against Britain.

Within his empire, Napoleon sought acceptance of certain revolutionary principles, including legal equality, religious toleration, and economic freedom. In the inner core and dependent states of his Grand Empire, Napoleon tried to destroy the old order. Nobility and clergy everywhere in these states lost their special privileges. He decreed equality of opportunity with offices open to talent, equality before the law, and religious toleration.

Napoleon hoped that his Grand Empire would last for centuries, but it collapsed almost as rapidly as it had been formed. As long as Britain ruled the waves, it was not subject to military attack. Napoleon hoped to invade Britain, but he could not overcome the British navy's decisive defeat of a combined French–Spanish fleet at Trafalgar in 1805. To defeat Britain, Napoleon turned to his **Continental System**. An alliance put into effect between 1806 and 1808, it attempted to prevent British goods from reaching the European continent in order to weaken Britain economically and destroy its capacity to wage war. But the Continental System failed. Allied states resented it, and some began to cheat and others to resist.

Napoleon also encountered new sources of opposition. His conquests made the French hated oppressors and aroused the patriotism of the conquered people. A Spanish uprising, aided by the British, kept a French force of 200,000 pinned down for years.

The Fall of Napoleon The beginning of Napoleon's downfall came in 1812 with his invasion of Russia. The refusal of the Russians to remain in the Continental System left Napoleon with little choice. Although aware of the risks in invading such a huge country, he knew that if the Russians were allowed to challenge the Continental System unopposed, other nations would follow suit. In June 1812, he led his Grand Army of more than 600,000 men into Russia. His hopes for victory depended on quickly defeating the Russian armies, but the Russian forces retreated and refused to give battle, torching their own villages to keep Napoleon's army from finding food. When the Russians did stop to fight at Borodino, Napoleon won an indecisive and costly victory. When the remaining troops of the Grand Army arrived in Moscow, they found the city ablaze. Lacking food and supplies, Napoleon abandoned Moscow late in October and made a retreat across Russia in terrible winter conditions. Only 40,000 of the original 600,000 men arrived back in Poland in January 1813.

This military disaster led other European states to rise up and attack the crippled French army. Paris was captured in March 1814, and Napoleon was sent into exile on the island of Elba off the coast of Italy. Meanwhile, the Bourbon monarchy was restored in the person of Louis XVIII, brother of the executed king. (Louis XVII, son of Louis XVI, had died in prison at age ten.) Bored on Elba, Napoleon slipped back into France. When troops were sent to capture him, Napoleon opened his coat and addressed them: "Soldiers of the 5th regiment, I am your Emperor. . . . If there is a man among you would kill his Emperor, here I am!" No one fired a shot. Shouting "Vive l'Empereur! Vive l'Empereur," the troops went over to his side, and Napoleon entered Paris in triumph on March 20, 1815. The powers that had defeated him pledged once more to fight him. Napoleon raised another army and moved to attack the allied forces stationed in what is now Belgium. At Waterloo on June 18, Napoleon met a combined British and Prussian army under the duke of Wellington and suffered a bloody defeat. This time, the victorious allies exiled him to Saint Helena, a small, forsaken island in the South Atlantic off the coast of Africa. Only the memory of Napoleon's reign continued to haunt French political life.

CHAPTER SUMMARY

In the Scientific Revolution, the Western world overthrew the medieval Ptolemaic worldview and arrived at a new conception of the universe: the sun at the center, the planets as material bodies revolving around the sun in elliptical  orbits, and an infinite rather than finite world. With the changes in the conception of "heaven" came changes in the conception of "Earth." Highly influenced by the new worldview created by the Scientific Revolution, the philosophes of the eighteenth century hoped to create a new society by using reason to discover the natural laws that governed it. They attacked traditional religion as the enemy and developed the new "sciences of man" in economics, politics, and education. Together, the Scientific Revolution of the seventeenth century and the Enlightenment of the eighteenth century constituted an intellectual revolution that laid the foundations for a modern worldview based on rationalism and secularism.

Everywhere in Europe at the beginning of the eighteenth century, the old order remained strong. Nobles, clerics, towns, and provinces all had privileges. Everywhere in the eighteenth century, monarchs sought to enlarge their bureaucracies to raise taxes to support large standing armies. The existence of these armies led to wars on a worldwide scale. Although the wars resulted in few changes in Europe, British victories enabled Great Britain to emerge as the world's greatest naval and colonial power. Meanwhile in Europe, increased demands for taxes to support these wars led to attacks on the old order and a desire for change not met by the ruling monarchs. At the same time, a growing population as well as changes in finance, trade, and industry created tensions that undermined the foundations of the old order.  Its inability to deal with these changes led to a revolutionary outburst at the end of the eighteenth century that marked the beginning of the end for the old order.

The revolutionary era of the late eighteenth century was a time of dramatic political transformations. Revolutionary upheavals, beginning in North America and continuing in France, spurred movements for political liberty and equality. The documents promulgated by these revolutions (the Declaration of Independence and the

Declaration of the Rights of Man and the Citizen) embodied the fundamental ideas of the Enlightenment and created a liberal political agenda based on a belief in popular sovereignty—the people as the source of political power—and the principles of liberty and equality. In theory, liberty meant freedom from arbitrary power as well as the freedom to think, write, and worship as one chose. Equality meant equality in rights, although it did not include equality between men and women.

REFLECTION QUESTIONS

Q What was the impact of the intellectual revolution of the seventeenth and eighteenth centuries on European society?

Q How was France changed by the revolutionary events between 1789 and 1799, and who benefited the most from these changes?

Q In what ways did Napoleon's policies reject the accomplishments of the French Revolution? In what ways did his policies strengthen those accomplishments?

CHAPTER TIMELINE

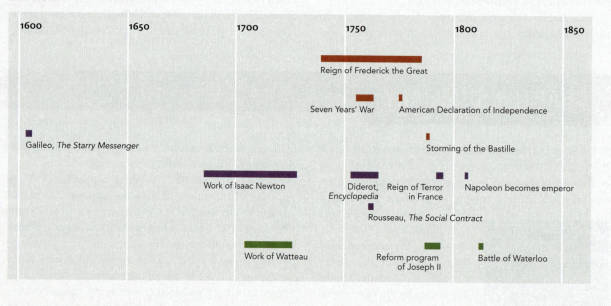

CHAPTER NOTES

1. Quoted in W. Doyle, *The Oxford History of the French Revolution* (Oxford, 1989), p. 184.

2. Quoted in L. Gershoy, *The Era of the French Revolution* (Princeton, N.J., 1957), p. 157.

3. Quoted in Doyle, *The Oxford History of the French Revolution*, p. 254.

MINDTAP
From Cengage

MindTap® is a fully online, highly personalized learning experience built upon Cengage Learning content. MindTap combines student learning tools—readings, multimedia, activities, and assessments—into a singular Learning Path that guides students through the course and helps students develop the critical thinking, analysis, and communication skills that are essential to academic and professional success.

PART IV

MODERN PATTERNS OF WORLD HISTORY (1800–1945)

THE PERIOD OF WORLD HISTORY from 1800 to 1945 was characterized by three major developments: the growth of industrialization, the rise of nationalism, and Western domination of the world. The three developments were, of course, interconnected. The Industrial Revolution became one of the major forces of change in the nineteenth century, leading Western civilization into an industrial era that has characterized the modern world ever since. Beginning in Britain, it spread to the European continent and the Western Hemisphere in the course of the nineteenth century. At the same time, the Industrial Revolution created the technological means, including new weapons, by which the West achieved domination over much of the rest of the world by the end of the nineteenth century. Moreover, the existence of competitive European nation-states after 1870 was undoubtedly a major determinant in the European states' intense scramble for overseas territory.

The advent of the industrial age had many lasting consequences for the modern world. On the one hand, nations that successfully passed through the process experienced a significant increase in material wealth. In many cases, the creation of advanced industrial societies led to stronger democratic institutions and enabled the majority of the population to enjoy a higher standard of living. On the other hand, not every consequence of the Industrial Revolution was beneficial. In the industrializing societies themselves, rapid economic change often led to widening disparities in the distribution of wealth and, with the decline in the pervasiveness of religious belief, a sense of rootlessness and alienation among much of the population.

The rise of nationalism was the second development that had a major impact on the era. Like the Industrial Revolution, nationalism originated in eighteenth-century Europe, where it was a product of the secularization of the age and the experience of the French revolutionary and Napoleonic eras. Although the concept provided the basis for a new sense of community and the rise of the modern nation-state, it also gave birth to ethnic tensions and hatreds that led to bitter disputes and civil strife and contributed to the competition that eventually erupted into world war.

Industrialization and the rise of national consciousness also transformed the nature of war itself. New weapons of mass destruction created the potential for a new kind of warfare that reached beyond the battlefield into the very heartland of the enemy's territory, while the concept of nationalism transformed war from the sport of kings to a matter of national honor and commitment.

IV.1

After the French Revolution, governments relied on mass conscription to defend the nation while their engines of destruction reached far into enemy territory to destroy the industrial base and undermine the will to fight. The two world wars of the twentieth century amply demonstrated this trend.

In the end, then, industrial power and nationalism—the very factors that had created the conditions for European global dominance—contained the seeds for the decline of that dominance. These seeds germinated during the 1930s when the Great Depression sharpened international competition and mutual antagonism and then sprouted in the ensuing conflict, which spanned the entire globe. By the time World War II came to an end, the once powerful countries of Europe were exhausted, leaving the door ajar for the emergence of two new global superpowers, the United States and the Soviet Union, and for the collapse of the Europeans' colonial empires.

The third development, Western expansion into the rest of the world, was connected to the development of both industrialization and nationalism. Europeans had begun to explore the world in the fifteenth century, but even as late as 1870, they had not yet completely penetrated North America, South America, Australia, or most of Africa. In Asia and Africa, with few exceptions, the Western presence was limited to trading posts. Between 1870 and 1914, however, Western civilization expanded into the rest of the Americas and Australia, and the bulk of Africa and Asia was divided into European colonies or spheres of influence. Two major events explain this remarkable expansion:

the migration of many Europeans to other parts of the world, a phenomenon resulting from population growth, and the revival of imperialism, a phenomenon made possible by the West's technological advances. Beginning in the 1880s, European states began an intense scramble for overseas territory. This revival of imperialism—the "new imperialism," some have called it—led Europeans to carve up Asia and Africa.

What was the overall economic effect of imperialism on the subject peoples? For most of the population in colonial areas, Western domination was rarely beneficial and often destructive. Although some merchants, large landowners, and traditional hereditary elites undoubtedly prospered under the expanding imperialistic economic order, the majority of colonial peoples, urban and rural alike, probably suffered considerable hardship as a result of the policies adopted by their foreign rulers.

Some historians point out, however, that for all its inequities, there was also a positive side to the colonial system. The expansion of markets and the beginnings of a modern transportation and communications network, while bringing few immediate benefits to the colonial peoples, offered considerable promise for future economic growth. At the same time, colonial peoples soon learned the power of nationalism, which would become a powerful force in the twentieth century for the rest of the world as nationalist revolutions moved through Asia, Africa, and the Middle East. Moreover, the exhaustive struggles of two world wars sapped the power of the European states, and the colonial powers no longer had the energy or the wealth to maintain their colonial empires after World War II.

Chapter Outline and Focus Questions

19-1 The Industrial Revolution and Its Impact

Q What were the basic features of the new industrial system created by the Industrial Revolution, and what effects did the new system have on urban life, social classes, family life, and standards of living?

19-2 The Growth of Industrial Prosperity

Q What was the Second Industrial Revolution, and what effects did it have on economic and social life? What were the main ideas of Karl Marx, and what role did they play in politics and the union movement in the late nineteenth and early twentieth centuries?

19-3 Reaction and Revolution: The Growth of Nationalism

Q What were the major ideas associated with conservatism, liberalism, and nationalism, and what role did each ideology play in Europe between 1800 and 1850? What were the causes of the revolutions of 1848, and why did these revolutions fail?

19-4 National Unification and the National State, 1848–1871

Q What actions did Cavour and Bismarck take to bring about unification in Italy and Germany, respectively, and what role did war play in their efforts?

19-5 The European State, 1871–1914

Q What general political trends were evident in the nations of western Europe in the late nineteenth and early twentieth centuries, and to what degree were those trends also apparent in the nations of central and eastern Europe? How did the growth of nationalism affect international affairs during the same period?

SuperStock

19.1 A Gathering of Statesmen at the Congress of Vienna

Critical Thinking

Q *In what ways was the development of industrialization related to the growth of nationalism?*

Connections to Today

Q *How do the locations of the centers of industrialization today compare with those during the Industrial Revolution, and how do you account for any differences?*

IN SEPTEMBER 1814, hundreds of foreigners began to converge on Vienna, the capital of the Austrian Empire. Many were members of European royalty—kings, archdukes, princes, and their wives—accompanied by their diplomatic advisers and scores of servants. Their congenial host was the Austrian emperor, Francis I, who never tired of regaling his guests with concerts, glittering balls, and sumptuous feasts. One participant remembered, "Eating, fireworks, public illuminations. For eight or ten days, I haven't been able to work at all. What a life!"

Of course, not every waking hour was spent in pleasure during this gathering of notables, known to history as the Congress of Vienna. The guests were also representatives of every state that had fought Napoleon, and their real business was to arrange a peace settlement after almost a decade of war. On June 8, 1815, they finally completed their task.

The forces of upheaval unleashed during the French revolutionary and Napoleonic wars were temporarily quieted in 1815 as rulers sought to restore stability by reestablishing much of the old order to a Europe ravaged by war. But the Western world had been changed, and it would not readily go back to the old system. New ideologies, especially liberalism and nationalism, products of the upheaval initiated in France, had become too powerful to be contained. The forces of change called forth revolts that periodically shook the West and culminated in a spate of revolutions in 1848. Some of the revolutions were successful; most were not. Yet by 1870, many of the goals sought by the liberals and nationalists during the first half of the nineteenth century seemed to have been achieved. National unity became a reality in Italy and Germany, and many Western states developed parliamentary features. Between 1870 and 1914, these newly constituted states experienced a time of great tension. Europeans engaged in a race for colonies that intensified existing antagonisms among the European states, while the creation of huge conscript armies and enormous military establishments heightened tensions among the major powers.

During the late eighteenth and early nineteenth centuries, another revolution—an industrial one—transformed the economic and social structure of Europe and spawned the industrial era that has characterized modern world history.

19-1 THE INDUSTRIAL REVOLUTION AND ITS IMPACT

Q **Focus Question:** What were the basic features of the new industrial system created by the Industrial Revolution, and what effects did the new system have on urban life, social classes, family life, and standards of living?

During the Industrial Revolution, Europe shifted from an economy based on agriculture and handicrafts to an economy based on manufacturing by machines and automated factories. The Industrial Revolution triggered an enormous leap in industrial production that relied largely on coal and steam, which replaced wind and water as new sources of energy to drive laborsaving machines. In turn, these machines called for new ways of organizing human labor to maximize the benefits and profits from the new machines. As factories replaced shop and home workrooms, large numbers of people moved from the countryside to the cities to work in the new factories. The creation of a wealthy industrial middle class and a huge industrial working class (or proletariat) substantially transformed traditional social relationships. Finally, the Industrial Revolution altered how people related to nature, ultimately creating an environmental crisis that came to be recognized as a danger to human existence itself in the twentieth century.

19-1a The Industrial Revolution in Great Britain

The Industrial Revolution began in Britain in the 1780s. Improvements in agricultural practices in the eighteenth century led to a significant increase in food production. British agriculture could now feed more people at lower prices with less labor; even ordinary families did not have to use most of their income to buy food, giving them the wherewithal to purchase manufactured goods. At the same time, rapid population growth in the second half of the eighteenth century provided a pool of surplus labor for the new factories of the emerging British industry.

In the course of its eighteenth-century wars, Great Britain had assembled a vast colonial empire at the expense of its leading rivals, the Dutch Republic and France. That empire's many markets gave British industrialists a ready outlet for their manufactured goods. British exports quadrupled from 1660 to 1760. Crucial to Britain's successful industrialization was the ability to produce the articles in greatest demand cheaply. The traditional methods of cottage industry could not keep up with the growing demand for cotton clothes throughout Britain and its vast colonial empire. Faced with this problem, British cloth manufacturers readily adopted the new methods of manufacturing that a series of inventions provided. In so doing, these individuals ignited the Industrial Revolution.

Changes in Textile Production   The invention of the flying shuttle enabled weavers to weave faster on a loom, thereby doubling their output. This created shortages of yarn until James Hargreaves's spinning jenny, perfected by 1768, allowed spinners to produce more yarn. Edmund Cartwright's loom, powered by water and invented in 1787, allowed the weaving of cloth to catch up with the

HISTORICAL VOICES

The Steam Engine and Cotton

Science & Technology

PRIOR TO THE INVENTION OF THE STEAM ENGINE, cotton was loomed by hand. In 1823, Richard Guest, an English economist, wrote of the advantages of steam weaving. It was not, however, advantageous for the handloom weavers; thousands lost their jobs as a result of the new invention.

Richard Guest, *A Compendious History of the Cotton-Manufacture*

The same powerful agent which so materially forwarded and advanced the progress of the Cotton Manufacture in the concluding party of the last century, has lately been further used as a substitute for manual labour, and the Steam Engine is now applied to the working of the loom as well as to the preparatory processes. . . .

It is a curious circumstance, that, when the Cotton Manufacture was in its infancy, all the operations, from the dress of the raw material to its being finally being turned out in the state of cloth, were completed under the roof of the weaver's cottage. The course of improved manufacture which followed, was to spin the yarn in factories and to weave it in cottages. . . . The Weaver's cottage with its rude apparatus of peg warping, hand card, hand wheels, and imperfect looms, was the Steam Loom factory in miniature. Those vast brick edifices in the vicinity of all the great manufacturing towns in the south of Lancashire, towering to the height of seventy or eighty feet, which strike the attention and excite the curiosity of the traveler, now perform the labors which formerly employed whole villages. In the Steam Loom factories, the cotton is carded, roved, spun, and woven into cloth, and the same quantum of labor is now performed in one of these structures which formerly occupied the industry of an entire district.

A very good Hand Weaver, a man twenty-five or thirty years of age, will weave two pieces of shirting per week, each twenty-four years long. . . . A Steam Loom Weaver, fifteen years of age, will in the same time weave seven similar pieces. A Steam Loom factory containing two hundred Looms, with the assistance of one hundred persons under twenty years of age, and of twenty-five men, will weave seven hundred pieces per week. To manufacture one hundred similar pieces per week by the hand, it would be necessary to employ at least one hundred and twenty-five Looms, because many of the Weavers are females, and have cooking, washing, cleaning and various other duties to perform; others of them are children and, consequently, unable to weave as much as the men.

Q *In what ways did the new steam loom transform the cotton industry? Who was excluded from this new form of industry?*

Source: Richard Guest, *A Compendious History of the Cotton-Manufacture* (Manchester, 1823), pp. 44–48.

spinning of yarn. It was now more efficient to bring workers to the machines and organize their labor collectively in factories located next to rivers, the source of power for these early machines.

The invention of the steam engine pushed the cotton industry to even greater heights of productivity. In the 1760s, a Scottish engineer, James Watt (1736–1819), built an engine powered by steam that could pump water from mines three times as quickly as previous engines. In 1782, Watt developed a rotary engine that could turn a shaft and thus drive machinery. Steam power could now be applied to spinning and weaving cotton, and before long, cotton mills using steam engines were multiplying across Britain. Fired by coal, these steam engines could be located anywhere (see Historical Voices, "The Steam Engine and Cotton").

The boost given to cotton textile production by these technological changes was readily apparent. In 1760, Britain had imported 2.5 million pounds of raw cotton, which was farmed out to cottage industries. In 1787, the British imported 22 million pounds of cotton; most of it was spun on machines, some of which were powered by water in large mills. By 1840, some 366 million pounds of cotton were being imported, making it Britain's most important product in value. By this time, British cotton goods were sold everywhere in the world.

Other Technological Changes The British iron industry was also radically transformed. Britain had always had large deposits of iron ore, but at the beginning of the eighteenth century, iron production had changed little since the Middle Ages and still depended heavily on charcoal. A better quality

A FIRST-CLASS TRAIN ON THE LIVERPOOL AND MANCHESTER RAIL-WAY, 1833.

A SECOND-CLASS TRAIN ON THE LIVERPOOL AND MANCHESTER RAIL-WAY, 1833.

19.2 Railroad Line from Liverpool to Manchester. The railroad line from Liverpool to Manchester, which opened in 1830, relied on steam locomotives. As is evident in this illustration, carrying passengers was the railroad's main business. First-class passengers rode in covered cars, second- and third-class passengers in open cars.

of iron was developed in the 1780s when Henry Cort developed a system called *puddling*, in which coke derived from coal was used to burn away impurities in pig iron (crude iron). A boom then ensued in the British iron industry. By 1852, Britain was producing almost 3 million tons of iron annually, more than the rest of the world combined.

The new high-quality wrought iron was in turn used to build new machines and ultimately new industries. In 1804, Richard Trevithick (TREV-uh-thik) pioneered the first steam-powered locomotive on an industrial rail line in southern Wales. It pulled ten tons of ore and seventy people at five miles per hour. Better locomotives soon followed. Engines built by George Stephenson and his son proved superior, and it was Stephenson's *Rocket* that was used on the first public railway line, which opened in 1830 and ran 32 miles from Liverpool to Manchester. *Rocket* sped along at sixteen miles per hour. Within twenty years, locomotives were traveling at fifty miles per hour. By 1840, Britain had almost 6,000 miles of railroads.

The railroad was important to the success and maturing of the Industrial Revolution. Railroads facilitated an entirely new industry, supporting jobs in upholstery, carriage-making, and glass production. The availability of a cheaper and faster means of transportation had a ripple effect on the growth of the industrial economy. As the prices of goods fell, markets grew larger; increased sales meant more factories and more machinery, thereby reinforcing the self-sustaining aspect of the Industrial Revolution—a development that marked a fundamental break with the traditional European economy. Continuous, self-sustaining economic growth came to be a fundamental characteristic of the new economy.

The Industrial Factory Another visible symbol of the Industrial Revolution was the factory (see the Comparative Illustration, "Textile Factories, West and East," p. 476). From its beginning, the factory created a new labor system. Factory owners wanted to use their new machines constantly. Workers were therefore obliged to work regular hours and in shifts to keep the machines producing at a steady rate. Early factory workers, however, came from rural areas, where peasant farmers were used to working hard at harvest time. But they were also used to periods of inactivity.

Early factory owners therefore had to institute a system of work discipline that would accustom employees to working regular hours and doing the same work over and over. Of course, such work was boring, and factory owners resorted to detailed regulations and tough methods to accomplish their goals. Adult workers were fined for a wide variety of minor infractions, including being a few minutes late for work, and workers could be dismissed for more serious misdoings, especially drunkenness, which courted disaster in the midst of dangerous machinery. Employers found that dismissals and fines worked well for adult employees; in a time when great population growth had produced large masses of unskilled labor, dismissal meant disaster. Children were less likely to understand the implications of dismissal, so they were disciplined more directly—often by beating. As the nineteenth century progressed, the second and third generations of workers came to view a regular workweek as a natural way of life.

By the mid-nineteenth century, Great Britain had become the world's first and richest industrial nation. Britain was the "workshop, banker, and trader of the world." It produced half of the world's coal and

Textile Factories, West and East

Science & Technology

THE DEVELOPMENT OF THE FACTORY changed the relationship between workers and employers as workers had to adjust to a new system of discipline that required them to work regular hours under close supervision.

Image 19.3a is an 1851 illustration that shows women working in a British cotton factory. The factory system came later to the rest of the world than it did to Britain. Image 19.3b shows one of the earliest industrial factories in Japan, the Tomioka silk factory, built in the 1870s. Note that although women are doing the work in both factories, the managers are men.

Q *What do you think were the major differences and similarities between British and Japanese factories?*

19.3a

19.3b

manufactured goods; in 1850, its cotton industry alone was equal in size to the industries of all other European countries combined.

19-1b The Spread of Industrialization

From Britain, industrialization spread to the continental countries of Europe and the United States, though at different times and speeds. First to be industrialized on the European continent were Belgium, France, and the German states. Their governments actively encouraged industrialization by, among other things, setting up technical schools to train engineers and mechanics and providing funds to build roads, canals, and railroads. By 1850, a network of iron rails had spread across Europe.

The Industrial Revolution also transformed the new nation in North America, the United States. In 1800, six of every seven American workers were farmers, and there were no cities with more than 100,000 people. By 1860, only 50 percent of American workers were farmers and nine U.S. cities had populations over 100,000. In sharp contrast to Britain, the United States was a large country. Thousands of miles of roads and canals were built linking east and west. Most important in the development of an American transportation system was the railroad, which was needed to transport the abundant raw materials found throughout the country. Beginning with 100 miles in 1830, by 1865 the United States was crisscrossed by more than 35,000 miles of railroad track. This transportation revolution turned the United States into a single massive market for the manufactured goods of the Northeast, the early center of American industrialization. By the end of the nineteenth century, with its growing manufacturing sector, abundant raw materials, and elaborate transportation system, the United States had become the world's second-largest industrial nation.

19-1c Limiting the Spread of Industrialization to the Rest of the World

Before 1870, the industrialization that was transforming western and central Europe and the United States did not extend in any significant way to the rest of the world (see Comparative Essay, "The Industrial Revolution," p. 478). Even in eastern Europe, industrialization lagged far behind. Russia, for example, was still largely rural and agricultural, ruled by an autocratic regime that preferred to keep peasants in serfdom.

In other parts of the world where they had established control (see Chapter 21), newly industrialized European states pursued a deliberate policy of preventing the growth of mechanized industry. India provides an excellent example. In the eighteenth century, India had been one of the world's greatest exporters of cotton cloth produced by hand labor, producing more than twenty-five times as much cotton cloth per year as England. By 1850, however, much of India fell under the control of the British East India Company. With British control came inexpensive textiles produced in British factories. The British intentionally prohibited the industrialization of India by cutting off credit, increasing land and rent prices, and raising transportation costs on goods that were not approved by British authorities. As the indigenous Indian textile industry declined, thousands of Indian spinners and handloom weavers lost their jobs, forcing many to turn to growing raw materials, such as cotton, wheat, and tea, for export to Britain, while buying British-made finished goods. The example of India was repeated elsewhere, as the rapidly industrializing nations of Europe worked to thwart the spread of the Industrial Revolution to their colonial dominions.

19-1d Social Impact of the Industrial Revolution

Eventually, the Industrial Revolution revolutionized the social life of Europe and the world. This change was already evident in the first half of the nineteenth century in the growth of cities and the emergence of new social classes.

Population Growth and Urbanization   The European population had already begun to increase in the eighteenth century, but the pace accelerated in the nineteenth century. Between 1750 and 1850, the total European population almost doubled, rising from 140 million to 266 million. The key to this population growth was a decline in death rates as wars and major epidemic diseases such as plague and smallpox became less frequent. Thanks to the increase in the food supply, more people were also better fed and more resistant to disease.

Throughout Europe, cities and towns grew dramatically in the first half of the nineteenth century, a phenomenon related to industrialization. By 1850, especially in Great Britain and Belgium, cities were rapidly becoming home to many industries. With the steam engine, factories could be located in urban centers where they had ready access to transportation facilities and large numbers of new arrivals from the country looking for work.

In 1800, Great Britain had one major city, London, with a population of 1 million, and six cities with populations between 50,000 and 100,000. Fifty years later, London's population had swelled to 2,363,000, and there were nine cities with populations of more than 100,000 and eighteen cities with populations between 50,000 and 100,000. More than 50 percent of the British population lived in towns and cities by 1850.

The dramatic growth of cities in the first half of the nineteenth century resulted in miserable living conditions for many inhabitants. Located in the center of most industrial towns were the row houses of the industrial workers. Rooms were small and frequently overcrowded. Sanitary conditions were appalling; sewers and open drains were common on city streets: "In the centre of this street is a gutter, into which the refuse of animal and vegetable matters of all kinds, the dirty water from the washing of clothes and of the houses, are all poured, and there they stagnate and putrefy."[1] Unable to deal with human excrement, early industrial cities smelled horrible and were extraordinarily unhealthy. Towns and cities were death traps: deaths outnumbered births in most large cities in the first half of the nineteenth century; only a constant influx of people from the country kept them alive and growing.

New Social Classes: The Industrial Middle Class   The rise of industrial capitalism produced a new middle-class group. The bourgeoisie was not new; it had existed since the emergence of cities in the Middle Ages. Originally, the bourgeois or burgher was a town dweller who was active as a merchant, official, artisan, lawyer, or man of letters. As wealthy townspeople bought land, the original meaning of the word *bourgeois* became lost, and the term came to include people involved in commerce, industry, and banking as well as professionals such as teachers, physicians, and government officials.

The Industrial Revolution

Science & Technology Why some societies were able to embark on the road to industrialization during the nineteenth century and others were not has long been debated. Some historians have pointed to the cultural characteristics of individual societies, such as the Protestant work ethic in parts of Europe or the tradition of social discipline and class hierarchy in Japan. Others have placed more emphasis on practical reasons. To historian Peter Stearns, for example, the availability of capital, natural resources, a network of trade relations, and navigable rivers all helped stimulate industrial growth in nineteenth-century Britain. By contrast, the lack of urban markets for agricultural goods (which reduced landowners' incentives to introduce mechanized farming) is sometimes cited as a reason for China's failure to set out on its own path toward industrialization.

To some observers, the ability of western European countries to exploit the resources of their colonies in Asia, Africa, and Latin America was crucial to their industrial success. In this view, the Age of Exploration led to the creation of a new "world system" characterized by the emergence of global trade networks and propelled by the rising force of European capitalism in pursuit of precious metals, markets, and cheap raw materials.

These views are not mutually exclusive. In his recent book *The Great Divergence: China, Europe, and the Making of the Modern World Economy*, Kenneth Pomeranz argued that coal resources and access to the cheap raw materials

of the Americas were both assets for Great Britain as it became the first to industrialize.

Clearly, this debate has no single answer. In any event, the coming of the industrial age had many lasting consequences for the world at large. On the one hand, the material wealth of nations that successfully passed through the process increased significantly. In many cases, the creation of advanced industrial societies strengthened democratic institutions and led to a higher standard of living for the majority of the population. It also helped reduce class barriers and bring about the emancipation of women from many of the legal and social restrictions that had characterized the previous era.

On the other hand, not every consequence of the Industrial Revolution was beneficial. In the industrializing societies themselves, rapid economic change often led to widening disparities in wealth and a sense of rootlessness and alienation among much of the population. Although some societies were able to manage these problems with a degree of success, others experienced a breakdown of social values and widespread political instability. In the meantime, the transformation of Europe into a giant factory sucking up raw materials and spewing manufactured goods out to the entire world had wrenching effects on traditional societies, whose own economic, social, and cultural foundations were forever changed by absorption into the new world order.

Q *What were the positive and negative consequences of the Industrial Revolution?*

HIP/Art Resource, NY

19.4 The Steam Engine. Pictured here is an early steam engine developed by James Watt. The steam engine revolutionized the production of cotton goods and helped usher in the factory system.

The new industrial middle class was made up of people who constructed factories, purchased machines, and figured out where the markets were. Their qualities included resourcefulness, single-mindedness, resolution, initiative, vision, ambition, and often, of course, greed. As

Jedediah Strutt, a cotton manufacturer said, "Getting of money . . . is the main business of the life of men." By 1850, in Britain at least, these entrepreneurs had formed a new business aristocracy that stemmed from the professional and industrial middle classes, especially as sons inherited successful businesses established by their fathers. As the new bourgeois bought great estates and acquired social respectability, they also sought political power, and in the course of the nineteenth century, their wealthiest members would merge with the old elites.

Members of the industrial middle class sought to reduce the barriers between themselves and the landed elite while simultaneously separating themselves from the laboring classes below. In the first half of the nineteenth century, the working class was actually a mixture of different groups, but factory workers came to form an industrial **proletariat** that constituted a majority of the working class in the course of the century.

New Social Classes: The Industrial Working Class

Early industrial workers faced wretched working conditions. Work shifts ranged from twelve to sixteen hours a day, six days a week, with a half hour for lunch and dinner. Workers had no security of employment and no minimum wage. The worst conditions were in the cotton mills where temperatures were especially debilitating. One report noted that "in the cotton-spinning work, these creatures are kept, fourteen hours in each day, locked up, summer and winter, in a heat of from eighty to eighty-four degrees." Mills were also dirty, dusty, and unhealthy.

Conditions in the coal mines were also harsh. Although steam-powered engines were used to lift coal to the top of the mines, inside the mines, men still had to dig the coal out while horses, mules, women, and children pulled coal carts on rails to the lift. Cave-ins, explosions, and gas fumes were a way of life. The cramped conditions—tunnels were often only three or four feet high—and constant dampness led to deformed bodies and ruined lungs.

Both children and women worked in large numbers in early factories and mines. Children had been an important part of the family economy in preindustrial times, working in the fields or carding and spinning wool at home. In the Industrial Revolution, however, exploitation of child labor increased because of children's unique qualifications. The owners of cotton factories found child labor especially helpful. Children had a particular delicate touch as spinners of cotton, and their small size enabled them to crawl under machines to gather loose cotton. Moreover, children were more easily trained to do factory work. Children made up an abundant and cheap supply of labor: they were paid only about one-sixth to one-third of what a man was paid.

By 1830, women and children made up two-thirds of the cotton industry's labor. In 1833, however, the Factory Act was passed, prohibiting the employment of children under the age of nine and restricting the working hours of those under eighteen. Child labor declined under the new law but did not disappear. In 1838, children under the age of eighteen still made up 29 percent of the total workforce in the cotton mills. As the number of children employed declined, women came to dominate the labor forces of the early factories, making up 50 percent of the labor force in textile (cotton and woolen) factories before 1870. They were mostly unskilled laborers and were paid half or less of what men received.

HISTORIANS DEBATE 19-1e **Did Industrialization Bring an Improved Standard of Living?**

During the first half of the nineteenth century, industrialization altered the lives of Europeans, especially the British, as they left their farms and moved to cities to work in factories. But did they experience a higher standard of living during this time? Some historians argue that industrialization increased employment and lowered the price of consumer goods, thus improving the way people lived. They also maintain that household income rose because several family members could now hold wage-paying jobs. Other historians argue that wage labor initially made life worse for many families and that employment in the early factories was highly volatile as employers quickly dismissed workers whenever demand declined. Families lived in cramped and unsanitary conditions in the early industrial cities and continued to spend most of their income on food and clothing. Most historians agree that members of the middle class were the real gainers in the early Industrial Revolution and that industrial workers had to wait until the second half of the nineteenth century to begin to reap the benefits of industrialization.

19-2 THE GROWTH OF INDUSTRIAL PROSPERITY

Q **Focus Questions:** What was the Second Industrial Revolution, and what effects did it have on economic and social life? What were the main ideas of Karl Marx, and what role did they play in politics and the union movement in the late nineteenth and early twentieth centuries?

After 1870, the Western world experienced a dynamic age of material prosperity. The new industries, new sources of energy, and new goods of the Second Industrial Revolution led people to believe that their material progress reflected human progress.

19-2a New Products

The first major change in industrial development between 1870 and 1914 was the substitution of steel for iron. New methods of shaping steel made it useful for constructing lighter, smaller, and faster machines and engines, as well as railways, ships, and armaments. In 1860, Great Britain, France, Germany, and Belgium produced 125,000 tons of steel; by 1913, the total was 32 million tons.

Electricity was a major new form of energy that could be easily converted into other forms of energy—such as heat, light, and motion—and it moved relatively effortlessly through space over transmitting wires. In the 1870s, the first commercially practical generators of electrical current were developed; by 1910, hydroelectric power stations and coal-fired steam-generating plants enabled homes and factories in whole neighborhoods to be tied into a single, common source of power.

Electricity spawned many inventions. The light bulb, developed independently by Thomas Edison in the United States and Joseph Swan, in Britain permitted homes and cities to be illuminated by electric lights. By the 1880s, streetcars and subways powered by electricity had appeared in major European cities. Electricity also transformed the factory. Conveyor belts, cranes, machines, and machine tools could all be powered by electricity and located anywhere. Similarly, a revolution in communications began when Alexander Graham Bell invented the telephone in 1876 and Guglielmo Marconi (gool-YEL-moh mahr-KOH-nee) sent the first radio waves across the Atlantic in 1901.

The development of the internal combustion engine, powered by oil and gasoline, provided a new source of power and gave rise to ocean liners as well as the airplane and automobile. In 1900, world production stood at 9,000 cars, but American Henry Ford revolutionized the automotive industry with the mass production of his Model T. By 1916, Ford's factories were producing 735,000 cars a year. In 1903, at Kitty Hawk, North Carolina, brothers Orville and Wilbur Wright made the first flight in a fixed-wing airplane. The first regular passenger air service was established in 1919.

19-2b New Patterns

Industrial production grew rapidly at this time because of the greatly increased sales of manufactured goods. An increase in real wages for workers after 1870, combined with lower prices for manufactured goods because of reduced transportation costs, made it easier for Europeans to buy consumer products. In the cities, the first department stores began to sell a host of new consumer goods made possible by the development of the steel and electrical industries. The desire to own sewing machines,

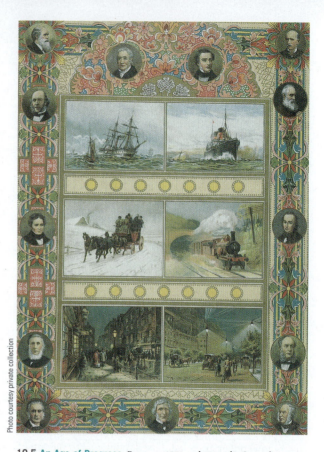

Photo courtesy private collection

19.5 An Age of Progress. Between 1871 and 1914, the Second Industrial Revolution led many Europeans to believe they were living in an age of progress when science would solve most human problems. This illustration is from a special issue of *The Illustrated London News* celebrating the Diamond Jubilee of Queen Victoria in 1897. On the left are scenes from 1837 when Victoria came to the British throne; on the right are scenes from 1897. The vivid contrast underscored the magazine's conclusion: "The most striking . . . evidence of progress during the reign is the ever increasing speed which the discoveries of physical science have forced into everyday life. Steam and electricity have conquered time and space to a greater extent during the last sixty years than all the preceding six hundred years witnessed."

clocks, bicycles, electric lights, and typewriters was rapidly generating a new consumer ethic that has continued to be a crucial part of the modern economy.

Not all nations benefited from the Second Industrial Revolution. Between 1870 and 1914, Germany replaced Great Britain as the industrial leader of Europe. Moreover, by 1900, Europe was divided into two economic zones. Great Britain, Belgium, France, the Netherlands, Germany, the western part of the Austro-Hungarian Empire, and northern Italy constituted an advanced industrialized core that had a high standard of living, decent systems of transportation, and relatively healthy and educated peoples (see Map 19.1). Another part of Europe, the backward and little industrialized area to the south and east, consisting of

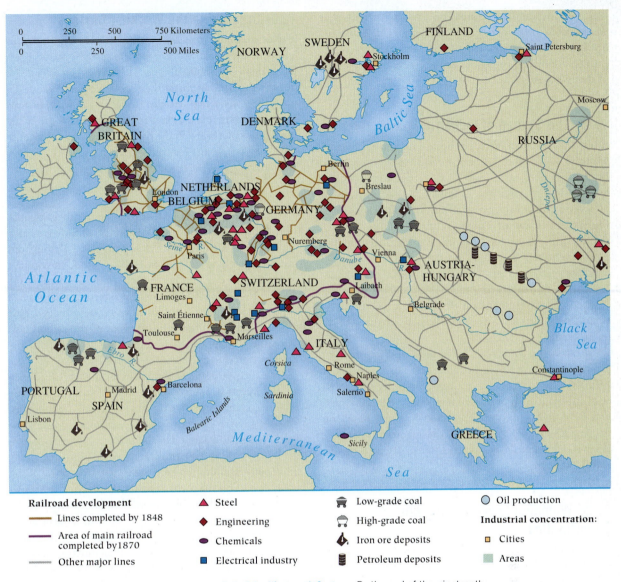

Railroad development		Steel		Low-grade coal		Oil production

Railroad development
— Lines completed by 1848
— Area of main railroad completed by 1870
···· Other major lines

▲ Steel
♦ Engineering
● Chemicals
■ Electrical industry

⛏ Low-grade coal
⛏ High-grade coal
⚒ Iron ore deposits
⬛ Petroleum deposits

○ Oil production

Industrial concentration:
◻ Cities
▨ Areas

Map 19.1 The Industrial Regions of Europe at the End of the Nineteenth Century. By the end of the nineteenth century, the Second Industrial Revolution—in steelmaking, electricity, petroleum, and chemicals—had spurred substantial economic growth and prosperity in western and central Europe; it also sparked economic and political competition between Great Britain and Germany.

Q *What correlation, if any, was there between industrial growth and political developments in the nineteenth century?*

southern Italy, most of Austria–Hungary, Spain, Portugal, the Balkan kingdoms, and Russia, was still largely agricultural and relegated by the industrial countries to providing food and raw materials.

19-2c Emergence of a World Economy

The economic developments of the late nineteenth century, combined with the transportation revolution that saw the growth of marine transport and railroads,

fostered a true world economy. By 1900, Europeans were receiving beef and wool from Argentina and Australia, coffee from Brazil, iron ore from Algeria, and sugar from Java. Until the Industrial Revolution, European countries had imported more from Asia than they had exported, but now foreign countries provided markets for the surplus manufactured goods of Europe. European capital was also invested abroad to develop railways, mines, electrical power plants, and banks. High rates of return, such as

11.3 percent on Latin American banking shares that were floated in London, provided plenty of incentive for investors. With its capital, industries, and military might, Europe dominated the world economy by the beginning of the twentieth century.

19-2d The Spread of Industrialization

After 1870, industrialization began to spread beyond western and central Europe and North America. Especially noticeable was its rapid development, fostered by governments, in Russia and Japan. A surge of industrialization began in Russia in the 1890s under the guiding hand of Sergei Witte (syir-GYAY VIT-uh), the minister of finance. Under Witte's direction, the government built 35,000 miles of railroad track by 1900 and produced a modern steel and coal industry, making Russia the fourth-largest producer of steel behind the United States, Germany, and Great Britain. At the same time, Russia was also turning out half of the world's oil production.

In Japan, the imperial government took the lead in promoting industry (see Chapter 22). The government financed industries, built railroads, brought foreign experts to train Japanese employees in new industrial techniques, and instituted a universal educational system based on applied science. By the end of the nineteenth century, Japan had developed key industries in tea, silk, armaments, and shipbuilding.

19-2e Women and Work: New Job Opportunities

During the nineteenth century, working-class organizations maintained that women should remain at home to bear and nurture children. Working-class men argued that keeping women out of industrial work would ensure the moral and physical well-being of families. In reality, however, when their husbands were unemployed, women had to do low-wage work at home or labor part-time in sweatshops to support their families.

The Second Industrial Revolution opened the door to new jobs for women. The development of larger industrial plants and the expansion of government services created a large number of service and white-collar jobs. The increased demand for white-collar workers at relatively low wages coupled with a shortage of male workers led employers to hire women. Women found new opportunities as telephone operators, typists, secretaries, file clerks, and salesclerks. Compulsory education necessitated more teachers, and the development of modern hospital services opened the way for an increase in nurses.

19-2f Organizing the Working Classes

The desire to improve their working and living conditions led many industrial workers to form socialist political parties and socialist trade unions. These emerged after 1870, but the theory that made them possible had been developed more than two decades earlier in the work of Karl Marx. **Marxism** made its first appearance on the eve of the revolutions of 1848 with the publication of a short treatise titled *The Communist Manifesto,* written by two Germans, Karl Marx (1818–1883) and Friedrich Engels (FREE-drikh ENG-ulz) (1820–1895).

Marxist Theory   Marx and Engels began their treatise with the statement that "the history of all hitherto existing society is the history of class struggles." Throughout history, oppressor and oppressed have "stood in constant opposition to one another."[2] One group of people—the oppressors—owned the means of production and thus had the power to control government and society. Indeed, government itself was but an instrument of the ruling class. The other group, which depended on the owners of the means of production, were the oppressed.

The **class struggle** continued in the industrialized societies of Marx's day. According to Marx, "Society as a whole is more and more splitting up into two great hostile camps, into two great classes directly facing each other: Bourgeoisie and Proletariat." Marx predicted that the struggle between the bourgeoisie and the proletariat would ultimately break into open revolution, "where the violent overthrow of the bourgeoisie lays the foundation for the sway of the proletariat." The fall of the bourgeoisie "and the victory of the proletariat are equally inevitable."[3] For awhile, the proletariat would form a dictatorship to reorganize the means of production, but then the state—itself an instrument of the bourgeois interests—would wither away. Because classes had arisen from the economic differences that would have been abolished, the end result would be a classless society (see Historical Voices, "The Classless Society," p. 483).

Socialist Parties   In time, Marx's ideas were picked up by working-class leaders who formed socialist parties. Most important was the German Social Democratic Party (Deutsche Sozialdemokratische Partei, or SPD), which emerged in 1875 and espoused revolutionary Marxist rhetoric while organizing itself as a mass political party competing in elections for the Reichstag (RYKHSS-tahk), the lower house of parliament. Once in the Reichstag, SPD delegates worked to achieve legislation to improve the condition of the working class. When it received 4 million votes in the 1912 elections, the SPD became the largest single party in Germany. Socialist parties also emerged in other European states.

The Classless Society

Family & Society   **IN** *THE COMMUNIST MANIFESTO,* Karl Marx and Friedrich Engels projected that the struggle between the bourgeoisie and the proletariat would end with the creation of a classless society. In this selection, they discuss the steps by which that classless society would be reached.

Karl Marx and Friedrich Engels, *The Communist Manifesto*

We have seen . . . that the first step in the revolution by the working class is to raise the proletariat to the position of ruling class. . . . The proletariat will use its political supremacy to wrest, by degrees, all capital from the bourgeoisie, to centralize all instruments of production in the hands of the State, i.e., of the proletariat organized as the ruling class; and to increase the total of productive forces as rapidly as possible.

Of course, in the beginning, this cannot be effected except by means of despotic inroads on the rights of property, and on the conditions of bourgeois production; by means of measures, therefore, which appear economically insufficient and untenable, but which, in the course of the movement, outstrip themselves, necessitate further inroads upon the old social order, and are unavoidable as a means of entirely revolutionizing the mode of production.

These measures will of course be different in different countries.

Nevertheless, in the most advanced countries, the following will be pretty generally applicable:

1. Abolition of property in land and application of all rents of land to public purposes.
2. A heavy progressive or graduated income tax.
3. Abolition of all right of inheritance. . . .
5. Centralization of credit in the hands of the State, by means of a national bank with State capital and an exclusive monopoly.
6. Centralization of the means of communication and transport in the hands of the State.
7. Extension of factories and instruments of production owned by the State. . . .
8. Equal liability of all to labor. Establishment of industrial armies, especially for agriculture.
9. Combination of agriculture with manufacturing industries; gradual abolition of the distinction between town and country, by a more equable distribution of the population over the country.
10. Free education for all children in public schools. Abolition of children's factory labor in its present form. . . .

When, in the course of development, class distinctions have disappeared, and all production has been concentrated in the whole nation, the public power will lose its political character. Political power, properly so called, is merely the organized power of one class for oppressing another. If the proletariat during its contest with the bourgeoisie is compelled, by the force of circumstances, to organize itself as a class, if, by means of a revolution, it makes itself the ruling class, and, as such, sweeps away by force the old conditions of production, then it will, along with these conditions, have swept away the conditions for the existence of class antagonisms and of classes generally, and will thereby have abolished its own supremacy as a class.

In place of the old bourgeois society, with its classes and class antagonisms, we shall have an association, in which the free development of each is the condition for the free development of all.

Q *How did Marx and Engels define the proletariat? The bourgeoisie? Why did Marxists come to believe that this distinction was paramount for understanding history? For shaping the future?*

Source: From *The Communist Manifesto* by Karl Marx and Friedrich Engels.

Marxist parties divided over the issue of **revisionism**. Pure Marxists believed in violent revolution that would bring the collapse of capitalism and socialist ownership of the means of production. But others known as *revisionists* rejected **revolutionary socialism** and argued that workers must organize mass political parties and work with other progressive elements to gain reforms. Evolution by democratic means, not revolution, would achieve the desired goal of socialism.

Another force working for evolutionary rather than revolutionary socialism was the development of trade unions. In Great Britain, unions won the right to strike in the 1870s. Soon after, factory workers began to organize into trade unions so that they could use the strike to improve their conditions. By 1900, British trade unions had 2 million members; by 1914, the number had risen to almost 4 million. Trade unions in the rest of Europe had varying degrees of success, but they had made considerable progress in bettering the living and working conditions of the laboring classes by the outbreak of World War I.

19-3 REACTION AND REVOLUTION: THE GROWTH OF NATIONALISM

Q **Focus Questions:** What were the major ideas associated with conservatism, liberalism, and nationalism, and what role did each ideology play in Europe between 1800 and 1850? What were the causes of the revolutions of 1848, and why did these revolutions fail?

Industrialization was a major force for change as it led the West into the machine-dependent modern world. Another major force for change was nationalism, which transformed the political map of Europe in the nineteenth century.

19-3a The Conservative Order

After the defeat of Napoleon, European rulers moved to restore much of the old order. This was the goal of the Great Powers—Great Britain, Austria, Prussia, and Russia—when they met at the Congress of Vienna in 1814 to arrange a final peace settlement after the Napoleonic wars. The leader of the congress was Austrian foreign minister Prince Klemens von Metternich (KLAY-menss fun MET-ayr-nikh) (1773–1859), who claimed he was guided at Vienna by the principle of **legitimacy**. To reestablish peace and stability in Europe, he considered it necessary to restore the legitimate monarchs who would preserve traditional institutions. This had already been done in France with the restoration of the Bourbon monarchy and in several other states, but it did not stop the Great Powers from grabbing territory—often from the smaller, weaker states (see Map 19.2).

The peace arrangements of 1815 were only the beginning of a conservative reaction determined to contain the liberal and nationalist forces unleashed by the French Revolution. Metternich and his kind were representatives

of the ideology known as **conservatism**. Most conservatives favored obedience to political authority, believed that organized religion was crucial to social order, hated revolutionary upheavals, and were unwilling to accept either the liberal demands for civil liberties and representative governments or the nationalistic aspirations generated by the French revolutionary era. After 1815, the political philosophy of conservatism was supported by hereditary monarchs, government bureaucracies, landowning aristocracies, and revived churches, both Protestant and Catholic. The conservative forces were dominant after 1815.

One method used by the Great Powers to maintain the new status quo they had constructed was the Concert of Europe, according to which Great Britain, Russia, Prussia, and Austria (and later France) agreed to convene periodically to take steps that would maintain the peace in Europe. Eventually, the Great Powers adopted a principle of **intervention**, asserting that they had the right to send armies into countries where there were revolutions to restore legitimate monarchs to their thrones.

19-3b Forces for Change

Although conservative governments throughout Europe strived to restore the old order after 1815, powerful forces for change—liberalism and nationalism—were also at work. **Liberalism** owed much to the eighteenth-century Enlightenment and the American and French Revolutions; it was based on the idea that people should be as free from restraint as possible.

Politically, liberals came to hold a common set of beliefs. Chief among them was the protection of civil liberties, or the basic rights of all people, which included equality before the law; freedom of assembly, speech, and the press; and freedom from arbitrary arrest. All of these freedoms should be guaranteed by a written document such as the American Bill of Rights. In addition to religious toleration for all, most liberals advocated separation of church and state. Liberals also demanded the right of peaceful opposition to the government in and out of parliament and the making of laws by a representative assembly (legislature) elected by qualified voters. Thus, many liberals believed in a constitutional monarchy or constitutional state with limits on the powers of government to prevent despotism and in written constitutions that would guarantee these rights. Liberals were not democrats, however. They thought that the right to vote and hold office should be open only to men of property. Liberals also believed in laissez-faire economic principles that rejected state interference in the regulation of wages and work hours. As a political philosophy, liberalism was adopted by middle-class men, especially industrial middle-class men, who favored voting

Map 19.2 Europe After the Congress of Vienna, 1815. The Congress of Vienna imposed order on Europe based on the principles of monarchical government and a balance of power. Monarchs were restored in France, Spain, and other states recently under Napoleon's control. Considerable territory changed hands, often at the expense of the small, weak states.

Q *How did Europe's major powers manipulate territory to decrease the probability that France could again threaten the European continent's stability?*

rights for themselves so they could share power with the landowning classes.

Nationalism was an even more powerful ideology for change. Nationalism arose out of an awareness of being part of a community that has common institutions, traditions, language, and customs. This community constitutes a "nation," and it would be the focus of the individual's primary loyalty. Nationalism did not become a popular force for change until the French Revolution. From then on, nationalists came to believe that each nationality should have its own government. Thus, the Germans, who were not united, wanted national unity in a German nation-state with one central government. Subject peoples such as the Hungarians wanted to establish their own autonomy rather than be subject to a German minority in the multi-national Austrian Empire.

Nationalism thus posed a threat to the existing political order. A united Germany, for example, would upset the balance of power established at Vienna in 1815, and an independent Hungarian state would mean the breakup of the Austrian Empire. Because many European states

were multinational, conservatives tried hard to repress the radical threat of nationalism. The conservative order dominated much of Europe after 1815, but the forces of liberalism and nationalism first generated by the French Revolution continued to grow as that second great revolution, the Industrial Revolution, expanded and brought in new groups of people who wanted change. In 1848, these forces for change erupted.

19-3c The Revolutions of 1848

Revolution in France was the spark for revolts in other countries. Even as the lower middle class, workers, and peasants were suffering from a severe industrial and agricultural depression, the government refused to lower the property qualification for voting, a policy that angered the disenfranchised members of the middle class. When the government of King Louis-Philippe (1830–1848) refused to make changes, opposition grew and finally overthrew the monarchy on February 24, 1848. A group of moderate and radical republicans established a provisional government and called for the election by universal male suffrage of a "constituent assembly" to draw up a new constitution.

The new constitution, ratified on November 4, 1848, established the Second Republic, with a single legislature elected to three-year terms by universal male suffrage and a president who was also elected by universal male suffrage to a four-year term. In the elections for the presidency held in December 1848, Charles Louis Napoleon Bonaparte (1808–1873), the nephew of the famous French ruler, won a resounding victory. Within four years, President Louis Napoleon would become Emperor Napoleon III and establish an authoritarian regime.

News of the 1848 revolution in France led to upheaval in central Europe as well (see Opposing Viewpoints, "Response to Revolution: Two Perspectives," p. 487). The Vienna settlement in 1815 had recognized the existence of thirty-eight sovereign states (called the Germanic Confederation) in what had once been the Holy Roman Empire. Austria and Prussia were the two Great Powers; the other states varied considerably in size. In 1848, cries for change caused many German rulers to promise constitutions, a free press, jury trials, and other liberal reforms. In Prussia, King Frederick William IV (1840–1861) agreed to establish a new constitution and work for a united Germany.

The promise of unity reverberated throughout the German states as governments allowed elections by universal male suffrage for deputies to an all-German parliament called the Frankfurt Assembly. Its purpose was to fulfill a liberal and nationalist dream—the preparation of a constitution for a new united Germany. But the assembly failed to achieve its goal. The members had no real means of compelling the German rulers to accept the constitution they had drawn up. German unification was not achieved; the revolution had failed.

The Austrian Empire needed only the news of the revolution in Paris to erupt in flames in March 1848. The Austrian Empire was a multinational state, containing at least eleven ethnically distinct peoples, including Germans, Czechs, Magyars (Hungarians), Slovaks, Romanians, Serbians, and Italians. The Germans, though only a quarter of the population, were economically dominant and played a leading role in government. The Hungarians, however, wanted their own legislature. In March, demonstrations in Buda, Prague, and Vienna led to the dismissal of Metternich, the Austrian foreign minister and arch symbol of the conservative order, who fled abroad. In Vienna, revolutionary forces took control of the capital and demanded a liberal constitution. Hungary was given its own legislature and a separate national army.

Austrian officials had made concessions to appease the revolutionaries, but they were determined to reestablish firm control. As in the German states, they were increasingly encouraged by the divisions between radical and moderate revolutionaries. By the end of October 1848, Austrian military forces had crushed the rebels in Vienna, but it was only with the assistance of a Russian army of 140,000 men that the Hungarian revolution was finally put down in 1849. The revolutions in the Austrian Empire had failed.

Revolutions in Italy also failed. The Congress of Vienna had established nine states in Italy, including the kingdom of Sardinia in the north ruled by the house of Savoy, the kingdom of the Two Sicilies (Naples and Sicily), the Papal States, a handful of small duchies, and the important northern provinces of Lombardy and Venetia (vuh-NEE-shuh), which were part of the Austrian Empire. Italy was largely under Austrian domination, but a new movement for Italian unity known as Young Italy led to initially successful revolts in 1848. By 1849, however, the Austrians had reestablished complete control over Lombardy and Venetia, and the old order also prevailed in the rest of Italy.

Throughout Europe in 1848–1849, moderate middle-class liberals and radical workers soon divided over their aims, and the failure of the revolutionaries to stay united soon led to the reestablishment of authoritarian regimes. In other parts of the Western world, revolutions took somewhat different directions (see Chapter 20).

19-3d Nationalism in the Balkans: The Ottoman Empire and the Eastern Question

The Ottoman Empire had long been in control of much of the Balkans in southeastern Europe. By the beginning of the nineteenth century, however, the Ottoman Empire was in decline, and authority over its outlying territories in the Balkans waned. As a result, European governments, especially those of Russia and Austria, began to take an active interest in the disintegration of the empire. The "Eastern Question," as it came to be called, troubled European diplomats throughout the century.

When the Russians invaded the Ottoman provinces of Moldavia (mohl-DAY-vee-uh) and Wallachia (wah-LAY-kee-uh), the Ottoman Turks declared war on Russia on October 4, 1853. The following year, on March 28, Great Britain and France, fearful of Russian gains, declared war on Russia. The Crimean War, as the conflict came to be called, was poorly planned and poorly fought. Heavy losses caused the Russians to sue for peace. By the Treaty of Paris in 1856, Russia agreed to allow Moldavia and Wallachia to be placed under the protection of all the Great Powers.

The Crimean War destroyed the Concert of Europe. Austria and Russia, the chief powers maintaining the status quo in the first half of the nineteenth century, were now enemies because Austria had failed to support Russia

Response to Revolution: Two Perspectives

Politics & Government **BASED ON THEIR POLITICAL BELIEFS,** Europeans responded differently to the specter of revolution that haunted Europe in the first half of the nineteenth century. The first excerpt is taken from a speech by Thomas Babington Macaulay (muh-KAHL-lee) (1800–1859), a historian and a member of the British Parliament. Macaulay spoke in Parliament on behalf of the Reform Act of 1832, which extended the right to vote to the industrial middle classes of Britain. A revolution in France in 1830 that had resulted in some gains for the upper bourgeoisie had influenced his belief that it was better to reform than to have a political revolution.

The second excerpt is taken from the *Reminiscences* of Carl Schurz (SHOORTS) (1829–1906). Like many liberals and nationalists in Germany, Schurz received the news of the 1848 revolution in France with great expectations for change in the German states. After the failure of the German revolution, Schurz emigrated to the United States and eventually became a U.S. senator for Missouri.

Thomas Babington Macaulay, Speech of March 2, 1831

My hon[orable] friend the member of the University of Oxford tells us that, if we pass this law, England will soon be a Republic. The reformed House of Commons will, according to him, before it has sat ten years, depose the King, and expel the Lords from their House. . . . His proposition is, in fact, this—that our monarchical and aristocratical institutions have no hold on the public mind of England; that these institutions are regarded with aversion by a decided majority of the middle class. . . . Now, sir, if I were convinced that the great body of the middle class in England look with aversion on monarchy and aristocracy, I should be forced, much against my will, to come to this conclusion, that monarchical and aristocratical institutions are unsuited to this country. Monarchy and aristocracy, valuable and useful as I think them, are still valuable and useful as means, and not as ends. The end of government is the happiness of the people; and I do not conceive that, in a country like this, the happiness of the people can be promoted by a form of government in which the middle classes place no confidence. . . . But, sir, I am fully convinced that the middle classes sincerely wish to uphold the royal prerogatives, and the constitutional rights of the Peers. . . .

But let us know our interest and our duty better. Turn where we may—within, around—the voice of great events is proclaiming to us, "Reform, that you may preserve." Now, therefore, while everything at home and abroad forebodes ruin to those who persist in a hopeless struggle against the spirit of the age; now, . . . take counsel, not of prejudice, not of party spirit . . . but of history, of reason. . . . If this Bill should be rejected, I pray to God that none of those who concur in rejecting it may ever remember their votes with unavailing regret, amidst the wreck of laws, the confusion of ranks, the spoliation of property, and the dissolution of social order.

Carl Schurz, *Reminiscences*

One morning, toward the end of February, 1848, I sat quietly in my attic-chamber, . . . when suddenly a friend rushed breathlessly into the room, exclaiming: "What, you sitting here! Do you not know what has happened?"

"No; what?"

"The French have driven away Louis Philippe and proclaimed the republic."

. . . We tore down the stairs, into the street, to the market-square. . . . Although it was still forenoon, the market was already crowded with young men talking excitedly. . . . What did we want there? This probably no one knew. But since the French had driven away Louis Philippe and proclaimed the republic, something of course must happen here, too. . . .

The next morning . . . [we were] impelled by a feeling that now we had something more important [than our classes] to do—to devote ourselves to the affairs of the fatherland. And this we did by seeking as quickly as possible again the company of our friends, in order to discuss what had happened and what was to come.

In these conversations, excited as they were, certain ideas and catchwords worked themselves to the surface, which expressed more or less the feelings of the people. Now had arrived in Germany the day for the establishment of "German Unity," and the founding of a great, powerful national German Empire. In the first line the convocation of a national parliament. Then the demands for civil rights and liberties, free speech, free press, the right of free assembly, equality before the law, a freely elected representation of the people with legislative power, responsibility of ministers, self-government of the communes, the right of the people to carry arms, the formation of a civic guard with elective officers, and so on—in short, that which was called a "constitutional form of government on a broad democratic basis." Republican ideas were at first only sparingly expressed. But the word *democracy* was soon on all tongues, and many, too, thought it a matter of course

(continued)

that if the princes should try to withhold from the people the rights and liberties demanded, force would take the place of mere petition. Of course the regeneration of the fatherland must, if possible, be accomplished by peaceable means. . . . I was dominated by the feeling that at last the great opportunity had arrived for giving to the German people the liberty which was their birthright and to the German fatherland its unity and greatness, and that it was now the first duty of every German to do and to sacrifice everything for this sacred object.

Q *What arguments did Macaulay use to support the Reform Act of 1832? Was he correct? Why or why not? Why was Carl Schurz so excited when he heard the news about the revolution in France? Do you think being a university student helps explain his reaction? Why or why not? What differences do you see in the approaches of these two writers? What do these selections tell you about the development of politics in the German states and Britain in the nineteenth century?*

Sources: Thomas Babington Macaulay, Speech of March 2, 1831. From *Speeches, Parliamentary and Miscellaneous* by Thomas B. Macaulay (New York: Hurst Co., 1853), vol. 1, pp. 20–21, 25–26. From *The Reminiscences of Carl Schurz* by Carl Schurz (New York: The McClure Co., 1907), vol. 1, pp. 112–113.

---

in the war. Defeated and humiliated by the obvious failure of its armies, Russia withdrew from European affairs for the next two decades. Disillusioned by its role in the war, Great Britain also pulled back from continental affairs. Austria, paying the price for its neutrality, was now without friends among the Great Powers. This new international situation opened the door for the unification of Italy and Germany.

19-4 NATIONAL UNIFICATION AND THE NATIONAL STATE, 1848–1871

Q **Focus Question:** What actions did Cavour and Bismarck take to bring about unification in Italy and Germany, respectively, and what role did war play in their efforts?

The revolutions of 1848 had failed, but many of the goals sought by liberals and nationalists during the first half of the nineteenth century were achieved within twenty-five years. Italy and Germany became nations, and constitutional monarchs now led many European states.

19-4a The Unification of Italy

The Italians were the first to benefit from the breakdown of the Concert of Europe. In 1850, Austria was still the dominant power on the Italian Peninsula. After the failure of the revolution of 1848–1849, more and more Italians looked to the northern Italian state of Piedmont, which was ruled by the house of Savoy, as their best hope to achieve a unified Italy. It was, however, doubtful that the little state could provide the necessary leadership until

King Victor Emmanuel II (1849–1878; 1861–1878 as king of Italy) named Count Camillo di Cavour (kuh-MEEL-oh dee kuh-VOOR) (1810–1861) prime minister in 1852.

Cavour pursued a policy of economic expansion that increased government revenues and enabled Piedmont to equip a large army. Then, allied with the French emperor, Napoleon III, Cavour defeated the Austrians and gained control of Lombardy. Cavour's success caused nationalists in some northern Italian states (Parma, Modena, and Tuscany) to overthrow their governments and join Piedmont.

Meanwhile in southern Italy, Giuseppe Garibaldi (joo-ZEP-pay gar-uh-BAHL-dee) (1807–1882), a dedicated Italian patriot, raised an army of a thousand volunteers called Red Shirts because of the color of their uniforms. Garibaldi's forces swept through Sicily and then crossed over to the mainland and began a victorious march up the Italian Peninsula. Naples and the kingdom of the Two Sicilies fell in September 1860. Ever the patriot, Garibaldi chose to turn over his conquests to Cavour's Piedmontese forces. On March 17, 1861, the new kingdom of Italy was proclaimed under a centralized government subordinated to the control of Piedmont and King Victor Emmanuel II. The task of unification was not yet complete, however.

CHRONOLOGY	The Unification of Italy
Victor Emmanuel II	1849–1878
Count Cavour becomes prime minister of Piedmont	1852
Garibaldi invades the Two Sicilies	1860
Kingdom of Italy is proclaimed	March 17, 1861
Italy annexes Venetia	1866
Italy annexes Rome	1870

Venetia in the north was taken from Austria in 1866. The Italian army annexed the city of Rome on September 20, 1870, and it became the new capital of the united Italian state.

19-4b The Unification of Germany

After the Frankfurt Assembly failed to achieve German unification in 1848–1849, Germans increasingly looked to Prussia for leadership in the cause of German unification. Prussia had become a strong, prosperous, and authoritarian state, with the Prussian king in firm control of both the government and the army. In 1862, King William I (1861–1888) appointed a new prime minister, Count Otto von Bismarck (OT-toh fun BIZ-mark) (1815–1898). Bismarck has often been portrayed as the ultimate realist, the foremost nineteenth-century practitioner of *Realpolitik* (ray-AHL-poh-lee-teek)—the "politics of reality." He said, "Not by speeches and majorities will the great questions of the day be decided—that was the mistake of 1848–1849—but by iron and blood."[4] Opposition to his domestic policy led Bismarck to favor an active foreign policy, which led to war and German unification.

After defeating Denmark with Austrian help in 1864 and gaining control over the duchies of Schleswig (SHLESS-vik) and Holstein (HOHL-shtyn), Bismarck goaded the Austrians into a war on June 14, 1866. The Austrians were barely defeated at Königgrätz (kur-nig-GRETS) on July 3, but Prussia now organized the northern German states into the North German Confederation. The southern German states, which were largely Catholic, remained independent but signed military alliances with Prussia out of fear of France, their western neighbor.

Prussia now dominated all of northern Germany, but Bismarck realized that France would never be content with

Map 19.3 The Unification of Italy

Map 19.4 The Unification of Germany

a strong German state to its east because of the potential threat to French security. Bismarck goaded the French into declaring war on Prussia on July 15, 1870. The Prussian armies advanced into France, and at Sedan (suh-DAHN) on September 2, 1870, they captured an entire French army and the French emperor Napoleon III himself. Paris capitulated on January 28, 1871. France had to give up the provinces of Alsace (al-SASS) and Lorraine (luh-RAYN) to the new German state, a loss that left the French burning for revenge.

Even before the war had ended, the southern German states had agreed to enter the North German Confederation. On January 18, 1871, in the Hall of Mirrors in Louis XIV's palace at Versailles, William I was proclaimed kaiser (KY-zur) (emperor) of the Second German Empire (the first was the medieval Holy Roman Empire). German unity had been achieved by the Prussian monarchy and the Prussian army. The Prussian leadership of German unification meant the triumph of authoritarian, militaristic values over liberal, constitutional sentiments in the development of the new German state. With its industrial resources and military might, the new state had become the strongest power on the European continent. A new European balance of power was at hand.

CHRONOLOGY	The Unification of Germany
King William I of Prussia	1861–1888
Danish War	1864
Austro–Prussian War	1866
Franco–Prussian War	1870–1871
German Empire is proclaimed	January 18, 1871

19.6 The Unification of Germany. Under Prussian leadership, a new German empire was proclaimed on January 18, 1871, in the Hall of Mirrors in the palace of Versailles after German forces under the command of Prussia had beaten France in a brief war. King William of Prussia became Emperor William I of the Second German Empire. Otto von Bismarck, who had been so instrumental in creating the new German state, is shown here resplendently attired in his white uniform and standing at the foot of the throne.

19-4c Nationalism and Reform: The European National State at Midcentury

Unlike nations on the European continent, Great Britain managed to avoid the revolutionary upheavals of the first half of the nineteenth century. In the early part of the century, Great Britain was governed by the aristocratic landowning classes that dominated both houses of Parliament. But in 1832, to avoid turmoil like that on the continent of Europe, Parliament passed a reform bill that increased the number of male voters by lowering the monetary requirements for voting, which chiefly benefited members of the industrial middle class (see Opposing Viewpoints, "Response to Revolution: Two Perspectives," p. 487). By allowing the industrial middle class to join the landed interests in ruling Britain, Britain avoided revolution in 1848.

In the 1850s and 1860s, the British liberal parliamentary system made both social and political reforms that enabled the country to remain stable. Another reason for Britain's stability was its continued economic growth

The Young Victoria

Watch *The Young Victoria* (2009), an imaginative but relatively realistic portrayal of the early struggles of the young woman who became Britain's longest-reigning monarch. Central to the film, however, is the romantic portrayal of the wooing of Victoria by her young German cousin, Prince Albert of Saxe-Coburg-Gotha (Rupert Friend), the nephew of the king of Belgium. The film accurately conveys the close bond and the deep and abiding love that developed between Victoria and Albert.

Q *How accurate is the film's portrayal of the young Victoria? As seen in the film, what character traits did the young queen possess that explain her ultimate success?*

Films/The Kobal Collection

MINDTAP See full-length Film & History feature in MindTap.
From Cengage

coupled with middle-class prosperity and improvements for the working classes as real wages for laborers increased more than 25 percent between 1850 and 1870. The British sense of national pride was well reflected in Queen Victoria (r. 1837–1901), whose sense of duty and moral respectability reflected the attitudes of her age, which has ever since been known as the Victorian Age (see Film & History, "*The Young Victoria*").

After the revolution of 1848, France moved toward a restored monarchy. Four years after his election as president, Louis Napoleon restored an authoritarian empire. On December 2, 1852, he assumed the title of Napoleon III (the first Napoleon had abdicated in favor of his son, Napoleon II, in 1814). The Second Empire had begun.

The first five years of Napoleon III's reign were a spectacular success. He took many steps to expand industrial growth. Government subsidies fostered the rapid construction of railroads as well as harbors, roads, and canals. The major French railway lines were completed during Napoleon III's reign, and iron production tripled. Napoleon III also undertook a vast reconstruction of the city of Paris. The medieval Paris of narrow streets and old city walls was destroyed and replaced by a modern Paris of broad boulevards, spacious buildings, an underground sewage system, a new public water supply, and gas streetlights.

In the 1860s, as opposition to his rule began to mount, Napoleon III began to liberalize his regime. He gave the Legislative Corps more say in affairs of state, including debate over the budget. Liberalization policies worked initially; in a plebiscite in May 1870 on whether to accept a new constitution that might have inaugurated a parliamentary regime, the French people gave Napoleon III a resounding victory. This triumph was short lived, however. War with Prussia in 1870 brought Napoleon III's ouster, and a republic was proclaimed.

Although nationalism was a major force in nineteenth-century Europe, one of the most powerful states, the Austrian Empire, managed to frustrate the desire of its numerous ethnic groups for self-determination. After the Habsburgs had crushed the revolutions of 1848–1849, they restored centralized, autocratic government. But Austria's defeat at the hands of the Prussians in 1866 forced the Austrians to deal with the fiercely nationalistic Hungarians.

The result was the negotiated **Ausgleich** (OWSS-glykh), or Compromise of 1867, which created the dual monarchy of Austria–Hungary. Each part of the empire now had its own constitution, its own legislature, its own governmental bureaucracy, and its own capital (Vienna for Austria and Budapest for Hungary). Holding the two states together were a single monarch—Francis Joseph (1848–1916), emperor of Austria and king of Hungary—and a common army, foreign policy, and system of finances. The Ausgleich did not, however, satisfy the other nationalities that made up the Austro–Hungarian Empire.

At the beginning of the nineteenth century, Russia was overwhelmingly rural, agricultural, and autocratic. The Russian imperial autocracy—based on soldiers, secret police, and repression—withstood the revolutionary fervor of the first half of the nineteenth century. But defeat in the Crimean War in 1856 led even staunch conservatives to realize that Russia was falling hopelessly behind the western European powers. Tsar Alexander II (1855–1881) decided to make serious reforms.

Serfdom was Russia's most burdensome problem. On March 3, 1861, Alexander issued his emancipation edict (see Historical Voices, "Emancipation: Serfs and Slaves," p. 492). Peasants were now free to own property and marry as they chose. But the redistribution of land instituted after emancipation was not favorable to them. The government provided land for the peasants by purchasing it from the landlords, but the landowners often kept the best lands. The peasants soon found that they had inadequate amounts of arable land to support themselves.

Nor were the peasants completely free. The state compensated the landowners for the land given to the peasants, but the peasants were to repay the state in long-term installments. To ensure that the payments were made, peasants were subjected to the authority of their *mir* (MEER), or village commune, which was collectively responsible for the payments to the government. Because the communes were responsible for the payments, they were reluctant to allow peasants to leave. Emancipation, then, led not to free, landowning peasants on the Western model but to unhappy, land-starved peasants who largely followed the old ways of agricultural production.

19-5 THE EUROPEAN STATE, 1871–1914

Focus Questions: What general political trends were evident in the nations of western Europe in the late nineteenth and early twentieth centuries, and to what degree were those trends also apparent in the nations of central and eastern Europe? How did the growth of nationalism affect international affairs during the same period?

Throughout much of Europe, the national state had become the focus of people's loyalties by 1870. Only in Russia, eastern Europe, Austria–Hungary, and Ireland did national groups still struggle for independence.

Within the major European states, considerable progress was made in achieving such liberal practices as constitutions and parliaments, but it was largely in the western European states that **mass politics** became a reality with the expansion of voting rights for men and the creation of mass political parties. At the same time, however, similar reforms were strongly resisted in parts of Europe where the old political forces remained strong.

19-5a Western Europe: The Growth of Political Democracy

By 1871, Great Britain had a functioning two-party parliamentary system. For the next fifty years, members of

Emancipation: Serfs and Slaves

Politics & Government   **ALTHOUGH OVERALL THEIR HISTORIES** have been quite different, Russia and the United States shared a common feature in the 1860s. They were the only states in the Western world that still had large enslaved populations (the Russian serfs were virtually slaves). The leaders of both countries issued emancipation proclamations within two years of each other. The first excerpt is taken from the imperial decree of March 3, 1861, which freed the Russian serfs. The second excerpt is from Abraham Lincoln's Emancipation Proclamation, issued on January 1, 1863.

Alexander II's Imperial Decree, March 3, 1861

By the grace of God, we, Alexander II, Emperor and Autocrat of all the Russias, King of Poland, Grand Duke of Finland, etc., to all our faithful subjects, make known:

Called by Divine Providence and by the sacred right of inheritance to the throne of our ancestors, we took a vow in our innermost heart to respond to the mission which is intrusted to us as to surround with our affection and our Imperial solicitude all our faithful subjects of every rank and of every condition. . . .

We thus came to the conviction that the work of a serious improvement of the condition of the peasants was a sacred inheritance bequeathed to us by our ancestors, a mission which, in the course of events, Divine Providence called upon us to fulfill. . . .

In virtue of the new dispositions above mentioned, the peasants attached to the soil will be invested within a term fixed by the law with all the rights of free cultivators. . . .

At the same time, they are granted the right of purchasing their close, and, with the consent of the proprietors, they may acquire in full property the arable lands and other appurtenances which are allotted to them as a permanent holding.

By the acquisition in full property of the quantity of land fixed, the peasants are free from their obligations toward the proprietors for land thus purchased, and they enter definitely into the condition of free peasant-landholders.

Lincoln's Emancipation Proclamation, January 1, 1863

Now therefore, I, Abraham Lincoln, President of the United States, by virtue of the power in me vested as Commander-in-Chief of the Army and Navy of the United States in time of actual armed rebellion against the authority and government of the United States, and as a fit and necessary war measure for suppressing such rebellion, do, on this 1st day of January, A.D. 1863, and in accordance with my purpose to do so, . . . order and designate as the States and parts of States wherein the people there of, respectively, are this day in rebellion against the United States the following, to wit:

Arkansas, Texas, Louisiana, . . . Mississippi, Alabama, Florida, Georgia, South Carolina, North Carolina, and Virginia. . . .

And by virtue of the power for the purpose aforesaid, I do order and declare that all persons held as slaves within said designated States and parts of States are, and henceforward shall be free; and that the Executive Government of the United States, including the military and naval authorities thereof, will recognize and maintain the freedom of said persons.

Q *What changes did Tsar Alexander II's emancipation of the serfs initiate in Russia? What effect did Lincoln's Emancipation Proclamation have on the southern "armed rebellion"? What reasons did each leader give for his action?*

Sources: From *Annual Register* (New York: Longmans, Green, 1861), p. 207. From *U.S. Statutes at large* (Washington, D.C., Government Printing Office, 1875), vol. 12, pp. 1268–1269.

---

the Liberal and Conservative Parties alternated in power. Aristocratic landowners and upper-middle-class business people dominated both parties. The parties competed in passing laws that expanded the right to vote. By 1918, all males over twenty-one and women over thirty could vote. Political democracy was soon accompanied by social welfare measures for the working class.

The growth of trade unions, which advocated more radical economic change, and the emergence in 1900 of the Labour Party, which dedicated itself to workers' interests, caused the Liberals, who held the government from 1906 to 1914, to realize they would have to create a program of social welfare or lose the workers' support. Therefore, they voted for a series of social reforms. The National Insurance Act of 1911 provided benefits for workers in case of sickness and unemployment. Additional legislation provided a small pension for those seventy and older. Although both the benefits and the tax increase were modest, they were the first hesitant steps toward the future British welfare state.

In France, the confusion that ensued after the collapse of the Second Empire finally ended in 1875 when an improvised constitution established the Third Republic, which lasted sixty-five years. France's parliamentary system was weak, however, because the existence of a dozen political parties forced the premier (or prime minister) to depend on a coalition of parties to stay in power. The Third Republic was notorious for its changes of government. Nevertheless, by 1914, the Third Republic commanded the loyalty of most French people.

19-5b Central and Eastern Europe: Persistence of the Old Order

The constitution of the new imperial Germany begun by Chancellor Otto von Bismarck in 1871 provided for a bicameral legislature. The lower house of the German parliament, the Reichstag, was elected by universal male suffrage, but it did not have ministerial responsibility. Government ministers were responsible to the emperor, not the parliament. The emperor also commanded the armed forces and controlled foreign policy and the bureaucracy.

During the reign of Emperor William II (1888–1918), Germany continued to be an "authoritarian, conservative, military-bureaucratic power state." By the end of William's reign, Germany had become the strongest military and industrial power on the European continent, but the rapid change had also helped produce a society torn between modernization and traditionalism. With the expansion of industry and cities came demands for true democracy. Conservative forces, especially the landowning nobility and industrialists, tried to block the movement for democracy by supporting William II's activist foreign policy. Expansion abroad, they believed, would divert people's attention from the yearning for democracy at home.

After the creation of the dual monarchy of Austria–Hungary in 1867, the Austrian part received a constitution that theoretically established a parliamentary system. In practice, however, Emperor Francis Joseph largely ignored parliament, ruling by decree when parliament was not in session. The problem of the various nationalities also remained unsolved. The German minority that governed Austria felt increasingly threatened by the Czechs, Poles, and other Slavic groups within the empire. Their agitation in the parliament for autonomy led prime ministers after 1900 to ignore the parliament and rely increasingly on imperial decrees to govern.

CHRONOLOGY	The National State, 1870–1914	
Great Britain		
Formation of Labour Party	1900	
National Insurance Act	1911	
France		
Republican constitution (Third Republic)	1875	
Germany		
Bismarck as chancellor	1871–1890	
Emperor William II	1888–1918	
Austria–Hungary		
Emperor Francis Joseph	1848–1916	
Russia		
Tsar Alexander III	1881–1894	
Tsar Nicholas II	1894–1917	
Russo–Japanese War	1904–1905	
Revolution	1905	

In Russia, the assassination of Alexander II in 1881 convinced his son and successor, Alexander III (1881–1894), that reform had been a mistake, and he lost no time in persecuting both reformers and revolutionaries. When Alexander III died, his weak son and successor, Nicholas II (1894–1917), began his rule with his father's conviction that the absolute power of the tsars should be preserved: "I shall maintain the principle of autocracy just as firmly and unflinchingly as did my unforgettable father."[5] But conditions were changing.

19.7 Nicholas II. The last tsar of Russia hoped to preserve the traditional autocratic ways of his predecessors. In this photograph, Nicholas II and his wife, Alexandra, are shown around 1907 with their four daughters and son on holiday on the deck of a ship.

Industrialization progressed rapidly in Russia after 1890, and with industrialization came factories, an industrial working class, and the development of socialist parties, including the Marxist Social Democratic Party and the Social Revolutionaries. Although repression forced both parties to go underground, the growing opposition to the regime finally exploded into revolution in 1905.

The military defeat of the Russians by the Japanese in 1904–1905 encouraged antigovernment groups to rebel against the tsarist regime. Nicholas II granted civil liberties and created a legislative assembly, the Duma (DOO-muh), whose members were elected directly by a broad franchise. But real constitutional monarchy proved short lived. By 1907, the tsar had curtailed the power of the Duma and relied again on the army and bureaucracy to rule Russia.

19-5c International Rivalries and the Winds of War

Between 1871 and 1914, Europe was mostly at peace. Wars did occur (including wars of conquest in the non-Western world), but none involved the great powers. Bismarck had realized in 1871 that the emergence of a unified Germany as the most powerful state on the European continent (see Map 19.5) had upset the balance of power established at Vienna in 1815. Fearful of a possible anti-German alliance

Map 19.5 Europe in 1871. German unification in 1871 upset the balance of power established at Vienna in 1815 and eventually led to a realignment of European alliances. By 1907, Europe was divided into two opposing camps: the Triple Entente of Great Britain, Russia, and France and the Triple Alliance of Germany, Austria–Hungary, and Italy.

Q *How was Germany affected by the formation of the Triple Entente?*

between France and Russia, and possibly even Austria, Bismarck made a defensive alliance with Austria in 1879. Three years later, this alliance was enlarged with the addition of Italy, which was angry with the French over conflicting colonial ambitions in North Africa. The Triple Alliance of 1882—Germany, Austria–Hungary, and Italy—committed the three powers to a defensive alliance against France. At the same time, Bismarck maintained a separate treaty with Russia.

When Emperor William II cashiered Bismarck in 1890 and took over direction of Germany's foreign policy, he embarked on an activist foreign policy dedicated to enhancing German power by finding, as he put it, Germany's rightful "place in the sun." One of his changes to Bismarck's foreign policy was dropping the treaty with Russia, which he viewed as being at odds with Germany's alliance with Austria. The ending of the alliance brought France and Russia together, and the two powers concluded a military alliance in 1894. During the next ten years, German policies caused the British to draw closer to France. By 1907, an alliance of Great Britain, France, and Russia—known as the Triple Entente (ahn-TAHNT)—stood opposed to the Triple Alliance of Germany, Austria–Hungary, and Italy. Europe became divided into two opposing camps that became more and more inflexible and unwilling to compromise. A series of crises in the Balkans between 1908 and 1913 set the stage for World War I.

Crisis in The Balkans   During the nineteenth century, the Balkan provinces of the Ottoman Empire had gradually gained their freedom, although the rivalry between Austria and Russia complicated the process. By 1878, Greece, Serbia, Romania, and Montenegro (mahn-tuh-NEE-groh)

Map 19.6 The Balkans in 1913

had become independent. Bulgaria, though not totally independent, was allowed to operate autonomously under Russian protection. Bosnia and Herzegovina (HAYRT-suh-guh-VEE-nuh) were placed under Austrian protection; Austria could occupy but not annex them.

Nevertheless, in 1908, Austria did annex the two Slavic-speaking territories. Serbia was outraged because the annexation dashed the Serbs' hopes of creating a large Serbian kingdom that would unite most of the southern Slavs. The Russians, as protectors of their fellow Slavs, supported the Serbs and opposed the Austrian action. Backed by the Russians, the Serbs prepared for war against Austria. At this point, William II intervened and demanded that the Russians accept Austria's annexation of Bosnia and Herzegovina or face war with Germany. Weakened from their defeat in the Russo-Japanese War in 1904–1905, the Russians backed down but vowed revenge. Two wars between the Balkan states in 1912–1913 further embittered the inhabitants of the region and generated more tensions among the Great Powers.

Serbia's desire to create a large Serbian kingdom remained unfulfilled. In their frustration, Serbian nationalists blamed the Austrians. Austria–Hungary was convinced that Serbia was a mortal threat to its empire and must at some point be crushed. As Serbia's chief supporters, the Russians were determined not to back down again in the event of a confrontation with Austria or Germany in the Balkans. The allies of Austria–Hungary and Russia were also determined to be more supportive of their respective allies in another crisis. By the beginning of 1914, two armed camps viewed each other with suspicion.

CHAPTER SUMMARY

In 1815, a conservative order had been reestablished throughout Europe, but the forces of liberalism and nationalism—unleashed by the French Revolution and now reinforced by the spread of industrialization—were pushing Europe into a new era of political and social change.

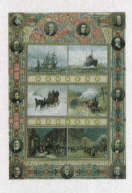

Industrialization spread rapidly from Great Britain to the European continent and the United States. As cities grew, the plight of Europe's new working class became the focus of new political philosophies, notably the work of Karl Marx, who sought to liberate the oppressed proletariat. At the same time, middle-class industrialists adopted the political philosophy of liberalism, espousing freedom in both politics and economic activity. By the mid-nineteenth century, nationalism threatened the status quo in divided Germany and Italy and the multiethnic Austrian Empire.

In 1848, revolutions erupted across the European continent. A republic with universal manhood suffrage was established in France, but it had given way to the Second Empire within four years. The Frankfurt Assembly worked to create a unified Germany, but it also failed. In the Austrian Empire, the liberal demands of the Hungarians and other nationalities were eventually put down. In Italy, too, uprisings against Austrian rule failed when conservatives regained control.

By 1871, nationalist forces had prevailed in Germany and Italy. The combined activities of Count Cavour and

Giuseppe Garibaldi finally led to the unification of Italy in 1870. Under the guidance of Otto von Bismarck, Prussia engaged in wars with Denmark, Austria, and France before it finally achieved the goal of German national unification in 1871. Reform characterized developments in other Western states. Austria created the dual monarchy of Austria–Hungary. Russia's defeat in the Crimean War led to reforms under Alexander II, which included the freeing of the Russian serfs.

Between 1871 and 1914, the functions of the national state began to expand as social insurance measures such as protection against illnesses and old age were adopted to appease the working masses. Liberal and democratic reforms, especially in western Europe, brought the possibility for greater participation in the political process. Nevertheless, large minority groups—especially in the multiethnic empires controlled by the Austrians, Ottomans, and Russians—had not achieved the goal of their own national states. Meanwhile, the collapse of the Ottoman Empire caused Russia and Austria to set their sights on territories in the Balkans. As Germany's power increased, the European nations formed new alliances that helped maintain a balance of power but also led to the creation of large armies. The alliances also generated tensions that were unleashed when Europeans were unable to resolve a series of crises in the Balkans and rushed into the catastrophic carnage of World War I.

REFLECTION QUESTIONS

Q What were the major similarities and differences between the First and Second Industrial Revolutions?

Q What were the chief ideas associated with liberalism and nationalism, and how were these ideas put into practice in Europe, Latin America, and Asia in the first half of the nineteenth century?

Q To what extent were the major goals of establishing liberal practices and achieving the growth of political democracy realized in Great Britain, France, Germany, Austria–Hungary, and Russia between 1871 and 1914?

CHAPTER TIMELINE

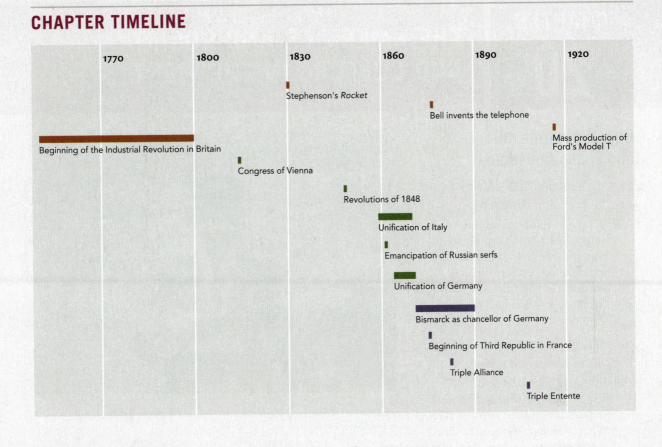

	1770	1800	1830	1860	1890	1920

Stephenson's *Rocket*

Bell invents the telephone

Mass production of Ford's Model T

Beginning of the Industrial Revolution in Britain

Congress of Vienna

Revolutions of 1848

Unification of Italy

Emancipation of Russian serfs

Unification of Germany

Bismarck as chancellor of Germany

Beginning of Third Republic in France

Triple Alliance

Triple Entente

CHAPTER NOTES

1. Quoted in E. Royston Pike, *Human Documents of the Industrial Revolution in Britain* (London, 1966), p. 315.
2. K. Marx and F. Engels, *The Communist Manifesto* (Harmondsworth, England, 1967), p. 80. Originally published in 1848.
3. Ibid., pp. 91, 94.
4. Quoted in L. L. Snyder, ed., *Documents of German History* (New Brunswick, N.J., 195S), p. 202.
5. Quoted in S. Galai, *The Liberation Movement in Russia, 1900–1905* (Cambridge, 1973), p. 26.

MINDTAP
From Cengage

MindTap® is a fully online, highly personalized learning experience built upon Cengage Learning content. MindTap combines student learning tools—readings, multimedia, activities, and assessments—into a singular Learning Path that guides students through the course and helps students develop the critical thinking, analysis, and communication skills that are essential to academic and professional success.

Chapter Outline and Focus Questions

20-1 Latin America in the Nineteenth and Early Twentieth Centuries

Q What role did liberalism and nationalism play in Latin America between 1800 and 1870? What were the major economic, social, and political trends in Latin America in the late nineteenth and early twentieth centuries?

20-2 The North American Neighbors: The United States and Canada

Q What role did nationalism and liberalism play in the United States and Canada between 1800 and 1870? What economic, social, and political trends were evident in the United States and Canada between 1870 and 1914?

20-3 The Emergence of Mass Society

Q What is meant by the term *mass society*, and what were its main characteristics?

20-4 Cultural Life: Romanticism and Realism in the Western World

Q What were the main characteristics of Romanticism and realism?

20-5 Toward the Modern Consciousness: Intellectual and Cultural Developments

Q What intellectual and cultural developments in the late nineteenth and early twentieth centuries "opened the way to a modern consciousness," and how did this consciousness differ from earlier worldviews?

20.1 Portrait of Toussaint L'Ouverture. L'Ouverture was leader of the Haitian independence movement.

Critical Thinking

Q *In what ways were the intellectual and cultural developments in the Western world between 1800 and 1914 related to the economic, social, and political developments?*

Connections to Today

Q *In the late nineteenth century, new work opportunities for women emerged, but many middle- and upper-class women were still expected to remain at home. What are the new opportunities and challenges for women today, and how do they compare with those in the nineteenth century?*

NATIONALISM—ONE OF THE MAJOR FORCES for change in Europe in the nineteenth century—also affected Latin America as colonial peoples there overthrew their Spanish and Portuguese masters and began to create new national states. An unusual revolution in Haiti preceded the main independence movements.

François-Dominique Toussaint L'Ouverture (frahn-SWAH-doh-muh-NEEK too-SANH loo-vayr-TOOR), the grandson of an African king, was born in 1746 as a slave in Saint-Domingue (san doh-MAYNG)—the western third of the island of Hispaniola, a French sugar colony. Educated by his godfather, Toussaint was able to amass a small private fortune through his own talents and the generosity of his French master. When black slaves in Saint-Domingue were inspired by news of the French Revolution and revolted in 1791, Toussaint became their leader. For years, Toussaint and his ragtag army struck at the French. By 1801, after his army had come to control Saint-Domingue, Toussaint assumed the role of ruler and issued a constitution that freed all slaves.

But Napoleon Bonaparte refused to accept Toussaint's control of France's richest colony and sent a French army of 23,000 men under General Leclerc (luh-KLAHR), his brother-in-law, to crush the rebellion. Although yellow fever took its toll on the French, their superior numbers and weapons enabled them to gain the upper hand. Toussaint was tricked into surrendering in 1802 by Leclerc's promise: "You will not find a more sincere friend than myself." Instead, Toussaint was arrested, put in chains, and shipped to France, where he died a year later in a dungeon. The western part of Hispaniola, now called Haiti, however, became the first independent state in Latin America when Toussaint's lieutenants drove out the French forces in 1804. Haiti was only one of several places in the Americas where new nations were formed during the nineteenth century. Indeed, nation building was prominent in North America as the United States and Canada expanded.

As national states in both the Western Hemisphere and Europe were evolving in the nineteenth century, significant changes were occurring in society and culture. The rapid economic changes of the nineteenth century led to the emergence of mass society in the Western world, which meant improvements for the lower classes, who benefited from the extension of voting rights, a better standard of living, and universal education. The coming of mass society also created new roles for the governments of nation-states, which now fostered national loyalty, created mass armies by conscription, and took more responsibility for public health and housing in their cities. Cultural and intellectual changes paralleled these social developments, and Western philosophers, writers, and artists began exploring modern cultural expressions that questioned traditional ideas and increasingly provoked a crisis of confidence after 1870.

20-1 LATIN AMERICA IN THE NINETEENTH AND EARLY TWENTIETH CENTURIES

Focus Questions: What role did liberalism and nationalism play in Latin America between 1800 and 1870? What were the major economic, social, and political trends in Latin America in the late nineteenth and early twentieth centuries?

The Spanish and Portuguese colonial empires in Latin America had been integrated into the traditional monarchical structure of Europe for centuries. When that structure was challenged, first by the ideas of the Enlightenment and then by the upheavals of the Napoleonic era, Latin America encountered the possibility of change. How it responded to that possibility, however, was determined in part by conditions unique to the region.

20-1a The Wars for Independence

By the end of the eighteenth century, the ideas of the Enlightenment and the new political ideals stemming from the successful revolution in North America were beginning to influence the creole elites (descendants of Europeans who became permanent inhabitants of Latin America). The principles of the equality of all people in the eyes of the law, free trade, and a free press proved highly attractive. Simón Bolívar (see-MOHN boh-LEE-var) (1783–1830) and José de San Martín (hoh-SAY day san mar-TEEN) (1778–1850), sons of creoles who became leaders of the independence movement, even went to European universities, where they imbibed the ideas of the Enlightenment (see Images 20.2a and 20.2b). These Latin American elites, joined by a growing class of merchants, especially resented the domination of their trade by Spain and Portugal.

Nationalistic Revolts in Latin America The creole elites soon began to use their new ideas to denounce the rule of the Iberian monarchs and the peninsulars (Spanish and Portuguese officials who resided in Latin America for political and economic gain). As Bolívar said in 1815, "It would be easier to have the two continents meet than to reconcile the spirits of Spain and America."[1] When Napoleon Bonaparte toppled the monarchies of Spain and Portugal, the authority of the Spaniards and Portuguese in their colonial empires was weakened, and a series of revolts

20.2a

20.2b

20.2a, 20.2b The Liberators of South America. José de San Martín and Simón Bolívar are hailed as the leaders of the South American independence movement. In the painting in Image 20.2a, San Martín is portrayed in the Andes. His forces liberated Argentina, Chile, and Peru from Spanish authority. The painting in Image 20.2b shows Bolívar leading his troops across the Andes in 1823 to fight in Peru. This depiction of impeccably uniformed troops moving in perfect formation through the snow of the Andes, by Chilean artist Franco Gomez, is highly unrealistic.

enabled most of Latin America to become independent between 1807 and 1825.

As already noted, the first revolt was actually a successful slave rebellion led by Toussaint L'Ouverture (1746–1803) on Hispaniola. The revolt resulted in the formation of Haiti as the first independent postcolonial state in Latin America in 1804.

Beginning in 1810, Mexico also experienced a revolt, fueled initially by the desire of the creole elites to over-throw the rule of the peninsulars. The first real hero of Mexican independence was Miguel Hidalgo y Costilla (mee-GEL ee-THAHL-goh ee kahs-TEE-yuh), a parish priest in a small village some 100 miles from Mexico City. Hidalgo, who had studied the French Revolution, roused the local Indians and mestizos, many of whom were suffering from a major famine, to free themselves from the Spanish. On September 16, 1810, a crowd of Indians and mestizos, armed with clubs, machetes, and a few guns, quickly formed a mob army and attacked

the Spaniards, shouting, "Long live independence and death to the Spaniards." But Hidalgo was not a good organizer, and his forces were soon crushed. A military court sentenced Hidalgo to death, but memory of his revolt lived on. In fact, September 16, the first day of the uprising, is celebrated as Mexico's Independence Day.

The participation of Indians and mestizos in Mexico's revolt against Spanish control frightened both creoles and peninsulars. Fearful of the masses, they cooperated in defeating the popular revolutionary forces. The elites—both creoles and peninsulars—then decided to over-throw Spanish rule as a way to preserve their own power. In 1821, they selected a creole military leader, Augustín de Iturbide (ah-goo-STEEN day ee-tur-BEE-day), as their leader and the first emperor of Mexico. The new govern-ment fostered neither political nor economic changes, and it soon became apparent that Mexican independence had benefited primarily the creole elites.

Independence movements elsewhere in Latin America were likewise the work of elites—primarily creoles—who overthrew Spanish rule and set up new governments they could dominate. José de San Martín of Argentina and Simón Bolívar of Venezuela, leaders of the independence movement, were both members of the creole elite, and both were hailed as the liberators of South America.

The Efforts of Bolívar and San Martín   Simón Bolívar has long been regarded as the George Washington of Latin America. Born into a wealthy Venezuelan family, he was introduced as a young man to the ideas of the Enlightenment. While in Rome in 1805 to witness the coronation of Napoleon as king of Italy, he committed himself to free his people from Spanish control. He vowed, "I swear before the God of my fathers, by my fathers themselves, by my honor and by my country, that my arm shall not rest nor my mind be at peace until I have broken the chains that bind me by the will and power of Spain."[2] When he returned to South America, Bolívar began to lead the bitter struggle for independence in Venezuela as well as other parts of northern South America. Although acclaimed as the "liberator" of Venezuela in 1813 by the people, not until 1821 did he definitively defeat Spanish forces there. He went on to liberate Colombia, Ecuador, and Peru. Already in 1819, he had become president of Venezuela, at the time part of a federation that included Colombia and Ecuador. But Bolívar was well aware of the difficulties in establishing stable republican governments in Latin America.

While Bolívar was busy liberating northern South America from the Spanish, José de San Martín was concentrating his efforts on the southern part of the continent. Son of a Spanish army officer in Argentina, San Martín himself went to Spain and pursued a military career in the Spanish army. In 1811, after serving twenty-two years, he learned of the liberation movement in his native Argentina, abandoned his military career in Spain, and returned to his homeland in March 1812. Argentina had already been freed from Spanish control, but San Martín believed that the Spaniards must be removed from all of South America if any nation was to remain free. In January 1817, he led his forces over the high Andes Mountains, an amazing feat in itself. Many of the soldiers suffered from lack of oxygen and severe cold while crossing mountain passes more than two miles above sea level. The arrival of San Martín's troops in Chile completely surprised the Spaniards, whose forces were routed at the Battle of Chacabuco (chahk-ah-BOO-koh) on February 12, 1817.

In 1821, San Martín moved on to Lima, Peru, the center of Spanish authority. Convinced that he would be unable to complete the liberation of all of Peru, San Martín welcomed the arrival of Bolívar and his forces. As he wrote to Bolívar, "For me it would have been the height of happiness to end the war of independence under the orders of a general to whom [South] America owes its freedom. Destiny orders it otherwise, and one must resign oneself to it."[3] Highly disappointed, San Martín left South America for Europe, where he remained until his death in 1850. Meanwhile, Bolívar took on the task of crushing the last significant Spanish army at Ayacucho (ah-ya-KOO-choh) on December 9, 1824. By then, Peru, Uruguay, Paraguay, Colombia, Venezuela, Argentina, Bolivia, and Chile had all become free states. In 1823, the Central American states became independent. In 1838–1839, they divided into five republics—Guatemala, El Salvador, Honduras, Costa Rica, and Nicaragua. Earlier, in 1822, the prince regent of Brazil had declared Brazil's independence from Portugal.

Independence and the Monroe Doctrine   In the early 1820s, only one major threat remained to the newly won independence of the Latin American states. Reveling in their success in crushing rebellions in Spain and Italy, the victorious continental European powers favored the use of troops to restore Spanish control in Latin America. This time, Britain's opposition to intervention prevailed. Eager to gain access to an entire continent for investment and trade, the British proposed joint action with the United States against European interference in Latin America. Distrustful of British motives, President James Monroe acted alone in 1823 and issued what is known as the *Monroe Doctrine*, which guaranteed the independence of the new Latin American nations and warned against further European intervention in the Americas. Even more important to Latin American independence than American words was Britain's navy. All of the continental European powers were reluctant to challenge British naval power, which stood between Latin America and any European invasion force.

20-1b The Difficulties of Nation Building

As Simón Bolívar had foreseen, the new Latin American nations (see Map 20.1), most of which began as republics, faced a number of serious problems between 1830 and 1870. The wars for independence themselves had resulted in a staggering loss of population, property, and livestock. At the same time, disputes arose between nations over their precise boundaries.

Map 20.1 Latin America in the First Half of the Nineteenth Century. Latin American colonies took advantage of Spain's weakness during the Napoleonic wars to fight for independence, beginning with Argentina in 1810 and spreading throughout the region over the next decade with the help of leaders such as Simón Bolívar and José de San Martín.

 How many South American countries are sources of rivers that feed the Amazon, and roughly what percentage of the continent is contained within the Amazon's watershed?

Political Difficulties   The new nations of Latin America established republican governments, but they had had no experience in ruling themselves. Because of insecurities prevailing after independence, strong leaders known as **caudillos** (kah-DEEL-yohz or kow-THEEL-yohz) came to power. Caudillos at the national level were generally one of two types. One type supported the elites and consisted of autocrats who controlled (and often abused) state revenues, used centralized power, and kept the new national states together. Sometimes they were also modernizers who built roads and canals, ports, and schools. These caudillos were usually supported by the Catholic church, the rural aristocracy, and the army, which emerged from the wars of independence as a powerful political force that often made and deposed governments. Many caudillos, in fact, were former army leaders.

In contrast, other caudillos were supported by the masses, became extremely popular, and served as instruments for radical change. Juan Manuel de Rosas (WAHN mahn-WEL day ROH-sas), for example, who led Argentina from 1829 to 1852, became extremely popular by favoring Argentine interests against foreigners.

Economic Patterns Although political independence brought economic independence, old patterns were quickly reestablished. Instead of Spain and Portugal, Great Britain now dominated the Latin American economy. British merchants arrived in large numbers, and British investors poured in funds, especially into the mining industry. Old trade patterns soon reemerged. Because Latin America served as a source of raw materials and foodstuffs for the industrializing nations of Europe and the United States, exports to the North Atlantic countries increased noticeably, especially wheat, tobacco, wool, sugar, coffee, and hides. At the same time, finished consumer goods, especially textiles, were imported in increasing quantities, causing a decline in industrial production in Latin America. Between 1870 and 1913, British investments—mostly in railroads, mining, and public utilities—constituted two-thirds of all foreign investment in Latin America. After 1913, however, the United States became the primary investor in the Latin American economy as well as the principle consumer of raw products. The emphasis on exporting raw materials and importing finished products ensured the ongoing domination of the Latin American economy by foreigners.

Social Conditions A fundamental underlying problem for all of the new Latin American nations was the persistent domination of society by the landed elites (see Historical Voices, "A Radical Critique of the Land Problem in Mexico," p. 504). Large estates remained an important aspect of Latin America's economic and social life. After independence, the size of these estates expanded even more. By 1848, the Sánchez Navarro (SAHN-ches nuh-VAH-roh) family in Mexico owned seventeen haciendas (hah-see-EN-duhz), or plantations, covering 16 million acres. Estates were often so large that they could not be farmed efficiently. As one Latin American newspaper put it, "The huge fortunes have the unfortunate tendency to grow even larger, and their owners possess vast tracts of land, which lie fallow and abandoned. Their greed for land does not equal their ability to use it intelligently and actively."[4] Landed elites ran governments, controlled courts, and maintained the system of debt peonage that provided large landowners with a supply of cheap labor. These landowners made enormous profits by concentrating on specialized crops for export such as coffee while the masses—left without land to grow basic food crops—lived in dire poverty.

20-1c Tradition and Change in the Latin American Economy and Society

After 1870, Latin America began to experience an era of rapid economic growth largely based on the export of a few basic commodities: wheat and beef from Argentina, coffee from Brazil, nitrates from Chile, coffee and bananas from Central America, and sugar and silver from Peru. These foodstuffs and raw materials were exchanged for finished goods—textiles, machines, and luxury goods—from Europe and the United States. Despite their economic growth, Latin American nations remained economic colonies of Western nations.

Old patterns also still largely prevailed in society. Rural elites dominated their estates and their workers. Although slavery was abolished by 1888, former slaves and their descendants were at the bottom of their society. The Indians remained poverty stricken.

One result of the new prosperity that came from increased exports was growth in the middle sectors of Latin American society—lawyers, merchants, shopkeepers, businesspeople, schoolteachers, professors, bureaucrats, and military officers. These middle sectors, which made up only 5 percent to 10 percent of the population, depending on the country, were hardly large enough in numbers to constitute a true middle class. Nevertheless, after 1900, the middle sectors continued to expand. They lived in the cities, sought education and decent incomes, and increasingly saw the United States as the model to emulate, especially in regard to industrialization and education.

As Latin American exports increased, so did the working class, and that in turn led to the growth of labor unions, especially after 1914. Radical unions often advocated the use of the general strike as an instrument for change. By and large, however, the governing elites succeeded in stifling the political influence of the working class by restricting workers' right to vote.

The need for industrial labor also led Latin American countries to encourage immigration from Europe. Between 1880 and 1914, 3 million Europeans, primarily Italians and Spaniards, settled in Argentina. More than 100,000 Europeans—mostly Italian, Portuguese, and Spanish—arrived in Brazil each year between 1891 and 1900.

As in Europe and the United States, industrialization led to urbanization, which was evident in the emergence of new cities and the rapid growth of old ones. Buenos Aires (the

A Radical Critique of the Land Problem in Mexico

Politics & Government

THE DOMINATION OF MEXICO by elites who owned large estates remained a serious problem throughout the nineteenth century. Conservatives, of course, favored the great estates as the foundation stones of their own political power—and even liberals shied away from any extremist attack on property rights. Nevertheless, there were strong voices of protest, as this excerpt from a speech delivered in 1857 by social liberal Ponciano Arriaga (pahn-SYAHN-oh ah-RYAH-guh) demonstrates. Arriaga's appeal went unheeded; conservatives called him a "communist."

Ponciano Arriaga, Speech to the Constitutional Convention of 1856–1857

One of the most deeply rooted evils of our country—an evil that merits the close attention of legislators when they frame our fundamental law—is the monstrous division of landed property.

While a few individuals possess immense areas of uncultivated land that could support millions of people, the great majority of Mexicans languish in a terrible poverty and are denied property, homes, and work. . . .

There are Mexican landowners who occupy (if one can give that name to a purely imaginary act) an extent of land greater than the areas of some of our sovereign states, greater even than that of one of several European states.

In this vast area, much of which lies idle, deserted, abandoned, awaiting the arms and labor of men, live four or five million Mexicans who know no other industry than agriculture, yet are without land or the means to work it, and who cannot emigrate in the hope of bettering their fortunes. They must either vegetate in idleness, turn to banditry, or accept the yoke of a landed monopolist who subjects them to intolerable conditions of life. . . .

How can a hungry, naked, miserable people practice popular government? How can we proclaim the equal rights of men and leave the majority of the nation in conditions worse than those of helots or pariahs? How can we condemn slavery in words, while the lot of most of our fellow citizens is more grievous than that of the black slaves of Cuba or the United States? . . .

With some honorable exceptions, the rich landowners of Mexico, or the administrators who represent them, resemble the feudal lords of the Middle Ages. On his seignorial land, . . . the landowner makes and executes laws, administers justice and exercises civil power, imposes taxes and fines, has his own jails and irons, metes out punishments and tortures, monopolizes commerce, and forbids the conduct without his permission of any business but that of the estate. The judges or officials who exercise on the hacienda the powers attached to public authority are usually the master's servants or tenants, his retainers, incapable of enforcing any law but the will of the master.

An astounding variety of devices are employed to exploit the peons or tenants, to turn a profit from their sweat and labor. They are compelled to work without pay even on days traditionally set aside for rest. They must accept rotten seeds or sick animals whose cost is charged to their miserable wages. . . . They must make all their purchases on the hacienda, using tokens or paper money that do not circulate elsewhere. At certain seasons of the year they are assigned articles of poor quality, whose price is set by the owner . . . , constituting a debt which they can never repay. They are forbidden to use pastures and woods, firewood and water, or even the wild fruit of the fields, save with the express permission of the master. In fine, they are subject to a completely unlimited and irresponsible power.

Q *What serious problems for Latin American politics were created by the concentration of land ownership in the hands of the elites? How did such large estates affect the structure of Latin American societies?*

Source: Excerpt from *Latin American Civilization* by Benjamin Keen, ed. (Boston: Houghton Mifflin, 1974), vol. 2, pp. 270–272.

"Paris" of South America) had 750,000 inhabitants by 1900 and 2 million by 1914—a fourth of Argentina's population.

20-1d Political Change in Latin America

Latin America also experienced a political transformation after 1870. Large landowners began to take a more direct interest in both national politics and governing. In Argentina and Chile, for example, landholding elites controlled the governments, and although they produced constitutions similar to those of the United States and European nations, they ensured they would maintain power by restricting voting rights.

20.3 Buenos Aires. Buenos Aires is called the "Paris" of South America for its use of neoclassical architecture influenced by European practices. The rapid urbanization of Buenos Aires is captured in this 1885 photograph of the Avenue Callao, which was designed to resemble the grand boulevards of Paris.

In some countries, large landowners supported dictators who would protect their interests. José de la Cruz Porfirio Díaz (hoh-SAY day lah KROOZ por-FEER-yoh DEE-ahs) (1830–1915), who ruled Mexico from 1876 to 1910, created a conservative, centralized government with the support of the army, foreign capitalists, large landowners, and the Catholic church. Nevertheless, there were forces for change in Mexico that led to revolution in 1910.

During Díaz's dictatorial regime, the real wages of the working class declined. Moreover, 95 percent of the rural population owned no land while around a thousand families owned almost all of Mexico. When a liberal landowner, Francisco Madero (frahn-SEES-koh muh-DERR-oh) (1873–1913), forced Díaz from power, he opened the door to a wider revolution. Madero's ineffectiveness triggered a demand for agrarian reform led by Emiliano Zapata (eh-mee-LYAH-noh zup-PAH-tuh) (1873–1919), who aroused the masses of landless peasants and began to seize the estates of the wealthy landholders. The ensuing revolution caused untold destruction to the Mexican economy. Finally, a new constitution in 1917 established a strong presidency, initiated land reform policies, established limits on foreign investors, and set an agenda for social welfare for workers.

By 1900, a new power had begun to wield its influence over Latin America. The United States, which had begun to emerge as a great world power, began to interfere in the affairs of its southern neighbors. As a result of the Spanish–American War (1898), Cuba became a U.S. protectorate, and Puerto Rico was annexed outright by the United States. American investments in Latin America soon followed; so did American resolve to protect these investments. Between 1898 and 1934, American military forces were sent to Cuba, Mexico, Guatemala, Honduras, Nicaragua, Panama, Colombia, Haiti, and the Dominican Republic to protect American interests. At the same time, the United States became the chief foreign investor in Latin America.

CHRONOLOGY	Latin America
Revolt in Mexico	1810
Bolívar and San Martín free most of South America	1810–1824
Augustín de Iturbide becomes emperor of Mexico	1821
Brazil gains independence from Portugal	1822
Monroe Doctrine	1823
Rule of Porfirio Díaz in Mexico	1876–1910
Mexican Revolution begins	1910

20-2 THE NORTH AMERICAN NEIGHBORS: THE UNITED STATES AND CANADA

Focus Questions: What role did nationalism and liberalism play in the United States and Canada between 1800 and 1870? What economic, social, and political trends were evident in the United States and Canada between 1870 and 1914?

While Latin America had been colonized by Spain and Portugal, the colonies established in North America were part of the British Empire and thus differed in various ways from their southern neighbors. Although they gained their freedom from the British at different times, both the United States and Canada emerged as independent and prosperous nations whose political systems owed much to British political thought. In the nineteenth century, both the United States and Canada faced difficult obstacles in achieving national unity.

20-2a The Growth of the United States

Ratified in 1789, the U.S. Constitution committed the United States to two of the major influences of the first half of the nineteenth century: liberalism and nationalism. Initially, this constitutional commitment to national unity was challenged by divisions over how much power the federal government and the individual states should have. A strong force for national unity came from the Supreme Court when John Marshall (1755–1835) was chief justice from 1801 to 1835. Marshall made the Supreme Court into an important national institution by asserting the right of the Court to overrule an act of Congress if the Court found it to be in violation of the Constitution. Under Marshall, the Supreme Court contributed further to establishing the supremacy of the national government by curbing the actions of state courts and legislatures.

The election of Andrew Jackson (1767–1845) as president in 1828 opened a new era in American politics, the era of mass democracy. The electorate was expanded by dropping property qualifications, and suffrage had been extended to almost all adult white males by the 1830s.

Slavery and the Coming of War By the mid-nineteenth century, however, the issue of slavery increasingly threatened American national unity. Both North and South had grown dramatically in population during the first half of the nineteenth century, but in different ways. The cotton economy and social structure of the South were based on the exploitation of enslaved black Africans and their descendants. Although the importation of new slaves had been barred in 1808, there were 4 million slaves in the South by 1860— four times the number sixty years earlier. The cotton economy depended on plantation-based slavery, and the South was determined to maintain its slaves. In the North, many people feared the spread of slavery into western territories. The issue first arose in the 1810s as new states were being created by the westward rush of settlers beyond the Mississippi. The free states of the North feared the prospect of a slave-state majority in the national government.

As polarization over the issue of slavery intensified, compromise became less feasible. When Abraham Lincoln, the man who had said in an 1858 speech in Illinois that "this government cannot endure permanently half slave and half free," was elected president in November 1860, the die was cast. As only the Republican Party's second presidential candidate, Lincoln carried only two of the 1,109 counties in the South; the Republican Party was not even on the ballot in ten Southern states. On December 20, 1860, a South Carolina convention voted to repeal the state's ratification of the U.S. Constitution. In February 1861, six more Southern states did the same, and a rival nation—the Confederate States of America— was formed. In April, fighting erupted between North and South.

The Civil War The American Civil War (1861–1865) was an extraordinarily bloody struggle, a foretaste of the type of total war to come in the twentieth century. More than 600,000 soldiers died, either in battle or from deadly infectious diseases spawned by filthy camp conditions. The northern—Union—forces enjoyed a formidable advantage in numbers of troops and material resources, but those assets were not decisive to Southerners. As they saw it, the Confederacy only had to defend the South from invasion, whereas the Union had to conquer the South. Southerners also believed that the dependence of manufacturers in the North and the European countries on Southern raw cotton would lead to antiwar sentiment in the North and support abroad for the South.

All of these Southern calculations meant little in the long run. Over a period of four years, the Union states mobilized their superior assets and gradually wore down the Confederate forces. As the war dragged on, it had the effect of radicalizing public opinion in the North. What began as a war to save the Union became a war against slavery. On January 1, 1863, Lincoln issued his Emancipation Proclamation, declaring most of the nation's slaves "forever free" (see Historical Voices, "Emancipation: Serfs and Slaves," in Chapter 19, p. 492). An increasingly effective Union blockade of the ports of the South, combined with a shortage of fighting men, made the Confederate cause desperate by the end of 1864. The final push of Union troops under General Ulysses S. Grant forced General Robert E. Lee's Confederate Army to surrender on April 9, 1865. Although problems lay ahead, the Union victory reunited the country and confirmed that the United States would thereafter again be "one nation, indivisible."

20-2b The Rise of the United States

Four years of bloody civil war had restored American national unity. The old South had been destroyed. One-fifth of its adult white male population had been killed, and 4 million black slaves had been freed. For awhile at least, a program of radical change in the South was attempted. The Thirteenth Amendment to the Constitution in 1865 formally abolished slavery, and the Fourteenth and Fifteenth Amendments extended citizenship to blacks and gave black men the right to vote. Radical Reconstruction in the early 1870s tried to create a new South based on the principle of the equality of black and white people, but the changes were soon mostly undone. Militia organizations such as the Ku Klux Klan used violence to discourage blacks from voting. After the war, white landowners made it difficult for newly freed slaves to purchase property, and a shortage of money led to a new system of sharecropping; a black family would work a specific piece of land in return for a share of the profit. The new sharecropping arrangement made blacks once again economically dependent on white landowners. New state laws made it nearly impossible for blacks to exercise their right to vote. By the end of the 1870s, supporters of white supremacy were back in power everywhere in the South.

Prosperity and Progressivism Between 1860 and 1914, the United States made the shift from an agrarian to a mighty industrial nation. American heavy industry stood unchallenged in 1900. In that year, the Carnegie Steel Company alone produced more steel than Great Britain's entire steel industry. Industrialization also led to urbanization. While 20 percent of Americans lived in cities in 1860, more than 40 percent did in 1900. Four-fifths of the population growth came from migration. Eight million to 10 million Americans moved from rural areas into the cities, and 14 million foreigners came from abroad.

The United States had become the world's richest nation and greatest industrial power. Yet serious questions remained about the quality of American life. In 1890, the richest 9 percent of Americans owned an incredible 71 percent of all wealth. Labor unrest over unsafe working conditions and a strict work discipline and periodic cycles of devastating unemployment led workers to organize. By the turn of the century, one national organization—the American Federation of Labor—had emerged as labor's dominant voice. Its lack of real power, however, was reflected in its membership figures. In 1900, it included only 8.4 percent of the American industrial labor force.

During the so-called Progressive Era after 1900, reform swept the United States. Efforts to improve living conditions in the cities included attempts to eliminate corrupt machine politics. At the state level, reforming governors sought to achieve clean government by introducing elements of direct democracy such as direct primaries for selecting nominees for public office. State governments also enacted economic and social legislation such as laws that governed hours, wages, and working conditions, especially for women and children.

State laws were ineffective in dealing with nationwide problems, however, and a Progressive movement soon developed at the national level. The Meat Inspection Act and Pure Food and Drug Act of 1906 provided for a limited degree of federal regulation of industrial practices. The presidency of Woodrow Wilson (1913–1921) witnessed the enactment of a graduated federal income tax and the establishment of the Federal Reserve System, which permitted the national government to play a role in important economic decisions formerly made by bankers. Like European nations, the United States was slowly adopting policies that broadened the functions of the state.

The United States as a World Power At the end of the nineteenth century, the United States began to expand abroad. The Samoan Islands in the Pacific became the first important American colony; the Hawaiian Islands were next. By 1887, American settlers had gained control of the sugar industry on the Hawaiian Islands. As more Americans settled in Hawai'i, they sought political power. The U.S. government sent Marines to "protect" American lives, and Hawai'i was annexed by the United States in 1898.

The defeat of Spain in the Spanish–American War in 1898 expanded the American Empire to include Cuba, Puerto Rico, Guam, and the Philippines. Although the Filipinos appealed for independence, the Americans refused to grant it. As President William McKinley said, the United States had a duty "to educate the Filipinos and uplift and Christianize them," a remarkable statement in view of the fact that Filipinos had mostly been Roman Catholics for centuries. It took three years and 60,000 troops to pacify the Philippines and establish U.S. control. By the beginning of the twentieth century, the United States had become another Western imperialist power.

20-2c The Making of Canada

North of the United States, the process of nation building was also making progress. Under the Treaty of Paris in 1763, Canada—or New France, as it was called—passed into the hands of the British. By 1800, most Canadians favored more autonomy, although the colonists disagreed on the form this autonomy should take. Upper Canada (now Ontario) was predominantly English speaking, whereas Lower Canada (now Quebec) was dominated by French Canadians. A dramatic increase in immigration to Canada from Great Britain (almost 1 million immigrants between 1815 and 1850) also fueled the desire for self-government.

In 1837, several Canadian groups rose in rebellion against British authority. Although the rebellions were crushed by the following year, the British government now began to seek ways to satisfy some Canadian demands. The U.S. Civil War proved to be a turning point. Fearful of American designs on Canada during the war, the British government finally capitulated to Canadian demands. In 1867, Parliament established the Dominion of Canada, with its own constitution. Canada now possessed a parliamentary system and

Map 20.2 Canada, 1914

ruled itself, although foreign affairs still remained under the control of the British government.

Canada faced problems of national unity between 1870 and 1914. At the beginning of 1870, the Dominion of Canada had only four provinces: Quebec, Ontario, Nova Scotia, and New Brunswick. With the addition of two more provinces in 1871—Manitoba and British Columbia—the Dominion now extended from the Atlantic Ocean to the Pacific. As the first prime minister, John Macdonald (1815–1891) moved to strengthen Canadian unity. He pushed for the construction of a transcontinental railroad, which was completed in 1885 and opened the western lands to industrial and commercial development. This also led to the incorporation of two more provinces—Alberta and Saskatchewan—into the Dominion of Canada in 1905.

Real unity was difficult to achieve, however, because of the distrust between the English-speaking majority and the French-speaking Canadians living primarily in Quebec. Wilfred Laurier (LOR-ee-ay), who became the first French Canadian prime minister in 1896, was able to reconcile Canada's two major groups and resolve the issue of separate schools for French Canadians. During Laurier's administration, industrialization boomed, especially the production of textiles, furniture, and railway equipment. Hundreds of thousands of immigrants, primarily from central and eastern Europe, also flowed into Canada. Many settled on lands in the west, thus helping populate Canada's vast territories.

CHRONOLOGY	The United States and Canada
The United States	
Election of Andrew Jackson	1828
Election of Abraham Lincoln and secession of South Carolina	1860
Civil War	1861–1865
Lincoln's Emancipation Proclamation	1863
Surrender of Robert E. Lee's Confederate Army	April 9, 1865
Spanish–American War	1898
Presidency of Woodrow Wilson	1913–1921
Canada	
Rebellions	1837–1838
Formation of the Dominion of Canada	1867
Transcontinental railroad	1885
Wilfred Laurier as prime minister	1896

20-3 THE EMERGENCE OF MASS SOCIETY

 Focus Question: What is meant by the term *mass society*, and what were its main characteristics?

Even as new states were developing in the Western Hemisphere in the nineteenth century, a new kind of society—a **mass society**—was emerging in Europe, especially in the second half of the nineteenth century, the result of rapid economic and social changes. For the lower classes, mass society brought voting rights, an improved standard of living, and access to education. At the same time, however, mass society also made possible the development of organizations that manipulated the populations of the **nation-states**. To understand this mass society, we need to examine some aspects of its structure.

20-3a The New Urban Environment

One of the most important consequences of industrialization and the population explosion of the nineteenth century was urbanization. In the course of the nineteenth century, more and more people came to live in cities. In 1800, city dwellers constituted 40 percent of the population in Britain, 25 percent in France and Germany, and only 10 percent in eastern Europe. By 1914, urban residents had increased to 80 percent of the population in Britain, 45 percent in France, 60 percent in Germany, and 30 percent in eastern Europe. The size of cities also expanded dramatically, especially in industrialized countries. Between 1800 and 1900, London's population grew from 960,000 to 6.5 million and Berlin's from 172,000 to 2.7 million.

Urban populations grew faster than the general population primarily because of the vast migration from rural areas to cities. But cities also grew faster in the second half of the nineteenth century because health and living conditions were improving as urban reformers and city officials used new technology to improve urban life. Following the reformers' advice, city governments set up boards of health to improve the quality of housing and instituted regulations requiring all new buildings to have running water and internal drainage systems.

Middle-class reformers also focused on the housing needs of the working class. Overcrowded, disease-ridden slums were seen as dangerous not only to physical health but also to the political and moral health of the entire nation. Early efforts to attack the housing problem emphasized the middle-class, liberal belief in the power of private enterprise. By the 1880s, as the number and size of cities continued to mushroom, governments concluded that private enterprise could not solve the housing crisis. In 1890, a British law empowered local town councils to construct cheap housing for the working classes. More and more, governments were stepping into areas of activity that they would not have touched earlier.

20-3b The Social Structure of Mass Society

At the top of European society stood a wealthy elite, constituting just 5 percent of the population but controlling between 30 percent and 40 percent of its wealth. In the course of the nineteenth century, landed aristocrats had joined with the most successful industrialists, bankers, and merchants (the wealthy upper middle class) to form a new elite. Marriage also united the two groups. Daughters of business tycoons gained titles, and aristocratic heirs gained new sources of cash. Members of this elite, whether aristocratic or middle class in background, assumed leadership roles in government bureaucracies and military hierarchies.

The middle classes included a variety of groups. Below the upper middle class was a group that included lawyers, doctors, and members of the civil service, as well as business managers, engineers, architects, accountants, and chemists benefiting from industrial expansion. Beneath this solid and comfortable middle group was a lower middle class of small shopkeepers, traders, manufacturers, and prosperous peasants.

Standing between the lower middle class and the lower classes were new groups of white-collar workers who were the product of the Second Industrial Revolution. They were the salespeople, bookkeepers, bank tellers, telephone operators, and secretaries. Though often paid little more than skilled laborers, these white-collar workers were committed to middle-class ideals of hard work, Christian morality, and propriety.

Below the middle classes on the social scale were the working classes, who constituted almost 80 percent of the European population. Many of them were landholding peasants, agricultural laborers, and sharecroppers, especially in eastern Europe. The urban working class included skilled artisans in such traditional trades as cabinetmaking, printing, and jewelry making, along with semiskilled laborers such as carpenters, bricklayers, and many factory workers. At the bottom of the urban working class stood the largest group of workers, the unskilled laborers. They included day laborers, who worked irregularly for extremely low wages, and large numbers of domestic servants, most of whom were women. Despite the new job opportunities, employment was unstable and wages were low, forcing many lower-class women to turn to prostitution to survive.

20-3c The Experiences of Women

In the nineteenth century, women remained legally inferior, economically dependent, and largely defined by family and household roles. Women struggled to change their status throughout the century.

Marriage and the Family Many women in the nineteenth century aspired to the ideal of femininity popularized

20.4 A Middle-class Family. Nineteenth-century middle-class moralists considered the family the fundamental pillar of a healthy society. The family was a crucial institution in middle-class life, and togetherness constituted one of the important ideals of the middle-class family. This painting by William P. Frith titled *Many Happy Returns of the Day* shows a family birthday celebration for a little girl in which grandparents, parents, and children are taking part. The servant at the left holds the presents for the little girl.

The family was the central institution of middle-class life. Men provided the family income while women focused on household and child care. The use of domestic servants in many middle-class homes was made possible by an abundant supply of cheap labor, and it reduced the amount of time middle-class women had to spend on household chores. At the same time, by reducing the number of children in the family, mothers could devote more time to child care and domestic leisure.

The middle-class family fostered an ideal of togetherness. The Victorians created the family Christmas with its Yule log, Christmas tree, songs, and exchange of gifts. In the United States, Fourth of July celebrations changed from drunken revels to family picnics by the 1850s.

Women in working-class families were more accustomed to hard work. Daughters in working-class families were expected to work until they married; even after marriage, they often did piecework at home to help support their families. For the children of the working classes, childhood was over by age nine or ten when they became apprentices or were employed at odd jobs.

Between 1890 and 1914, however, family patterns among the working class began to change. High-paying jobs in heavy industry and improvements in the standard of living made it possible for working-class families to depend on the income of husbands and the wages of grown children. By the early twentieth century, some working-class mothers could afford to stay at home, following the pattern of middle-class women.

by writers and poets. Alfred Lord Tennyson's poem *The Princess* expressed it well:

> *Man for the field and woman for the hearth:*
> *Man for the sword and for the needle she:*
> *Man with the head and woman with the heart:*
> *Man to command and woman to obey;*
> *All else confusion.*

This traditional characterization of the sexes, based on socially defined gender roles, was elevated to the status of universal male and female attributes in the nineteenth century. As the chief family wage earners, men worked outside the home for pay, while women were left with the care of the family, for which they were paid nothing. For most of the century, marriage was viewed as the only honorable career available to most women.

The most significant development in the modern family was the decline in the number of offspring born to the average woman. Although some historians attribute the decline to more widespread use of coitus interruptus, or male withdrawal before ejaculation, others have emphasized female control of family size through abortion and even infanticide or abandonment. That a change in attitude occurred was apparent in the development of a movement to increase awareness of birth control methods. Europe's first birth control clinic opened in Amsterdam in 1882.

The Movement for Women's Rights Modern European feminism, or the movement for women's rights, had its beginnings during the French Revolution, when some women advocated equality for women based on the doctrine of natural rights. In the 1830s, many women in the United States and Europe worked together in several reform movements and argued for the right of women to divorce and own property. These early efforts were not overly successful; women did not gain the right to their own property until 1870 in Britain, 1900 in Germany, and 1907 in France.

Divorce and property rights were only a beginning for the women's movement, however. Some middle- and upper-middle-class women gained access to higher education, and others sought entry into occupations dominated by men. The first to fall was teaching. As medical training was largely closed to women, they sought alternatives in the development of nursing. Nursing pioneers included British nurse Florence Nightingale, whose efforts during the Crimean War (1854–1856), along with those of Clara Barton in the American Civil War (1861–1865), transformed nursing into a profession of trained, middle-class "women in white."

By the 1840s and 1850s, the movement for women's rights had entered the political arena with the call for equal political rights. Many feminists believed that the right to vote was the key to all other reforms to improve the position of women. **Suffragists** had one basic aim: the right of women to full citizenship in the nation-state.

The British women's movement was the most vocal and active in Europe. In 1903, Emmeline Pankhurst (PANK-hurst) (1858–1928) and her daughters, Christabel and Sylvia, founded the Women's Social and Political Union, which enrolled mostly middle- and upper-class women. The members of Pankhurst's organization realized the value of the media and staged unusual publicity stunts to call attention to their demands. Derisively labeled "suffragettes" by male politicians, they pelted government officials with eggs, chained themselves to lampposts, smashed the windows of department stores on fashionable shopping streets, burned railroad cars, and went on hunger strikes in jail (see Film & History, "*Suffragette*").

Before World War I, the demands for women's rights were being heard throughout Europe and the United States, although only in Norway and some American states did women receive the right to vote before 1914. It would take the dramatic upheaval of World War I before male-dominated governments capitulated on this basic issue. At the same time, at the turn of the twentieth century, many "new women" became prominent. These women rejected traditional feminine roles (see Opposing Viewpoints, "Advice to Women: Two Views," p. 512) and sought new freedom outside the household and new roles other than those of wives and mothers.

20-3d Education in an Age of Mass Society

Education in the early nineteenth century was primarily for the elite or the wealthier middle class, but between 1870 and 1914 most Western governments began to offer at least primary education to both boys and girls between ages six and twelve. States also assumed responsibility for

⊡ FILM & HISTORY

Suffragette

Watch *Suffragette* (2015), a British historical period film about the suffragist movement in Britain. The film revolves around the activities of the fictitious character Maud Watts, who slowly becomes involved in suffragette activities, especially after hearing a speech by Emmeline Pankhurst, the leader of the suffragist movement, who argues that it is "deeds, not words" that will get women the right to vote. Maud becomes increasingly radicalized as a result of violent police activity against the women.

Q *How accurate is the film's presentation of the activities of the suffragettes? What role does police violence play in the movement for women's rights?*

Focus Features/Courtesy Everett Collection

MINDTAP See full-length Film & History feature in MindTap.
From Cengage

better training of teachers by establishing teacher-training schools. By the beginning of the twentieth century, many European states, especially in northern and western Europe, were providing state-financed primary schools, salaried and trained teachers, and free, compulsory elementary education.

Why did Western nations make this commitment to **mass education**? One reason was industrialization. The new firms of the Second Industrial Revolution demanded skilled labor. Both boys and girls with an elementary education had new possibilities of jobs beyond their villages or small towns, including white-collar jobs

Advice to Women: Two Views

Family & Society **INDUSTRIALIZATION HAD A STRONG IMPACT** on middle-class women as strict gender-based social roles became the norm. Men worked outside the home to support the family, while women provided for the needs of their children and husband at home. In the first selection, *Woman in Her Social and Domestic Character* (1842), Elizabeth Poole Sanford gives advice to middle-class women on their proper role and behavior.

Although a majority of women probably followed the nineteenth-century middle-class ideal, an increasing number of women fought for women's rights. The second selection is taken from the third act of Henrik Ibsen's 1879 play *A Doll's House,* in which the character Nora Helmer declares her independence from her husband's control.

Elizabeth Poole Sanford, *Woman in Her Social and Domestic Character*

The changes wrought by Time are many. . . .

It is thus that the sentiment for woman has undergone a change. The romantic passion which once almost deified her is on the decline; and it is by intrinsic qualities that she must now inspire respect. . . . But if there is less of enthusiasm entertained for her, the sentiment is more rational, and, perhaps, equally sincere; for it is in relation to happiness that she is chiefly appreciated.

And in this respect it is, we must confess, that she is most useful and most important. Domestic life is the chief source of her influence; and the greatest debt society can owe to her is domestic comfort. . . . A woman may make a man's home delightful, and may thus increase his motives for virtuous exertion. She may refine and tranquilize his mind—may turn away his anger or allay his grief. Her smile may be the happy influence to gladden his heart, and to disperse the cloud that gathers on his brow. And in proportion to her endeavors to make those around her happy, she will be esteemed and loved.

Nothing is so likely to conciliate the affections of the other sex as a feeling that woman looks to them for support and guidance. In proportion as men are themselves superior, they are accessible to this appeal. On the contrary, they never feel interested in one who seems disposed rather to offer than to ask assistance. There is, indeed, something unfeminine in independence. It is contrary to nature, and therefore it offends. . . . A really sensible woman feels her dependence. She does what she can; but she is conscious of inferiority, and therefore grateful for support. She knows that she is the weaker vessel, and that as such she should receive honor. In this view, her weakness is an attraction, not a blemish.

Henrik Ibsen, *A Doll's House*

NORA: Yes, it's true, Torvald. When I was living at home with Father, he told me his opinions and mine were the same. If I had different opinions, I said nothing about them, because he would not have liked it. He used to call me his doll-child and played with me as I played with my dolls. Then I came to live in your house.

HELMER: What a way to speak of our marriage!

NORA *(Undisturbed):* I mean that I passed from Father's hands into yours. You arranged everything to your taste and I got the same tastes as you; or pretended to—I don't know which—both, perhaps; sometimes one, sometimes the other. When I look back on it now, I seem to have been living here like a beggar, on handouts. I lived by performing tricks for you, Torvald. . . . I must stand quite alone if I am ever to know myself and my surroundings; so I cannot stay with you.

HELMER: You are mad! I shall not allow it! I forbid it!

NORA: It's no use your forbidding me anything now. I shall take with me only what belongs to me; from you I will accept nothing, either now or later. . . .

HELMER: Forsake your home, your husband, your children! And you don't consider what the world will say.

NORA: I can't pay attention to that. I only know that I must do it.

HELMER: This is monstrous! Can you forsake your holiest duties?

NORA: What do you consider my holiest duties?

HELMER: Need I tell you that? Your duties to your husband and children.

NORA: I have other duties equally sacred.

HELMER: Impossible! What do you mean?

NORA: My duties toward myself.

HELMER: Before all else you are a wife and a mother.

NORA: That I no longer believe. Before all else I believe I am a human being just as much as you are—or at least that I should try to become one. I know that most people agree with you, Torvald, and that they say so in books. But I can no longer be satisfied with what most people say and what is in books. I must think things out for myself and try to get clear about them.

Q *According to Elizabeth Sanford, what is the proper role of women? What forces in nineteenth-century European society merged to shape Sanford's understanding of "proper" gender roles? In Ibsen's play, what challenges does Nora Helmer make to Sanford's view of the proper role and behavior of wives? Why is her husband so shocked? Why did Ibsen title this play A Doll's House?*

Sources: From Elizabeth Poole Sanford, *Woman in Her Social and Domestic Character* (Boston: Otis, Broaders & Co., 1842), pp. 5–7,15–16. From *Henrik Ibsen, A Doll's House*, Act III, 1879, as printed in *Roots of Western Civilization* by Wesley D. Camp, John Wiley & Sons, 1983.

in railways and subways, post offices, banking and shipping firms, teaching, and nursing. Mass education furnished the trained workers industrialists needed. For most students, elementary education led to apprenticeship and jobs.

The chief motive for mass education, however, was political. The expansion of suffrage created the need for a more educated electorate. In parts of Europe where the Catholic Church remained in control of education, implementing a mass education system reduced the influence of the church over the electorate. Even more important, however, mass compulsory education instilled patriotism and nationalized the masses, providing an opportunity for even greater national integration. As people lost their ties to local regions and even to religion, nationalism supplied a new faith (see Comparative Essay, "The Rise of Nationalism," p. 514).

Compulsory elementary education created a demand for teachers, and most of them were women. Many men viewed teaching children as an extension of women's "natural role" as nurturers of children. Moreover, females were paid lower salaries, in itself a considerable incentive for governments to encourage the establishment of teacher-training institutes for women. The first female colleges were really teacher-training schools. Not until the beginning of the twentieth century were women permitted to enter male-dominated universities.

20-3e Leisure in an Age of Mass Society

With the Industrial Revolution came new forms of leisure. Work and leisure became opposites as leisure came to be viewed as what people do for fun after work. The new leisure hours created by the industrial system—evening hours after work, weekends, and eventually a week or two in the summer—largely determined the contours of the new **mass leisure**.

New technology created novel experiences for leisure such as the Ferris wheel at amusement parks, and the subways and streetcars of the 1880s meant that even the working classes were no longer dependent on neighborhood facilities and could make their way to athletic games, amusement parks, and dance halls. Railroads could take people to the beaches on weekends.

By the late nineteenth century, team sports had also developed into another important form of mass leisure. Unlike old rural games, which were spontaneous and often chaotic activities, new sports were strictly organized with sets of rules and officials to enforce them. These rules were the products of organized athletic groups such as the English Football Association (1863) and the American Bowling Congress (1895). The development of urban transportation systems made possible the construction of stadiums where thousands could attend, making mass spectator sports into a big business. Attendance at the British soccer cup final increased from 2,000 in 1872 to 100,000 in 1901.

20-4 CULTURAL LIFE: ROMANTICISM AND REALISM IN THE WESTERN WORLD

 Focus Question: What were the main characteristics of Romanticism and realism?

At the end of the eighteenth century, a new intellectual movement known as **Romanticism** emerged to challenge the ideas of the Enlightenment. The Enlightenment stressed reason as the chief means for discovering truth. Although the Romantics by no means disparaged reason, they tried to balance its use by stressing the importance of feeling, emotion, and imagination as sources of knowing.

The Rise of Nationalism

Politics & Government Like the Industrial Revolution, the concept of nationalism originated in eighteenth-century Europe, where it was the product of a variety of factors, including the spread of printing and the replacement of Latin with vernacular languages, the secularization of the age, and the experience of the French revolutionary and Napoleonic eras. The French were the first to show what a nation in arms could accomplish, but peoples conquered by Napoleon soon created their own national armies. At the beginning of the nineteenth century, peoples who had previously focused their identity on a locality or a region, on loyalty to a monarch or to a particular religious faith, now shifted their political allegiance to the idea of a nation, based on ethnic, linguistic, or cultural factors. This idea had explosive consequences: by 1920, the world's three largest multi-ethnic states—imperial Russia, Austria–Hungary, and the Ottoman Empire—had all given way to many individual nation-states.

The idea of establishing political boundaries on the basis of ethnicity, language, or culture had a broad appeal throughout Western civilization, but it also had unintended consequences. Although the concept provided the basis for a new sense of community that was tied to liberal thought in the first half of the nineteenth century, it also gave birth to ethnic tensions and hatred in the second half of the century that resulted in bitter disputes and contributed to the competition between nation-states that eventually erupted into world war. Following the lead of the radical government in Paris during the French Revolution, other governments took full advantage of the rise of a strong national consciousness and transformed war into a demonstration of national honor and commitment. Universal schooling enabled states to arouse patriotic enthusiasm and create national unity. Most soldiers who joyfully went to war in 1914 were convinced that their nation's cause was just.

Although the concept of nationalism was initially the product of conditions in modern Europe, it soon spread to other parts of the world. A few societies such as Vietnam had already developed a strong sense of national identity, but most of the peoples in Asia and Africa lived in multiethnic and multireligious communities and were not yet ripe for the spirit of nationalism. As we shall see, the first attempts to resist European colonial rule were often based on religious or ethnic identity rather than on the concept of denied nationhood. But the imperialist powers, which at first benefited from the lack of political cohesion among their colonial subjects, eventually reaped what they had sowed. As the colonial peoples became familiar with Western concepts of democracy and self-determination, they too began to manifest a sense of common purpose that helped knit together the different elements in their societies to oppose colonial regimes and create the conditions for the emergence of future nations. For good or ill, the concept of nationalism had now achieved global proportions.

The Art Archive/Museo Civico, Modigliana, Italy/Collection Dagli Orti

20.5 Giuseppe Garibaldi. Garibaldi was a dedicated patriot and an outstanding example of the Italian nationalism that led to the unification of Italy by 1870.

Q *What is nationalism? How did it arise, and what impact did it have on the history of the nineteenth and twentieth centuries?*

20-4a The Characteristics of Romanticism

Many Romantics had a passionate interest in the past. They revived medieval Gothic architecture and left European country sides adorned with pseudomedieval castles and cities bedecked with grandiose neo-Gothic cathedrals, city halls, and parliamentary buildings. Literature, too, reflected this historical consciousness. The novels of Walter Scott (1771–1832) became European best sellers in the first half of the nineteenth century. In *Ivanhoe*, Scott sought to evoke the clash between Saxon and Norman knights in medieval England; it became one of his most popular works.

Many Romantics also had a deep attraction to the exotic and unfamiliar. In an exaggerated form, this preoccupation gave rise to **Gothic literature**. Chilling examples include Mary Shelley's *Frankenstein* and Edgar Allan Poe's short stories of horror. Some Romantics even tried to bring the unusual into their own lives by experimenting with cocaine, opium, and hashish to achieve drug-induced altered states of consciousness.

To the Romantics, poetry was the direct expression of the soul and therefore ranked above all other literary forms. Romantic poetry gave full expression to one of the most important characteristics of Romanticism: love of nature, which was especially evident in the poetry of William Wordsworth (1770–1850). His experience of nature was almost mystical as he claimed to receive "authentic tidings of invisible things":

> One impulse from a vernal wood
> May teach you more of man,
> Of Moral Evil and of good,
> Than all the sages can.[5]

Romantics believed that nature served as a mirror into which humans could look to learn about themselves.

Like the literary arts, the visual arts were also deeply affected by Romanticism. To Romantic artists, all artistic expression was a reflection of the artist's inner feelings; a painting should mirror the artist's vision of the world and be the instrument of his own imagination.

The early life experiences of Caspar David Friedrich (kass-PAR dah-VEET FREED-rikh) (1774–1840) left him with a lifelong preoccupation with God and nature. Friedrich painted landscapes with an interest that transcended the mere presentation of natural details. His portrayals of mountains shrouded in mist, gnarled trees bathed in moonlight, and the stark ruins of monasteries surrounded by withered trees all conveyed a feeling of mystery and mysticism. For Friedrich, nature was a manifestation of divine life, as is evident in *The Wanderer Above the Sea of Fog*. To Friedrich, the artistic process depended on the use of an unrestricted

20.6 Caspar David Friedrich, *The Wanderer Above the Sea of Fog.* German artist Caspar David Friedrich sought to express in painting his own mystical view of nature. "The divine is everywhere," he once wrote, "even in a grain of sand." In this painting, a solitary wanderer is shown from the back gazing at mountains covered in fog. Overwhelmed by the all-pervasive presence of nature, the figure expresses the human longing for infinity.

imagination that could only be achieved through inner vision.

20-4b A New Age of Science

With the Industrial Revolution came a renewed interest in basic scientific research. By the 1830s, new scientific discoveries led to many practical benefits as science had an ever-greater impact on European life.

In biology, Frenchman Louis Pasteur (LWEE pass-TOOR) (1822–1895) developed the germ theory of disease, which had enormous practical applications in the development of modern scientific medical practices. In chemistry in the 1860s, Russian Dmitri Mendeleev (di-MEE-tree men-duh-LAY-ef) (1834–1907) classified all the material elements then known on the basis of their atomic weights and provided the systematic foundation for the periodic law.

The popularity of scientific and technological achievement produced a widespread acceptance of the scientific method as the only path to objective truth and objective reality. This in turn undermined the faith of many people in religious revelation. It is no accident that the nineteenth century was an age of increasing **secularization**, evident in the belief that truth was to be found in the concrete material existence of human beings. No one did more to create a picture of humans as material beings that were simply part of the natural world than Charles Darwin.

In 1859, Charles Darwin (1809–1882) published *On the Origin of Species by Means of Natural Selection*. The basic idea of this book was that all plants and animals had evolved over a long period of time from earlier and simpler forms of life, a principle known as **organic evolution**. In every species, he argued, "many more individuals of each species are born than can possibly survive." This results in a "struggle for existence." Darwin believed that some organisms were more adaptable to the environment than others, a process he called **natural selection**. Those that were naturally selected for survival ("survival of the fit") reproduced and thrived. The unfit did not survive and their lines became extinct. The fit who survived passed on small variations that enhanced their survival until, from Darwin's point of view, a new and separate species emerged.

Oskar Reinhart Collection, Winterthur, Switzerland/The Bridgeman Art Library

20.7 Gustave Courbet, *The Stonebreakers.* As largely developed by French painters, realism aimed at a lifelike portrayal of the daily activities of ordinary people. Gustave Courbet was the most famous of the realist artists. As is evident in *The Stonebreakers,* he sought to portray things as they really appear. He shows an old road builder and his young assistant in their tattered clothes, engrossed in their dreary work of breaking stones to construct a road.

20-4c Realism in Literature and Art

The name **realism** was first applied in 1850 to describe a new style of painting and soon spread to literature. The literary realists of the mid-nineteenth century rejected Romanticism. They wanted to deal with ordinary characters from actual life rather than Romantic heroes in exotic settings. They also sought to avoid emotional language by using close observation and precise description, an approach that led them to write novels rather than poems.

The leading novelist of the 1850s and 1860s, Frenchman Gustave Flaubert (goo-STAHV floh-BAYR) (1821–1880), perfected the realist novel. His *Madame Bovary* (1857) was a straightforward description of barren and sordid provincial life in France (see Historical Voices, "Flaubert and an Image of Bourgeois Marriage," p. 517). Emma Bovary is trapped in a marriage to a drab provincial doctor. Impelled by the images of romantic love she has read about in novels, she seeks the same thing for herself in adulterous love affairs but is ultimately driven to suicide.

In art, too, realism became dominant after 1850. Gustave Courbet (goo-STAHV koor-BAY) (1819–1877), the

most famous visual artist of the realist school, reveled in realistic portrayals of everyday life. His subjects were factory workers, peasants, and the wives of saloon keepers. "I have never seen either angels or goddesses, so I am not interested in painting them," he exclaimed. One of his famous works, *The Stonebreakers,* painted in 1849, shows two road workers engaged in the deadening work of breaking stones to build a road. Courbet did not romanticize the laborers' work; instead he used browns and grays to convey the dreariness of the task. This representation of human misery was a scandal to those who objected to Courbet's "cult of ugliness."

20-5 TOWARD THE MODERN CONSCIOUSNESS: INTELLECTUAL AND CULTURAL DEVELOPMENTS

Q **Focus Question:** What intellectual and cultural developments in the late nineteenth and early twentieth centuries "opened the way to a modern consciousness," and how did this consciousness differ from earlier worldviews?

Flaubert and an Image of Bourgeois Marriage

Art & Ideas IN *MADAME BOVARY*, Gustave Flaubert portrays the tragic life of Emma Rouault, a farm girl whose hopes of escape from provincial life are dashed after she marries a doctor, Charles Bovary. After her initial attempts to find happiness in her domestic life, Emma seeks refuge in affairs and extravagant shopping. In this excerpt, Emma expresses her restlessness and growing boredom with her new husband. Flaubert's detailed descriptions of everyday life make *Madame Bovary* one of the seminal works of realism.

Gustave Flaubert, *Madame Bovary*

Charles's conversation was as flat as a sidewalk, with everyone's ideas walking through it in ordinary dress, arousing neither emotion, nor laughter, nor dreams. He had never been curious, he said, the whole time he was living in Rouen to go see a touring company of Paris actors at the theater. He couldn't swim, or fence, or shoot, and once he couldn't even explain to Emma a term about horseback riding she had come across in a novel.

But a man should know everything, shouldn't he? Excel in many activities, initiate you into the excitements of passion, into life's refinements, into all its mysteries? Yet this man taught nothing, knew nothing, hoped for nothing. He thought she was happy, and she was angry at him for this placid stolidity, for this leaden serenity, for the very happiness she gave to him.

Sometimes she would draw. Charles was always happy watching her lean over her drawing board. . . . As for the piano, the faster her fingers flew over it, the more he marveled. She struck the keys with aplomb and ran from one end of the keyboard to the other without a stop. . . .

On the other hand, Emma did know how to run the house. She sent patients statements of their visits in well-written letters that didn't look like bills. When some neighbor came to dine on Sundays, she managed to offer some tasty dish. . . . All this reflected favorably on Bovary.

Charles ended up thinking all the more highly of himself for possessing such a wife. In the living room he pointed with pride to her two small pencil sketches that he had mounted in very large frames and hung against the wallpaper on long green cords.

He would come home late, at ten o'clock, sometimes at midnight. Then he would want something to eat and Emma would serve him because the maid was asleep. . . . He would report on all the people he had met one after the other, ... and, content with himself, would eat the remainder of the stew, peel his cheese, bite into an apple, empty the decanter, then go to sleep, lying on his back and snoring. . . .

And yet, in line with the theories she admired, she wanted to give herself up to love. In the moonlight of the garden she would recite all the passionate poetry she knew by heart and would sing melancholy adagios to him with sighs, but she found herself as calm afterward as before and Charles didn't appear more amorous or moved because of it.

After she had several times struck the flint on her heart without eliciting a single spark,... she convinced herself without difficulty that Charles's passion no longer offered anything extravagant. His effusions had become routine; he embraced her at certain hours. It was one habit among others, like the established custom of eating dessert after the monotony of dinner.

Q *What does this passage reveal about bourgeois life in France during the mid-nineteenth century? What does the passage tell us about the roles of women during this time? How did Charles fail to live up to Emma's expectations of romantic love?*

Source: From Gustave Flaubert, *Madame Bovary*, trans. by M. Marmur (New York: Penguin Press, 1964), 39–43.

Before 1914, many people in the Western world continued to believe in the values and ideals that had been generated by the Scientific Revolution and the Enlightenment. The idea that human beings could improve themselves and achieve a better society seemed to be proved by a rising standard of living, urban comforts, and mass education. It was easy to think that the human mind could make sense of the universe. Between 1870 and 1914, though, radically new ideas challenged these optimistic views and opened the way to a modern consciousness.

20-5a A New Physics

Science was one of the chief pillars underlying the optimistic and rationalistic view of the world that many Westerners shared in the nineteenth century. Supposedly based on hard facts and cold reason, science offered a certainty of belief in the orderliness of nature. The new physics dramatically altered that perspective.

Throughout much of the nineteenth century, Westerners adhered to the mechanical conception of the universe postulated by the classic physics of Isaac Newton.

In this perspective, the universe was viewed as a giant machine in which time, space, and matter were objective realities that existed independently of the observers. Matter was thought to be composed of indivisible and solid material bodies called *atoms*.

Albert Einstein (YN-styn) (1879–1955), a German-born patent officer working in Switzerland, questioned this view of the universe. In 1905, Einstein published his special theory of relativity, which stated that space and time are not absolute but relative to the observer. Neither space nor time had an existence independent of human experience. As Einstein later explained simply to a journalist: "It was formerly believed that if all material things disappeared out of the universe, time and space would be left. According to the **relativity theory**, however, time and space disappear together with the things."[6] Einstein concluded that matter was nothing but another form of energy. His epochal formula $E = mc^2$—stating that each particle of matter is equivalent to its mass times the square of the velocity of light—was the key theory explaining the vast energies contained within the atom. It led to the atomic age.

20-5b Sigmund Freud and the Emergence of Psychoanalysis

At the turn of the twentieth century, Viennese physician Sigmund Freud (SIG-mund or ZIG-munt FROID) (1856–1939) advanced a series of theories that undermined optimism about the rational nature of the human mind. Freud's thought, like the new physics, added to the uncertainties of the age. His major ideas were published in 1900 in *The Interpretation of Dreams*.

According to Freud, human behavior was strongly determined by the unconscious, by past experiences and internal forces of which people were largely oblivious. For Freud, human behavior was no longer truly rational but rather instinctive or irrational. He argued that painful and unsettling experiences were blotted from conscious awareness but still continued to influence behavior because they had become part of the unconscious (see Historical Voices, "Freud and the Concept of Repression," p. 519). Repression of these thoughts began in childhood. Freud devised a method known as **psychoanalysis** through which a psychotherapist and patient could probe deeply into the memory and retrace the chain of repression all the way back to its childhood origins. When the conscious mind was made aware of the unconscious and its repressed contents, the patient's psychic conflict was resolved.

Map 20.3 Palestine in 1900

20-5c The Impact of Darwin: Social Darwinism and Racism

In the second half of the nineteenth century, scientific theories were sometimes wrongly applied to achieve other ends. For example, Charles Darwin's principle of organic evolution was applied to the social order as **Social Darwinism**, the belief that societies were organisms that evolved through time from a struggle with their environment. Such ideas were used in a radical way by rabid nationalists and racists. In their pursuit of national greatness, extreme nationalists insisted that nations, too, were engaged in a "struggle for existence" in which only the fittest survived.

Anti-Semitism Anti-Semitism had a long history in European civilization, but as a result of the ideals of the Enlightenment and the French Revolution in the nineteenth century, Jews were increasingly granted legal equality in many European countries. Many Jews now left the ghetto and became assimilated into the cultures around them. Many became successful as bankers, lawyers, scientists, scholars, journalists, and stage performers.

These achievements represent only one side of the picture, however. In Germany and Austria during the 1880s and 1890s, conservatives founded right-wing anti-Jewish parties that used anti-Semitism to win the votes of traditional lower-middle-class groups who felt threatened by the new economic forces of the times. The worst treatment of Jews at the turn of the century, however, occurred in eastern Europe, where 72 percent of the world's Jewish population lived. Russian Jews were forced to live in certain regions of the country, and persecutions and pogroms were widespread. Hundreds of thousands of Jews decided to emigrate to escape the persecution.

Many Jews went to the United States, although some moved to Palestine, which soon became the focus of a Jewish nationalist movement called **Zionism**. For many Jews, Palestine—the land of ancient Israel—had long been the land of their dreams. Settlement in Palestine was difficult, however, because it was then part of the Ottoman Empire, which was opposed to Jewish immigration. Despite the problems, the First Zionist Congress, which met in Switzerland in 1897, proclaimed as its aim the creation of a "home in Palestine secured by public law" for the Jewish people. In 1900, around a thousand Jews migrated to Palestine, and the trickle rose to some 3,000 a year between 1904 and 1914, keeping the Zionist dream alive.

Freud and the Concept of Repression

Art & Ideas SIGMUND FREUD'S PSYCHOANALYTICAL THEORIES resulted from his attempt to understand the world of the unconscious. This excerpt is taken from one of five lectures given in 1909 in which Freud described how he arrived at his theory of the role of repression. Although Freud valued science and reason, his theories of the unconscious produced a new image of the human being as governed less by reason than by irrational forces.

Sigmund Freud, *The Origin and Development of Psychoanalysis*

But I did not give [the technique of encouraging patients to reveal forgotten experiences] up without drawing definite conclusions from the data which I had gained. I had substantiated the fact that the forgotten memories were not lost.

They were in the possession of the patient, ready to emerge and form associations with his other mental content, but hindered from becoming conscious, and forced to remain in the unconscious by some sort of a force. The existence of this force could be assumed with certainty, for in attempting to drag up the unconscious memories into the consciousness of the patient, in opposition to this force, one got the sensation of his own personal effort striving to overcome it. One could get an idea of this force, which maintained the pathological situation, from the resistance of the patient.

It is on this idea of resistance that I based my theory of the psychic processes of hystericals. It had been found that in order to cure the patient it was necessary that this force should be overcome. Now with the mechanism of the cure as a starting point, quite a definite theory could be constructed. These same forces, which in the present situation as resistances opposed the emergence of the forgotten ideas into consciousness, must themselves have caused the forgetting, and repressed from consciousness the pathogenic experiences. I called this hypothetical process "repression" and considered that it was proved by the undeniable existence of resistance.

But now the question arose: what were those forces, and what were the conditions of this repression, in which we were now able to recognize the pathogenic mechanism of hysteria? A comparative study of the pathogenic situations, which the cathartic treatment has made possible, allows us to answer this question. In all those experiences, it had happened that a wish had been aroused, which was in sharp opposition to the other desires of the individual, and was not capable of being reconciled with the ethical, aesthetic and personal pretensions of the patient's personality. There had been a short conflict, and the end of this inner struggle was the repression of the idea that presented itself to consciousness as the bearer of this irreconcilable wish. This was, then, repressed from consciousness and forgotten. The incompatibility of the idea in question with the "ego" of the patient was the motive of the repression, the ethical and other pretensions of the individual were the repressing forces. The presence of the incompatible wish, or the duration of the conflict, had given rise to a high degree of mental pain; this pain was avoided by the repression. This latter process is evidently in such a case a device for the protection of the personality.

Q *According to Freud, how did he discover the existence of repression? What function does repression perform?*

Source: From *The American Journal of Psychology*, Vol. 21, No. 2 (April 1910), pp. 192–199.

20-5d The Culture of Modernity

The revolution in physics and psychology was paralleled by a revolution in literature and the arts. Before 1914, writers and artists were rebelling against the traditional literary and artistic styles that had dominated European cultural life since the Renaissance. The changes they produced have since been called **modernism**.

At the beginning of the twentieth century, a group of writers known as the *symbolists* caused a literary revolution. Primarily interested in writing poetry and strongly influenced by the ideas of Freud, the symbolists believed that an objective knowledge of the world was impossible. The external world was not real but only a collection of symbols that reflected the true reality of the individual human mind.

The period from 1870 to 1914 was one of the most fertile in the history of art. By the late nineteenth century, artists were seeking new forms of expression.

Experience an interactive version of this period in ❖ MINDTAP

Painting, West and East

Art & Ideas **BERTHE MORISOT**, the first female painter to join the impressionists, developed her own unique style. Her gentle colors and strong use of pastels are especially evident in *Young Girl by the Window* (Image 20.8a). The French impressionist style also spread abroad. One of the most outstanding Japanese artists of the time was Kuroda Seiki (koor-OH-duh SAY-kee) (1866–1924), who returned from nine years in Paris to open a Western-style school of painting in Tokyo. Image 20.8b is his *Under the Trees*, an excellent example of the fusion of contemporary French impressionist painting with the Japanese tradition of courtesan prints.

Q *What differences and similarities do you notice in these two paintings?*

20.8a

Erich Lessing/Art Resource, NY

20.8b

Christie's Images Ltd./SuperStock

The preamble to modern painting can be found in **impressionism**, a movement that originated in France in the 1870s when a group of artists rejected the studios and museums and went out into the countryside to paint nature directly.

One important impressionist artist was American-born painter Mary Cassatt (1844–1926). Cassatt studied at the Pennsylvania Academy of the Fine Arts before moving to Paris to renew her studies. Her time in Paris was interrupted by the Franco–Prussian War. Following her return to Paris in 1871, Cassatt began exhibiting with the impressionists. In 1890, she attended an exhibit of Japanese prints at the École des Beaux Arts and created a series of ten works that capture the "Japonisme" style (see Comparative Illustration, "Painting, West and East"). Near the end of her life, she lamented the refusal of men to take her work seriously: "I don't think there has ever been a man who treated a woman as an equal, and that's all I would have asked, for I know I'm worth as much as they."[7]

In the 1880s, a new movement known as **postimpressionism** arose in France and soon spread to other European countries. Perhaps the most famous postimpressionist was the tortured and tragic figure Vincent

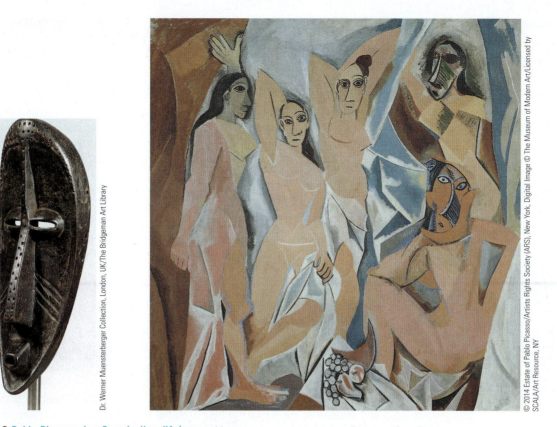

20.9 Pablo Picasso, *Les Demoiselles d'Avignon* Pablo Picasso, a major pioneer and activist of modern art, experimented with a remarkable variety of modern styles. *Les Demoiselles d'Avignon* (1907) was the first great example of Cubism, which one art historian has called "the first style of [the twentieth] century to break radically with the past." Geometrical shapes replace traditional forms, forcing the viewer to re-create reality in his or her own mind. The head next to the painting reflects Picasso's attraction to aspects of African art, as is evident from the mask shown at the left.

van Gogh (van GOH or vahn GOK) (1853–1890). For van Gogh, art was a spiritual experience. He was especially interested in color and believed it could act as its own form of language.

By the beginning of the twentieth century, the belief that the task of art was to represent "reality" had lost much of its meaning. The growth of photography gave artists one reason to reject realism. Invented in the 1830s, photography became popular and widespread after 1888 when George Eastman created the first Kodak camera for the mass market. What was the point of an artist doing what a camera did better? Unlike the camera, which could only mirror reality, artists could create reality.

By 1905, one of the most important figures in modern art was just beginning his career. Pablo Picasso (PAHB-loh pi-KAH-soh) (1881–1973) was from Spain but settled in Paris in 1904. Picasso was extremely flexible and painted in a remarkable variety of styles. He was instrumental in the development of a new style called **cubism** that used

geometrical designs as visual stimuli to re-create reality in the viewer's mind.

Pablo Picasso, a major pioneer and activist of modern art, experimented with a remarkable variety of modern styles. *Les Demoiselles d'Avignon* (lay dem-wah-ZEL dah-vee-NYONH) was the first great example of cubism, which one art historian called "the first style of this [twentieth] century to break radically with the past." Geometrical shapes replace traditional forms, forcing viewers to re-create reality in their own minds. The head at the upper right of the painting reflects Picasso's attraction to aspects of African art, as is evident from the mask included at the left.

The modern artist's flight from "visual reality" reached a high point in 1910 with the beginning of **abstract painting**. A Russian who worked in Germany, Vasily Kandinsky (vus-YEEL-yee kan-DIN-skee) (1866–1944) was one of its founders. Kandinsky sought to avoid representation altogether. He believed that art should speak directly to the soul. To do so, it must avoid any reference to visual reality and concentrate on line and color.

CHAPTER SUMMARY

Since the sixteenth century, much of the Western Hemisphere had been under the control of Great Britain, Spain, and Portugal. But between 1776 and 1826, an age of revolution in the Atlantic world led to the creation of the United States and nine new nations in Latin America. Canada and other nations in Latin America followed in the course of the nineteenth century. This age of revolution was an expression of the force of nationalism, which had first emerged as a political ideology at the end of the eighteenth century.

Influential, too, were the ideas of the Enlightenment that had made an impact on intellectuals and political leaders in both North and South America.

The new nations that emerged in the Western Hemisphere did not, however, develop without challenges to their national unity. Latin American nations often found it difficult to establish stable republics and resorted to strong leaders who used military force to govern. Although Latin American nations achieved political independence, they soon found themselves economically dependent on Great Britain as well as their northern neighbor. The United States dissolved into four years of bloody civil war before reconciling, and Canada achieved only questionable unity owing to distrust between the English-speaking majority and the French-speaking minority.

By the second half of the nineteenth century, much of the Western world was experiencing a new mass society in which the lower classes in particular benefited from the right to vote, a higher standard of living, and new schools that provided them with some education. New forms of mass transportation, combined with new work patterns, enabled large numbers of people to enjoy weekend trips to amusement parks and seaside resorts as well as participate in new mass leisure activities.

The cultural revolutions before 1914 produced anxiety and a crisis of confidence in Western civilization. Albert Einstein showed that time and space were relative to the observer, that matter was simply another form of energy, and that the old Newtonian view of the universe was no longer valid. Sigmund Freud added to the uncertainties of

the age with his argument that human behavior was governed not by reason but by the unconscious. Some intellectuals used the ideas of Charles Darwin to argue that in the struggle of race and nations, only the fittest survive. Collectively, these new ideas helped create a modern consciousness that questioned most Europeans' optimistic faith in reason, the rational structure of nature, and the certainty of progress. As we shall see in Chapter 23, the devastating experiences of World War I would turn this culture of uncertainty into a way of life after 1918.

REFLECTION QUESTIONS

Q What were the similarities and dissimilarities in the development of Latin American nations, the United States, Canada, and China in the nineteenth century?

Q How were the promises and problems of the new mass society reflected in education, leisure, and the experiences of women?

Q How is modernism evident in literature and the arts between 1870 and 1914? How do these literary and artistic products reflect the political and social developments of the age?

CHAPTER TIMELINE

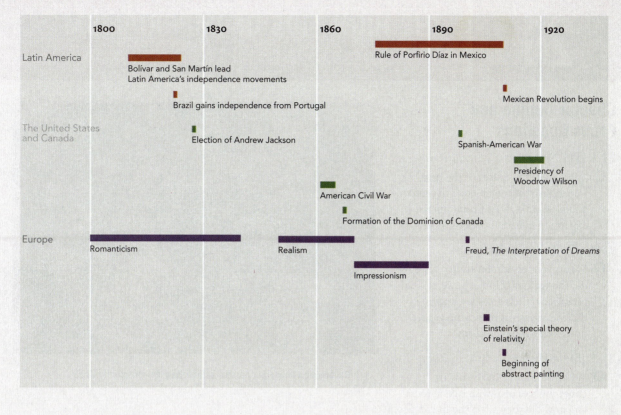

	1800	1830	1860	1890	1920
Latin America					

Latin America

Bolívar and San Martín lead
Latin America's independence movements

Brazil gains independence from Portugal

Rule of Porfirio Díaz in Mexico

Mexican Revolution begins

The United States and Canada

Election of Andrew Jackson

Spanish-American War

Presidency of Woodrow Wilson

American Civil War

Formation of the Dominion of Canada

Europe

Romanticism

Realism

Freud, *The Interpretation of Dreams*

Impressionism

Einstein's special theory of relativity

Beginning of abstract painting

CHAPTER NOTES

1. Quoted in J. C. Chasteen, *Americanos: Latin America's Struggle for Independence* (Oxford, 2008), p. 122.
2. Quoted in P. Bakewell, *A History of Latin America* (Oxford, 1997), p. 367.
3. Quoted in M. C. Eakin, *The History of Latin America: Collision of Cultures* (New York, 2007), p. 188.
4. Quoted in E. B. Burns, *Latin America: A Concise Interpretive History,* 4th ed. (Englewood Cliffs, N.J., 1986), p. 116.
5. W. Wordsworth, "The Tables Turned," in M. Arnold, ed., *Poems of Wordsworth* (London, 1963), p. 138.
6. Quoted in A. E. E. McKenzie, *The Major Achievements of Science,* vol. 1 (New York, 1960), p. 310.
7. Quoted in A. Higonnet, *Berthe Morisot's Images of Women* (Cambridge, Mass., 1992), p. 19.

MINDTAP
From Cengage

MindTap® is a fully online, highly personalized learning experience built upon Cengage Learning content. MindTap combines student learning tools—readings, multimedia, activities, and assessments—into a singular Learning Path that guides students through the course and helps students develop the critical thinking, analysis, and communication skills that are essential to academic and professional success.

Chapter Outline and Focus Questions

21.1 Revere the conquering heroes: establishing British rule in Africa

Critical Thinking

Q *What were the consequences of the new imperialism of the nineteenth century for the colonies of the European powers? How should the imperialist countries be evaluated in terms of their motives and stated objectives?*

Connections to Today

Q *Based on the definition of imperialism contained in this chapter, do you think it is fair to conclude that there continue to be imperialist nations in the world today?*

THERE IS A STATUE OF CECIL RHODES on the campus of Oriel College at Oxford University. Rhodes, an industrialist and diamond magnate who became prime minister of the Cape Colony in the 1890s, was one of the most prominent proponents of British imperialist expansion at the end of the nineteenth century. Eventually, he used some of his wealth to endow the famous Rhodes Scholarships, which provide financial support for deserving students from all over the world to attend Oxford University.

In the fall of 2015, a group of students at Oxford organized protests demanding that Rhodes's statue be removed on the grounds that he was responsible for the enslavement of millions of Africans. To them, he embodied the worst aspects of European colonial rule over the non-Western world. Although similar protests at the University of Cape Town in South Africa had been successful, the student demands at Oxford were eventually denied, as opponents argued that Rhodes had been an important historical figure and a major benefactor for the cause of education—whatever his faults.

The protest movements at Oxford and Cape Town brought into sharp relief the complex debate over the motives and consequences of a century of Western imperialism. For Rhodes and like-minded contemporaries, European colonial rule had been a necessary step in the arduous task of bringing modern civilization to backward peoples around the world whatever its limitations. To critics, in the words of one of the recent protesters, Rhodes was responsible for "stealing land, massacring tens of thousands of black Africans, imposing a regime of unspeakable labor exploitation in the diamond mines and devising pro-apartheid policies."[1]

Behind all this rhetoric lies an incontrovertible historical fact. Through the efforts of Rhodes and his contemporaries, Western colonialism spread throughout much of the non-Western world during the nineteenth and early twentieth centuries. Spurred by the demands of the Industrial Revolution, a few powerful Western states—notably Great Britain, France, Germany, Russia, and the United States—competed avariciously for consumer markets and raw materials for their expanding economies. By the end of the nineteenth century, virtually all of the traditional societies in Asia and Africa were under direct or indirect colonial rule. As the new century began, the Western imprint of Asian and African societies appeared to be a permanent feature of the political and cultural landscape, for better or for worse.

21-1 THE SPREAD OF COLONIAL RULE

Q **Focus Question:** What were the causes of the new imperialism of the nineteenth century, and how did it differ from imperial expansion in earlier periods of history?

In the nineteenth century, a new phase of Western expansion into Asia and Africa began. Whereas before 1800, European aims in the East could be summed up as "Christians and spices" and Western gold and silver were exchanged for cloves, silk, and porcelain, now European nations began to view Asian and African societies as markets for the prodigious output of European factories and as sources of the raw materials needed to fuel the Western industrial machine. This relationship between the West and African and Asian societies has been called the **new imperialism** (see Comparative Essay, "Imperialisms Old and New," p. 526).

21-1a The Motives

The reason for this change, of course, was the Industrial Revolution. Industrializing countries in the West needed vital raw materials that were not available at home, as well as reliable markets for the goods produced in their factories. The latter factor became increasingly crucial as producers discovered that their home markets could not absorb their entire output and that they had to export to make a profit. When consumer demand lagged, economic depression threatened.

The relationship between colonialism and national survival was expressed directly by French politician Jules Ferry (ZHOOL feh-REE) in 1885. A policy of "abstinence," he warned, would set France on "the broad road to decadence" and initiate its decline into a "third or fourth-rate power." British imperialists agreed, convinced by the theory of Social Darwinism that only the fit are victorious and survive in the struggle between nations. As British professor of mathematics Karl Pearson argued in 1900, "The path of progress is strewn with the wrecks of nations; traces are everywhere to be seen of the [slaughtered remains] of inferior races. . . . Yet these dead people are, in very truth, the stepping stones on which mankind has arisen to the higher intellectual and deeper emotional life of today."[2]

For some advocates, colonialism had a moral purpose, whether to promote Christianity or to build a better world. British colonial official Henry Curzon (CURR-zun) argued that the British Empire "was under Providence, the greatest instrument for good that the world has seen." To Cecil Rhodes, the most famous empire builder of his day, the extraction of material wealth from the colonies was only a secondary matter. "My ruling purpose," he remarked, "is the extension of the British Empire."[3] That British Empire, on which, as the saying went, "the sun never set," was the envy of its rivals and was viewed as the primary source of British global dominance during the second half of the nineteenth century.

21-1b The Tactics

With changes in European motives for colonization came a shift in tactics. Earlier, European states had generally been satisfied to deal with existing independent states rather than

COMPARATIVE ESSAY

Imperialisms Old and New

Interaction & Exchange Originally, the word *imperialism* (derived from the Latin word "to command") was used to describe certain types of political entities. An empire was larger than a kingdom and comprised more than one nation or people, all ruled by an emperor who represented one dominant ethnic or religious group within the territory. Good examples include the Roman Empire, the Chinese empire, the Mongol Empire in Central Asia, the empires of Ghana and Mali in West Africa, and the Inka Empire in South America. See Image 21.2.

In the nineteenth century, as Western expansion into Asia and Africa gathered strength, it became fashionable to call that process *imperialism* as well. In this instance, the expansion was motivated by the efforts of capitalist states in the West to seize markets, capture cheap raw materials, and find lucrative avenues for investment in the countries beyond Western civilization. Eventually, it resulted in the creation of colonies ruled by the imperialist powers. In this interpretation, the primary motives behind imperial expansion were economic. In his influential book *Imperialism: A Study*, published in 1902, British political economist John A. Hobson promoted this view, maintaining that modern imperialism was a direct consequence of the modern industrial economy.

As historians began to analyze the phenomenon, however, many became convinced that the motivations of the imperial powers were not simply economic. As Hobson himself conceded, economic concerns were inevitably tinged with political overtones and questions of national grandeur and moral purpose. To nineteenth-century Europeans, economic wealth, national status, and political power went hand in hand with the possession of a colonial empire. To global strategists, colonies brought tangible benefits in balance-of-power politics as well as economic profits, and many nations pursued colonies as much to gain advantage over their rivals as to acquire territory for its own sake.

After World War II, when colonies throughout Asia and Africa were gradually replaced by independent nations, a new term, *neocolonialism*, appeared to describe the situation in which imperialist nations ceded formal political independence to their former colonies but continued to exercise control by various political and economic means. Hence, many critics argue, Western imperialism has not disappeared in the former colonial territories but has simply found other ways to maintain its influence. We will discuss this issue further in Part V.

21.2 Gateway to India. Built in the Roman imperial style by the British to commemorate the visit to India of King George V and Queen Mary in 1911, the Gateway to India was erected at the water's edge in the harbor of Bombay (now Mumbai), India's greatest port city. For thousands of British citizens arriving in India, the Gateway to India was the first view of their new home and a symbol of the power and majesty of the British raj.

Q *What were the principal motives of the major trading nations for seizing colonies in Asia and Africa in the late nineteenth century?*

attempting to establish direct control over vast territories. There had been exceptions, where state power was at the point of collapse (as in India), where European economic interests were especially intense (as in Latin America and the East Indies), or where there was no centralized authority (as in North America and the Philippines). But for the most part, the Western presence had been limited to controlling regional trade networks and establishing a few footholds where foreigners could carry on trade and missionary activity.

After 1800, the demands of industrialization in Europe created a new set of dynamics. Maintaining access to raw materials such as tin and rubber and setting up markets for European products required more extensive control over colonial territories. As competition for colonies increased, the colonial powers sought to solidify their hold over their territories to protect them from attack by their rivals. After 1880, the quest for colonies became a scramble as all the major European states, now joined by the United States and Japan, engaged in a global land grab. In many cases, economic interests were secondary to security concerns or the demands of national prestige.

By 1900, almost every society in Africa and Asia was either under full colonial rule or, as in China and the Ottoman Empire, at a point of virtual collapse. Only a handful of states—including Thailand, Afghanistan, Iran, Ethiopia, and Japan—managed to escape internal disintegration or subjection to colonial rule.

21-2 THE COLONIAL SYSTEM

 Focus Question: What types of administrative systems did the various colonial powers establish in their colonies, and how did these systems reflect the general philosophy of colonialism?

Once they had control of most of the world, the colonial powers set out to achieve their primary objective—to exploit the natural resources of the subject areas and open up markets for manufactured goods and capital investment from the mother country. In some cases, that goal could be realized in cooperation with local political elites, whose loyalty could be earned or purchased by economic rewards or by confirming them in their positions of authority and status in a new colonial setting. Sometimes, however, this policy of **indirect rule** was not feasible because local leaders refused to cooperate with their colonial masters or even actively resisted. In such cases, the imperialists resorted to **direct rule**, removing the local elites from power and replacing them with officials from the mother country.

In general, the societies most likely to actively resist colonial conquest were those with a long tradition of national cohesion and independence such as Burma (now Myanmar) and Vietnam in Asia and the African Muslim states in northern Nigeria and Morocco. In those areas, the colonial powers encountered more resistance and consequently tended to dispense with local collaborators and govern directly. In some parts of Africa, the Indian subcontinent, and the Malay Peninsula, where the local authorities, for whatever reason, were willing to collaborate with the imperialist powers, indirect rule was more common.

21-2a The Philosophy of Colonialism

To justify their rule, the colonial powers appealed in part to the time-honored maxim "Might makes right." That attitude received pseudoscientific validity from the concept of Social Darwinism, which maintained that only societies that aggressively adapted to changing circumstances would survive and prosper in a world governed by the Darwinian law of "survival of the fittest" (see Image 21.3).

Some people, however, were uncomfortable with such a brutal view of the law of nature and sought a moral justification for imperialism that appeared to benefit the victim. Here again, Social Darwinism pointed the way. By bringing the benefits of Western democracy, capitalism, and Christianity to tradition-ridden societies, the colonial powers were enabling primitive peoples to adapt to the challenges of the modern world. Buttressed by such comforting theories, sensitive Westerners could ignore the brutal aspects of colonialism and persuade themselves that in the long run, the results would be beneficial for both sides (see Opposing Viewpoints, "White Man's Burden, Black Man's Sorrow," p. 529). Few were as adept at describing this "civilizing mission" as the French governor-general of French Indochina, Albert Sarraut (ahl-BAYR sah-ROH). While admitting that colonialism was originally an "act of force" undertaken for profit, he insisted that by redistributing Earth's wealth the colonial process would result in a better life for all: "Is it just, is it legitimate that such [an uneven distribution of resources] should be indefinitely prolonged? . . . No! . . . Humanity is distributed throughout the globe. No race, no people has the right or power to isolate itself egotistically from the movements and necessities of universal life." Guilt, in this interpretation, was transferred from the conqueror to the victim.[4]

But what if historically and culturally the societies of Asia and Africa were fundamentally different from those of the West and could not or would not be persuaded to transform themselves along Western lines? In that case, a policy of cultural transformation could not be expected to succeed and could even lead to disaster.

Assimilation or Association? In fact, colonial theorists never decided the issue on a consistent basis. The French, who were most inclined to philosophize about the problem, adopted the terms **assimilation** (which implied an effort to transform colonial societies in the Western image) and **association** (implying collaboration with local elites while leaving local traditions alone) to describe the two alternatives and then proceeded to vacillate between them. French policy in Indochina, for example, began as one of association but switched to assimilation under pressure from those who felt that colonial powers owed a debt to their subject peoples. But assimilation (which in any case was never accepted as feasible or desirable by many colonial officials)

21.3 The Company Resident and His Puppet. The British East India Company gradually replaced the sovereigns of the once-independent Indian states with puppet rulers who carried out the company's policies. Here we see the company's resident dominating a procession in Tanjore in 1825, while the Indian ruler, Sarabhoji, follows like an obedient shadow. As a boy, Sarabhoji had been educated by European tutors and had filled his life and home with English books and furnishings.

aroused resentment among the local population, many of whom opposed the destruction of their native traditions. In the end, the French abandoned the attempt to justify their presence and resorted to ruling by force of arms.

Other colonial powers had little interest in the dilemma. The British, whether out of a sense of pragmatism or of racial superiority, refused to entertain the possibility of assimilation and treated their subject peoples as culturally and racially distinct. In formulating its policy in the Philippines, the United States straddled the issue by adopting a policy of assimilation in theory but often neglecting to put it in practice. In the remainder of the chapter, we will analyze the advent of the age of the era of imperialism in terms of its effect on different parts of the world.

21-3 INDIA UNDER THE BRITISH RAJ

Focus Question: What were some of the major consequences of British rule in India, and how did they affect the Indian people?

By 1800, the once glorious empire of the Mughals (MOO-guls) had been reduced by British military power to a shadow of its former greatness. During the next decades, the British consolidated their control over the Indian subcontinent. Some territories were taken over directly, first by the East India Company and later by the British crown. Others were ruled indirectly through their local maharajas (mah-huh-RAH-juhs) and rajas (RAH-juhs).

21-3a Colonial Reforms

As the territory under British rule expanded, colonial officials in India turned to matters of governance. Order and stability were introduced to a society that had been rent by civil war. A relatively honest and efficient government was put in place that in many respects operated to the benefit of the average Indian. One benefit was the heightened attention given to education. A new school system was established to train the children of Indian elites, and the British civil service examination was introduced (see Historical Voices, "Indian in Blood, English in Taste and Intellect," p. 530). The instruction of young girls also expanded, primarily to make them better wives and mothers for the educated male population. In 1875, a Madras (muh-DRAS or muh-DRAHS) medical college accepted its first female student.

British rule also brought an end to some of the more inhumane aspects of Indian tradition. The practice of *sati*

White Man's Burden, Black Man's Sorrow

 Art & Ideas **ONE OF THE JUSTIFICATIONS FOR MODERN IMPERIALISM** was the notion that the allegedly "more advanced" white peoples had the moral responsibility to raise "ignorant" indigenous peoples to a higher level of civilization. Few captured this notion better than British poet Rudyard Kipling (1865–1936) in his famous poem "The White Man's Burden." His appeal, directed to the United States, became one of the most famous verses in the English-speaking world.

That sense of moral responsibility, however, was often misplaced or, even worse, laced with hypocrisy. All too often, the consequences of imperial rule were detrimental to almost everyone living under colonial authority. Few observers described the destructive effects of Western imperialism on the African people as well as Edmund Morel, a British journalist whose book *The Black Man's Burden* pointed out some of the more harmful aspects of colonialism in the Belgian Congo. The brutal treatment of Congolese workers involved in gathering rubber, ivory, and palm oil for export aroused an international outcry and in 1903 led to the formation of a commission under British consul Roger Casement to bring about reforms.

Rudyard Kipling, "The White Man's Burden"

Take up the White Man's burden—
Send forth the best ye breed—
Go bind your sons to exile
To serve your captives' need;
To wait in heavy harness,
On fluttered folk and wild—
Your new-caught sullen peoples,
Half-devil and half-child.
Take up the White Man's burden—
In patience to abide,
To veil the threat of terror
And check the show of pride;
By open speech and simple,
An hundred times made plain
To seek another's profit,
And work another's gain.
Take up the White Man's burden—

The savage wars of peace—
Fill full the mouth of Famine
And bid the sickness cease;
And when your goal is nearest
The end for others sought,
Watch Sloth and heathen
Folly Bring all your hopes to nought.

Edmund Morel, *The Black Man's Burden*

It is [the Africans] who carry the "Black man's burden." They have not withered away before the white man's occupation. Indeed . . . Africa has ultimately absorbed within itself every Caucasian and, for that matter, every Semitic invader, too. In hewing out for himself a fixed abode in Africa, the white man has massacred the African in heaps. The African has survived, and it is well for the white settlers that he has. . . .

What the partial occupation of his soil by the white man has failed to do; what the mapping out of European political "spheres of influence" has failed to do; what the Maxim and the rifle, the slave gang, labour in the bowels of the earth and the lash, have failed to do; what imported measles, smallpox and syphilis have failed to do; whatever the overseas slave trade failed to do; the power of modern capitalistic exploitation, assisted by modern engines of destruction, may yet succeed in accomplishing.

For from the evils of the latter, scientifically applied and enforced, there is no escape for the African. Its destructive effects are not spasmodic; they are permanent. In its permanence resides its fatal consequences. It kills not the body merely, but the soul. It breaks the spirit. It attacks the African at every turn, from every point of vantage. It wrecks his polity, uproots him from the land, invades his family life, destroys his natural pursuits and occupations, claims his whole time, enslaves him in his own home.

Q *According to Kipling, why should Western nations take up the "white man's burden"? What was the "black man's burden," in the eyes of Edmund Morel?*

Sources: From Rudyard Kipling, "The White Man's Burden," *McClure's Magazine* 12 (February. 1899). From Edmund Morel, *Black Man's Burden*, Metro Books, 1972.

HISTORICAL VOICES

Indian in Blood, English in Taste and Intellect

 THOMAS BABINGTON MACAULAY (1800–1859) was named a member of the Supreme Council of India in the early 1830s. In that capacity, he was responsible for drawing up a new educational policy for British subjects in the area. In his *Minute on Education*, he considered the claims of English and various local languages to become the vehicle for educational training and decided in favor of the former. It is better, he argued, to teach Indian elites about Western civilization so as "to form a class who may be interpreters between us and the millions whom we govern; a class of persons, Indian in blood and color, but English in taste, in opinions, in morals, and in intellect." Later Macaulay became a prominent historian. The debate in India over the relative benefits of English and the various Indian languages continues today.

Thomas Babington Macaulay, *Minute on Education*

We have a fund to be employed as government shall direct for the intellectual improvement of the people of this country. The simple question is, what is the most useful way of employing it?

All parties seem to be agreed on one point, that the dialects commonly spoken among the natives of this part of India contain neither literary or scientific information, and are, moreover so poor and rude that, until they are enriched from some other quarter, it will not be easy to translate any valuable work into them. . . .

What, then, shall the language [of education] be? One half of the Committee maintain that it should be the English. The other half strongly recommend the Arabic and Sanskrit. The whole question seems to me to be, which language is the best worth knowing?

I have no knowledge of either Sanskrit or Arabic—but I have done what I could to form a correct estimate of their value. I have read translations of the most celebrated Arabic and Sanskrit works. I have conversed both here and at home with men distinguished by their proficiency in the Eastern tongues. I am quite ready to take the Oriental learning at the valuation of the Orientalists themselves. I have never found one among them who could deny that a single shelf of a good European library was worth the whole native literature of India and Arabia . . .

It is, I believe, no exaggeration to say, that all the historical information which has been collected from all the books written in the Sanskrit language is less valuable than what may be found in the most paltry abridgments used at preparatory schools in England. In every branch of physical or moral philosophy the relative position of the two nations is nearly the same.

Q *How did Macaulay justify the teaching of the English language in India? How might a critic have responded?*

Source: From Speeches by *Lord Macaulay, With His Minute on Indian Education* by Thomas B. MacAuley. AMS Press, 1935.

(suh-TEE) was outlawed, and widows were legally permitted to remarry. The British also attempted to put an end to the endemic brigandage (known as *thuggee*, which gave rise to the English word *thug*) that had plagued travelers in India since time immemorial. Railroads, the telegraph, and the postal service were introduced to India shortly after they appeared in Great Britain. Work began on the main highway from Calcutta to Delhi (DEL-ee) in 1839 (see Map 21.1), and the first rail network in northern India was opened in 1853.

21-3b The Costs of Colonialism

In fact, the Indian people paid a high price for the peace and stability brought by the British **raj** (RAHJ) (from the Indian *raja*, or prince). Perhaps the most flagrant cost was economic. Although British entrepreneurs and a small percentage of the local population reaped financial benefits from British rule, it brought hardship to millions in both the cities and the rural areas. The introduction of British textiles put thousands of Bengali women out of work and severely damaged the local textile industry.

In rural areas, the British adopted the *zamindar* (zuh-meen-DAHR) system (see Chapter 16) in the misguided expectation that it would facilitate the collection of taxes and create a new landed gentry, who could become the conservative foundation of imperial rule as it had in Britain. But the local gentry took advantage of this new authority to increase taxes and force the less fortunate peasants to become tenants or lose their land entirely. British officials also made few efforts during the nineteenth century to introduce democratic institutions or values. As one senior political figure remarked in Parliament in 1898,

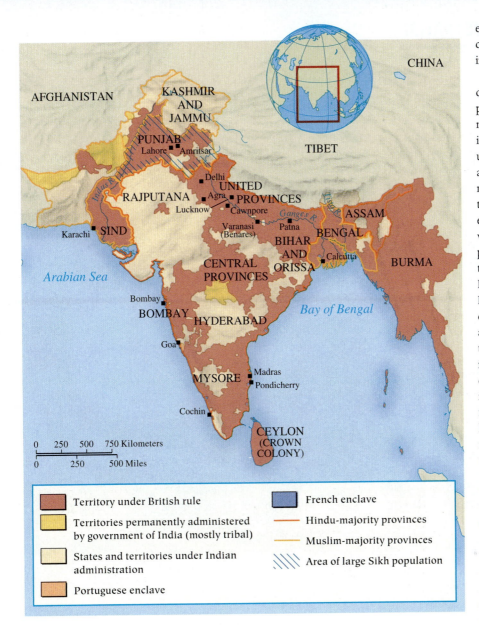

Legend:
- Territory under British rule
- Territories permanently administered by government of India (mostly tribal)
- States and territories under Indian administration
- Portuguese enclave
- French enclave
- Hindu-majority provinces
- Muslim-majority provinces
- Area of large Sikh population

Map 21.1 India Under British Rule, 1805–1931. This map shows the different forms of rule that the British applied in India under their control.

Q *Where were the major cities of the subcontinent located, and under whose rule did they fall?*

emergence of other vital new commercial and manufacturing operations.

Foreign rule also had a psychological effect on the Indian people. Although many colonial officials sincerely tried to improve the lot of the people under their charge, British arrogance and contempt for native tradition cut deeply into the pride of many Indians, especially those of high caste, who were accustomed to a position of superior status in their own country. Educated Indians trained in the Anglo–Indian school system for a career in the civil service, as well as Eurasians born to mixed marriages, often imitated the behavior and dress of their rulers, speaking English, eating Western food, and taking up European leisure activities, but many rightfully wondered where their true cultural loyalties lay (see Comparative Illustration, "Cultural Influences, East and West," p. 532). This cultural collision was poignantly described in the novel *A Passage to India* by British writer E. M. Forster, which related the story of a visiting Englishwoman who becomes interested in the Indian way of life, much to the dismay of the local European community (see Film & History, *A Passage to India*, p. 533).

democratic institutions "can no more be carried to India by Englishmen . . . than they can carry ice in their luggage."[5]

The British also did little to bring modern science and technology to India. Some limited industrialization took place, notably in the manufacturing of textiles and jute (used in making rope). The first textile mill opened in 1856. Seventy years later, there were eighty mills in the city of Bombay (now Mumbai) alone. Nevertheless, the lack of local capital and the advantages given to British imports prevented the

21-4 COLONIAL REGIMES IN SOUTHEAST ASIA

Q **Focus Question:** Which Western countries were most active in seeking colonial possessions in Southeast Asia, and what were their motives in doing so?

Cultural Influences, East and West

Interaction & Exchange | **WHEN EUROPEANS MOVED INTO ASIA** in the nineteenth century, some Asians began to imitate European customs for prestige or social advancement. Seen in Image 21.4a, for example, is a young Vietnamese during the 1920s dressed in Western sports clothes, learning to play tennis. Sometimes, however, the cultural influence went the other way. In Image 21.4b, an English nabob, as European residents in India were often called, apes the manner of an Indian aristocrat, complete with harem and hookah, the Indian water pipe. The paintings on the wall, however, are in the European style.

Q *Compare and contrast the artistic styles of these two paintings. What message do they send to the viewer?*

21.4a

21.4b

In 1800, only two societies in Southeast Asia were under effective colonial rule: the Spanish Philippines and the Dutch East Indies. During the nineteenth century, however, European interest in Southeast Asia increased rapidly; by 1900, virtually the entire area was under colonial domination (see Map 21.2).

21-4a "Opportunity in the Orient": Colonial Takeover in Southeast Asia

The process of colonial takeover began after the Napoleonic Wars when the British, by agreement with the Dutch, abandoned their claims to territorial possessions in the East Indies in return for a free hand in the Malay Peninsula. In 1819, colonial administrator Stamford Raffles founded a new British colony on the island of Singapore at the tip of the peninsula (see Image 21.5). Singapore became a major stopping point for traffic to and from China and other commercial centers in the region.

During the next decades, the pace of European penetration into Southeast Asia accelerated. The British attacked southern Burma in 1826 and eventually established control there, arousing fears in France that the British might acquire a monopoly of trade in South China. In 1858, the French launched an attack against Vietnam. Though it was not a total success, the Nguyen (NGWEN) Dynasty in Vietnam was ultimately forced to cede some territories. A generation later, French rule was extended over the remainder of the country. By 1900, French seizure of neighboring Cambodia and Laos had led to the creation of the French-ruled Indochinese Union.

After the French conquest of Indochina, Thailand—then known as Siam—was the only remaining independent state on the Southeast Asian mainland, with its new capital at Bangkok. Under the astute leadership of two remarkable rulers—King Mongkut (MAHNG-koot) (r. 1851–1868) and his son, King Chulalongkorn (CHOOluh-lahng-korn) (r. 1868–1910)—the Thais attempted to introduce Western learning and maintain relations with the major European powers without undermining internal stability or inviting an imperialist attack. In 1896, the British and the French agreed to preserve Thailand as an independent buffer zone between their possessions in Southeast Asia.

The final piece in the colonial edifice in Southeast Asia was put in place during the Spanish–American War in 1898 (see Chapter 20), when U.S. naval forces under Commodore George Dewey defeated the Spanish fleet in Manila Bay. Although one U.S. congressman, Senator Beveridge of Indiana, portrayed the takeover of the islands as a sacred mission "to lead in the regeneration of the world," a more immediate reason was that the Americans (like the Spanish before them) found the islands a convenient jumping-off point for their China trade (see Chapter 22).[6]

Not all Filipinos agreed with Senator Beveridge's portrayal of the situation. Guerrilla forces under the leadership of Emilio Aguinaldo (ay-MEEL-yoh ah-gwee-NAHLdoh) fought bitterly against U.S. troops to establish their independence from both Spain and the United States. But

Map 21.2 Colonial Southeast Asia. This map shows the spread of European colonial rule into Southeast Asia from the sixteenth century to the end of the nineteenth. Initially seized by the Portuguese in 1511, Malacca was taken by the Dutch in the seventeenth century and then by the British 100 years later.

Q *What was the significance of Malacca?*

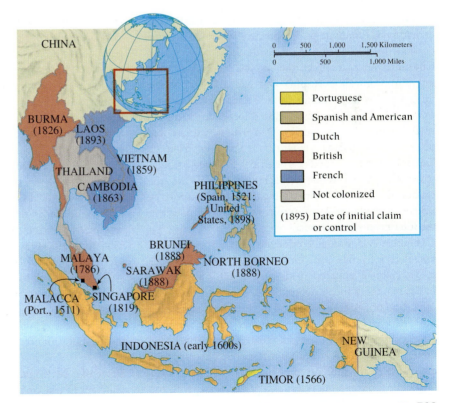

21.5 Government Hill in Singapore. After the occupation of the strategic island of Singapore by the British in 1819, the one-time pirate haven rapidly emerged as a major transit point for British shipping between the Indian Ocean and the South China Sea and as a home to a rich mixture of peoples, who came to work as merchants, urban laborers, and craftsmen in the new imperial marketplace. The multiracial character of the colony is evident in this mid-nineteenth-century painting by a British artist. People of various ethnic backgrounds stroll on Government Hill, with the busy harbor in the background.

America's first war in Asia was a success, and the bulk of the resistance collapsed in 1901. The United States had its stepping-stone to the rich markets of China.

21-4b The Nature of Colonial Rule

In Southeast Asia, the colonial powers were primarily concerned with economic profit and tried wherever possible to work with local elites to facilitate the exploitation of natural resources. Indirect rule was less costly than training European administrators and had a less corrosive impact on the local culture. In the Dutch East Indies, for example, colonial officials entrusted local administration to the indigenous aristocracy, who maintained law and order and collected taxes in return for a payment from the Dutch East India Company. The British followed a similar practice in Malaya. While establishing direct rule over the crucial commercial centers of Singapore and Malacca, the British allowed local Muslim rulers to maintain power in the interior of the peninsula.

Indirect rule, though convenient and inexpensive, was not always feasible. In some instances, local resistance to the colonial conquest made such a policy impossible. In Burma, the staunch opposition of the royal court and other traditionalist forces caused the British to abolish the monarchy and administer the country directly through their colonial government in India. In Indochina, the French used both direct and indirect means. They imposed direct rule on the southern provinces in the Mekong River Delta but governed the north as a protectorate, with the emperor retaining titular authority from his palace in Hué (HWAY). The French adopted a similar policy in Cambodia and Laos, where local rulers were left in charge with French advisers to counsel them.

Democratic Reforms Whatever method was used, the colonial regimes were slow to create democratic institutions. The first legislative councils and assemblies were composed almost exclusively of European residents in the colonies. The first representatives from the indigenous population were wealthy and politically conservative. When Southeast Asians complained, colonial officials reluctantly agreed to broaden the franchise. The French official Albert Sarraut advised patience in awaiting the full benefits of colonial policy: "I will treat you like my younger brothers, but do not forget that I am the older brother. I will slowly give you the dignity of humanity."[7]

Colonial officials were also slow to adopt educational reforms. Although the introduction of Western education was one of the justifications of colonialism, it soon became clear that educating local elites could backfire. Colonial societies often had few jobs for lawyers, engineers, and architects, leading to a mass of unemployed intellectuals ready to take out their frustrations on the colonial regime. As one French official noted in voicing his opposition to increasing the number of schools in Vietnam, educating the locals meant not "one coolie less, but one rebel more."

Economic Development Colonial powers were equally reluctant to take up the "white man's burden" in the area of economic development. As we have seen, their primary goals were to secure cheap raw materials and maintain markets for manufactured goods. Colonial policy, therefore, concentrated on exporting raw materials—teakwood from Burma; rubber and tin from Malaya; spices, tea and coffee, and palm oil from the East Indies; and sugar and copra (the meat of the coconut) from the Philippines.

In some Southeast Asian colonial societies, a measure of industrial development did take place to meet the needs of the European population and local elites. Major manufacturing cities such as Rangoon in lower Burma, Batavia (buh-TAY-vee-uh) on the island of Java, and Saigon (sy-GAHN) in French Indochina grew rapidly. Most large industrial and commercial establishments were owned and managed by Europeans, however, or by Indian or Chinese merchants in some cases.

Colonialism and the Countryside   Despite the growth of an urban economy, the vast majority of people continued to farm the land. Many continued to live by subsistence agriculture, but the colonial policy of emphasizing cash crops for export also led to the creation of a plantation agriculture in which peasants worked for poverty-level wages on rubber, sugar, and tea plantations owned by Europeans. Many laborers were "shanghaied" (an English term that described the practice of recruiting workers by the use of force, alcohol, or drugs, which was common among the docks and streets of Shanghai) to work on the plantations, where conditions were often so inhumane that thousands died. High taxes imposed by colonial governments to pay for administrative costs or improvements in the local infrastructure were a heavy burden for poor peasants.

The economic situation was made even more difficult by the dramatic growth of the population as improved sanitation and medical treatment resulted in lower rates of infant mortality. The population of the island of Java, for example, increased from around 1 million in the precolonial era to some 40 million at the end of the nineteenth century. Under these conditions, the rural areas could no longer support the growing populations, and many young people fled to the cities to seek jobs in factories or shops.

As in India, colonial rule brought some benefits to Southeast Asia. It led to the beginnings of a modern economic infrastructure and to what is sometimes called a "modernizing elite" dedicated to the creation of an advanced industrialized society. The development of an export market helped create an entrepreneurial class in rural areas. This happened, for example, on the outer islands of the Dutch East Indies (such as Borneo and Sumatra), where small growers of rubber trees, palm trees for oil, coffee, tea, and spices began to share in the profits of the colonial enterprise. But most of the profits from the development of export products were repatriated to the colonial mother country, while displaced peasants fleeing to the cities found little opportunity for employment. Many were left with seasonal employment, with one foot on the farm and the other in the factory. The old world was being destroyed—and the new one had yet to be born.

21-5 EMPIRE BUILDING IN AFRICA

Focus Question: What factors were behind the "scramble for Africa," and what impact did it have on the continent?

Before 1800, European economic interests in Africa had been relatively limited because there was little incentive to penetrate the interior or politically take over the coastal areas. The slave trade, the main source of European profit during the eighteenth century, could be carried on by using African rulers and merchants as intermediaries. Disease, political instability, the lack of transportation, and the generally unhealthy climate all deterred Europeans from more extensive efforts in Africa. The situation began to change in the nineteenth century as the growing need for industrial materials created a reason for the imperialist countries to increase their economic presence in the continent.

21-5a From Slavery to "Legitimate Trade" in Africa

As the new century dawned, the slave trade was in decline, in part because of the efforts of humanitarians in several European countries. Dutch merchants effectively ceased trafficking in slaves in 1795, and the Danes stopped in 1803. In 1808, the slave trade was declared illegal in both Great Britain and the United States. The British began to apply pressure on other nations to follow suit, and most did so after the end of the Napoleonic Wars in 1815, although the illegal smuggling of slaves continued for many years (see Historical Voices, "Tragedy at Caffard Cove," p. 536).

CHRONOLOGY	Imperialism in Asia	
Stamford Raffles arrives in Singapore	1819
British attack lower Burma	1826
British rail network opens in northern India	1853
Sepoy Rebellion	1857
French attack Vietnam	1858
British and French agree to neutralize Thailand	1896
Commodore Dewey defeats Spanish fleet in Manila Bay	1898
French create Indochinese Union	1900

Tragedy at Caffard Cove

Interaction & Exchange

THE SLAVE TRADE WAS DECLARED ILLEGAL in France in 1818, but the clandestine shipment of Africans to the Americas continued for many years afterward. At the same time, slavery was widely tolerated in the French colonies, especially in the Caribbean, where sugar plantations on the islands of Guadeloupe and Martinique depended on cheap labor for their profits. Not until 1849 was slavery abolished throughout the French Empire.

Among the tragic events that characterized the shipment of slaves to the Americas (often called the "Middle Passage"), few are as poignant as the incident described in the passage below, which took place in 1830 on the island of Martinique. The text, which includes passages from the original official report of the incident, is taken from a memorial erected at the site many years later. Laurent Valère, a local sculptor, erected fifteen statues to commemorate the victims. The name of the ship and the name and nationality of the ship's captain, as well as the ultimate fate of the surviving victims, remain a mystery to this day.

The Caffard Memorial

Around noon on the 8th of April 1830, a sailing ship [was observed] carrying out odd maneuvers off the coast of [the town of] Diamant [on the southern coast of Martinique]; at about five p.m. [the vessel] cast anchor off the dangerous coast of nearby Caffard Cove. François Dizac, a resident of the neighborhood and manager of the Plage du Diamant, a plantation owned by the Count de Latournelle, realized that the ship's situation was perilous, but a heavy swell prevented him from launching a boat to warn the captain that the vessel was in imminent danger of running aground. He therefore sent signals that the captain either could not, or chose not, to acknowledge.

At 11 P.M. that evening, anguished cries and cracking sounds suddenly began to shatter the silence of the night. Dizac and a party of slaves from the nearby plantation rushed promptly to the scene, only to encounter a horrifying sight: the ship had been dashed on the rocks and its passengers thrown into the fury of the raging seas. The rescuers on shore then observed a large number of panic-stricken males clinging desperately to the ship's foremast, which suddenly broke in two, tossing them into the foam or onto the rocks. Broken masts lying on the rocks, fragments of torn sails floating alongside ropes caught in the reef where the ship itself lay on the rocks all provided visual evidence of the frightful incident that had just occurred.

Forty-six bodies, four of whom were white males, were lying amidst the rocks. . . . "I ordered the bodies of the black victims to be buried at a short distance from the shore, then directed that those of the white males be carried to the cemetery of Diamant parish, where they received a Christian burial. I was then taken to the cabin of a certain Borromé, a free man of color, where those black castaways who had been rescued from the shipwreck had been given temporary shelter. Among the victims, six were found to be in such poor condition that they could not be taken to the Latournelle plantation. The other 80 survivors were handed over to the naval authorities at Fort Royal. In all, 86 African captives, of whom 60 were women or girls, were rescued out of a ship's 'cargo' estimated at nearly 300 persons.

"I ordered the interrogation of the surviving black castaways by interpreters, and it became clear from their testimony that the ship had been at sea for four months, and that most of the white sailors on board had died during the crossing [of the Atlantic], and that an additional 70 blacks had died from illness and had been thrown overboard during the voyage. Another 260 individuals remained on the ship when it was sunk off the coast of Diamant. . . . Only a few males had thus survived, since all of them were shackled together in the ship's hold with irons on their feet at the time of the wreck."

At that point, a legal issue was raised: what should be done with the surviving castaways who, although they could not be classified as slaves under existing law (since they were victims of illegal trade), yet could not be considered in this colony as men and therefore couldn't be freed. In May 1830, the Privy Council of Martinique ordered that the captured Negroes were to be shipped to Cayenne [the capital of French Guiana] in order to avoid having in the [French] West Indies a special class of people who could not be classified either as slaves or as free individuals. . . .

Thus, in July 1830, a second deportation followed the first, adding to the ordeal of the [African] slaves who had survived the shipwreck at Caffard Cove.

Q *How were the surviving victims of the shipwreck at Caffard Cove dealt with by the government authorities in Martinique? Under what provisions of the law was the decision reached?*

Source: Association de Sauvegarde du Patrimoine du Diamant. Text by Merlande, Moanda Saturnin, historian. Translation from the original French by the author.

At first, the institution of slavery was left untouched where it already existed, but as the demand for slaves began to decline over the course of the century, Europeans became more interested in so-called legitimate trade. Exports of peanuts, timber, hides, and palm oil from West Africa increased substantially during the first decades of the nineteenth century, and imports of textile goods and other manufactured products rose.

European governments also began to push for a more permanent presence along the coast. During the early nineteenth century, the British established settlements along the Gold Coast and in Sierra Leone, where they set up agricultural plantations for freed slaves who had returned from the Western Hemisphere or had been liberated by British ships while en route to the Americas. A similar haven for ex-slaves was developed with the assistance of the United States in Liberia. The French occupied the area around the Senegal River near Cape Verde, where they attempted to develop peanut plantations.

The European presence in West Africa led to the emergence of a new class of Africans educated in Western culture and often employed by Europeans. Many became Christians, and some studied in European or American universities. At the same time, tensions were increasing between Europeans and some African governments. Most African states were able to maintain their independence from this creeping European encroachment, called the **informal empire** by some historians, but the prospects for the future were ominous. When local groups attempted to organize to protect their interests, the British stepped in and annexed the coastal states as the British colony of Gold Coast in 1874. At about the same time, the British extended an informal protectorate over warring ethnic groups in the Niger River Delta.

21-5b Imperialist Shadow over the Nile

A similar process was under way in the Nile Valley. There had long been interest in shortening the trade route to the East by digging a canal across the isthmus separating the Mediterranean from the Red Sea. In 1798, Napoleon had unsuccessfully invaded Egypt in an effort to cement French power in the eastern Mediterranean and open a faster route to India. French troops landed in Egypt and destroyed the ramshackle Mamluk (MAM-look) regime, but the British counterattacked and destroyed the French fleet. The British restored the Mamluks

to power, but in 1805 Muhammad Ali (1769–1849), an Ottoman army officer, seized control.

During the next three decades, Muhammad Ali introduced a series of reforms to bring Egypt into the modern world. He modernized the army, set up a public education system (supplementing the traditional religious education provided in Muslim schools), and sponsored the creation of a small industrial sector producing refined sugar, textiles, munitions, and even ships. Muhammad Ali also extended Egyptian authority southward into the Sudan and eastward into Arabia, Syria, and northern Iraq and even threatened to seize Istanbul itself. To prevent the possible collapse of the Ottoman Empire, the British and the French recognized Muhammad Ali as the hereditary **pasha** (PAH-shuh) of Egypt under the loose authority of the Ottoman government.

The growing economic importance of the Nile Valley, along with the development of steam navigation, made the heretofore visionary plans for a Suez canal more urgent. In 1869, construction of the canal was completed under the direction of Ferdinand de Lesseps (fer-DEE-nahn duh le-SEPS), a French entrepreneur. The project brought little immediate benefit to Egypt, however. The construction cost thousands of lives and left the Egyptian government deep in debt, forcing it to depend increasingly on foreign financial support. When an army revolt against growing foreign influence broke out in 1881, the British stepped in to protect their investment (they had bought Egypt's canal company shares in 1875) and established an informal protectorate that would last until World War I. (See Map 21.3.)

Rising discontent in the Sudan added to Egypt's growing internal problems. In 1881, Muslim cleric Muhammad Ahmad (AH-mahd) (1844–1885), who was widely known as the Mahdi (MAH-dee) (in Arabic, the "rightly guided one"), led a religious revolt that brought much of the Upper Nile River Valley under his control. Famous British general Charles Gordon led a military force to Khartoum (kahr-TOOM) to restore Egyptian authority, but his besieged army was captured in 1885 by the Mahdi's troops thirty-six hours before a British rescue mission reached Khartoum. Gordon himself died in the battle.

The weakening of Turkish rule in the Nile Valley had a parallel to the west, where local viceroys in Tripoli, Tunis, and Algiers had begun to establish their autonomy.

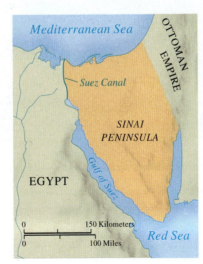

Map 21.3 The Suez Canal

In 1830, the French, on the pretext of protecting shipping from pirates, seized the area surrounding Algiers and integrated it into the French Empire. In 1881, the French imposed a protectorate on neighboring Tunisia; only Tripoli and Cyrenaica (seer-uh-NAY-uh-kuh), the territories constituting modern Libya, remained under Turkish rule.

21-5c Arab Merchants and European Missionaries in East Africa

As always, events in East Africa followed their own distinctive pattern. While the Atlantic slave trade was in decline, demand for slaves was increasing on the other side of the continent because of the growth of plantation agriculture in the region. The French introduced sugar to the island of Réunion (ray-yoo-NYAHN) early in the century, and plantations of cloves (introduced from the Moluccas) were established under Omani Arab ownership on the island of Zanzibar (ZAN-zi-bar). Zanzibar itself became the major shipping port along the east coast during the early nineteenth century, and the sultan of Oman, who had reasserted Arab suzerainty over the region after the collapse of Portuguese authority, established his capital there in 1840.

The tenacity of the slave trade in East Africa—Zanzibar was now the largest slave market in Africa—drew Christian missionaries to the region during the middle of the

century. The most renowned was Scottish doctor David Livingstone (1813–1873), who arrived in Africa in 1841. Because Livingstone spent much of his time exploring the interior of the continent, discovering Victoria Falls in the process, he was occasionally criticized for being more explorer than missionary. But Livingstone was convinced that it was his divinely appointed task to bring Christianity to the continent, and his passionate opposition to slavery did much to win British public support for the abolitionist cause. Public outcries caused the British to redouble their efforts to bring the slave trade to an end; shortly after Livingstone's death in 1873, the slave market at Zanzibar was finally closed as the result of pressure from London (see Image 21.6).

21-5d Bantus, Boers, and British in the South

Nowhere in Africa did the European presence grow more rapidly than in the south. During the eighteenth century, the Boers (BOORS or BORS), Afrikaans-speaking farmers descended from the original Dutch settlers of the Cape Colony, began to migrate eastward. After the British seized the cape during the Napoleonic Wars, the Boers' eastward migration intensified, culminating in the Great Trek of the mid-1830s. In part, the Boers' departure was provoked by the British attitude toward the local population. Slavery was abolished in the British Empire in 1834, and the British government was generally more sympathetic to the rights of the local African population than were the Afrikaners (ah-fri-KAH-nurz), many of whom believed that white superiority was ordained by God. Eventually, the Boers formed their own independent republics— the Orange Free State and the South African Republic, usually called the Transvaal (trans-VAHL) (see Map 21.4).

Although the Boer occupation of the eastern territory was initially facilitated by internecine warfare among the local inhabitants, the new settlers met some resistance. In the early nineteenth

21.6 Zanzibar: Entrepôt of East Africa. For centuries, the island of Zanzibar was one of the most important trading posts along the coast of East Africa. It was not only an active entrepôt for exchanging goods between inland areas in the continent of Africa and regions throughout the Indian Ocean but also a center of the mixed Afro–Arabian Swahili culture that flourished up and down the coast. By the end of the eighteenth century, Zanzibar took on a new importance, as clove trees, imported secretly from the Spice Islands by European adventurers, were planted throughout the island. For years, it also served as a center for the slave trade as captives from the African mainland were shipped to purchasers throughout the Middle East.

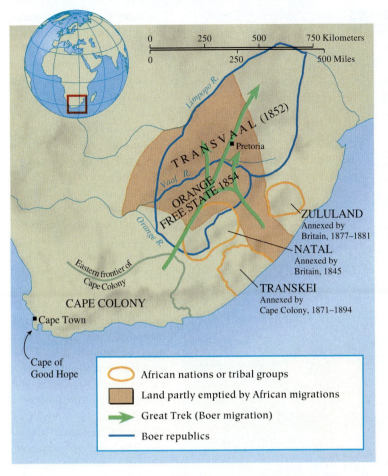

Map 21.4 The Struggle for Southern Africa. European settlers from the Cape Colony expanded into adjacent areas of southern Africa during the nineteenth century. The arrows indicate the routes taken by the Afrikaans-speaking Boers.

Q *Who were the Boers, and why did they migrate eastward?*

century, the Zulus (ZOO-looz), a Bantu people led by a talented ruler named Shaka (SHAH-kuh), engaged in a series of wars with the Europeans that ended only when Shaka was overthrown.

21-5e The Scramble for Africa

At the beginning of the 1880s, most of Africa was still independent. European rule was limited to the fringes of the continent such as Algeria, the Gold Coast, and South Africa. Other areas like Egypt, lower Nigeria, Senegal (sen-ni-GAHL), and Mozambique (moh-zam-BEEK) were under loose protectorates. But the pace of European penetration was accelerating.

The scramble began in the mid-1880s when several European states, including Belgium, France, Germany, and Great Britain, engaged in a feeding frenzy to seize a piece

of the African cake before the plate had been picked clean. By 1900, virtually all of the continent had been placed under some form of European rule. The British consolidated their authority over the Nile Valley and seized additional territories in East Africa (see Map 21.3). The French advanced eastward from Senegal into the central Sahara. They also occupied Madagascar and other territories in West and Central Africa. The Germans claimed the hinterland opposite Zanzibar, as well as coastal strips in West and Southwest Africa, and King Leopold (LAY-oh-polt) II (1835–1909) of Belgium claimed the Congo for his own personal use. Italy entered the contest in 1911–1912 and seized the territories that constitute modern Libya.

What had sparked the imperialist hysteria that brought an end to African independence? Although trade between Europe and Africa had increased, it was probably not sufficient by itself to justify the risks and expense of conquest. More important than economic interests were the rivalries among the European states that led them to engage in imperialist takeovers out of fear that if they did not, then another state would. As one British diplomat remarked, a protectorate at the mouth of the Niger River would be an "unwelcome burden," but a French protectorate there would be "fatal." Hence, as in Southeast Asia, statesmen felt compelled to obtain colonies as a hedge against future actions by European rivals. Notably, the British solidified their control over the entire Nile Valley to protect the Suez Canal from the French (see Map 21.5).

Another consideration might be called the "missionary factor," as European missionaries lobbied for colonial takeovers to facilitate their efforts to convert the African population. The concept of Social Darwinism and the "white man's burden" persuaded many that they had a duty to introduce the African people to the benefits of Western civilization. Even David Livingstone believed that missionary work and economic development had to go hand in hand, pleading with his fellow Europeans to introduce the "three C's" (Christianity, commerce, and civilization) to the continent. How much easier that task would be if African peoples were under benevolent European rule!

There were more prosaic reasons as well. Advances in Western technology and European superiority in

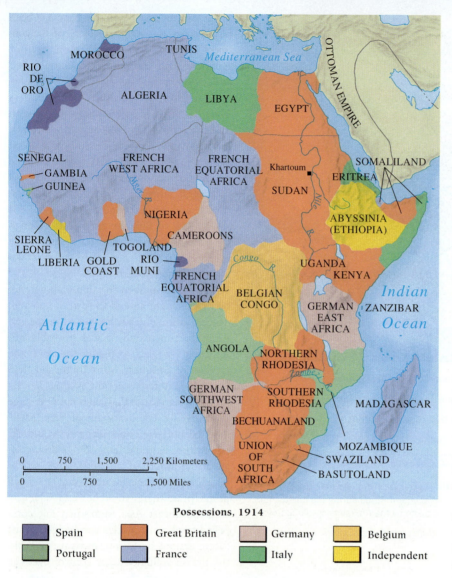

0	750	1,500		2,250 Kilometers			
0		750		1,500 Miles			

Possessions, 1914

Spain	Great Britain	Germany	Belgium
Portugal	France	Italy	Independent

Map 21.5 Africa in 1914. By the start of the twentieth century, virtually all of Africa was under some form of European rule. The territorial divisions established by colonial powers on the continent of Africa on the eve of World War I are shown here.

Q *Which European countries possessed the most colonies in Africa? Why did Ethiopia remain independent?*

firearms made it easier than ever for a small European force to defeat superior numbers. Furthermore, life expectancy for Europeans living in Africa had improved. With the discovery that quinine (made from the bark of the cinchona tree) could provide partial immunity from malaria, the mortality rate for Europeans living in Africa dropped dramatically. By the end of the century, European residents in tropical Africa faced only slightly higher risks of death by disease than individuals living in Europe.

Under these circumstances, King Leopold of Belgium used missionary activities as an excuse to claim vast territories in the Congo River basin. Belgium, he said, as "a small country, with a small people," needed a colony to enhance its image.[8] The royal land grab set off a race among European nations to stake claims throughout sub-Saharan Africa. Leopold ended up with the territories south of the Congo River, while France occupied areas to the north. Rapacious European adventurers established plantations in the new Belgian Congo to grow rubber, palm oil, and other valuable export products. Conditions for African workers were so abysmal that an international outcry led in 1903 to the formation of a commission under British consul Roger Casement to investigate. The commission's report, released in 1904, helped bring about reforms.

Meanwhile, in East Africa, Germany annexed the colony of Tanganyika (tan-gan-YEE-kuh). To avert violent clashes among the Great Powers, German Chancellor Otto von Bismarck convened a conference in Berlin in 1884 to set ground rules for future annexations of African territory. Like the famous Open Door Note 15 years later (see Chapter 22), the conference combined high-minded resolutions with a hardheaded recognition of practical interests. The delegates called for free commerce in the Congo and along the Niger River as well as for further efforts to end the slave trade. At the same time, the participants recognized the inevitability of the imperialist dynamic, agreeing only that future annexations of African territory should not be recognized until effective occupation had been demonstrated (see Image 21.7). No African delegates were present at the conference.

21.7 Legacy of Shame. By the mid-nineteenth century, most European nations had prohibited the trade in African slaves, but slavery continued to exist in Africa well into the next century. The most flagrant example was in the Belgian Congo, where the mistreatment of conscript laborers led to a popular outcry and the formation of a commission to investigate and recommend reforms. Shown here a young African male in manacles is a poignant symbol of the cruelties that took place as rapacious colonial powers seized control of the continent.

Over the next few years, African territories were annexed without provoking a major confrontation between the Western powers, but in 1898 Britain and France reached the brink of conflict at Fashoda (fuh-SHOH-duh), a small town in the Sudan. The French had been advancing eastward across the Sahara with the objective of controlling the regions around the Upper Nile River. British and Egyptian troops then marched southward to head off the French. After a tense face-off, the French government backed down, and British authority over the area was secured.

21-5f Colonialism in Africa

Having seized Africa in what could almost be described as a fit of hysteria, the European powers had to decide what to do with it. With economic concerns relatively limited except for isolated areas like the gold mines in the Transvaal and copper deposits in the Belgian Congo,

interest in Africa declined, and most European governments settled down to govern their new territories with the least effort and expense possible. In many cases, this meant a form of indirect rule similar to what the British used in the princely states in India.

Indirect Rule   For British administrators, the stated goal of indirect rule was to preserve African political traditions. The desire to limit cost was one reason for this approach, but it may also have been the result of the conviction that Africans were inherently inferior and thus incapable of adopting European customs and institutions. In any event, indirect rule entailed relying on existing political elites and institutions. In some areas, the British simply asked a local ruler to formally accept British authority.

Nigeria offers a case in point. British officials maintained the central administration, but local authority was assigned to local chiefs, with British district officers serving as intermediaries. The local authorities were expected to maintain law and order and to collect taxes. Local customs were generally left undisturbed, although slavery was abolished. A dual legal system was instituted that applied African laws to Africans and European laws to foreigners.

The situation was somewhat different in East Africa, especially in Kenya, which had a relatively large European population attracted by the temperate climate in the central highlands. The local colonial authorities had encouraged white settlers to migrate to the area as a means of promoting economic development. Fertile farmlands in the central highlands were reserved for Europeans, while specified reserve lands were set aside for Africans. The presence of a substantial European minority affected Kenya's political development. The white settlers sought self-government and dominion status similar to that granted to Canada and Australia. The British government, however, was not willing to risk provoking racial tensions with the African majority and agreed only to establish separate government organs for the European and African populations.

In southern Africa, an even higher percentage of European settlers were divided between the English-speaking and Afrikaner elements. After gold and diamonds were discovered in the Boer republic of the Transvaal, Cecil Rhodes, prime minister of the Cape Colony, attempted to bring the Transvaal under British rule, and the so-called Boer War broke out between Britain and the Boer republics in 1899. Guerrilla resistance by the Boers was fierce, but the vastly superior forces of the British were able to prevail by 1902. To compensate the Afrikaners for the loss of independence, the British government agreed that only whites would vote in the now essentially self-governing colony.

In 1910, the British agreed to the creation of the independent Union of South Africa, which combined the old were eligible to run for office and to serve in the French National Assembly, and a few were appointed to high positions in the colonial administration. Such policies reflected the conviction of the French in the superiority of Gallic culture as well as the malleability of human nature. With the proper instruction, Africans could become almost like the French.

High Colonialism   After World War I, European colonial policy in Africa entered a more formal phase that historians call **high colonialism**. The colonial enterprise was viewed more formally as a moral and social responsibility, a "sacred trust" to be maintained by the colonial powers until Africans became capable of self-government. Greater attention was placed on economic development to enable local economics to become more self-sufficient. Social services were to be improved, including education, medicine and sanitation, and communications. More Africans were appointed to serve in colonial administrations, although rarely in positions of responsibility. At the same time, race consciousness probably increased. Segregated clubs, schools, and churches were established as more European officials brought their wives and began to raise families in the colonies.

European feelings of superiority to their African subjects led to countless examples of cruelty. Although the institution of slavery was discouraged, African workers were often subjected to harsh conditions as they were put to use promoting the cause of imperialism.

Cape Colony and Natal (nuh-TAHL) with the Boer republics. The new union adopted a representative government, but only for the European population, and areas reserved for African settlers were subordinated directly to the crown. Formal British rule was also extended to the lands south of the Zambezi River, which were eventually divided into the territories of Northern and Southern Rhodesia. The latter attracted many British immigrants, and after a popular referendum it became a crown colony in 1922.

Direct Rule   Some European nations governed all of their African possessions through a form of direct rule. The prototype was the French system, which reflected the centralized administrative system used in France. At the top was a French governor-general, who was appointed from Paris. At the provincial level, French commissioners were assigned to deal with local administrators, who were required to be conversant in French. The goal was to assimilate their African subjects into French culture rather than preserving their local traditions. Africans

Women in Colonial Africa   The colonial era had a mixed impact on the rights and status of women in Africa. Sexual relationships changed profoundly, sometimes in ways that could justly be described as beneficial. Colonial governments attempted to bring an end to forced marriage, bodily mutilation such as the clitoridectomy (clit-er-ih-DEK-toh-mee), and polygamy. Missionaries introduced women to Western education and encouraged them to organize to defend their interests.

But the colonial system had unfavorable consequences as well. Previously, African women had benefited from the matrilineal system and their traditional role as primary agricultural producers. Under colonialism, European settlers not only took the best land for themselves but also tended to deal exclusively with males, encouraging them to develop lucrative cash crops using new techniques while women were restricted to traditional farming methods. In British colonies, Victorian attitudes of female subordination led to restrictions on women's freedom, and positions in government they formerly held were now closed to them.

21-6 THE EMERGENCE OF ANTICOLONIALISM

 Focus Question: How did the subject peoples respond to colonialism, and what role did nationalism play in their response?

Thus far we have looked at the colonial enterprise primarily from the point of view of the colonial powers. Equally important is the way the subject peoples reacted to the experience. In the final section of this chapter, we will deal with the initial response, which can be usefully described as the stage of "traditional resistance." Later, colonized peoples began to turn to the European concept of nationalism as a means to preserve their ethnic, cultural, or religious identity. We will deal with that stage in Chapter 24.

21-6a Stirrings of Nationhood

As noted previously, nationalism involves an awareness of being part of a community that possesses common institutions, traditions, language, and customs (see Comparative Essay, "The Rise of Nationalism," in Chapter 20, p. 514). In the nineteenth century, few societies in Asia and Africa met such criteria. Most contained a variety of ethnic, religious, and linguistic communities, each with its own sense of cultural and national identity. In fact, the very terms *nation* and *nationalism* were foreign concepts imported from the West. Before the colonial era, most traditional societies in Africa and Asia were formed on the basis of religious beliefs, ethnic or tribal loyalties, or devotion to hereditary monarchies. Although individuals in some countries may have identified themselves as members of a particular national group, others viewed themselves as subjects of a king, members of a lineage group, or adherents to a particular religion.

The advent of European colonialism brought the consciousness of modern nationhood to many of these societies. The creation of colonies with defined borders and a powerful central government led to the weakening of local ethnic and religious loyalties. The introduction of Western ideas of citizenship and representative government—even though they usually were not replicated in the colonies themselves—produced a desire for participation in the affairs of government. Not surprisingly, the introduction of a new and foreign elite class based on alleged racial or cultural superiority aroused a shared sense of resentment among the subject peoples. By the first quarter of the twentieth century, political

movements dedicated to the overthrow of colonial rule and the creation of modern nations had arisen throughout much of the non-Western world.

Modern nationalism in most countries suffering from colonial rule then was both a product of colonialism and a reaction to it. But a sense of nationhood does not emerge full-blown in a society. The rise of modern nationalism is a process that begins among a few members of the educated elite (most commonly among articulate professionals such as lawyers, teachers, journalists, and doctors) and then spreads gradually—through mobilization or rising literacy rates—to the mass of the population. Even after national independence has been realized, it is often questionable whether a mature sense of nationhood has been created because local ethnic, linguistic, or religious ties often continue to predominate over loyalty to the larger community (see Chapter 29).

21-6b Traditional Resistance: A Precursor to Nationalism

The beginnings of modern nationalism in Asia and Africa can be found in the initial resistance by indigenous peoples to the colonial conquest. Although such resistance was essentially motivated by the desire to defend traditional institutions and thus was not strictly "nationalist," it did reflect an incipient awareness of nationhood in that it aimed to protect the homeland from the invader. After independence was achieved, the governments of such new nations often hailed early resistance movements as the precursors of twentieth-century nationalist movements. Thus, traditional resistance to colonial conquest may be viewed as the first stage in the development of modern nationalism.

Such resistance took various forms. For the most part, it was led by the existing ruling elites, although in some instances traditionalists continued their opposition even after resistance by the indigenous rulers had ceased. In India, for example, many local leaders fought against the expansion of British rule even after the virtual collapse of the Mughal Dynasty. Some like the Deccan leader Haider Ali used guerrilla tactics with considerable success. Similarly, after the decrepit monarchy in Vietnam had been defeated by a French attack on the capital of Hanoi in 1884, civilian and military officials set up an independent organization called Can Vuong (kahn VWAHNG) (literally, "save the king") and continued their own resistance campaign without imperial sanction (see Image 21.8).

Sometimes traditional resistance to Western penetration took the form of peasant revolts. In traditional Asian societies, peasant discontent over high taxes, official

21.8 The French Seizure of North Vietnam. In the late 1850s, the French seized control of the southern part of Vietnam in the Mekong River Delta and transformed it into the French colony of Cochin China. In the summer of 1884, the French sought to complete their conquest of Vietnam by seizing the Red River Delta. In this painting by a Vietnamese artist, French troops prepare for an attack on the port city of Haiphong (Hy-PHONG) in preparation for an advance toward the Vietnamese capital of Hanoi. Eventually the entire country was occupied, and the northern part of Vietnam—renamed Tonkin—became a French protectorate

corruption, rising debt, and famine had often led to uprisings. Under colonialism, rural conditions frequently deteriorated as population density increased and peasants were driven off the land to make way for plantation agriculture. Angry peasants then vented their frustration at the foreign invaders. For example, in Burma, the Buddhist monk Saya San (SAH-yuh SAHN) led a widespread peasant uprising against the British. Similar unrest occurred in India, where zamindars and rural villagers alike resisted government attempts to increase tax revenues. A peasant uprising took place against the French occupation of Algeria in 1840.

Opposition to Colonial Rule in Africa   Because of Africa's sheer size and its ethnic, religious, and linguistic diversity, resistance to the European invaders was often sporadic and uncoordinated, but fierce nonetheless. The uprising led by the Mahdi in the Sudan was only the most dramatic example. In South Africa, the Zulus engaged in a bitter war of resistance to Boer colonists arriving from the Cape Colony. Later they fought against the British occupation of their

territory and were not finally subdued until the end of the century. In West Africa, the Ashanti ruling class led a bitter struggle against the British with broad-based popular support. But perhaps the most horrendous example of colonial oppression was in South-West Africa (today Namibia), where the indigenous Herero peoples, aided by their Namaqua allies, launched an uprising in 1904 against the presence of German occupation troops in the territory. After fierce battles, German forces drove the surviving resistance fighters into the Namibian Desert, where up to 100,000 died of exposure or starvation.

Resistance to the colonial conquest, therefore, was fairly widespread. The lack of modern weapons was decisive, however, and African forces eventually suffered defeat throughout the continent. The most fearsome weapon in the hands of the Europeans was the Maxim gun, the first recoil-operated machine gun, which had been invented by the American Hiram Stevens in 1883. In the hands of colonial authorities it enabled European troops to defeat adversaries many times their own size (in the widely-quoted words of the British poet Hilaire Belloc: "Whatever happens, we have got. The Maxim gun, and they have not")

The one exception was in Ethiopia, where, at the Battle of Adowa (AH-doo-wah) in 1896, the army of Emperor Menelik II (MEN-il-ik) was able to fend off an Italian invasion force with firearms purchased from several European countries and thus preserve the country's national independence well into the next century (see Image 21.9).

The Sepoy Uprising   Perhaps the most famous revolt against European authority in the mid-nineteenth century was that of the **sepoys** (SEE-poiz) in India. The sepoys (from the Turkish *sipahis*, cavalrymen or soldiers) were Indian troops hired by the East India Company to protect British interests. Unrest within Indian units of the colonial army had been common since early in the century,

21.9 The Battle of Adowa. During the 1890s, ambitious Italian leaders—their country only recent reunited—sought to follow the example of their European counterparts by creating their own colony in East Africa. After forcing the kingdom of Ethiopia to cede territories along the coast, in the winter of 1896 they determined to complete their conquest of the entire country. But on March 1, Ethiopian forces armed with European firearms inflicted a major defeat on the Italian army near the town of Adowa. In the ensuing Treaty of Addis Ababa, Italy formally recognized Ethiopian independence. The victory inspired African resistance leaders for decades, as well as the anonymous artists of this painting, which shows Ethiopian forces, led by their patron St. George on his white horse, matched against their Italian adversaries.

Like the Sepoy Uprising, traditional resistance movements usually met with little success. Peasants armed with pikes and spears were no match for Western armies possessing the most terrifying weapons then known to human society. In a few cases, such as the revolt of the Mahdi at Khartoum, the local peoples were able to defeat the invaders temporarily. But such successes were rare, and the late nineteenth century witnessed the seemingly inexorable march of the Western powers, armed with terrifying modern weapons, to mastery of the globe.

The Path of Collaboration

Not all Asians and Africans reacted to a colonial takeover by choosing the path of violent resistance. Some found elements to admire in Western civilization and compared it favorably with their own traditional practices and institutions. Even in sub-Saharan Africa, where the colonial record was often at its most brutal, some elites supported the imposition of colonial authority.

The decision to collaborate with the colonial administration was undoubtedly often motivated by self-interest. In those cases, the collaborators might be treated with scorn or even hostility by their contemporaries, especially those who had chosen resistance. On occasion, however, the decision was reached only after painful consideration of the alternatives. Whatever the circumstances, the decision often divided friends and families, as occurred with two onetime childhood friends in central Vietnam, when one chose resistance and the other collaboration (see Opposing Viewpoints, "To Resist or Not to Resist," p. 546).

Not all colonial subjects, of course, felt required to choose between resistance and collaboration. Most simply lived out their lives without engaging in the political arena. Even so, in some cases their actions affected their country's future. A prime example was Ram Mohan Roy (RAHM moh-HUHN ROI). A brahmin from Bengal (ben-GAHL), Roy founded the Brahmo Samaj (BRAH-moh suh-MAHJ) (Society of Brahma) in 1828 to help his fellow Hindus defend their faith against verbal attacks from British acquaintances. Roy was by no means a hidebound traditionalist. He

when it had been sparked by economic issues, religious sensitivities, or nascent anticolonial sentiment. In 1857, new tensions erupted when the British adopted the new Enfield rifle for use by sepoy infantrymen. The rifle was a muzzleloader that used paper cartridges covered with animal fat and lard; because the cartridge had to be bitten off, it broke strictures against high-class Hindus' eating animal products and Muslim prohibitions against eating pork. Protests among sepoy units in northern India were initially ignored by British authorities and soon turned into a full-scale mutiny, supported by uprisings in rural districts in various parts of the country. But the movement lacked clear goals, and discord between Hindus and Muslims prevented them from coordinating operations. Although the Indian troops fought bravely and outnumbered the British six to one, they were poorly organized, and the British forces (often supplemented by loyalist sepoy units) suppressed the rebellion.

Still, the revolt frightened the British and led to several reforms. The proportion of Indian troops in the army was reduced, and precedence was given to ethnic groups likely to be loyal to the British such as the Sikhs (SEEKS or see-ikhz) of Punjab (pun-JAHB) and the Gurkhas (GUR-kuhz), an upland people from Nepal (nuh-PAHL). The British also decided to suppress the final remnants of the hapless Mughal Dynasty, which had supported the mutiny, and turned responsibility for the administration of the subcontinent over to the crown.

To Resist or Not to Resist

Interaction & Exchange

HOW TO RESPOND TO COLONIAL RULE could be an excruciating problem for political elites in many Asian countries because resistance often seemed futile while often adding to the suffering of the indigenous population. Hoang Cao Khai (HWANG cow KY) and Phan Dinh Phung (FAN din FUNG) were members of the Confucian scholar-gentry from the same village in Vietnam. Yet they reacted in dramatically different ways to the French conquest of their country. Their exchange of letters, reproduced here, illustrates the dilemmas they faced.

Hoang Cao Khai's Letter to Phan Dinh Phung

Soon, it will be seventeen years since we ventured upon different paths of life. How sweet was our friendship when we both lived in our village. . . . At the time when the capital was lost and after the royal carriage had departed, you courageously answered the appeals of the King by raising the banner of righteousness. It was certainly the only thing to do in those circumstances. No one will question that.

But now the situation has changed and even those without intelligence or education have concluded that nothing remains to be saved. How is it that you, a man of vast understanding, do not realize this? . . . You are determined to do whatever you deem righteous. . . . But though you have no thoughts for your own person or for your own fate, you should at least attend to the sufferings of the population of a whole region. . . .

Until now your actions have undoubtedly accorded with your loyalty. May I ask however what sin our people have committed to deserve so much hardship? I would understand your resistance, did you involve but your family for the benefit of a large number. As of now, hundreds of families are subject to grief; how do you have the heart to fight on? I venture to predict that, should you pursue your struggle, not only will the population of our village be destroyed but our entire country will be transformed into a sea of blood and a mountain of bones. It is my hope that men of your superior morality and honesty will pause a while to appraise the situation.

Reply of Phan Dinh Phung to Hoang Cao Khai

In your letter, you revealed to me the causes of calamities and of happiness. You showed me clearly where advantages and disadvantages lie. All of which sufficed to indicate that your anxious concern was not only for my own security but also for the peace and order of our entire region. I understood plainly your sincere arguments.

I have concluded that if our country has survived these past thousand years when its territory was not large, its army not strong, its wealth not great, it was because the relationships between king and subjects, fathers and children, have always been regulated by the five moral obligations. In the past, the Han, the Sung, the Yuan, the Ming time and again dreamt of annexing our country and of dividing it up into prefectures and districts within the Chinese administrative system. But never were they able to realize their dream. Ah! if even China, which shares a common border with our territory, and is a thousand times more powerful than Vietnam, could not rely upon her strength to swallow us, it was surely because the destiny of our country had been willed by Heaven itself.

The French, separated from our country until the present day by I do not know how many thousand miles, have crossed the oceans to come to our country. Wherever they came, they acted like a storm, so much so that the Emperor had to flee. The whole country was cast into disorder. Our rivers and our mountains have been annexed by them at a stroke and turned into a foreign territory.

How can the French not be aware of all the suffering that the rural population has had to endure? Under these circumstances, is it surprising that families should be disrupted and the people scattered?

My friend, if you are troubled about our people, then I advise you to place yourself in my position and to think about the circumstances in which I live. You will understand naturally and see clearly that I do not need to add anything else.

Q *Explain briefly the reasons advanced by each writer to justify his actions. Which argument do you think would have earned more support from contemporaries? Why?*

Source: From Truong Buu Lam, *Patterns of Vietnamese Response to Foreign Intervention*, Monograph Series No. 11. Southeast Asian Studies, Yale University, 1967. Dist. By Celler Book Shop, Detroit, MI.

opposed such practices as sati and recognized the benefit of introducing the best aspects of European culture into Indian society. He probably had no intention of promoting Indian independence by his action, but by encouraging his countrymen to defend their traditional values against the onslaught of Western civilization he helped promote the first stirrings of nationalist sentiment in nineteenth-century India.

HISTORIANS DEBATE ### 21-6c Imperialism: Drawing Up The Balance Sheet

Few periods of history are as controversial as the era of imperialism. To defenders of the colonial enterprise like the poet Rudyard Kipling, imperialism was the "white man's burden," a disagreeable but necessary phase in the evolution of human society, lifting up the toiling races from tradition to modernity and bringing an end to poverty, famine, and disease (see earlier Opposing Viewpoints "White Man's Burden, Black Man's Sorrow," p. 529).

Critics take exception to such views, portraying imperialism as a tragedy of major proportions. The insatiable drive of the advanced economic powers for access to raw materials and markets created an exploitative environment that transformed the vast majority of colonial peoples into a permanent underclass while restricting the benefits of modern technology to a privileged few. In this view, Kipling's "white man's burden" was dismissed as a hypocritical gesture to hoodwink the naïve and salve the guilty feelings of those who recognized imperialism for what it was—a savage act of rape.

The issue continues to inspire debate among historians in our own day. Defenders of the colonial enterprise sometimes concede there were gross inequities in the system but that there was a positive side as well. The expansion of markets and the beginnings of a modern transportation and communications network, while bringing few immediate benefits to the colonial peoples, laid the groundwork for future economic growth. At the same time, the introduction of the rule of law and new ways of looking at human freedom, the relationship between the individual and society, and democratic principles set the stage for the adoption of such ideas after the restoration of independence following World War II. Finally, the colonial experience offered a new approach to the traditional relationship between men and women. Although colonial rule was by no means uniformly beneficial to women in African and Asian societies, growing awareness of the struggle for equality by women in the West gave them a weapon to use against long-standing barriers of custom and legal discrimination.

Between these two seemingly irreconcilable views, where does the truth lie? This chapter has contended that neither extreme position is justified. In fact, the consequences of colonialism have been more complex than either defenders or critics would have us believe. Although colonial peoples received little immediate benefit, overall the imperialist era brought about a vast expansion of the international trade network and created at least the potential for societies throughout Africa and Asia to play an active and rewarding role in the new global economic arena. If, as historian William McNeill believes, the introduction of new technology through cross-cultural encounters is the driving force of change in world history, then Western imperialism, whatever its faults, helped open the door to such change, much as the rise of the Arab Empire and the Mongol invasions hastened the process of global economic development in earlier periods.

Still, the critics have a point. Although colonialism introduced the peoples of Asia and Africa to new technology and the expanding global marketplace, it was unnecessarily brutal in its application and all too often failed to realize the exalted claims of its promoters. Existing economic networks—often potentially valuable as a foundation for later economic development—were ruthlessly swept aside to provide markets for Western manufactured goods. Potential sources of local industrialization were nipped in the bud to avoid competition for factories in Amsterdam, London, Pittsburgh, or Manchester. Promises to provide training in Western democratic ideals and practices were ignored out of fear that the recipients might use them as weapons against the ruling authorities.

The fundamental weakness of colonialism, then, was that it was ultimately based on the self-interests of the colonial powers. When those interests collided with the needs of the colonial peoples, those of the former always triumphed. However sincerely the David Livingstones, Albert Sarrauts, and Albert Beveridges of the world were convinced of the rightness of their civilizing mission, the ultimate result was to deprive colonial peoples of the right to make their own choices about their own destiny. Sophisticated age-old societies that could have been left to respond to the technological revolution in their own way were squeezed dry of precious national resources under the false guise of a "civilizing mission." As sociologist Clifford Geertz remarked in his book *Agricultural Involution: The Processes of Ecological Change in Indonesia*, the tragedy is not that the colonial peoples suffered through the colonial era but that they suffered for nothing.

By the first quarter of the twentieth century, virtually all of Africa and a good part of South and Southeast Asia were under some form of colonial rule. With the advent of the age of imperialism, a global economy was finally  established, and the domination of Western civilization over the civilizations of Africa and Asia appeared to be complete.

The imperialist rush for colonies did not take place without opposition. In most areas of the world, local governments and peoples resisted the onslaught, sometimes to the bitter end. But with few exceptions, they were unable to overcome the fearsome new warships and firearms that the Industrial Revolution in Europe had brought into being. Although the material benefits and democratic values of the occupying powers aroused admiration from observers in much of the colonial world, in the end it was weapons more than ideas that ushered in the age of imperialism.

Africa and southern Asia were not the only areas of the world that were buffeted by the winds of Western expansionism in the late nineteenth century. The nations of eastern Asia, Latin America, and the Middle East were also affected in significant ways. The consequences of Western political, economic, and military penetration varied substantially from one region to another, however, and therefore require separate treatment. The experience of East Asia will be dealt with in the next chapter. Those of Latin America and the Middle East will be discussed in Chapter 24. In these areas, new rivals—notably the United States, Russia, and Japan—entered the scene and played  active roles in the process. By the end of the nineteenth century, the rush to secure colonies had circled the world.

REFLECTION QUESTIONS

Q What arguments have been advanced to justify the European takeover of societies in Asia and Africa during the latter part of the nineteenth century? To what degree are such arguments justified?

Q The colonial powers adopted two basic philosophies in seeking to govern their conquered territories in Asia and Africa—assimilation and association. What were the principles behind these philosophies, and how did they work in practice? Which do you believe was more successful?

Q How did the forms of imperialism applied by the advanced industrial powers in the nineteenth century compare with earlier examples of imperial rule as established throughout history? How would you draw up the balance sheet?

CHAPTER TIMELINE

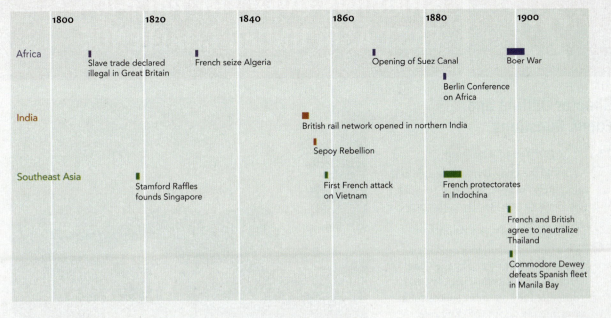

	1800	1820	1840	1860	1880	1900

Africa
- Slave trade declared illegal in Great Britain
- French seize Algeria
- Opening of Suez Canal
- Boer War
- Berlin Conference on Africa

India
- British rail network opened in northern India
- Sepoy Rebellion

Southeast Asia
- Stamford Raffles founds Singapore
- First French attack on Vietnam
- French protectorates in Indochina
- French and British agree to neutralize Thailand
- Commodore Dewey defeats Spanish fleet in Manila Bay

CHAPTER NOTES

1. Quoted in *The New York Times*, January 30, 2016.

2. K. Pearson, *National Life from the Standpoint of Science* (London, 1905), p. 184. The comment by Jules Ferry is from W. Baumgart, *Imperialism: The Idea and Reality of British and French Colonial Expansion, 1880–1914* (Oxford, 1982), p. 73.

3. Quoted in H. Braunschwig, *French Colonialism, 1871–1914* (London, 1961), p. 80.

4. Quoted in G. Garros, *Forceries Humaines* (Paris, 1926), p. 21.

5. Cited in B. Schwartz's review of D. Cannadine's *Ornamentalism: How the British Saw Their Empire,* in *The Atlantic,* November 2001, p. 135.

6. Quoted in R. Bartlett, ed., *The Record of American Diplomacy: Documents and Readings in the History of American Foreign Relations* (New York, 1952), p. 385.

7. Quoted in L. Roubaud, *Vietnam: La Tragédie Indochinoise* (Paris, 1926), p. 80.

8. Quoted in T. Pakenham, *The Scramble for Africa* (New York, 1991), p. 13.

MINDTAP
From Cengage

MindTap® is a fully online, highly personalized learning experience built upon Cengage Learning content. MindTap combines student learning tools—readings, multimedia, activities, and assessments—into a singular Learning Path that guides students through the course and helps students develop the critical thinking, analysis, and communication skills that are essential to academic and professional success.

Chapter Outline and Focus Questions

22-1 The Decline of the Qing

Q Why did the Qing Dynasty decline and ultimately collapse, and what role did the Western powers play in this process?

22-2 Chinese Society in Transition

Q What political, economic, and social reforms were instituted by the Qing Dynasty during its final decades, and why were they not more successful in reversing the decline of Qing rule?

22-3 A Rich Country and a Strong State: The Rise of Modern Japan

Q To what degree was the Meiji Restoration a "revolution," and to what extent did it succeed in transforming Japan?

The Art Archive/British Museum, London/Eileen Tweedy

22.1 The Macartney mission to China, 1793

Critical Thinking

Q *How did China and Japan each respond to Western pressures in the nineteenth century, and what implications did their different responses have for each nation's history?*

Connections To Today

Q *What lessons can developing nations today learn from the experiences encountered by China and Japan during the period covered in this chapter?*

BRITISH EMISSARY LORD MACARTNEY had arrived in Beijing in 1793 with a caravan loaded with gifts for the emperor. Flags provided by the Chinese proclaimed in Chinese characters that the visitor was an "ambassador bearing tribute from the country of England." But the gifts were in vain, for Macartney's request for an increase in trade between the two countries was flatly rejected, and he left Beijing with nothing to show for his efforts. Not until half a century later would the Qing Dynasty—at the point of a gun—agree to the British demand for an expansion of commercial ties.

In fact, the Chinese emperor Qianlong had responded to his visitor's requests with polite but poorly disguised condescension. To Macartney's proposal that a British ambassador be stationed in Beijing, the emperor replied that such a request was "not in harmony with the state system of our dynasty and will definitely not be permitted." He also rejected the British envoy's suggestion that regular trade relations be established between the two countries. We receive all sorts of precious things as gifts from the myriad nations, replied the Celestial Emperor.

"Consequently," he added, "there is nothing we lack, as your principal envoy and others have themselves observed. We have never set much store on strange or ingenious objects, nor do we need more of your country's manufactures."

Historians have often viewed the failure of Macartney's mission as a reflection of the disdain of Chinese rulers toward their counterparts in other countries and their serene confidence in the superiority of Chinese civilization in a world inhabited by barbarians. From his serene position in the heart of the Forbidden City in Beijing, the emperor's attitude certainly appeared justified because China at that moment seemed to be at the height of its power. From our perspective today, however, Qianlong's confidence was undoubtedly misplaced because, as the eighteenth century came to an end, China faced a growing challenge not only from the escalating power and ambitions of the West but also from its own internal weakness. When insistent British demands for the right to carry out trade and missionary activities in China were rejected, Britain resorted to force and gave Qing troops a sound thrashing in the Opium War that broke out in 1839. A humiliated China was finally forced to open its doors.

22-1 THE DECLINE OF THE QING

Q **Focus Question:** Why did the Qing Dynasty decline and ultimately collapse, and what role did the Western powers play in this process?

In 1800, the Qing (CHING) or Manchu Dynasty was at the height of its power. China had experienced a long period of peace and prosperity under the rule of two great emperors, Kangxi (kang-SHEE) and Qianlong (CHAN-loong). Its borders were secure, and its culture and intellectual achievements were the envy of the world. Its rulers, hidden behind the walls of the Forbidden City in Beijing (bay-ZHING), had every reason to describe their patrimony as the "Central Kingdom." But a little more than a century later, humiliated and harassed by the black ships and big guns of the Western powers, the Qing Dynasty, the last in a series that had endured for more than 2,000 years, collapsed in the dust (see Map 22.1).

The primary reason for the rapid decline and fall of the Qing Dynasty was once assumed to be the intense pressure applied by the Western powers. Now, however, most historians believe that internal changes played a major role in the dynasty's collapse and that at least some of its problems during the nineteenth century were self-inflicted.

Actually, both explanations have some validity. Like so many of its predecessors, after an extended period of growth, the Qing Dynasty began to experience the familiar dynastic ills of official corruption, peasant unrest, and incompetence at court. Such weaknesses were probably exacerbated by the rapid growth in population. The long era of peace, the introduction of new crops such as maize and sweet potatoes from the Americas, and the cultivation of new, fast-ripening strains of rice enabled the Chinese population to double in size between 1550 and 1800 and to reach the unprecedented level of 400 million by the end of the nineteenth century. With land pressure intensifying even without the Western powers, the Qing were probably destined to repeat the fate of their imperial predecessors. The ships, guns, and ideas of the foreigners simply highlighted the growing weakness of the dynasty and likely hastened its demise. In doing so, Western imperialism exerted an indelible impact on the history of modern China—but as a contributing but not causal factor.

22-1a Opium and Rebellion

By 1800, Europeans had been in contact with China for more than 200 years, but Western traders were limited to a small commercial outlet at Canton. This arrangement was not acceptable to the British, however. They not only chafed at being restricted to a tiny enclave but also had a growing appetite for Chinese tea that was creating a severe balance-of-payments problem. After the failure of Macartney's mission in 1793, a second mission in 1816 managed only to worsen the already strained relations between the two countries. The British solution to the problem was opium. A product more addictive than tea, opium had been grown in southwestern China for centuries, but it had been used primarily for medicinal purposes. Now opium grown in northeast India was carried to China in British ships, creating popular demand for the addictive product in China despite an official prohibition on its use. Soon bullion was flowing out of the Chinese imperial treasury into the pockets of British merchants.

The Qing court in Beijing became concerned and in 1839 assigned the imperial official Lin Zexu (LIN dzeh-SHOO) (1785–1850) the task of curtailing the opium trade. Lin appealed to Queen Victoria on both moral and practical grounds, threatening to prohibit the sale of rhubarb (widely used as a laxative in nineteenth-century Europe) to Great Britain if she did not respond. But moral principles paled before the lure of commercial profits, and the British continued to promote the opium trade, arguing that if the Chinese did not want the opium, they did not have to buy it. Lin Zexu attacked on three fronts, imposing

Map 22.1 The Qing Empire. Shown here is the Qing Empire at the height of its power in the late eighteenth century, together with its shrunken boundaries at the moment of dissolution in 1911.

 How do China's tributary states on this map differ from those in Map 17.2? Which of them fell under the influence of foreign powers during the nineteenth century?

penalties on smokers, arresting dealers, and seizing supplies from importers as they attempted to smuggle the drug into China. The last tactic caused his downfall. When he blockaded the foreign factory area in Canton to force traders to hand over their opium, the British government, claiming that it could not permit British subjects "to be exposed to insult and injustice," launched a naval expedition to punish the Qing and force them to open China to foreign trade.[1]

The Opium War The Opium War (1839–1842) lasted three years and demonstrated the superiority of British firepower and military tactics. British warships destroyed Chinese coastal and river forts and seized the offshore island of Zhoushan (JOE-shahn) near the mouth of the Yangzi River. Imperial officials contemptuously dismissed

the threat from what they viewed as a small and insignificant nation (see Historical Voices, "An Insignificant and Detestable Race," p. 553). In response, a British fleet sailed virtually unopposed up the Yangzi to Nanjing (nan-JING) and cut off the supply of "tribute grain" from southern to northern China. The Qing finally agreed to British terms. In the Treaty of Nanjing in 1842, the Chinese agreed to open five coastal ports to British trade, limit tariffs on imported British goods, grant extraterritorial rights to British citizens in China, and pay a substantial indemnity to cover the costs of the war. China also agreed to cede the island of Hong Kong (dismissed by a senior British official as a "barren rock") to Great Britain. Nothing was said in the treaty about the opium trade, which continued unabated until it was brought under control through Chinese government efforts in the early twentieth century.

HISTORICAL VOICES

An Insignificant and Detestable Race

WHEN THE EUROPEAN POWERS BEGAN TO THREATEN MILITARY ACTION to force the Qing court to open Chinese borders to foreign commerce, imperial officials initially found it difficult to take the threat seriously. Such small and insignificant countries, they reasoned, could pose no serious challenge to the august and powerful Chinese Empire. Such was the case at the outset of the Opium War, when Qing officials like the author of the excerpt printed here complacently anticipated a rapid victory over the British naval forces in South China. Basing their confidence on China's presumed technological and cultural superiority, their expectations were quickly dashed. As it turned out, it would be decades before the imperial court fully realized the immensity of the threat to the ultimate survival of the Qing Dynasty.

A Memorial to the Emperor

The English barbarians are an insignificant and detestable race, trusting entirely to their strong ships and large guns; but the immense distance they have traversed will render the arrival of . . . supplies impossible, and their soldiers, after a single defeat, being deprived of provisions, will become dispirited and lost. Though it is . . . true that their guns are destructive, . . . in the attack on our harbors they will be too elevated, and their aim . . . rendered unsteady by the waves; while we in our forts, with larger pieces, can more steadily return the fire. Notwithstanding the riches of their government, the people are poor, and unable to contribute to the expenses of an army at such a distance. Granted that their vessels are their homes, and that in them they defy wind and weather, still they require a great draft of water; and, since our coasts are beset with shoals, they will certainly, without the aid of native pilots, run ashore . . . . Though waterproof, their ships are not fireproof, and we may therefore easily burn them. The crews will not be able to withstand the ravages of our climate, and surely waste away by degrees; . . . Without, therefore, despising the enemy, we have no cause to fear them . . .

> **Q** *In what respects do you believe that the author of this memorial underestimated the threat posed by British forces to the security of the Chinese Empire?*

Source: H. F. MacNair, *Modern Chinese History: Selected Readings* (Shanghai: Commercial Press Ltd., 1923), p. 136, reproduced in F. Schurmann and Orville Schell (eds.), *Imperial Reader: The Decline of the Last Dynasty and the Origins of Modern China* (New York, 1967), pp. 146–147.

Although the Opium War has traditionally been considered the beginning of modern Chinese history, it was probably not viewed that way at the time (see Image 22.2, p. 554). This was not the first time that a ruling dynasty had been forced to make concessions to foreigners, and the opening of five coastal ports to the British hardly constituted a serious threat to the empire. Although a few concerned Chinese argued that the court should learn more about European civilization, others contended that China had nothing to learn from the barbarians and that borrowing foreign ways would undercut the purity of Confucian civilization.

For the time being, then, the Qing attempted to deal with the foreigners in the traditional way of playing them off against each other. Concessions granted to the British were offered to other Western nations, including the United States, and soon foreign concession areas were operating in treaty ports along the Chinese coast from Canton to Shanghai (SHANG-hy).

The Taiping Rebellion In the meantime, however, the Qing's failure to deal with internal economic problems led to a major peasant revolt that shook the foundations of the empire. On the surface, the Taiping (TYping) ("Great Peace") Rebellion owed something to the Western incursion; the leader of the uprising, Hong Xiuquan (HOONG shee-oo-CHWAHN), a failed examination candidate, was a Christian convert who viewed himself as a younger brother of Jesus and hoped to establish what he referred to as a "Heavenly Kingdom of Supreme Peace." But the rebellion also had many local causes. The rapid increase in population forced millions of peasants to eke out a living as sharecroppers or landless laborers. Official corruption and incompetence led to the whipsaw of increased taxes and a decline in government services; even the Grand Canal was allowed to silt up, hindering the shipment of grain. In 1853, the rebels seized Nanjing, but that proved to be their high-water mark. Plagued by factionalism, the rebellion gradually

22.2 The Opium War. Waged between China and Great Britain between 1839 and 1842, the Opium War was China's first conflict with a European power. Lacking modern military technology, the Chinese suffered a humiliating defeat. In this painting, heavily armed British steamships destroy unwieldy Chinese junks along the Chinese coast. The steamship in the right background is the *HMS Nemesis*. Built in 1839, it was Britain's first iron-hulled steamship, and its ability to navigate shallow coastal waters inspired Chinese defenders to dub it "the devil ship." China's humiliation at sea was a legacy of its rulers' lack of interest in maritime matters since the middle of the fifteenth century when Chinese junks were among the most advanced sailing ships in the world.

lost momentum and was finally suppressed in 1864, but by then more than 25 million people had reportedly been killed, the vast majority of them civilians.

22-1b The Taiping Rebellion

One reason for the dynasty's failure to deal effectively with the internal unrest was its continuing difficulties with Western imperialists. In 1856, the British and the French, still smarting from the restrictions on trade and on their missionary activities, launched a new series of attacks and seized Beijing in 1860. As punishment, British troops

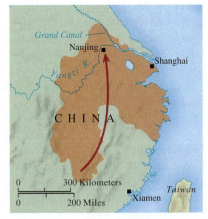

Map 22.2 The Taiping Rebellion

destroyed the imperial summer palace outside the city. In the ensuing Treaty of Tianjin (TYAHN-jin), the Qing agreed to humiliating new concessions: the legalization of the opium trade, the opening of additional ports to foreign trade, and the cession of the peninsula of Kowloon (KOW-loon) (opposite the island of Hong Kong) to the British (see Map 22.3). Additional territories in the north were ceded to Russia.

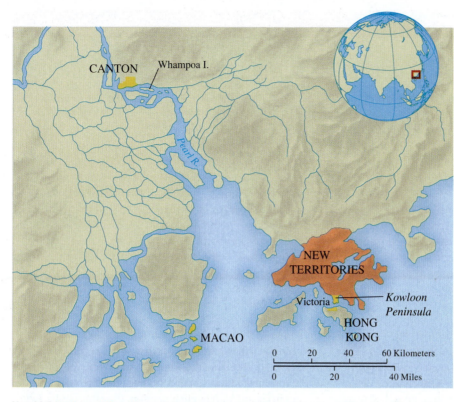

Map 22.3 Canton and Hong Kong. This map shows the estuary of the Pearl River in southern China, an important area of early contact between China and Europe.

Q *What was the importance of Canton? What were the New Territories, and when were they annexed by the British?*

22-1c Efforts at Reform

By the late 1870s, the old dynasty was well on the road to internal disintegration. To fend off the Taiping Rebellion, the Qing had had to rely on armed forces under regional command, but now many of these regional commanders refused to disband their units and continued to collect local taxes for their own use. The dreaded pattern of imperial breakdown, so familiar in Chinese history, was beginning to appear again.

Finally, the court began to listen to reform-minded officials, who advocated a new policy called **self-strengthening** in which Western technology would be adopted while Confucian principles and institutions were maintained intact. This policy, popularly known by its slogan "East for Essence, West for Practical Use," remained China's guiding standard for nearly a quarter of a century. Some even called for reforms in education and in China's hallowed political institutions (see Opposing Viewpoints, "Practical Learning or Confucian Essence: The Debate over Reform," p. 556).

22-1d The Climax of Imperialism

For the time being, the more cautious arguments won the day. During the last quarter of the nineteenth century, the Qing attempted to modernize the military and build an industrial base without disturbing the essential elements of traditional Chinese civilization. Railroads, weapons arsenals, and shipyards were built, but the value system remained unchanged.

In the end, the results spoke for themselves. During the last decades of the century, European penetration of China intensified. Rapacious imperialists began to bite off the outer edges of the empire. The Gobi Desert north of the Great Wall, Central Asia, and Tibet, all inhabited by non-Chinese peoples and never fully assimilated into the Chinese empire, were gradually lost. In the north and northwest, the main beneficiary was Russia, which forced the court to cede territories north of the Amur (ah-MOOR) River in Siberia. Competition between Russia and Great Britain prevented either power from seizing Tibet outright, but it did enable Tibetan authorities to revive their local autonomy. In the south, British and French advances in mainland Southeast Asia removed Burma (now Myanmar) and Vietnam from their traditional status as vassals to the Qing court. Even more ominous were the foreign spheres of influence in the Chinese heartland, where local commanders were willing to sell exclusive commercial, railroad-building, or mining privileges.

The disintegration of the Qing Dynasty accelerated as the century came to an end. In 1894, the Qing went to war with Japan over Japanese incursions into the Korean Peninsula, which threatened China's long-held suzerainty over the area (see section 22-3c, "Joining the Imperialist Club," p. 568). The Chinese were roundly defeated, confirming to some critics the failure of the policy of self-strengthening by halfway measures. In 1897, Germany, a new entry in the race for spoils in East Asia, used the murder of two German missionaries by

Practical Learning or Confucian Essence: The Debate over Reform

 Politics & Government

BY THE LAST QUARTER OF THE NINETEENTH CENTURY, Chinese officials and intellectuals had become increasingly alarmed at the country's inability to counter the steady pressure emanating from the West. Some, like the journalist Wang Tao (1828–1897), asserted that nothing less than a full-scale reform of Chinese society was required, including the adoption of the Western concept of political rights and democratic institutions. Others, like the scholar-official Zhang Zhidong (1837–1909), countered that such values and institutions would not work in China, and that the adoption of Western technology and science would be sufficient to protect the country from collapse. These two excerpts display the depth of disagreement between the two opposing views.

Zhang Zhidong, *Rectification of Political Rights*

The doctrine of people's rights will bring us not a single benefit but a hundred evils. Are we going to establish a parliament? Among the Chinese scholars and people there are still many today who are content to be vulgar and rustic. They are ignorant of the general situation of the world, they do not understand the basic system of the state. They have not the most rudimentary ideas about foreign countries – about the schools, the political systems, military training, and manufacture of armaments. Even supposing the confused and clamorous people are assembled in one house, for every one of them who is clear-sighted, there will be a hundred others whose vision is beclouded; they will converse at random and talks if in a dream—what use will it be? . . . .

Wang Tao, *A General History of France*

Since the National Assembly is established as a public body, not a private one, the people all submit to it. It is like this in all the countries of Europe . . . Under such a [system], those above and those below are at peace with one another and the monarch and his subjects share in the governing.. Things can go on for a long time, without getting to the point where people suffer from tyrannical administration and popular support is lost through the avarice and cruelty [of the officials]. For the members of both the upper and the lower assemblies are chosen entirely by the public, and from the time they first put themselves forward [as candidate] they must display fairness and rectitude in order to win. If they should at some point do something that is improper, in flagrant violation of public sentiment and not in accord with popular opinion, the same people who elected them can also remove them. Thus, even if they are inclined to turn a deaf ear to people's criticisms, there are definite bounds to their misconduct . . . .

Q *Why does journalist Wang Tao believe that the reforms he proposes are necessary? What are Zhang Zhidong's criticisms of such reforms?*

Sources: From Ssu-yu Teng and John K. Fairbank, *China's Response to the West: A Documentary Survey, 1839–1923* (Cambridge: Harvard University Press, 1954), p. 167. From Paul Cohen, *Between Tradition and Modernity: Wang T'ao and Reform in Late Ch'ing China* (Cambridge: Harvard University Press, 1974, p. 221, citing Fa-kuo chih-lueh (A General History of France, 1890.

Chinese rioters as a pretext to demand territories in the Shandong (SHAHN-doong) Peninsula. The imperial court granted the demand, setting off a scramble for territory (see Map 22.4). Russia demanded the Liaodong (LYOW-doong) Peninsula with its ice-free port at Port Arthur, and Great Britain obtained a 100-year lease on the New Territories adjacent to Hong Kong as well as a coaling station in northern China.

The government responded with yet another spasmodic effort at reform. In 1898, progressive Confucian scholar Kang Youwei (KAHNG yow-WAY) won the support of the young Guangxu (gwahng-SHOO) emperor for a comprehensive reform program patterned after recent measures in Japan. But when the emperor issued edicts calling for political, administrative, and educational reforms, they were opposed by conservatives, who saw little advantage and much risk in copying the West. The new program was also opposed by the emperor's aunt, the Empress Dowager Cixi (TSE-shee) (1835–1908) (see Image 22.3, p. 558). Cixi had begun her career as a concubine to an earlier emperor. After his death, she became a dominant force at court and in 1878 placed her infant nephew, the future Guangxu emperor, on the throne. For two decades, she ruled in his name as regent. With the aid of conservatives in the army, she arrested and executed several of the reformers and had the emperor incarcerated in the palace. With Cixi's palace coup, the One Hundred Days of reform came to an end.

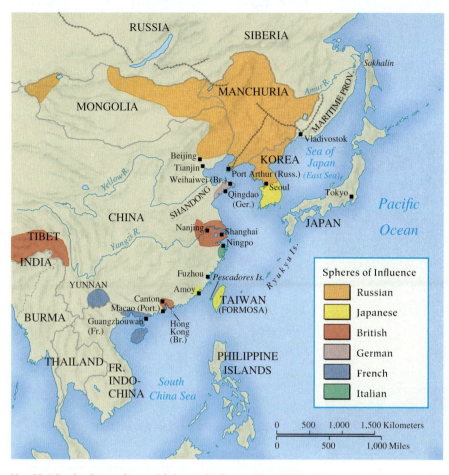

Map 22.4 Foreign Possessions and Spheres of Influence About 1900. At the end of the nineteenth century, China was being carved up like a melon by foreign imperialist powers.

Q Which of the areas marked on the map were removed from Chinese control during the nineteenth century?

expression of intent) quelled fears in Britain, France, Germany, and Russia that other powers would take advantage of the dynasty's weakness to dominate the China market.

The Boxer Rebellion Although the Open Door brought a measure of sanity to imperialist meddling in East Asia, it unfortunately came too late to stop the explosion known as the Boxer Rebellion. The Boxers, so-called because of the physical exercises they performed (similar to the more martial forms of tai chi), were a secret society operating primarily in rural areas in northern China. Provoked by a damaging drought and high unemployment caused in part by foreign activity (the introduction of railroads and steamships, for example, undercut the livelihood of barge workers on the rivers and canals), groups of Boxers attacked foreign residents and besieged the foreign legation quarter in Beijing until an international expeditionary force arrived in the late summer of 1900. As punishment, the foreign troops destroyed temples in the capital suburbs, and the Chinese government was compelled to pay a heavy indemnity to the foreign governments involved in suppressing the uprising. (See Image 22.4, p. 558.)

Opening The Door During the next two years, foreign pressure on the dynasty intensified. The British hoped to avert a total collapse of the Qing Dynasty, so with their encouragement U.S. Secretary of State John Hay proposed in 1899 that the imperialist powers join together to ensure equal access to the China market for all states and to guarantee the territorial and administrative integrity of the Chinese empire. Though probably motivated more by the U.S. preference for open markets than by a benevolent wish to protect China, the **Open Door Notes** had the practical effect of reducing the imperialist hysteria over access to China. That obsession, a product of decades of mythologizing among Western commercial interests about the 400 million potential Chinese customers, had accelerated at the end of the century as fear of China's imminent collapse increased. The "gentlemen's agreement" about the Open Door (it was not a treaty, but merely a nonbinding

22-1e The Collapse of the Old Order

During the next few years, the old dynasty tried desperately to reform itself. The empress dowager had long resisted change but now embraced several reforms. The venerable civil service examination system was replaced by a new educational system based on the Western model. In 1905, a commission was formed to study constitutional changes; over the next years, legislative assemblies were established at the provincial level, and elections for a national assembly were held in 1910.

Such moves helped shore up the dynasty temporarily, but history shows that the most dangerous period for an authoritarian system is when it begins to reform itself, because change breeds instability and performance rarely

22.3 The Empress Dowager Cixi. The role of Empress Dowager Cixi in policy formulation has been the focus of intense debate among historians in recent years, with some biographers taking issue with the prevailing view that she was a ruthless opponent of institutional reform in China. Complicating the issue is the fact that women who played an active role in politics routinely received critical treatment by Chinese historians. After the disastrous Boxer Rebellion, Cixi sought to improve her image in the Western world and turned to the modern medium of photography to do so. In this photograph taken in 1903, she appeared in an elaborate costume in a traditional Chinese setting, but her casual stance was apparently intended to soften her image among foreign observers.

22.4 Justice or mercy? Uncle Sam decides. In the summer of 1900, Chinese rebels known as Boxers besieged Western embassies in the imperial capital of Beijing. Western nations, including the United States, dispatched troops to North China to rescue their compatriots. In this cartoon, which appeared in a contemporary American newsmagazine, China figuratively seeks pardon from a stern Uncle Sam.

matches rising expectations. Such was the case in China. The new provincial elite— merchants, professionals, and reform-minded gentry—became impatient with the slow pace of change and was disillusioned to find that the new assemblies were to be primarily advisory. The reforms also had little meaning for peasants, artisans, miners, and transportation workers, whose standard of living was being eroded by rising taxes and official venality. Rising rural unrest was an ominous sign of deep-seated resentment.

The Rise Of Sun Yat-Sen The first stirrings of future revolution appeared during the last decade of the nineteenth

CHRONOLOGY	China in the Era of Imperialism
Lord Macartney's mission to China	1793
Opium War	1839–1842
Taiping rebels seize Nanjing	1853
Taiping Rebellion suppressed	1864
Cixi becomes regent for nephew, the Guangxu emperor	1878
Sino–Japanese War	1894–1895
One Hundred Days reform	1898
Open Door policy	1899
Boxer Rebellion	1900
Commission to study constitution formed	1905
Deaths of Cixi and the Guangxu emperor	1908
Revolution in China	1911

HISTORICAL VOICES

Program for a New China

 Politics & Government IN 1905, SUN YAT-SEN united a number of anti-Manchu groups into a single patriotic organization called the Revolutionary Alliance (Tongmenghui). The new organization eventually formed the core of his Guomindang (**gwoh-min-DAHNG**), or Nationalist Party. This excerpt is from the organization's manifesto, published in 1905 in Tokyo. Note that Sun believed that the Chinese people were not ready for democracy and required a period of tutelage to prepare them for the final era of constitutional political government. This was a formula that would be adopted by many other political leaders in Asia and Africa after World War II.

Sun Yat-sen, *Manifesto for the Tongmenghui*

By order of the Military Government, . . . the Commander-in-Chief of the Chinese National Army proclaims the purposes and platform of the Military Government to the people of the nation:

1. *Drive out the Tartars:* The Manchus of today were originally the eastern barbarians beyond the Great Wall. They frequently caused border troubles during the Ming Dynasty; then when China was in a disturbed state they , conquered China, and enslaved our Chinese people. . . . The extreme cruelties and tyrannies of the Manchu government have now reached their limit. With the righteous army poised against them, we will overthrow that government, and restore our sovereign rights.
2. *Restore China:* China is the China of the Chinese. The government of China should be in the hands of the Chinese. After driving out the Tartars we must restore our national state. . . .

3. *Establish the Republic:* Our revolution is based on equality, in order to establish a republican government. All our people are equal and all enjoy political rights. . . .
4. *Equalize land ownership:* The [wealth of our country] is to be shared equally by all the people of the nation. We [will] create a socialist state, where each family within the empire can be well supported, each person satisfied, and no one fail to secure employment. . . .

The above four points will be carried out in three steps in due order. The first period is government by military law. Evils like the oppression of the government, the greed and graft of officials, . . . —shall all be exterminated. Evils in social customs, such as the keeping of slaves, the cruelty of foot binding, the spread of the poison of opium, should also all be prohibited. . . .

The second period is that of government by a provisional constitution. When military law is lifted in each *hsien* [district], the Military Government shall return the right of self-government to the local people. . . .

The third period will be government under the constitution. Six years after the provisional constitution has been enforced a constitution shall be made. The military and administrative powers of the Military Government shall be annulled; the people shall elect the president, and elect the members of parliament to organize the parliament.

Q *How do Sun Yat-sen's proposals compare with those advanced by Wang Tao earlier in this chapter? Can Sun be described as a Chinese nationalist?*

Source: From Ssu-yu Teng and John K. Fairbank, *China's Response to the West: A Documentary Survey, 1839–1923* (New York, 1970), pp. 227–228, citing *Chung-shan chuan-shu* (The Complete Works of Sun Yat-sen), pp. 227–229.

---

century with the formation of the Revive China Society by the young radical Sun Yat-sen (SOON yaht-SEN) (1866–1925). Born in a village south of Canton, Sun was educated in Hawai'i and returned to China to practice medicine. Soon he turned his full attention to the ills of Chinese society.

At first, Sun's efforts yielded few positive results, but in 1905 he managed to unite radical groups from across China in the so-called Revolutionary Alliance, or Tongmenghui (toong-meng-HWAY). Its program was based

on Sun's **three people's principles** of nationalism (meaning primarily the elimination of Qing rule over China), democracy, and people's livelihood (see Historical Voices, "Program for a New China"). Although the organization was small and relatively inexperienced, it benefited from rising popular discontent.

The Revolution of 1911 In October 1911, Sun's followers launched an uprising in the industrial center of Wuhan (WOO-HAHN) in central China. With Sun traveling

Experience an interactive version of this period in **MINDTAP**   *22-1 The Decline of the Qing* ■ **559** in the United States, the insurrection lacked leadership, but when the central government was slow to react, local insurgent forces took measures into their own hands. The dynasty was now in a state of virtual collapse: the empress dowager had died in 1908, one day after her nephew, and the throne was occupied by China's "last emperor," the infant Puyi (POO-YEE). In desperation, the imperial regent called on General Yuan Shikai (yoo-AHN shee-KY) to suppress the rebellion. He opportunistically abandoned the Qing and acted on his own behalf. In negotiations with the revolutionaries, he agreed to serve as president of a new Chinese republic. The old dynasty and the age-old system that it had attempted to preserve were no more.

HISTORIANS DEBATE 22-1f Was the 1911 Revolution a Success or a Failure?

In these circumstances, some historians have argued that China would have been better served had the old dynasty been allowed to follow the path of gradual reform that had been inaugurated during the first decade of the new century. No doubt it is true that Sun Yat-sen's program had only limited relevance to conditions in China. It had been based primarily on Western liberal democratic principles aimed at the urban middle class. That class had provided the driving force for the capitalist democratic revolutions in Western Europe and North America in the late eighteenth and nineteenth centuries, but its counterpart in China was too small to form the basis for a new political order. The vast majority of the Chinese people still lived on the land. Sun had hoped to win their support with a land reform program, but few peasants were aware of it and rural participation in the 1911 revolution was minimal. In failing to provide a set of ideas that could arouse the active support of the impoverished millions of Chinese, Sun and his followers had brought about less a revolution than merely a collapse of the old order. Under the weight of imperialism and its own internal weaknesses, the old dynasty had crumbled before new political and social forces were ready to fill the vacuum.

Still, to argue that the old dynasty could have done better is hypothetical at best. What China experienced in 1911 was part of a historical process that was bringing down traditional empires across the globe, both in regions threatened by Western imperialism and within Europe itself (see Chapter 23). Like its counterparts, the Qing Dynasty had responded to the forces of industrialization, technological change, and popular participation in the political process with hesitation and reluctance, and its attempts at reform were too little and too late. All paid the supreme price for their folly.

22-2 CHINESE SOCIETY IN TRANSITION

Focus Question: What political, economic, and social reforms were instituted by the Qing Dynasty during its final decades, and why were they not more successful in reversing the decline of Qing rule?

Although the growing Western presence in China during the late nineteenth and early twentieth centuries obviously had a major impact on Chinese society, the country was already in a state of transition when the European penetration began to accelerate in the mid-nineteenth century. Manufacturing and trade were growing, particularly in the cities, where a national market for such commodities as oil, copper, salt, tea, and porcelain had developed. In the countryside, new crops introduced from abroad significantly increased food production and aided population growth. The Chinese economy had never been more productive or more complex.

22-2a The Economy: The Drag of Tradition

Whether these changes by themselves in the absence of outside intervention would have led to an industrial revolution and a capitalist economy on the Western model is impossible to know. Certainly, several obstacles would have made it difficult for China to embark on the Western path if it had wished to do so.

First, although industrial production was on the rise, it was still based almost entirely on traditional methods. There was no uniform system of weights and measures, and the banking system was still primitive by European standards. Although paper money had been invented by the Chinese centuries earlier (see Chapter 10), its use was still relatively limited. The transportation system, which had been neglected since the end of the Yuan Dynasty, was increasingly chaotic. There were few paved roads, and the Grand Canal, long the most efficient means of carrying goods from north to south, was silting up. As a result, merchants had to rely more and more on the coastal route, where they faced increased competition from foreign shipping.

Second, although foreign concession areas along the coast provided a conduit for the importation of Western technology and manufacturing methods, the Chinese borrowed less for such purposes than they might have. Foreign enterprises could not legally operate in China until the last decade of the nineteenth century, and their methods had little influence beyond the concession areas in the coastal cities. Chinese efforts to imitate Western methods, notably in shipbuilding and weapons manufacture, often suffered from inefficiency and mismanagement. Equally serious problems persisted in the countryside. The rapid increase in population had led to smaller plots and burgeoning numbers of tenant farmers. Whether per capita food consumption was on the decline is not clear from the available evidence, but apparently rice as a staple of the diet was increasingly being replaced by less nutritious foods, many of which depleted the soil, already under pressure from the dramatic increase in population. Some farmers benefited from switching to commercial agriculture to supply the markets of the growing coastal cities, but the shift entailed a sizable investment. Many farmers went so deeply into debt that they eventually lost their land. In the meantime, the traditional patron–client relationship was frayed as landlords moved to the cities to take advantage of the glittering urban lifestyle introduced by the West.

Some of these problems can undoubtedly be ascribed to the challenges presented by the growing Western presence. But the imperial court's hesitant response suggests that the most important obstacle was at the top: Qing officials often seemed overwhelmed by the combination of external pressure and internal strife. At a time when other traditional societies such as Russia, the Ottoman Empire, and Japan were making vigorous attempts to modernize their economies, the Qing court, along with much of the elite class, still exhibited an alarming degree of complacency.

22-2b The Impact of Imperialism

In any event, with the advent of the imperialist era, the question of whether China left to itself would have experienced an industrial revolution became academic. Imperialism caused serious distortions in the local economy that resulted in massive changes in Chinese society during the twentieth century. Whether the Western intrusion was beneficial or harmful is still debated to this day. The Western presence undoubtedly accelerated the development of the Chinese economy in some ways: the introduction of modern means of production, transport, and communications; the creation of a larger export market; and the steady integration of the Chinese market into the global economy. To many Westerners at the time, it was self-evident that such changes would ultimately benefit the Chinese people (see Comparative Essay, "Imperialism and the Global Environment," p. 562). In their view, by supplying (in the catch phrase of the day) "oil for the lamps of China," the West was providing a backward society with an opportunity to move up a notch or two on the ladder of human evolution.

Not everyone agreed. Critics of the colonial enterprise contended that Western imperialists hindered the process of structural change in preindustrial societies by thwarting the rise of a local industrial and commercial sector to maintain colonies as markets for Western manufactured goods and sources of cheap labor and materials. Had the West not intervened, they argued, China would have found its own road to the creation of an advanced industrial society.

Many historians today would say that both explanations are too simplistic. By shaking China out of its traditional mind-set, imperialism accelerated the change that had begun in the late Ming and early Qing periods and forced the Chinese to adopt new ways of thinking and acting. At the same time, China paid a heavy price in the destruction of its local industry while many of the profits flowed abroad. Although industrial revolution is inevitably a painful process, the Chinese found the experience doubly painful because it was foisted on them from the outside.

22-2c Daily Life in Qing China

In 1800, daily life for most Chinese was not substantially different from what it had been centuries earlier. Most were farmers, whose lives were governed by the harvest cycle, village custom, and family ritual. Their roles in society were fixed by the time-honored principles of Confucian social ethics. Male children, at least the more fortunate ones, were educated in the Confucian classics, while females remained in the home or in the fields. All children were expected to obey their parents, and all wives to submit to their husbands.

A visitor to China a hundred years later would have seen a distinctly different society, although one still recognizably Chinese. Change was most striking in the coastal cities, where the educated and affluent had been affected by the Western presence. Confucian social institutions and behavioral norms were beginning to decline in influence, while those of Europe and North America were on the ascendant. Change was much less noticeable in the countryside, but the customary bonds had been frayed even there.

Some of the change can be traced to the educational system. During the nineteenth century, the importance of a Confucian education was waning, with as many as half of all degree holders purchasing their degrees. After 1906, when the government abolished the civil service examinations, a Confucian education ceased to be the key to a successful career, and Western-style education became more desirable. The old dynasty attempted to establish an educational system on the Western model with universal education at the elementary level. The effect was greatest in the cities, where public schools, missionary schools, and other private institutions educated a new generation of Chinese with little knowledge of or respect for the past. The impact was much weaker in the countryside, where local inertia and lack of funds undercut the effort.

Imperialism and the Global Environment

Earth & Environment Beginning in the late nineteenth century, European states engaged in an intense scramble for overseas territory. This "new imperialism," as it is termed by historians, led to the carving up of independent Asian and African states and the creation of European colonial empires. Within these empires, the new rulers exercised complete political control over the indigenous societies and redrew political boundaries to meet their needs. In Africa, for example, in drawing the boundaries that separated one colony from another (boundaries that often became the boundaries of the modern countries of Africa), Europeans ignored existing political, linguistic, or religious divisions and frequently divided distinctive communities into different colonies or included two mutually hostile communities within the same colony.

To organize these new colonies to meet their own needs in the global marketplace, European colonial authorities paid little attention to the economic requirements of their colonial subjects. Urban areas were dramatically altered to serve as a hub for a new commercial and manufacturing economy. Workers were recruited, often by force, to serve the needs of Western-owned companies that drilled for oil and dug mines for gold, tin, iron ore, and copper, a process that resulted in enormous profits for colonial interests but inevitably transformed and often scarred the natural landscape.

Rural landscapes were even more dramatically altered by Europe's demand for cash crops. Throughout vast regions of Africa, Asia, and colonial territories in the Western Hemisphere, woodlands were cleared to make way for plantations where crops for export could be cultivated. In Ceylon (modern Sri Lanka) and India, the British cut down vast tropical forests to plant row upon row of tea bushes. The Dutch razed forests in the East Indies to plant palm oil plantations and cinchona trees (quinine, a derivative of cinchona bark, had been discovered to cure malaria). In Indochina, the French replaced extensive forests with rubber, tea, and coffee plantations. Local workers, who were usually paid pitiful wages by their European overseers, provided the labor for all of these vast plantations.

In many areas, precious farmland was turned over to the cultivation of cash crops, thus making it more difficult to feed growing populations. In the Dutch East Indies, farmers were forced to plow up some of their rice fields to make way for the cultivation of sugar. In West Africa, overplanting of cash crops damaged fragile grasslands and turned parts of the Sahel (suh-HAYL or suh-HEEL) into a wasteland.

During the era of new imperialism, the commercial exploitation of the Asian and African environments redounded almost entirely to the benefit of the colonial powers themselves. After the restoration of independence, however, many of the new states of Asia and Africa found it to their advantage to continue the process of extracting raw materials and cultivating cash crops as a means of improving their balance of payments. The profits from such activities are now beginning to benefit members of the local population, but the damage to the environment continues. The new enemy is thus not the imperialist powers themselves, but the industrial revolution that they unleashed over two centuries ago.

Liszt Collection/Alamy

22.5 The First Chinese Railroad. Few Western technological innovations were as controversial in late-nineteenth-century China as the railroad. Not only was it viewed as a threat to traditional forms of transportation—the cart and the barge—but the belching steam engines and even the train tracks were believed to disturb the graves and spirits of ancestors. Shown here is a drawing of the first train leaving the railroad station in Shanghai, already a city dominated by Western interests in 1876.

Q *How did the effects of imperialism on the environment in colonial countries compare with the impact of the Industrial Revolution in Europe and North America?*

Changing Roles For Women The status of women was also in transition. During the mid-Qing era, women were still expected to remain in the home. Their status as useless sex objects was painfully symbolized by the practice of foot binding, which had probably originated among court entertainers in the Tang Dynasty. By the mid-nineteenth century, more than half of all adult women probably had bound feet (see Image 22.6).

During the second half of the century, signs of change began to appear. Women began to seek employment in factories—notably in cotton mills and in the newly mechanized silk industry established in Shanghai in the 1890s. Some women participated in the Taiping Rebellion and the Boxer movement, and a few fought beside men in the 1911 revolution. Qiu Jin (chee-oo JIN), a well-known female revolutionary, wrote a manifesto calling for women's liberation and then organized a revolt against the Qing government, only to be captured and executed in 1907 at age thirty-two.

By the end of the century, educational opportunities for women began to appear for the first time, as Christian missionaries opened some girls' schools, mainly in the foreign concession areas. Although only a small number of women were educated in these schools, they had a significant impact as progressive intellectuals began to argue that ignorant women produced ignorant children. In 1905, the court announced plans to open public schools for girls, but few such schools ever materialized. The government also began to take steps to discourage foot binding but with only minimal success initially.

22-3 A RICH COUNTRY AND A STRONG STATE: THE RISE OF MODERN JAPAN

Q **Focus Question:** To what degree was the Meiji Restoration a "revolution," and to what extent did it succeed in transforming Japan?

When the nineteenth century began, the Tokugawa (tohkoo-GAH-wah) Shogunate had ruled the Japanese islands for 200 years. It had united the country, which had virtually disintegrated under its predecessors. It had driven out foreign traders and missionaries and reduced its contacts with the Western world. The Tokugawa maintained formal relations only with Korea, although informal trading links with Dutch and Chinese merchants continued at Nagasaki (nah-gah-SAH-kee). Isolation, however, did not mean stagnation. Although the vast majority of Japanese still depended on agriculture for their livelihood, a vigorous manufacturing and commercial sector had begun to emerge during the long period of peace and prosperity. As a result, Japanese society had begun to undergo deep-seated changes, and traditional class distinctions were becoming blurred.

By the end of the eighteenth century, however, there were signs that the Tokugawa system was beginning to come apart, just as the medieval order in Europe had started to disintegrate at the beginning of the Renaissance. Factionalism and corruption plagued the central bureaucracy, while rural unrest provoked by a series of poor harvests brought about by bad weather swept the countryside. Farmers fled to the towns, where anger was already rising as a result of declining agricultural incomes and shrinking stipends for the samurai. Many samurai lashed out at the perceived incompetence and corruption of the government. In response, the bakufu (buh-KOO-foo or bah-KOO-fuh) became

Private Collection/The Bridgeman Art Library

22.6 Women with Bound Feet. To ensure the best possible marriages for their daughters, upper-class families began to perform foot binding during the Song Dynasty. Eventually, the practice spread to all social classes in China. Although small feet were supposed to denote a woman of leisure, most Chinese women with bound feet contributed to the labor force, working mainly in textiles and handicrafts to supplement the family income. The two young women shown here are clearly from an upper-class family and are being taken for an outing on a rickshaw.

increasingly rigid, persecuting its critics and attempting to force fleeing peasants back to their lands.

Under these conditions, the government intensified its efforts to limit contacts with the outside world, driving away foreign ships that were prowling along the Japanese coast in increasing numbers. For years, Japan had financed its imports of silk and other needed products from other countries in Asia with the output of its silver and copper mines. But as these mines became exhausted during the eighteenth century, the bakufu cut back on foreign trade while encouraging the domestic production of goods that had previously been imported. Thus, the Tokugawa sought to adopt a policy of **sakoku** (sah-KOH-koo), or closed country, even toward the Asian neighbors with which Japan had once had active relations.

22-3a Opening to the World

To the Western powers, Japan's refusal to open its doors to Western goods was an affront and a challenge. Convinced that the expansion of trade would benefit all nations, Western nations began to approach Japan in the hope of opening up the kingdom to foreign interests.

The first to succeed was the United States. American steamships crossing the northern Pacific needed a fueling station before proceeding to China. In 1853, four American warships under Commodore Matthew C. Perry arrived in Edo Bay (now Tokyo Bay) with a letter from President Millard Fillmore asking for the opening of foreign relations between the two countries (see Image 22.7). A few months later, Perry returned with a larger fleet for an answer. In his

The Art Archive/British Museum

22.7 Black Ships in Tokyo Bay. The arrival of a U.S. fleet commanded by Commodore Matthew Perry in 1853 caused consternation among many Japanese observers, who were intimidated by the size and ominous presence of the American ships. This nineteenth-century woodblock print shows curious Japanese paddling out to greet the arrivals.

absence, Japanese officials had hotly debated the issue. Some argued that contacts with the West would be politically and morally disadvantageous to Japan, while others pointed to U.S. military superiority and recommended concessions. For the shogunate in Edo (EHdoh), the black guns of Perry's ships proved decisive, and Japan agreed to the Treaty of Kanagawa (kah-nah-GAH-wah), which provided for the return of ship-wrecked American sailors, the opening of two ports, and the establishment of a U.S. consulate in Japan. In 1858, U.S. Consul Townsend Harris negotiated a more elaborate commercial treaty calling for the opening of several more ports, the exchange of ministers, and the granting of extraterritorial privileges for U.S. residents in Japan. Similar treaties were soon signed with several European nations.

The opening of relations with the Western barbarians was highly unpopular in some quarters, particularly in regions distant from the shogunate headquarters in Edo. Resistance was especially strong in the key southern territories of Satsuma (sat-SOO-muh) and Choshu (CHOH-shoo), both of which had strong military traditions. In 1863, the "Sat-Cho" alliance forced the hapless shogun to promise to end relations with the West. The shogun eventually reneged on the agreement, but the rebels soon had their own problems. When Choshu troops fired on Western ships in the Strait of Shimonoseki (shee-mohnoh-SEK-ee), the Westerners fired back and destroyed the Choshu fortifications. The incident reinforced the rebellious samurais' antagonism toward the West and convinced them of the need to build up their own military. Having done so, they demanded the shogun's resignation and the restoration of the emperor's power. In January 1868, rebel armies attacked the shogun's palace in Kyoto and proclaimed the restored authority of the emperor. After a few weeks, resistance collapsed, and the venerable shogunate system came to an end.

22-3b The Meiji Restoration

Although the victory of the Sat-Cho faction appeared on the surface to be a triumph of tradition over change, the new leaders soon realized that Japan must change to survive. Accordingly, they embarked on a policy of comprehensive reform that would lay the foundations of a modern industrial nation within a generation.

The symbol of the new era was the young emperor himself, who had taken the reign name *Meiji* (MAY-jee) ("enlightened rule") on ascending the throne in 1867. Although the post-Tokugawa period was termed a "restoration," the Meiji ruler, who shared the Sat-Cho group's newly adopted modernist outlook, was controlled by the new leadership just as the shogun had controlled his predecessors. In tacit recognition of the real source of political power, the new capital was located at Edo (now renamed

22.8 The Meiji Emperor. In 1868, reformist elements overthrew the Tokugawa Shogunate and launched an era of rapid modernization in Japanese society. The young Emperor Meiji, who had mounted the throne the previous year, became the symbol of Japan's effort to transform itself along Western lines. Although the emperor traditionally played no military role in Japanese society, the young monarch is shown here in a manner that may have been designed to convey the martial character of the new Japan.

Tokyo, "eastern capital"), and the imperial court was moved to the shogun's palace in the center of the city (see Image 22.8).

The Transformation of Japanese Politics The new leaders launched a comprehensive reform of Japanese political institutions. They moved first to abolish the remnants of the old order and strengthen executive power in their hands. To undercut the power of the daimyo (DYM-yoh), hereditary privileges were abolished in 1871, and the great lords lost title to their lands. As compensation, they were given government bonds and were named governors of the territories formerly under their control. The samurai, comprising some 8 percent of the total population, received a lump-sum payment to replace their traditional stipends, but they were forbidden to wear the sword, the symbol of their hereditary status.

The Meiji modernizers then set out to create a modern political system on the Western model. In the Charter Oath of 1868, they promised to create a new deliberative assembly within the framework of continued imperial rule. They also called for the implementation of reforms based on international practices to "strengthen the foundations of imperial rule." The key posts in the new government were dominated by modernizing samurai, eventually known as the *genro* (gen-ROH or GEN-roh), or elder statesmen, from the Sat-Cho clique.

During the next two decades, the Meiji government undertook a systematic study of Western political systems. A commission under Prince Ito Hirobumi (eeTOH HEE-roh-BOO-mee) traveled to several Western countries, including Great Britain, Germany, Russia, and the United States, to observe their political systems. Several factions scuffled for precedence over which system to adopt. Some favored a model that would vest supreme authority in the parliament as the representative of the people, while others called for a balance of power between the legislative and executive branches, with a nod to the latter.

The Constitution of 1890   In the end, the latter model emerged victorious. The Meiji Constitution, which was adopted in 1890, was based on the Bismarckian model with authority vested in the executive branch; the imperialist faction was pacified by the statement that the constitution was the gift of the emperor. The Meiji oligarchs would handpick the cabinet. The upper house of parliament would be appointed and have equal legislative powers with the lower house, called the Diet, whose members would be elected. The core ideology of the state, called the **kokutai** (koh-kuh-TY), or national polity, embodied the concept of the uniqueness of the Japanese system based on the supreme authority of the emperor. The ancient practice of Shinto was transformed into a virtual national religion, and its traditional ceremonies were performed at all important events in the imperial court.

The result was a system that was democratic in form but despotic in practice, modern in appearance but still traditional in keeping power in the hands of a ruling oligarchy. The system permitted the traditional elites to retain their influence and economic power while acquiescing in the emergence of new institutions and values.

Meiji Economics   With the end of the daimyo domains, the government needed a new system of landownership that would transform the rural population from indentured serfs into yeoman farmers. Accordingly, it enacted a land reform program that redefined the domain lands as the private property of the tillers while compensating the previous owners with government bonds. A new land tax, set at an annual rate of 3 percent of the land's estimated value, was imposed to raise revenue for the government. The tax proved to be a lucrative source of income for the government, but it was onerous for the farmers, who had previously paid a fixed percentage of their harvest to the landowner. In bad years, many peasants were unable to pay their taxes and were forced to sell their lands to wealthy neighbors. Eventually, the government reduced the tax to 2.5 percent of the land value. Still, by the end of the century, around 40 percent of all farmers were tenants.

With its budget needs secured, the government turned to the promotion of industry with the objective of guaranteeing Japan's survival against the challenge of Western imperialism. Building on the growing industrial economy that existed under the Tokugawa, the Meiji reformers provided massive stimulus in the form of financial subsidies, training, foreign advisers, improved transport and communications, and a universal educational system emphasizing applied science. Unlike China, Japan relied little on foreign capital.

During the late Meiji era, Japan's industrial sector began to grow. Besides tea and silk, key industries included weaponry, shipbuilding, and sake (SAHkee) (fermented rice wine). From the start, the distinctive feature of the Meiji model was the intimate relationship between government and private business. Once an individual enterprise or industry was on its feet, it was turned over entirely to private ownership, although the government often continued to play some role.

There was a certain logic to Meiji economic policy. Industrial growth was subsidized by funds provided by the new land tax, but because the tax imposed severe hardships on the peasants, many fled to the cities, where they provided an abundant source of cheap labor. As in Europe during the early Industrial Revolution, workers toiled for long hours in the coal mines and textile mills, often under horrendous conditions. Reportedly, coal miners on a small island in Nagasaki harbor worked naked in temperatures up to 130 degrees Fahrenheit. If they tried to escape, they were shot.

Building a Modern Social Structure   By the late Tokugawa era, the rigidly hierarchical social order was beginning to disintegrate. Rich merchants were buying their way into the ranks of the samurai, and Japanese of all classes were abandoning their rice fields and moving into the cities. Nevertheless, community and hierarchy still formed the basis of society. The lives of all Japanese were determined by their membership in various social organizations—their family, village, and social class. Membership in a particular social class determined a person's occupation and social relationships with others. Women in particular were constrained by the "**three obediences**": child to father, wife to husband, and widow to son. Husbands could easily obtain a divorce, but wives could not (allegedly, a husband could divorce his wife if she drank too much tea or talked too

HISTORICAL VOICES

The Rules of Good Citizenship in Meiji Japan

Politics & Government

AFTER SEIZING POWER from the Tokugawa Shogunate in 1868, the new Japanese leaders turned their attention to the creation of a new political system that would bring the country into the modern world. After exploring various systems in use in the West, a constitutional commission decided to adopt the system used in imperial Germany because of its paternalistic character. To promote civic virtue and obedience among the citizenry, the government then drafted an imperial rescript that was to be taught to every schoolchild in the country. The rescript instructed all children to obey their sovereign and place the interests of the community and the state above their own personal desires.

Imperial Rescript on Education, 1890

Know ye, Our subjects:

Our Imperial Ancestors have founded Our Empire on a basis broad and everlasting, and have deeply and firmly implanted virtue; Our subjects ever united in loyalty and filial piety have from generation to generation illustrated the beauty thereof. This is the glory of the fundamental character of Our Empire, and herein also lies the source of Our education. Ye, Our subjects, be filial to your parents, affectionate to your brothers and sisters; as husbands and wives be harmonious, as friends true; bear yourselves in modesty and moderation; extend your benevolence to all; pursue learning and cultivate arts, and thereby develop intellectual faculties and perfect moral powers; furthermore, advance public good and promote common interests; always respect the Constitution and observe the laws; should emergency arise, offer yourselves courageously to the State; and thus guard and maintain the prosperity of Our Imperial state; and thus guard and maintain the prosperity of Our Imperial Throne coeval with heaven and earth. So shall ye not only be Our good and faithful subjects, but render illustrious the best traditions of your forefathers.

The way here set forth is indeed the teaching bequeathed by Our Imperial Ancestors, to be observed alike by Their Descendants and the subjects, infallible for all ages and true in all places. It is Our wish to lay it to heart in all reverence, in common with you, Our subjects, that we may all attain to the same virtue.

Q *According to the Imperial Rescript, what was the primary purpose of education in Meiji Japan? How did these goals compare with those in China and the West?*

Source: Dairoku, Kikuchi. "The Imperial Rescript on Education (1890)." 2–3 in *Japanese Education*. London: John Murray, 1909.

---

much). Marriages were arranged, and the average age at marriage for females was sixteen years old. Females did not share inheritance rights with males, and few received any education outside the family.

The Meiji reformers destroyed much of the traditional social system. With the abolition of hereditary rights in 1871, the legal restrictions of the past were brought to an end with a single stroke. Special privileges for the aristocracy were abolished, as were the legal restrictions on the *eta* (AY-tuh), the traditional slave class (numbering some 400,000 in the 1870s). Another key focus of the reformers was the army. The Sat-Cho reformers had been struck by the weakness of the Japanese forces in clashes with Western powers and set out to create a military that could compete in the modern world. The old feudal army based on the traditional warrior class was abolished, and an imperial army based on universal conscription was formed in 1871.

Education also underwent major changes. Recognizing the need for universal education including technical subjects, Meiji leaders adopted the American model of a three-tiered system culminating in a series of universities and specialized institutes. Bright students were sent to study abroad, and foreign scholars were invited to Japan to teach in the new schools, where much of the content was inspired by Western models. In another break with tradition, women for the first time were given an opportunity to get an education.

These changes were included in the Imperial Rescript on Education that was issued in 1890, but the rescript also emphasized the traditional Confucian virtues of filial piety and loyalty to the state (see Historical Voices, "The Rules of Good Citizenship in Meiji Japan"). One reason for issuing the Imperial Rescript was concern that Western individualistic ideas might dilute the traditional Japanese emphasis on responsibility to the community.

Indeed, Western ideas and fashions had become the rage in elite circles, and the ministers of the first Meiji government were known as the "dancing cabinet" because of their addiction to Western-style ballroom dancing. Young people began to imitate the clothing styles, eating habits, and social practices of their European and American counterparts.

Traditional Values and Women's Rights Nevertheless, the self-proclaimed transformation of Japan into a "modern society" by no means detached the country entirely from its traditional moorings. Although an educational order in 1872 provided women the first opportunity to receive an education, conservatives soon began to impose restrictions and bring about a return to more traditional social relationships. Traditional values were given a firm legal basis in the constitution of 1890, which restricted the franchise to males and defined individual liberties as "subject to the limitations imposed by law," and by the Civil Code of 1898, which deemphasized individual rights and treated women within the context of their role in the family.

Still, changes were under way as women began to play a crucial role in the nation's effort to modernize. Urged by their parents to augment the family income, as well as by the government to fulfill their patriotic duty, young girls went en masse to work in textile mills. From 1894 to 1912, women represented 60 percent of the Japanese labor force. Thanks to them, by 1914, Japan was the world's leading exporter of silk and dominated cotton manufacturing. Without the revenues earned from textile exports, Japan might have required an infusion of foreign capital to develop its heavy industry and military.

Japanese women received few rewards for their contribution, however. In 1900, new regulations prohibited women from joining political organizations or attending public meetings. Beginning in 1905, a group of independent-minded women petitioned the Japanese parliament to rescind this restriction. Although the regulation was not repealed until 1922, calls for women's rights were increasingly heard.

22-3c Joining the Imperialist Club

Traditionally, Japan had not been an expansionist country, but now the Japanese began to emulate the Western approach to foreign affairs as well as Western domestic policies. This is perhaps not surprising. The Japanese felt particularly vulnerable in the global economic arena. Small in territory, lacking in resources, and densely populated, they had no natural outlet for expansion. To observant Japanese, the lessons of history were clear. Western nations had amassed wealth and power not only because of their democratic systems and high level of education but also because of their colonies. The Japanese began their program of territorial expansion close to home (see Map 22.5). In 1874, after a brief conflict with China, Japan

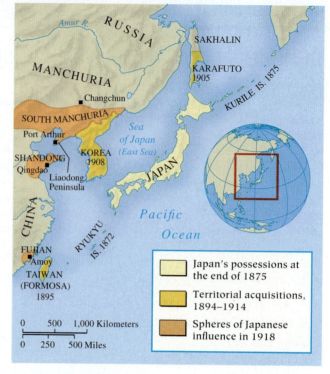

Map 22.5 Japanese Overseas Expansion During the Meiji Era. Beginning in the late nineteenth century, Japan ventured beyond its home islands and became an imperialist power. The extent of Japanese colonial expansion through World War I is shown here.

Q *Which parts of imperial China came under Japanese influence?*

was able to claim suzerainty over the Ryukyu (RYOO-kyoo) Islands, long tributary to the Chinese empire. Two years later, Japanese naval pressure forced Korea to open three ports to Japanese commerce.

During the early nineteenth century, Korea had followed Japan's example and attempted to isolate itself from outside contact except for periodic tribute missions to China. Christian missionaries, mostly Chinese or French, were vigorously persecuted. But Korea's problems were basically internal. In the early 1860s, a peasant revolt partly inspired by the Taiping Rebellion in China caused considerable devastation before being crushed in 1864. In succeeding years, the Choson Dynasty sought to strengthen the country by returning to traditional values and fending off outside intrusion, but rural poverty and official corruption remained rampant. A U.S. fleet sought to open the country in 1871 but was driven off with considerable loss of life.

Korea's most persistent suitor, however, was Japan, which was determined to bring an end to Korea's dependency status with China and modernize it along Japanese lines. In 1876, Korea agreed to open three ports to Japanese commerce in return for Japanese recognition of Korean

Two Views of the World

Interaction & Exchange

DURING THE NINETEENTH CENTURY, China's hierarchical way of looking at the outside world came under severe challenge, not only from European countries avid for new territories in Asia but also from the rising power of Japan, which accepted the Western view that a colonial empire was the key to national greatness. Japan's first objective was Korea, long a dependency of China, and in 1894 the competition between China and Japan in the peninsula led to war. The following declarations of war by the rulers of the two countries are revealing. Note the Chinese use of the derogatory term *Wojen* ("dwarf people") in referring to the Japanese.

Declaration of War Against China

Korea is an independent state. She was first introduced into the family of nations by the advice and guidance of Japan. It has, however, been China's habit to designate Korea as her dependency, and both openly and secretly to interfere with her domestic affairs. [When the recent uprising in Korea broke out], China despatched troops . . . , alleging that her purpose was to [assist her dependency]. We, in virtue of the treaty concluded [by Japan] with Korea in 1882, [sent our Japanese troops] to that country.

Wishing to procure for Korea freedom . . . and thereby to maintain . . . peace [in the region] . . . , Japan invited China's cooperation for the accomplishment of [this objective]. But China, advancing various pretexts, declined Japan's proposal. . . . Such conduct on the part of China is [a threat to the Japanese empire and] a menace to the permanent peace and tranquility of the Orient. . . . In this situation, . . . we find it impossible to avoid a formal declaration of war against China.

Declaration of War Against Japan

Korea has been our tributary for the past two hundred odd years. She has given us tribute all this time, which is a matter known to the world. [When the recent rebellion broke out in Korea] we, in sympathy with our small tributary . . . , ordered [our emissary Li Hongzhang] to send troops to Korea; and the rebels immediately scattered. But the *Wojen*, without any cause whatever, suddenly sent their troops to Korea . . . , reinforcing them constantly . . . [They also]forced the Korean king to change his system of government. . . .

As Japan has violated the treaties and not observed international laws, and is now running rampant with her false and treacherous actions commencing hostilities herself, . . . we therefore desire to [inform] the world that we have . . . followed the paths of philanthropy and perfect justice throughout the whole complications, while the *Wojen* . . . have broken all the laws of nations and treaties which it passes our patience to bear with. Hence we commanded [our emissary] to give strict orders to our various armies to hasten with all speed to root the *Wojen* out of their lairs.

Q Compare the worldviews of China and Japan at the end of the nineteenth century, as expressed in these declarations. Which point of view do you find more persuasive?

Sources: From MacNair, *Modern Chinese History*, pp. 530–534, quoted in Franz Schurmann and Orville Schell, eds., *The China Reader: Imperial China* (New York: Vintage, 1967), pp. 251–259.

independence. During the 1880s, Sino–Japanese rivalry over Korea intensified. When a new peasant rebellion broke out in Korea in 1894, China and Japan intervened on opposite sides (see Opposing Viewpoints, "Two Views of the World"). During the war, the Japanese navy destroyed the Chinese fleet and seized the Manchurian city of Port Arthur. In the Treaty of Shimonoseki, the Chinese were forced to recognize the independence of Korea and cede Taiwan (TY-WAHN) and the Liaodong Peninsula with its strategic naval base at Port Arthur to Japan.

Shortly thereafter and under pressure from the European powers, the Japanese returned the Liaodong Peninsula to China, but in the early twentieth century they went back on the offensive. Rivalry with Russia over influence in Korea led to increasingly strained relations between the two countries. In 1904, Japan launched a surprise attack on the Russian naval base at Port Arthur, which Russia had taken from China in 1898. The Japanese armed forces were weaker, but Russia faced difficult logistical problems along its new Trans-Siberian Railway and severe political instability at home. In 1905, after Japanese warships sank almost the entire Russian fleet off the coast of Korea, the Russians agreed to a humiliating peace, ceding the Liaodong Peninsula back to Japan, as well as

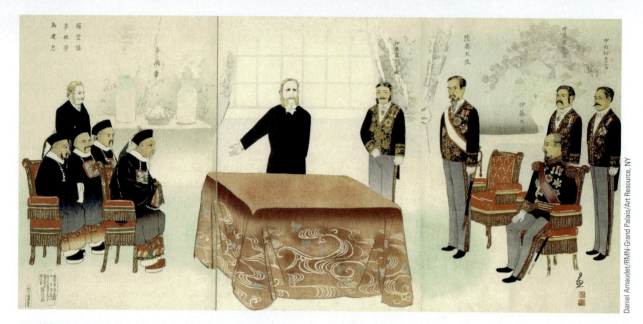

22.9 Total Humiliation. Whereas China had persevered in hiding behind the grandeur of its past, Japan had embraced the West, modernizing politically, militarily, and culturally. China's humiliation at the hands of its newly imperialist neighbor is evident in this scene painted by a Japanese artist, where the differences in dress and the body posture of the officials negotiating the treaty after the war reflect China's disastrous defeat by the Japanese in 1895.

southern Sakhalin (SAK-uh-leen) and the Kurile (KOOR-il or koo-REEL) Islands. Russia also agreed to abandon its political and economic influence in Korea and southern Manchuria, which now came increasingly under Japanese control. The Japanese victory stunned the world, including the colonial peoples elsewhere in Asia, who now began to realize that the white race was not necessarily invincible.

During the next few years, the Japanese consolidated their position in northeastern Asia, annexing Korea in 1908 as an integral part of Japan. When the Koreans protested, Japanese reprisals resulted in thousands of deaths. The United States was the first to recognize the annexation in return for Tokyo's declaration of respect for U.S. authority in the Philippines. In 1908, the United States recognized Japanese interests in the region in return for Japanese acceptance of the principles of the Open Door. But mutual suspicion between the two countries was growing, sparked in part by U.S. efforts to restrict immigration from all Asian countries.

22-3d Japanese Culture in Transition

The wave of Western technology and ideas that entered Japan in the second half of the nineteenth century greatly altered traditional Japanese culture. Dazzled by European literature, Japanese authors began translating and imitating the imported models. Experimenting with Western verse, Japanese poets were influenced by such styles as symbolism

and later by Dadaism (DAHduh-iz-um) and surrealism, although some traditional poetry was still composed.

Western artistic and architectural techniques and styles were also adopted on a massive scale. Japanese architects created huge buildings of steel and reinforced concrete adorned with Greek columns and cupolas, and artists produced oil paintings reflecting the European concern with depth perception and shading.

Cultural exchange also went from East to West as Japanese arts and crafts, porcelains, textiles, fans, folding screens, and woodblock prints became the vogue in Europe and North America. Japanese art influenced Western painters such as Vincent van Gogh, Edgar Degas (duh-GAH), and James Whistler, who experimented with flatter compositional perspectives and unusual poses. Japanese gardens, with their exquisite attention to the positioning of rocks and falling water, became especially popular.

After the initial period of mass absorption of Western art, a reaction occurred at the end of the nineteenth century as many artists returned to pre-Meiji techniques. In 1889, the Tokyo School of Fine Arts (today the Tokyo National University of Fine Arts and Music) was founded to promote traditional Japanese art. Over the next decades, Japanese art underwent a dynamic resurgence, reflecting the nation's emergence as a prosperous and powerful state. Although some Japanese artists attempted to synthesize native and foreign techniques, others found inspiration in past artistic traditions.

22.10 The Ginza in downtown Tokyo. This 1877 woodblock print shows the Ginza, a major commercial thoroughfare in downtown Tokyo, with modern brick buildings and a horse-drawn streetcar. The centerpiece and focus of public attention is a new electric streetlight. In combining traditional form with modern content, this painting symbolizes the unique ability of the Japanese to borrow ideas from abroad while preserving much of the essence of their traditional culture.

22-3e The Meiji Restoration: A Revolution from Above

Japan's transformation from a feudal agrarian society to an industrializing, technologically advanced society in little more than half a century has frequently been described by outside observers (if not by the Japanese themselves) as an almost miraculous change. Some historians, however, have questioned this characterization, pointing out that the achievements of the Meiji leaders were spotty at best. In *Japan's Emergence as a Modern State*, Canadian historian E. H. Norman lamented that the **Meiji Restoration** was an "incomplete revolution" because it did not end the economic and social inequities of feudal society or enable the common people to participate fully in the governing process. Although the genro were enlightened in many respects, they were also despotic and elitist, and the distribution of wealth remained as unequal as it had been under the old system.[2]

It has also been noted that Japan's transformation into a major industrial nation was by no means complete by the beginning of the new century. Until at least the outbreak of World War I in 1914, the majority of manufactured goods were produced by traditional cottage industries rather than by modern factories. The integration of the Japanese economy into the global marketplace was also limited, and foreign investment played a much smaller role than in most comparable economies in the West.

Although these criticisms are persuasive, most of them could also be applied to many other societies going through the early stages of industrialization. In any event, from an economic perspective, the Meiji Restoration was certainly one of the great success stories of modern times. The Meiji leaders not only put Japan firmly on the path to the creation of Asia's first advanced industrial economy but also managed to initiate the process of transforming Japan's traditional political system while removing the unequal treaty provisions that had been imposed at midcentury. Japanese achievements are especially impressive when compared with the difficulties experienced by China, which was not only unable to bring about significant changes in its traditional society but also had not even reached a consensus on the need to do so. Japan's achievements more closely resemble those of Europe, but whereas the West needed a

CHRONOLOGY	Japan and Korea in the Era of Imperialism
Commodore Perry arrives in Tokyo Bay	1853
Townsend Harris Treaty	1858
Fall of Tokugawa Shogunate	1868
U.S. fleet fails to open Korea	1871
Feudal titles abolished in Japan	1871
Japanese imperial army formed	1871
Meiji Constitution adopted	1890
Imperial Rescript on Education	1890
Treaty of Shimonoseki awards Taiwan to Japan	1895
Russo–Japanese War	1904–1905
Korea annexed by Japan	1908

century and a half to achieve significant industrial development, the Japanese realized it in forty years.

One of the distinctive features of Japan's transition from a traditional to a modern society was that it took place for the most part without violence or the kind of social or political revolution that occurred in so many other countries. The Meiji Restoration, which began the process, has been called a "revolution from above," a comprehensive restructuring of Japanese society by its own ruling group.

HISTORIANS DEBATE **What Explains Japanese Uniqueness?** The differences between the Japanese response to the West and the responses of China and many other nations in the region have sparked considerable debate among students of comparative history. In this and previous chapters, we have already discussed some of the reasons why China—along with most other countries in Asia and Africa—had not yet entered an industrial revolution of its own by the end of the nineteenth century. The puzzle then becomes, why was Japan apparently uniquely positioned to make the transition to an advanced industrial economy?

Some historians have argued that Japan's success was partly the result of good fortune. Lacking abundant natural resources, it was exposed to less pressure from the West than many of its neighbors. That argument is problematic, however, and would probably not have been accepted by Japanese observers at the time. Nor does it explain why nations under considerably less pressure, such as Laos and Nepal, did not advance even more quickly. All in all, the luck hypothesis is not especially persuasive.

Some explanations have already been suggested in this book. Japan's unique geographic position was certainly a factor. China, a continental nation with a heterogeneous ethnic composition, was distinguished from its neighbors by its Confucian culture. By contrast, Japan was an island nation, ethnically and linguistically homogeneous, and it had never been conquered. Unlike the Chinese or many other peoples in the region, the Japanese had little to fear from cultural change in terms of its effect on their national identity. The fact that the emperor, the living symbol of the nation, had adopted change ensured that his subjects could follow in his footsteps without fear.

In addition, several other factors may have played a role. Japanese values, with their emphasis on practicality and military achievement, may have contributed. Finally, the Meiji also benefited from the fact that the pace of urbanization and commercial and industrial development had already begun to quicken under the Tokugawa. Having already lost their traditional feudal role and much of the revenue from their estates, the Japanese aristocracy—daimyo and samurai alike—could discard sword and kimono and don modern military uniforms or Western business suits and still feel comfortable in both worlds. In effect, Japan was ripe for change, and nothing could have been more suitable as an antidote for the collapsing old system than the Western emphasis on wealth and power. It was a classic example of challenge and response.

The Fusion of East and West The final product was an amalgam of old and new, Japanese and foreign, which formed a new civilization that was still uniquely Japanese. As we shall soon see, however, there were some undesirable consequences. Because Meiji politics was essentially despotic, Japanese leaders were able to fuse key traditional elements such as the warrior ethic and the concept of feudal loyalty with the dynamics of modern industrial capitalism to create a state totally dedicated to the possession of material wealth and national power. This combination of kokutai and capitalism, which one scholar has described as a form of "Asian fascism," was highly effective but explosive in its international manifestation. Like modern Germany, which also entered the industrial age directly from feudalism, Japan eventually engaged in a policy of repression at home and expansion abroad to achieve its national objectives. In Japan, as in Germany, it took defeat in war to disconnect the drive for national development from the feudal ethic and bring about the transformation to a pluralistic society dedicated to living in peace and cooperation with its neighbors.

CHAPTER SUMMARY

Few areas of the world resisted the Western incursion as stubbornly and effectively as East Asia. Although military, political, and economic pressure by the European powers was relatively intense during this era, two of the main states in the area were able to retain their independence while the third—Korea—was temporarily absorbed by one of its larger neighbors. Why the Chinese and the Japanese were able to prevent a total political and military takeover by foreign powers is an interesting question. One key reason was that both had a long history as well-defined states with a strong sense of national community and territorial cohesion. Although China had frequently been conquered, it had retained its sense of unique culture and identity. Geography, too, was in its favor. As a continental nation, China was able to survive partly because of its sheer size. Japan possessed the advantage of an island location.

Even more striking, however, are the different ways in which the two states attempted to deal with the challenge. The Japanese chose to face the problem in a pragmatic manner, borrowing foreign ideas and institutions that appeared to be of value and at the same time were not in conflict with traditional attitudes and customs. China, however, agonized over the issue for half a century while conservative elements fought a desperate battle to retain a maximum of the traditional heritage intact.

This chapter has discussed some of the possible reasons for those differences. In retrospect, it is difficult to avoid the conclusion that the Japanese approach was more effective. Whereas the Meiji leaders were able to set in motion an orderly transition from a traditional to an advanced society, in China the old system collapsed in disorder, leaving chaotic conditions that were still not rectified a generation later. China would pay a heavy price for its failure to respond coherently to the challenge.

But the Japanese "revolution from above" was by no means an unalloyed success. Ambitious efforts by Japanese leaders to carve out a share in the spoils of empire led to escalating conflict with China as well as with rival Western powers and in the early 1940s to global war. We will deal with that issue in Chapter 25. Meanwhile, in Europe, a combination of old rivalries and the effects of the Industrial Revolution were leading to a bitter regional conflict that eventually engulfed the entire world.

REFLECTION QUESTIONS

Q What were some of the key reasons why the Meiji reformers were so successful in launching Japan on the road to industrialization? Which of those reasons also applied to China under the Qing?

Q What impact did colonial rule have on the environment in the European colonies in Asia and Africa during the nineteenth century? Did some of these same factors apply in China and Japan?

Q How did Western values and institutions influence Chinese and Japanese social mores and traditions during the imperialist era?

CHAPTER TIMELINE

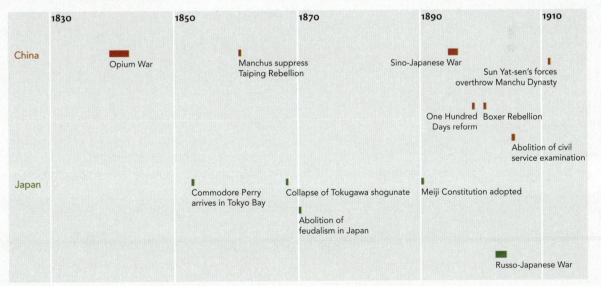

CHAPTER NOTES

1. H. B. Morse, *The International Relations of the Chinese Empire*, vol. 2 (London, 1910–1918), p. 622.

2. Quoted in J. W. Dower, ed., *The Origins of the Modern Japanese State: Selected Writings of E. H. Norman* (New York, 1975), p. 13.

MindTap® is a fully online, highly personalized learning experience built upon Cengage Learning content. MindTap combines student learning tools—readings, multimedia, activities, and assessments—into a singular Learning Path that guides students through the course and helps students develop the critical thinking, analysis, and communication skills that are essential to academic and professional success.

Chapter Outline and Focus Questions

23-1 The Road to World War I

Q What were the long-range and immediate causes of World War I?

23-2 The Great War

Q Why did the course of World War I turn out to be so different from what the belligerents had expected? How did World War I affect the belligerents' governmental and political institutions, economic affairs, and social life?

23-3 Crisis in Russia and the End of the War

Q What were the causes of the Russian Revolution of 1917, and why did the Bolsheviks prevail in the civil war and gain control of Russia?

23-4 An Uncertain Peace

Q What problems did Europe and the United States face in the 1920s?

23-5 In Pursuit of a New Reality: Cultural and Intellectual Trends

Q How did the cultural and intellectual trends of the post–World War I years reflect the crises of the time as well as the lingering effects of the war?

Critical Thinking

Q *What was the relationship between World War I and the Russian Revolution?*

Connections to Today

Q *What lessons from the outbreak of World War I are of value in considering international relations today?*

Universal History Archive/UIG/Getty Images

23.1 British Infantrymen Prepare to Advance During the Battle of the Somme

ON JULY 1, 1916, BRITISH AND FRENCH INFANTRY FORCES attacked German defensive lines along a twenty-five-mile front near the Somme (SUHM) River in France. Each soldier carried almost seventy pounds of equipment, making it "impossible to move much quicker than a slow walk." German machine guns soon opened fire: "We were able to see our comrades move forward in an attempt to cross No-Man's Land, only to be mown down like meadow grass," recalled one British soldier. "I felt sick at the sight of this carnage and remember weeping." In one day, more than 21,000 British soldiers died. After six months of fighting, the British had advanced 5 miles; 1 million British, French, and German soldiers had been killed or wounded.

English war correspondent Philip Gibbs described what he saw in the German trenches that the British forces overran:

Victory! . . . . Some of the German dead were young boys, too young to be killed for old men's crimes, and others might have been old or young. One could not tell because they had no faces, and were just masses of raw flesh in rags of uniforms. Legs and arms lay separate without any bodies thereabout.

575

World War I (1914–1918) was the defining event of the twentieth-century Western world. Overwhelmed by the size of its battles, the extent of its casualties, and its impact on all facets of life, contemporaries referred to it simply as the "Great War." The Great War was all the more disturbing to Europeans because it came after a period that many believed to have been an age of progress. Material prosperity and a fervid belief in scientific and technological advances had convinced many people that the world stood on the verge of creating the utopia that humans had dreamed of for centuries. Historian Arnold Toynbee expressed what the era before the war had meant to his generation:

> [We had expected] that life throughout the world would become more rational, more humane, and more democratic and that, slowly, but surely, political democracy would produce greater social justice. We had also expected that the progress of science and technology would make mankind richer, and that this increasing wealth would gradually spread from a minority to a majority. We had expected that all this would happen peacefully. In fact we thought that mankind's course was set for an earthly paradise.[1]

After 1918, it was no longer possible to maintain naive illusions about the progress of Western civilization. As World War I was followed by revolutionary upheavals, the mass murder machines of totalitarian regimes, and the destructiveness of World War II, it became all too apparent that instead of a utopia, Western civilization had become a nightmare. World War I and the revolutions it spawned can properly be seen as the first stage in the crisis of the twentieth century.

23-1 THE ROAD TO WORLD WAR I

Focus Question: What were the long-range and immediate causes of World War I?

On June 28, 1914, the heir to the Austrian throne, Archduke Francis Ferdinand, was assassinated in the Bosnian city of Sarajevo (sar-uh-YAY-voh). Although this event precipitated the confrontation between Austria and Serbia that led to World War I, underlying forces had been propelling Europeans toward armed conflict for a long time.

23-1a Nationalism and Internal Dissent

The system of nation-states that emerged in Europe in the second half of the nineteenth century (see Map 23.1) had led to intense competition. Rivalries over colonies and trade intensified during an era of frenzied imperialist expansion, while the division of Europe's great powers into two loose alliances—Germany, Austria, and Italy on one side and France, Great Britain, and Russia on the other—only added to the tensions. The series of crises that tested these alliances in the 1900s and early 1910s had left European states embittered, eager for revenge, and willing to go to war to preserve the power of their national states.

The growth of nationalism in the nineteenth century had yet another serious consequence. Not all ethnic groups had achieved the goal of nationhood. Slavic minorities in the Balkans and the multiethnic Habsburg Empire, for example, still dreamed of creating their own national states. So did the Irish in the British Empire and the Poles in the Russian Empire.

National aspirations, however, were not the only source of internal strife at the beginning of the twentieth century. Socialist labor movements had grown more powerful and were increasingly inclined to use strikes—even violent ones—to achieve their goals. Some conservative leaders, alarmed at the increase in labor strife and class division, even feared that European nations were on the verge of revolution. Did these statesmen opt for war in 1914 because they believed that "prosecuting an active foreign policy," as some Austrian leaders expressed it, would smother "internal troubles"? Some historians have argued that the desire to suppress internal disorder may have encouraged some leaders to take the plunge into war in 1914.

23-1b Militarism

The growth of large mass armies after 1900 not only heightened the existing tensions in Europe but also made it inevitable that any war would be extremely destructive. **Conscription**—obligatory military service—had been established as a regular practice in most Western countries before 1914 (the United States and Britain were major exceptions). European military machines had doubled in size between 1890 and 1914. The Russian army was the largest, with 1.3 million men, but the French and Germans were not far behind, with 900,000 each. The British, Italian, and Austrian armies numbered between 250,000 and 500,000 soldiers.

Militarism, however, involved more than just large armies. As armies grew, so did the influence of military leaders, who drew up vast and complex plans for quickly mobilizing millions of men and enormous quantities of supplies in the event of war. Fearful that changing these plans would cause chaos in the armed forces, military leaders insisted that the plans not be altered. In the crises during the summer of 1914, the generals' lack of flexibility

Map 23.1 **Europe in 1914.** By 1914, two alliances dominated Europe: the Triple Entente of Britain, France, and Russia and the Triple Alliance of Germany, Austria–Hungary, and Italy. Russia sought to bolster fellow Slavs in Serbia, whereas Austria–Hungary was intent on increasing its power in the Balkans and thwarting Serbia's ambitions. Thus, the Balkans became the flash point for World War I.

Q *Which nonaligned nations were positioned between the two alliances?*

determined to create a large, independent Slavic state in the Balkans, and Austria–Hungary, which had its own Slavic minorities to contend with, was equally set on preventing that possibility. Many Europeans perceived the inherent dangers in this explosive situation. The British ambassador to Vienna wrote in 1913:

> Serbia will some day set Europe by the ears, and bring about a universal war on the Continent. . . . I cannot tell you how exasperated people are getting here at the continual worry which that little country causes to Austria under encouragement from Russia. . . . It will be lucky if Europe succeeds in avoiding war as a result of the present crisis. The next time a Serbian crisis arises . . . , I feel sure that Austria–Hungary will refuse to admit of any Russian interference in the dispute and that she will proceed to settle her differences with her little neighbor by herself.[2]

It was against this backdrop of mutual distrust and hatred that the events of the summer of 1914 were played out.

forced European political leaders to make decisions for military instead of political reasons.

23-1c The Outbreak of War: Summer 1914

Militarism, nationalism, and the desire to stifle internal dissent may all have played a role in the coming of World War I, but the decisions made by European leaders in the summer of 1914 directly precipitated the conflict. It was another crisis in the Balkans that forced this predicament on European statesmen.

As we have seen, states in southeastern Europe had struggled to free themselves from Ottoman rule in the course of the nineteenth and early twentieth centuries. But the rivalry between Austria–Hungary and Russia for domination of these new states created serious tensions in the region. By 1914, Serbia, supported by Russia, was

The Assassination of Francis Ferdinand: What was the "Blank Check"? The assassination of Austrian Archduke Francis Ferdinand and his wife, Sophia, on June 28, 1914, was carried out by a Bosnian activist who worked for the Black Hand, a Serbian terrorist organization dedicated to the creation of a pan-Slavic kingdom. Although the Austrian government did not know whether the Serbian government had been directly involved in the archduke's assassination, it saw an opportunity to "render Serbia innocuous once and for all by a display of force," as the Austrian foreign minister put it. Fearful of Russian intervention on Serbia's behalf, Austrian leaders sought the backing of their German allies. Emperor William II and his chancellor responded with the infamous "blank check," their assurance that

Austria–Hungary could rely on Germany's "full support," even if "matters went to the length of a war between Austria–Hungary and Russia." Much historical debate has focused on this "blank check" extended to the Austrians. Did the Germans realize that an Austrian–Serbian war could lead to a wider war? If so, did they actually want one? Historians are still divided on the answers to these questions.

Declarations of War Strengthened by German support, Austrian leaders issued an ultimatum to Serbia on July 23 in which they made such extreme demands that Serbia had little choice but to reject some of them to preserve its sovereignty. Austria then declared war on Serbia on July 28. Although the Austrians had hoped to keep the war limited to Serbia and Austria to ensure their success in the Balkans, Russia was determined to support Serbia's cause. Thus, on July 28, Tsar Nicholas II ordered partial mobilization of the Russian army against Austria. The Russian general staff informed the tsar that their mobilization plans were based on a war against both Germany and Austria simultaneously. They could not execute partial mobilization without creating chaos in the army. Consequently, the Russian government ordered full mobilization of the Russian army on July 29, knowing that the Germans would consider this an act of war against them. Germany quickly responded with an ultimatum that the Russians must halt their mobilization within twelve hours. When the Russians ignored it, Germany declared war on Russia on August 1.

At this stage of the conflict, German war plans determined whether France would become involved in the war. Under the guidance of General Alfred von Schlieffen (AHL-fret fun SHLEEfun), chief of staff from 1891 to 1905, the German general staff had devised a military plan based on the assumption of a two-front war with France and Russia because the two powers had formed a military alliance in 1894. The Schlieffen Plan called for a minimal troop deployment against Russia while most of the German army would make a rapid invasion of France before Russia could become effective in the east or before the British could cross the English Channel to help France. This meant invading France by advancing through neutral Belgium, with its level coastal plain on which the army could move faster than on the rougher terrain to the southeast. After the planned quick defeat of the French, the German army

expected to redeploy to the east against Russia. Under the Schlieffen Plan, Germany could not mobilize its troops solely against Russia and therefore declared war on France on August 3 after issuing an ultimatum to Belgium on August 2 demanding the right of German troops to pass through Belgian territory. On August 4, Great Britain declared war on Germany, officially over this violation of Belgian neutrality but in fact over the British desire to maintain world power. As one British diplomat argued, if Germany and Austria were to win the war, "what would be the position of a friendless England?" By August 4, all the great powers of Europe were at war.

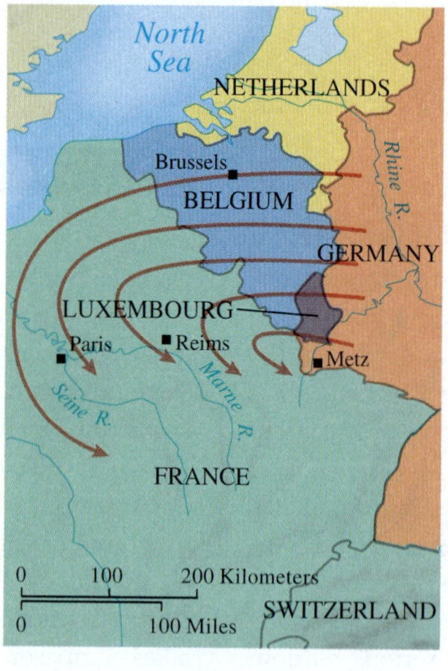

23-2 THE GREAT WAR

Focus Questions: Why did the course of World War I turn out to be so different from what the belligerents had expected? How did World War I affect the belligerents' governmental and political institutions, economic affairs, and social life?

Before 1914, many political leaders had been convinced that war involved so many political and economic risks that it was not worth fighting. Others had believed that "rational" diplomats could control any situation and prevent the outbreak of war. At the beginning of August 1914, both prewar illusions were shattered, but the new illusions that replaced them soon proved equally foolish.

23-2a 1914–1915: Illusions and Stalemate

Europeans went to war in 1914 with great enthusiasm (see Historical Voices, "The Excitement of War," p. 579). Government propaganda had been successful in stirring up national antagonisms before the war. Now in August 1914, the urgent pleas of governments for defense against aggressors found many receptive ears in every belligerent nation. A new set of illusions also fed the enthusiasm for war. In August 1914, almost everyone believed that the war would be over in a few weeks. People were reminded that the major battles in European wars since 1815 had ended in a matter of weeks. Both the soldiers who exuberantly boarded the trains for the war front in August

Map 23.2 The Schlieffen Plan

The Excitement of War

Politics & Government **THE INCREDIBLE OUTPOURING** of patriotic enthusiasm that greeted the declaration of war at the beginning of August 1914 demonstrated the power that nationalistic feeling had attained at the beginning of the twentieth century. Many Europeans seemingly believed that the war had given them a higher purpose, a renewed dedication to the greatness of their nations. These selections are taken from three sources: the autobiography of Stefan Zweig (SHTE-fahn TSVYK), an Austrian writer; the memoirs of Robert Graves, a British writer; and a letter by a German soldier, Walter Limmer, to his parents.

Stefan Zweig, *The World of Yesterday*

The next morning I was in Austria. In every station placards had been put up announcing general mobilization. The trains were filled with fresh recruits, banners were flying, music sounded, and in Vienna I found the entire city in a tumult. . . . There were parades in the street, flags, ribbons, and music burst forth everywhere, young recruits were marching triumphantly, their faces lighting up at the cheering. . . .

And to be truthful, I must acknowledge that there was a majestic, rapturous, and even seductive something in this first outbreak of the people from which one could escape only with difficulty. And in spite of all my hatred and aversion for war, I should not like to have missed the memory of those days. As never before, thousands and hundreds of thousands felt what they should have felt in peace time, that they belonged together. A city of two million, a country of nearly fifty million, in that hour felt that they were participating in world history, in a moment which would never recur. . . . All differences of class, rank, and language were flooded over at that moment by the rushing feeling of fraternity. . . .

What did the great mass know of war in 1914, after nearly half a century of peace? They did not know war, they had hardly given it a thought. It had become legendary, and distance had made it seem romantic and heroic. They still saw it in the perspective of their school readers and of paintings in museums; brilliant cavalry attacks in glittering uniforms, the fatal shot always straight through the heart, the entire campaign a resounding march of victory—"We'll be home at Christmas," the recruits shouted laughingly to their mothers in August of 1914. . . .

Robert Graves, *Goodbye to All That*

I had just finished with Charterhouse and gone up to Harlech, when England declared war on Germany. A day or two later I decided to enlist. In the first place, though the papers predicted only a very short war—over by Christmas at the outside—I hoped that it might last long enough to delay my going to Oxford in October, which I dreaded. Nor did I work out the possibilities of getting actively engaged in the fighting, expecting garrison service at home, while the regular forces were away. In the second place, I was outraged to read of the Germans' cynical violation of Belgian neutrality. Though I discounted perhaps twenty percent of the atrocity details as wartime exaggeration, that was not, of course, sufficient.

Walter Limmer, Letter to His Parents

In any case I mean to go into this business. . . . That is the simple duty of every one of us. And this feeling is universal among the soldiers, especially since the night when England's declaration of war was announced in the barracks. We none of us got to sleep till three o'clock in the morning, we were so full of excitement, fury, and enthusiasm. It is a joy to go to the Front with such comrades. We are bound to be victorious! Nothing else is possible in the face of such determination to win.

Q *What do these excerpts reveal about the motivations of people to join and support World War I? Do the passages reveal anything about the power of nationalism in Europe in the early twentieth century?*

Sources: From *The World of Yesterday* by Stefan Zweig, translated by Helmut Ripperger. Translation copyright 1943 by the Viking. Press, Inc. Robert Graves, *Good-Bye to All That* (New York: Anchor, 1958). From *German Students' War Letters*, edited by Philipp Witkop, Translated by A. F. Wedd. Originally published in 1929 by Methuen. Pine Street Books © 2002.

1914 and the jubilant citizens who bombarded them with flowers when they departed believed that the warriors would be home by Christmas.

German hopes for a quick end to the war rested on a military gamble. The Schlieffen Plan called for the German army to proceed through Belgium into northern France with a vast circling movement that would sweep around Paris and surround most of the French army. But the German advance was halted only twenty miles from Paris at the First Battle of the Marne (September 6–10). The war quickly turned into a stalemate because neither the Germans nor the French could dislodge each other from the trenches they had been digging for shelter (see Map 23.2).

In contrast to the western front, the war in the east was marked by much more mobility, although the cost in lives was equally enormous. At the beginning of the war, the Russian army moved into eastern Germany but was decisively defeated at the Battles of Tannenberg on August 30 and the Masurian Lakes on September 15. The Russians were no longer a threat to German territory.

The Austrians, Germany's allies, fared less well initially. They had been defeated by the Russians in Galicia (guh-LISH-ee-uh) and thrown out of Serbia as well. To

Eastern Front:

- Battle site, 1914
- Russian advances, 1914–1916
- Deepest German penetration
- Brest-Litovsk boundary, 1918

Western Front:

- Farthest German advance, September 1914
- German offensive, March–July 1918
- Winter, 1914–1915
- Armistice line

- German advances
- Allied advances
- (CRIMEA) Regions of national states

Map 23.3 World War I, 1914–1918. This map shows how greatly the western and eastern fronts of World War I differed. After initial German gains in the west, the war became bogged down in trench warfare, with little change in the battle lines between 1914 and 1918. The eastern front was marked by considerable mobility, with battle lines shifting by hundreds of miles.

Q *How do you explain the difference in the two fronts?*

make matters worse, the Italians betrayed the Germans and Austrians and entered the war on the Allied side by attacking Austria in May 1915. (France, Great Britain, and Russia were called the Allied Powers, or Allies.) By this time, the Germans had come to the aid of the Austrians. A German–Austrian army routed the Russian army in Galicia and pushed the Russians back 300 miles into their own territory. Russian casualties stood at 2.5 million killed, captured, or wounded; the Russians had almost been knocked out of the war. Buoyed by their success, the Germans and Austrians, joined by the Bulgarians in September 1915, attacked and eliminated Serbia from the war.

23-2b 1916–1917: The Great Slaughter

The successes in the east enabled the Germans to move back to the offensive in the west. The early trenches dug in 1914, which stretched from the English Channel to the frontiers of Switzerland, had by now become elaborate systems of defense. Both lines of trenches were protected by barbed-wire entanglements 3 feet to 5 feet high and 30 yards wide, concrete machine-gun nests, and mortar batteries, supported farther back by heavy artillery. Troops lived in holes in the ground, separated from each other by a so-called no-man's land.

The unexpected development of **trench warfare** on the western front baffled military leaders, who had been trained to fight wars of movement and maneuver. Periodically, the high command on either side would order an offensive that would begin with an artillery barrage to flatten the enemy's barbed wire and leave the enemy in a state of shock. After "softening up" the enemy in this fashion, a mass of soldiers would climb out of their trenches with fixed bayonets and hope to work their way toward the enemy trenches. The attacks rarely worked because the machine gun put hordes of men advancing unprotected across open fields at a severe disadvantage. In 1916 and 1917, millions of young men were sacrificed in the search for the elusive break-through. In ten months at Verdun (ver-DUHN) in 1916, 700,000 men lost their lives over a few miles of terrain.

Warfare in the trenches of the western front produced unimaginable horrors (see Film & History, *Paths of Glory*; and Historical Voices, "The Reality of War: The Views of British Poets," p. 582). Battlefields were hellish landscapes of barbed wire, shell holes, mud, and injured and dying men. The introduction of poison gas in 1915 produced new forms of injuries. As one British writer described them:

> I wish those people who write so glibly about this being a holy war could see a case of mustard gas . . . could see the poor things burnt and blistered all over with great

mustard-coloured suppurating blisters with blind eyes all sticky . . . and stuck together, and always fighting for breath, with voices a mere whisper, saying that their throats are closing and they know they will choke.[3]

Soldiers in the trenches also lived with the persistent presence of death. Because combat went on for months, soldiers had to carry on in the midst of countless dead bodies and the remains of men dismembered by artillery barrages. Many soldiers remembered the stench of decomposing bodies and the swarms of rats that grew fat in the trenches.

Soldiers on the western front did not spend all of their time on the frontline or in combat when they were on the frontline. An infantryman spent one week out of every month in the frontline trenches, one week in the reserve lines, and the remaining two weeks somewhere behind the lines in rest camps where he might at least have a roof over his head in a wooden hut. But there was not much

The Reality of War: The Views of British Poets

PERHAPS NO ONE CAPTURED the horrors of trench warfare and the use of poison gas better than British poets who served on the frontlines of the war. Most notorious are Wilfred Owen and Siegfried Sassoon, both of whom served on the western front and had firsthand knowledge of the conditions suffered by frontline soldiers. The first poem is "Dulce et Decorum Est," in which Owen uses striking descriptions to question why anyone would die fighting for one's country. The second poem, "Suicide in the Trenches," is by Sassoon and depicts the conditions in the trenches.

Wilfried Owen, "Dulce et Decorum Est"

Bent double, like old beggars under sacks,
Knock-kneed, coughing like hags, we cursed through sludge,
Till on the haunting flares we turned out backs,
And towards our distant rest began to trudge.
Men marched asleep. Many had lost their boots,
But limped on, blood-shod. All went lame, all blind;
Drunk with fatigue; deaf even to the hoots
Of gas-shells dropping softly behind.

Gas! GAS! Quick, boys!-An ecstasy of fumbling
Fitting the clumsy helmets [gas masks] just in time,
But someone still was yelling out and stumbling
And flound'ring like a man in fire or lime.
Dim though the misty panes and thick green light,
As under a green sea, I saw him drowning.

In all my dreams before my helpless sight
He plunges at me, guttering, choking, drowning.
If in some smothering dreams, you too could pace

Behind the wagon that we flung him,
And watch the white eyes writhing in his face,
His hanging face, like a devil's sick of sin,
If you could hear, at every jolt, the blood
Come gargling from the froth-corrupted lungs
Bitter as the cud
Of vile, incurable shores on innocent tongues,
My friend, you would not tell with such high zest
To children ardent [keen] for some desperate glory,
The old Lie: Dulce et decorum est
Pro patria mori.[4]

Siegfried Sassoon, "Suicide in the Trenches"

I knew a simple soldier boy
Who grinned at life in empty joy,
Slept soundly through the lonesome dark,
And whistled early with the lark.

In winter trenches, cowed and glum,
With crumps and lice and lack of rum,
He put a bullet through his brain.
No one spoke of him again.

You smug-faced crowds with kindling eye
Who cheer when soldier lads march by,
Sneak home and pray you'll never know
The hell where youth and laughter go.

Q *What impressions of trench warfare do you learn from these two poems? Why would characterize them as antiwar poems?*

Source: www.PoemHunter.com, The World's Poetry Archive.

---

rest; drills in the morning and games in the afternoon were aimed at keeping soldiers fit. There was at least light entertainment in the evening: concerts, popular songs, and comedic sketches.

23-2c The Widening of the War

As another response to the stalemate on the western front, both sides looked for new allies who might provide a winning advantage. The Ottoman Empire had already come into the war on Germany's side in August 1914. Russia, Great Britain, and France declared war on the Ottoman Empire in November. Although the Allies attempted to open a Balkan front in April 1915 by landing forces at Gallipoli (gah-LIP-poh-lee), a peninsula southwest of Constantinople, Bulgaria's entry into the war on the side of the Central Powers (as Germany, Austria–Hungary, and the Ottoman Empire were called) and a disastrous campaign at Gallipoli caused them to withdraw.

A Global Conflict Because the major European powers controlled colonial empires in other parts of the world, the war in Europe soon became a world conflict (see the Comparative Illustration, "Soldiers from Around the World," p. 583). In the Middle East, British officer

Soldiers from Around the World

Politics & Government

ALTHOUGH WORLD WAR I BEGAN IN EUROPE, it soon became a global conflict fought in different areas of the world and with soldiers from all parts of the globe. France, especially, recruited troops from its African colonies to fight in Europe. Shown in Image 23.2a are French Senegalese troops arriving in France in 1915; they would later fight in the Marne campaign on the western front. Image 23.2b shows a group of German soldiers in their machine-gun nest on the western front.

Q *What do these photographs reveal about the nature of World War I and the role of African troops in the conflict?*

Private Collection/Archives Charmet/The Bridgeman Art Library

23.2a

General Photographic Agency/Hulton Archive/Getty Images

23.2b

T. E. Lawrence (1888–1935), who came to be known as Lawrence of Arabia, incited Arab princes to revolt against their Ottoman overlords in 1917. In 1918, British forces from Egypt and Mesopotamia destroyed the rest of the Ottoman Empire in the Middle East. For their Middle East campaigns, the British mobilized forces from India, Australia, and New Zealand.

The Allies also took advantage of Germany's preoccupation in Europe and lack of naval strength to seize German colonies in Africa. The first British shots of World War I were actually fired in Africa when British African troops moved into the German colony of Togoland near the end of August 1914. But in East Africa, German commander Colonel Paul von Lettow-Vorbeck

Experience an interactive version of this period in ⁙ MINDTAP

(POWL fun LEH-toh-FOR-bek) managed to keep his African troops fighting one campaign after another for four years; he did not surrender until two weeks after the armistice ended the war in Europe.

In the battles in Africa, Allied governments drew mainly on African soldiers, but some states, especially France, also recruited African troops to fight in Europe. The French drafted more than 170,000 West African soldiers, many of whom fought in the trenches on the western front. African troops were also used as occupation forces in the German Rhineland at the end of the war. Around 80,000 Africans were killed or injured in Europe, where they were often at a distinct disadvantage because of the unfamiliar terrain and climate.

Hundreds of thousands of Africans were also used for labor, especially for carrying supplies and building roads and bridges. In East Africa, both sides drafted Africans as carriers for their armies. More than 100,000 of these workers died from disease and starvation resulting from neglect.

The immediate impact of World War I in Africa was the extension of colonial rule because Germany's African colonies were simply transferred to the winning powers, especially the British and the French. But the war also had unintended consequences for the Europeans. African soldiers who had gone to war for the Allies—especially those who left Africa and fought in Europe—became politically aware and began to advocate political and social equality. As one African who had fought for the French said, "We were not fighting for the French, we were fighting for ourselves [to become] French citizens."[5] Moreover, educated African elites, who had aided their colonial overlords in enlisting local peoples to fight, did so in the belief that they would be rewarded with citizenship and new political possibilities after the war. When their hopes were frustrated, they soon became involved in anticolonial movements (see Chapter 24).

In East Asia and the Pacific, Japan joined the Allies on August 23, 1914, primarily to seize control of German territories in Asia. As one Japanese statesman declared, the war in Europe was "divine aid . . . for the development of the destiny of Japan."[6] The Japanese took possession of German territories in China, as well as German-occupied islands in the Pacific. New Zealand and Australia quickly joined the Japanese in conquering the German-held parts of New Guinea.

Entry of the United States   Most important to the Allied cause was the entry of the United States into the war. American involvement grew out of the naval conflict between Germany and Great Britain. Britain used its superior naval power to maximum effect by setting up a naval blockade of Germany. Germany retaliated by imposing a counterblockade that it enforced by the use of unrestricted submarine warfare. Strong American protests over the German sinking of passenger liners, especially the British ship *Lusitania* on May 7, 1915, when more than 100 Americans lost their lives, forced the German government to suspend unrestricted submarine warfare in September 1915.

In January 1917, however, eager to break the deadlock in the war, the Germans decided on another military gamble by returning to unrestricted submarine warfare. This change in strategy brought the United States into the war on April 6, 1917. Although U.S. troops did not arrive in Europe in large numbers until the following year, the entry of the United States into the war gave the Allied Powers a psychological boost when they needed it.

The year 1917 had not been good for them. Allied offensives on the western front were disastrously defeated. The Italian armies were smashed in October, and the Bolshevik Revolution in Russia in November (see section 23-3a, "The Russian Revolution," p. 586) led to Russia's withdrawal from the war and left Germany free to concentrate entirely on the western front. The cause of the Central Powers looked favorable, although war weariness in the Ottoman Empire, Bulgaria, Austria–Hungary, and Germany was beginning to take its toll. The home front was rapidly becoming a cause for as much concern as the war front.

23-2d The Home Front: The Impact of Total War

The prolongation of World War I made it a **total war** that affected the lives of all citizens, however remote they might be from the battlefields. The need to organize masses of men and matériel for years of combat (Germany alone had 5.5 million men in active units in 1916) led to increased centralization of government powers, economic regimentation, and manipulation of public opinion to keep the war effort going.

Political Centralization and Economic Regimentation
Because the war was expected to be short, little thought had been given to long-term wartime needs. Governments had to respond quickly, however, when the war machines failed to achieve their knockout blows and made ever greater demands for men and matériel. To meet these needs, governments expanded their powers. Countries drafted tens of millions of young men for that elusive breakthrough to victory.

Throughout Europe, wartime governments expanded their powers over their economies. Free-market capitalistic systems were temporarily shelved as governments experimented with price, wage, and rent controls; rationed food supplies and materials; and nationalized transportation systems and industries. Under total war mobilization, the distinction between soldiers at war and civilians at home was narrowed. In the view of political leaders, all citizens constituted a national army.

Control of Public Opinion As the Great War dragged on and casualties mounted, the patriotic enthusiasm that had marked the early days of the conflict waned. By 1916, there were numerous signs that civilian morale was beginning to crack under the pressure of total war. Governments took strenuous measures to fight the growing opposition to the war. Even parliamentary regimes resorted to an expansion of police powers to stifle internal dissent. The British Parliament, for example, passed the Defence of the Realm Act, which allowed public authorities to arrest dissenters and charge them as traitors. Newspapers were censored, and sometimes publication was even suspended.

Wartime governments also made active use of propaganda to arouse enthusiasm for the war. At first, public officials needed to do little to achieve this goal. The British and French, for example, exaggerated German atrocities in Belgium and found that their citizens were only too willing to believe these accounts. But as the war dragged on and morale sagged, governments were forced to devise new techniques for stimulating declining enthusiasm.

Women in the War Effort World War I also created new roles for women. With so many men fighting at the front, women were called on to assume jobs and responsibilities that had not been open to them before. These included clerical jobs that only small numbers of women had held earlier. In Britain, for example, the number of women who worked in banking rose from 9,500 to 64,000 over the course of the war. Overall, 1,345,000 women in Britain obtained new jobs or replaced men during the war.

Women were also now employed in jobs that had been considered beyond the "capacity of women." These included such occupations as chimney sweeps, truck drivers, farm laborers, and factory workers in heavy industry (see Historical Voices, "Women in the Factories," p. 586). In Germany, 38 percent of the workers in the Krupp (KROOP) armaments works in 1918 were women. Nevertheless, despite the noticeable increase in women's wages that resulted from government regulations, women working at

Archive Images/Alamy

23.3 British Recruiting Poster. As the conflict persisted month after month, governments resorted to active propaganda campaigns to generate enthusiasm for the war. In this British recruiting poster, the government encourages men to "enlist now" to preserve their country. By 1916, the British were forced to adopt compulsory military service.

industrial jobs were still being paid less than men at the end of the war.

Even worse, women's place in the workforce was far from secure. Both men and women seemed to assume that many of the new jobs for women were only temporary. At the end of the war, governments moved quickly to remove women from the jobs they had encouraged them to take earlier, and wages for women who remained employed were lowered.

Nevertheless, in some countries, the role played by women in the wartime economies had a positive impact on the women's movement for social and political emancipation. The most obvious gain was the right to vote, which was granted to women in Britain in January 1918 and in Germany and Austria immediately after the war.

Women in the Factories

Family & Society **DURING WORLD WAR I**, women were called on to assume new job responsibilities, including factory work. In this selection, Naomi Loughnan, a young, upper-middle-class woman, describes the experiences in a munitions plant that considerably broadened her perspective on life.

Naomi Loughnan, "Munition Work"

We little thought when we first put on our overalls and caps and enlisted in the Munition Army how much more inspiring our life was to be than we had dared to hope. . . . Our long days are filled with interest, and with the zest of doing work for our country in the grand cause of Freedom. As we handle the weapons of war we are learning great lessons of life. In the busy, noisy workshops we come face to face with every kind of class, and each one of these classes has something to learn from the others. . . .

Engineering mankind is possessed of the unshakable opinion that no woman can have the mechanical sense. If one of us asks humbly why such and such an alteration is not made to prevent this or that drawback to a machine, she is told, with a superior smile, that a man has worked her machine before her for years, and that therefore if there were any improvement possible it would have been made. As long as we do exactly what we are told and do not attempt to use our brains, we give entire satisfaction, and are treated as nice, good children. Any swerving from the easy path prepared for us by our males arouses the most scathing contempt in their manly bosoms. . . . Women have, however, proved that their entry into the munition world has increased the output. Employers who forget things personal in their patriotic desire for large results are enthusiastic over the success of women in the shops. But their workmen have to be handled with the utmost tenderness and caution lest they should actually imagine it was being suggested that women could do their work equally well, given equal conditions of training—at least where muscle is not the driving force. . . .

The coming of the mixed classes of women into the factory is slowly but surely having an educative effect upon the men. "Language" is almost unconsciously becoming subdued. There are fiery exceptions, who make our hair stand up on end under our close-fitting caps, but a sharp rebuke or a look of horror will often straighten out the most savage. . . . It is grievous to hear the girls also swearing and using disgusting language. Shoulder to shoulder with the children of the slums, the upper classes are having their eyes opened at last to the awful conditions among which their sisters have dwelt. Foul language, immorality, and many other evils are but the natural outcome of over-crowding and bitter poverty. . . . Sometimes disgust will overcome us, but we are learning with painful clarity that the fault is not theirs whose actions disgust us, but must be placed to the discredit of those other classes who have allowed the continued existence of conditions which generate the things from which we shrink appalled.

Q *What did Naomi Loughnan learn about men and lower-class women while working in the munitions factory? What did she learn about herself?*

Source: From "Munition Work" by Naomi Loughnan in Gilbert Stone, ed., *Women War Workers* (London: George Harrap and Company, 1971), pp. 25, 35, 38.

23-3 CRISIS IN RUSSIA AND THE END OF THE WAR

Q **Focus Question:** What were the causes of the Russian Revolution of 1917, and why did the Bolsheviks prevail in the civil war and gain control of Russia?

By 1917, total war was creating serious domestic turmoil every belligerent European state. One, however, was experiencing the kind of complete collapse that others were predicting might happen throughout Europe. Out of Russia's collapse came the Russian Revolution.

23-3a The Russian Revolution

Tsar Nicholas II was an autocratic ruler who relied on the army and the bureaucracy to uphold his regime. World War I magnified Russia's problems and challenged the tsarist government as Russian industry was unable to produce the weapons needed for the war. Russian armies suffered incredible losses. Between 1914 and 1916, 2 million soldiers were killed, and another 4 million to 6 million were wounded or captured.

In the meantime, Tsar Nicholas II was increasingly insulated from events by his German-born wife, Alexandra, a well-educated woman who had fallen under the sway of Rasputin (rass-PYOO-tin), a Siberian peasant whom the tsarina regarded as a holy man because he alone seemed able to stop the bleeding of her hemophiliac son, Alexis. Rasputin's influence made him a power behind the throne, and he did not hesitate to interfere in government affairs. As the leadership at the top experienced a series of military and economic disasters, the middle class, aristocrats, peasants, soldiers, and workers grew more and more disenchanted with the tsarist regime. Even conservative aristocrats who supported the monarchy felt the need to do something to reverse the deteriorating situation. For a start, they assassinated Rasputin in December 1916. By then it was too late to save the monarchy, which fell quickly at the beginning of March 1917.

The March Revolution

In early 1917, a series of strikes led by working-class women broke out in the capital city of Petrograd (formerly St. Petersburg). A few weeks earlier, the government had introduced bread rationing in the capital city after the price of bread had skyrocketed. Many of the women who stood in the lines waiting for bread were also factory workers who had put in twelve-hour days. The Russian government soon became aware of the volatile situation in the capital. One police report stated: "Mothers of families, exhausted by endless standing in line at stores, distraught over their half-starving and sick children, are today perhaps closer to revolution than [the liberal opposition leaders] and of course they are a great deal more dangerous because they are the combustible material for which only a single spark is needed to burst into flame."[7] On March 8, a day celebrated since 1910 as International Women's Day, around 10,000 Petrograd women marched in parts of the city demanding "peace and bread." Soon other workers joined the women, and together they called for a general strike that succeeded in shutting down all factories in the city on March 10. Nicholas ordered his troops to disperse the crowds by shooting them if necessary, but large numbers of the soldiers soon joined the demonstrators. The Duma (DOO-muh), or legislative body, which the tsar had tried to dissolve, met anyway and on March 12 declared that it was assuming governmental responsibility. It established a Provisional Government on March 15; the tsar abdicated the same day.

The Provisional Government, which came to be led in July by Alexander Kerensky (kuh-REN-skee), decided to carry on the war to preserve Russia's honor—a major blunder because it satisfied neither workers nor peasants, who above all wanted an end to the war. The Provisional Government also faced another authority, the **soviets**, or councils of workers' and soldiers' deputies. The Petrograd soviet had been formed in March 1917; at the same time, soviets sprang up spontaneously in army units, factory towns, and rural areas. The soviets represented the more radical interests of the lower classes and were largely composed of socialists of various kinds. One group—the Bolsheviks (BOHL-shuhviks)—came to play a crucial role.

Lenin and the Bolshevik Revolution

The Bolsheviks were a small faction of Russian Social Democrats who had come under the leadership of Vladimir Ulianov (VLAD-ih-meer ool-YA-nuf), known to the world as Lenin (LEH-nin) (1870–1924). Under Lenin's direction, the Bolsheviks became a party dedicated to violent revolution. He believed that only a revolution could destroy the capitalist system and that a "vanguard" of activists must form a small party of well-disciplined professional revolutionaries to accomplish this task. Between 1900 and 1917, Lenin spent most of his time in exile in Switzerland. When the Provisional Government was set up in March 1917, he believed that an opportunity for the Bolsheviks to seize power had come. Just weeks later, the German military's high command, which hoped to create disorder in Russia, shipped Lenin to Russia in a "sealed train" by way of Finland.

Lenin believed that the Bolsheviks must work to gain control of the soviets of soldiers, workers, and peasants and then use them to overthrow the Provisional Government. At the same time, the Bolsheviks sought mass support through promises geared to the needs of the people: an end to the war, redistribution of all land to the peasants, the transfer of factories and industries from capitalists to committees of workers, and the relegation of government power from the Provisional Government to the soviets. Three simple slogans summed up the Bolshevik program: "Peace, Land, Bread," "Worker Control of Production," and "All Power to the Soviets."

By the end of October, the Bolsheviks had achieved a slight majority in the Petrograd and Moscow soviets. The number of party members had also grown from 50,000 to 240,000. With fervid revolutionary Leon Trotsky (TRAHT-skee) (1877–1940) as chairman of the Petrograd soviet, Lenin and the Bolsheviks were in a position to seize power in the name of the soviets. During the night of November 6, pro-soviet and pro-Bolshevik forces took control of Petrograd. The Provisional Government quickly collapsed, with little bloodshed. The following

23.4a

23.4b

23.4a, 23.4b Lenin and Trotsky. Vladimir Lenin and Leon Trotsky were important figures in the Bolsheviks' successful seizure of power in Russia. In Image 23.4a, Lenin addresses a rally in Moscow in 1917. Image 23.4b shows Trotsky, who became commissar of war in the new regime, haranguing his troops.

Keystone/Hulton Archive/Getty Images

Underwood & Underwood/Historical/Corbis

night, the All-Russian Congress of Soviets, representing local soviets from all over the country, affirmed the transfer of power. At the second session, on the night of November 8, Lenin announced the new Soviet government, the Council of People's Commissars, with himself as its head.

But the Bolsheviks, soon renamed the Communists, still had a long way to go. For one thing, Lenin had promised peace, and he realized that would not be an easy task because of the humiliating losses of Russian territory that it would entail. There was no real choice, however. On March 3, 1918, Lenin signed the Treaty of Brest-Litovsk (BREST-li-TUFFSK) with Germany and gave up eastern Poland, Ukraine, and the Baltic provinces. He had promised peace to the Russian people, but real peace did not come. The country soon sank into civil war.

Civil War There was great opposition to the new Communist regime, not only from groups loyal to the tsar but also from bourgeois and aristocratic liberals and anti-Leninist socialists. In addition, thousands of Allied troops were eventually sent to different parts of Russia in the hope of bringing Russia back into the war.

Between 1918 and 1921, the Communist (Red) Army was forced to fight on many fronts. The first serious threat to the Communists came from Siberia, where White (anti-Communist) forces attacked westward and advanced almost to the Volga River. Attacks also came from the Ukrainians in the southwest and from the Baltic regions. In mid-1919, White forces swept through Ukraine and advanced almost to Moscow before being pushed back. The disunity of the anti-Communist forces seriously weakened their efforts. Political differences created distrust among the Whites and prevented them from cooperating effectively with each other. By 1920, the major White forces had been defeated, and Ukraine had been retaken. The next year, the Communist regime regained control over the independent nationalist governments in the Caucasus: Georgia, Russian Armenia, and Azerbaijan (az-ur-by-JAHN).

What helped Lenin and the Bolsheviks triumph over what once seemed to be overwhelming forces? For one thing, the Red Army became a well-disciplined fighting force largely because of the organizational genius of Leon Trotsky. As commissar of war, Trotsky reinstated the draft and insisted on rigid discipline; soldiers who deserted or refused to obey orders were summarily executed.

The Communists also succeeded in translating their revolutionary faith into practical instruments of power. A policy of **war communism**, for example, was used to ensure regular supplies for the Red Army. War communism included the nationalization of banks and most industries, the forcible requisition of grain from peasants, and the centralization of state power under Bolshevik control. Another Bolshevik instrument was "revolutionary terror." A new Red secret police known as the Cheka (CHEK-uh) instituted the Red Terror, which aimed at nothing less than the destruction of all who opposed the new regime.

Finally, the intervention of foreign armies enabled the Communists to appeal to the powerful force of Russian patriotism. Appalled by the takeover of power in Russia by the radical Communists, the Allied Powers intervened. At one point, more than 100,000 foreign troops—mostly Japanese, British, American, and French—were stationed on Russian soil. This intervention by the Allies enabled the Communist government to appeal to patriotic Russians to fight the attempts of foreigners to control their country.

By 1921, the Communists were in control of Russia. In the course of the civil war, the Communist regime had also transformed Russia into a bureaucratically centralized state dominated by a single party. It was a state that was largely hostile to the Allied Powers that had sought to assist the Communists' enemies in the civil war.

23-3b The Last Year of the War

For Germany, the withdrawal of the Russians in March 1918 offered renewed hope for a favorable end to the war. The victory over Russia persuaded Erich von Ludendorff (LOO-dun-dorf) (1865–1937), who guided German military operations, and most German leaders to make one final military gamble—a grand offensive in the west to break the military stalemate. The German attack was launched in March and lasted into July, but an Allied counterattack supported by the arrival of 140,000 fresh American troops defeated the Germans at the Second Battle of the Marne on July 18. Ludendorff's gamble had failed.

On September 29, 1918, General Ludendorff informed German leaders that the war was lost and insisted that the government sue for peace at once. Implicit among the Allied demands, however, was the abdication of the emperor. But Kaiser William II refused to abdicate. When German officials discovered, however, that the Allies were unwilling to make peace with the autocratic imperial

CHRONOLOGY	World War I
	1914
Battle of Tannenberg	August 26–30
First Battle of the Marne	September 6–10
Battle of Masurian Lakes	September 15
	1915
Battle of Gallipoli begins	April 25
Italy declares war on Austria–Hungary	May 23
	1916
Battle of Verdun	February 21–December 18
	1917
United States enters the war	April 6
	1918
Last German offensive	March 21–July 18
Second Battle of the Marne	July 18
Allied counteroffensive	July 18–November 10
Armistice between Allies and Germany	November 11

government, they instituted reforms to create a liberal government. Meanwhile, popular demonstrations broke out throughout Germany. William II capitulated to public pressure and abdicated on November 9, and the Socialists under Friedrich Ebert (FREED-rikh AY-bert) (1871–1925) announced the establishment of a republic. Two days later, on November 11, 1918, the new German government agreed to an armistice. The way in which the war ended, with German armies still fighting outside Germany, later led German nationalists, especially Adolf Hitler (see Chapter 25), to argue that the German army had not been defeated but stabbed in the back by the "Jewish–Marxist" civilians who had established the republic. Moreover, at the end of World War II, the Allied armies would be sure to occupy defeated Germany rather than repeat the experience of World War I. The Great War was over, but the revolutionary forces set in motion by the war were not yet exhausted.

The Casualties of the War World War I devastated European civilization. Between 8 million and 9 million soldiers died on the battlefields; another 22 million were wounded. Many of those who survived the war died later from war injuries or lived on without arms or legs or with other forms of mutilation. The birthrate in many European countries declined noticeably as a result of the death or maiming of so many young men. World War I also created a lost generation of war veterans who had become accustomed to violence and who would later band together in support of Mussolini and Hitler in their bids for power.

Nor did the killing affect only soldiers. Untold numbers of civilians died from war injuries or starvation. In 1915, using the excuse of a rebellion by the Armenian minority and their supposed collaboration with the Russians, the Turkish government began systematically to kill Armenian men and expel women and children. Within seven months, 600,000 Armenians had been killed, and 500,000 had been deported. Of the latter, 400,000 died while marching through the deserts and swamps of Syria and Mesopotamia. By September 1915, an estimated 1 million Armenians were dead, the victims of genocide.

23-3c The Peace Settlement

In January 1919, the delegations of twenty-seven victorious Allied nations gathered in Paris to conclude a final settlement of the Great War. Over a period of years, the reasons for fighting World War I had been transformed from selfish national interests to idealistic principles.

No one expressed these principles better than U.S. President Woodrow Wilson (1856–1924). Wilson's proposals for a truly just and lasting peace included "open covenants of peace, openly arrived at" instead of secret diplomacy; the reduction of national armaments to a "point consistent with domestic safety"; and the self-determination of people so that "all well-defined national aspirations shall be accorded the utmost satisfaction." As the spokesman for a new world order based on democracy and international cooperation, Wilson was enthusiastically cheered by many Europeans when he arrived in Europe for the peace conference at the palace of Versailles. Wilson's rhetoric on self-determination also inspired peoples in the colonial world in Africa, Asia, and the Middle East, and it was influential in developing anticolonial nationalist movements in these areas (see Chapter 24).

Wilson soon found, however, that more practical motives guided other states at the Paris Peace Conference. The secret treaties and agreements that had been made before the war could not be totally ignored. National interests also complicated the deliberations of the conference. David Lloyd George (1863–1945), prime minister of Great Britain, had won a decisive electoral victory in December 1918 on a platform of making the Germans pay for this dreadful war.

France's approach to peace was primarily determined by considerations of national security. To Georges Clemenceau (ZHORZH kluh-mahn-SOH) (1841–1929), the feisty premier of France who had led his country to victory, the French people had borne the brunt of German aggression. They deserved revenge and security against future German aggression (see Opposing Viewpoints, "Two Voices of Peacemaking," p. 591).

The most important decisions at the Paris Peace Conference were made by Wilson, Clemenceau, and Lloyd George. In the end, only compromise made it possible to achieve a peace settlement. Wilson's wish that the creation of an international peacekeeping organization be the first order of business was granted, and the conference adopted the principle of the League of Nations on January 25, 1919. In return, Wilson agreed to make compromises on territorial arrangements to guarantee the establishment of the league, believing that a functioning league could later rectify bad arrangements.

The Treaty of Versailles   The final peace settlement consisted of five separate treaties with the defeated nations—Germany, Austria, Hungary, Bulgaria, and Turkey. The Treaty of Versailles with Germany, signed on June 28, 1919, was by far the most important one. The Germans considered it a harsh peace and were particularly unhappy with Article 231, the War Guilt Clause, which declared Germany (and Austria) responsible for starting the war and ordered Germany to pay reparations for all the damage endured by Allied governments and their people.

The military and territorial provisions of the treaty also rankled Germans. Germany had to reduce its army to 100,000 men, cut back its navy, and eliminate its air force. German territorial losses included the return of Alsace and Lorraine to France and sections of Prussia to the new Polish state (see Map 23.4). German land west and as far as thirty miles east of the Rhine was established as a demilitarized zone and stripped of all armaments or fortifications to serve as a barrier to any future German military moves westward against France. Outraged by the "dictated peace," the new German government complained but accepted the treaty.

The Other Peace Treaties   The separate peace treaties made with the other Central Powers extensively redrew the map of Eastern Europe. Many of these changes merely ratified what the war had already accomplished. Both the German and Russian Empires lost considerable

Two Voices of Peacemaking

Politics & Government

WHEN THE ALLIED POWERS MET IN PARIS IN JANUARY 1919, it soon became apparent that the victors had different opinions on the kind of peace they expected. The first selection is an excerpt from a speech by Woodrow Wilson in which the American president presented his idealistic goals for a peace based on justice and reconciliation.

The second selection is from a book by French leader Georges Clemenceau, whose vision of peacemaking was quite different from Wilson's. The French sought revenge and security. In this selection from his book *Grandeur and Misery of Victory*, Clemenceau revealed his fundamental dislike and distrust of Germany.

Woodrow Wilson, Speech, May 26, 1917

We are fighting for the liberty, the self-government, and the undictated development of all peoples, and every feature of the settlement that concludes this war must be conceived and executed for that purpose. Wrongs must first be righted and then adequate safeguards must be created to prevent their being committed again. . . .

No people must be forced under sovereignty under which it does not wish to live. No territory must change hands except for the purpose of securing those who inhabit it a fair chance of life and liberty. No indemnities must be insisted on except those that constitute payment for manifest wrongs done. No readjustments of power must be made except such as will tend to secure the future peace of the world and the future welfare and happiness of its peoples.

And then the free peoples of the world must draw together in some common covenant, some genuine and practical cooperation that will in effect combine their force to secure peace and justice in the dealings of nations with one another.

Georges Clemenceau, *Grandeur and Misery of Victory*

War and peace, with their strong contrasts, alternate against a common background. For the catastrophe of 1914 the Germans are responsible. Only a professional liar would deny this. . . .

What after all is this war, prepared, undertaken, and waged by the German people, who flung aside every scruple of conscience to let it loose, hoping for a peace of enslavement under the yoke of a militarism, destructive of all human dignity? It is simply the continuance, the recrudescence, of those never-ending acts of violence by which the first savage tribes carried out their depredations with all the resources of barbarism. . . .

I have sometimes penetrated into the sacred cave of the Germanic cult, which is, as every one knows, the *Bierhaus* [beer hall]. A great aisle of massive humanity where there accumulate, amid the fumes of tobacco and beer, the popular rumblings of a nationalism upheld by the sonorous brasses blaring to the heavens the supreme voice of Germany, *Deutschland über alles! Germany above everything!* Men, women, and children, all petrified in reverence before the divine stoneware pot, brows furrowed with irrepressible power, eyes lost in a dream of infinity, mouths twisted by the intensity of willpower, drink in long draughts the celestial hope of vague expectations.

Q *How did the peacemaking aims of Wilson and Clemenceau differ? How did their different views affect the deliberations of the Paris Peace Conference and the nature of the final peace settlement?*

Sources: Excerpts from *The Public Papers of Woodrow Wilson: War and Peace*, edited by Ray Stannard Baker. Copyright 1925, 1953 by Edith Bolling Wilson. From *Georges Clemenceau, Grandeur and Misery of Victory* (New York: Harcourt, 1930), pp. 105, 107, 280.

territory in Eastern Europe, and the Austro–Hungarian Empire disappeared altogether. New nation-states emerged from the lands of these three empires: Finland, Latvia, Estonia, Lithuania, Poland, Czechoslovakia, Austria, and Hungary. Territorial rearrangements were also made in the Balkans. Serbia formed the nucleus of a new southern Slavic state called Yugoslavia that combined Serbs, Croats, and Slovenes under a single monarch.

Although the Paris Peace Conference was supposedly guided by the principle of self-determination, the mixtures of peoples in eastern Europe made it impossible to draw boundaries along neat ethnic lines. As a result of compromises, virtually every eastern European state was left

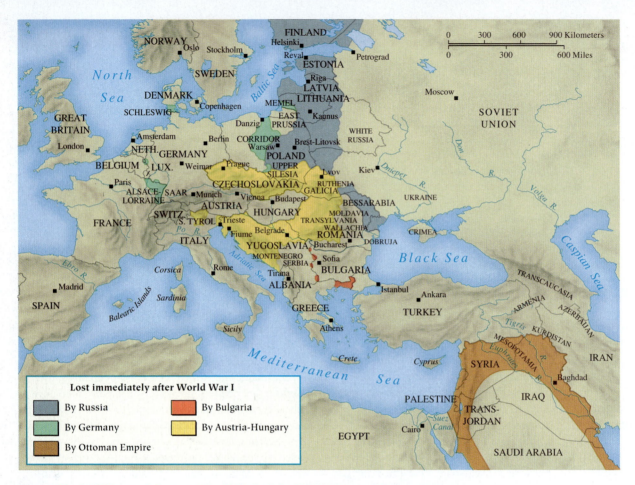

Map 23.4 Territorial Changes in Europe and the Middle East after World War I. The victorious Allies met in Paris to determine the shape and nature of postwar Europe. At the urging of U.S. President Woodrow Wilson, many nationalist aspirations of former imperial subjects were realized with the creation of several new countries from the prewar territory of Austria–Hungary, Germany, Russia, and the Ottoman Empire.

Q *What new countries emerged in Europe and the Middle East?*

with a minorities problem that could lead to future conflicts. Germans in Poland; Hungarians, Poles, and Germans in Czechoslovakia; Hungarians in Romania; and the combination of Serbs, Croats, Slovenes, Macedonians, and Albanians in Yugoslavia all became sources of later conflict.

Yet another centuries-old empire, the Ottoman Empire, was dismembered by the peace settlement after the war. To gain Arab support against the Ottoman Turks during the war, the Western Allies had promised to recognize the independence of Arab

Map 23.5 The Middle East in 1919

states in the Middle Eastern lands of the Ottoman Empire. But the imperialist habits of Western nations died hard. After the war, France was given control of Lebanon and Syria, and Britain received Iraq and Palestine (including Trans-Jordan). Officially, both acquisitions were called **mandates**, a system whereby a nation officially administered a territory on behalf of the League of Nations. The system of mandates could not hide the fact that the principle of national self-determination at the Paris Peace Conference was largely for Europeans.

23-4 AN UNCERTAIN PEACE

 Focus Question: What problems did Europe and the United States face in the 1920s?

Four years of devastating war had left many Europeans with a profound sense of despair and disillusionment. The Great War indicated to many people that something was dreadfully wrong with Western values. In *The Decline of the West*, German writer Oswald Spengler (1880–1936) reflected this disillusionment when he emphasized the decadence of Western civilization and posited its collapse.

23-4a The Search for Security

The peace settlement at the end of World War I had tried to fulfill the nineteenth-century dream of nationalism by creating new boundaries and new states. From its inception, however, this peace settlement had left nations unhappy and eager to revise it.

U.S. President Woodrow Wilson had recognized that the peace treaties contained unwise provisions that could serve as new causes for conflicts, and he had placed many of his hopes for the future in the League of Nations. The league, however, was not particularly effective in maintaining the peace. The failure of the United States to join the league in a backlash of isolationist sentiment undermined its effectiveness from the beginning. Moreover, the league could use only economic sanctions to halt aggression.

France's search for security between 1919 and 1924 was founded primarily on a strict enforcement of the Treaty of Versailles. This tough policy toward Germany began with the issue of reparations, the payments that the Germans were supposed to make to compensate for war damage. In April 1921, the Allied Reparations Commission settled on a sum of 132 billion marks ($33 billion) for German reparations that was to be paid in annual installments of 2.5 billion (gold) marks. The new German republic made its first payment in 1921, but by the following year, the German government faced financial troubles and announced that it was unable to pay more. Outraged, the French government sent troops to occupy the Ruhr Valley, Germany's chief industrial and mining center. If the Germans would not pay reparations, the French would collect reparations in kind by operating and using the Ruhr's mines and factories.

Both Germany and France suffered from the French occupation of the Ruhr. The German government adopted a policy of passive resistance to French occupation that was largely financed by printing more paper money. This only intensified the inflationary pressures that had already begun in Germany by the end of the war. The German mark became worthless, and economic disaster fueled political upheavals. All nations, including France, were happy to cooperate with the American suggestion for a new conference of experts to reassess the reparations problem.

In August 1924, an international commission produced a new plan for reparations. The Dawes Plan, named after the American banker who chaired the commission, reduced the reparations and stabilized Germany's payments on the basis of its ability to pay. The Dawes Plan also opened the door to heavy American investments in Europe that helped create a new era of European prosperity between 1924 and 1929.

With prosperity came a new age of European diplomacy. In 1925, a spirit of cooperation was fostered by the foreign ministers of Germany and France, Gustav Stresemann (GOOS-tahf SHTRAY-zuh-mahn) and Aristide Briand (ah-ruh-STEED bree-AHNH), when they concluded the Treaty of Locarno (loh-KAHR-noh) guaranteeing Germany's new western borders with France and Belgium. Although Germany's new eastern borders with Poland were conspicuously absent from the agreement, the Locarno pact was viewed by many as the beginning of a new era of European peace. The spirit of Locarno was based on little real substance, however, because Germany lacked the military power to alter its western borders.

23-4b The Great Depression

Almost as devastating as the two world wars in the first half of the twentieth century was the economic collapse that ravaged the world in the 1930s. Two events set the stage for the Great Depression: a downturn in domestic economic activities and an international financial crisis created by the collapse of the American stock market in 1929.

Already in the mid-1920s, prices for agricultural goods were beginning to decline rapidly because of overproduction of basic commodities such as wheat. During the war, farmers in North and South America had expanded food production to meet the demands of the warring European nations. After the war, these farmers did not curtail production, expecting that Europe would not recover from the damage of the war. By 1927, European production had returned to prewar levels, precipitating a sharp decline in commodity prices. Commodity prices fell by 30 percent between 1924 and 1929.

In addition to domestic economic troubles, much of the European prosperity between 1924 and 1929

23.5 The Great Depression: Bread Lines in Paris. The Great Depression devastated the European economy and had serious political repercussions. Because of its more balanced economy, France did not feel the effects of the depression as quickly as other European countries. By 1931, however, even France was experiencing lines of unemployed people at free-food centers.

had been built on American bank loans to Germany. The crash of the U.S. stock market in October 1929 led panicky American investors to withdraw many of their funds from Germany and other European markets. The withdrawal of funds seriously weakened the banks of Germany and other central European states. By 1931, trade was slowing down, industrialists were cutting back production, and unemployment was increasing as the ripple effects of international bank failures had a devastating impact on domestic economies.

Economic depression was by no means a new phenomenon in European history, but the depth of the economic downturn after 1929 fully justifies the label of "Great Depression." During 1932, the worst year of the depression, one British worker in four was unemployed; in Germany, 6 million people, or 40 percent of the labor force, were out of work. Unemployed and homeless people filled the streets of cities throughout the advanced industrial world.

The economic crisis also had unexpected social repercussions. Women were often able to secure low-paying jobs as servants, housecleaners, or laundresses, while many men remained unemployed, either begging on the streets or staying at home to do household tasks. Many unemployed men, resenting this reversal of traditional gender roles, were open to the shrill cries of demagogues with simple solutions to the economic crisis.

Governments seemed powerless to deal with the crisis. The classic liberal remedy for depression was a deflationary policy of balanced budgets, which involved cutting costs by lowering wages and raising tariffs to exclude other countries' goods from home markets, but this policy only served to worsen the economic crisis and cause even greater mass discontent. This in turn led to serious political repercussions. Increased government activity in the economy was one reaction. Another effect was a renewed interest in Marxist doctrines. Many asked, hadn't Marx predicted that capitalism would destroy itself through overproduction? Communism took on new popularity, especially with workers and intellectuals. Finally, the Great Depression increased the attractiveness of simplistic dictatorial solutions, especially from a new movement known as *fascism*. Everywhere, democracy seemed on the defensive in the 1930s (see Chapter 25).

23-4c The Democratic States

After World War I, Great Britain went through a period of serious economic difficulties. During the war, Britain had lost many of the markets for its industrial products, especially to the United States and Japan. The postwar decline of such staple industries as coal, steel, and textiles led to a rise in unemployment, which reached the 2 million mark in 1921. But Britain soon rebounded and from 1925 to 1929 experienced an era of renewed prosperity.

By 1929, however, Britain faced the growing effects of the Great Depression. A national government (a coalition of Liberals and Conservatives) claimed credit for bringing Britain out of the worst stages of the depression, primarily by using the traditional policies of balanced budgets and protective tariffs. British politicians had largely ignored the new ideas of a Cambridge economist, John Maynard Keynes (KAYNZ) (1883–1946), who published his *General Theory of Employment, Interest and Money* in 1936. He condemned the traditional view that in a free economy, depressions should be left to work themselves out. Keynes argued that unemployment stemmed not from overproduction but from a decline in demand and maintained that demand could be increased by putting people back to work constructing highways and public buildings, even if governments had to go into debt to pay for these public works, a concept known as **deficit spending**.

After the defeat of Germany, France had become the strongest power on the European continent, but no French government seemed capable of solving the country's financial problems between 1921 and 1926. Like other European countries, though, France did experience a period of relative prosperity between 1926 and 1929.

Because it had a more balanced economy than other nations, France did not begin to feel the full effects of the Great Depression until 1932. Then economic instability soon had political repercussions. During a nineteen-month period in 1932 and 1933, six different cabinets were formed as France faced political chaos. Finally, in June 1936, a coalition of leftist parties—Communists, Socialists, and Radicals—formed a new government, the Popular Front, but its policies failed to solve the problems of the depression. By 1938, the French were experiencing a serious decline of confidence in their political system.

After the imperial Germany of William II had come to an end in 1918 with Germany's defeat in World War I, a German democratic state known as the Weimar (VY mar) Republic was established. From its beginnings, Weimar was plagued by a series of problems. The republic had no truly outstanding political leaders and faced serious economic difficulties. In 1922 and 1923, Germany experienced runaway inflation; widows, orphans, the retired elderly, army officers, teachers, civil servants, and others who lived on fixed incomes all watched their monthly stipends become worthless and their lifetime savings disappear. Their economic losses increasingly pushed the middle class to the rightist parties that were hostile to the republic. To make matters worse, after a period of prosperity from 1924 to 1929, Germany faced the Great Depression. Unemployment increased to 3 million in March 1930 and 4.4 million by December of the same year. The depression paved the way for the rise of extremist parties.

After Germany, no Western nation was more affected by the Great Depression than the United States. By 1932, U.S. industrial production fell to 50 percent of what it had been in 1929. By 1933, there were 15 million unemployed. Under these circumstances, Democrat Franklin Delano Roosevelt (1882–1945) was able to win a landslide electoral victory to the presidency in 1932. He and his advisers pursued a policy of active government intervention in the economy that came to be known as the New Deal. Economic intervention included a stepped-up program of public works, such as the Works Progress Administration, which was established in 1935 and employed between 2 million and 3 million people who worked at building bridges, roads, post offices, and airports. In 1935, the Social Security Act created a system of old-age pensions and unemployment insurance.

The New Deal provided some social reform measures, but it did not solve the unemployment problems of the Great Depression. In May 1937, during what was considered a period of full recovery, American unemployment still stood at 7 million.

23-4d Socialism in Soviet Russia

The civil war in Russia had taken an enormous toll of life. Lenin had pursued a policy of war communism, but peasants began to sabotage the program by hoarding food once the war was over. A great famine between 1920 and 1922, caused by drought, claimed as many as 5 million lives. Industrial collapse paralleled the agricultural disaster. By 1921, industrial output was only 20 percent of its 1913 levels. Russia was exhausted. A peasant banner proclaimed, "Down with Lenin and horseflesh, Bring back the Tsar and pork." As Leon Trotsky said, "The country, and the government with it, were at the very edge of the abyss."[8]

In March 1921, Lenin pulled Russia back from the abyss by adopting his **New Economic Policy** (NEP), a modified version of the old capitalist system. Peasants were now allowed to sell their produce openly. Retail stores and small industries that employed fewer than twenty employees could now operate under private ownership, although heavy industry, banking, and mines remained in the hands of the government.

In 1922, Lenin and the Communists formally created a new state called the Union of Soviet Socialist Republics, known as the USSR by its initials or the Soviet Union by its shortened form. Already by that year, a revived market and a good harvest had brought the famine to an end; Soviet agricultural production climbed to 75 percent of its prewar level.

Lenin's death in 1924 inaugurated a struggle for power among the seven members of the Politburo (POL-itbyoor-oh), the institution that had become the leading organ of the party. The Politburo was severely divided over the future direction of the country. The Left, led by Leon Trotsky, wanted to end the NEP, launch Russia on the path of rapid industrialization, and spread the revolution abroad. Another group in the Politburo, called the Right, rejected the cause of world revolution and wanted instead to concentrate on constructing a socialist state. This group also favored a continuation of Lenin's NEP.

These ideological divisions were underscored by an intense personal rivalry between Leon Trotsky and Joseph Stalin (1879–1953). In 1924, Trotsky held the post of commissar of war and was the leading spokesman for the Left in the Politburo. Stalin was content to hold the dull bureaucratic job of party general secretary while other Politburo members held party positions that enabled them to display their brilliant oratorical abilities. Stalin was skillful at avoiding allegiance to either the Left or Right factions in the Politburo. He was also a good organizer (his fellow Bolsheviks called him "Comrade Index-Card") and used his post as party general secretary to gain complete control of the Communist Party. Trotsky was expelled from the party in 1927. By 1929, Stalin had succeeded in eliminating the Bolsheviks of the revolutionary era from the Politburo and establishing a dictatorship.

23-5 IN PURSUIT OF A NEW REALITY: CULTURAL AND INTELLECTUAL TRENDS

Q **Focus Question:** How did the cultural and intellectual trends of the post–World War I years reflect the crises of the time as well as the lingering effects of the war?

The enormous suffering and the deaths of almost 10 million people during the Great War had shaken society to its foundations. As they tried to rebuild their lives, Europeans wondered what had gone wrong with Western civilization. The Great Depression only added to the desolation left behind by the war.

Political and economic uncertainties were paralleled by social innovations. The Great War had served to break down many traditional middle-class attitudes, especially toward sexuality. In the 1920s, women's physical appearance changed dramatically. Short skirts, short hair, the use of cosmetics that were once thought to be the preserve of prostitutes, and the new practice of sun tanning gave women a new image. This change in physical appearance, which stressed more exposure of a woman's body, was also accompanied by frank discussions of sexual matters. In 1926, Dutch physician Theodor van de Velde (TAY-oh-dor vahn duh VEL-duh) published *Ideal Marriage: Its Physiology and Technique*, which became an international bestseller. Van de Velde described female and male anatomy, discussed birth control techniques, and glorified sexual pleasure in marriage.

23-5a Nightmares and New Visions

Uncertainty also pervaded the cultural and intellectual achievements of the postwar years. Artistic trends were largely a working out of the implications of prewar developments. Abstract painting, for example, became ever more popular (see Comparative Essay, "A Revolution in the Arts," p. 597). In addition, prewar fascination with the absurd and the unconscious content of the mind seemed even more appropriate after the nightmare landscapes of World War I battlefronts. This gave rise to both the Dada movement and surrealism.

Dadaism (DAH-duh-iz-um) attempted to enshrine the purposelessness of life; revolted by the insanity of life, especially the mass destruction of World War I, Dadaists tried to give absurdity an expression by creating "antiart." The 1918 Berlin Dada manifesto maintained that "Dada is the international expression of our times, the great rebellion of artistic movements." Many Dadaists assembled pieces of junk (wire, string, rags, scraps of newspaper, nails, washers) into collages, believing they were transforming the refuse of their culture into art. In the hands of Hannah Höch (HURKH) (1889–1978), Dada became an instrument to comment on women's roles in the new mass culture.

Perhaps more important as an artistic movement was **surrealism**, which sought a reality beyond the material, sensible world and found it in the world of the unconscious through the portrayal of fantasies, dreams, or nightmares. Spaniard Salvador Dalí (sahl-vah-DOR dah-LEE) (1904–1989) became the high priest of surrealism and in his mature phase became a master of representational surrealism. Dalí portrayed recognizable objects entirely divorced from their normal context. By placing objects into unrecognizable relationships, Dalí created a disturbing world in which the irrational became tangible.

23-5b Probing the Unconscious

The interest in the unconscious evident in surrealism was also apparent in the development of new literary techniques that emerged in the 1920s. One of its most apparent manifestations was the "stream of consciousness" technique in which the writer presented an interior monologue or a report of the innermost thoughts of each character. One example of this genre was written by Irish exile James Joyce (1882–1941). His *Ulysses*, published in 1922, told the story of one day in the life of ordinary people in Dublin by following the flow of their inner dialogue.

German writer Hermann Hesse (hayr-MAHN HESS-uh) (1877–1962) dealt with the unconscious in a different fashion. His novels reflected the influence of new psychological theories and Eastern religions and focused on, among other things, the spiritual loneliness of modern human beings in a mechanized urban society. Hesse's novels made a large impact on German youth in the 1920s. He won the Nobel Prize for Literature in 1946.

A Revolution in the Arts

Art & Ideas The period between 1880 and 1930 witnessed a revolution in the arts throughout Western civilization. Fueled in part by developments in physics and psychology, artists and writers rebelled against the traditional belief that the task of art was to represent "reality" and experimented with innovative new techniques so they might approach reality from a totally fresh perspective.

From impressionism and expressionism to cubism, abstract art, Dadaism, and surrealism, painters seemed intoxicated with the belief that their canvases would help reveal the radically changing world. Especially after the cataclysm of World War I, which shattered the image of a rational society, artists sought an absolute freedom of expression, confident that art could redefine humanity in the midst of chaos. Other arts soon followed their lead: James Joyce turned prose on its head by focusing on his characters' innermost thoughts, and Arnold Schönberg (AR-nawlt SHURN-bayrk) created atonal music by using a scale composed of twelve notes that were independent of any tonal key.

This revolutionary spirit had already been exemplified by Pablo Picasso's *Les Demoiselles d'Avignon*, painted in 1907. Picasso used geometrical designs to create a new reality and appropriated non-Western cultural resources, including African masks, in the desire to revitalize Western art.

Another example of the revolutionary approach to art was the decision by French artist Marcel Duchamp (mar-SEL duh-SHAHN) to enter a porcelain urinal in a 1917 art exhibit held in New York City. By signing it and giving it the title *Fountain*, Duchamp proclaimed that he had transformed the urinal into a work of art, thus declaring that art was whatever the artist proclaimed as art. Dadaist artist Kurt Schwitters (KOORT SCHVIT-urz) brought together postage stamps, old handbills, streetcar tickets, newspaper scraps, and pieces of cardboard to form his works of art.

Such intentionally irreverent acts demystified the nearly sacred reverence that had traditionally been attached to works of art. Essentially, Duchamp and others claimed that anything under the sun could be selected as a work of art because the mental choice itself equaled the act of artistic creation. Therefore, art need not be a manual construct; it need only be a mental conceptualization. This liberating concept opened the floodgates of the art world, allowing artists of the new century to swim in this free-flowing, exploratory torrent.

23.6 Kurt Schwitters, *Der Harz*. Kurt Schwitters became identified with the Dada movement when he began to create his collages. He wrote in 1928, "Fundamentally I cannot understand why one is not able to use in a picture, exactly in the same way as commercially made color . . . all the old junk which piles up in closets or the rubbish heaps."

Q *How was the revolution in the arts between 1880 and 1930 related to the political, economic, and social developments of the same period?*

For much of the Western world, the best way to find (or escape) reality was through mass entertainment. The 1930s represented the heyday of the Hollywood studio system, which in the single year of 1937 turned out nearly 600 feature films. Supplementing the movies were cheap paperback books and radio that brought sports, soap operas, and popular music to the masses. The increased size of audiences and the ability of radio and cinema, unlike the printed word, to provide an immediate mass experience added new dimensions to mass culture.

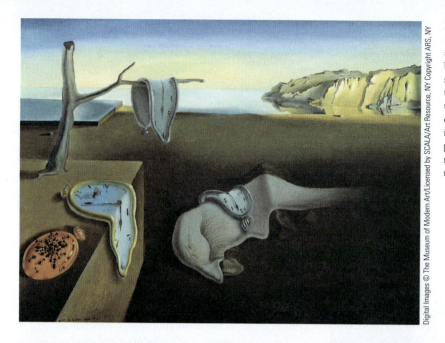

23.7 Salvador Dalí, *The Persistence of Memory*. Surrealism was an important artistic movement in the 1920s. Influenced by the theories of Freudian psychology, surrealists sought to reveal the world of the unconscious, or the "greater reality" that they believed existed beyond the world of physical appearances. As is evident in this painting, Salvador Dalí sought to portray the world of dreams by painting recognizable objects in unrecognizable relationships.

CHAPTER SUMMARY

The assassination of Archduke Francis Ferdinand of Austria–Hungary in the summer of 1914 in the Bosnian capital of Sarajevo led within six weeks to a major war among the major powers of Europe. The Germans drove the Russians back in the east, but in the west a stalemate developed with trenches defended by barbed wire and machine guns extending from the Swiss border to the English Channel. After German submarine attacks, the United States entered the war in 1917, but even from the beginning of the war, battles also took place in the African colonies of the European belligerents as well as in the East, making this a truly global war.

Unprepared for war, Russia soon faltered and collapsed, resulting in a revolution against the tsar. But the new Provisional Government in Russia also soon failed, enabling the revolutionary Bolsheviks of V. I. Lenin to seize power. Lenin established a dictatorship and made a costly peace with Germany. After American troops entered the war, the German government collapsed, leading to an armistice on November 11, 1918.

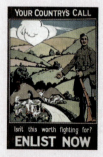

World War I was the defining event of the twentieth century. The incredible destruction and the deaths of almost 10 million people undermined the whole idea of progress.

World War I was also a total war that required a mobilization of resources and populations and increased the centralization of government power. Civil liberties such as freedom of the press, speech, and assembly were circumscribed in the name of national security. Governments' need to plan the distribution of goods restricted economic freedom. World War I made the practice of strong central authority a way of life.

Finally, World War I ended the age of European hegemony over world affairs. In 1917, the Russian Revolution had laid the foundation for the creation of a new Eurasian power, the Soviet Union, and the United States had entered the war. The waning of the European age was not immediately evident to all, however, because it was clouded by American isolationism and the withdrawal of the Soviets from world affairs while they nurtured the growth of their own socialist system. These developments, though temporary, created a political vacuum in Europe that all too soon would be filled by the revival of German power.

Although World War I had destroyed the liberal optimism of the prewar era, many people in the 1920s still hoped that the progress of Western civilization could somehow be restored. These hopes proved largely unfounded. Feeling vulnerable to another invasion,

France sought to weaken Germany. European recovery, largely the result of American loans and investments, ended with the onset of the Great Depression at the end of the 1920s. Democratic states such as Great Britain, France, and the United States spent much of the 1930s trying to recover from the depression. In the Soviet Union, Lenin's New Economic Policy helped stabilize the economy, but on his death a struggle for power ensued that ended with the establishment of a dictatorship under Joseph Stalin.

REFLECTION QUESTIONS

Q What nation, if any, was the most responsible for causing World War I? Why?

Q How did Lenin and the Bolsheviks manage to seize and hold power despite their small numbers?

Q Q How was World War I the first global war?

CHAPTER TIMELINE

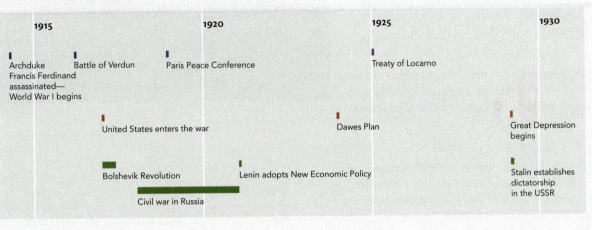

1915	1920	1925	1930
Archduke Francis Ferdinand assassinated—World War I begins	Battle of Verdun	Paris Peace Conference	Treaty of Locarno
	United States enters the war	Dawes Plan	Great Depression begins
	Bolshevik Revolution	Lenin adopts New Economic Policy	Stalin establishes dictatorship in the USSR
	Civil war in Russia		

CHAPTER NOTES

1. A. Toynbee, *Surviving the Future* (New York, 1971), pp. 106–107.
2. Quoted in J. Remak, "1914—The Third Balkan War: Origins Reconsidered," *Journal of Modern History* 43 (1971): 364–365.
3. Quoted in J. M. Winter, *The Experience of World War I* (New York, 1989), p. 142.
4. From an ode by Horace: "It is sweet and right to die for your country."
5. Quoted in H. Strachan, *The First World War* (New York, 2004), pp. 94–95.
6. Quoted in ibid., p. 72.
7. Quoted in W. M. Mandel, *Soviet Women* (Garden City, N.Y., 1975), p. 43.
8. Quoted in I. Howe, ed., *The Basic Writings of Trotsky* (London, 1963), p. 162.

MINDTAP
From Cengage

MindTap® is a fully online, highly personalized learning experience built upon Cengage Learning content. MindTap combines student learning tools—readings, multimedia, activities, and assessments—into a singular Learning Path that guides students through the course and helps students develop the critical thinking, analysis, and communication skills that are essential to academic and professional success.

CHAPTER 24

NATIONALISM, REVOLUTION, AND DICTATORSHIP: ASIA, THE MIDDLE EAST, AND LATIN AMERICA FROM 1919 TO 1939

Chapter Outline and Focus Questions

Critical Thinking

Q *How did the societies discussed in this chapter deal with the political, economic, and social challenges that they faced after World War I, and how did these challenges differ from one region to another?*

Connections to Today

Q *Do nationalist movements in various parts of the world today face any of the same challenges faced by their counterparts in the early twentieth century? If so, what are they?*

24.1 Struggle for the Banner

IN THE SPRING OF 1913, Bolshevik leader V. I. Lenin wrote an article in the party newspaper *Pravda* on the awakening of Asia. "Was it so long ago," he asked his readers, "that China was considered typical of the lands that had been standing still for centuries? Today China is a land of seething political activity, the scene of a virile social movement and of a democratic upsurge." Similar conditions, he added, were spreading the democratic revolution to other parts of Asia—to Turkey, Persia, and China. Ferment was even on the rise in British India.[1]

A year later, the Great War erupted, and Lenin, like millions of his contemporaries, turned his eyes to events in Europe. In February 1917, riots in the streets of Petrograd (the old St. Petersburg) marked the onset of the Russian Revolution. By the end of the year, the Bolsheviks were in power in Moscow. For the next few years, Lenin and his colleagues were preoccupied with consolidating their control over the vast territories of the old tsarist Russian empire.

But Lenin's earlier prediction about the underlying conditions beyond the borders of Europe had been prescient: during the two decades following the end of World War I, a wave of unrest against internal tyranny and external domination was unleashed throughout many parts of Asia, Africa, and Latin America. With the infant Soviet state virtually surrounded by its capitalist enemies, Lenin now concluded that the oppressed masses of Asia and Africa were potential allies in the bitter struggle against the brutal yoke of world imperialism. For the next two decades, Soviet leaders in Moscow turned their attention to China and other parts of Asia in an effort to ride what they hoped would be a mounting wave of revolt against foreign domination. That mounting wave of unrest is the focus of our attention in this chapter.

24-1 THE RISE OF NATIONALISM

Focus Questions: What were the various stages in the rise of nationalist movements in Asia and the Middle East? How did their experience compare with that of nationalist movements in nineteenth-century Europe?

Although the West had emerged from World War I relatively intact, its political and social foundations and its self-confidence had been severely undermined. Within Europe, doubts about the viability of Western civilization were widespread, especially among the intellectual elite. These doubts were quick to reach perceptive observers elsewhere and contributed to a rising tide of unrest against Western political domination throughout the colonial and semicolonial world. That unrest took various forms but was most evident in increasing worker activism, rural protests, and a new sense of national identity in recently colonized societies. In areas of Asia and Latin America where independent states had successfully resisted the Western onslaught, the discontent fostered by the war and later by the Great Depression led to a loss of confidence in democratic institutions and the rise of political dictatorships.

24-1a Modern Nationalism

The first stage of resistance to the West in Asia (see Chapters 21 and 22) had resulted in humiliation and failure in many countries and must have led many Western observers to conclude that the colonized peoples lacked the strength and know-how to create modern states and govern their own destinies. In fact, however, the struggle against imperial rule was just beginning, as a new phase in the process—the rise of modern nationalism—began to take shape at the beginning of the twentieth century.

It was the product of the convergence of several factors. The most vocal source of anticolonialist sentiment was a new urban middle class of Westernized intellectuals. In many cases, these merchants, petty functionaries, clerks, students, and professionals had been educated in Western-style schools. A few had spent time in the West. Many spoke European languages, wore Western clothes, and worked in occupations identified with the rise of modern industrial societies in the West.

The results were paradoxical. On the one hand, this "new class" admired Western culture and sometimes harbored a deep contempt for traditional ways. On the other hand, many strongly resented foreigners and their arrogant contempt for colonized peoples. Though eager to introduce Western ideas and institutions into their own society, these intellectuals were dismayed at the gap between ideal and reality, theory and practice, in colonial policy. Although Western political thought exalted democracy, equality, and individual freedom, such concepts were virtually nonexistent in the colonies.

Equality in economic opportunity and social life was also noticeably lacking in colonial areas. Normally, the middle classes did not suffer in the same manner as impoverished peasants or menial workers, but they, too, had complaints. They were usually relegated to low-level jobs in the government or business and were paid less than Europeans in similar positions. The superiority of the Europeans was expressed in a variety of ways, including "whites only" clubs and the use of the familiar form of the language (normally used by adults to children) when addressing the locals.

Under these conditions, many of the new urban educated class were highly ambivalent about their colonial masters and the civilization they represented. Out of this mixture of hope and resentment emerged the first stirrings of modern nationalism in Asia and North Africa. During the first quarter of the century, in colonial and semicolonial societies from the Suez Canal to the Pacific Ocean, people began to organize political parties and movements seeking reforms or the restoration of independence.

Religion and Nationalism At first, many of the leaders of these movements did not focus clearly on the importance of nationhood but were motivated primarily to defend indigenous economic interests or religious beliefs. In Burma, for example, the first expression of modern nationalism came from students at the University of Rangoon, who protested against official persecution of the Buddhist religion and British lack of respect for local religious traditions (such as failing to remove footwear when entering a Buddhist temple). The protesters adopted the name

Thakin (TAHK-in), a polite term in the Burmese language meaning "lord" or "master," thereby emphasizing their demand for the right to rule themselves. Only in the 1930s did the Thakins begin to focus specifically on national independence.

In the Dutch East Indies, Sarekat (SAR-eh-kaht) Islam (Islamic Association) was established in 1911 as a self-help society among Muslim merchants to fight against domination of the local economy by Chinese interests. Eventually, activist elements realized that the problem was not the Chinese merchants, most of whom were Buddhists, but the colonial presence itself. In the 1920s, Sarekat Islam was transformed into the Nationalist Party of Indonesia, which focused on national independence. Like the Thakins in Burma, this party would lead the country to independence after World War II.

Independence or Modernization? The Nationalist Quandary Building a new nation, however, requires more than a shared sense of grievances against a foreign invader. A host of other issues also had to be resolved. Should independence or modernization be the primary objective? If the colonial regime was viewed as a source of needed reforms in a highly decrepit traditional society, then a gradualist approach made sense. But if it was seen primarily as an impediment to change, the first priority was to bring it to an end. The vast majority of patriotic individuals were convinced that their societies must adopt much of the Western way of life to survive, yet many were equally determined that the local culture would not, and should not, become a carbon copy of the West. What was the national identity, after all, if it did not incorporate some traditional elements?

One important reason to retain some traditional values was being able to provide ideological symbols that the common people could understand and rally around. Though aware that they needed to enlist the mass of the population in the common struggle, many urban intellectuals had themselves become alienated from their own cultural traditions and had difficulty communicating with the rural populations who did not understand such unfamiliar concepts as democracy and nationhood. As Indonesian intellectual Sutan Sjahrir (SOO-tan syah-REER) lamented, many Westernized intellectuals had more in common with their colonial rulers than with the people

in the villages (see Historical Voices, "The Dilemma of the Intellectual," p. 603). As one French colonial official remarked in some surprise to a French-educated Vietnamese reformist, "Why, Monsieur, you are more French than I am!"

24-1b Gandhi and the Indian National Congress

Nowhere in the colonial world were these issues debated more vigorously than in India. Before the Sepoy Uprising (see Chapter 21), Indian efforts had focused mainly on the question of religious identity, as had been the case with the Brahmo Samaj in the 1820s. But in the latter half of the nineteenth century, a stronger sense of national consciousness began to arise, provoked by the conservative policies and racial arrogance of British colonial authorities.

The first Indian nationalists were almost invariably upper class and educated. Many were from urban areas such as Bombay (now Mumbai), Madras (now Chennai), and Calcutta (now Kolkata). At first, many tended to prefer reform to revolution and believed that India needed modernization before taking on the challenges of independence. Such reformists did have some effect. In the 1880s, the government promised a measure of self-government, but all too often such efforts were sabotaged by local British officials.

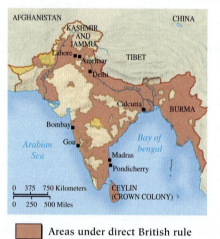

Areas under direct British rule

Map 24.1 British India Between the Wars

The slow pace of reform convinced many Indian nationalists that relying on British benevolence was futile. In 1885, a small group of Indians, with some British participation, met in Bombay to form the Indian National Congress (INC). Although they hoped to speak for all India, most were high-class, English-trained Hindus. Like their reformist predecessors, INC members did not demand immediate independence and called for reforms to end traditional abuses such as child marriage and sati. At the same time, they demanded a share in the governing process and more spending on economic development and less on military campaigns along the frontier. The British responded with a few concessions, but change was glacially slow.

The INC also had difficulty reconciling religious differences within its ranks. Its stated goal was self-determination for all Indians regardless of class or religion, but many of its leaders were Hindu and inevitably reflected Hindu concerns. In the first decade of

The Dilemma of the Intellectual

Interaction & Exchange   **SUTAN SJAHRIR (1909–1966) WAS A PROMINENT LEADER** of the Indonesian nationalist movement who briefly served as prime minister of the Republic of Indonesia in the 1950s. Like many Western-educated Asian intellectuals, he was tortured by the realization that by education and outlook he was closer to his colonial masters—in his case, the Dutch—than to his own people. He wrote the following passage in a letter to his wife in 1935 and later included it in his book *Out of Exile*.

Sutan Sjahrir, *Out of Exile*

Am I perhaps estranged from my people? . . . Why are the things that contain beauty for them and arouse their gentler emotions only senseless and displeasing for me? In reality, the spiritual gap between my people and me is certainly no greater than that between an intellectual in Holland . . . and the undeveloped people of Holland. . . . The difference is rather . . . that the intellectual in Holland does not feel this gap because there is a portion—even a fairly large portion—of his own people on approximately the same intellectual level as himself. . . .

This is what we lack here. Not only is the number of intellectuals in this country smaller in proportion to the total population—in fact, very much smaller—but in addition, the few who are here do not constitute any single entity in spiritual outlook, or in any spiritual life or single culture whatsoever. . . . It is for them so much more difficult than for the intellectuals in Holland. In Holland they build—both consciously and unconsciously—on what is already there. . . . Even if they oppose it, they do so as a method of application or as a starting point.

In our country this is not the case. Here there has been no spiritual or cultural life, and no intellectual progress for centuries. There are the much-praised Eastern art forms but what are these except bare rudiments from a feudal culture that cannot possibly provide a dynamic fulcrum for people of the twentieth century? . . . Our spiritual needs are needs of the twentieth century; our problems and our views are of the twentieth century . . . . Our inclination is no longer toward the mystical, but toward reality, clarity, and objectivity. . . .

We intellectuals here are much closer to Europe or America than we are to the Borobudur or Mahabharata or to the primitive Islamic culture of Java and Sumatra. . . .

So, it seems, the problem stands in principle. It is seldom put forth by us in this light, and instead most of us search unconsciously for a synthesis that will leave us internally tranquil. We want to have both Western science and Eastern philosophy, the Eastern "spirit," in the culture. But what is this Eastern spirit? It is, they say, the sense of the higher, of spirituality, of the eternal and religious, as opposed to the materialism of the West. I have heard this countless times, but it has never convinced me.

Q   *Why did Sutan Sjahrir feel estranged from his own culture? What was his answer to the challenges faced by his country in coming to terms with the modern world?*

Source: From *Out of Exile* by Soetan Sjahrir and Charles Wolf, Jr. (New York: The John Day Company, Inc., 1949), pp. 66–68.

---

the twentieth century, the Muslim League was created to represent the interests of the millions of Muslims in Indian society.

Nonviolent Resistance   In 1915, a young Hindu lawyer returned from South Africa to become active in the INC. He transformed the movement and galvanized India's struggle for independence and identity. Mohandas Gandhi (moh-HAHN-dus GAHN-dee) was born in 1869 in Gujarat (goo-juh-RAHT) in western India, the son of a government minister. After studying law in London, in 1893 he went to South Africa to work in a law firm serving Indian émigrés working as laborers there. He soon became aware of the racial prejudice and exploitation experienced by Indians living in the territory and tried to organize them to protect their interests.

On his return to India, Gandhi became active in the independence struggle, setting up a movement based on nonviolent resistance—the Hindi term was *satyagraha* (SUHT-yuh-grah-hah), meaning "hold fast to the truth"—to try to force the British to improve the lot of the poor and grant independence to India. His goals were to convert the British to his views while simultaneously strengthening the unity and sense of self-respect of his compatriots. When the British sought to suppress dissent, Gandhi urged his followers to refuse to obey British regulations. He began to manufacture his own clothes, dressing in a simple dhoti (DOH-tee) made of coarse homespun cotton, and he adopted the spinning wheel as a symbol of Indian resistance to British textile imports.

Gandhi combined his anticolonial activities with an appeal to the spiritual instincts of all Indians. Though he had been born and raised a Hindu and his ideas were shaped by historical Hindu themes, his universalist approach to the idea of God transcended individual religion. In a speech in 1931, he described God as "an indefinable mysterious power that pervades everything . . . , an unseen power which makes itself felt and yet defies all proof."[2]

Gandhi, now increasingly known as *Mahatma* (mah-HAHT-muh), India's "Great Soul," organized mass protests to achieve his aims, but in 1919 they got out of hand and led to violence and British reprisals. British troops killed hundreds of unarmed protesters in the city of Amritsar (am-RIT-sur) in northwestern India. Gandhi was horrified at the violence and briefly retreated from active politics. Nevertheless, he was arrested for his role in the protests and spent several years in prison.

In Gandhi's absence, the political situation continued to evolve. In 1921, the British passed the Government of India Act, transforming the heretofore advisory Legislative Council into a bicameral parliament, two-thirds of whose members would be elected. Similar bodies were created at the provincial level. In a stroke, 5 million Indians were enfranchised. But such reforms were no longer enough for many members of the INC, who wanted to push aggressively for full independence. The British exacerbated the situation by increasing the salt tax and prohibiting the Indian people from manufacturing or harvesting their own salt. Gandhi, now released from prison, returned to his earlier policy of **civil disobedience** by joining several dozen supporters in a 240-mile walk to the sea, where he picked up a lump of salt and urged Indians to ignore the law. Gandhi and many other members of the INC were arrested.

Organizations to promote women's rights had been established in India shortly after 1900, and Indian women played an active role in the movement. Women accounted for about 20,000—nearly 10 percent—of all those arrested for taking part in demonstrations during the interwar period. Women marched, picketed foreign shops, and promoted the spinning and wearing of homemade cloth. By the 1930s, women's associations were also actively promoting social reforms, including women's education, the introduction of birth control devices, the abolition of child marriage, and universal suffrage. In 1929, the Sarda Act raised the minimum age of marriage to fourteen.

New Leaders for New Challenges In the 1930s, a new figure entered the movement in the person of Jawaharlal Nehru (juh-WAH-hur-lahl NAY-roo) (1889–1964), son of an earlier INC leader. Educated in the law in Great Britain and a brahmin by birth, Nehru personified the new Anglo–Indian politician: secular, rational, upper class, and intellectual. In fact, he appeared to be everything that Gandhi was not. With his emergence, the independence movement embarked on two paths, religious and secular, Indian and Western, traditional and modern. The dual character of the INC leadership may well have strengthened the movement by bringing together the two primary impulses behind the desire for independence: elite nationalism and the primal force of Indian traditionalism. But it portended trouble for the nation's new leadership in defining India's future path (see Comparative Illustration, "Masters and Disciples," p. 605). In the meantime, Muslim discontent with Hindu dominance over the INC was increasing. In 1940, the Muslim League called for the creation of a separate state of Pakistan ("land of the pure") based on Islamic principles in Muslim majority areas of the country (see Opposing Viewpoints, "Islam in the Modern World: Two Views," p. 606). As strife between Hindus and Muslims increased, many Indians came to realize with sorrow (and some British colonialists with satisfaction) that British rule was all that stood between peace and civil war.

24-1c Revolt in the Middle East

In the Middle East as in Europe, World War I hastened the collapse of old empires. The Ottoman Empire, which had dominated the eastern Mediterranean since the seizure of Constantinople in 1453, had been growing weaker, troubled by government corruption, the declining effectiveness of the sultans, and the loss of territory in the Balkans and southwestern Russia. In North Africa, Ottoman authority, tenuous at best, had disintegrated in the nineteenth century, enabling the French to seize Algeria and Tunisia and the British to establish a protectorate over the Nile River Valley.

Twilight of the Ottoman Empire Reformist elements in Istanbul, to be sure, had tried periodically to resist the trend, but military defeats continued: Greece declared its independence, and Ottoman power eroded steadily in the Middle East. A rising sense of nationality among Serbs, Armenians, and other minority peoples threatened the stability and cohesion of the empire. In the 1870s, a new generation of reformers seized power in Istanbul and pushed through a constitution that created a legislative assembly representing all peoples in the state. But the sultan they placed on the throne suspended the new charter and attempted to rule by traditional authoritarian means.

By the end of the century, the defunct 1876 constitution had become a symbol of change for reformist

Masters and Disciples

Politics & Government **WHEN THE FOUNDERS OF NATIONALIST MOVEMENTS** passed leadership over to their successors, the result was often a change in the strategy and tactics of the organizations. When Jawaharlal Nehru (Image 24.2a on the left) replaced Mahatma Gandhi (wearing a simple Indian dhoti rather than the Western dress favored by his colleagues) as leader of the Indian National Congress, the movement adopted a more secular posture. In China, Chiang Kai-shek (Image 24.2b, standing) took Sun Yat-sen's Nationalist Party in a more conservative direction after Sun's death in 1925.

 How do these four leaders compare in terms of their roles in furthering political change in their respective countries?

24.2a

24.2b

elements who were now grouped together under the name **Young Turks**. They found support in the army and administration and among Turks living in exile. In 1908, the Young Turks forced the sultan to restore the constitution, and he was removed from power the following year. Shortly after, the army stepped in.

The final blow came in World War I, when the Ottoman government allied with Germany in the hope of driving the British from Egypt and restoring Ottoman rule over the Nile Valley. In response, the British declared an official protectorate over Egypt and, aided by the efforts of the dashing if eccentric British adventurer T. E. Lawrence (popularly known as "Lawrence of Arabia"), sought to undermine Ottoman rule in the Arabian Peninsula by encouraging Arab nationalists there (see Film & History, *Lawrence of Arabia*, p. 607). In 1916, the local governor of Mecca declared Arabia independent from Ottoman rule, while British troops advanced from Egypt to seize Palestine (see Map 24.2, p. 607). In October 1918, having suffered more than 300,000 casualties during the war, the Ottoman Empire negotiated an armistice with the Allied Powers.

Islam in the Modern World: Two Views

Politics & Government

AS PART OF HIS PLAN to transform Turkey into a modern society, Mustafa Kemal Atatürk sought to free his country from what he considered to be outdated practices imposed by traditional beliefs. The first selection is from a speech in which he proposed bringing an end to the caliphate, which had been in the hands of Ottoman sultans since the formation of the empire. But not all Muslims wished to move in the direction of a more secular society. Mohammed Iqbal (ik-BAHL), a well-known Muslim poet in colonial India, was a prominent advocate for the creation of a separate state for Muslims in South Asia. The second selection is from an address he presented to the All-India Muslim League in December 1930, explaining the rationale for his proposal.

Atatürk, Speech to the Assembly (October 1924)

The sovereign entitled Caliph was to maintain justice among the three hundred million Muslims on the terrestrial globe, to safeguard the rights of these peoples, to prevent any event that could encroach upon order and security, and confront every attack which the Muslims would be called upon to encounter from the side of other nations. It was to be part of his attributes to preserve by all means the welfare and spiritual development of Islam. . . .

If the Caliph and Caliphate, as they maintained, were to be invested with a dignity embracing the whole of Islam, ought they not to have realized in all justice that a crushing burden would be imposed on Turkey, on her existence; her entire resources and all her forces would be placed at the disposal of the Caliph? . . .

For centuries our nation was guided under the influence of these erroneous ideas. But what has been the result of it? Everywhere they have lost millions of men. "Do you know," I asked, "how many sons of Anatolia have perished in the scorching deserts of the Yemen? Do you know the losses we have suffered in holding Syria and Egypt and in maintaining our position in Africa? And do you see what has come out of it? Do you know?"

"New Turkey, the people of New Turkey, have no reason to think of anything else but their own existence and their own welfare. She has nothing more to give away to others."

Mohammed Iqbal, Speech to the All-India Muslim League (1930)

It cannot be denied that Islam, regarded as an ethical ideal plus a certain kind of polity—by which expression I mean a social structure regulated by a legal system and animated by a specific ethical ideal—has been the chief formative factor in the life history of the Muslims of India. It has furnished those basic emotions and loyalties which gradually unify scattered individuals and groups and finally transform them into a well-defined people. Indeed it is no exaggeration to say that India is perhaps the only country in the world where Islam, as a people-building force, has worked at its best. In India, as elsewhere, the structure of Islam as a society is almost entirely due to the working of Islam as a culture inspired by a specific ethical ideal. What I mean to say is that Muslim society, with its remarkable homogeneity and inner unity, has grown to be what it is under the pressure of the laws and institutions associated with the culture of Islam.

Communalism in its higher aspect, then, is indispensable to the formation of a harmonious whole in a country like India. The units of Indian society are not territorial as in European countries. India is a continent of human groups belonging to different religions. Their behavior is not at all determined by a common race consciousness. Even the Hindus do not form a homogeneous group. The principle of European democracy cannot be applied to India without recognizing the fact of communal groups. The Muslim demand for the creation of a Muslim India within India is, therefore, perfectly justified. . . .

I therefore demand the formation of a consolidated Muslim State in the best interests of India and Islam.

For India it means security and peace resulting from an internal balance of power; for Islam an opportunity to rid itself of the stamp that Arabian imperialism was forced to give it, to mobilize its law, its education, its culture, and to bring them into closer contact with its own original spirit and with the spirit of modern times.

Q *Why did Mustafa Kemal believe that the caliphate no longer met the needs of the Turkish people? Why did Mohammed Iqbal believe that a separate state for Muslims in India would be required? How did he attempt to persuade non-Muslims that this would be to their benefit as well?*

Sources: From *Ataturk's Speech to the Assembly*, pp. 432–433. A speech delivered by Ghazi Mustafa Kemal, President of the Turkish Republic, October 1927. From *Sources of Indian Tradition*, Vol. 2, 2e, by Stephen Hay, pp. 218–222. Copyright 1988 by Columbia University Press. Reprinted with permission of the publisher.

The geographical shape of the modern Middle East was formed at the end of World War I when eccentric British military officer T. E. Lawrence led Arab tribesmen in revolt against the territories of the declining Ottoman Empire in the region. The epic story was put in film in *Lawrence of Arabia* (1962) by legendary director David Lean, and the lead character was played with panache by Irish actor Peter O'Toole.

Q *How were the boundaries of the Middle East affected by the treaties enacted at the end of World War I?*

Everett Collection, Inc.

Mustafa Kemal and the Modernization of Turkey

During the next years, the tottering empire began to fall apart as the British and the French made plans to divide Ottoman territories in the Middle East and the Greeks won Allied approval to seize the western parts of the Anatolian Peninsula for their dream of re-creating the substance of the old Byzantine Empire. The impending collapse energized key elements in Turkey under the leadership of a war hero, Colonel Mustafa Kemal (moos-tah-FAH kuh-MAHL) (1881–1938), who had successfully defended the Dardanelles against the British during World War I. Now he

resigned from the army and convoked a national congress that called for the creation of an elected government and the preservation of the empire's remaining territories in a new republic of Turkey. Establishing his capital at Ankara (AN-kuh-ruh), Kemal drove the Greeks from the Anatolian Peninsula and persuaded the British to agree to a new treaty. In 1923, the last Ottoman sultan fled the country, which was now declared a Turkish republic. The Ottoman Empire had come to an end.

During the next few years, President Mustafa Kemal, now popularly known as Atatürk (ah-tah-TIRK), or "Father Turk," attempted to transform Turkey into a modern secular republic. The trappings of a democratic system were put in place with the centerpiece an elected Grand National Assembly, but the president was relatively intolerant of opposition and harshly suppressed critics. Turkish nationalism was emphasized, and the Turkish language, now written in the Roman alphabet, was shorn of many of its Arabic elements. Popular education was emphasized, old aristocratic titles such as *pasha* and *bey* were abolished, and all Turkish citizens were given family names in the European style.

Atatürk also took steps to modernize the economy, overseeing the establishment of a light industrial sector producing textiles, glass, paper, and cement and instituting a five-year plan on the Soviet model to provide for state direction over the economy. Atatürk was no admirer of Soviet communism, however, and the Turkish economy can be better described as a form of state capitalism. He also established training institutions and model farms in an effort to modernize the agricultural sector, although such reforms had little effect on the predominantly conservative peasantry.

Perhaps the most significant aspect of Atatürk's reform program was his attempt to break the power of the Islamic clerics and transform Turkey into a secular state. The caliphate was formally abolished in 1924 (see Opposing Viewpoints, "Islam in the Modern World: Two Views," p. 606), and shari'a (Islamic law) was replaced by a revised version of the Swiss law code. The fez (the brimless cap worn by Turkish Muslims) was abolished as a form of headdress, and women were discouraged from wearing the traditional Islamic veil. Women received the right to vote in 1934 and were legally equal to men in all aspects of marriage and inheritance.

Map 24.2 The Middle East After World War I

24.3 Mustafa Kemal Atatürk. War hero Mustafa Kemal took the initiative in creating the republic of Turkey. As president, Atatürk ("Father Turk") worked hard to transform Turkey into a modern secular state by restructuring the economy, adopting Western dress, and breaking the powerful hold of Islamic traditions. He is now reviled by Muslim fundamentalists for his opposition to an Islamic state. In this photograph, Atatürk (at left in civilian clothes) hosts the shah of Persia during his visit to Turkey in 1934.

Education and the professions were now open to citizens of both genders, and some women even began to participate in politics. All citizens were given the right to convert to another religion at will.

Mustafa Kemal Atatürk's legacy was enormous. Although not all of his reforms were widely accepted in practice, especially by devout Muslims, most of the changes he introduced were retained after his death in 1938. In virtually every respect, the Turkish republic was the product of his determined efforts to create a modern Turkish nation.

Modernization in Iran

In the meantime, a similar process was under way in Persia. Under the Qajar (kuh-JAHR) Dynasty (1794–1925), the country had not been particularly successful in resisting Russian advances in the Caucasus or resolving its domestic problems. To secure themselves from foreign influence, the Qajars moved the capital from Tabriz to Tehran (teh-RAHN), which lies in a mountainous area south of the Caspian Sea. During the mid-nineteenth century, one modernizing shah

Map 24.3 Iran Under the Pahlavi Dynasty

attempted to introduce political and economic reforms but faced resistance from tribal and religious forces, which were predominantly Shi'ite. Increasingly, the dynasty turned to Russia and Great Britain to protect itself from its own people.

Eventually, the growing foreign presence led to the rise of a Persian nationalist movement. Supported by Shi'ite religious leaders, opposition to the regime rose steadily among both peasants and merchants in the cities, and popular pressure forced the shah to grant a constitution on the Western model in 1906.

As in the Ottoman Empire and the Qing Dynasty in China, however, the modernizers had moved too soon—before their power base was secure. With the support of the Russians and the British, the shah regained control, while the two foreign powers began to divide the country into separate spheres of influence. One reason for the foreign interest in Persia was the discovery of oil reserves there in 1908. Over the next years, oil exports increased rapidly, with the bulk of the profits going to British investors.

In 1921, Reza Khan (ree-ZAH KAHN) (1878–1944), an officer in the Persian army, led a mutiny that seized power in Tehran. Four years later, the new Pahlavi (PAH-luh-vee) Dynasty, with Reza Khan as shah, replaced the now defunct Qajar Dynasty. During the next few years, Reza Khan imitated the example of Atatürk in Turkey, introducing reforms to strengthen the central government, modernize the civilian and military bureaucracy, and establish a modern economic infrastructure. In 1935, he officially changed the name of the nation to Iran.

Unlike Atatürk, Reza Khan did not attempt to destroy the power of Islamic beliefs, but he did encourage the establishment of a Western-style educational system and forbade women to wear the veil in public. To strengthen Iranian nationalism and reduce the power of Islam, Reza Khan attempted to popularize the symbols and beliefs of pre-Islamic times. Like his Qajar predecessors, however, he was hindered by strong foreign influence. When the Soviet Union and Great Britain decided to send troops into the country during World War II, he resigned in protest and died three years later.

Nation Building in Iraq

Another consequence of the collapse of the Ottoman Empire was the emergence of a new political entity along the Tigris and Euphrates Rivers, once the heartland of ancient empires. Lacking defensible borders and sharply divided along ethnic and religious lines—a Shi'ite majority in rural areas, a vocal Sunni minority in the cities, and a largely Kurdish population in the northern mountains—the region had been under Ottoman rule since the seventeenth century. During World War I, British forces occupied the area from Baghdad southward to the Persian Gulf to protect the oil-producing regions in neighboring Iran from a German takeover.

Although the British claimed to have arrived as liberators, in 1920 the League of Nations placed the country under British control as the mandate of Iraq. Civil unrest and growing anti-Western sentiment rapidly dispelled any plans for the emergence of an independent government. In 1921, the British turned titular control of Iraq over to a monarchy under the titular authority of King Faisal (FY-suhl) of Syria, a descendant of the Prophet Muhammad. Faisal relied for support primarily on the politically more sophisticated urban Sunni population, although they represented less than a quarter of the population. The discovery of oil near Kirkuk (kir-KOOK) in 1927 increased the value of the area to the British, who had made the shift from coal to oil for their warships during World War I and now needed secure access to the rich oil fields of the Middle East. Faced with rising unrest throughout the country, Great Britain granted formal independence to the kingdom of Iraq in 1932, although British advisers retained a strong influence over the fragile government.

The Rise of Arab Nationalism
As we have seen, the Arab uprising inspired by T. E. Lawrence during World War I helped bring about the demise of the Ottoman Empire. There had been resistance to Ottoman rule in the Arabian Peninsula since the eighteenth century when the devoutly Muslim Wahhabi (wuh-HAH-bee) sect attempted to drive out outside influences and cleanse Islam of corrupt practices that had developed in past centuries. The revolt was eventually suppressed, but Wahhabi influence persisted.

World War I offered an opportunity for the Arabs to throw off the shackles of Ottoman rule, but when the Arab leaders in Mecca declared their independence in 1916 they were to be sorely disappointed. At the close of the war, the British and French created several mandates in the area under the supervision of the League of Nations (see Chapter 23). Iraq was assigned to the British; Syria and Lebanon (the two areas were separated so that Christian peoples in Lebanon could be placed under Christian administration) were given to the French.

In the early 1920s, Ibn Saud (IB-un sah-OOD) (1880–1953), a Wahhabi leader and descendant of the family that had led the eighteenth-century revolt, united Arab tribes in the northern part of the Arabian Peninsula and drove out the remnants of Ottoman rule. Devout and gifted, Ibn Saud

won broad support among Arab tribal peoples and established the kingdom of Saudi Arabia throughout much of the peninsula in 1932.

At first, the new kingdom, consisting essentially of the vast desert wastes of central Arabia, was desperately poor and depended on the income from Muslim pilgrims visiting the holy sites in Mecca and Medina. But during the 1930s, American companies began to explore for oil, and Standard Oil made a successful strike at Dhahran (dah-RAHN) on the Persian Gulf in 1938. Soon an Arabian–American oil conglomerate, popularly called Aramco, was established, and the isolated kingdom was suddenly inundated by Western oilmen and untold wealth.

The Issue of Palestine
The land of Palestine—once the home of the Jews but now inhabited primarily by Muslim Arabs—was made a separate mandate and immediately became a thorny problem for the British. In 1897, Austrian-born journalist Theodor Herzl (TAY-ohdor HAYRT-sul) (1860–1904) had convened an international conference in Switzerland that led to the creation of the World Zionist Organization (WZO). Its aim was to create a homeland in Palestine for the Jewish people, who had long been dispersed throughout Europe, North Africa, and the Middle East (see Historical Voices, "The Zionist Case for Palestine," p. 610).

Over the next decade, Jewish immigration into Palestine, then under Ottoman rule, increased with WZO support. By the outbreak of World War I, some 85,000 Jews lived in Palestine, representing about 15 percent of the total population. In 1917, responding to appeals from British chemist Chaim Weizmann (KY-im VYTS-mahn), British foreign secretary Lord Arthur Balfour (BAL-foor) issued a declaration saying Palestine was to be a national home for the Jews. The Balfour Declaration, which was later confirmed by the League of Nations, was ambiguous on the legal status of the territory and promised that the rights of non-Jewish peoples currently living in the area would not be undermined. But Arab nationalists were incensed. How could a national home for the Jewish people be established in a territory where the majority of the population was Muslim?

CHRONOLOGY	The Middle East Between the Wars
Balfour Declaration on Palestine	1917
Reza Khan seizes power in Persia	1921
End of Ottoman Empire and establishment of a republic in Turkey	1923
Rule of Mustafa Kemal Atatürk in Turkey	1923–1938
Beginning of Pahlavi Dynasty in Iran	1925
Establishment of kingdom of Saudi Arabia	1932

The Zionist Case for Palestine

Politics & Government

AFTER THE BRITISH GOVERNMENT issued the famous Balfour Declaration in 1917 recognizing the right of the Jewish people to a Jewish homeland in Palestine, the Zionist organization presented a memorandum to the delegates at the Paris Peace Conference in February 1919. The memorandum, excerpted here, sought to make the case for a Jewish home in Palestine as the Great Powers assembled to discuss the future of onetime Ottoman holdings in the Middle East.

Memorandum to the Peace Conference in Versailles

The Historic Title

The claims of the Jews with regard to Palestine rest upon the following main considerations:

1. The land is the historic home of the Jews; there they achieved their greatest development; from the centre, through their agency, there emanated spiritual and moral influences of supreme value to mankind. By violence they were driven from Palestine, and through the ages they have never ceased to cherish the longing and the hope of a return.

2. In some parts of the world, and particularly in Eastern Europe, the conditions of life of millions of Jews are deplorable. Forming often a congested population, denied the opportunities which would make a healthy development possible, the need of fresh outlets is urgent, both for their own sake and the interests of the population of other races, among whom they dwell. Palestine would offer one such outlet. To the Jewish masses it is the country above all others in which they would most wish to cast their lot. By the methods of economic development to which we shall refer later, Palestine can be made now, as it was in ancient times, the home of a prosperous population many times as numerous as that which now inhabits it.

3. Palestine is not large enough to contain more than a proportion of the Jews of the world. The greater part of the fourteen millions or more scattered throughout all countries must remain in their present localities, and it will doubtless be one of the cares of the Peace Conference to ensnare for them, wherever they have been oppressed, as for all peoples, equal rights and humane conditions. A Jewish National Home in Palestine will, however, be of high value to them also. Its influence will permeate the Jewries of the world, it will inspire these millions, hitherto often despairing, with a new hope; it will hold out before their eyes a higher standard; it will help to make them even more useful citizens in the lands in which they dwell.

4. Such a Palestine would be of value also to the world at large, whose real wealth consists in the healthy diversities of its civilizations.

5. Lastly, the land itself needs redemption. Much of it is left desolate. Its present condition is a standing reproach. Two things are necessary for that redemption—a stable and enlightened Government, and an addition to the present population which shall be energetic, intelligent, devoted to the country, and backed by the large financial resources that are indispensable for development. Such a population the Jews alone can supply.

 What are the key points included in this excerpt of a memorandum in defense of the idea of a Jewish state in Palestine?

Source: David Hunter Miller, *My Diary at the Conference of Paris* (New York, 1924), V, pp. 15–29, as printed in Akram F. Khater, *Sources in the History of the Modern Middle East*, 2nd ed. (Cengage, 2011), pp. 152–153.

After World War I, more Jewish settlers began to arrive in Palestine in response to the promises made in the Balfour Declaration. As tensions between the new arrivals and existing Muslim residents began to escalate, the British tried to restrict Jewish immigration into the territory while Arab voices rejected the concept of a separate state. In a bid to relieve Arab sensitivities, Great Britain created the separate emirate of Trans-Jordan out of the eastern portion of Palestine. After World War II, it would become the independent kingdom of Jordan. The stage was set for the conflicts that would take place in the region after World War II.

The British in Egypt Great Britain had maintained a loose protectorate over Egypt since the mid-nineteenth century, although the area remained nominally under Ottoman rule. London formalized its protectorate in 1914 to protect the Suez Canal and the Nile Valley from possible seizure by the Central Powers. After the war, however, nationalist

24.4 European Jewish Refugees. After the 1917 Balfour Declaration promised a Jewish homeland in Palestine, increasing numbers of European Jews emigrated there. Their goal was to build a new life in a Jewish land. Like the refugees aboard this ship, they celebrated as they reached their new homeland. The sign reads, "Keep the gates open, we are not the last"—a reaction to British efforts to slow the pace of Jewish immigration in response to protests by Muslim residents of Palestine.

elements became restive and formed the Wafd (WAHFT) Party, a secular organization dedicated to the creation of an independent Egypt based on the principles of representative government. The Wafd received the support of many middle-class Egyptians who, like Atatürk in Turkey, hoped to meld Islamic practices with the secular tradition of the modern West. This modernist form of Islam did not have broad appeal outside the cosmopolitan centers, however, and in 1928 the Muslim cleric Hasan al-Bana (hah-SAHN al-BAN-ah) organized the Muslim Brotherhood, which demanded strict adherence to the teachings of the prophet as set forth in the Qur'an. The Brotherhood rejected Western ways and sought to create a new Egypt based firmly on the precepts of shari'a. By the 1930s, the organization had as many as 1 million members.

24-1d Nationalism and Revolution

Before the Russian Revolution, "Westernization" to most intellectuals in Asia and Africa referred to the capitalist democratic civilization of Western Europe and the United States, not the doctrine of social revolution developed by Karl Marx. Until 1917, Marxism was generally regarded as a utopian idea rather than a concrete system of government. Moreover, Marxism appeared to have little relevance to conditions in Asia and Africa. Orthodox Marxist

doctrine, after all, declared that a communist society would arise only from the ashes of an advanced capitalism that had already passed through an industrial revolution. From the perspective of Marxist historical analysis, most societies in Asia and Africa were still at the feudal stage of development; they lacked the economic conditions and political awareness to achieve a socialist revolution that would bring the working class to power. Finally, the Marxist view of nationalism and religion had little appeal in the non-Western world. Marx believed that nationhood and religion were false ideas that diverted the oppressed masses from the critical issues of class struggle. Instead, Marx stressed an "internationalist" outlook based on class consciousness and the eventual creation of a classless society with no artificial divisions based on culture, nation, or religion.

Lenin and the East The situation began to change after the Russian Revolution. Lenin's Bolsheviks had demonstrated that a revolutionary party espousing Marxist principles could overturn a corrupt, outdated system and launch a new experiment dedicated to ending human inequality and achieving a paradise on Earth. In 1920, Lenin proposed a new revolutionary strategy designed to relate Marxist doctrine and practice to non-Western societies (see the vignette at the beginning of this chapter). His reasons were not entirely altruistic. Soviet Russia, surrounded by capitalist powers, desperately needed allies in its struggle to survive in a hostile world. To Lenin, the anticolonial movements emerging in North Africa, Asia, and the Middle East after World War I were natural allies of the beleaguered new regime in Moscow. Lenin was convinced that only the ability of the imperialist powers to find markets, raw materials, and sources of capital investment in the non-Western world kept capitalism alive. If the tentacles of capitalist influence in Asia and Africa could be severed, imperialism would weaken and collapse.

Establishing such an alliance was not easy, however. Most nationalist leaders in colonial countries belonged to the urban middle class, and had no interest in promoting the concept of a comprehensive revolution to create a totally egalitarian society. In addition, many still adhered to traditional religious beliefs and were opposed to the atheistic principles of classic Marxism. To provide restive colonial peoples with the Bolshevik alternative, Lenin called for the creation of an organization to train agents who would then be dispatched across the world to carry the message of Marxism beyond the bounds of industrialized Europe. The primary instrument of this effort was the **Communist International**, or **Comintern** for short. Formed in 1919 at Lenin's prodding, the Comintern was a worldwide organization of Communist parties dedicated to world revolution. At its headquarters in Moscow, agents from around the world were trained in the precepts of world communism and then sent back to their countries to form Marxist parties and promote social revolution. By the end of the 1920s, almost every colonial or semicolonial society in Asia had a party based on Marxist principles. The Soviets had less success in the Middle East, where Marxism appealed mainly to minorities such as Jews and Armenians in the cities, and in black Africa, where Soviet strategists in any case felt that conditions were not sufficiently advanced for the creation of Communist organizations.

Of course, the new doctrine's appeal was not the same in all non-Western societies. In Confucian societies such as China and Vietnam, where traditional beliefs and practices had been badly discredited by their failure to counter the Western challenge, communism provided uprooted intellectuals with a new secular ideology and rapidly became a major factor in the anticolonial movement. In heavily Buddhist and Muslim societies, where traditional religion remained strong and was a cohesive factor in the resistance movement, communism had less success. To maximize their appeal and minimize potential conflict with traditional ideas, some Communist parties sought to forge temporary alliances with more moderate antiimperialist groups. In so doing, they found it necessary to adapt Marxist doctrine to indigenous values and institutions. In the Middle East, for example, the Ba'ath (BAHTH) Party in Syria adopted a hybrid socialism combining Marxism with Arab nationalism. In Africa, radical intellectuals talked vaguely of a uniquely "African road to socialism." In French Indochina, the Vietnamese revolutionary Hô Chi Minh sought to clothe the radical objectives of his party behind the screen of a national liberation movement allegedly designed to promote Vietnamese independence (see Chapter 26).

24-2 REVOLUTION IN CHINA

Q **Focus Question:** What challenges did China encounter between the two world wars, and what solutions did the Nationalists and the Communists propose to solve them?

Overall, revolutionary Marxism had its greatest impact in China, where a group of young radicals founded the Chinese Communist Party (CCP) in 1921. The rise of the CCP was a product of the failed revolution of 1911. When political forces are too weak or too divided to consolidate their power during a period of instability, the military usually steps in to fill the vacuum. In China, Sun Yat-sen (SOON yaht-SEN) and his colleagues had accepted General Yuan Shikai (yoo-AHN shee-KY) as president of the new Chinese republic in 1911 because they lacked the military force to compete with his control over the army. But some had misgivings about Yuan's intentions. As one remarked in a letter to a friend, "We don't know whether he will be a George Washington or a Napoleon."

As it turned out, he was neither. Showing little comprehension of the new ideas sweeping into China from the West, Yuan ruled in a traditional manner, reviving Confucian rituals and institutions and eventually attempting to found a new imperial dynasty. Yuan's dictatorial inclinations rapidly led to clashes with Sun's party, now renamed the Guomindang (gwoh-min-DAHNG), or Nationalist Party. When Yuan dissolved the new parliament, the Nationalists launched a rebellion. When it failed, Sun Yat-sen fled to Japan.

Yuan was strong enough to brush off the challenge from the revolutionary forces but not strong enough to turn back the clock of history. He died in 1916 and was succeeded by one of his military subordinates. For the next several years, China slipped into semianarchy as the power of the central government disintegrated and military warlords seized power in the provinces.

24-2a Mr. Science and Mr. Democracy: The New Culture Movement

In the meantime, discontent with existing conditions continued to rise. The most vocal protests came from radical intellectuals, who were now convinced that political change could not take place until the Chinese people were more familiar with trends in the outside world. Braving the displeasure of Yuan and his successors, intellectuals at Peking University launched the **New Culture Movement**, which was aimed at abolishing the remnants of the old system and introducing Western values and institutions. Through their classrooms and newly established progressive magazines and newspapers, the intellectuals introduced a host of new ideas from the philosophy of Friedrich Nietzsche (FREED-rikh NEE-chuh) to the feminist plays of Henrik Ibsen. Educated Chinese youths were soon chanting "Down with Confucius and sons" and talking of a new era dominated by "Mr. Sai" (Mr. Science) and "Mr. De" (Mr. Democracy). No one was a greater defender of free thought and speech than the chancellor of Peking University, Cai Yuanpei (TSY yoo-wahn-PAY): "Regardless of what school of thought a person may adhere to, so long as that person's ideas are justified and conform to reason and have not been passed by through the process of natural selection, although there may be controversy, such ideas have a right to be presented."[3] It is not surprising that such views were not appreciated by conservative army officers, one of whom threatened to lob artillery shells into the university to destroy the poisonous new ideas.

Soon, however, the intellectuals' discontent was joined by a growing protest against Japan's efforts to expand its influence on the mainland. Early in the twentieth century, Japan had taken advantage of the Qing's decline to extend its domination over Manchuria and Korea (see Chapter 22). In 1915, the Japanese government insisted that Yuan Shikai accept twenty-one demands that would have given Japan a virtual protectorate over the Chinese government and economy. Yuan was able to fend off the most far-reaching demands by arousing popular outrage in China, but at the Paris Peace Conference four years later, Japan received Germany's sphere of influence in Shandong (shahn-DOONG) Province as a reward for its support of the Allied cause in World War I. On hearing that the Chinese government had accepted the decision, patriotic students demonstrated in Beijing and other major cities on May 4, 1919. Although this May Fourth Movement did not lead to the restoration of Shandong to Chinese rule, it did alert the politically literate population to the threat to national survival and the incompetence of the warlord government.

24-2b The Nationalist–Communist Alliance

By 1920, central authority had almost ceased to exist in China. Two competing political forces now began to emerge from the chaos: Sun Yat-sen's Nationalist Party and the CCP. Following Lenin's strategy, Comintern agents advised the CCP to link up with the more experienced Nationalists. Sun Yat-sen needed the expertise and diplomatic support that Soviet Russia could provide because his antiimperialist rhetoric had alienated many Western powers. In 1923, the two parties formed an alliance to oppose the warlords and drive the imperialist powers out of China.

For three years, the two parties submerged their mutual suspicions and mobilized a revolutionary army to march north and seize control over China. The so-called Northern Expedition began in the summer of 1926 (see Map 24.1). By the following spring, revolutionary forces were in control of all Chinese territory south of the Yangzi River, including the major river ports of Wuhan (WOO-HAHN) and Shanghai (SHANG-hy). But tensions between the two parties now surfaced. Sun Yat-sen had died in 1925 and was succeeded as head of the Nationalist Party by his military subordinate, Chiang Kai-shek (ZHANG ky-SHEK) (see Comparative Illustration, "Masters and Disciples," p. 605). Chiang feigned support for the alliance with the Communists but actually planned to destroy them. In April 1927, he struck against the Communists in Shanghai, killing thousands. After the massacre, most of the Communist leaders went into hiding in the city, attempting to revive the movement in its traditional base among the urban working class. Some party members, however, led by a young Communist organizer, Mao Zedong [mow zee-DOONG ("ow" as in "how")], fled to the hilly areas south of the Yangzi River.

Unlike most CCP leaders, Mao was convinced that the Chinese revolution must be based not on workers in the big cities but on the impoverished peasants in the countryside. The son of a prosperous farmer, Mao served as an agitator in villages in his native province of Hunan (HOO-NAHN) during the Northern Expedition in 1926. At that time, he wrote a report to the party leadership suggesting that the CCP support peasant demands for a land revolution (see Historical Voices, "A Call for Revolt," p. 614). But his superiors refused, fearing that such radical policies would destroy the alliance with the Nationalists.

24-2c The Nanjing Republic

In 1928, Chiang Kai-shek founded a new Chinese republic at Nanjing, and over the next three years he sought to reunify China by a combination of military operations and inducements to various northern warlords to join his movement. He also attempted to put an end to the Communists, rooting them out of their urban base in Shanghai and their rural redoubt in the hills of Jiangxi (JAHNG-shee) Province. He apparently succeeded in the first task in 1931 when, under pressure from Chiang Kai-shek's security services, most CCP leaders were forced to flee Shanghai for Mao's base in Jiangxi Province in southern China. Three years later, Chiang's troops surrounded the Communist headquarters, forcing Mao's young Red Army to embark on the famous Long March, an arduous journey of thousands of miles on foot to the provincial town of Yan'an (yuh-NAHN) in northern China (see Map 24.4).

Meanwhile, Chiang was trying to build a new nation. When the Nanjing Republic was established in 1928, Chiang publicly declared his commitment to Sun Yat-sen's Three People's Principles. In 1918, Sun had written about the all-important second stage of "political tutelage":

> China . . . needs a republican government just as a boy needs school. As a schoolboy must have good teachers and helpful friends, so the Chinese people, being for the first time under republican rule, must have a farsighted revolutionary government for their training. This calls for the period of political tutelage, which is a necessary transitional stage from monarchy to republicanism. Without this, disorder will be unavoidable.[4]

A Call for Revolt

Politics & Government

IN THE FALL OF 1926, Nationalist and Communist forces moved north from Canton on their Northern Expedition in an effort to defeat the warlords. The young Communist Mao Zedong accompanied revolutionary troops into his home province of Hunan, where he submitted a report to the CCP Central Committee calling for a massive peasant revolt against the ruling order. The report shows his confidence that peasants could play an active role in the Chinese revolution despite the skepticism of many of his colleagues.

Mao Zedong, "The Peasant Movement in Hunan"

During my recent visit to Hunan I made a firsthand investigation of conditions. . . . In a very short time, . . . several hundred million peasants will rise like a mighty storm, . . . a force so swift and violent that no power, however great, will be able to hold it back. They will smash all the trammels that bind them and rush forward along the road to liberation. They will sweep all the imperialists, warlords, corrupt officials, local tyrants, and evil gentry into their graves. Every revolutionary party and every revolutionary comrade will be put to the test, to be accepted or rejected as they decide. There are three alternatives. To march at their head and lead them? To trail behind them, gesticulating and criticizing? Or to stand in their way and oppose them? Every Chinese is free to choose, but events will force you to make the choice quickly.

The main targets of attack by the peasants are the local tyrants, the evil gentry and the lawless landlords, but in passing they also hit out against patriarchal ideas and institutions, against the corrupt officials in the cities and against bad practices and customs in the rural areas.

. . . As a result, the privileges which the feudal landlords enjoyed for thousands of years are being shattered to pieces. . . . With the collapse of the power of the landlords, the peasant associations have now become the sole organs of authority, and the popular slogan "All power to the peasant associations" has become a reality.

The peasants' revolt disturbed the gentry's sweet dreams. When the news from the countryside reached the cities, it caused immediate uproar among the gentry. . . . From the middle social strata upwards to the Kuomintang [Nationalist] right-wingers, there was not a single person who did not sum up the whole business in the phrase, "It's terrible!" . . . Even quite progressive people said, "Though terrible, it is inevitable in a revolution." In short, nobody could altogether deny the word "terrible." But . . . the fact is that the great peasant masses have risen to fulfill their historic mission. . . . What the peasants are doing is absolutely right; what they are doing is fine! "It's fine!" is the theory of the peasants and of all other revolutionaries. Every revolutionary comrade should know that the national revolution requires a great change in the countryside. The Revolution of 1911 did not bring about this change, hence its failure. This change is now taking place, and it is an important factor for the completion of the revolution. Every revolutionary comrade must support it, or he will be taking the stand of counterrevolution.

Q *Why did Mao Zedong believe that rural peasants could help bring about a social revolution in China? How does his vision compare with the reality of the Bolshevik Revolution in Russia?*

Source: From *Selected Works of Mao Tse-Tung* (London: Lawrence and Wishart, Ltd., 1954), Vol. 1, pp. 21–23.

In keeping with Sun's program, Chiang announced a period of political indoctrination to prepare the Chinese people for constitutional government. In the meantime, the Nationalists would use their power to carry out a land reform program and modernize the industrial sector.

But it would take more than paper plans to create a new China. There were faint signs of an impending industrial revolution in the major urban centers, but most people in the countryside, drained by warlord exactions and civil strife, were still grindingly poor and overwhelmingly illiterate. A Westernized urban middle class had begun to emerge and formed the natural constituency of the Nanjing government. But this new Westernized elite, preoccupied with individual advancement and material accumulation, had few links with the peasants or the rickshaw drivers "running in this world of suffering" in the words of a Chinese poet. Some critics dismissed Chiang and his chief followers as "banana Chinese"—yellow on the outside, white on the inside.

The Best of East and West Aware of the difficulty of introducing exotic foreign ideas into a culturally

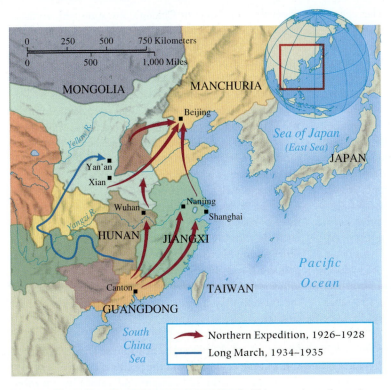

Map 24.4 **The Northern Expedition and the Long March.** This map shows the routes taken by the combined Nationalist–Communist forces during the Northern Expedition of 1926–1928. The blue arrow indicates the route taken by Communist units during the Long March led by Mao Zedong.

Q *Where did Mao establish his new headquarters?*

24.5 Mao Zedong on the Long March. In 1934, Communist leader Mao Zedong led his bedraggled forces on the Long March from southern China to Yan'an in the hills south of the Gobi Desert. The epic journey has ever since been celebrated as a symbol of the party's willingness to sacrifice for the revolutionary cause. In this photo, Mao rides a white horse as he accompanies his followers on the march. Reportedly, he was the only participant allowed to ride a horse.

Experience an interactive version of this period in MINDTAP

conservative society, Chiang attempted to synthesize modern Western ideas with traditional Confucian values of hard work, obedience, and moral integrity. Through the New Life Movement, sponsored by his Wellesley College-educated wife, Meiling Soong (may-LING SOONG), Chiang sought to propagate traditional Confucian social ethics such as propriety and righteousness while rejecting what he considered the excessive individualism and material greed of Western capitalism.

Unfortunately for Chiang, the effort to meld the best of East and West would be no easy task because Confucian ideas—at least in their institutional form—had been widely discredited by the failure of the traditional system to solve China's festering problems. Moreover, with only a tenuous hold over the provinces, a growing Japanese threat in the north, and a world suffering from the Great Depression, Chiang was facing strong headwinds internally and externally. To make matters worse, he lacked the political sensitivity and popular support of his mentor, Sun Yat-sen. Fearing Communist influence and distrusting many of his warlord rivals, Chiang repressed all opposition and censored free expression, thereby alienating many intellectuals and political moderates. Because the urban middle class and the landed gentry were his natural political constituency, he shunned programs that would lead to a redistribution of wealth, thus disappointing the vast majority of his constituents, many of whom had felt few benefits from nearly a century of dynastic decline and imperialist interference.

24-2d "Down with Confucius and Sons": Economic, Social, and Cultural Change in Republican China

The transformation of the old order that had begun at the end of the Qing era continued during the early Chinese republic. Unfortunately, for many of the reasons already mentioned, success was disappointingly slow.

Industrial and Agricultural Development The centerpiece of an advanced economy is a modern manufacturing and commercial sector. Unfortunately, the Nanjing government had little success in promoting industrial development, which grew at an average annual rate of only 1 percent or so during the first decade of its existence. Although mechanization had begun to replace manual labor in some traditional industries like textile manufacturing, three-quarters of all industrial goods were still manually produced in the early 1930s. Traditional exports like silk and tea were hard hit by the Great Depression. In the countryside, as well, success was fleeting. A land reform program was enacted in 1930, but it was sabotaged by wealthy landowners—among Chiang's most loyal supporters—and had little impact in reducing rural poverty. Farmers were often victimized by the endemic conflict in the countryside as well as by high taxes imposed by local warlords. Although similar conditions in Meiji Japan had led to the flight of rural migrants to join the growing labor market in the cities, there was no such option in early twentieth century China.

As we have seen, some of the new government's problems can be ascribed to its own missteps. Much of the national wealth was in the hands of senior officials and close subordinates of the ruling elite. High military expenses—a product of Chiang's obsession with eradicating the CCP—consumed half the budget, and distressingly few funds were devoted to social and economic development. Meanwhile, Chiang and his ruling circle appeared oblivious to the need to take decisive steps to alleviate conditions in the countryside. Still, it is only fair to note that the Nanjing Republic was fated to make its effort to install the foundations of a modern industrial economy in a historically inhospitable climate marked by high global tariffs and vanishing investment funds. Under the best of circumstances, the Nanjing government was faced with an enormous challenge in dealing with Chia's deep-seated economic and social problems. The deadly combination of internal disintegration and foreign pressure now began to coincide with the virtual collapse of the global economic order during the Great Depression and the rise of militant political forces in Tokyo determined to extend Japanese influence and power in an unstable Asia. These forces and the turmoil they unleashed will be examined in the next chapter.

Social Changes Changes in Chinese society followed shifts in the economy and the political culture. By 1915, the assault on the old system and values by educated youth was intense. The main focus of the attack was the Confucian concept of the family—in particular, filial piety and the subordination of women. Young people insisted on the right to choose their own mates and their own careers. Women began to demand rights and opportunities equal to those enjoyed by men (see Comparative Essay "Out of the Doll's House," p. 618). More broadly, progressives called for an end to the concept of duty to the community and praised the Western individualist ethos. Popular short story writer Lu Xun (loo SHUN) attracted attention when he criticized the Confucian concept of family as a "man-eating" system that degraded humanity. In a famous short story titled "Diary of a Madman," the protagonist remarks:

24.6 The Bund in Shanghai. When several Chinese coastal cities were opened up to Western commercial interests after the Opium War, the Europeans and the Americans viewed Shanghai, on a lower branch of the Yangzi River, as the centerpiece of their efforts to enter the rich Chinese market. Several foreign concession areas were established along the Huangpu River, and a row of imposing Western-style buildings, including banks, customs houses, and upscale hotels were eventually constructed along the embankment known to Westerners as the Bund. Long a symbol of Western power in China, the Bund—shown here in the 1920s—retains its historic image in the new China today.

I remember when I was four or five years old, sitting in the cool of the hall, my brother told me that if a man's parents were ill, he should cut off a piece of his flesh and boil it for them if he wanted to be considered a good son. I have only just realized that I have been living all these years in a place where for four thousand years they have been eating human flesh.[5]

Such criticisms did have some beneficial results. During the early republic, the tyranny of the old family system began to decline, at least in urban areas, under the impact of economic changes and the urgings of the New Culture intellectuals. Women began to escape their cloistered existence and seek education and employment. Free choice in marriage became commonplace among affluent families in the cities, where the teenage children of Westernized elites aped the clothing, social habits, and even musical tastes of their contemporaries in Europe and the United States.

But, as a rule, the new individualism and women's rights did not penetrate to the textile factories, where more than 1 million women worked in conditions resembling slave labor, or to the villages, where traditional attitudes and customs still held sway. Arranged marriages continued to be the rule rather than the exception, and concubinage remained common. According to a survey taken in the 1930s, more than two-thirds of marriages even among urban couples had been arranged by their parents (see Historical Voices, "An Arranged Marriage," p. 619).

A New Culture   Nowhere was the struggle between traditional and modern more visible than in the area of culture. Beginning in the New Culture era, radical reformists criticized traditional culture as the symbol and instrument of feudal oppression. During the 1920s and 1930s, Western literature and art became highly popular, especially among the urban middle class. Traditional culture continued to prevail among more conservative elements, however, and some intellectuals argued for a new art that would synthesize the best of Chinese and foreign culture. But the most creative artists were interested in imitating foreign trends, whereas traditionalists were more concerned with preservation.

CHRONOLOGY	Revolution in China
May Fourth demonstrations	1919
Formation of Chinese Communist Party	1921
Death of Sun Yat-sen	1925
Northern Expedition	1926–1928
Establishment of Nanjing Republic	1928
Long March	1934–1935

24-3 JAPAN BETWEEN THE WARS

Focus Question: How did Japan address the challenges of nation building in the first decades of the twentieth century, and why did democratic institutions not take hold more effectively?

During the first two decades of the twentieth century, Japan made remarkable progress toward the creation of an advanced society on the Western model. The political system based on the Meiji Constitution of 1890 began to evolve along Western pluralistic lines, and a multiparty system took shape. The economic and social reforms launched during the Meiji era led to increasing prosperity and the development of a modern industrial and commercial sector.

24-3a Experiment in Democracy

During the first quarter of the twentieth century, Japanese political parties expanded their popular following and became increasingly competitive. Individual pressure groups began to appear, along with an independent press and a bill of rights. The influence of the old ruling oligarchy, the genro, had not yet been significantly challenged, however, nor had that of its ideological foundation, the kokutai (koh-kuh-TY).

These fragile democratic institutions were able to survive throughout the 1920s, often called the era of **Taisho** (TY-SHOH) **democracy**, from the reign title of the emperor. During this period, the military budget was reduced, and a suffrage bill enacted in 1925 granted the vote to all Japanese males. Although women were still disenfranchised, many women were active in the labor movement and in campaigning for social reforms.

But the era was also marked by growing social turmoil, and two opposing forces within the system were gearing up to challenge the prevailing wisdom. On the left, a Marxist labor movement began to take shape in the early 1920s. On the right, ultranationalist groups called for a rejection of Western models of development and a more militant approach to realizing national objectives.

This cultural conflict between old and new, indigenous and foreign, was reflected in literature. The Japanese, their self-confidence restored after the victories over China and Russia, launched an age of cultural creativity in the early twentieth century. Fascination with Western literature gave birth to a striking new genre called the "I novel." Defying traditional Japanese reticence, some authors reveled in self-exposure with confessions of their innermost

Out of the Doll's House

Family & Society In Henrik Ibsen's play *A Doll's House* (1879), Nora Helmer informs her husband, Torvald, that she will no longer accept his control over her life and announces her intention to leave home to start her life anew (see Chapter 20's Opposing Viewpoints, "Advice to Women: Two Views," p. 510). When the outraged Torvald cites her sacred duties as wife and mother, Nora replies that she has other duties just as sacred—those to herself. "I can no longer be satisfied with what most people say," she declares. "I must think things out for myself."

To Ibsen's contemporaries, such remarks were revolutionary. In nineteenth-century Europe, the traditional characterization of the sexes, which were based on gender-defined social roles, had been elevated to a universal law. As family wage earners, men went off to work while women stayed home to care for home and family. Women were advised to accept their lot and play their role as effectively and gracefully as possible. In other parts of the world, women generally had even fewer rights. Often, as in traditional China, they were viewed as sex objects.

The ideal, however, did not always match reality. With the advent of the Industrial Revolution, many women, especially those in the lower classes, were driven by the need for supplemental income to seek employment outside the home. Some women were inspired by the ideals of human dignity and freedom expressed during the Enlightenment and the French Revolution, and they began to protest against a tradition of female inferiority that had long kept them in a "doll's house" of male domination and to claim equal rights before the law.

The movement to liberate women first gained ground in English-speaking countries such as Great Britain and the United States, but it gradually spread to the European continent and then to colonies in Africa and Asia. By the early twentieth century, women's liberation movements were under way in parts of North Africa, the Middle East, and East Asia, calling for access to education, equal treatment before the law, and the right to vote. In China, a small minority of educated women began to agitate for equal rights with men.

Progress, however, was often agonizingly slow, especially in societies where traditional values had not been undermined by the Industrial Revolution. Colonialism had also been a double-edged sword, as the sexist bias of European officials combined with indigenous traditions of male superiority to marginalize women even further. As men moved to the cities to exploit opportunities provided by the colonial administration, women were left to cope with their traditional responsibilities in the villages, often without the safety net of male support that had sustained them during the precolonial era.

With the advent of nationalist movements, the drive for women's rights in many colonial societies was subordinated to the goal of national independence. In some instances, too, women's liberation movements were led by educated elites who failed to take note of the concerns of working-class women.

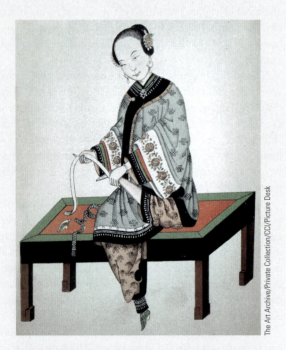

The Art Archive/Private Collection/CCI/Picture Desk

24.7 The Chinese "Doll's House." A woman in traditional China binding her feet.

Q *To what extent, if at all, did women benefit from the policies applied by the Europeans in their colonies?*

An Arranged Marriage

Family & Society

UNDER WESTERN INFLUENCE, Chinese social customs changed dramatically for many urban elites in the interwar years. A vocal women's movement campaigned aggressively for universal suffrage and an end to sexual discrimination. Some progressives called for free choice in marriage and divorce and even for free love. By the 1930s, the government had taken some steps to free women from patriarchal marriage constraints, but life was generally unaffected in the villages, where traditional patterns held sway. This often created severe tensions between older and younger generations, as this passage from a novel by popular twentieth-century writer Ba Jin (BAH JIN)shows.

Ba Jin, *Family*

Brought up with loving care, after studying with a private tutor for a number of years, Chueh-hsin entered middle school. . . . [H]e graduated four years later at the top of his class. He was very interested in physics and chemistry and hoped to study abroad, in Germany. His mind was full of beautiful dreams. At that time he was the envy of his classmates.

In his fourth year at middle school, he lost his mother. His father later married again, this time to a younger woman who had been his mother's cousin. Chueh-hsin was aware of his loss, for he knew full well that nothing could replace the love of a mother. But her death left no irreparable wound in his heart; he was able to console himself with rosy dreams of his future. Moreover, he had someone who understood him and could comfort him—his pretty cousin Mei, "mei" for "plum blossom."

But then, one day, his dreams were shattered, cruelly and bitterly shattered. The evening he returned home carrying his diploma, the plaudits of his teachers and friends still ringing in his ears, his father called him into his room and said:

"Now that you've graduated, I want to arrange your marriage. Your grandfather is looking forward to having a great-grandson, and I, too, would like to be able to hold a grandson in my arms. You're old enough to be married; I won't feel easy until I fulfill my obligation to find you a wife. Although I didn't accumulate much money in my years away from home as an official, still I've put by enough for us to get along on. My health isn't what it used to be; I'm thinking of spending my time at home and having you help me run the household affairs. All the more reason you'll be needing a wife. I've already arranged a match with the Li family. The thirteenth of next month is a good day. We'll announce the engagement then. You can be married within the year. . . . "

Chueh-hsin did not utter a word of protest, nor did such a thought ever occur to him. He merely nodded to indicate his compliance with his father's wishes. But after he returned to his own room, and shut the door, he threw himself down on his bed, covered his head with the quilt and wept. He wept for his broken dreams.

He was deeply in love with Mei, but now his father had chosen another, a girl he had never seen, and said that he must marry within the year. . . .

He cried his disappointment and bitterness. But the door was closed and Chueh-hsin's head was beneath the bedding. No one knew. He did not fight back, he never thought of resisting. He only bemoaned his fate. But he accepted it. He complied with his father's will without a trace of resentment. But in his heart he wept for himself, wept for the girl he adored—Mei, his "plum blossom."

Q *Why does Chueh-hsin comply with the wishes of his father in the matter of his marriage? Why were arranged marriages so prevalent in traditional China?*

Source: Excerpt from "Family" by Ba Jin. Copyright © 1964 Foreign Languages Press, 24 Baiwanzhuang Rd., Beijing 10037, P.R. China.

thoughts. Others found release in the "proletarian literature" movement of the early 1920s. Inspired by Soviet literary examples, these authors wanted literature to serve socialist goals and improve the lives of the working class. Finally, some Japanese writers blended Western psychology with Japanese sensibility in exquisite novels reeking with nostalgia for the old Japan. One well-known example is *Some Prefer Nettles* (1929) by Junichiro Tanizaki (jun-ih-CHEE-roh tan-ih-ZAH-kee), which delicately juxtaposed the positive aspects of both traditional and modern Japan. By the 1930s, however, military censorship increasingly inhibited free literary expression.

24-3b A Zaibatsu Economy

Japan also continued to make impressive progress in economic development. Spurred by rising domestic demand and continued government investment in the economy, the production of raw materials tripled between 1900 and 1930, and industrial production increased more than twelvefold. Much of the increase went into exports, and Western manufacturers began to complain about competition from the Japanese.

As often happens, rapid industrialization was accompanied by some hardship and rising social tensions. In the Meiji model, various manufacturing processes were concentrated in a single enterprise, the **zaibatsu** (zy-BAHTsoo), or financial clique. Some of these firms were existing companies that had the capital and the foresight to move into new areas. Others were formed by enterprising samurai, who used their status and managerial experience to good account in a new environment. Whatever their origins, these firms, often with official encouragement, developed into large conglomerates that controlled major segments of the Japanese economy. By 1937, the four largest zaibatsu—Mitsui (MIT-swee), Mitsubishi (mit-soo-BEE-shee), Sumitomo (soo-mee-TOH-moh), and Yasuda (yah-SOO-duh)—controlled 21 percent of the banking industry, 26 percent of mining, 35 percent of shipbuilding, 38 percent of commercial shipping, and more than 60 percent of paper manufacturing and insurance.

This concentration of power and wealth in a few industrial combines created problems in Japanese society. In the first place, it resulted in the emergence of a dual economy: on the one hand, a modern industry was characterized by up-to-date methods and massive government subsidies; on the other hand, a traditional manufacturing sector was characterized by conservative methods and small-scale production techniques.

Concentration of wealth also led to growing economic inequalities. As we have seen, economic growth had been achieved at the expense of the peasants, many of whom fled to the cities to escape rural poverty. That labor surplus benefited the industrial sector, but the urban proletariat was still poorly paid and ill-housed. A rapid increase in population (the total population of the Japanese islands increased from an estimated 43 million in 1900 to 73 million in 1940) led to food shortages and rising unemployment. In the meantime, those left on the farm continued to suffer. As late as the beginning of World War II, an estimated one-half of all Japanese farmers were tenants.

24-3c Shidehara Diplomacy

A final problem for Japanese leaders in the post-Meiji era was the familiar dilemma of finding sources of raw materials and foreign markets for the nation's manufactured goods. Before World War I, Japan had dealt with the problem by seizing territories such as Taiwan, Korea, and southern Manchuria and transforming them into colonies or protectorates. That policy had begun to arouse apprehension in China. As we have seen, Japanese demands for Shandong Province at the Paris Peace Conference in 1919 aroused massive protests in China.

The United States was especially concerned about Japanese aggressiveness. Although it had been less active than some European states in pursuing colonies in the Pacific, it had a strong interest in keeping the area open for U.S. commercial activities. In 1922, the United States convened in Washington, D.C., a major conference of nations with interests in the Pacific to discuss problems of regional security. The Washington Conference led to agreements on several issues, but the major accomplishment was a nine-power treaty recognizing the territorial integrity of China and the Open Door. The other participants induced Japan to accept these provisions by accepting its special position in Manchuria.

During the remainder of the 1920s, Japan attempted to play by the rules laid down at the Washington Conference. Known as *Shidehara* (shee-deh-HAH-rah) diplomacy, after the foreign minister (and later prime minister) who attempted to carry it out, this policy sought to achieve Japanese interests in Asia through diplomatic and economic means. But this approach came under severe pressure as Japanese industrialists began to move into new areas such as chemicals, mining, and the manufacturing of appliances and automobiles. Because such industries needed resources not found in abundance locally, the Japanese government came under increasing pressure to find new sources abroad.

The Rise of Militant Nationalism   In the early 1930s, with the onset of the Great Depression and growing tensions in the international arena, nationalist forces rose to dominance in the Japanese government. The changes that occurred in the 1930s, which we shall discuss in Chapter 25, were not in the constitution or the institutional structure, which remained essentially intact, but in the composition and attitudes of the ruling group. Party leaders during the 1920s had attempted to realize Tokyo's aspirations within the existing global political and economic framework. The military officers and ultranationalist politicians who dominated the government in the 1930s were convinced that the diplomacy of the 1920s had failed and advocated a more aggressive approach to protecting national interests in a brutal and competitive world.

24-3d Taisho Democracy: An Aberration?

The dramatic shift in Japanese political culture that occurred in the early 1930s has caused some historians to question the breadth and depth of the trend toward democratic practices in the 1920s. Was Taisho democracy merely a fragile attempt at comparative liberalization in a framework dominated by the Meiji vision of empire and kokutai? Or was the militant nationalism of the 1930s an aberration brought on by the Great Depression, which caused the inexorable emergence of democracy in Japan to stall?

Clearly, there is no simple answer to these questions. A process of democratization was taking place in Japan during the first decades of the twentieth century but without shaking the essential core of the Meiji concept of the state. When the "liberal" approach of the 1920s failed to solve the problems of the day, political forces deeply imbedded in Japanese society expressed growing concerns about the government's current policies in Asia and continued to believe in Japanese uniqueness. With the shallow roots of the democracy movement exposed, the shift toward a more aggressive approach became virtually inevitable.

Still, the course of Japanese history after World War II (see Chapter 30) suggests that the emergence of multiparty democracy in the 1920s was not an aberration but a natural consequence of evolutionary trends in Japanese society. The seeds of democracy nurtured during the Taisho era were nipped in the bud by the cataclysmic effects of the Great Depression. In the more conducive climate after World War II, however, a democratic system suitably adjusted to Japanese soil reached full flower.

24-4 NATIONALISM AND DICTATORSHIP IN LATIN AMERICA

Q **Focus Questions:** What problems did the nations of Latin America face in the interwar years? To what degree were they a consequence of foreign influence?

Although the nations of Latin America had emerged from colonial rule during the nineteenth century, they continued to experience the effects of global events as the new century got under way.

24-4a A Changing Economy

At the beginning of the twentieth century, virtually all of Latin America—except the three Guianas, British Honduras, and some of the Caribbean islands—had achieved independence (see Map 24.5). The economy of the region was based largely on the export of foodstuffs and raw materials. Some countries relied on exports of only one or two products. Argentina, for example, exported primarily beef and wheat; Chile, nitrates and copper; Brazil and the Caribbean nations, sugar; and the Central American states, bananas. A few reaped large profits from these exports, but the returns were meager for the majority of the population.

The Role of the Yankee Dollar World War I led to a decline in European investment in Latin America and a rise in the U.S. role in local economies. By the late 1920s, the United States had replaced Great Britain as the foremost source of investment in Latin America. Unlike the British, however, U.S. investors put their funds directly into production enterprises, causing large segments of the area's export industries to fall into American hands. Several Central American states, for example, were popularly labeled "banana republics" because of the power and influence of the U.S.-owned United Fruit Company. American firms also dominated the copper mining industry in Chile and Peru and the oil industry in Mexico, Peru, and Bolivia.

24-4b The Effects of Dependency

During the late nineteenth century, most governments in Latin America had been increasingly dominated by landed or military elites who controlled the mass of the population—mostly impoverished peasants—by the blatant use of military force. Authoritarianism increased during the 1930s as domestic instability caused by the effects of the Great Depression led to the creation of dictatorships throughout the region. This trend was especially evident in Argentina and Brazil and to a lesser degree in Mexico—three countries that together possessed more than half of the land and wealth of Latin America.

Argentina The political domination of Argentina by an elite minority often had disastrous effects. The Argentine government, controlled by landowners who had benefited from the export of beef and wheat, was slow to recognize the importance of establishing a local industrial base. In 1916, Hipólito Irigoyen (ee-POH-lee-toh ee-ree-GOH-yen) (1852–1933), head of the Radical Party, was elected president on a program to improve conditions for the middle and lower classes. Little was achieved, however, as the party became increasingly corrupt and drew closer to large landowners. In 1930, the army overthrew Irigoyen's government and reestablished the power of the landed class. But their efforts failed to revive the previous export economy or suppress the growing influence of the labor unions.

0 500 1,000 1,500 Kilometers
0   500   1,000 Miles

MEXICO
BRITISH HONDURAS
HONDURAS
Caribbean Sea
NICARAGUA
BRITISH
GUIANA
COSTA
RICA
Caracas
VENEZUELA
DUTCH
GUIANA
North
Atlantic
Ocean
PANAMA
Bogotá
FRENCH
GUIANA
EL SALVADOR
COLOMBIA
GUATEMALA
Quito
ECUADOR
PERU
Lima
BRAZIL
La Paz
BOLIVIA
PARAGUAY
Río de
Janeiro
South
Pacific
Ocean
CHILE
Asunción
ARGENTINA
URUGUAY
Santiago
Buenos
Aires
Montevideo
South
Atlantic
Ocean
Falkland
Islands (U.K.)
South Georgia
Island (U.K.)

Map 24.5 Latin America in the First Half of the Twentieth Century. Shown here are the boundaries dividing the countries of Latin America after the independence movements of the nineteenth century.

Q *Which areas remained under European rule?*

Brazil Brazil followed a similar path. In 1889, the army replaced the Brazilian monarchy with a republic, but it was controlled by landed elites, many of whom derived their wealth from vast rubber and coffee plantations. Exports of Brazilian rubber dominated the world market until just before World War I. When it proved easier to produce rubber in Southeast Asia, however, Brazilian exports suddenly

collapsed, leaving the economy of the Amazon River basin in ruins.

As in Argentina, the ruling oligarchy ignored the importance of establishing an urban industrial base. When the Great Depression ravaged profits from coffee exports, a wealthy rancher, Getúlio Vargas (zhi-TOO-lyoo VAHR-guhs) (1883–1954), seized power. At first he sought to appease workers by instituting labor reforms such as a minimum wage and an eight-hour day. Eventually, however, influenced by the success of fascist regimes in Europe, he ruled the country as president from 1930 to 1945.

Mexico After dictator Porfirio Díaz (por-FEER-yoh DEE-ahs) was ousted from power in 1910 (see Chapter 20), Mexico entered a state of turbulence that lasted for years. The ineffective leaders who followed Díaz were unable to solve the country's economic problems or bring an end to the civil strife. In southern Mexico, the landless peasants responded eagerly to Emiliano Zapata (ee-mee-LYAH-noh zup-PAH-tuh) (1879–1919) when he called for agrarian reform and began to seize the haciendas of wealthy landholders.

For the next several years, Zapata and rebel leader Pancho Villa (pahn-CHOH VEE-uh) (1878–1923), who operated in the northern state of Chihuahua (chih-WAH-wah), became an important political force by calling for measures to redress the grievances of the poor. But neither man fully grasped the challenges facing the country, and power eventually gravitated to a more moderate group of reformists around the Constitutionalist Party. They were intent on breaking the power of the great landed families

24.8 Emiliano Zapata. Deep-seated poverty in the southern state of Chiapas led one of its own, the young militant Emiliano Zapata, to organize his followers to launch a revolt against wealthy landowners in southern Mexico. After his demands for widespread land reform were rejected, Zapata joined forces with the northern rebel leader Pancho Villa and was killed in a battle with government troops in 1923.

and U.S. corporations, but without engaging in radical land reform or the nationalization of property. After a bloody conflict that cost the lives of thousands, the moderates consolidated power, and in 1917 they promulgated a new constitution that established a strong presidency, initiated land reform, established limits on foreign investment, and set an agenda for social welfare programs.

CHRONOLOGY	Latin America Between the Wars
Hipólito Irigoyen becomes president of Argentina	1916
Argentinian military overthrows Irigoyen	1930
Rule of Getúlio Vargas in Brazil	1930–1945
Beginning of Good Neighbor policy	1933
Presidency of Lázaro Cardenas in Mexico	1934–1940

In 1920, Constitutionalist Party leader Alvaro Obregón (AHL-vah-roh oh-bree-GAHN) assumed the presidency and began to carry out his reform program. But real change did not take place until the presidency of General Lázaro Cárdenas (LAH-zah-roh KAHR-day-nahss) (1895–1970) in 1934. Cardenas ordered the redistribution of 44 million acres of land controlled by landed elites and seized control of the oil industry, which had hitherto been dominated by major U.S. oil companies. In 1933, in a bid to improve relations with Latin American countries, U.S. President Franklin D. Roosevelt had announced the **Good Neighbor policy**, which renounced the use of U.S. military force in the region. Now Roosevelt refused to intervene, and eventually Mexico agreed to compensate U.S. oil companies for their lost property. It then set up PEMEX, a governmental organization, to run the oil industry.

24-4c Latin American Culture

The first half of the twentieth century witnessed a dramatic increase in literary activity in Latin America. Much of it reflected the region's ambivalent relationship with Europe and the United States. While experimenting with imported modernist styles, many authors also used native themes and social issues to express Latin America's unique identity and its physical separation from the rest of the world. In *The Underdogs* (1915), for example, Mariano Azuela (mahr-YAHN-oh ah-SWAY-luh) (1873–1952) presented a sympathetic but not uncritical portrait of the Mexican Revolution. In *Don Segundo Sombra* (1926), Ricardo Guiraldes (ree-KAHR-doh gwee-RAHL-dess) (1886–1927) celebrated the life of the gaucho (cowboy), defining Argentina's hope and strength as the enlightened management of its fertile earth. Finally, in *Dona Barbara* (1929), Romulo Gallegos (ROH-moo-loh gay-YAY-gohs) (1884–1969) wrote in a similar vein about his native Venezuela.

Latin American artists followed their literary counterparts in joining the modernist movement in Europe, yet they too were eager to celebrate the emergence of a new regional and national essence. In Mexico, where the government provided financial support for painting murals on public buildings, artist Diego Rivera (DYAY-goh rih-VAIR-uh) (1886–1957) began to produce a monumental style of mural art that served two purposes: to illustrate the national past by portraying Aztec legends and folk customs and to popularize a political message in favor of realizing the social goals of the Mexican Revolution. His wife, Frida Kahlo (FREE-duh KAH-loh) (1907–1954), incorporated surrealist whimsy in her own paintings, many of which were portraits of herself and her family.

The turmoil brought about by World War I not only destroyed several major Western empires and redrew the map of Europe but also opened the door to political and social upheavals elsewhere in the world. In the Middle East, the decline and fall of the Ottoman Empire led to the creation of the secular republic of Turkey. The state of Saudi Arabia emerged in the Arabian Peninsula, and Palestine became a source of tension between newly arrived Jewish immigrants and long-time Muslim residents.

Other parts of Asia and Africa also witnessed the rise of movements for national independence. In many cases, these movements were spearheaded by local leaders who had been educated in Europe or the United States. In India, Mahatma Gandhi and his campaign of civil disobedience played a crucial role in his country's bid to be free of British rule. Communist movements also began to emerge in Asian societies as radical elements sought new methods of bringing about the overthrow of Western imperialism. Japan continued to follow its own path to modernization, which, although economically successful, took a menacing turn during the 1930s.

Between 1919 and 1939, China experienced a dramatic struggle to establish a modern nation. Two dynamic political organizations—the Nationalists and the Communists—competed for legitimacy as the rightful heirs of the old order. They initially formed an alliance

in an effort to defeat their common adversaries, but cooperation ultimately turned to conflict. The Nationalists under Chiang Kai-shek emerged supreme, but Chiang found it difficult to control the remnants of the warlord regime in China, and the Great Depression undermined his efforts to build an industrial nation.

During the interwar years, the nations of Latin America faced severe economic problems because of their dependence on exports. Increasing U.S. investments in Latin America contributed to growing hostility toward the powerful neighbor to the north. The Great Depression forced the region to begin developing new industries, but it also led to the rise of authoritarian governments, some of them modeled after the fascist regimes of Italy and Germany.

By demolishing the remnants of their old civilization on the battlefields of World War I, Europeans had inadvertently encouraged the subject peoples of their vast colonial empires to begin their own movements for national independence. The process was by no means completed in the two decades following the end of World War I, but the bonds of imperial rule had been severely strained. Once Europeans began to weaken themselves in the even more destructive conflict of World War II, the hopes of African and Asian peoples for national independence and freedom could at last be realized. It is to that devastating world conflict that we must now turn.

REFLECTION QUESTIONS

Q In what ways did Japan's political system and social structure in the interwar years combine modern and traditional elements? How successful was the attempt to create a modern political system while retaining indigenous traditions of civil obedience and loyalty to the emperor?

Q During the early twentieth century, did conditions for women change for the better or for the worse in the countries discussed in this chapter? Why?

Q Communist parties were established in many Asian societies in the years immediately following the Bolshevik Revolution. How successful were these parties in winning popular support and achieving their goals?

CHAPTER TIMELINE

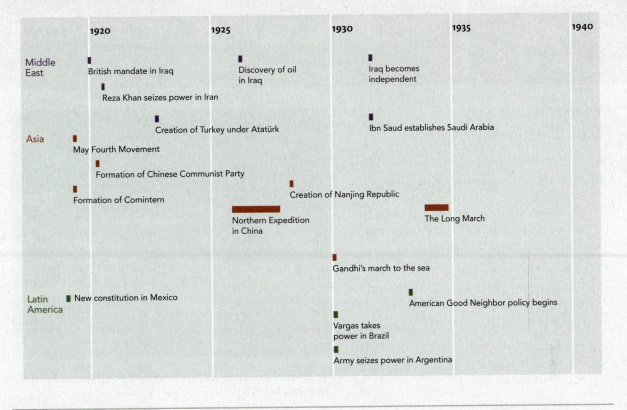

	1920	1925	1930	1935	1940
Middle East	British mandate in Iraq / Reza Khan seizes power in Iran	Discovery of oil in Iraq	Iraq becomes independent		
Asia	May Fourth Movement / Formation of Chinese Communist Party / Formation of Comintern	Creation of Turkey under Atatürk / Northern Expedition in China	Ibn Saud establishes Saudi Arabia / Creation of Nanjing Republic / Gandhi's march to the sea	The Long March	
Latin America	New constitution in Mexico		Vargas takes power in Brazil / Army seizes power in Argentina	American Good Neighbor policy begins	

CHAPTER NOTES

1. V. I. Lenin, "The Awakening of Asia," in *The Awakening of Asia: Selected Essays* (New York, 1963–1968), p. 22.
2. Speech by Mahatma Gandhi, delivered in London in September 1931 during his visit for the first Roundtable Conference.
3. Ts'ai Yuan-p'ei, "Ta Lin Ch'in-nan Han," in *Ts'ai Yuan-p'ei Hsien-sheng Ch'uan-chi* [Collected Works of Mr. Ts'ai Yuan-p'ei] (Taipei, 1968), pp. 1057–1058.
4. Quoted in W. T. de Bary et al., eds., *Sources of Chinese Tradition* (New York, 1963), p. 783.
5. Lu Xun, "Diary of a Madman," in *Selected Works of Lu Hsun*, vol. 1 (Peking, 1957), p. 20.

MINDTAP From Cengage

MindTap® is a fully online, highly personalized learning experience built upon Cengage Learning content. MindTap combines student learning tools—readings, multimedia, activities, and assessments—into a singular Learning Path that guides students through the course and helps students develop the critical thinking, analysis, and communication skills that are essential to academic and professional success.

Chapter Outline and Focus Questions

Critical Thinking

Q *What was the relationship between World War I and World War II, and how did the ways in which the wars were fought differ?*

Connections to Today

Q *In what ways are the results of World War II still having an impact today?*

25.1 Adolf Hitler Salutes Soldiers Marching in Nuremberg During the Party Rally in 1938

Hugo Jaeger/Timepix/Time Life Pictures/Getty Images

ON FEBRUARY 3, 1933, three days after he had been appointed chancellor of Germany, Adolf Hitler met secretly with Germany's leading generals. He revealed to them his desire to remove the "cancer of democracy," create a new authoritarian leadership, and forge a new domestic unity. All Germans would need to realize that "only a struggle can save us and that everything else must be subordinated to this idea." Because Germany's living space was too small for its people, Hitler said, Germany must rearm and prepare for "the conquest of new living space in the east and its ruthless Germanization." Even before he had consolidated his power, Adolf Hitler had a clear vision of his goals, and their implementation meant another war.

World War II in Europe was clearly Hitler's war. Although other countries may have helped make the war possible by not resisting Hitler earlier, it was Nazi Germany's actions that made World War II inevitable.

But World War II was more than just Hitler's war. It was, in fact, two separate and parallel conflicts, one provoked by the ambitions of Germany in Europe and the other by the ambitions of Japan in Asia. In the early 1930s, the United States and major European nations raised the tariffs they imposed on Japanese imports in a desperate effort to protect local businesses and jobs. In response, militant groups in Tokyo began to argue that Japan must obtain what it could not secure by peaceful means by violent action. By 1941, when the United States became embroiled in both wars, the two had merged into a single global conflict.

Although World War I had been described as a total war, World War II was even more so and was fought on a scale unheard of in history. Almost everyone in the warring countries was involved in one way or another: as soldiers; as workers in wartime industries; as ordinary citizens subject to invading armies, military occupation, or bombing raids; as refugees; or as victims of mass extermination. The world had never witnessed such widespread human-induced death and destruction.

25-1 RETREAT FROM DEMOCRACY: DICTATORIAL REGIMES

Focus Questions: What are the characteristics of so-called totalitarian states, and to what degree were these characteristics present in Fascist Italy, Nazi Germany, and Stalinist Russia? To what extent was Japan a totalitarian state?

The rise of dictatorial regimes in the 1930s had a great deal to do with the coming of World War II. By 1939, only two major states in Europe—France and Great Britain—remained democratic. Italy and Germany had succumbed to the political movement called **fascism**, and Soviet Russia under Joseph Stalin had moved toward repressive totalitarianism. A host of other European states and Latin American countries adopted authoritarian structures of various kinds, and a militarist regime in Japan moved that country down the path to war. What had happened to Woodrow Wilson's claim that World War I had been fought to make the world safe for democracy? Actually, World War I turned out to have had the opposite effect.

HISTORIANS DEBATE 25-1a **The Retreat from Democracy: Did Europe Have Totalitarian States?**

The postwar expansion of the electorate made mass politics a reality and seemed to enhance the spread of democracy in Europe. But the war itself had created conditions that led the new mass electorate to distrust democracy and move toward a more favorable view of radicalized politics.

Many postwar societies were badly divided, especially along class lines. Gender divisions also weakened social cohesion. At the same time, fears about a declining population because of the war led many male political leaders to encourage women who had taken new jobs during the war to return to their traditional roles of wives and mothers. The Great Depression also deepened social conflict. Increasing numbers of people felt victimized—first by the war and now by socioeconomic conditions that seemed beyond their control. Postwar politics became more and more polarized, and moderate centrist parties that supported democracy soon found themselves with fewer allies as people became increasingly radicalized politically and supported the extremes of left-wing communism or right-wing fascism. In the 1920s, Italy had become the first fascist state, and the Soviet Union moved toward a repressive Communist state. In the 1930s, a host of other European states adopted authoritarian structures of various kinds. Is it justified to call any of them **totalitarian states**?

The word *totalitarian* was first used by Benito Mussolini (buh-NEE-toh moos-suh-LEE-nee) in Italy to describe his new fascist state. "Fascism is totalitarian," he declared. Many historians eventually applied the term to both Nazi Germany and the Soviet Union. Especially during the Cold War between the United States and the Soviet Union in the 1950s and 1960s, Western leaders were inclined to refer to both the Soviet Union and the Eastern European states that had been brought under Soviet control as "totalitarian."

What did these historians think were the characteristics of a totalitarian state? Totalitarian regimes, it was argued, extended the functions and power of the central state far beyond what they had been in the past. The totalitarian state expected the active loyalty and commitment of its citizens to the regime's goals and used modern mass propaganda techniques and high-speed modern communications to conquer the minds and hearts of its subjects. The total state aimed to control not only the economic, political, and social aspects of life but also its intellectual and cultural life. The purpose of that control was the active involvement of the masses in the achievement of the regime's goal—whether it be war, a socialist state, or a thousand-year reich (RYKH). Moreover, the totalitarian state was led by a single leader and a single party and ruthlessly rejected the liberal ideal of limited government power and constitutional guarantees of individual freedoms. Indeed, individual freedom was subordinated to the collective will of the masses as organized and determined for them by a leader. Furthermore, modern technology gave these states unprecedented ability to use police controls to enforce their wishes on their subjects.

By the 1970s and 1980s, however, revisionist historians were questioning the usefulness of the term *totalitarian* and regarded it as crude and imprecise. Certainly, regimes such as Fascist Italy, Nazi Germany, and the Soviet Union sought total control, but these states exhibited significant differences, and none was successful in establishing total control of its society.

Nevertheless, these three states did transcend traditional political labels and led to some rethinking of these labels. Fascism in Italy and Nazism in Germany grew out of extreme rightist preoccupations with nationalism and, in the case of Germany, with racism and corporatist economic policies. Communism in the Soviet Union emerged out of Marxist socialism, a radical leftist program with collectivist economic policies. Thus, extreme right-wing and left-wing regimes no longer appeared to be at opposite ends of the political spectrum but came to be viewed as similar to each other in at least some respects.

25-1b The Birth of Fascism

In the early 1920s, Benito Mussolini (1883–1945) bestowed on Italy the first successful fascist movement in Europe. In 1919, Mussolini, a veteran of World War I, had established a new political group, the Fascio di Combattimento (FASH-ee-oh dee com-bat-ee-MEN-toh) (League of Combat), which won support from middle-class industrialists who were fearful of working-class agitation and large landowners who objected to strikes by farmers. Mussolini also perceived that Italians were angry over Italy's failure to receive more territory after World War I and the perceived failures of the socialist government in handling the postwar crises. The movement gained momentum as Mussolini's nationalist rhetoric and the middle-class fear of socialism, Communist revolution, and disorder made the Fascists seem more and more attractive. On October 29, 1922, after Mussolini and the fascists threatened to march on Rome if they were not given power, King Victor Emmanuel (1900–1946) capitulated and made Mussolini prime minister of Italy.

By 1926, Mussolini had established the institutional framework for a fascist dictatorship. The prime minister was made "head of government" with the power to legislate by decree. A law empowered the police to arrest and confine anybody for both nonpolitical and political crimes without pressing charges. In 1926, all antifascist parties were outlawed, and a secret police force was established. By the end of the year, Mussolini ruled Italy as Il Duce (eel DOO-chay), the leader.

Mussolini conceived of the fascist state as totalitarian: "Fascism is totalitarian, and the Fascist State, the synthesis and unity of all values, interprets, develops and gives strength to the whole life of the people."[1] Although Mussolini tried to create a police state, it was not particularly effective. Likewise, the Italian fascists were rarely able to exercise control over all forms of mass media,

including newspapers, radio, and cinema so they could use propaganda as an instrument to integrate the masses into the state. Most commonly, fascist propaganda was disseminated through simple slogans such as "Mussolini is always right," which was plastered on walls all over Italy.

The fascists portrayed the family as the pillar of the state and women as the basic foundation of the family. "Woman into the home" became the fascist slogan. Women were to be homemakers and baby producers, "their natural and fundamental mission in life," according to Mussolini, for population growth was viewed as an indicator of national strength. Employment outside the home might distract women from conception.

Despite the instruments of repression, the use of propaganda, and the creation of numerous fascist organizations, Mussolini never achieved the degree of control attained in Hitler's Germany or Stalin's Soviet Union. Mussolini and the Fascist Party never completely destroyed the old power structure, and they were soon overshadowed by a much more powerful fascist movement to the north.

25-1c Hitler and Nazi Germany

In 1923, a small rightist party led by an obscure Austrian rabble-rouser named Adolf Hitler (1889–1945) attempted to seize power in southern Germany in a notorious event known as the Beer Hall Putsch. Although the effort failed, the attempt to overthrow the Bavarian government brought Hitler and the Nazis to national prominence.

Hitler's Rise to Power, 1919–1933 At the end of World War I, after four years of service on the western front, Hitler joined the obscure German Workers' Party, one of several right-wing extreme nationalist parties in Munich. By the summer of 1921, Hitler had assumed control of the party, which he renamed the National Socialist German Workers' Party (Nationalsozialistische Deutsche Arbeiterpartei) or Nazi Party for short (from the pronunciation of the first two syllables of the German name). Hitler's own oratorical skills were largely responsible for attracting an increasing number of followers. Hitler's early speeches warned the German people of a potential threat of a Bolshevik revolution in Germany while promoting the myth that the Communist Party was supported by the Jews. In this way, Hitler aligned his anti-Semitic ideology with his political opponents. In two years, membership reached 55,000, including 15,000 in the party militia known as the the Sturmabteilung (SHTOORM-ap-tyloonk) or SA (German for "Storm Troops").

Overconfident, Hitler staged an armed uprising against the government in Munich in November 1923. The Beer Hall Putsch was quickly crushed, and Hitler was sentenced to prison. During his brief stay in jail, he wrote Mein Kampf (myn KAHMPF) (*My Struggle*), an autobiographical account of his movement and its underlying ideology. In the book, extreme German nationalism, virulent anti-Semitism, and anticommunism are linked together by a Social Darwinian theory of struggle that stresses the right of superior nations to Lebensraum (LAY-benz-rown) ("living space") through territorial expansion and the right of superior individuals to secure authoritarian leadership over the masses. After his release from prison, Hitler reorganized the Nazi Party and began to compete for votes with the other political parties. By 1929, the Nazis had a national party organization.

Three years later, the Nazi Party had 800,000 members and had become the largest party in the Reichstag (RYKHSS-tahk), Germany's national legislature. The country's economic difficulties were a crucial factor in the Nazis' rise to power. Unemployment rose dramatically from 4 million in 1931 to 6 million by the winter of 1932. Claiming to stand above all differences, Hitler promised he would create a new Germany free of class differences and party infighting. His appeal to national pride, national honor, and traditional militarism struck receptive chords in his listeners. After attending one of Hitler's rallies, a schoolteacher in Hamburg said: "When the speech was over, there was roaring enthusiasm and applause. . . . Then he went—How many look up to him with touching faith as their savior, their deliverer from unbearable distress."[2]

Increasingly, the right-wing elites of Germany—the industrial magnates, landed aristocrats, military establishment, and higher bureaucrats— came to see Hitler as the man who had the mass support to establish a right-wing, authoritarian regime that would save Germany and their privileged positions from a Communist takeover. Because the Nazi Party had the largest share of seats in the Reichstag, President Paul von Hindenburg was under pressure and agreed to allow Hitler to become chancellor (on January 30, 1933) and form a new government.

Within two months, Hitler had laid the foundations for the Nazis' complete control over Germany. The crowning step in Hitler's "legal seizure" of power came on March 23 when the Reichstag passed the Enabling Act by a two-thirds vote. The Enabling Act would give the government the right to issue laws without the consent of the Reichstag. This legislation empowered the government to dispense with constitutional forms for four years while it issued laws to deal with the country's problems.

With their new source of power, the Nazis acted quickly to bring all institutions under party control. The civil service was purged of Jews and democratic elements, concentration camps were established for opponents of the new regime, trade unions were dissolved, and all political parties except the Nazis were abolished. By the end of the summer of 1933, Hitler and the Nazis had established the foundations for a totalitarian state. When Hindenburg died on August 2, 1934, the office of Reich president was abolished, and Hitler became *der Führer* (FYOOR-ur) (the leader)—sole ruler of Germany.

The Nazi State, 1933–1939 Having smashed the parliamentary state, Hitler now felt the real task was at hand: developing the "total state." Hitler's goal was the development of an Aryan racial state that would dominate Europe and possibly the world for generations to come. Hitler stated:

> We must develop organizations in which an individual's entire life can take place. Then every activity and every need of every individual will be regulated by the collectivity represented by the party. There is no longer any arbitrary will, there are no longer any free realms in which the individual belongs to himself. . . . The time of personal happiness is over.[3]

25.2 The Nazi Mass Spectacle. Hitler and the Nazis made clever use of mass spectacles to rally the German people behind the ruling regime. These mass demonstrations evoked intense enthusiasm, as is evident in this photograph of Hitler arriving at the Bückeberg (BOOK-uh-bayrk) near Hamelin for the Harvest Festival in 1937. Almost 1 million people were present for the celebration.

Hugo Jaeger/Timepix/Time Life Pictures/Getty Images

The Nazis pursued the realization of this totalitarian ideal in a variety of ways. Mass demonstrations and spectacles were employed to integrate the German nation into a collective fellowship and to mobilize it as an instrument for Hitler's policies. These mass demonstrations, especially the party rallies that were held in Nuremberg every September, combined the symbolism of a religious service with the merriment of a popular amusement and usually evoked mass enthusiasm and excitement (see Film & History, *Triumph of the Will*).

In the economic sphere, Hitler and the Nazis also worked to establish control. Hitler's ideological objective of creating a pure Aryan nation established economic policies that forced Jewish owners out of business rather than attacking business itself as the socialists had done in Russia. *Aryanization*, the policy of the Nazi state to eliminate Jews from the economy, forced Jews to sell their businesses at lowered rates. Beginning in 1933, Jews who emigrated and wished to transfer capital abroad were subject to a 20-percent fee levied by the German Gold Discount Bank; by 1938 this fee was raised to 90 percent. Although the regime garnished billions from Jewish-owned businesses and property, the regime used public works projects and "pump-priming" grants to private construction firms to foster employment and end the depression. However, rearmament undoubtedly contributed far more to solving the unemployment problem. Unemployment, which had stood at 6 million in 1932, dropped to 2.6 million in 1934 and less than 500,000 in 1937. This was an important factor in convincing many Germans to accept the new regime despite its excesses.

For Germans who needed coercion, the Nazi state had its instruments of terror and repression. Especially important were the *Schutzstaffel* (SHOOTS-shtah-fuhn) (guard squadrons), known simply as the SS. Under the direction of Heinrich Himmler (1900–1945), the SS came to control all of the regular and secret police forces. Himmler and the SS functioned on the basis of two principles: terror and ideology. Terror included the instruments of repression and murder: secret police, criminal police, concentration camps, and later execution squads and death camps for the extermination of the Jews. For Himmler, the primary goal of the SS was to further the Aryan "master race."

The creation of the Nazi total state also affected women. Women played a crucial role in the Aryan racial state as bearers of the children who would bring about the triumph of the Aryan race. To the Nazis, the differences between men and women were natural: men were destined to be warriors and political leaders; women were to be wives and mothers.

The Nazi total state was intended to be an Aryan racial state. From its beginning, the Nazi Party reflected Hitler's strong anti-Semitic beliefs. Once in power, the Nazis translated anti-Semitic ideas into anti-Semitic policies. In September 1935, at the annual party rally in Nuremberg, the Nazis announced new racial laws that excluded German Jews from German citizenship and forbid marriages and extramarital relations between Jews and German citizens.

A more violent phase of anti-Jewish activity took place in 1938 and 1939. It was initiated on November 9–10, 1938, with the infamous *Kristallnacht* (kri-STAHL-nahkht), or night of shattered glass. The assassination of a secretary in the German embassy in Paris became the excuse for a Nazi-led rampage against the Jews in which synagogues were burned, 7,000 Jewish businesses were destroyed, and at least 100 Jews were killed. Jews were barred from all

 FILM & HISTORY

Triumph of the Will

Watch *Triumph of the Will* (1934), one of the best-known films of Nazi Germany, a documentary directed by Leni Riefenstahl (LAY-nee REE-fuhn-shtahl), an actress who turned to directing in 1932. Adolf Hitler invited her to make a film about the 1934 Nuremberg party rally. In filming this party day of unity—as it was called—Hitler was trying to demonstrate, in the wake of the purge of the SA on June 30, that the Nazi Party was strongly united behind its leader.

Q *In what ways is the film a piece of propaganda aimed at conveying to viewers the power of National Socialism? Riefenstahl maintained that it was "a pure historical film." Why was she criticized for that view?*

Universal History Archive/Getty Images

MINDTAP See full-length Film & History feature in MindTap.
From Cengage

public buildings and prohibited from owning or working in any retail store.

25-1d The Stalinist Era in the Soviet Union

Joseph Stalin made a significant shift in economic policy in 1928 when he launched the centralized control of the entire economy with his first five-year plan. Its real goal was nothing less than the transformation of the agrarian Soviet Union into an industrial country virtually overnight. Instead of consumer goods, the first five-year plan emphasized maximum production of capital goods and armaments and succeeded in quadrupling the production of heavy machinery and doubling oil production. Between 1928 and 1937, during the first two five-year plans, annual steel production increased from 4 million to 18 million tons.

Rapid industrialization was accompanied by an equally rapid collectivization of agriculture. Its goal was to eliminate private farms and push people onto collective farms. When peasants resisted strongly, hoarding crops and killing livestock, Stalin only stepped up the program. By 1934, Russia's 26 million family farms had been collectivized into 250,000 units. The Russian state took ownership of all farms, exiling or imprisoning large landowners and leaving peasants with small plots of land for themselves while forcing them to farm the land for the state. This was done at tremendous cost because Stalin did not hesitate to starve the peasants to force them to comply with the policy of collectivization, especially in Ukraine, where 2.9 million died. Moreover, perhaps 10 million peasants died in the artificially created famines of 1932 and 1933. The only concession Stalin made to the peasants was to allow each collective farm worker to have one tiny, privately owned garden plot.

To achieve his goals, Stalin strengthened the party bureaucracy under his control. Those who resisted were sent into forced-labor camps in Siberia. Stalin's desire for sole control of decision making also led to purges of the Old Bolsheviks. Between 1936 and 1938, the most prominent Old Bolsheviks were put on trial and condemned to death. During this same time, Stalin undertook a purge of army officers, diplomats, union officials, party members, intellectuals, and numerous ordinary citizens. An estimated 8 million Russians were arrested, and millions died in Siberian labor camps. Stalin became one of the greatest mass murderers in human history.

The Stalinist era also reversed much of the permissive social legislation of the early 1920s. Advocating complete equality of rights for women, the Communists had made divorce and abortion easy to obtain while also encouraging women to work outside the home and set their own moral standards. After Stalin came to power, the family was praised as a miniature collective in which parents were responsible for inculcating values of duty, discipline, and hard work. Abortion was outlawed, and divorced fathers who failed to support their children were fined heavily.

25-1e The Rise of Militarism in Japan

The rise of militarism in Japan resulted from the growing influence of militant forces at the top of the political hierarchy. In the early 1930s, confrontations with China in Manchuria combined with the onset of the Great Depression to bring an end to the fragile stability of the immediate postwar years.

The depression had a disastrous effect on Japan because many European countries, along with the United States, raised stiff tariff walls against cheap Japanese imports to protect their struggling domestic industries. The ensuing economic slowdown imposed a heavy burden on the fragile democracy in Japan, and the political parties were no longer able to stem the growing influence of militant nationalist elements. Extremist patriotic organizations began to terrorize Japanese society by assassinating businessmen and public figures identified with the policy of conciliation toward the outside world. Some argued that Western-style political institutions should be replaced by a new system that would return to traditional Japanese values and imperial authority. Their message of "Asia for the Asians" became increasingly popular as the Great Depression convinced many Japanese that capitalism was unsuitable for Japan.

During the mid-1930s, the influence of the military and extreme nationalists over the government steadily increased. National elections continued to take place, but cabinets were dominated by the military or advocates of Japanese expansionism. In February 1936, junior army officers led a coup, briefly occupying the Diet building in Tokyo and assassinating several members of the cabinet. The ringleaders were quickly tried and convicted of treason but under conditions that further strengthened the influence of the military.

25-2 THE PATH TO WAR

Q **Focus Question:** What were the underlying causes of World War II, and what specific steps taken by Nazi Germany and Japan led to war?

Only twenty years after the "war to end war," the world plunged back into the nightmare. The efforts at collective security in the 1920s proved meaningless in view of the growth of Nazi Germany and the rise of militant Japan.

25-2a The Path to War in Europe

World War II in Europe had its beginnings in the ideas of Adolf Hitler, who believed that only so-called Aryans were capable of building a great civilization. To Hitler, Germany needed more land to support a larger population and be a great power. Already in the 1920s, in the second volume of *Mein Kampf*, Hitler had indicated that a National Socialist regime would find this land to the east—in Russia.

On March 9, 1935, in defiance of the Treaty of Versailles, Hitler announced the creation of an air force and one week later the introduction of a military draft that would expand Germany's army from 100,000 to 550,000 troops. Hitler's unilateral repudiation of the Versailles treaty brought a swift reaction as France, Great Britain, and Italy condemned Germany's action and warned against future aggressive steps, but nothing concrete was done.

Meanwhile, Hitler gained new allies. In October 1935, Benito Mussolini had committed Fascist Italy to imperial expansion by invading Ethiopia. In October 1936, Hitler and Mussolini concluded an agreement that recognized their common interests, and Mussolini referred publicly to the new Rome–Berlin axis one month later. Also in November, Germany and Japan (the rising military power in the Far East) concluded their Anti-Comintern Pact and agreed to maintain a common front against communism.

By 1937, Germany was once more a "world power," as Hitler proclaimed. Hitler was convinced that neither the French nor the British would provide much opposition to his plans and decided in 1938 to move to achieve one of his long-time goals: union with Austria. By threatening Austria with invasion, Hitler coerced the Austrian chancellor into putting Austrian Nazis in charge of the government. The new government promptly invited German troops to enter Austria and assist in maintaining law and order. One day later, on March 13, 1938, after his triumphal return to his native land, Hitler formally annexed Austria to Germany.

Hitler's next objective was the destruction of Czechoslovakia, and he believed that France and Britain would not use force to defend that nation. He was right again. On September 15, 1938, Hitler demanded the cession of the Sudetenland (soo-DAY-tun-land) (an area in northwestern Czechoslovakia inhabited largely by ethnic Germans) to Germany and expressed his willingness to risk "world war" if he was refused. Instead of objecting, the British, French, Germans, and Italians—at a hastily arranged conference at Munich—reached an agreement that met all of Hitler's demands (see Opposing Viewpoints, "The Munich Conference," p. 633). German troops were allowed to occupy the Sudetenland. Increasingly, Hitler was convinced of his own infallibility, and he was by no means been satisfied at Munich. In March 1939, Hitler occupied all the Czech lands (Bohemia and Moravia), while the Slovaks, with Hitler's encouragement, declared their independence of the Czechs and became a puppet state (Slovakia) of Nazi Germany. On the evening of March 15, 1939, Hitler triumphantly declared in Prague that he would be known as the greatest German of them all.

At last, the Western states reacted to Hitler's threat. When Hitler began to demand the return of Danzig (which had been made a free city by the Treaty of Versailles to serve as a seaport for Poland) to Germany, Britain offered to protect Poland in the event of war. At the same time, both France and Britain realized that only the Soviet Union was powerful enough to help contain Nazi aggression and began political and military negotiations with Stalin and the Soviets.

Meanwhile, Hitler pressed on. To preclude an alliance between the West and the Soviet Union, which would open the danger of a two-front war, Hitler negotiated his own nonaggression pact with Stalin and shocked the world with its announcement on August 23, 1939. The treaty with the Soviet Union gave Hitler the freedom to attack Poland. He told his generals: "Now Poland is in the position in which I wanted her. . . . I am only afraid that at the last moment some swine or other will yet submit to me a plan for mediation."[4] He need not have worried. On September 1, German forces invaded Poland; two days later, Britain and France declared war on Germany. Europe was again at war.

25-2b The Path to War in Asia

During the mid-1920s, Japan had maintained a strong military and economic presence in Manchuria, an area in northeastern China controlled by a Chinese warlord. Then in September 1931, Japanese military officers stationed in the area launched a coup to bring about a complete Japanese takeover of the region. Despite worldwide protests from the League of Nations, which eventually condemned the seizure, Japan steadily strengthened its control over Manchuria, renaming it Manchukuo (man-CHOOkwoh), and then began to expand into northern China.

For the moment, Chiang Kai-shek attempted to avoid a direct confrontation with Japan so that he could deal with the Communists, whom he considered the greater threat. When clashes between Chinese and Japanese troops broke out, he sought to appease the Japanese by granting them the authority to administer areas in northern China. But as the Japanese moved steadily southward, popular protests in Chinese cities against Japanese aggression intensified. In December 1936, Chiang ended his military efforts against the Communists in Yan'an and formed a

The Munich Conference

Politics & Government

AT THE MUNICH CONFERENCE, the leaders of France and Great Britain capitulated to Hitler's demands on Czechoslovakia. Although British Prime Minister Neville Chamberlain defended his actions at Munich as necessary for peace, another British statesman, Winston Churchill, characterized the settlement at Munich as "a disaster of the first magnitude."

Winston Churchill, Speech to the House of Commons, October 5, 1938

I will begin by saying what everybody would like to ignore or forget but which must nevertheless be stated, namely, that we have sustained a total and unmitigated defeat, and that France has suffered even more than we have. . . . The utmost my right honorable Friend the Prime Minister . . . has been able to gain for Czechoslovakia and in the matters which were in dispute has been that the German dictator, instead of snatching his victuals from the table, has been content to have them served to him course by course. . . . And I will say this, that I believe the Czechs, left to themselves and told they were going to get no help from the Western Powers, would have been able to make better terms than they have got. . . .

We are in the presence of a disaster of the first magnitude which has befallen Great Britain and France. Do not let us blind ourselves to that. . . .

And do not suppose that this is the end. This is only the beginning of the reckoning. This is only the first sip, the first foretaste of a bitter cup which will be proffered to us year by year unless by a supreme recovery of moral health and martial vigor, we arise again and take our stand for freedom as in the olden time.

Neville Chamberlain, Speech to the House of Commons, October 6, 1938

That is my answer to those who say that we should have told Germany weeks ago that, if her army crossed the border of Czechoslovakia, we should be at war with her. We had no treaty obligations and no legal obligations to Czechoslovakia. When we were convinced, as we became convinced, that nothing any longer would keep the Sudetenland within the Czechoslovakian State, we urged the Czech Government as strongly as we could to agree to the cession of territory, and to agree promptly. . . . It was a hard decision for anyone who loved his country to take, but to accuse us of having by that advice betrayed the Czechoslovakian State is simply preposterous. What we did was to save her from annihilation and give her a chance of new life as a new State, which involves the loss of territory and fortifications, but may perhaps enable her to enjoy in the future and develop a national existence under a neutrality and security comparable to that which we see in Switzerland today. Therefore, I think the Government deserve the approval of this House for their conduct of affairs in this recent crisis which has saved Czechoslovakia from destruction and Europe from Armageddon.

Q *What were the opposing views of Churchill and Chamberlain on the Munich Conference? Why did they disagree so much? With whom do you agree? Why?*

Sources: From *Parliamentary Debates, House of Commons* (London: His Majesty's Stationery Office, 1938), vol. 339, pp. 361–369. From Neville Chamberlain, *In Search of Peace* (New York: Putnam, 1939), pp. 215, 217.

---

new united front against the Japanese. When Chinese and Japanese forces clashed at the Marco Polo Bridge south of Beijing in July 1937, China refused to apologize and hostilities spread.

Japan had not planned to declare war on China, but neither side would compromise, and the 1937 incident eventually turned into a major conflict. The Japanese advanced up the Yangzi River Valley and seized the Chinese capital of Nanjing in December, but Chiang Kai-shek refused to capitulate and moved his government upriver to Hankou (HAHN-kow). When the Japanese seized that city, he retreated to Chongqing (chung-CHING) in remote Sichuan (suh-CHWAHN) Province and kept his capital there for the remainder of the war.

Japanese strategists had hoped to force Chiang to join a Japanese-dominated "New Order" in East Asia comprising Japan, Manchuria, and China. This was part of a larger Japanese plan to seize Soviet Siberia and its rich resources and create a new "Monroe Doctrine for Asia" under which Japan would guide its Asian neighbors on the path to development and prosperity (see Historical Voices, "Japan's Justification for Expansion," p. 634). After all, who better to instruct Asian societies on modernization than the one Asian country that had already achieved it?

Japan's Justification for Expansion

 Politics & Government **ADVOCATES OF JAPANESE EXPANSION** justified their proposals by claiming both economic necessity and moral imperatives. Note the familiar combination of motives in this passage written by an extremist military leader in the late 1930s.

Hashimoto Kingoro on the Need for Emigration and Expansion

We have already said that there are only three ways left to Japan to escape from the pressure of surplus population, . . . namely emigration, advance into world markets, and expansion of territory. The first door, emigration, has been barred to us by the anti-Japanese immigration policies of other countries. The second door, advance into world markets, is being pushed shut by tariff barriers and the abrogation of commercial treaties. What should Japan do when two of the three doors have been closed against her?

It is quite natural that Japan should rush upon the last remaining door.

It may sound dangerous when we speak of territorial expansion, but the territorial expansion of which we speak does not in any sense of the word involve the occupation of the possessions of other countries, the planting of the Japanese flag thereon, and the declaration of their annexation to Japan. It is just that since the Powers have suppressed the circulation of Japanese materials and merchandise abroad, we are looking for some place overseas where Japanese capital, Japanese skills and Japanese labor can have free play, free from the oppression of the white race.

We would be satisfied with just this much. What moral right do the world powers who have themselves closed to us the two doors of emigration and advance into world markets have to criticize Japan's attempt to rush out of the third and last door? . . .

At the time of the Manchurian incident, the entire world joined in criticism of Japan. They said that Japan was an untrustworthy nation. . . . But the military action taken by Japan was not in the least a selfish one. Moreover, we do not recall ever having taken so much as an inch of territory belonging to another nation. The result of this incident was the establishment of the splendid new nation of Manchuria. The Powers are still discussing whether or not to recognize this new nation, but regardless of whether or not other nations recognize her, the Manchurian Empire has already been established, and now, seven years after its creation, the empire is further consolidating its foundations with the aid of its friend, Japan.

And if it is still protested that our actions in Manchuria were excessively violent, we may wish to ask the white race just which country it was that sent warships and troops to India, South Africa, and Australia and slaughtered innocent natives, bound their hands and feet with iron chains, lashed their backs with iron whips, proclaimed these territories as their own, and still continues to hold them to this very day.

Q *What arguments did Hashimoto Kingoro make in favor of Japanese territorial expansion? What was his reaction to the condemnation of Japan by Western nations?*

Source: From *Sources of Japanese Tradition* by William Theodore de Bary. Copyright © 1958 by Columbia University Press.

During the late 1930s, Japan began to cooperate with Nazi Germany on the assumption that the two countries would ultimately launch a joint attack on the Soviet Union and divide its resources between them. But when Germany surprised the world by signing a nonaggression pact with the Soviets in August 1939, Japanese strategists were compelled to reevaluate their long-term objectives. The Japanese were not strong enough to defeat the Soviet Union alone and so began to shift their eyes southward to the vast resources of Southeast Asia—the oil of the Dutch East Indies, the rubber and tin of Malaya, and the rice of Burma and Indochina.

A move southward, of course, would risk war with the European colonial powers and the United States. When Japan demanded the right to occupy airfields and exploit economic resources in French Indochina in the summer of 1940, the United States warned the Japanese that it would cut off the sale of oil and scrap iron unless Japan withdrew from the area and returned to its 1931 borders.

The Japanese viewed the American threat of retaliation as an obstacle to their long-term objectives. Japan badly needed oil and scrap iron from the United States. Should they be cut off, Japan would have to find them elsewhere. The Japanese were thus caught in a vise. To obtain

25.3 A Japanese Victory March in China. After consolidating its authority over Manchuria, Japan began to expand into northern China. Direct hostilities between Japanese and Chinese forces began in 1937. This photograph shows a Japanese victory march in Shanghai at the beginning of December 1937. By 1939, Japan had conquered most of eastern China.

guaranteed access to natural resources that were necessary to fuel the Japanese military machine, Japan must risk being cut off from its current source of raw materials that would be needed in the event of a conflict. After much debate, Japan decided to launch a surprise attack on American and European colonies in Southeast Asia in the hope of a quick victory that would evict the United States from the region.

25-3 WORLD WAR II

> **Q Focus Question:** What were the main events of World War II in Europe and Asia?

Unleashing an early form of **blitzkrieg** (BLITZ-kreeg), or "lightning war," Hitler stunned Europe with the speed and efficiency of the German attack. Armored columns or panzer divisions (a panzer division was a strike force of some 300 tanks and accompanying forces and supplies)

supported by airplanes broke quickly through Polish lines and encircled the bewildered Polish troops. Conventional infantry units then moved in to hold the newly conquered territory. Within four weeks, Poland had surrendered. On September 28, 1939, Germany and the Soviet Union officially divided Poland between them.

25-3a Europe at War

After a winter of waiting and no military actions coming from England and France, Hitler resumed the war on April 9, 1940, with another blitzkrieg against Denmark and Norway (see Map 25.1). One month later, on May 10, the Germans launched their attack on the Netherlands, Belgium, and France. The main assault through Luxembourg and the Ardennes Forest was completely unexpected by the French and British forces. German panzer divisions broke through weak French defensive positions and raced across northern France, splitting the Allied armies and trapping French troops and the entire British army on the beaches of Dunkirk. Only by heroic efforts did the British achieve a gigantic evacuation of 330,000 Allied troops. The French capitulated on June 22. German armies occupied some three-fifths of France while the French hero of World War I, Marshal Henri Pétain (AHN-ree pay-TAHN), established an authoritarian regime—known as Vichy (VISH-ee) France—over the remaining area in the south (see Map 25.1). Germany was now in control of western and central Europe, but Britain still had not been defeated.

Hitler realized that an amphibious invasion of Britain would be possible only if Germany gained control of the air. At the beginning of August 1940, the German air force, or Luftwaffe (LOOFT-vahf-uh), launched a major offensive against British air and naval bases, harbors, communication centers, and war industries. The British fought back doggedly, supported by an effective radar system that gave them early warning of German attacks. Nevertheless, the British air force suffered critical losses by the end of August and was probably only saved by a change in Hitler's strategy. In September, in retaliation for a British attack on Berlin, Hitler ordered a shift from military targets to massive bombing of British cities to break British morale. The British rebuilt their air strength quickly and were soon inflicting major losses on Luftwaffe bombers. By the end of September, Germany had lost the Battle of Britain, and the invasion of Britain had to be postponed.

Although he had no desire for a two-front war, Hitler became convinced that Britain was remaining in the war only because it expected Soviet support. If the Soviet Union were smashed, Britain's last hope would be eliminated. Although the invasion of the Soviet Union was

 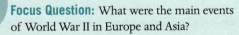

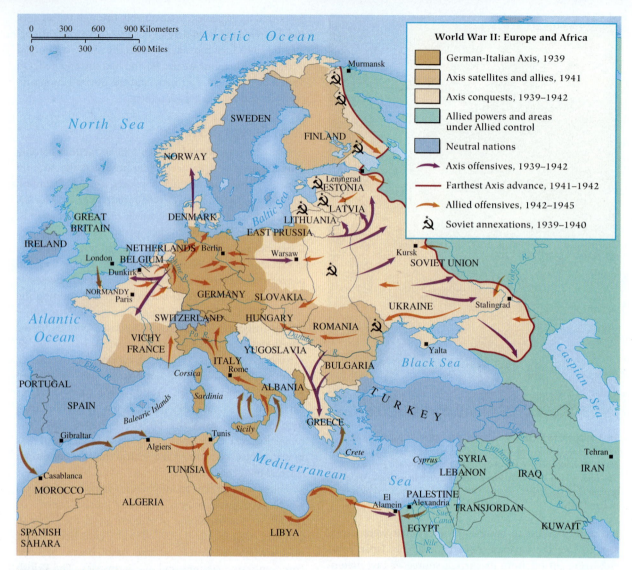

Map 25.1 World War II in Europe and North Africa. With its fast and effective military, Germany quickly overwhelmed much of western Europe. Hitler had overestimated his country's capabilities, however, and underestimated those of his foes. By late 1942, his invasion of the Soviet Union was failing, and the United States had become a major factor in the war. The Allies successfully invaded Italy in 1943 and France in 1944.

Q *Which countries were neutral, and how did geography help make their neutrality an option?*

scheduled for spring 1941, the attack was delayed because of problems in the Balkans. Hitler had already obtained the political cooperation of Hungary, Bulgaria, and Romania, but Mussolini's disastrous invasion of Greece in October 1940 exposed Hitler's southern flank to British air bases in Greece. To secure his Balkan flank, German troops seized both Yugoslavia and Greece in April. Feeling reassured, Hitler turned to the east and invaded the Soviet Union on June 22, 1941.

The massive attack stretched out along a 1,800-mile front. German troops advanced rapidly, capturing 2 million

Soviet soldiers. By November, one German army group had swept through Ukraine and a second was besieging Leningrad; a third approached within twenty-five miles of Moscow, the Soviet capital. An early winter and unexpected Soviet resistance, however, brought a halt to the German advance. For the first time in the war, German armies had been stopped. A Soviet counterattack in December 1941 came as an ominous ending to the year for the Germans. By that time, another of Hitler's decisions—the declaration of war on the United States—turned another European conflict into a global war.

25-3b Japan at War

On December 7, 1941, Japanese carrier-based aircraft attacked the U.S. naval base at Pearl Harbor in the Hawaiian Islands, then an American territory. The same day, other Japanese units launched assaults on the Philippines and began advancing toward the British colony of Malaya (see Map 25.2). Shortly thereafter, Japanese forces invaded the Dutch East Indies and occupied many islands in the Pacific Ocean. By the spring of 1942, almost all of Southeast Asia and much of the western Pacific had fallen into Japanese hands. Japan declared the establishment of the Greater East Asia Co-Prosperity Sphere, putting the entire region under Japanese tutelage and announcing its intention to liberate the colonial areas of Southeast Asia from Western colonial rule. For the moment, however, Japan needed the resources of the region for its war machine and placed the countries under its own rule on a wartime basis.

Japanese leaders had hoped their lightning strike at American bases would destroy the U.S. Pacific fleet and persuade President Franklin D. Roosevelt to accept Japanese domination of the Pacific. But the attack on Pearl Harbor galvanized American opinion and won broad support for Roosevelt's war policy. The United States

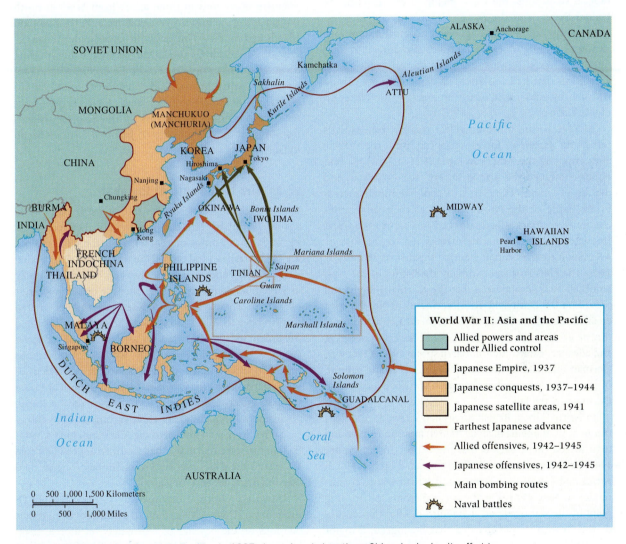

Map 25.2 World War II in Asia and the Pacific. In 1937, Japan invaded northern China, beginning its effort to create a Greater East-Asia Co-Prosperity Sphere. Further expansion led the United States to end iron and oil sales to Japan. Deciding that war with the United States was inevitable, Japan engineered a surprise attack on Pearl Harbor.

Q *Why was control of the islands in the western Pacific of great importance to both the Japanese and the Allies?*

now joined with European nations and Nationalist China in a combined effort to defeat Japan. Believing that American involvement in the Pacific would render the United States ineffective in the European theater of war, Hitler declared war on the United States four days after Pearl Harbor.

25-3c The Turning Point of the War, 1942–1943

The entry of the United States into the war created a coalition (the Grand Alliance) that ultimately defeated the Axis Powers (Germany, Italy, and Japan). To overcome mutual suspicions, the three major Allies—Britain, the United States, and the Soviet Union—agreed to stress military operations while ignoring political differences. At the beginning of 1943, the Allies also agreed to fight until the Axis Powers surrendered unconditionally, a decision that had the effect of cementing the Grand Alliance by making it nearly impossible for Hitler to divide his foes.

As 1942 began, however, defeat was far from Hitler's mind. As Japanese forces advanced into the Pacific after crippling the American naval fleet at Pearl Harbor, Hitler continued the war in Europe against Britain and the Soviet Union. The Germans continued their success in the Battle of the North Atlantic as their submarines continued to attack Allied ships carrying supplies to Great Britain. German submarine attacks led to the loss of 4.5 million tons of shipping during the first six months of 1942. The Germans were winning the battles of the seas. Until fall 1942, it appeared that the Germans might still prevail on the battlefield. Reinforcements in North Africa enabled the Afrika Korps under General Erwin Rommel (RAHM-ul) to break through the British defenses in Egypt and advance toward Alexandria. In spring 1942, a renewed German offensive in the Soviet Union led to the capture of the entire Crimea, but the war had turned against the Germans by the fall.

In North Africa, British forces had stopped Rommel's troops at El Alamein (ell ah-lah-MAYN) in summer 1942 and then forced them back across the desert. In November 1942, British and American forces invaded French North Africa and forced the German and Italian troops to surrender in May 1943. On the eastern front, the turning point of the war occurred at Stalingrad. After the capture of the Crimea, Hitler decided that Stalingrad, a major industrial center on the Volga, should be taken next. Between November 1942 and February 1943, German troops were stopped, then encircled, and finally forced to surrender on February 2, 1943 (see Historical Voices, "A German Soldier at Stalingrad," p.639). The entire German Sixth Army of 300,000 men was lost. By February 1943, German forces in the Soviet Union were back to their positions of June 1942.

The tide of battle in the Far East also turned dramatically in 1942. In the Battle of the Coral Sea on May 7–8, 1942, American naval forces stopped the Japanese advance and temporarily relieved Australia of the threat of invasion. On June 4 at the Battle of Midway Island, American carrier planes destroyed all four attacking Japanese aircraft carriers and established American naval superiority in the Pacific. The victory came at a high cost: around two-fifths of the American planes were shot down in the encounter. By fall 1942, Allied forces were beginning to gather for offensive operations in three areas: from bases in north Burma and India into the rest of Burma; in the Solomon Islands and on New Guinea, with forces under the direction of American General Douglas MacArthur moving toward the Philippines; and across the Pacific, where combined U.S. Army, Marine, and Navy forces would mount attacks against Japanese-held islands. After a series of bitter engagements in the waters of the Solomon Islands from August to November 1942, Japanese fortunes began to fade.

25-3d The Last Years of the War

By the beginning of 1943, the tide of battle had turned against Germany, Italy, and Japan. After Axis forces had surrendered in Tunisia on May 13, 1943, the Allies crossed the Mediterranean and carried the war to Italy. After taking Sicily, Allied troops began the invasion of mainland Italy in September. In the meantime, after the ouster and arrest of Benito Mussolini, a new Italian government offered to surrender to Allied forces. But the Germans liberated Mussolini and then set him up as the head of a puppet German state in northern Italy while German troops moved in and occupied much of Italy. The new defensive lines established by the Germans in the hills south of Rome were so effective that the Allied advance up the Italian Peninsula was a painstaking affair accompanied by heavy casualties. Rome did not fall to the Allies until June 4, 1944. By that time, the Italian war had assumed a secondary role anyway as the Allies prepared to open their long-awaited "second front" in western Europe.

Under the direction of American General Dwight D. Eisenhower (1890–1969), the Allies landed five assault divisions on the beaches of Normandy on June 6, 1944, in history's greatest naval invasion. An initially indecisive German response enabled the Allied forces to establish a beachhead. Within three months, they had landed 2 million men and a half-million vehicles that pushed inland and broke through German defensive lines.

A German Soldier at Stalingrad

 Politics & Government THE SOVIET VICTORY AT STALINGRAD was a major turning point in World War II. This excerpt comes from the diary of a German soldier who fought and died in the Battle of Stalingrad. His dreams of victory and a return home with medals were soon dashed by the realities of Soviet resistance.

Diary of a German Soldier

Today, after we'd had a bath, the company commander told us that if our future operations are as successful, we'll soon reach the Volga, take Stalingrad, and then the war will inevitably soon be over. Perhaps we'll be home by Christmas.

July 29. The company commander says the Russian troops are completely broken, and cannot hold out any longer. To reach the Volga and take Stalingrad is not so difficult for us. The Führer knows where the Russians' weak point is. Victory is not far away. . . .

August 10. The Führer's orders were read out to us. He expects victory of us. We are all convinced that they can't stop us.

August 12. This morning outstanding soldiers were presented with decorations. Will I really go back to Elsa without a decoration? I believe that for Stalingrad the Führer will decorate even me. . . .

September 4. We are being sent northward along the front toward Stalingrad. We marched all night and by dawn had reached Voroponovo Station. We can already see the smoking town. It's a happy thought that the end of the war is getting nearer. That's what everyone is saying. . . .

September 8. Two days of nonstop fighting. The Russians are defending themselves with insane stubbornness. Our regiment has lost many men. . . .

September 16. Our battalion, plus tanks, is attacking the [grain storage] elevator, from which smoke is pouring—the grain in it is burning; the Russians seem to have set light

25.4a

25.4b

25.4a, 25.4b The Battle of Stalingrad. The Battle of Stalingrad was a major turning point on the eastern front. Shown in Image 25.4a is a German infantry platoon in the ruins of a tractor factory they had captured in the northern part of Stalingrad. This victory took place on October 15, 1942, at a time when Hitler still believed he was winning the Battle for Stalingrad. That belief was soon dashed as a Soviet counteroffensive in November led to a total defeat for the Germans. Image 25.4b shows thousands of captured soldiers being marched across frozen Soviet soil to prison camps. The soldiers in white fur hats are Romanian. Fewer than 6,000 captured soldiers survived to go home; the remainder—almost 85,000 prisoners—died in captivity.

(continued)

to it themselves. Barbarism. The battalion is suffering heavy losses. . . .

October 10. The Russians are so close to us that our planes cannot bomb them. We are preparing for a decisive attack. The Führer has ordered the whole of Stalingrad to be taken as rapidly as possible. . . .

October 22. Our regiment has failed to break into the factory. We have lost many men; every time you move you have to jump over bodies. . . .

November 10. A letter from Elsa today. Everyone expects us home for Christmas. In Germany everyone believes we already hold Stalingrad. How wrong they are. If they could only see what Stalingrad has done to our army. . . .

November 21. The Russians have gone over to the offensive along the whole front. Fierce fighting is going on. So, there it is—the Volga, victory, and soon home to our families! We shall obviously be seeing them next in the other world.

November 29. We are encircled. It was announced this morning that the Führer has said: "The army can trust

me to do everything necessary to ensure supplies and rapidly break the encirclement."

December 3. We are on hunger rations and waiting for the rescue that the Führer promised. . . .

December 14. Everybody is racked with hunger. Frozen potatoes are the best meal, but to get them out of the ice-covered ground under fire from Russian bullets is not so easy. . . .

December 26. The horses have already been eaten. I would eat a cat; they say its meat is also tasty. The soldiers look like corpses or lunatics, looking for something to put in their mouths. They no longer take cover from Russian shells; they haven't the strength to walk, run away, and hide. A curse on this war!

Q *What did this soldier believe about the Führer? Why? What was the source of his information? Why is the battle for Stalingrad considered a major turning point in World War II?*

Source: From Vasili Chuikov, *The Battle of Stalingrad* (Grafton Books).

After the breakout, Allied troops moved south and east and liberated Paris by the end of August. By March 1945, they had crossed the Rhine River and advanced farther into Germany. At the end of April 1945, Allied armies in northern Germany moved toward the Elbe River, where they finally linked up with the Soviets. The Soviets had come a long way since the Battle of Stalingrad in 1943. In the summer of 1943, they soundly defeated German forces at the Battle of Kursk (KOORSK) (July 5–12), the greatest tank battle of World War II. Soviet forces then began a relentless advance westward. The Soviets had reoccupied Ukraine by the end of 1943 and lifted the siege of Leningrad and moved into the Baltic states by the beginning of 1944. Advancing along a northern front, Soviet troops occupied Warsaw in January 1945 and entered Berlin in April. Meanwhile, Soviet troops also swept along a southern front through Hungary, Romania, and Bulgaria.

In January 1945, Hitler had moved into a bunker fifty-five feet under Berlin to direct the final stages of the war. Hitler committed suicide on April 30, two days after Mussolini had been shot by partisan Italian forces.

25.5 The Liberation of Paris. Paris was liberated by Allied forces in August 1944. Shown here in a hand-colored photograph are young French women with American soldiers sitting in front of the Eiffel Tower.

AGIP (RDA)/Bridgeman Images

On May 7, German commanders surrendered. The war in Europe was over.

Defeat of Japan   The war in Asia continued. Beginning in 1943, American forces had gone on the offensive and proceeded, slowly at times, across the Pacific. American forces took an increasing toll on enemy resources, especially at sea and in the air. Especially devastating to the Japanese were the losses they sustained at the Battle of Leyte Gulf in the Philippines, the largest naval battle of World War II. Combined American and Australian naval forces caused such heavy losses of Japanese ships that the Japanese navy was unable to sail to battle in any significant way.

As Allied military power drew inexorably closer to the main Japanese islands in the first months of 1945, President Harry Truman, who had succeeded to the presidency on the death of Franklin Roosevelt in April, had an excruciatingly difficult decision to make. Should he use atomic weapons to bring the war to an end without the necessity of an Allied invasion of the Japanese homeland? At the time, only

two bombs had been developed, and their effectiveness had not been demonstrated. As the world knows, Truman answered that question in the affirmative. The first bomb was dropped on the city of Hiroshima (hee-roh-SHEE-muh) on August 6. Three days later, a second bomb was dropped on Nagasaki (nahgah-SAH-kee). Japan surrendered unconditionally on August 14. World War II was finally over.

25-4 THE NEW ORDER

 Focus Question: What was the nature of the new orders that Germany and Japan attempted to establish in the territories they occupied?

The initial victories of the Germans and the Japanese had given them the opportunity to create new orders in Europe and Asia. Both followed policies of ruthless domination of their subject peoples.

25-4a The New Order in Europe

In 1942, the Nazi Empire stretched across continental Europe from the English Channel in the west to the outskirts of Moscow in the east. Nazi-occupied Europe was largely organized in one of two ways. Some areas such as western Poland were directly annexed by Nazi Germany and made into German provinces. The rest of occupied Europe was administered by German military or civilian officials in combination with different degrees of indirect control from collaborationist regimes.

Because the conquered lands in the east contained the living space for German expansion and were populated in Nazi eyes by racially inferior Slavic peoples, Nazi administration there was considerably more ruthless than in the west. Soon after the conquest of Poland, Heinrich Himmler, a strong believer in Nazi racial ideology and the leader of the SS, was put in charge of German resettlement plans in the east. Himmler's task was to evacuate the inferior Slavic peoples and replace them with Germans, a policy first applied to the new German provinces created from the lands of western Poland. One million Poles were uprooted and dumped in southern Poland. Hundreds of thousands of ethnic Germans (descendants of Germans who had migrated years earlier from Germany to different parts of southern and eastern Europe) were encouraged to colonize designated areas in Poland. By 1942, 2 million ethnic Germans had been settled in Poland.

Labor shortages in Germany led to a policy of ruthless mobilization of foreign labor for Germany. In 1942, a special office was created to recruit labor for German farms and industries. By summer 1944, 7 million foreign workers—20 percent of the labor force—were laboring in Germany. At the same time, another 7 million workers were supplying forced labor in their own countries.

25-4b The Holocaust

No aspect of the Nazi new order was more terrifying than the deliberate attempt to exterminate the Jews of Europe. Racial struggle was a key element in Hitler's ideology and meant to him a clearly defined conflict of opposites: the Aryans, creators of human cultural development, against the Jews, parasites who were trying to destroy the Aryans. Himmler and the SS organization closely shared Hitler's racial ideology. The SS was given responsibility for what the Nazis called their **Final Solution** to the "Jewish problem"—the annihilation of the Jewish people. After the defeat of Poland, the SS ordered the **Einsatzgruppen** (YN-zahtz-groop-un), or special strike forces, to round up all Polish Jews and concentrate them in ghettos established in several Polish cities.

In June 1941, the Einsatzgruppen were given new responsibilities as mobile killing units. These SS death squads followed the regular army's advance into Russia. Their job was to round up Jews in their villages and execute and bury them in mass graves, often giant pits dug by the victims themselves before they were shot. Such constant killing produced morale problems among the SS executioners.

Although it has been estimated that as many as 1 million Jews were killed by the Einsatzgruppen, this approach to solving the Jewish problem was soon perceived to be inadequate. So the Nazis opted for the systematic annihilation of the European Jewish population in death camps. Jews from countries occupied by Germany (or sympathetic to Germany) were rounded up, packed like cattle into freight trains, and shipped to Poland, where six extermination centers were built for this purpose. The largest and most famous was Auschwitz-Birkenau (OW-shvitz-BEER-kuhnow). Medical technicians chose Zyklon B (the commercial name for hydrogen cyanide) as the most effective gas for quickly killing large numbers of people in gas chambers designed to look like shower rooms to facilitate the cooperation of the victims.

The death camps were up and running by spring 1942; by the summer, Jews were also being shipped from France, Belgium, and the Netherlands. Even as the Allies were making significant advances in 1944, Jews were being shipped from Greece and Hungary. A harrowing experience awaited the Jews when they arrived at one of the six death camps. Rudolf Hess (HESS), commandant at Auschwitz-Birkenau, described it:

> We had two SS doctors on duty at Auschwitz to examine the incoming transports of prisoners. The prisoners would be marched by one of the doctors who would make spot decisions as they walked by. Those who

were fit for work were sent into the camp. Others were sent immediately to the extermination plants. Children of tender years were invariably exterminated since by reason of their youth they were unable to work. . . . At Auschwitz we endeavored to fool the victims into thinking that they were to go through a delousing process. Of course, frequently they realized our true intentions and we sometimes had riots and difficulties due to that fact.[5]

Approximately 30 percent of the arrivals at Auschwitz were sent to a labor camp; the remainder went to the gas chambers. After they had been gassed, the bodies were burned in specially built crematoria. The victims' goods and even their bodies were used for economic gain. Women's hair was cut off, collected, and used to stuff mattresses or make cloth. Altogether, the Germans killed between 5 million and 6 million Jews, more than 3 million of them in the death camps. Around 90 percent of the Jewish populations of Poland, the Baltic countries, and Germany were exterminated. Overall, the Holocaust was responsible for the death of nearly two of every three Jews in Europe (see Historical Voices, "Heinrich Himmler: 'We Had the Moral Right,'" p. 643).

The Nazis were also responsible for the death by shooting, starvation, or overwork of at least another 9 million to 10 million people. Because the Nazis also considered the Romani (gypsies) of Europe a race containing alien blood (like the Jews), they were systematically rounded up for extermination. Around 40 percent of Europe's 1 million Romani were killed in the death camps. The leading elements of the "subhuman" Slavic peoples—the clergy, intelligentsia, civil leaders, judges, and lawyers—were also arrested and deliberately killed. Probably an additional 4 million Poles, Ukrainians, and Byelorussians lost their lives as slave laborers for Nazi Germany, and 3 million to 4 million Soviet prisoners of war were killed in captivity.

25-4c The New Order in Asia

Once the takeover was completed, Japanese war policy in the occupied areas in Asia became essentially defensive as Japan hoped to use its new possessions to meet its burgeoning needs for raw materials such as tin, oil, and rubber, and also as an outlet for Japanese manufactured goods. To provide an organizational structure for the arrangement, Japanese leaders set up the Greater East Asia Co-Prosperity Sphere, a self-sufficient economic community designed to provide mutual benefits to the occupied areas and the home country.

The Japanese conquest of Southeast Asia had been accomplished under the slogan "Asia for the Asians." Japanese officials in the occupied territories quickly promised that independent governments would be

Heinrich Himmler: "We Had the Moral Right"

Politics & Government ALTHOUGH NAZI LEADERS WERE RELUCTANT to talk openly about their attempted destruction of the Jews of Europe, when they did, they had no qualms about justifying it. Heinrich Himmler, the leader of the SS, assumed responsibility for executing the Holocaust and in 1943 gave a remarkable speech to the leaders of the SS in Poznan, Poland.

Heinrich Himmler, Speech to SS Leaders

I also want to talk to you, quite frankly, on a very grave matter. Among yourselves it should be mentioned quite frankly, and yet we will never speak of it publicly. I mean the clearing out of the Jews, extermination of the Jewish race. It's one of those things it is easy to talk about—"The Jewish race is being exterminated," says one party member, "that's quite clear, it's in our program—elimination of the Jews, and we're doing it, exterminating them." And then they come, 80 million worthy Germans, and each one had his decent Jew. Of course, the others are vermin, but this one is an A-1 Jew. Not one of those who talk this way has witnessed it, not one of those who talk this way has witnessed it, not one of them has been through it. Most of you must know what it means when 100 corpses are lying

side by side, or 500 or 1000. To have stuck it out and at the same time . . . to have remained decent fellows, that is what has made us hard. This is a page of glory in our history which has never been written and is never to be written, . . . We have taken from them what wealth they had. I have issued a strict order, . . . that this wealth should, as a matter of course, be handed over to [Germany] without reserve. We have taken none of it for ourselves. . . . We had the moral right, we had the duty to our people, to destroy this people which wanted to destroy us. But we have not the right to enrich ourselves with so much as a fur, a watch, a mark, or a cigarette or anything else. Because we have exterminated a bacterium we do not want, in the end, to be infected by the bacterium and die of it. I will not see so much as a small area of sepsis appear here or gain a hold. Wherever it may form, we will cauterize it. Although however, we can say, that we have fulfilled this most difficult duty for the love of our people. And our spirit our soul, our character has not suffered injury from it.

Q *How does Himmler justify the Holocaust? What is wrong with his argument, and how does it demonstrate the danger of ideological rigidity?*

Source: *Nazi Conspiracy and Aggression* (Washington, D.C.,1946), 4:563–564.

established under Japanese tutelage. Such governments were eventually established in Burma, the Dutch East Indies, Vietnam, and the Philippines.

In fact, however, real power rested with the Japanese military authorities in each territory, and the local Japanese military command was directly subordinated to the army general staff in Tokyo. The economic resources of the colonies were exploited for the benefit of the Japanese war machine, and natives were recruited to serve in local military units or conscripted to work on public works projects. In some cases, the people living in the occupied areas were subjected to severe hardships.

At first, many Southeast Asian nationalists took Japanese promises at face value and agreed to cooperate with their new masters. But as the exploitative nature of Japanese occupation policies became clear, sentiment turned against the new order. Japanese officials sometimes unwittingly provoked such attitudes by their arrogance and contempt for local customs.

Like German soldiers in occupied Europe, Japanese military forces often had little respect for the lives of their subject peoples. In their conquest of Nanjing, China, in 1937, Japanese soldiers had devoted several days to killing, raping, and looting. After the surrender of Japan in 1945, all documents relating to the conquest of Nanjing were destroyed. The degree to which the massacre took place and the number of victims is still a point of contention between China and Japan. Japanese military forces also sent almost 800,000 Koreans overseas to Japan for forced labor. Tens of thousands of women from Korea and the Philippines were forced to be "comfort women" (prostitutes) for Japanese troops. Japan has still not taken responsibility for the sexual enslavement of Korean women, and protests continue today in Japan and Korea over the issue of recognition and compensation for the victims. The Japanese also made extensive use of both prisoners of war and local peoples as laborers on construction projects for the war effort.

25-5 THE HOME FRONT

 Focus Question: What were conditions like on the home front for the major belligerents in World War II?

World War II was even more of a total war than World War I. Fighting was much more widespread and covered most of the world. The number of civilians killed was also far higher.

25-5a Mobilizing the People: Three Examples

The initial defeats of the Soviet Union led to drastic emergency mobilization measures that affected the civilian population. As the German army made its rapid advance into Soviet territory, the factories in the western part of the Soviet Union were dismantled and shipped to the interior—to the Urals, western Siberia, and the Volga region. Machines were set down on bare earth, and walls went up around them as workers began their work.

Stalin called the widespread military and industrial mobilization of the nation a "battle of machines," and the Soviets won by producing 78,000 tanks and 98,000 artillery pieces. In 1943, fully 55 percent of Soviet national income went for war matériel compared to 15 percent in 1940 (see the Comparative Essay, "Paths to Modernization," p. 645).

Soviet women played a major role in the war effort. Women and girls were enlisted for work in industries, mines, and railroads. Overall the number of women working in industry increased almost 60 percent. Soviet women were also expected to dig antitank ditches and work as air raid wardens. In addition, the Soviet Union was the only country in World War II to use women as combatants. Soviet women functioned as snipers and as crews in bomber squadrons.

In August 1914, Germans had enthusiastically cheered their soldiers marching off to war; in September 1939, the streets were quiet. Many Germans were apathetic or, even worse for the Nazi regime, had a foreboding of disaster. Hitler was keenly aware of the importance of the home front. He believed that the collapse of the home front in World War I had caused Germany's defeat. To avoid a repetition of that experience, he adopted economic policies that may actually have cost Germany the war.

To maintain the morale of the home front during the first two years of the war, Hitler refused to cut production of consumer goods or increase the production of armaments. After German defeats on the Russian front

and the American entry into the war, however, the situation changed. Early in 1942, Hitler finally ordered a massive increase in armaments production and the size of the army. Hitler's architect, Albert Speer (AHL-bert SHPAYR), was made minister for armaments and munitions in 1942. By eliminating waste and rationalizing procedures, Speer was able to triple the production of armaments between 1942 and 1943, despite intense Allied bombing raids. Speer's urgent plea for a total mobilization of resources for the war effort went unheeded, however. Fearful of civilian morale problems that would undermine the home front, Hitler refused any dramatic cuts in the production of consumer goods. A total mobilization of the economy was not implemented until 1944, but it was too late by that time.

The war caused a reversal in Nazi attitudes toward women. Nazi resistance to female employment declined as the war progressed and more and more men were called up for military service. But the number of women working in industry, agriculture, commerce, and domestic service increased only slightly. In September 1944, 14.9 million women were employed, compared with 14.6 million in May 1939. Many women, especially those of the middle class, resisted regular employment, particularly in factories.

Wartime Japan was a highly mobilized society. To guarantee its control over all national resources, the government set up a planning board to control prices, wages, the use of labor, and the allocation of resources. Traditional habits of obedience and hierarchy, buttressed by the concept of imperial divinity, were emphasized to encourage citizens to sacrifice their resources and sometimes their lives for the national cause. The system culminated in the final years of the war when young Japanese were encouraged to volunteer en masse to serve as pilots in deadly suicide missions—known as *kamikaze* (kah-mi-KAH-zee) or "divine wind" attacks—against U.S. battleships.

Women's rights too were to be sacrificed to the greater national cause. Already by 1937, Japanese women were being exhorted to fulfill their patriotic duty by bearing more children and espousing the slogans of the Greater Japanese Women's Association. Japan was extremely reluctant to mobilize women on behalf of the war effort, however. General Hideki Tojo (hee-DEK-ee TOH-joh), prime minister from 1941 to 1944, opposed female employment, arguing that "the weakening of the family system would be the weakening of the nation. . . . We are able to do our duties only because we have wives and mothers at home."[6] Instead of using women to meet labor shortages, the Japanese government brought in Korean and Chinese laborers.

Paths to Modernization

Politics & Government

To the casual observer, the most important feature of the first half of the twentieth century was the rise of a virulent form of competitive nationalism that began in Europe and ultimately led to two destructive world wars. Behind the scenes, however, another competition was taking place over the most effective path to modernization.

The traditional approach in which modernization was fostered by an independent urban merchant class had been adopted by Great Britain, France, and the United States and led to the emergence of democratic societies on the capitalist model. In the second approach, which was adopted in the late nineteenth century by imperial Germany and Meiji Japan, modernization was carried out by traditional elites in the absence of a strong independent bourgeois class. Both Germany and Japan relied on strong government intervention to promote the growth of national wealth and power, and modernization in both nations led ultimately to the formation of fascist and militarist regimes during the depression years of the early 1930s.

The third approach, which was selected by Vladimir Lenin after the Bolshevik Revolution in 1917, was designed to carry out an industrial revolution without going through an intermediate capitalist stage. Under the guidance of the Communist Party in the almost total absence of an urban middle class, an advanced industrial

25.6 The Soviet Path to Modernization. One aspect of the Soviet effort to create an advanced industrial society was the collectivization of agriculture, which included the rapid mechanization of food production. In this photograph, peasants are watching a new tractor at work.

society would be created by destroying the concept of private property. Although Lenin's plans ultimately called for the "withering away of the state," the party adopted totalitarian methods to eliminate enemies of the revolution and carry out the changes needed to create a future classless utopia.

Q *What were the three major paths to modernization in the first half of the twentieth century?*

25-5b The Frontline Civilians: The Bombing of Cities

Bombing was used in World War II against nonhuman military targets, enemy troops, and civilian populations. The bombing of civilians made World War II as devastating for noncombatants as it was for frontline soldiers. A small number of bombing raids in the last year of World War I had given rise to the argument that public outcry over the bombing of civilian populations would be an effective way to coerce governments into making peace. Consequently, European air forces began to develop long-range bombers in the 1930s.

The sustained use of civilian bombing failed to support the theory. Beginning in early September 1940, the German Luftwaffe subjected London and many other British cities and towns to nightly air raids, making the Blitz (as the British called the German air raids) a national experience. Londoners took the first heavy blows but kept up their morale, setting the standard for the rest of the British population (see Comparative Illustration, "The Bombing of Civilians, East and West," p. 646).

The British failed to learn from their own experience, however. Prime Minister Winston Churchill and his advisers believed that destroying German communities would break civilian morale and bring victory. Major bombing raids began in 1942. On May 31, 1942, Cologne became the first German city to be subjected to an attack by a thousand bombers. Bombing raids added an element of terror to circumstances already made difficult by growing shortages of food, clothing, and fuel. Germans especially feared incendiary bombs, which ignited firestorms that swept destructive paths through the cities. The ferocious

The Bombing of Civilians, East and West

Family & Society

THE MOST DEVASTATING BOMBING of civilians in World War II came near the end of the war when the United States dropped atomic bombs on the Japanese cities of Hiroshima and Nagasaki. Image 25.7a is a panoramic view of Hiroshima after the bombing that shows the incredible devastation produced by the atomic bomb. Image 25.7b shows a street in Clydebank, near Glasgow in Scotland, the day after the city was bombed by the Germans in March 1941. Only seven of the city's 12,000 houses were left undamaged; 35,000 of the 47,000 inhabitants became homeless overnight.

Q *What was the rationale for bombing civilian populations? Did such bombing achieve its goal?*

25.7a

Keystone/Hulton Archive/Getty Images

J. R. Eyerman/Time Life Pictures/Getty Images

25.7b

bombing of Dresden from February 13 to 15, 1945, created a firestorm that may have killed as many as 35,000 inhabitants and refugees.

Germany suffered enormously from Allied bombing raids. Millions of buildings were destroyed, and possibly half a million civilians died from the raids. Nevertheless, it is highly unlikely that Allied bombing sapped the morale of the German people. Instead Germans, whether pro-Nazi or anti-Nazi, fought on stubbornly, often driven simply by a desire to live. Nor did the bombing destroy Germany's industrial capacity. The Allied strategic bombing survey revealed that the production of war matériel actually increased between 1942 and 1944.

In Japan, the bombing of civilians reached a horrendous new level with the use of the first atomic bomb. Attacks on Japanese cities by the new American B-29 Superfortresses, the biggest bombers of the war, had begun on November 24, 1944. By summer 1945, many of Japan's industries had been destroyed, along with one-fourth of its dwellings. After President Truman and his advisers decided that Japanese fanaticism during an invasion might mean a million American casualties, they decided to drop the newly developed atomic bomb on Hiroshima and Nagasaki. The destruction was incredible. Of 76,000 buildings near the hypocenter of the explosion in Hiroshima, 70,000 were flattened, and 140,000 of the city's 400,000 inhabitants had died by the end of 1945. Over the next five years, another 50,000 perished from the effects of radiation. The dropping of the atomic bomb on Hiroshima on August 6, 1945, announced the dawn of the nuclear age.

25-6 AFTERMATH OF THE WAR

Q Focus Questions: What were the costs of World War II? How did World War II affect the European nations' colonial empires? How did the Allies' visions of the postwar world differ, and how did these differences contribute to the emergence of the Cold War?

World War II was the most destructive war in history. Much had been at stake. Nazi Germany followed a worldview based on racial extermination and the enslavement of millions to create an Aryan racial empire. Fueled by extreme nationalist ideals, the Japanese also pursued dreams of empire in Asia that led to mass murder and untold devastation. Fighting the Axis Powers in World War II required the mobilization of millions of ordinary men and women in the Allied countries who struggled to preserve a different way of life. As Winston Churchill once put it, "War is horrible, but slavery is worse."

25-6a The Costs of World War II

The costs of World War II were enormous. At least 21 million soldiers died. Civilian deaths were even greater and are now estimated at around 40 million, of whom more than 28 million were Russian and Chinese. The Soviet Union experienced the greatest losses: 10 million soldiers and 19 million civilians. In 1945, millions of people around the world faced starvation: in Europe, 100 million people depended on food relief of some kind.

Millions of people had also been uprooted by the war and became "displaced persons." Europe alone may have had 30 million displaced persons, many of whom found it hard to return home. In Asia, millions of Japanese were returned from the former Japanese empire to Japan, and thousands of Korean forced laborers returned to Korea.

Devastation was everywhere. Most areas of Europe had been damaged or demolished. China was in shambles after eight years of conflict, the Philippines had suffered heavy damage, and large sections of major cities in Japan had been destroyed in air raids. The economies of most

belligerents, with the exception of the United States, were left drained and on the brink of disaster.

25-6b The Impact of Technology

Before World War II, theoretical science and technology were largely separated. Pure science was the domain of university professors who were far removed from the practical technological concerns of technicians and engineers. But during World War II, governments recruited university scientists to develop new weapons and practical instruments of war. In 1940, British physicists played a crucial role in the development of an improved radar system that helped defeat the German air force in the Battle of Britain. German scientists created self-propelled rockets and jet airplanes to keep Hitler's hopes alive for a miraculous turnaround in the war. The computer, too, was a wartime creation. British mathematician Alan Turing designed a primitive computer to assist British intelligence in breaking the secret codes of German ciphering machines. The most famous product of wartime scientific research was the atomic bomb, which was created by a team of American and European scientists under the guidance of American physicist J. Robert Oppenheimer. Obviously, most wartime devices were created for destructive purposes, but it is worth noting that computers and jet airplanes could easily be adapted for peacetime use.

25-6c World War II and the European Colonies: Decolonization

As we saw in Chapter 24, movements for independence had begun in earnest in Africa and Asia in the years between World War I and World War II. After World War II, these movements grew even louder. The ongoing subjugation of peoples by colonial powers seemed at odds with the goals the Allies had pursued in overthrowing the repressive regimes of Germany, Italy, and Japan. Then, too, indigenous peoples everywhere took up the call for national self-determination and expressed their determination to fight for independence.

The ending of the European powers' colonial empires did not come easily, however. In 1941, Churchill had said, "I have not become His Majesty's Chief Minister in order to preside over the liquidation of the British Empire." Britain and France in particular seemed reluctant to let go of their colonies, but for a variety of reasons both eventually gave in to the obvious—the days of empire were over.

During the war, the Japanese had already humiliated the Western states by overrunning their colonial empires.

In addition, colonial soldiers who had fought on behalf of the Allies (India, for example, had contributed large numbers of troops to the British Indian Army) were well aware that Allied war aims included the principle of self-determination for the peoples of the world. Equally important to the process of **decolonization**, the power of the European states had been destroyed by the exhaustive struggles of World War II. The greatest empire builder, Great Britain, no longer had the energy or wealth to maintain its empire. Given this combination of circumstances, a rush of decolonization swept the world after the war (see the chapters in Part V).

25-6d The Allied War Conferences

The total victory of the Allies in World War II was not followed by a real peace but by the emergence of a new conflict known as the **Cold War** that dominated world politics until the end of the 1980s. The Cold War grew out of military, political, and ideological differences, especially between the Soviet Union and the United States, that became apparent at the Allied war conferences held in the last years of the war.

Stalin, Roosevelt, and Churchill, the leaders of the Big Three of the Grand Alliance, met at Tehran, the capital of Iran, in November 1943 to decide the future course of the war. Stalin and Roosevelt argued successfully for an American–British invasion of the European continent through France, which they scheduled for spring 1944. This meant that Soviet and British-American forces would meet in defeated Germany along a north–south dividing line and that Soviet forces would most likely liberate Eastern Europe. The Allies also agreed to a partition of postwar Germany.

By the time of the conference at Yalta in southern Russia in February 1945, Germany's defeat was a foregone conclusion. The Western powers now faced the reality of 11 million Red Army soldiers taking possession of Eastern and Central Europe. Deeply suspicious of the Western powers, Stalin desired a buffer to protect the Soviet Union from possible future Western aggression. At the same time, however, Stalin was eager to obtain economically important resources and strategic military positions. Roosevelt by this time was moving toward the idea of self-determination for Europe. The Grand Alliance approved a declaration to assist liberated European nations in the creation of "democratic institutions of their own choice."

At Yalta, Roosevelt sought Russian military help against Japan. The atomic bomb was not yet a certainty, and American military planners feared the possibility of heavy losses in amphibious assaults on the Japanese home islands. Roosevelt therefore agreed to Stalin's price for military assistance against Japan: Soviet possession of Sakhalin and the Kurile Islands, as well as two warm-water ports and railroad rights in Manchuria.

The creation of the United Nations was a major American concern at Yalta. Roosevelt hoped to ensure the participation of the Big Three powers in a postwar international organization before difficult issues divided them into hostile camps. Both Churchill and Stalin eventually accepted Roosevelt's plans for a United Nations organization and set the first meeting for San Francisco in April 1945.

The issues of Germany and Eastern Europe were treated less decisively. The Big Three reaffirmed that Germany must surrender unconditionally and created four occupation zones (see Map 25.3). A compromise was also worked out in regard to Poland. Stalin agreed to free elections in the future to determine a new government. But the issue of free elections in Eastern Europe caused a serious rift between the Soviets and the Americans. In principle, Eastern European governments were to be freely elected, but they were also supposed to be pro-Soviet. This attempt to reconcile two irreconcilable goals was doomed to failure; this soon became evident at the next conference of the Big Three.

The Potsdam Conference of July 1945 began under a cloud of mistrust. Roosevelt had died on April 12 and was succeeded as president by Harry Truman. At Potsdam, Truman demanded free elections throughout Eastern Europe. Stalin responded, "A freely elected government in any of these East European countries would be anti-Soviet, and that we cannot allow."[7] After a bitterly fought and devastating war, Stalin sought absolute military security. To him, it could be gained only by the presence of Communist states in Eastern Europe. By the middle of 1945, only an invasion by Western forces could undo developments in Eastern Europe, and few people favored such a policy.

As the war slowly receded into the past, the reality of conflicting ideologies had reappeared. Many in the West interpreted Soviet policy as part of a worldwide Communist conspiracy. The Soviets viewed Western, especially American, policy as nothing less than global capitalist expansionism or, in Leninist terms, economic imperialism. In March 1946, in a speech to an American audience, former British Prime Minister Winston Churchill declared that "an iron curtain" had "descended across the continent," dividing Germany and Europe into two hostile camps. Stalin branded Churchill's speech a "call to war with the Soviet Union." Only months after the world's most devastating conflict had ended, the world seemed once again to be bitterly divided in the Cold War.

Map 25.3 **Territorial Changes in Europe After World War II.** In the last months of World War II, the Red Army occupied much of Eastern Europe. Stalin sought pro-Soviet satellite states in the region as a buffer against future invasions from Western Europe, whereas Britain and the United States wanted democratically elected governments. Soviet military control of the territory settled the question.

Q *Which country gained the greatest territory at the expense of Germany?*

CHAPTER SUMMARY

BETWEEN 1933 AND 1939, Europeans watched as Adolf Hitler rebuilt Germany into a great military power. During that same period, Japan fell under the influence of military leaders who conspired with right-wing forces to push a program of expansion. The ambitions of Germany in Europe and Japan in Asia led to a global conflict that became the most devastating war in human history.

The Axis nations—Germany, Italy, and Japan—proved victorious during the first two years of the war. By 1942, the war had begun to turn in favor of the Allies, an

Experience an interactive version of this period in MINDTAP

alliance of Great Britain, the Soviet Union, and the United States. The Japanese advance was ended at the naval battles of the Coral Sea and Midway in 1942. In February 1943, the Soviets won the Battle of Stalingrad and began a push westward. By mid-1943, Germany and Italy had been driven out of North Africa; in June 1944, Rome fell to the Allies, and an Allied invasion force landed in Normandy in France. After the Soviets linked up with British and American forces in April 1945, Hitler committed suicide, and the war in Europe came to an end. After atomic bombs were dropped on Hiroshima and Nagasaki in August 1945, the war in Asia also ended.

During its domination of Europe, the Nazi Empire brought death and destruction to many people, especially Jews and others whom the Nazis considered racially inferior. The Japanese New Order in Asia, while claiming to promote "Asia for the Asians," also brought exploitation, severe hardship, and often death for the peoples under Japanese control. All sides bombed civilian populations, making the war as devastating for civilians as for frontline soldiers.

If Hitler had been successful, the Nazi New Order—built on authoritarianism, racial extermination, and the brutal oppression of peoples—would have meant a triumph of barbarism and the end of freedom and equality, which, however imperfectly realized, had become important ideals in Western civilization.

The Nazis lost, but only after tremendous sacrifices and costs. Much of European civilization lay in ruins. Europeans now watched helplessly as the two new superpowers created by the two world wars took control of their destinies. Even before the last battles had been fought, the United States and the Soviet Union had arrived at different visions of the postwar European world: their differences gave rise to a new and potentially even more devastating conflict known as the Cold War.

REFLECTION QUESTIONS

Q How do you account for the early successes of the Germans from 1939 to 1941?

Q How did the Nazis and the Japanese attempt to establish new orders in Europe and Asia after their military victories, and what were the results of their efforts?

Q How did the attempt to arrive at a peace settlement after World War II lead to the beginnings of a new conflict known as the Cold War?

CHAPTER TIMELINE

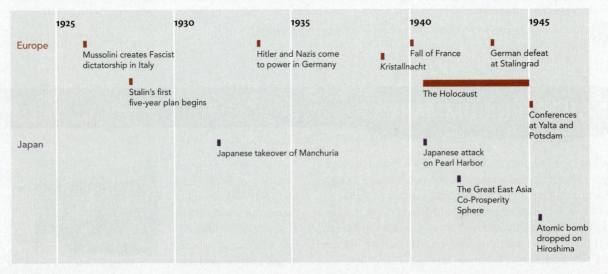

CHAPTER NOTES

1. B. Mussolini, "The Doctrine of Fascism," in A. Lyttleton, ed., *Italian Fascisms* (London, 1973), p. 42.
2. Quoted in J. J. Spielvogel, *Hitler and Nazi Germany: A History*, 5th ed. (Upper Saddle River, N.J., 2005), p. 60.
3. Quoted in J. Fest, *Hitler*, trans. R. Winston and C. Winston (New York, 1974), p. 418.
4. *Documents on German Foreign Policy*, ser. D, vol. 7 (London, 1956), p. 204.
5. *Nazi Conspiracy and Aggression*, vol. 6 (Washington, D.C., 1946), p. 789.
6. Quoted in J. Campbell, *The Experience of World War II* (New York, 1989), p. 143.
7. Quoted in N. Graebner, *Cold War Diplomacy*, 1945–1960 (Princeton, N.J., 1962), p. 117.

MINDTAP
From Cengage

MindTap® is a fully online, highly personalized learning experience built upon Cengage Learning content. MindTap combines student learning tools—readings, multimedia, activities, and assessments—into a singular Learning Path that guides students through the course and helps students develop the critical thinking, analysis, and communication skills that are essential to academic and professional success.

PART V

TOWARD A GLOBAL CIVILIZATION? THE WORLD SINCE 1945

AS WORLD WAR II CAME TO AN END, the survivors of that bloody struggle felt encouraged to face the future with a cautious measure of optimism. There was modest reason to hope that the bitter rivalry that had marked relations among the Western powers would finally be put to an end and that the wartime alliance of the United States, Great Britain, and the Soviet Union could be maintained into the postwar era. If so, the march toward a more prosperous future for the peoples of the world could resume.

It soon became clear that this vision of global peace and prosperity would face many severe challenges in the postwar era. On the one hand, the Western capitalist nations managed to recover from the economic depression that had led into World War II and advanced to a level of economic prosperity never seen before. Equally important, Germany and Japan—the two restless powers most responsible for unleashing the carnage of the recent war—were fully reintegrated into the world community.

On the other hand, the prospects for a stable, peaceful world and an end to balance-of-power politics were undercut by the emergence of a grueling and sometimes tense ideological struggle between the socialist and capitalist camps, a competition headed by the only remaining great powers, the Soviet Union and the United States. Many observers feared that the rivalry could only end in a new and even more destructive war. In the meantime, the postwar Soviet domination of Eastern Europe, both

political and economic, seemed so complete that many people doubted it could ever be undone.

In the meantime, the peoples of Africa and Asia had their own reasons for cautious optimism as World War II came to a close. In the Atlantic Charter promulgated in the summer of 1941, Franklin Roosevelt and Winston Churchill had set forth a joint declaration of their peace aims and called for the self-determination of all peoples. Although some colonial powers eventually proved reluctant to divest themselves of their colonies, the war had severely undermined the stability of the colonial order, and within a few years most colonies in Asia had received their independence. Africa followed a decade or two later.

Broadly speaking, the leaders of these newly liberated countries set forth three goals at the outset of independence. First, they wanted to throw off the shackles of Western economic domination and ensure material prosperity for all of their citizens. Second, they wanted to introduce new political institutions that would enhance the right of self-determination of their peoples. Third, they wanted to develop a sense of common nationhood within the population and establish secure territorial boundaries. To achieve these goals, some sought to follow a capitalist or a moderately socialist path toward economic development. Others opted for autocratic rule or the Marxist–Leninist model represented by the Soviet Union. Regardless of which path was chosen, the initial results were often disappointing. Much of Africa and Asia remained economically dependent on the advanced industrial nations. Some societies faced severe problems of urban and rural poverty. Others were rent by bitter internal conflicts.

What had happened to tarnish their bright dream of political stability and economic affluence? The dominant school of thought among many Western scholars and government officials at the time was known as **modernization theory**. Modernization theorists took the

V.1

view that the problems faced by the newly independent countries were a consequence of the difficult transition from a traditional to a modern society. Although most newly independent countries were expected to follow a path toward the creation of modern industrial societies on the capitalist model, they would need both time and substantial amounts of economic and technological assistance from the West to complete the journey.

As it turned out, modernization theory had only limited success in the practical arena (see Chapter 30), and it soon came under attack from a new generation of scholars and analysts who argued that the responsibility for continued political unrest and economic underdevelopment in the postcolonial world lay not with the countries themselves but with their continued domination by former colonial powers. In this view, which is known as **dependency theory**, the countries of Asia, Africa, and Latin America were the victims of the international marketplace in which high prices were charged for the manufactured goods of the West while low prices were paid to the preindustrial countries for their raw material exports. Efforts by such countries to build up their industrial sectors and move into the stage of self-sustaining growth were hampered by foreign control of many of their resources via European and American-owned corporations. To end this "neocolonial" relationship, dependency theory advocates argued, developing societies should reduce their economic ties with the West and institute a policy of economic self-reliance, thereby taking control over their own destinies.

Either way, it was clear that most newly independent African and Asian countries faced severe challenges in forging new political cultures responsive to their citizens' needs. After flirting with the Western liberal democratic model, many turned from pluralistic political systems to military dictatorships or one-party governments that redefined the concept of democracy to fit their own preferences. It was clear that the difficulties in building democratic political institutions in developing societies had been underestimated.

But perhaps the most daunting of all the challenges facing the new nations of Asia and Africa was that of establishing a common national identity. Many of these new states were a composite of various ethnic, religious, and linguistic groups that found it difficult to agree on common symbols of nationalism or national values. The process of establishing an official language and delineating territorial boundaries left over from the colonial era created difficulties in many countries. Internal conflicts spawned by deep-rooted historical and ethnic hatreds have proliferated throughout the world, causing vast numbers of people to move across state boundaries in migrations as large as any since the great migrations of the thirteenth and fourteenth centuries.

In 1991, the Cold War suddenly came to an end. The Soviet Union disintegrated into multiple independent nations, and its Eastern European satellites began to join the rest of Europe, itself newly transformed into a European Union. Many Asian countries successfully surmounted age-old challenges and entered an era of peaceful development, political pluralism, and self-sustaining growth. The elimination of communication and trade barriers began to create a more global society in which consumer products, culture, and ideas were rapidly disseminated from one end of the world to the other.

But globalization has created its own challenges. Intense competition over trade markets has led to areas of economic hardship, even in the advanced countries of the West, and sown the seeds of growing doubts over the benefits of a world order based on the principle of free trade. Bitter internal conflicts in some regions have provoked waves of mass migration that threaten the stability of their neighbors and inspire impassioned debate over the concept of open societies with open borders. Meanwhile, the invention of new communications technology arouses violent controversy in some countries and sparks tension and even armed conflict between supporters and opponents of traditional values.

At first, the end of the Cold War brought about a new wave of optimism that what some dubbed a "New World Order" was in the offing. Today a more sober view prevails as the rivalry among the major world powers has intensified in tone while prospects for the advent of a peaceful and prosperous globalized society have grown dimmer. In a chastened world where rising expectations are longer taken for granted, even the once widespread consensus on the superiority of democratic institutions and values has begun to unravel. As we continue our collective journey into the new century, the challenges that faced the world at the end of World War II remain unresolved.

Chapter Outline and Focus Questions

26-1 *The Collapse of the Grand Alliance*

Q Why were the United States and the Soviet Union suspicious of each other after World War II, and what events between 1945 and 1949 heightened the tensions between the two nations?

26-2 *Cold War in Asia*

Q How and why did Mao Zedong and the Communists come to power in China, and what were the Cold War implications of their triumph?

26-3 *From Confrontation to Coexistence*

Q What events led to the era of coexistence in the 1960s, and to what degree did each side contribute to the reduction in international tensions?

26-4 *An Era of Equivalence*

Q Why did the Cold War briefly flare up again in the 1980s, and why did it come to a definitive end at the end of the decade?

26.1 Winston Churchill: A Call to Arms

Imperial War Museum/The Art Archive/Picture Desk

Critical Thinking

Q *How have historians answered the question of whether the United States or the Soviet Union bears the primary responsibility for the Cold War, and what evidence can be presented on each side of the issue?*

Connections to Today

Q *Are the challenges facing the world today a product of the Cold War, or did the latter serve to distract world leaders from facing those challenges?*

ON MARCH 5, 1946, the former British prime minister and war leader Winston Churchill gave a speech before invited guests—including U.S. President Harry S. Truman—at Westminster College, in Fulton, Missouri. His remarks shook the world. Although it had been only six months since the surrender of Imperial Japan had marked the end of World War II, Churchill expressed serious foreboding about the future. The bright vision of peace and prosperity that had followed the end of the war, he warned, was threatened by the specter of a new era of confrontation among the wartime allies, three members of a grand alliance who only a year previously had pledged at Yalta and Potsdam to inaugurate a new era of global peace.

Churchill did not mince words. The threat, he declared, had been unilaterally provoked by the Soviet Union. Contrary to Stalin's commitment at Yalta to allow all peace-loving forces in Eastern Europe to take part in new national elections, Soviet occupation leaders had installed pro-Soviet regimes throughout the region and suppressed any and all political parties and groups that did not express subservience to Moscow. As a result, Churchill warned, "an iron curtain has descended across the continent" from the shores of the Baltic Sea to the Adriatic, dividing Germany and Europe itself into two hostile camps. Only the determined mutual cooperation of Moscow's two major wartime allies—the United States and the United Kingdom—could prevent the danger of an outbreak of a new war from becoming a reality. On the other side of Earth, Churchill's words ran loud and clear. In Moscow, Soviet leader Joseph Stalin retorted that Churchill's speech was nothing less than "a call to war with the Soviet Union." The Cold War had begun.

The unravelling of the Grand Alliance had not been long in coming. Within months after the German surrender, the mutual trust among the Allies—if it had ever truly existed—rapidly disintegrated, and the dream of a stable peace was replaced by the specter of a potential nuclear holocaust. The United Nations, envisioned by its founders as a mechanism for adjudicating international disputes, became mired in partisan bickering. As the Cold War between Moscow and Washington intensified, Europe was divided into two armed camps, while the two superpowers glared at each other across a deep ideological divide while holding the survival of the entire world in their hands.

26-1 THE COLLAPSE OF THE GRAND ALLIANCE

Focus Question: Why were the United States and the Soviet Union suspicious of each other after World War II, and what events between 1945 and 1949 heightened the tensions between the two nations?

As Winston Churchill had pointed out, the problems started in Europe. At the end of the war, by Allied agreement Soviet military forces occupied much of Eastern Europe and the Balkans, while U.S. and other Allied forces secured the western part of the European continent. Roosevelt had hoped that free elections, administered promptly by "democratic and peace-loving forces," would lead to democratic governments that were responsive to the local population throughout the region. But it soon became clear that the Soviet Union interpreted the Yalta agreement differently. When Soviet occupation authorities began the process of forming a new Polish government, Stalin refused to accept the Polish government in exile—which was headquartered in London during the war and composed partly of landed aristocrats who harbored a deep distrust of the Soviet Union—and instead set up a provisional government composed of Communists who had spent the war in Moscow. Just before the close of the war, noncommunist resistance forces inside Poland had initiated hostilities against the Nazi occupation regime in anticipation of assistance from approaching Soviet armies, but that assistance never came. Thousands were eventually executed by Soviet troops or security police. Roosevelt complained to Stalin about Soviet actions in Poland but eventually agreed reluctantly to a compromise whereby two members of the London government were included in the new Communist regime. A week later, Roosevelt was dead of a cerebral hemorrhage, and Stalin felt emboldened to do much as he pleased.

26-1a Soviet Domination of Eastern Europe

Similar developments took place in every state occupied by Soviet troops. Coalitions of all political parties (except fascist or right-wing parties) were formed to run governments, but the Communist Party in each coalition had assumed the lion's share of power within a year or two. Key posts in each government were occupied by loyal Communists, and members of other parties who appeared hostile to Communist rule were declared fascist and incarcerated. It was then just a short step to the establishment of one-party Communist governments. Between 1945 and 1947, Communist governments became firmly entrenched in East Germany, Bulgaria, Romania, Poland, and Hungary. In Czechoslovakia, with its strong tradition of democratic institutions, the Communists did not achieve their goals until 1948. After the Czech elections of 1946, the Communist Party shared control of the government with the non-Communist parties. When the latter appeared likely to win new elections early in 1948, the Communists seized control of the government on February 25. All other parties were dissolved, and the Communist leader Klement Gottwald (KLEM-ent GUT-vald) (1896–1953) became the new president of Czechoslovakia.

Yugoslavia was a notable exception to the pattern of Soviet dominance in Eastern Europe. The Communist Party there had led resistance to the Nazis during the war and easily assumed power when the war ended. Josip Broz (yaw-SEEP BRAWZ), known as "Tito" (TEE-toh) (1892–1980), the leader of the Communist resistance movement, appeared to be a loyal Stalinist. After the war, however, he moved to establish an independent Communist state. Stalin hoped to take control of Yugoslavia, but Tito refused to capitulate to Stalin's demands and gained the support of the people (and some sympathy in the West) by portraying the struggle as one of Yugoslav national freedom. In 1958, the Yugoslav party congress asserted that Yugoslav Communists did not see themselves as deviating from communism, only from Stalinism. They considered their more decentralized system—in which workers managed themselves and local communes exercised some political power—closer to the Marxist–Leninist ideal.

To Stalin (who had once boasted, "I will shake my little finger, and there will be no more Tito"), the creation of pliant pro-Soviet regimes throughout Eastern Europe to serve as a buffer zone against the capitalist West may simply have been his interpretation of the Yalta peace agreement as well as a reward for sacrifices suffered during the war. If the Soviet leader had any intention of promoting future Communist revolutions in Western Europe—and there is evidence that he did—such developments would have to await the appearance of a new capitalist crisis a decade or more into the future. Lenin had always maintained that revolutions come in waves, and the ever-cautious Stalin was willing to wait for the next one to come along.

26-1b Descent of the Iron Curtain

In any case, Stalin had no need to worry: the United States was in no mood to take direct action to prevent Soviet domination of Eastern Europe. Although public suspicion of Moscow's intentions grew rapidly, especially among the millions of Americans who had relatives living in the region, the desire for peace was strong within the war-weary public, who wanted no more than to "bring the boys home" from abroad. Winston Churchill's stirring words in Fulton, Missouri, were clearly aimed at warning the American people that a return to isolationism would be a dangerous error.

As it turned out, the first threat of a direct U.S.–Soviet confrontation took place in the Middle East. During World War II, British and Soviet troops had been stationed in Iran to prevent Axis occupation of that country's rich oil fields. Both nations had promised to withdraw their forces after

Map 26.1 Eastern Europe in 1948

the war, but at the end of 1945 there were ominous signs that Moscow might attempt to use its troops as a bargaining chip to annex Iran's northern territories—known as Azerbaijan (az-ur-by-JAHN)—into the Soviet Union. When the government of Iran, with strong U.S. support, threatened to take the issue to the United Nations, the Soviets backed down and removed their forces from that country in the spring of 1946.

26-1c The Truman Doctrine

A civil war in Greece created another potential arena for confrontation between the superpowers and a challenge for the Truman administration to take a stand. The president agreed with Churchill on the need for unity among democratic nations in the face of the Soviet threat, and the opportunity to act appeared when guerrilla forces supported by Marshall Tito took up arms against the pro-Western government in Athens. The British had initially assumed primary responsibility for promoting postwar reconstruction in the eastern Mediterranean, but in 1947 economic problems caused the Labour government of Prime Minister Clement Attlee to withdraw from the active role it had been playing in both Greece and Turkey. Alarmed by British weakness and the danger of Soviet expansion into the eastern Mediterranean, the White House responded with the **Truman Doctrine**, according to which the United States would provide financial aid to countries that were threatened by Communist expansion (see Historical Voices, "The Truman Doctrine," p. 657). If the Soviets were not stopped in Greece, Truman argued, then the United States would have to confront the spread of communism throughout the free world. As Dean Acheson, the U.S. secretary of state, explained, "Like apples in a barrel infected by disease, the corruption of Greece would infect Iran and all the East . . . likewise Africa . . . Italy . . . France. . . . Not since Rome and Carthage has there been such a polarization of power on this earth."[1]

The somewhat apocalyptic tone of Acheson's statement was intentional. Not only were the American people in no mood for foreign adventures, but also members of the U.S. Congress—in Republican hands for the first time in a decade—were in an isolationist frame of mind. Only the prospect of a dire threat from abroad, the president's advisers concluded, could persuade the nation to take action. The tactic worked, and Congress voted to provide the aid Truman had requested.

The Truman Doctrine

 Politics & Government **IN 1947, THE BATTLE LINES IN THE COLD WAR** had been clearly drawn. This excerpt is taken from a speech by President Harry Truman to the U.S. Congress in which he justified his request for aid to Greece and Turkey. Truman expressed the urgent need to contain the expansion of communism.

Truman's Speech to Congress, March 12, 1947

The peoples of a number of countries of the world have recently had totalitarian regimes forced upon them against their will. The Government of the United States has made frequent protests against coercion and intimidation, in violation of the Yalta agreement, in Poland, Rumania, and Bulgaria. I must also state that in a number of other countries there have been similar developments.

At the present moment in world history nearly every nation must choose between alternative ways of life. The choice is too often not a free one.

One way of life is based upon the will of the majority, and is distinguished by free institutions, representative government, free elections, guarantees of individual liberty, freedom of speech and religion, and freedom from political oppression.

The second way of life is based upon the will of a minority forcibly imposed upon the majority. It relies upon terror and oppression, a controlled press and radio, fixed elections, and the suppression of personal freedoms.

I believe that it must be the policy of the United States to support free peoples who are resisting attempted subjugation by armed minorities or by outside pressures.

I believe that we must assist free peoples to work out their own destinies in their own way.

I believe that our help should be primarily through economic and financial aid which is essential to economic stability and orderly political processes. . . . I therefore ask the Congress for assistance to Greece and Turkey in the amount of $400,000,000.

Q *How did President Truman defend his request for aid to Greece and Turkey? What role did this decision play in intensifying the Cold War?*

Source: From U.S. Congress, Congressional Record, 80th Congress, 1st Session (Washington, D.C.: U.S. Government Printing Office, 1947), Vol. 93, p. 1981.

As it turned out, the administration's suspicion that Moscow was actively supporting the insurgent movement in Greece was unfounded. Stalin was actually unhappy with Tito's role in promoting the conflict, not only because he suspected that the latter was attempting to create his own sphere of influence in the Balkans, but also because it risked provoking a direct confrontation between Moscow and Washington in an area that was clearly within the Western sphere of influence. "The rebellion in Greece," Stalin declared, "must be crushed."[2]

26-1d The Marshall Plan

The White House, however, was unaware of Stalin's cautious stance and, with public concern in the United States about Soviet intentions at new heights, the proclamation of the Truman Doctrine was followed in June 1947 by the European Recovery Program, better known as the **Marshall Plan**, which provided $13 billion in U.S. assistance for the economic recovery of war-torn Europe. Underlying the program was the belief that the economic recovery of Europe would insulate the peoples of that continent against the appeal of international communism.

From the Soviet perspective, the Marshall Plan was another example of capitalist imperialism, a thinly veiled attempt to buy the support of the smaller European countries for a U.S. effort to encircle the Soviet Union. A Soviet spokesperson described the United States as the "main force in the imperialist camp" whose ultimate goal was "the strengthening of imperialism, preparation for a new imperialist war, a struggle against socialism and democracy, and the support of reactionary and antidemocratic, profascist regimes and movements." Although the White House declared that the Marshall Plan was open to the Soviet Union and its Eastern European satellite states, Soviet leaders viewed the offer as a devious capitalist ploy and refused to participate. Under heavy pressure from Moscow, Eastern European governments did so as well. The Soviets were in no position to compete financially with the United States, however, and could do little to counter the Marshall Plan except tighten their control in Eastern Europe.

26-1e Europe Divided

By 1947, the split in Europe between East and West had become a fact of life. At the end of World War II, the United States had favored a quick end to its commitments in Europe. But American fears of Soviet aims caused the United States to play an increasingly important role in European affairs. In an article in *Foreign Affairs* in July 1947, George Kennan, a well-known U.S. diplomat with much knowledge of Soviet affairs, advocated a policy of **containment** against further aggressive Soviet moves. Kennan favored the "adroit and vigilant application of counter-force at a series of constantly shifting geographical and political points, corresponding to the shifts and maneuvers of Soviet policy." When the Soviets blockaded Berlin in 1948, containment of the Soviet Union became formal U.S. policy.

The Berlin Blockade   The fate of Germany had become a source of heated contention between East and West. Aside from **denazification** (dee-naht-sih-fuh-KAY-shun) and the partitioning of Germany (and Berlin) into four occupied zones (Soviet, U.S., British, and French), the Allied Powers had agreed on little with regard to the conquered nation. The Soviet Union, hardest hit by the war, took reparations from Germany by pillaging German industry. By the summer of 1946, 200 chemical, paper, and textile factories in the East German zone had been shipped to the Soviet Union. At the same time, the German Communist Party—vigorously suppressed under the Nazi regime—was reestablished under the control of veteran apparatchik Walter Ulbricht (VAHL-tuh OOL-brikkt) (1893–1973), and it was soon in charge of the political reconstruction of the Soviet zone in eastern Germany.

Although the foreign ministers of the four occupying powers kept meeting in an attempt to arrive at a final peace treaty with Germany, they moved further and further apart. At the same time, the British, French, and the United States gradually began to merge their zones economically and by February 1948 drew up plans for the formation of a national government. In an effort to secure all of Berlin and halt the creation of a West German government, the Soviet Union imposed a blockade of West Berlin that prevented all land traffic from entering the city's western zones through Soviet-controlled territory in East Germany.

The Western powers faced a dilemma. Direct military confrontation seemed dangerous, and no one wished to risk World War III. Therefore, an attempt to break

Map 26.2 Berlin at the Start of the Cold War

through the blockade with tanks and trucks was ruled out. The solution was to deliver supplies for the city's inhabitants by plane. At its peak, the Berlin Airlift flew thirteen thousand tons of supplies daily into Berlin. The Soviets, also not wanting war, did not interfere and finally lifted the blockade in May 1949. The blockade of Berlin had severely increased tensions between the United States and the Soviet Union and brought about the separation of Germany into two states. The Federal Republic of Germany (FRG) was formally created from the three Western zones in September 1949, and a month later the separate German Democratic Republic (GDR) was established in East Germany. Berlin remained a divided city and the source of much contention between East and West.

Nato and the Warsaw Pact   The search for security in the new world of the Cold War also led to the formation of military alliances. The North Atlantic Treaty Organization (NATO) was formed in April 1949 when Belgium, Denmark, France, Great Britain, Iceland, Italy, Luxembourg, the Netherlands, Norway, and Portugal signed a treaty with the United States and Canada. Every power agreed to provide mutual assistance if any one of them was attacked. A few years later, Greece, Turkey, and West Germany joined NATO.

Moscow and its new Eastern European allies soon followed suit. In 1949, they formed the Council for Mutual Economic Assistance (COMECON) for economic cooperation. Then in 1955, Albania, Bulgaria, Czechoslovakia, East Germany, Hungary, Poland, Romania, and the Soviet Union organized a formal military alliance, the Warsaw Pact. Once again, Europe was tragically divided into hostile alliance systems (see Map 26.3).

HISTORIANS DEBATE

26-1f Who Started the Cold War?

There has been considerable historical debate over who bears responsibility for starting the Cold War. In the 1950s, most scholars in the West contended that the bulk of the blame must fall on the shoulders of Stalin, whose determination to impose Soviet rule on Eastern Europe snuffed out hopes for freedom and self-determination there and aroused justifiable fears of Communist expansion in the West. During the next decade, however, revisionist historians in the West—influenced in part by their hostility to U.S. policies in Southeast Asia—began to argue that the fault lay primarily in

Keystone/Hulton Archives/Getty Images

26.2 A City Divided. In 1948, U.S. planes airlifted supplies into Berlin to break the blockade that Soviet troops had imposed to isolate the city. Shown here is Checkpoint Charlie, which was located at the boundary between the U.S. and Soviet zones of Berlin, just as Soviet roadblocks are about to be removed. The banner at the entrance to the Soviet sector ironically reads, "The sector of freedom greets the fighters for freedom and right of the Western sectors."

Washington, where Truman and his anti-Communist advisers abandoned the precepts of Yalta and sought to encircle the Soviet Union with a tier of pliant U.S. client states. More recently, many historians have adopted a more nuanced view, noting that both the United States and the Soviet Union took unwise steps that contributed to rising tensions at the end of World War II.

The root of the problem was that both nations were working within a framework conditioned by the past. The rivalry between the two superpowers ultimately stemmed from their different historical perspectives and irreconcilable political ambitions. As we have seen, intense competition for political and military supremacy had long been a regular feature of Western civilization. The United States and the Soviet Union were heirs to that European tradition of power politics, and it should come as no surprise that two such different systems would seek to extend their way of life to the rest of the world. Because of its need to secure its western border, the Soviet Union was not prepared to give up the advantages it had gained in Eastern Europe

from Germany's defeat. But neither were Western leaders prepared to accept without protest the establishment of a system of Soviet satellites that not only threatened the security of Western Europe but also deeply offended Western sensibilities because of its blatant disregard of the Western concept of human rights.

This does not necessarily mean that both sides bear equal responsibility for starting the Cold War. Some revisionist historians have claimed that the U.S. doctrine of containment was an unnecessarily provocative action that aroused Stalin's suspicions and drove him into a position of hostility toward the West. This charge lacks credibility. Although the Soviets were understandably concerned that the United States might use its monopoly of nuclear weapons to attempt to intimidate them (Stalin himself was quoted as saying that the atomic bomb was "a good weapon for threatening people with weak nerves"), information now available from the Soviet archives makes it increasingly clear that Stalin's suspicions of the West were rooted in his Marxist–Leninist worldview and long predated Washington's enunciation of the doctrine of containment.[3] As his foreign minister, Vyacheslav Molotov, once remarked, Soviet policy was inherently aggressive and would be triggered whenever the opportunity offered. Although Stalin apparently had no master plan to advance Soviet power into Western Europe, he was undoubtedly prepared to make every effort to do so once the next revolutionary wave arrived. Under the circumstances, Western leaders were fully justified in reacting to this possibility by strengthening their own lines of defense.

On the other hand, a case can be made that in deciding to respond to the Soviet challenge in a primarily military manner, Western leaders overreacted and virtually guaranteed that the Cold War would be transformed into an arms race that could conceivably result in a new and uniquely destructive war. George Kennan, the original architect of the doctrine of containment, had initially proposed a primarily political approach and eventually disavowed the means by which the containment strategy was carried out.

Map 26.3 **The New European Alliance Systems During the Cold War.** This map shows postwar Europe as it was divided during the Cold War into two contending power blocs, the NATO alliance and the Warsaw Pact. Major military and naval bases are indicated by symbols on the map.

Q *Where on the map was the "Iron Curtain"?*

26-2 COLD WAR IN ASIA

Focus Question: How and why did Mao Zedong and the Communists come to power in China, and what were the Cold War implications of their triumph?

The Cold War was somewhat slower to make its appearance in Asia. At Yalta, Stalin had formally agreed to enter the Pacific War against Japan three months after the close of the conflict with Germany. As a reward for Soviet participation in the struggle against Japan, Roosevelt promised that Moscow would be granted "preeminent interests" in Manchuria (reminiscent of the interests possessed by imperial Russia before its defeat by Japan in 1904–1905) and be allowed to establish a Soviet naval base at Port Arthur. In return, Stalin promised to sign a treaty of alliance with the Republic of China (ROC), thus implicitly committing the Soviet Union not to aid the Chinese Communists in a possible future civil war. Although many observers would later question Stalin's sincerity in making such a commitment to the vocally anti-Communist Chiang Kai-shek, for Moscow the decision probably had a logic of its own. Stalin had no particular liking for the independent-minded Mao Zedong and indeed did not anticipate an early Communist victory in any civil war in China. Only an agreement with Chiang could provide the Soviet Union with a strategically vital economic and political presence in northern China.

The Truman administration was equally reluctant to get embroiled in a confrontation with Moscow over the unfolding events in East Asia. Doubts about Chiang Kai-shek's prospects ran high in Washington, and as we shall see, many key U.S. policy makers hoped to avoid a deeper involvement in China by brokering a compromise agreement between Chiang and his Communist rival, Mao. Despite these commitments, the Allied agreements soon broke down, and East Asia was sucked into the vortex of the Cold War by the end of the 1940s. The root of the problem lay in the underlying weakness of Chiang's regime, which threatened to create a political vacuum in East Asia that both Moscow and Mao Zedong's Communist forces headquartered in Yan'an would be tempted to fill.

26-2a The Chinese Civil War

As World War II came to an end in the Pacific, relations between the government of Chiang Kai-shek and its powerful U.S. ally had become frayed. Although Roosevelt had hoped that the ROC would be the keystone of his plan for peace and stability in Asia after the war, U.S. officials became disillusioned with the corruption of Chiang's government and his unwillingness to risk his forces against the Japanese

(Chiang hoped to save them for use against the Communists after the war in the Pacific ended). Hence, China was no longer the object of Washington's close attention as the war came to a close. Nevertheless, U.S. military and economic aid to China had been substantial, and at the war's end the new Truman administration still hoped it could rely on Chiang to support U.S. postwar goals in the region.

While Chiang Kai-shek wrestled with Japanese aggression and problems of national development, the Communists were building up their strength in northern China. To enlarge their political base, they carried out a "mass line" policy (a term in Communist jargon that meant responding to the needs of the mass of the population), reducing land rents and confiscating the lands of wealthy landlords. By the end of World War II, 20 million to 30 million Chinese citizens were living under the administration of the Communists, and their People's Liberation Army (PLA), as it was now called, included nearly 1 million troops.

As the war came to an end, world attention began to focus on the prospects for renewed civil strife in China. Members of a U.S. liaison team stationed in Yan'an (yuh-NAHN) were impressed by the performance of the Communists, and some recommended that the United States should support them or at least remain neutral in a possible conflict between Communists and Nationalists for control of China. The Truman administration, though skeptical of Chiang's ability to forge a strong and prosperous country, felt that it was necessary to keep the ROC in power in China and hoped to work out a peaceful solution through the formation of a multiparty coalition government under Chiang Kai-shek's leadership.

The Communist Triumph From the outset, the chances for success appeared doubtful. By 1946, full-scale war between the Nationalist government (now reinstalled in Nanjing) and the Communists resumed. Initially, most of the fighting took place in Manchuria, which had been occupied during the war by Japanese troops. As the war came to an end, newly arrived Communist units began to surround Nationalist forces who had been sent north to occupy the major cities. Now Chiang Kai-shek's errors came home to roost. In the countryside, millions of peasants had become attracted to the Communists by promises of land and social justice and flocked to serve under their banners. In the cities, middle-class Chinese, normally hostile to communism, were alienated by Chiang's brutal suppression of all dissent and his government's inability to slow the ruinous rate of inflation or solve the economic problems it caused. By the end of 1947, almost all of Manchuria was under Communist control (see Map 26.4).

The Truman administration reacted to the spread of Communist power in China with acute discomfort.

Experience an interactive version of this period in ✷ MINDTAP

Map 26.4 **The Chinese Civil War.** After the close of the Pacific war in 1945, the Nationalist Chinese government and the Chinese Communists fought a bitter civil war that ended with a Communist victory in 1949. The path of the Communist advance is shown on the map.

Q *Where did Chiang Kai-shek's government retreat to after its defeat?*

Washington had no desire to see a Communist government on the mainland, but it had little confidence in Chiang Kai-shek's ability to realize Roosevelt's dream of a strong, united, and prosperous China. In December 1945, President Truman sent General George C. Marshall to China in a last-ditch effort to bring about a peaceful settlement, but anti-Communist elements in the Republic of China resisted U.S. pressure to create a coalition government with the Chinese Communist Party (CCP). During the next two years, the United States gave limited military support to Chiang's regime but refused to commit U.S. power to guarantee its survival. The administration's hands-off policy deeply angered many members of Congress, who charged that the White House was "soft on communism" and called for increased military assistance to the Nationalist government.

With morale dropping in the cities, Chiang's troops began to defect to the Communists. Sometimes whole divisions, officers as well as ordinary soldiers, changed sides. By 1948, the PLA was advancing south out of Manchuria and had encircled Beijing. Communist troops took the old imperial

26.3 **Mao Zedong and Chiang Kai-shek Exchange a Toast.** After World War II, the United States sent General George C. Marshall to China in an effort to prevent civil war between Chiang Kai-shek's government and Mao Zedong's Communists. Marshall's initial success was symbolized by this toast between Mao (at the left) and Chiang. But suspicion ran too deep, and soon conflict ensued, leading to a Communist victory in 1949. Chiang's government retreated to the island of Taiwan. Today the Communist government in China offers qualified praise for Chiang Kai-shek for his steadfast resistance to the Japanese during World War II.

Who Lost China?

Politics & Government

IN 1949, WITH CHINA ABOUT TO FALL under the control of the Communists, President Truman instructed the State Department to prepare a "white paper" report explaining why the U.S. policy of seeking to avoid a Communist victory in China had failed. The authors of the paper concluded that responsibility lay at the door of Nationalist Chinese leader Chiang Kai-shek and that there was nothing the United States could have done to alter the result. Most China observers today would accept that assessment, but it did little at the time to deflect criticism of the administration for "selling out" the interests of our ally in China.

U.S. State Department White Paper on China, 1949

When peace came the United States was confronted with three possible alternatives in China: (1) it could have pulled out lock, stock, and barrel; (2) it could have intervened militarily on a major scale to assist the Nationalists to destroy the Communists; and (3) it could, while assisting the Nationalists to assert their authority over as much of China as possible, endeavor to avoid a civil war by working for a compromise between the two sides.

The first alternative would, and I believe American public opinion at the time so felt, have represented an abandonment of our international responsibilities and of our traditional policy of friendship for China before we had made a determined effort to be of assistance. The second alternative policy, while it may look attractive theoretically, in retrospect, was wholly impracticable. The Nationalists had been unable to destroy the Communists during the ten years before the war. Now after the war the Nationalists were . . . weakened, demoralized, and unpopular. They had quickly dissipated their popular support and prestige in the areas liberated from the Japanese by the conduct of their civil and military officials.

The Communists on the other hand were much stronger than they had ever been and were in control of most of North China. Because of the ineffectiveness of the Nationalist forces, which was later to be tragically demonstrated, the Communists probably could have been dislodged only by American arms. It is obvious that the American people would not have sanctioned such a colossal commitment of our armies in 1945 or later. We therefore came to the third alternative policy whereunder we faced the facts of the situation and attempted to assist in working out a modus vivendi which would avert civil war but nevertheless preserve and even increase the influence of the National Government. . . .

The distrust of the leaders of both the Nationalist and Communist Parties for each other proved too deep-seated to permit final agreement, notwithstanding temporary truces and apparently promising negotiations. The Nationalists, furthermore, embarked in 1946 on an overambitious military campaign in the face of warnings by General Marshall that it not only would fail but would plunge China into economic chaos and eventually destroy the National Government. . . .

The unfortunate but inescapable fact is that the ominous result of the civil war in China was beyond the control of the government of the United States. Nothing that this country did or could have done within the reasonable limits of its capabilities could have changed that result; nothing that was left undone by this country has contributed to it. It was the product of internal Chinese forces, forces which this country tried to influence but could not. A decision was arrived at within China, if only a decision by default.

Q *How did the authors of the white paper explain the Communist victory in China? According to this argument, what actions might have prevented it?*

Source: From *United States Relations with China* (Washington, D.C., Dept. of State, 1949), pp. iii–xvi.

---

capital, crossed the Yangzi the following spring, and occupied the commercial hub of Shanghai (see Map 26.4). During the next few months, Chiang's government and 2 million of his followers fled to Taiwan, which the Japanese had returned to Chinese control after World War II. From the imperial gate in front of the Forbidden City, Party Chairman Mao Zedong declared the formation of a new People's Republic of China (PRC), with its capital at Beijing.

With the Communist victory in China, Asia became a major theater of the Cold War and an integral element in American politics. In a white paper issued by the Department of State in the fall of 1949, the Truman administration placed most of the blame for the debacle on Chiang Kai-shek's regime (see Historical Voices, "Who Lost China?"). Republicans in Congress, however, disagreed, arguing that Roosevelt had betrayed Chiang

Kai-shek at Yalta by granting privileges in Manchuria to the Soviet Union. In their view, Soviet troops had hindered the dispatch of Nationalist forces to the area and provided the PLA with weapons to use against their rivals.

In later years, sources in Moscow and Beijing made it clear that the Soviet Union actually provided little assistance to the CCP in its postwar struggle against the Nanjing regime. In fact, Stalin—probably concerned at the prospect of a military confrontation with the United States—advised Mao against undertaking the effort. Although PLA forces undoubtedly received some assistance from Soviet occupation troops in Manchuria, their victory ultimately stemmed from conditions inside China. Nevertheless, the White House felt required to respond to the charge by critics that it was ignoring the Communist threat in Asia. During the spring of 1950, under pressure from Congress and public opinion to define U.S. interests in Asia, the Truman administration adopted a new national security policy that implied the United States would take whatever steps were necessary to stem the further expansion of communism in the region. Containment had come to East Asia.

26-2b The New China

From their new capital of Beijing, China's Communist leaders probably hoped that their accession to power in 1949 would bring about at least a temporary reduction of tensions in the region and permit their new government to concentrate on domestic goals. But their desire for peace was tempered by their determination to erase a century of humiliation at the hands of imperialist powers and to restore the traditional outer frontiers of the empire. In addition to recovering territories that had been part of the Qing Empire such as Manchuria, Taiwan, Tibet, and Xinjiang (SHIN-jyahng)—the desolate region that had recently come under the influence of Imperial Russia—the new regime in Beijing also hoped to restore Chinese influence in former tributary areas such as Korea and Vietnam.

It soon became clear that these two goals were not always compatible. Negotiations between Mao and Stalin were held in Moscow in January 1950. Although tense, they led to grudging Soviet recognition of Chinese sovereignty over Manchuria and Xinjiang (SHIN-jyahng), although the Soviets managed to retain a measure of economic influence in both areas. Chinese troops occupied Tibet in 1950 and brought it under Chinese administration for the first time in more than a century. But in Korea and Taiwan, China's efforts to re-create the imperial buffer zone offshore were more complicated and threatened to provoke new conflicts with foreign powers (see Image 26.4).

26.4 **A Pledge of Eternal Friendship.** After the Communist victory in the Chinese civil war, Chairman Mao Zedong traveled to Moscow, where in 1950 he negotiated a treaty of friendship and cooperation with the Soviet Union. The poster shown here trumpets the results of the meeting: "Long live and strengthen the unbreakable friendship and cooperation of the Soviet and Chinese peoples!" The two leaders, however, did not get along. Mao reportedly complained to colleagues that obtaining assistance from Stalin was "like taking meat from a tiger's mouth."

The problem of Taiwan was a consequence of the Cold War. As the civil war in China came to an end, the Truman administration appeared determined to avoid entanglement in China's internal affairs and initially indicated that it would not seek to prevent a Communist takeover of the island, although it had now become the headquarters of Chiang Kai-shek's Republic of China. But as tensions between the United States and the new government in Beijing escalated during the winter of 1949–1950, influential figures in the United States began to argue that Taiwan was crucial to U.S. defense strategy in the Pacific.

26-2c The Korean War

The sudden outbreak of war in Korea was the final step that brought the Cold War to East Asia. After the Sino–Japanese War in 1894–1895, long-time Chinese tributary Korea had fallen increasingly under the rival influences of Japan and Russia. After the Japanese defeated the Russians in 1905, Korea became an integral part of the Japanese empire and remained so until 1945. Japanese rule had been deeply unpopular, and the removal of Korea from Japanese control became one of the stated objectives of the Allies in World War II. On the eve of the Japanese surrender in August 1945, the Soviet Union and the United States agreed to divide the country into two separate occupation zones at the 38th parallel. They originally planned to hold national elections after the restoration of peace to reunify Korea under an independent government, but as U.S.–Soviet relations deteriorated, two separate governments emerged in Korea, a Communist-led Democratic People's Republic of Korea in the north and an anti-Communist Republic of Korea in the south.

Tensions between the two governments ran high along the dividing line, and with the apparent approval of Stalin, North Korean troops invaded the south on June 25, 1950. The Truman administration immediately ordered U.S. naval and air forces to support South Korea, and the United Nations Security Council (with the Soviet delegate absent to protest the United Nation's refusal to assign China's seat to the new government in Beijing) passed a resolution calling on member nations to jointly resist the invasion, a measure in line with the security provisions of the United Nations Charter. By September, UN forces under the command of U.S. General Douglas MacArthur marched northward across the 38th parallel with the aim of unifying Korea under a single, non-Communist government.

President Truman worried that by approaching the Chinese border at the Yalu (YAH-loo) River, the UN troops could trigger Chinese intervention, but MacArthur assured him that China would not respond. In November, however, Chinese "volunteer" forces intervened in force on the side of North Korea and drove the UN troops southward in disarray. A static defense line was eventually established near the original dividing line at the 38th parallel (see Map 26.5), although the war continued.

To U.S. officials, the outbreak of war in Korea—along with a buildup of PLA forces on the mainland across from Taiwan—was clear evidence that China intended to promote communism throughout Asia. To counter such a possibility, President Truman dispatched the U.S. Seventh Fleet to the Taiwan Strait to prevent a possible Chinese invasion of the island. In Beijing, however, the decision to enter the war in Korea was probably motivated primarily by the fear that hostile U.S. forces might be stationed on the Chinese frontier and perhaps even launch an attack across the border. MacArthur intensified such fears by calling publicly for air attacks on Manchurian cities in preparation for an attack on Communist China.

The consequences of the Korean War were particularly unfortunate for China. The war not only hardened Western attitudes against the new regime and led to China's isolation from the major capitalist powers for two decades but also strengthened the U.S. commitment to the Nationalist

Map 26.5 The Korean Peninsula. With tensions between the two Koreas on the rise, North Korean forces crossed the 38th parallel in a sudden invasion of the south in June 1950. Shown here is the cease-fire line that brought an end to the war in 1953.

Q *What is the significance of the Yalu River in the Cold War?*

government in Taiwan as the only legal representative of the Chinese people and led the Truman administration to support its retention of China's seat on the UN Security Council. As a result, China was cut off from all forms of economic and technological assistance and was forced to rely almost entirely on the Soviet Union, with which it had signed a pact of friendship and cooperation in early 1950.

26-2d Conflict in Indochina

During the mid-1950s, China sought to build contacts with the nonsocialist world. A cease-fire agreement brought the Korean War to a de facto end in July 1953, and China signaled its desire to live in peaceful coexistence with other independent countries in the region. But a relatively minor conflict now began to intensify on China's southern flank in French Indochina. The struggle had begun after World War II when the Indochinese Communist Party led by Ho Chi Minh (HOH CHEE MIN) (1890–1969), at the head of a multiparty nationalist alliance called the Vietminh (vee-et-MIN) Front, seized power in northern and central Vietnam.

After abortive negotiations between Hô's government and the returning French, war broke out in December 1946. French forces occupied the cities and the densely populated lowlands while the Vietminh took refuge in the mountains.

For three years, the Vietminh waged a "people's war" of national liberation from colonial rule, gradually increasing in size and effectiveness. At the time, however, the conflict in Indochina attracted relatively little attention from world leaders, who viewed the events there as only one aspect of the transition to independence of colonial territories in postwar Asia. The Truman administration was uneasy about Hô's long-standing credentials as a Soviet agent but was equally reluctant to anger anticolonialist elements in the region by intervening on behalf of the French. Moscow had even less interest in the issue. Stalin—still hoping to see the Communist Party come to power in Paris—ignored Hô's request for recognition of his movement as the legitimate representative of the national interests of the Vietnamese people.

But what had begun as an anticolonial struggle by the Vietminh Front against the French became entangled in the Cold War after the CCP came to power in China. In early 1950, Beijing began to provide military assistance to the Vietminh to burnish its revolutionary credentials and protect its own borders from hostile forces. The Truman administration, increasingly concerned that a revolutionary "Red tide" was sweeping through the region, decided to provide financial and technical assistance to the French while pressuring them to prepare for an eventual transition to independent non-Communist governments in Vietnam, Laos, and Cambodia.

Despite growing U.S. involvement in the war, Vietminh forces continued to gain strength. With casualties mounting and the French public tired of fighting the "dirty war" in Indochina, the French had agreed to hold peace talks with the Vietminh in May 1954. The day before the peace conference convened in Geneva, Switzerland, Vietminh forces overran the French bastion at Dien Bien Phu, which was close to the border with Laos. The humiliating defeat weakened French resolve to maintain a presence in Indochina. In July, the two sides agreed to a settlement. Vietnam was temporarily divided into a Communist northern half known as the Democratic Republic of Vietnam (DRV) and a non-Communist southern

Map 26.6 Indochina After 1954

half based in Saigon (sy-GAHN) (now Ho Chi Minh City) that eventually came to be known as the Republic of Vietnam (RVN). A demilitarized zone separated the two at the 17th parallel. Elections were to be held two years later to create a unified government. Cambodia and Laos were both declared independent under neutral governments, and French forces were withdrawn from all three countries (see Map 26.6).

China had played an active role in bringing about the settlement and clearly hoped it would reduce tensions in the area, but subsequent efforts to improve relations between China and the United States foundered on the issue of Taiwan. In the fall of 1954, the United States signed a mutual security treaty with the Republic of China guaranteeing U.S. military support in case of an invasion of Taiwan. When Beijing demanded U.S. withdrawal from Taiwan as the price for improved relations, diplomatic talks between the two countries collapsed.

26-3 FROM CONFRONTATION TO COEXISTENCE

Q **Focus Question:** What events led to the era of coexistence in the 1960s, and to what degree did each side contribute to the reduction in international tensions?

The decade of the 1950s opened with the world teetering on the edge of a nuclear holocaust. The Soviet Union had detonated its first nuclear device in 1949, and the two great global blocs—capitalist and socialist—viewed each other across an ideological divide that grew increasingly bitter with each passing year. Yet as the decade drew to a close, a measure of sanity crept into the Cold War, and the leaders of the major world powers began to seek ways to coexist in a peaceful and stable world (see Map 26.7).

The first clear sign of change occurred after Stalin's death in early 1953. His successor, Georgy Malenkov (gyee-OR-gyee muh-LENkawf) (1902–1988), openly hoped to improve relations with the Western powers in order to reduce defense expenditures and shift government spending to growing consumer needs. Nikita Khrushchev (nuh-KEE-tuh KHROOSH-chawf) (1894–1971), who replaced

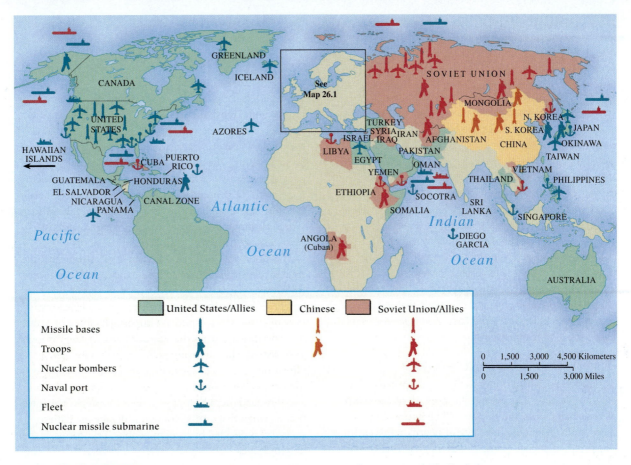

Map 26.7 The Global Cold War. This map shows the location of the major military bases and missile sites maintained by the three contending power blocs at the height of the Cold War.

Q *Which continents were the most heavily armed? Why?*

Malenkov in 1955, continued his predecessor's efforts to reduce tensions with the West and improve the living standards of the Soviet people.

In an adroit public relations touch, in 1956 Khrushchev promoted an appeal for a policy of **peaceful coexistence** with the West (see Historical Voices, "A Plea for Peaceful Coexistence," p. 668). In 1955, he had surprisingly agreed to negotiate an end to the postwar occupation of Austria by the victorious allies and allow the creation of a neutral country with strong cultural and economic ties with the West. He also called for a reduction in defense expenditures and reduced the size of the Soviet armed forces.

26-3a Ferment in Eastern Europe

At first, Western leaders were suspicious of Khrushchev's motives, especially in light of events that were taking place in Eastern Europe. For Moscow, the key to security along the western frontier of the Soviet Union was the string of Eastern European satellite states that had been assembled in the aftermath of World War II (see Map 26.3). Once Communist domination had been ensured, a series of "little Stalins" put into power by Moscow instituted Soviet-type five-year plans that emphasized heavy industry rather than consumer goods, the collectivization of agriculture, and the nationalization of industry. They also appropriated the political tactics that Stalin had perfected in the Soviet Union, eliminating all non-Communist parties and establishing the classical institutions of repression—the secret police and military forces. Dissidents were tracked down and thrown into prison, and "national Communists" who resisted total subservience to the Soviet Union were charged with treason in mass show trials and executed.

Despite these repressive efforts, discontent became increasingly evident in several Eastern European countries. Hungary, Poland, and Romania harbored bitter

A Plea for Peaceful Coexistence

Interaction & Exchange

SOVIET LEADER VLADIMIR LENIN had contended that war between the socialist and imperialist camps was inevitable because the imperialists would never give up without a fight. That assumption had probably guided Joseph Stalin, who told colleagues shortly after World War II that a new war would break out in fifteen to twenty years. But Stalin's successor, Nikita Khrushchev, feared that a new world conflict could result in a nuclear holocaust and contended that the two sides must learn to coexist, although peaceful competition would continue. In this speech given in Beijing in 1959, Khrushchev attempted to persuade the Chinese to accept his views. But Chinese leaders argued that the "imperialist nature" of the United States would never change and countered that the crucial area of competition was in the Third World, where "people's wars" would bring down the structure of imperialism.

Khrushchev's Speech to the Chinese, 1959

Comrades! Socialism brings to the people peace— that greatest blessing. The greater the strength of the camp of socialism grows, the greater will be its possibilities for successfully defending the cause of peace on this earth. The forces of socialism are already so great that real possibilities are being created for excluding war as a means of solving international disputes. . . .

When I spoke with President Eisenhower— and I have just returned from the United States of America—I got the impression that the President of the U.S.A.—and not a few people support him—understands the need to relax international tension. . . .

There is only one way of preserving peace—that is the road of peaceful coexistence of states with different social systems. The question stands thus: either peaceful coexistence or war with its catastrophic consequences. Now, with the present relation of forces between socialism and capitalism being in favor of socialism, he who would continue the "cold war" is moving towards his own destruction. . . .

It is not at all because capitalism is still strong that the socialist countries speak out against war, and for peaceful coexistence. No, we have no need of war at all. If the people do not want it, even such a noble and progressive system as socialism cannot be imposed by force of arms. The socialist countries therefore, while carrying through a consistently peace-loving policy, concentrate their efforts on peaceful construction; they fire the hearts of men by the force of their example in building socialism, and thus lead them to follow in their footsteps. The question of when this or that country will take the path to socialism is decided by its own people. This, for us, is the holy of holies.

Q *Why did Nikita Khrushchev feel that the conflict between the socialist and capitalist camps that Lenin had predicted was no longer inevitable?*

Source: Khrushchev's Speech to the Chinese, 1959. From G. F. Hudson et al., eds., *The Sino–Soviet Dispute* (New York: Frederick Praeger, 1961), pp. 61–63, cited in *Peking Review*, No. 40, 1959.

---

memories of past Russian domination and suspected that Stalin, under the guise of proletarian internationalism, was seeking to revive the empire of the tsars. For the vast majority of peoples in Eastern Europe, the imposition of so-called people's democracies (a term invented by Moscow to refer to societies in the early stage of socialist transition) resulted in economic hardship and severe threats to the most basic political liberties. The first indications of unrest appeared in East Berlin, where popular riots broke out against Communist rule in 1953. The riots eventually subsided, but the virus had spread to neighboring countries.

In Poland, public demonstrations against an increase in food prices in 1956 escalated into widespread protests against the regime's economic policies, restrictions on the freedom of Catholics to practice their religion, and the continued presence of Soviet troops (as called for by the Warsaw Pact) on Polish soil. In a desperate effort to defuse the unrest, the party turned to Wladyslaw Gomulka (vlah-DIS-lahf goh-MOOL-kuh) (1905–1982), a popular figure who had previously been demoted for his "nationalist" tendencies. When Gomulka took steps to ease the crisis, Khrushchev flew to Warsaw to warn him against adopting policies that could undermine the political dominance of the party and weaken security links with the Soviet Union. After a tense confrontation, Poland agreed to remain in the Warsaw Pact and to maintain the sanctity of party rule; in return, Gomulka was authorized to adopt domestic reforms, such as easing restrictions on religious practice and ending the policy of forced collectivization in rural areas.

The Hungarian Revolution The developments in Poland sent shock waves throughout the region. The impact was strongest in neighboring Hungary, where the methods of the local "little Stalin," Mátyás Rákosi (MAH-tyash RAH-koh-see) (1892–1971), were so brutal that he had been summoned to Moscow for a lecture. In late October 1956, student-led popular riots broke out in the capital of Budapest and soon spread to other towns and villages throughout the country. Rákosi was forced to resign and was replaced by Imre Nagy (IM-ray NAHJ) (1896–1958), a national Communist who attempted to satisfy popular demands without arousing the anger of Moscow. Unlike Gomulka, however, Nagy was unable to contain the zeal of leading members of the protest movement, who sought major political reforms and the withdrawal of Hungary from the Warsaw Pact. On November 1, Nagy promised free elections, which would probably have brought an end to Communist rule given the mood of the country. After a brief moment of uncertainty, Moscow decided on firm action. Soviet troops, recently withdrawn at Nagy's request, returned to Budapest and installed a new government under the more pliant party leader János Kádár (YAH-nush KAH-dahr) (1912–1989). As Kádár rescinded many of Nagy's measures, Nagy sought refuge in the Yugoslav embassy. A few weeks later, he left the embassy under the promise of safety but was quickly arrested, convicted of treason, and executed (see Opposing Viewpoints, "Soviet Repression in Eastern Europe: Hungary, 1956," p. 670).

Different Roads to Socialism The dramatic events in Poland and Hungary graphically demonstrated the vulnerability of the Soviet satellite system in Eastern Europe, and many observers throughout the world anticipated that the United States would intervene on behalf of freedom fighters in Hungary: after all, the Eisenhower administration had promised that it would "roll back communism," and radio broadcasts by the U.S.-sponsored Radio Liberty and Radio Free Europe had encouraged the peoples of Eastern Europe to rise up against Soviet domination. In reality, Washington was well aware that U.S. intervention could lead to nuclear war and limited itself to protests against Soviet brutality in crushing the uprising.

The year of discontent was not without consequences, however. Soviet leaders now recognized that Moscow could maintain control over its satellites in Eastern Europe only by granting them the leeway to adopt domestic policies appropriate to local conditions. Khrushchev had already embarked on this path in 1955 when he assured Tito that there were "different roads to socialism." Some Eastern European Communist leaders now took Khrushchev at his word and adopted reform programs to make socialism more palatable to their subject populations. Even Kádár,

derisively labeled the "butcher of Budapest," managed to preserve many of Nagy's reforms to allow a measure of capitalist incentive and freedom of expression in Hungary.

Crisis Over Berlin But in the late 1950s, a new crisis erupted over the status of Berlin. The Soviet Union had launched its first intercontinental ballistic missile in August 1957, arousing U.S. fears of a missile gap between the United States and the Soviet Union. Khrushchev attempted to take advantage of the U.S. frenzy over missiles to solve the problem of West Berlin, which had remained an "island of prosperity" inside the relatively poverty-stricken state of East Germany. Many East Germans sought to escape to West Germany by fleeing through West Berlin, a serious blot on the credibility of the GDR and a potential source of instability in East–West relations. In November 1958, Khrushchev announced that unless the West removed its forces from West Berlin within six months, he would turn over control of the access routes to the East Germans. Unwilling to accept an ultimatum that would have abandoned West Berlin to the Communists, U.S. President Dwight D. Eisenhower and the West stood firm, and Khrushchev eventually backed down.

Despite such periodic crises in East–West relations, there were tantalizing signs that an era of true peaceful coexistence between the two power blocs could be achieved. In 1958, Khrushchev visited the United States and had a brief but friendly encounter with President Eisenhower at Camp David, the presidential retreat in northern Maryland. To defuse tensions, the United States and the Soviet Union initiated a cultural-exchange program. While Leningrad's Kirov Ballet appeared at theaters in the United States, Benny Goodman and the film *West Side Story* played in Moscow. Yet the tensions behind

---

⊡ FILM & HISTORY

Bridge of Spies

Bridge of Spies (2015) produced by filmmaker Steven Spielberg, provides a dramatic account of the shooting down of a U.S. reconnaissance plane over the Soviet Union in 1960 and the tangled events that led to the release of pilot Francis Gary Powers two years later.

Q *How did the shooting down of the U.S. spy plane affect U.S.–Soviet relations?*

MINDTAP From Cengage See full-length Film & History feature in MindTap.

Soviet Repression in Eastern Europe: Hungary, 1956

Interaction & Exchange

DEVELOPMENTS IN POLAND IN 1956 inspired the Communist leaders of Hungary to begin to extricate their country from Soviet control. But there were limits to Khrushchev's tolerance, and he sent Soviet troops to crush Hungary's movement for independence. The first selection is a statement by the Soviet government justifying its use of troops, and the second is the brief and tragic final statement from Imre Nagy, the Hungarian leader.

Statement of the Soviet Government, October 30, 1956

The Soviet Government regards it as indispensable to make a statement in connection with the events in Hungary.

The course of the events has shown that the working people of Hungary, who have achieved great progress on the basis of their people's democratic order, correctly raise the question of the necessity of eliminating serious shortcomings in the field of economic building, the further raising of the material wellbeing of the population, and the struggle against bureaucratic excesses in the state apparatus.

However, this just and progressive movement of the working people was soon joined by forces of black reaction and counterrevolution, which are trying to take advantage of the discontent of part of the working people to undermine the foundations of the people's democratic order in Hungary and to restore the old landlord and capitalist order.

The Soviet Government and all the Soviet people deeply regret that the development of events in Hungary has led to bloodshed. On the request of the Hungarian People's Government the Soviet Government consented to the entry into Budapest of the Soviet Army units to assist the Hungarian People's Army and the Hungarian authorities to establish order in the town.

The Last Message of Imre Nagy, November 4, 1956

This fight is the fight for freedom by the Hungarian people against the Russian intervention, and it is possible that I shall only be able to stay at my post for one or two hours. The whole world will see how the Russian armed forces, contrary to all treaties and conventions, are crushing the resistance of the Hungarian people. They will also see how they are kidnapping the Prime Minister of a country which is a Member of the United Nations, taking him from the capital, and therefore it cannot be doubted at all that this is the most brutal form of intervention. I should like in these last moments to ask the leaders of the revolution, if they can, to leave the country. I ask that all that I have said in my broadcast, and what we have agreed on with the revolutionary leaders during meetings in Parliament, should be put in a memorandum, and the leaders should turn to all the peoples of the world for help and explain that today it is Hungary and tomorrow, or the day after tomorrow, it will be the turn of other countries because the imperialism of Moscow does not know borders, and is only trying to play for time.

Q *How did the United States and its allies respond to the events in Hungary? Why did the United States decide not to intervene in support of the dissident forces?*

Source: From *Department of State Bulletin*, Nov. 12, 1956, pp. 746–747.

---

the Cold War were never far beneath the surface. In July 1959, when Vice President Richard Nixon attended a U.S. Cultural Exhibit in Moscow, he and Khrushchev sparred publicly over the alleged superiority of the capitalist and socialist ways of life in what came to be called the Kitchen Debate.

26-3b Rivalry in the Third World

Yet Khrushchev could rarely avoid the temptation to gain an advantage over the United States in the competition for influence throughout the world, a posture that exacerbated the unstable relationship between the two global superpowers. Unlike Stalin, who had exhibited a profound distrust of all foreign and domestic political figures who did not slavishly follow his lead, Khrushchev viewed the dismantling of colonial regimes in Asia, Africa, and Latin America as a potential advantage for the Soviet Union. When neutralist leaders such as Jawaharlal Nehru in India, Tito in Yugoslavia, and Sukarno (soo-KAHR-noh) in Indonesia founded the **Nonaligned Movement** in 1955 to provide an alternative to the two major power blocs, Khrushchev took every opportunity to promote Soviet

26.5 The Kitchen Debate. During the late 1950s, the United States and the Soviet Union sought to defuse Cold War tensions by encouraging cultural exchanges between the two countries. On one occasion, U.S. Vice President Richard M. Nixon visited Moscow in conjunction with the arrival of an exhibit to introduce U.S. culture and society to the Soviet people. Here Nixon lectures Soviet Communist Party chief Nikita Khrushchev on the technology of the U.S. kitchen. On the other side of Nixon (far right) is future Soviet president Leonid Brezhnev.

interests in the Third World (as the nonaligned countries of Asia, Africa, and Latin America were now popularly called). Khrushchev openly sought alliances with strategically important neutralist countries such as India, Indonesia, and Egypt as Washington's ability to influence events at the United Nations began to wane.

In January 1961, just as John F. Kennedy (1917–1963) assumed the U.S. presidency, relations between Moscow and Washington remained tense, as the shooting down of a U.S. reconnaissance plane over Soviet territory had provoked a war of words between the two capitals and provided the Soviet leader with a pretense to cancel a planned summit meeting with President Eisenhower (see Film & History, *Bridge of Spies*, p. 669). Shortly after Kennedy took office, Khrushchev unnerved the new president at an informal summit meeting in Vienna by declaring that the Soviet Union would provide active support to national liberation movements throughout the world. There were rising fears in Washington of Soviet meddling in such sensitive trouble spots as Southeast Asia, where insurgent activities in Indochina continued to simmer; in Central Africa, where the pro-Soviet tendencies of radical leader Patrice Lumumba (puh-TREES loo-MOOM-buh) (1925–1961) aroused deep suspicion in Washington; and in the Caribbean, where a little-known left-wing Cuban revolutionary named Fidel Castro threatened to transform his country into an advanced base for Soviet expansion in the Americas.

26-3c The Cuban Missile Crisis and the Move Toward Détente

In 1959, Fidel Castro (fee-DELL KASS-troh) (1927–2016) overthrew Cuban dictator Fulgencio Batista (full-JEN-see-oh bah-TEES-tuh) and established a Soviet-supported totalitarian regime. As tensions increased between the new government in Havana and the United States, the Eisenhower administration broke relations with Cuba and drafted plans to overthrow Castro, who reacted by drawing closer to Moscow.

Soon after taking office in early 1961, Kennedy approved a plan drafted during Eisenhower's administration to support an invasion of Cuba by anti-Castro exiles. But the attempted landing in April at the Bay of Pigs in southern Cuba was an utter failure. At Castro's invitation, the Soviet Union then began secretly to station nuclear missiles in Cuba within striking distance of the American mainland. When U.S. intelligence discovered the presence of the Soviet missiles in Cuba in early fall 1962 and spotted a Soviet fleet carrying more missiles heading toward Havana, Kennedy decided to dispatch U.S. warships into the Atlantic to prevent the fleet from reaching its destination.

This approach to the problem was risky but had the benefit of providing the two sides with time to find a peaceful solution. After a tense standoff during which the two countries came frighteningly close to a direct nuclear confrontation (the Soviet missiles already in Cuba were launch ready), Khrushchev finally sent a conciliatory letter to Kennedy agreeing to turn back the fleet if Kennedy pledged not to invade Cuba. In a secret concession not revealed until many years later, the president also promised to dismantle U.S. nuclear missiles in Turkey. To the world, however (and to an angry Castro), it appeared that Kennedy had bested Khrushchev. "We were eyeball to eyeball," noted U.S. Secretary of State Dean Rusk, "and they blinked."

The ghastly realization that the world might have faced annihilation in a matter of days profoundly affected both sides. A communication hotline between Moscow and Washington was installed in 1963 to expedite rapid communication between the two superpowers in time of crisis. In the same year, the two powers agreed to ban nuclear tests in the atmosphere, a step that served to lessen tensions between the two nations.

26-3d The Sino–Soviet Dispute

Nikita Khrushchev had launched his slogan of peaceful coexistence as a means of improving relations with the capitalist powers; ironically, one result of the campaign was to undermine Moscow's ties with its close ally China. During Stalin's lifetime, Beijing had accepted the Soviet Union as the acknowledged leader of the socialist camp. After Stalin's death, however, relations began to deteriorate. Part of the reason may have been Mao Zedong's contention that he, as the most experienced Marxist leader, should now be acknowledged as the most authoritative voice within the socialist community. But another determining factor was that just as Soviet policies were moving toward moderation, China's policies were becoming more radical.

Several other issues were involved, including territorial disputes along the Sino–Soviet border and China's unhappiness with limited Soviet economic assistance. But the key sources of disagreement involved ideology and the Cold War. Chinese leaders were convinced that the successes of the Soviet space program confirmed that the socialists were now technologically superior to the capitalists (the East Wind, trumpeted the Chinese official press, had triumphed over the West Wind), and they urged Khrushchev to go on the offensive to promote world revolution. Specifically, China wanted Soviet assistance in retaking Taiwan from Chiang Kai-shek. But Khrushchev was trying to improve relations with the West and rejected Chinese demands for support against Taiwan.

By the end of the 1950s, the Soviet Union had begun to remove its advisers from China, and the dispute broke into the open in 1961. Increasingly isolated in the global arena, China voiced its hostility to what Mao described as the "urban industrialized countries" (which included the Soviet Union) and portrayed itself as the leader of the "rural underdeveloped countries" of Asia, Africa, and Latin America in a global struggle against imperialist oppression. In effect, China had applied Mao Zedong's concept of people's war in an international framework.

26-3e The Second Indochina War

In the meantime, a new source of Cold War friction was opening up in Southeast Asia with the renewed outbreak of war in Indochina. The Eisenhower administration had opposed the peace settlement at Geneva in 1954, which divided Vietnam temporarily into two separate regroupment zones, specifically because the provision for future national elections opened the possibility that the entire country would come under Communist rule. But Eisenhower had been unwilling to introduce U.S. military forces to continue the conflict without the full support of the British and the French, who preferred to seek a negotiated settlement. In the end, Washington promised not to break the provisions of the agreement but refused to commit itself to the results. It now proceeded to provide aid to the new Republic of Vietnam in the south, which was led by the veteran anti-Communist politician Ngo Dinh Diem (NGHOH din DEE-em).

Bolstered by U.S. assistance, the new Saigon regime began to root out dissidents. With the tacit approval of the United States, Diem refused to hold the national elections called for by the Geneva Accords. It was widely anticipated, even in Washington, that the Communists would win such elections. In 1959, the Communist government in Hanoi, despairing of the peaceful unification of the country under its rule, decided to return to a policy of revolutionary war in the south. To provide an image of political legitimacy, Hanoi sponsored the formation of a new political organization designed to win the support of a wide spectrum of the population in the south. Called the National Front for the Liberation of South Vietnam (NLF), it purported to be an independent organization representing the interests of the South Vietnamese people, but it was actually under the secret but firm leadership of high-ranking Communists in the DRV (see Opposing Viewpoints, "Confrontation in Southeast Asia," p. 673).

By 1963, South Vietnam was on the verge of collapse. Diem's autocratic methods and inattention to severe economic inequality had alienated much of the population, and revolutionary forces, popularly known as the **Viet Cong** (Vietnamese Communists) and supported by the Communist government in North Vietnam, expanded their influence throughout much of the country. In the fall of 1963, with the approval of the Kennedy administration, senior military officers overthrew the Diem regime. But factionalism kept the new military leadership from reinvigorating the struggle against the insurgent forces, and the situation in South Vietnam continued to deteriorate. By early 1965, the Viet Cong, their ranks now swelled by military units infiltrating from North Vietnam, were on the verge of seizing control of the entire country. In March, President Lyndon Johnson decided to send U.S. combat troops to South Vietnam to prevent the total defeat of the anti-Communist government in Saigon. Over the next three years, U.S. troop levels steadily increased as the White House counted on U.S. firepower to persuade Ho Chi Minh to abandon his quest to unify Vietnam under Communist leadership.

Confrontation in Southeast Asia

 Politics & Government

IN DECEMBER 1960, the NLF was born. Composed of political and social leaders opposed to the anticommunist government, it operated under the direction of the Communist regime in North Vietnam and served as the formal representative of revolutionary forces in the south throughout the remainder of the Vietnam War. When President Lyndon B. Johnson began to dispatch U.S. combat troops to Vietnam to prevent a Communist victory there in spring 1965, the NLF issued the declaration presented in the first selection. The second selection is from a speech that Johnson gave at Johns Hopkins University in April 1965 in response to the NLF.

Statement of the National Front for the Liberation of South Vietnam (1965)

American imperialist aggression against South Vietnam and interference in its internal affairs have now continued for more than ten years. More American troops and supplies, including missile units, Marines, B-57 strategic bombers, and mercenaries from South Korea, Taiwan, the Philippines, Australia, Malaysia, etc., have been brought to South Vietnam. . . .

The Saigon puppet regime, paid servant of the United States, is guilty of the most heinous crimes. These despicable traitors, these boot-lickers of American imperialism, have brought the enemy into our country. They have brought to South Vietnam armed forces of the United States and its satellites to kill our compatriots, occupy and ravage our sacred soil and enslave our people.

The Vietnamese, the peoples of all Indo-China and Southeast Asia, supporters of peace and justice in every part of the world, have raised their voice in angry protest against this criminal unprovoked aggression of the United States imperialists.

In the present extremely grave situation, the South Vietnam National Liberation Front considers it necessary to proclaim anew its firm and unswerving determination to resist the U.S. imperialists and fight for the salvation of our country. . . . [It] will continue to rely chiefly on its own forces and potentialities, but it is prepared to accept any assistance, moral and material, including arms and other military equipment, from all the socialist countries, from nationalist countries, from international organizations, and from the peace-loving peoples of the world.

Lyndon B. Johnson, "Peace Without Conquest"

The world as it is in Asia is not a serene or peaceful place.

The first reality is that North Viet-Nam has attacked the independent nation of South Viet-Nam. Its object is total conquest.

Of course, some of the people of South Viet-Nam are participating in attack on their own government. But trained men and supplies, orders and arms, flow in a constant stream from north to south.

This support is the heartbeat of the war.

And it is a war of unparalleled brutality. Simple farmers are the targets of assassination and kidnapping. Women and children are strangled in the night because their men are loyal to their government. And helpless villages are ravaged by sneak attacks. Large-scale raids are conducted on towns, and terror strikes in the heart of cities. . . .

Why are these realities our concern? Why are we in South Viet-Nam?

We are there because we have a promise to keep. Since 1954 every American President has offered support to the people of South Viet-Nam. We have helped to build, and we have helped to defend. Thus, over many years, we have made a national pledge to help South Viet-Nam defend its independence.

Our objective is the independence of South Viet-Nam, and its freedom from attack. We want nothing for ourselves—only that the people of South Viet-Nam be allowed to guide their own country in their own way. We will do everything necessary to reach that objective. And we will do only what is absolutely necessary.

Q *How did the NLF justify its claim to represent the legitimate aspirations of the people of South Vietnam? What was President Johnson's counterargument?*

Sources: From *New Times* (March 27, 1965), pp. 36–40. From Lyndon B. Johnson, "Peace Without Conquest" speech, April 1965 from *Public Papers of the Presidents of the United States: Lyndon B. Johnson, 1965.* Volume I, entry 172, pp. 394–399. Washington D.C.: Government Printing Office, 1966.

War in the Rice Paddies

 Politics & Government **THE FIRST STAGE OF THE VIETNAM WAR** consisted primarily of guerrilla conflict as Viet Cong insurgents relied on guerrilla tactics to bring down the U.S.–supported government in Saigon. In 1965, however, President Lyndon Johnson ordered U.S. combat troops into South Vietnam (Image 26.6a) in a desperate bid to prevent a Communist victory in that beleaguered country. The Communist government in North Vietnam responded in kind, sending its own regular forces down the Ho Chi Minh Trail to confront U.S. troops on the battlefield. In Image 26.6b, North Vietnamese troops storm the U.S. Marine base at Khe Sanh (KAY SARN), near the demilitarized zone, in 1968, the most violent year of the war. Although U.S. military commanders believed that helicopters would be a key factor in defeating the insurgent forces in Vietnam, this was one instance when technological superiority did not produce a victory on the battlefield.

Q *How do you think helicopters were used to assist U.S. operations in South Vietnam? Why didn't their use result in a U.S. victory?*

26.6a

26.6b

The Vietnam Conflict in the Cold War Chinese and Soviet leaders observed the gradual escalation of the conflict in South Vietnam with mixed feelings. The Chinese were undoubtedly pleased to have a firm Communist ally— one that had in many ways followed the path of Mao Zedong—just beyond their southern frontier. Yet they were concerned that bloodshed in South Vietnam might enmesh China in a new conflict with the United States. Beijing had a further concern that a powerful and ambitious DRV might wish to extend its influence throughout mainland Southeast Asia, an area that China considered its own backyard.

Both Moscow and Beijing therefore tiptoed delicately through the minefield of the Indochina conflict. As the war escalated in 1964 and 1965, Soviet leaders assured Washington that they had no interest in seeing the Indochinese conflict escalate into a Great Powers confrontation. For its part, Beijing publicly announced that the Chinese people fully supported their comrades seeking national liberation but privately assured Washington that China would not directly enter the conflict unless U.S. forces threatened its southern border. Beijing also refused to cooperate fully with Moscow in shipping Soviet goods to North Vietnam through Chinese territory.

Despite its dismay at the lack of full support from China, the Communist government in North Vietnam responded to U.S. escalation by infiltrating more of its own regular troops into the South, and the war had reached a stalemate by 1968. The Communists were not strong enough to overthrow the government in Saigon, whose weakness was shielded by the presence of half a million U.S. troops, but President Johnson was reluctant to engage in all-out war on North Vietnam for fear of provoking a global nuclear conflict. In the fall, after the Communist-led Tet offensive undermined claims of progress in Washington and aroused intense antiwar protests in the United States, peace negotiations began in Paris.

Quest for Peace Richard Nixon (1913–1994) came into the White House in 1969 on a pledge to bring an honorable end to the Vietnam War. With U.S. public opinion sharply divided on the issue, he began to withdraw U.S. troops while continuing to hold peace talks in Paris. But the centerpiece of his strategy was to improve relations with China and thus undercut Chinese support for the North Vietnamese war effort. During the 1960s, relations between Moscow and Beijing had reached a point of extreme tension, and thousands of troops were stationed on both sides of their long common frontier. To intimidate their Communist rivals, Soviet sources hinted that they might launch a preemptive strike to destroy Chinese nuclear facilities in Xinjiang. Sensing an opportunity to split the two one-time allies, Nixon sent his emissary, Henry Kissinger, on a secret trip to China. Responding to assurances that the United States was determined to withdraw from Indochina and hoping to improve relations with the mainland regime, Chinese leaders invited President Nixon to visit China in early 1972. Nixon accepted, and the two sides agreed to set aside their differences over Taiwan to pursue a better mutual relationship.

The Fall of Saigon Incensed at the apparent betrayal by their close allies, North Vietnamese leaders decided to seek a negotiated settlement of the war in an effort to bring about the final withdrawal of U.S. combat forces from the RVN. In January 1973, a peace treaty was signed in Paris calling for the removal of all U.S. forces from South Vietnam. In return, the Communists agreed to halt military operations and negotiate to resolve their differences with the Saigon regime. But negotiations between north and south over the political settlement soon broke down, and the Communists resumed the offensive in early 1975. At the end of April, under a massive assault by North Vietnamese military forces, the South Vietnamese government surrendered. A year later, the country was unified under Communist rule.

The Communist victory in Vietnam was a severe humiliation for the United States, but its strategic impact was limited because of the new U.S.–China relationship. During the next decade, Sino–American relations continued to improve. In 1979, diplomatic ties were established between the two countries under an arrangement whereby the United States renounced its mutual security treaty with

the Republic of China in return for a pledge from China to seek reunification with Taiwan by peaceful means. By the end of the 1970s, China and the United States had forged a "strategic relationship" in which they would cooperate against the common threat of Soviet hegemony in Asia.

Why had the United States failed to achieve its objective of preventing a Communist victory in Vietnam? Dean Rusk, U.S. secretary of state during the 1960s, later commented that Washington had underestimated the determination of its adversary in Hanoi and overestimated the patience of the American people. No doubt both points are valid, but deeper reflection suggests that another factor was equally important: the United States had overestimated the capacity of its client state in South Vietnam to defend itself against a disciplined adversary. Although many South Vietnamese fought bravely in the effort to prevent a Communist takeover, their leaders in Saigon lacked the determination and the vision to support their efforts. In subsequent years, it became a crucial lesson to the Americans on the perils of nation building.

26-4 AN ERA OF EQUIVALENCE

Q Focus Question: Why did the Cold War briefly flare up again in the 1980s, and why did it come to a definitive end at the end of the decade?

When the Johnson administration sent U.S. combat troops to South Vietnam in 1965, Washington's main concern was with Beijing, not Moscow. By the mid-1960s, U.S. officials viewed the Soviet Union as an essentially conservative power that was more concerned with protecting its vast empire than with expanding its borders. In fact, U.S. policy makers periodically sought Soviet assistance in seeking a peaceful settlement of the Vietnam War. As long as Khrushchev was in power, they found a receptive ear in Moscow. Khrushchev was firmly dedicated to promoting peaceful coexistence (at least on his terms) and had no desire to risk a confrontation with the United States in far-off Southeast Asia.

Such was not the case with his successors. After October 1964, when Khrushchev was replaced by a new leadership headed by party chief Leonid Brezhnev (leeoh-NYEET BREZH-neff) (1906–1982) and Prime Minister Alexei Kosygin (uh-LEK-say kuh-SEE-gun) (1904–1980), Soviet attitudes about Vietnam became more ambivalent. On the one hand, the new Soviet leaders had no desire to see the Vietnam conflict poison relations between the Great Powers. On the other hand, Moscow was eager to demonstrate its support for the North Vietnamese to deflect

Chinese charges that the Soviet Union had betrayed the interests of the oppressed peoples of the world. As a result, Soviet officials publicly voiced sympathy for the U.S. predicament in Vietnam but put no pressure on their allies to bring an end to the war. Indeed, the Soviet Union became Hanoi's main supplier of advanced military equipment in the final years of the war.

26-4a The Brezhnev Doctrine

In the meantime, new Cold War tensions were brewing in Eastern Europe, where discontent with Stalinist policies in the so-called people's democracies continued to fester after the 1956 crackdown by Soviet troops in Hungary. Although some countries in the region had begun to make the transition from peasant societies to industrial economies, the local standard of living remained relatively stagnant (as the popular saying had it, "We pretend to work, and they pretend to pay us"), while individual freedoms continued to be severely restricted. This was especially the case in Czechoslovakia, where popular discontent with the regime's Stalinist policies was on the rise. The country had not shared in the thaw of the mid-1950s and remained under the rule of hardliner Antonín Novotný (AHN-toh-nyeen NOH-vaht-nee) (1904–1975), who had been installed in power by Stalin himself. By the late 1960s, however, Novotný's policies had led to widespread popular alienation, and Alexander Dubček (DOOB-check) (1921–1992) was elected first secretary of the Communist Party in 1968 with the support of intellectuals and reformist party members. He immediately attempted to create what was popularly called "socialism with a human face," relaxing restrictions on freedom of speech and the press and the right to travel abroad. Economic reforms were announced, and party control over all aspects of society was reduced. A period of euphoria erupted that came to be known as the "Prague Spring."

It proved to be short-lived. Encouraged by Dubček's actions, some Czechs called for more far-reaching reforms, including neutrality and withdrawal from the Soviet bloc. To forestall the spread of this "spring fever," the Soviet Red Army, supported by troops from other Warsaw Pact states, invaded Czechoslovakia in August 1968 and crushed the reform movement (see Image 26.7). Gustav Husák (goo-STAHV HOO-sahk) (1913–1991), a committed Stalinist, replaced Dubček and restored the old order, while Moscow attempted to justify its action by issuing the so-called **Brezhnev Doctrine**, according to which the Soviet Union was justified in intervening to prevent any of its satellites from straying too far from Marxist–Leninist orthodoxy.

In East Germany as well, Stalinist policies continued to hold sway. Led by Walter Ulbricht, the ruling Communist government in East Germany had consolidated its position in the early 1950s and became a faithful Soviet satellite. Industry was nationalized and agriculture collectivized. After the 1953 workers' revolt was crushed by Soviet tanks, a steady flight of East Germans to West Germany ensued, primarily through the city of Berlin. This exodus of mostly skilled laborers, numbering an estimated 3 million by 1961

26.7 The Prague Spring. When moderate elements in the Communist Party of Czechoslovakia led by Alexander Dubček sought to force the resignation of the Stalinist leader Antonin Novotny and create "socialism with a human face," Leonid Brezhnev in Moscow ordered Soviet tanks into the streets of Prague to suppress the movement. Popular protests against the Soviet intervention erupted into the streets of the city, but were ultimately futile when Alexander Dubček and his followers were forced to resign.

AFP/Getty Images

("Soon only party chief Ulbricht will be left," remarked one Soviet observer sardonically), created economic problems and in 1961 led the East German government to erect a wall separating East Berlin from West Berlin (known officially as "the democratic anti-fascist protection wall"), as well as even more fearsome barriers along the entire border with West Germany.

Although the Berlin Wall was a public relations disaster, it stemmed the flow of refugees from the eastern zone into West Berlin, while the GDR succeeded in developing the strongest economy among the Soviet Union's Eastern European satellites. In 1971, Ulbricht was succeeded by Erich Honecker (AY-reekh HON-nek-uh) (1912–1994), a party hardliner. Propaganda increased, and the use of the Stasi (SHTAHsee), the secret police, became a hallmark of Honecker's virtual dictatorship. Honecker ruled unchallenged for the next eighteen years.

26-4b An Era of Détente

With the situation in Eastern Europe temporarily stabilized, Moscow continued to pursue peaceful coexistence with the West during the early 1970s and adopted a generally cautious posture in foreign affairs. As a result, a new age in Soviet–American relations emerged, often referred to as **détente** (day-TAHNT), a French term meaning a reduction of tensions between the two sides. One symbol of détente was the 1972 Anti-Ballistic Missile (ABM) Treaty, often called SALT I (for Strategic Arms Limitation Talks) in which the two nations agreed to limit the size of their ABM systems.

The U.S. objective in pursuing the treaty was to make it unlikely that either superpower could win a nuclear exchange by launching a preemptive strike against the other. Nixon administration officials believed that a policy of "equivalence," in which the two sides had roughly equal power, was the best way to avoid a nuclear confrontation. Détente was pursued in other ways as well. When President Nixon took office in 1969, he sought to increase trade and cultural contacts with the Soviet Union. His purpose was to set up a series of "linkages" in U.S.–Soviet relations that would persuade Moscow of the economic and social benefits of maintaining good relations with the West.

The Helsinki Accords were a symbol of that new relationship. Signed in 1975 by the United States, Canada, and every European nation on both sides of the Iron Curtain, these accords recognized all borders in Europe that had been established since the end of World War II, thereby formally acknowledging for the first time the Soviet sphere of influence in Eastern Europe. The Helsinki Accords also committed the signatories to recognize and protect the human rights of their citizens, a clear effort by the Western

CHRONOLOGY	The Cold War to 1980
Truman Doctrine	1947
Formation of NATO	1949
Soviet Union explodes first nuclear device	1949
Communists come to power in China	1949
Nationalist government retreats to Taiwan	1949
Korean War	1950–1953
Geneva Conference ends Indochina War	1954
Warsaw Pact created	1955
Khrushchev calls for peaceful coexistence	1956
Sino–Soviet dispute breaks into the open	1961
Cuban Missile Crisis	1962
SALT I treaty signed	1972
Nixon's visit to China	1972
Fall of South Vietnam	1975
Soviet invasion of Afghanistan	1979

states to improve the performance of the Soviet Union and its allies in that arena. Under U.S. President Jimmy Carter (b. 1924), protection of human rights became one of the most important objectives in U.S. foreign policy.

26-4c Renewed Tensions in the Third World

Ironically, however, just at the point when U.S. involvement in Vietnam came to an end and relations with China began to improve, relations with the Soviet Union began to sour. There were several reasons. Some U.S officials had become increasingly concerned about perceived aggressive new tendencies in Soviet foreign policy, notably in Africa, where Soviet activities were on the rise. Moscow sought influence in Somalia, across the Red Sea from South Yemen, and in neighboring Ethiopia, where a Marxist regime took control. In Angola, once a colony of Portugal, an insurgent movement supported by Cuban troops came to power.

In 1979, concerns about Soviet expansionism shifted to the Middle East, where Soviet troops were sent across the border into Afghanistan to protect a newly installed Marxist regime facing internal resistance from fundamentalist Muslims. Some observers suspected that the ultimate objective of the Soviet advance into hitherto neutral Afghanistan was to extend Soviet power into the oil fields of the Persian Gulf. To deter such a possibility, the White House promulgated the Carter Doctrine, which stated that the United States would use its military power to safeguard Western access to the oil reserves in the Middle East if necessary. In fact, sources in Moscow later disclosed that the Soviet advance had little to do with the oil of the Persian Gulf but was an effort to increase Soviet influence in a region increasingly beset by Islamic fervor. Soviet officials feared that Islamic activism could spread to the Muslim populations in the Soviet republics in Central Asia and were confident that the United States was too distracted by the so-called **Vietnam syndrome** (the public fear of U.S. involvement in another Vietnam-type conflict) to respond.

A second reason for growing suspicion of the Soviet Union in the United States was the fear among some U.S. defense analysts that the Soviet Union had abandoned the policy of equivalence and was seeking strategic superiority in nuclear weapons. Accordingly, they argued for a substantial increase in U.S. defense spending. Such charges, combined with evidence of Soviet efforts in Africa and the Middle East and reports of the persecution of Jews and dissidents in the Soviet Union, helped undermine public support for détente in the United States. These changing attitudes were reflected in the failure of the Carter administration to obtain congressional approval of a new arms limitation agreement (SALT II), which was signed with the Soviet Union in 1979.

26-4d Countering the Evil Empire

The early years of the administration of President Ronald Reagan (1911–2004) witnessed a return to the harsh rhetoric, if not all of the harsh practices, of the Cold War. President Reagan's anti-Communist credentials were well known. In a speech given shortly after his election in 1980, he referred to the Soviet Union as an "evil empire" and frequently voiced his suspicion of Soviet motives in foreign affairs. In an effort to eliminate perceived Soviet advantages in strategic weaponry, the White House began a military buildup that stimulated a renewed arms race. In 1982, the Reagan administration introduced the nuclear-tipped cruise missile that was able to fly at low altitudes, making it difficult to detect by enemy radar. Reagan also became an ardent exponent of the Strategic Defense Initiative, which was nicknamed **Star Wars**. The intention of this proposed defense system was not only to create a space shield that could destroy incoming missiles but also to force Moscow into an arms race that it could not hope to win.

Competition between the United States and the Soviet Union continued to fester in various areas of the world. In Central America, the Reagan administration provided military assistance to an anti-Communist guerrilla movement (the **Contras**) against the revolutionary Sandinista

(san-duh-NEES-tuh) regime in Nicaragua. In Afghanistan, the White House provided weapons to fundamentalist Muslim insurgents in a bid to entangle the Soviet Union in its own quagmire. Like the Vietnam War, the conflict in Afghanistan resulted in heavy Soviet casualties and demonstrated that the influence of a superpower was limited in the face of strong nationalist, guerrilla-type opposition.

26-4e The End of the Cold War

In 1985, Mikhail Gorbachev (meek-HAYL GOR-buhchawf) (b. 1931) was elected secretary of the Communist Party of the Soviet Union. During Brezhnev's last years and the brief tenures of his two successors (see Chapter 27), the Soviet Union had entered an era of serious economic decline, and the dynamic new party chief was well aware that drastic changes would be needed to rekindle

26.8 Reagan and Gorbachev in Reykjavik. With the election of Mikhail Gorbachev as party general secretary in 1985, Moscow and Washington began to explore the means to reduce tensions between the two Great Powers. In October 1986, Gorbachev and U.S. President Ronald Reagan held a summit meeting in Reykjavik, the capital of Iceland, to explore issues of concern to both sides. Although no agreements resulted from the meeting, the atmospherics from the meeting resulted in a new era of good feeling and soon led to meaningful agreements on arms control and a reduction of tensions in the Cold War.

the dreams that had inspired the Bolshevik Revolution. During the next few years, he launched a program of restructuring known as *perestroika* (per-uh-STROI-kuh) to revitalize the Soviet system. As part of that program, he set out to improve relations with the United States and the rest of the capitalist world. When he met with President Reagan in Reykjavik (RAY-kyuh-vik), the capital of Iceland, the two leaders agreed to set aside their ideological differences and seek cooperation in several areas (see Image 26.8, p. 678).

Eastern Europe: From Satellites to New Nations

Gorbachev's desperate effort to rescue the Soviet Union from collapse was too little and too late. In 1989, popular demonstrations against Communist rule broke out across Eastern Europe. As before, Poland was the first to react to events. In the late 1970s, an independent labor union called **Solidarity** was created under the leadership of Lech Walesa (LEK wah-WENT-sah) (b. 1943). Sensing a threat to its monopoly of power, the Warsaw regime sought to suppress the movement, but as it continued to grow in popularity communist leaders reluctantly agreed to grant the union legal stature. In December 1990, national elections elevated Walesa to the presidency of Poland. Moscow took no action to reverse the verdict.

Similar trends were at work in neighboring Czechoslovakia, where a hardline regime under Gustav Husák had used repressing methods to maintain power. In 1977, dissident intellectuals inspired by the Helsinki Accords formed an organization called Charter 77 as a vehicle for protest against violations of human rights. Dissident activities continued to grow during the 1980s, and when massive demonstrations broke out in several cities in 1989 the Husák regime collapsed. At the end of December, he was replaced by Václav Havel (VATS-laf HAV-el) (1936-2011), a playwright who had been a leading figure in Charter 77.

But the most dramatic events took place in East Germany, where a persistent economic slump and the ongoing oppression by the Honecker regime led to widespread protests and the flight of refugees to neighboring countries during the summer and fall of 1989. Capitulating to popular pressure, a midlevel communist official ordered the opening of the border with West Berlin on November 9th. The Berlin Wall, the most tangible symbol of the Cold War, became the site of a massive celebration (see Image 26.9). Most of the wall was dismantled by joyful Germans from both sides of the border. In March 1990, free elections led to the formation of a non-Communist government

Agencja Fotograficzna Caro / Alamy

26.9 The Fall of the Berlin Wall. As communist regimes in Eastern Europe began to crumble during the summer and fall of 1989, popular protests broke out in East Berlin to demand the destruction of the Berlin Wall. In early November, when local communist officials in the eastern zone appeared uncertain over how to deal with the crisis, crowds of Berliners on both sides of the barrier took measures into their own hands. With the fall of the Berlin Wall, one of the most repugnant symbols of the Cold War had been relegated into history.

Experience an interactive version of this period in ⁕ MINDTAP

Global Village or Clash of Civilizations?

As the Cold War came to an end in 1991, policy makers, scholars, and political pundits began to forecast the emergence of a "new world order." One hypothesis put forth by political philosopher Francis Fukuyama was that the decline of communism signaled that the industrial capitalist democracies of the West had triumphed in the world of ideas and were now poised to remake the rest of the world in their own image. In line with this hypothesis, many observers began to predict that technological advances were transforming the world into a vast "global village" in which age-old traditions and prejudices would be replaced by a new world civilization supported by a world marketplace of values, goods, and services.

Not everyone agreed with this optimistic assessment of the world situation. In *The Clash of Civilizations and the Remaking of the World Order*, historian Samuel P. Huntington suggested that the post-Cold War era, far from marking the triumph of Western ideals, would be characterized by increased global fragmentation and a "clash of civilizations" based on ethnic, cultural, or religious differences. According to Huntington, the twenty-first century would be dominated by disputatious cultural blocs in East Asia, Western Europe and the United States, Eurasia, and the Middle East. The dream of a universal order—a global village—dominated by Western values, he concluded, was a fantasy.

Recent events have lent some support to Huntington's hypothesis. The collapse of the Soviet Union eventually led to the emergence of an atmosphere of conflict and tension all along the perimeter of the old Soviet Empire. The terrorist attack on the United States in September 2001 set the advanced nations of the West and much of the Muslim world on a collision course, while the Western concept of democracy is under challenge in many parts of the world. As for the new economic order, public anger at the impact of globalization has reached disturbing levels in many countries, leading to a growing demand for self-protection and group identity in an impersonal and rapidly changing world.

Are we then headed toward multiple power blocs divided by religion and culture as Huntington predicted? His thesis is indeed a useful corrective to the complacent tendency of many observers to view Western civilization as the zenith of human achievement. By dividing the world into competing cultural blocs, however, Huntington underestimated the centrifugal forces at work within the various regions of the world. As the industrial and technological revolutions spread across the face of Earth, their impact is measurably stronger in some societies than in others, thereby intensifying historical rivalries in a given region while establishing links between individual societies and counterparts in other parts of the world. In recent years, for example, Japan has had more in common with the United States than with its traditional neighbor China.

The most likely scenario for the next few decades, then, is more complex than either the global village hypothesis or its rival, the clash of civilizations. The twenty-first century will be characterized by simultaneous trends toward globalization and fragmentation as the thrust of technology and information transforms societies and gives rise to counter-reactions among societies seeking to preserve a group identity and sense of meaning and purpose in a confusing world.

William J. Duiker

26.10 Ronald McDonald in Indonesia. This giant statue welcomes young Indonesians to a McDonald's restaurant in Jakarta, the capital city. McDonald's food chain symbolizes the globalization of today's world civilization.

Q *How has the recent global economic recession affected the issues discussed in this essay?*

in the GDR that soon began negotiations with West Germany over a program of political and economic reunification.

The contagion in Prague, Warsaw, and Berlin soon spread to other countries in the region, and in 1991 the final piece toppled when the Soviet Union, for 70 years an apparently permanent fixture on the global scene, suddenly disintegrated. In its place arose fifteen new nations. The Cold War was over (see Chapter 27).

26-4f The Revenge of History

The end of the Cold War seduced many observers into a vision of a new world order that would be characterized by peaceful cooperation and increasing prosperity. Sadly, such hopes have not been realized. A bitter civil war in the Balkans in the mid-1990s and the rise of militant Islam in the Middle East have graphically demonstrated that under the surface of the Cold War, old fault lines of national, religious, and ethnic hostility have not abated. Growing tensions in U.S.–China relations and the flare-up between Russia and the Western democracies over the status of Ukraine suggests that the bitter rivalries behind the Cold War may themselves be ready to return with a vengeance. In the meantime, other issues beyond the daily headlines—the growing threat to the global environment, the gap between rich and poor nations, and tensions unleashed by the migration of peoples—have begun to resurface (see Comparative Essay "Global Village or Clash of Civilizations?" p. 680). These events will be discussed in greater detail in the chapters that follow.

CHAPTER SUMMARY

At the end of World War II, a new conflict threatened as the two superpowers, the United States and the Soviet Union, began to compete for political domination. This ideological division soon spread throughout the world as the United States fought in Korea and Vietnam to prevent the spread of communism, promoted by the new Maoist government in China, while the Soviet Union used its influence to prop up pro-Soviet regimes in Asia, Africa, Eastern Europe, and Latin America.

What had begun, then, as a confrontation across the great divide of the "Iron Curtain" in Europe eventually took on global significance, much as the major European powers had jostled for position and advantage in Africa and eastern Asia before World War I. As a result, both Moscow and Washington became entangled in areas that in themselves had little importance in terms of real national security interests.

As the twentieth century wore on, however, there were tantalizing signs of a thaw in the Cold War. In 1979, China and the United States established mutual diplomatic relations, a consequence of Beijing's decision to focus on domestic reform and stop supporting wars of national liberation in Asia. Six years later, the ascent of Mikhail Gorbachev to leadership in the Soviet Union, which culminated in the dissolution of the Soviet Union in 1991, brought an end to almost half a century of bitter rivalry between the world's two superpowers.

The Cold War thus ended without the horrific vision of a mushroom cloud. Unlike the earlier rivalries that had resulted in two world wars, this time the antagonists had gradually come to realize that the struggle for supremacy could be carried out in the political and economic arena rather than on the battlefield. And in the final analysis, it was not military superiority, but political, economic, and cultural factors that brought about the triumph of Western civilization over the Marxist vision of a classless utopia. The world's policy makers could now shift their focus to other problems of mutual concern.

REFLECTION QUESTIONS

Q This chapter has described the outbreak of the Cold War as virtually inevitable given the ambitions of the two superpowers and their ideological differences. Do you agree? How might the Cold War have been avoided?

Q What disagreements brought about an end to the Sino–Soviet alliance in 1961? Which factors appear to have been most important?

Q How did the wars in Korea and Vietnam relate to the Cold War and affect its course?

CHAPTER TIMELINE

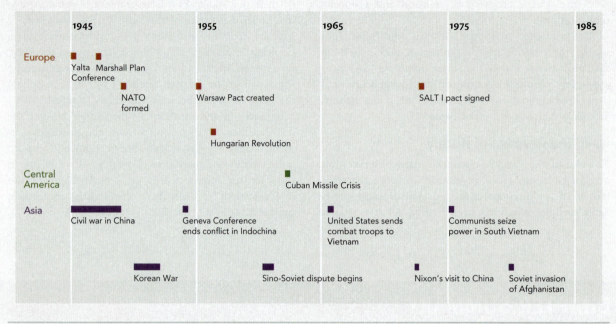

	1945	1955	1965	1975	1985

Europe
Yalta Conference — Marshall Plan
NATO formed
Warsaw Pact created
SALT I pact signed
Hungarian Revolution

Central America
Cuban Missile Crisis

Asia
Civil war in China
Geneva Conference ends conflict in Indochina
United States sends combat troops to Vietnam
Communists seize power in South Vietnam
Korean War
Sino-Soviet dispute begins
Nixon's visit to China
Soviet invasion of Afghanistan

CHAPTER NOTES

1. Quoted in J. M. Jones, *The Fifteen Weeks (February 21–June 5, 1947)*, 2d ed. (New York, 1964), pp. 140–141.
2. Quoted in M. Glenny, *The Balkans: Nationalism, War, and the Great Powers* (New York, 1999), pp. 543–544.
3. Quoted in Freeman Dyson, "Churchill, Love, and the Bomb" in *The New York Review of Books*, April 24, 2014, p. 46.

Chapter Outline and Focus Questions

William J. Duiker

27.1 Shopping in Moscow

Critical Thinking

Q *Why has communism survived in China when it failed to survive in Eastern Europe and Russia? Are Chinese leaders justified in claiming that without party leadership, the country would fall into chaos?*

Connections to Today

Q *Do China's successes in raising the standard of living of the Chinese people since the 1980s compensate for the continuing lack of individual freedom in the People's Republic of China today? If not, why not?*

ACCORDING TO KARL MARX, capitalism is a system that involves the exploitation of man by man; under socialism, it is the other way around. That wry joke was typical of popular humor in post–World War II Moscow, where the dreams of a future utopia had faded in the grim reality of life in the Soviet Union.

For the average Soviet citizen after World War II, few images better symbolized the shortcomings of the Soviet system than a long line of people queuing up outside an official state store selling consumer goods. Because the command economy was so inefficient, items of daily use were chronically in such short supply that when a particular item became available, people often lined up immediately to buy several for themselves and their friends. Sometimes, when people saw a line forming, they would automatically join the queue without even knowing what item was available for purchase!

Despite the evident weaknesses of the centralized Soviet economy, the Communist monopoly on power seemed secure, as did Moscow's hold over its client states in Eastern Europe. In fact, for three decades after the end of World War II, the Soviet Empire appeared to be a permanent feature of the international landscape. But by the early 1980s, it was clear that there were cracks in the Kremlin wall. The Soviet economy was stagnant, minority nationalities were restive, and Eastern European leaders were increasingly emboldened to test the waters of the global capitalist marketplace. In the United States, newly elected President Ronald Reagan boldly predicted the imminent collapse of the "evil empire."

Within less than three years (1989–1991), the Soviet Union ceased to exist as a nation. Russia and other former Soviet republics declared their separate independence, Communist regimes in Eastern Europe were toppled, and the long-standing division of postwar Europe came to an end. Although some Communist parties survived the demise of the system, their monopolies ended, and they must now compete with other parties for power.

The fate of communism in China has been quite different. Despite some turbulence, communism has survived in China, even as that nation takes giant strides toward becoming an economic superpower. Yet as China's leaders struggle to bring the nation into the modern age, many of the essential principles of Marxist–Leninist dogma have been tacitly abandoned.

27-1 THE POSTWAR SOVIET UNION

Q **Focus Questions:** How did Nikita Khrushchev change the system that the Soviet dictator Joseph Stalin had put in place before his death in 1953? Were his changes successful? Why or why not?

At the end of World War II, the Soviet Union was one of the world's two superpowers, and its leader, Joseph Stalin, was in a position of strength. He and his Soviet colleagues were now in control of a vast empire that included Eastern Europe, much of the Balkans, and new territory gained from Japan in East Asia (see Map 27.1).

27-1a From Stalin to Khrushchev

World War II had devastated the Soviet Union. Nearly 30 million citizens lost their lives, and cities such as Kiev (KEE-yev), Kharkov (KHAR-kawf), Stalingrad, and Leningrad had suffered enormous physical destruction. As the lands that had been seized by German forces were liberated, the Soviet government turned its attention to restoring their economic structures. Nevertheless, in 1945, agricultural production was only 60 percent and steel output only 50 percent of prewar levels. The Soviet people faced difficult conditions: ill-housed and poorly clothed, they worked longer hours and ate less than before the war.

Stalinism in Action In the immediate postwar years, the Soviet Union removed goods and materials from occupied Germany and extorted valuable raw materials from its satellite states in Eastern Europe (see Map 27.1). To stimulate industrial growth, Stalin applied the method he had used in the 1930s—the exploitation of Soviet labor. Working hard for little pay and for few consumer goods, Soviet workers were expected to produce goods for export with little in return for themselves. The earnings from exports could then be used to purchase machinery and Western technology. Because millions of men had died during the war, much of this tremendous workload fell on Soviet women, who performed almost 40 percent of the heavy manual labor.

The pace of economic recovery in the years immediately after the war was impressive. By 1947, industrial production had returned to 1939 levels. New power plants, canals, and giant factories were built, and industrial enterprises and oil fields were established in Siberia and Soviet Central Asia. Consumer goods, however, remained scarce as Soviet citizens were still being asked to suffer for a better tomorrow. Heavy industry grew at a rate three times that of personal consumption. Moreover, the housing shortage was acute, with living conditions especially difficult in the overcrowded cities.

Looming over the postwar Soviet scene was the country's dominant leader, Joseph Stalin. With his power enforced by several hundred thousand secret police and an estimated 9 million Soviet citizens in Siberian concentration camps, his position was secure. His morbid suspicions of potential rivals extended to even his closest colleagues, causing them to become completely cowed. As he remarked mockingly on one occasion, "When I die, the imperialists will strangle all of you like a litter of kittens."[1]

The Rise and Fall of Khrushchev Stalin died—presumably of natural causes—in 1953 and, after some bitter infighting within the party leadership, was succeeded by Georgy Malenkov, a veteran administrator and member of the Politburo (POL-it-byoor-oh), the party's governing body. But Malenkov's reform goals did not necessarily appeal to key groups, including the army, the Communist Party, the managerial elite, and the security services (now known as the Committee on Government Security, or KGB). By 1955, power had shifted to his chief rival, the new party general secretary, Nikita Khrushchev.

Once in office, Khrushchev moved vigorously to boost the performance of the Soviet economy and revitalize Soviet society. To free the national economy from the stranglehold of the central bureaucracy, he abolished dozens of government ministries and split up the party and government apparatus. Khrushchev also sought to

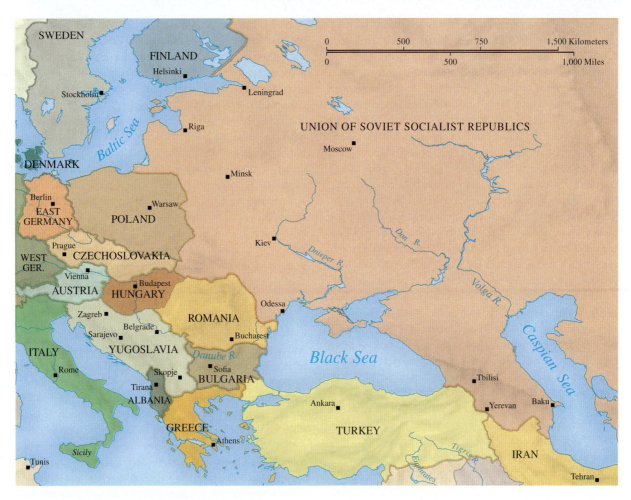

Map 27.1 Eastern Europe and the Soviet Union. After World War II, the boundaries of Eastern Europe were redrawn as a result of Allied agreements reached at the Tehran and Yalta conferences. This map shows the new boundaries that were established throughout the region, placing Soviet power at the center of Europe.

Q *How had the boundaries changed from the prewar era?*

SPUTNIK/Alamy

27.2 The Portals of Doom. Perhaps the most feared location in the Soviet Union was Lubyanka Prison, an ornate prerevolutionary building in the heart of Moscow. Taken over by the Bolsheviks after the 1917 revolution, it became the headquarters of the Soviet secret police (the Cheka, later to be known as the KGB). Here many Soviet citizens accused of "counterrevolutionary acts" were imprisoned and executed. The figure on the pedestal is that of Felix Dzerzhinsky, first director of the Cheka. After the disintegration of the Soviet Union, the statue was removed, although some Muscovites now want it returned to its original resting place.

rejuvenate the stagnant agricultural sector by increasing profit incentives and opening "virgin lands" in Soviet Kazakhstan (ka-zak-STAN or kuh-zahk-STAHN) to bring thousands of acres of new land under cultivation.

An innovator by nature, Khrushchev had to overcome the inherently conservative instincts of the Soviet bureaucracy as well as those of the mass of the population. His plan to remove the "dead hand" of the state, however laudable in intent, alienated much of the official class, and his effort to split the party angered those who saw it as the central force in the Soviet system. Khrushchev's agricultural schemes inspired similar opposition. His effort to persuade Russians to eat more corn (an idea he had apparently picked up during a visit to the United States) earned him the mocking nickname "Cornman." The industrial growth rate, which had soared in the early 1950s, now declined dramatically from 13 percent in 1953 to 7.5 percent in 1964.

Khrushchev was probably best known for his policy of **de-Stalinization**. Khrushchev had risen in the party hierarchy as a Stalin protégé, but he had been deeply disturbed by his mentor's excesses and, once in a position of authority, moved to excise the Stalinist legacy from Soviet society. The campaign began at the Party Congress in February 1956, when Khrushchev gave a long speech criticizing some of Stalin's major shortcomings. The speech had not been intended for public distribution, but it was quickly leaked to the Western press and created a sensation throughout the world (see Historical Voices, "Khrushchev Denounces Stalin," p. 687). Under Khrushchev's instructions, thousands of prisoners were released from concentration camps.

Khrushchev's personality, however, did not endear him to higher Soviet officials, who frowned at his tendency to crack jokes and play the clown. Foreign policy failures further damaged Khrushchev's reputation among his colleagues (see Chapter 26). While he was on vacation in 1964, a special meeting of the Politburo voted him out of office (because of "deteriorating health") and forced him into retirement.

27-1b The Brezhnev Years (1964–1982)

The ouster of Nikita Khrushchev in October 1964 vividly demonstrated the challenges that would be encountered by any leader sufficiently bold to try to reform the Soviet system. Leonid Brezhnev (1906–1982), the new party chief, was undoubtedly aware of these realities, and his long tenure in power was marked above all by the desire to avoid changes that might provoke instability either at home or abroad. Himself a product of the Soviet system, Brezhnev had entered the ranks of the party leadership under Stalin; although he was not a particularly avid believer in party ideology, he was no partisan of reform.

Still, Brezhnev sought stability in the domestic arena. He and his prime minister, Alexei Kosygin (1904–1980), undertook what might be described as a program of "de-Khrushchevization," returning the responsibility for long-term planning to the central ministries and reuniting the Communist Party apparatus. Despite cautious attempts to stimulate the stagnant agricultural sector, they made no effort to revise the basic system of collective farms. In the industrial sector, the regime launched a series of reforms designed to give factory managers (themselves employees of the state) more responsibility for setting prices, wages, and production quotas. These "Kosygin reforms" had little effect, however, because of stubborn resistance from the bureaucracy.

A Controlled Society Brezhnev also initiated a significant retreat from Khrushchev's policy of de-Stalinization. Criticism of the "Great Leader" had angered conservatives both within the party hierarchy and among the public at large, many of whom still revered Stalin as a hero and a defender of Russia against Nazi Germany. Early in Brezhnev's reign, Stalin's reputation began to revive. Although his alleged shortcomings were not totally ignored, he was now described in the official press as "an outstanding party leader" who had been primarily responsible for the successes achieved by the Soviet Union.

The regime also adopted a more restrictive policy toward dissidents in Soviet society. Critics of the Soviet system such as physicist Andrei Sakharov (ahn-DRAY SAH-kuh-rawf) (1921–1989) were harassed and arrested or, like famous writer Alexander Solzhenitsyn (sohl-zhuh-NEET-sinh), forced to leave the country. The media were controlled by the state and presented only what the state wanted people to hear. The government made strenuous efforts to prevent the Soviet people from being exposed to harmful foreign ideas, especially modern art, literature, and contemporary Western rock music. When the Summer Olympic Games were held in Moscow in 1980, Soviet newspapers advised citizens to keep their children indoors to prevent them from being polluted with "bourgeois" ideas passed on by foreign visitors. For citizens of Western democracies, such a political atmosphere would seem highly oppressive, but for the Russian people an emphasis on law and order was an accepted aspect of everyday life inherited from the tsarist period. It was firmly enshrined in the Soviet constitution, which subordinated individual freedom to the interests of the state. Conformity was the rule in virtually every corner of Soviet society from the educational system (characterized at all levels by rote memorization and political indoctrination) to child rearing (it was forbidden, for example, to be left-handed)

Khrushchev Denounces Stalin

Politics & Government **THREE YEARS AFTER STALIN'S DEATH,** new Soviet Premier Nikita Khrushchev addressed the Twentieth Congress of the Communist Party and denounced the former Soviet dictator for his crimes. This denunciation was the beginning of a policy of de-Stalinization. When Khruschev's comments were secretly leaked to Western news organizations, excited debate followed in countries around the world but great consternation was felt by conservative elements in the Soviet Union. One member of the Congress reportedly died of a heart attack shortly after the speech.

Khrushchev Addresses the Twentieth Party Congress, February 1956

A lot has been said about the cult of the individual and about its harmful consequences. . . . The cult of the person of Stalin . . . became at a certain specific stage the source of a whole series of exceedingly serious and grave perversions of Party principles, of Party democracy, of revolutionary legality.

Stalin absolutely did not tolerate collegiality in leadership and in work and . . . practiced brutal violence, not only toward everything which opposed him, but also toward that which seemed to his capricious and despotic character, contrary to his concepts.

Stalin abandoned the method of ideological struggle for that of administrative violence, mass repressions and terror. . . . Arbitrary behavior by one person encouraged and permitted arbitrariness in others. Mass arrests and deportations of many thousands of people, execution without trial and without normal investigation created conditions of insecurity, fear, and even desperation.

Stalin showed in a whole series of cases his intolerance, his brutality, and his abuse of power. . . . He often chose the path of repression and annihilation, not only against actual enemies, but also against individuals who had not committed any crimes against the Party and the Soviet government. . . .

Many Party, Soviet, and economic activists who were branded in 1937 and 1938 as "enemies" were actually never enemies, spies, wreckers, and so on, but were always honest communists; they were only so stigmatized, and often, no longer able to bear barbaric tortures, they charged themselves (at the order of the investigative judges-falsifiers) with all kinds of grave and unlikely crimes.

This was the result of the abuse of power by Stalin, who began to use mass terror against the Party cadres. . . . Stalin put the Party and the NKVD [the Soviet police agency] up to the use of mass terror when the exploiting classes had been liquidated in our country and when there were no serious reasons for the use of extraordinary mass terror. The terror was directed . . . against the honest workers of the Party and the Soviet state. . . .

Stalin was a very distrustful man, sickly, suspicious. . . . Everywhere and in everything he saw "enemies," "two-facers," and "spies." Possessing unlimited power, he indulged in great willfulness and choked a person morally and physically. A situation was created where one could not express one's own will. When Stalin said that one or another would be arrested, it was necessary to accept on faith that he was an "enemy of the people." What proofs were offered? The confession of the arrested. . . . How is it possible that a person confesses to crimes that he had not committed? Only in one way—because of application of physical methods of pressuring him, tortures, bringing him to a state of unconsciousness, deprivation of his judgment, taking away of his human dignity.

Q *What were the key charges that Khrushchev made against Stalin? Can it be said that Khrushchev corrected these problems?*

Source: From *Congressional Record*, 84th Congress, 2nd Session, Vol. 102, Part 7, pp. 9389–9402 (June 4, 1956).

and even to yearly vacations (most workers took their vacations at resorts run by their employer, where the daily schedule of activities was highly regimented). Young Americans studying in the Soviet Union reported that their Soviet friends were often shocked to hear U.S. citizens criticizing the U.S. president.

A Stagnant Economy Soviet leaders also failed to achieve their objective of revitalizing the national economy. Although growth rates during the 1950s had been impressive (prompting Khrushchev during a reception at the Kremlin in the 1950s to chortle to an American guest, "We will bury you"), under Brezhnev industrial growth declined to an annual rate of less than 4 percent in the early 1970s and less than 3 percent in the period from 1975 to 1980. Successes in the agricultural sector were equally meager.

One reason for the stagnation of the Soviet economy was the absence of incentives. Salary structures offered little reward for hard labor and extraordinary achievement. Pay differentials operated in a much narrower range than in most Western societies, and there was little danger of being dismissed. According to the Soviet constitution, every Soviet citizen was guaranteed an opportunity to work.

There were exceptions to the general rule. Athletic achievement was highly prized, and a gymnast of Olympic stature would be rewarded in terms of prestige and lifestyle. Senior officials did not receive high salaries but were provided with countless perquisites, such as access to foreign goods, official automobiles with a chauffeur, and entry into prestigious institutions of higher learning for their children.

An Aging Leadership

Brezhnev died in November 1982 and was succeeded by Yuri Andropov (YOOR-ee ahn-DRAHP-awf) (1914–1984), head of the Soviet secret services. During his brief tenure as party chief, Andropov was a vocal advocate of reform, but little had been done to change the system when he died after only a few months in office. He was succeeded, in turn, by a mediocre party stalwart, the elderly Konstantin Chernenko (kuhn-stuhn-TEEN chirn-YEN-koh) (1911–1985). With the Soviet system in crisis, Moscow seemed stuck in a time warp.

27-1c Cultural Expression in the Soviet Union

In his occasional musings about the future Communist utopia, Karl Marx had predicted that a new classless society would replace the exploitative and hierarchical systems of feudalism and capitalism. In their free time, workers would produce a new advanced culture that was proletarian in character and egalitarian in content.

The reality in the post–World War II Soviet Union was somewhat different. All forms of literary and scientific expression were dependent on the state and expected to follow the party line. Historians, philosophers, and social scientists all grew accustomed to quoting Marx, Lenin, and, above all, Stalin as their chief authorities. Novels and plays, too, were supposed to portray Communist heroes and their efforts to create a better society. No criticism of existing social conditions was permitted. Some areas of intellectual activity were virtually abolished; the science of genetics disappeared, and few movies were made during Stalin's final years.

27.3 Stalinist Heroic: An Example of Socialist Realism. Under Stalin and his successors, art was assigned the task of indoctrinating the Soviet population on public virtues such as hard work, loyalty to the state, and patriotism. Grandiose statuary erected to commemorate the heroic efforts of the Red Army during World War II appeared in every Soviet city. Here is an example in Minsk, today the capital of Belarus.

These restrictions, however, did not prevent the emergence of significant Soviet literature, although authors paid a heavy price if they alienated Soviet authorities. Boris Pasternak (buh-REESS PASS-tur-nak) (1890–1960), who began his literary career as a poet, won the Nobel Prize for Literature in 1958 mainly for his celebrated novel *Doctor Zhivago*, which was written between 1945 and 1956 and published in Italy in 1957. But the Soviet government condemned Pasternak's anti-Soviet tendencies, banned the novel, and would not allow him to accept the prize. The author had alienated the authorities by describing a society scarred by the excesses of Bolshevik revolutionary zeal.

Alexander Solzhenitsyn (sohl-zhih-NEET-sin) (1918–2008) created an even greater furor than Pasternak. Solzhenitsyn had spent eight years in forced-labor camps for criticizing Stalin, and his *One Day in the Life of Ivan Denisovich*, one of the works that won him the Nobel Prize in 1970, was an account of life in those camps (see Historical Voices, "One Day in the of Ivan Denisovich," p. 689). Khrushchev allowed the book's publication as part of his de-Stalinization campaign. Solzhenitsyn then wrote *The Gulag Archipelago*, a detailed indictment of the whole system of Soviet oppression. Soviet authorities expelled Solzhenitsyn from the Soviet Union in 1973.

27-1d Social Changes

According to Marxist doctrine, state control of industry and the elimination of private property were supposed to lead to a classless society. Although that ideal was never achieved, it did have important social consequences.

One Day in the Life of Ivan Denisovich

 ON NOVEMBER 20, 1962, a Soviet magazine published a work by Alexander Solzhenitsyn that unleashed a literary and political furor. The short novel related one day in the life of its chief character, Ivan Denisovich, at a Siberian concentration camp, to which he had been sentenced at the end of World War II for supposedly spying for the Germans while a Soviet soldier. This excerpt narrates the daily journey from the prison camp to a work project through the subzero cold of Siberia. Many Soviets identified with Ivan as a symbol of the suffering they had endured under Stalin.

Alexander Solzhenitsyn, *One Day in the Life of Ivan Denisovich*

There were escort guards all over the place. They flung a semicircle around the column on its way to the power station, their machine guns sticking out and pointing right at your face. And there were guards with gray dogs. One dog bared its fangs as if laughing at the prisoners. The escorts all wore short sheepskins, except for half a dozen whose coats trailed the ground. The long sheepskins were interchangeable: they were worn by anyone whose turn had come to man the watchtowers.

And once again as they brought the squads together the escort recounted the entire power-station column by fives. . . .

Out beyond the camp boundary the intense cold, accompanied by a headwind, stung even Shukhov's face, which was used to every kind of unpleasantness. Realizing that he would have the wind in his face all the way to the power station, he decided to make use of his bit of rag. To meet the contingency of a headwind he, like many other prisoners, had got himself a cloth with a long tape on each end. The prisoners admitted that these helped a bit. Shukhov covered his face up to the eyes, brought the tapes around below his ears, and fastened the ends together at the back of his neck. Then he covered his nape with the flap of his hat and raised his coat collar. The next thing was to pull the front flap of the hat down into his brow. Thus in front only his eyes remained unprotected. He fixed his coat tightly at the waist with the rope. Now everything was in order except for his hands, which were already stiff with cold (his mittens were worthless). He rubbed them, he clapped them together, for he knew that in a moment he'd have to put them behind his back and keep them there for the entire march.

The chief of the escort guard recited the "morning prayer," which every prisoner was heartily sick of:

"Attention, prisoners. Marching orders must be strictly obeyed. Keep to your ranks. No hurrying, keep a steady pace. No talking. Keep your eyes fixed ahead and your hands behind your backs. A step to right or left is considered an attempt to escape and the escort has orders to shoot without warning. Leading guards, on the double."

The two guards in the lead of the escort must have set out along the road. The column heaved forward, shoulders swaying, and the escorts, some twenty paces to the right and left of the column, each man at a distance of ten paces from the next, machine guns held at the ready, set off too.

Q *What was the author's purpose in writing this literary work? How did it contribute to Khrushchev's destalinization program?*

Source: Alexander Solzhenitsyn, *One Day in the Life of Ivan Denisovich* (tr. by Ralph Parker), translation copyright 1963 by E.P. Dutton and Victor Gollancz, Ltd.. Copyright renewed in 1991 by Penguin USA and Victor Gollancz Ltd.

The desire to create a classless society, for example, led to noticeable changes in education. In their effort to weaken the influence of traditional elites, children of manual laborers were given preference in both job opportunities and education. This led to the emergence of a new privileged class composed of party members, government officials, and professional groups. The new elite not only possessed political power but also received special privileges, including the right to purchase high-quality goods in special stores, access to good housing and medical treatment, and advantages in education for their children.

The regime also did not measure up in terms of its treatment of women. Although women did have greater opportunities in the workforce and even in the professions (women constituted 51 percent of the labor force in 1980, including 50 percent of engineers, 80 percent of doctors, and 75 percent of teachers), pay scales were unequal—and the chief administrators in hospitals and schools were still men. Moreover, although women made up half of the workforce, they remained tied to their traditional roles in the home. Most women had to work what became known as the "double shift." After working eight hours in their jobs, they returned home to do the housework and care for the children. They might also spend two hours a day in long lines at several stores waiting to buy food and clothes.

Nearly three-quarters of a century after the Bolshevik Revolution, then, the Marxist dream of an advanced, egalitarian society was still far away. Although in some respects conditions in the socialist camp were a distinct improvement over those before World War II, many problems and inequities were as intransigent as ever.

27-2 THE DISINTEGRATION OF THE SOVIET EMPIRE

Focus Questions: What were the key components of perestroika espoused by Mikhail Gorbachev during the 1980s? Why did perestroika fail?

On the death of Konstantin Chernenko in 1985, party leaders selected the talented and youthful Soviet official Mikhail Gorbachev to succeed him. The new Soviet leader had shown early signs of promise. Born into a peasant family in 1931, Gorbachev earned a good school record that enabled him to study law at the University of Moscow. After graduating in 1955, he moved up quickly in the ranks of the party and in 1978 became a member of the Central Committee in Moscow. Two years later, he became a full member of the ruling Politburo.

In Moscow, Gorbachev began to realize the immensity of Soviet problems and the crucial need for massive reform to transform the system. During a visit to Canada in 1983, he discovered to his astonishment that Canadian farmers worked hard on their own initiative. "We'll never have this for fifty years," he reportedly remarked.[2] On his return to Moscow, he set in motion a series of committees to evaluate the situation and recommend measures to improve the system.

27-2a The Gorbachev Era

With his election as party general secretary in 1985, Gorbachev sought to take earlier reforms to their logical conclusions. The cornerstone of his program was *perestroika* (per-uh-STROI-kuh), or "restructuring." At first, it meant only a reordering of economic policy, as Gorbachev called for the beginning of a market economy with limited free enterprise and some private property (see

Comparative Illustration, "Sideline Industries: Creeping Capitalism in a Socialist Paradise," p. 691). But Gorbachev soon perceived that in the Soviet system, the economic sphere was intimately tied to the social and political spheres. Any efforts to reform the economy without political or social reform would be doomed to failure. As a result, a key component of perestroika was *glasnost* (GLAHZ-nohst), or "openness." Soviet citizens and officials were encouraged to openly discuss the strengths and weaknesses of the Soviet Union. The arts also benefited from the new policy, and previously banned works were now published and motion pictures were allowed to depict negative aspects of Soviet life. Music based on Western styles such as jazz and rock could now be performed openly. Religious activities, long banned by the authorities, were once again tolerated.

Political reforms were equally revolutionary. In June 1987, the principle of two-candidate elections was introduced; previously, voters had been presented with only one candidate. A year later, Gorbachev called for the creation of a new Soviet parliament, the Congress of People's Deputies, whose members were to be chosen in competitive elections. It convened in 1989, the first such meeting in the nation since 1918. Early in 1990, Gorbachev legalized the formation of other political parties and struck out Article 6 of the Soviet constitution, which guaranteed the "leading role" of the Communist Party. Hitherto, the position of first secretary of the party was the most important post in the Soviet Union, but as the Communist Party became less closely associated with the state, the powers of this office diminished. Gorbachev attempted to consolidate his power by creating a new state presidency, and in March 1990 he became the Soviet Union's first president.

End of Empire One of Gorbachev's most serious problems stemmed from the character of the Soviet Union. The Union of Soviet Socialist Republics was a truly multiethnic country, containing 92 nationalities and 112 recognized languages. Previously, the iron hand of the Communist Party, centered in Moscow, had kept a lid on the centuries-old ethnic tensions that had periodically erupted throughout the history of the region. As Gorbachev released this iron grip, ethnic groups throughout the Soviet Union began to call for sovereignty of the republics and independence from Russian-based rule from Moscow.

On March 11, 1990, the tiny Soviet Republic of Lithuania announced its independence from Soviet rule. When authorities in Moscow declared the announcement null and void, the Lithuanians ignored the statement. For the next several months, Gorbachev struggled to cope with the challenges unleashed by

Sideline Industries: Creeping Capitalism in a Socialist Paradise

Politics & Government

IN THE LATE 1980S, Communist leaders in both the Soviet Union and China began to encourage their citizens to engage in private commercial activities as a means of reviving moribund economies. In Image 27.4a, a Soviet farmworker displays fruits and vegetables on a street corner in Odessa, a seaport on the Black Sea. In Image 27.4b, a Chinese woman sells her dumplings to passersby in Shandong Province. As her smile suggests, the Chinese took up the challenge of entrepreneurship with much greater success and enthusiasm than their Soviet counterparts did.

Q *Why did Chinese citizens adopt capitalist reforms in the countryside more enthusiastically than their Soviet counterparts?*

William J. Duiker

27.4b

William J. Duiker

27.4a

---

his reforms while seeking to appease conservative forces who complained about the growing disorder within the country. The effort was futile. Ukraine voted for independence on December 1, 1991. A week later, the leaders of Russia, Ukraine, and Belarus (bell-uh-ROOSS) announced that the Soviet Union had "ceased to exist" and would be replaced by a "commonwealth of independent states." Gorbachev resigned on December 25, 1991, and turned over his responsibilities as commander in chief to Boris Yeltsin (YELT-sun) (1931–2007), the president of Russia. By the end of 1991, one of the largest empires in world history had come to an end, and a new era had begun in its lands (see Chapter 28).

Experience an interactive version of this period in MINDTAP

HISTORIANS DEBATE 27-2b **Why Did the Soviet Union Collapse?**

What caused the sudden disintegration of the Soviet system? Some historians argue that the ambitious defense policies adopted by the Reagan administration forced Moscow into an arms race that it could not afford and that ultimately led to the collapse of the Soviet economy. This contention has some superficial plausibility, because Soviet leaders did indeed react to Reagan's Star Wars program by increasing their own defense expenditures, which put a strain on the Soviet budget. And President Reagan was also prescient for having recognized the vulnerability of the Soviet system at a time when most analysts doubted that it would collapse any time in the near future.

Still, most knowledgeable observers believe that the fall of the Soviet Union was primarily a consequence of conditions inherent in the system, several of which have been pointed out in this chapter. For decades, leaders in the Kremlin had disguised or ignored the massive inefficiencies in the Soviet economy. In the 1980s, time began to run out. The perceptive Mikhail Gorbachev tried to stem the decline by instituting radical reforms, but by then it was too late.

An additional factor should also be considered. One of the most vulnerable aspects of the Soviet Union was its multiethnic character, with only a little more than half of the total population composed of ethnic Russians. Many of the minority nationalities were becoming increasingly restive and were demanding more autonomy or even independence for their regions. In the eyes of some astute observers, it was such demands—more than the state of the economy—that brought about the final collapse of the system. The Soviet Empire died at least partly from imperial overreach.

27-3 THE EAST IS RED: CHINA UNDER COMMUNISM

Q **Focus Question:** What were Mao Zedong's chief goals for China, and what policies did he institute to try to achieve them?

A revolution is not a dinner party, or writing an essay, or painting a picture, or doing embroidery; it cannot be so refined, so leisurely and gentle, so temperate and kind, courteous, restrained, and magnanimous. A revolution

is an insurrection, an act of violence by which one class overthrows another.[3]

These words were written in 1926, a time when the Communists—in cooperation with Chiang Kai-shek's Nationalist Party—were embarked on their Northern Expedition to defeat the warlords and reunify China. The young revolutionary Mao Zedong was warning his colleagues that the road to victory in the struggle to build a Communist society would be arduous and would inevitably involve acts of violence against the class enemy.

In the fall of 1949, China was at peace for the first time in twelve years. The newly victorious Communist Party under the leadership of Chairman Mao Zedong now turned its attention to consolidating its power base and healing the wounds of war. Its long-term goal was to construct a socialist society, but its leaders realized that popular support for the revolution was based on the party's platform of honest government, land reform, social justice, and peace rather than on the utopian goal of a classless society. Accordingly, the new regime temporarily set aside Mao Zedong's stirring exhortation of 1926 and adopted a moderate program of political and economic recovery known as New Democracy.

27-3a New Democracy

With **New Democracy**—which was patterned roughly after Lenin's New Economic Policy in Soviet Russia in the 1920s (see Chapter 23)—the new Chinese leadership tacitly recognized that time and extensive indoctrination would be needed to convince the Chinese people of the superiority of socialism. In the meantime, the party would rely on capitalist profit incentives to spur productivity. Manufacturing and commercial firms were permitted to remain under private ownership, although with stringent government regulations. To win the support of the poorer peasants, who made up the majority of the population, a land-redistribution program was adopted, but the collectivization of agriculture was postponed.

In several key respects, New Democracy was a success. Although the land reform program was marked by considerable violence—thousands if not millions of better-off farmers lost their lands, their personal property, and sometimes their lives—some two-thirds of peasant households in the country received land and thus had reason to be grateful to the new regime (see Historical Voices, "Land Reform in the Countryside," p. 693). Spurred by official tolerance for capitalist activities and the end of internal conflict, the national economy began to rebound, although agricultural production still lagged

Land Reform in the Countryside

Family & Society

ONE OF THE GREAT ACHIEVEMENTS of the new Communist regime in China was the land-reform program, which resulted in the distribution of farmland to almost two-thirds of the rural population. The program consequently won the gratitude of millions of Chinese. But it also had a dark side as local land reform tribunals routinely convicted "wicked landlords" of crimes against the people and then put them to death. The following passage, written by a foreign observer, describes the process in one village.

Revolution in a Chinese Village

T'ien-ming [a Party cadre] called all the active young cadres and the militiamen of Long Bow [village] together and announced to them the policy of the county government, which was to confront all enemy collaborators and their backers at public meetings, expose their crimes, and turn them over to the county authorities for punishment. He proposed that they start with Kuo Te-yu, the puppet village head. Having moved the group to anger with a description of Te-yu's crimes, T'ien-ming reviewed the painful life led by the poor peasants during the occupation and recalled how hard they had all worked and how as soon as they harvested all the grain the puppet officials, backed by army bayonets, took what they wanted, turned over huge quantities to the Japanese devils, forced the peasants to haul it away, and flogged those who refused.

As the silent crowd contracted toward the spot where the accused man stood, T'ien-ming stepped forward. . . . "This is our chance. Remember how we were oppressed. The traitors seized our property. They beat us and kicked us. . . .

"Let us speak out the bitter memories. Let us see that the blood debt is repaid. . . ."

He paused for a moment. The peasants were listening to every word but gave no sign as to how they felt. . . .

"Come now, who has evidence against this man?"

Again there was silence.

Kuei-ts'ai, the new vice-chairman of the village, found it intolerable. He jumped up [and] struck Kuo Te-yu on the jaw with the back of his hand. "Tell the meeting how much you stole," he demanded. . . .

The people in the square waited fascinated as if watching a play. They did not realize that in order for the plot to unfold they themselves had to mount the stage and speak out what was on their minds.

That evening T'ien-ming and Kuei-ts'ai called together the small groups of poor peasants from various parts of the village and sought to learn what it was that was really holding them back. They soon found the root of the trouble was fear of the old established political forces, and their military backers. . . .

Emboldened by T'ien-ming's words, other peasants began to speak out. They recalled what Te-yu had done to them personally. Several vowed to speak up and accuse him the next morning. . . .

On the following day the meeting was livelier by far. It began with a sharp argument as to who would make the first accusation, and T'ien-ming found it difficult to keep order. Before Te-yu had a chance to reply to any questions, a crowd of young men, among whom were several militiamen, surged forward ready to beat him.

Q *What was the Communist Party's purpose in carrying out land reform in China? How did the tactics employed here support that strategy?*

Source: From Richard Solomon, *Mao's Revolution and the Chinese Political Culture*, pp. 198–199. Copyright © 1971 Center for Chinese Studies, University of Michigan.

---

behind both official targets and the growing population, which was increasing at an annual rate of more than 2 percent.

27-3b The Transition to Socialism

In 1953, party leaders launched the nation's first five-year plan (patterned after similar Soviet plans), which called for substantial increases in industrial output. Lenin had believed that mechanization would induce Russian peasants to join collective farms, which could better afford to purchase expensive farm machinery because of the collective farms' greater size and efficiency. But the difficulty of providing tractors and reapers for millions of rural villages eventually convinced Mao that it would take years, if not decades, for China's infant industrial base to meet the needs of a modernizing agricultural sector. He, therefore, decided to begin collectivization immediately in the hope that collective farms would increase food production and release land, labor, and capital for the industrial sector. Accordingly, beginning in 1955, virtually all private farmland was collectivized (although peasant families were allowed to retain small private plots), and most businesses and industries were nationalized.

Collectivization was achieved without provoking the massive peasant unrest that had taken place in the Soviet Union during the 1930s, but the desired production increases did not materialize. In 1958, at Mao's insistent urging, party leaders approved a more radical program known as the **Great Leap Forward**. Existing rural collectives, normally the size of a traditional village, were combined into vast "people's communes," each containing more than 30,000 people. These communes were to be responsible for all administrative and economic tasks at the local level. The party's official slogan promised "Hard work for a few years, happiness for a thousand."[4]

The communes were a disaster. Administrative bottlenecks, bad weather, and peasant resistance to the new system (which, among other things, attempted to eliminate work incentives and destroy the traditional family as the basic unit of Chinese society) combined to drive food production downward, and over the next few years, as many as 15 million people may have died of starvation. In 1960, the experiment was essentially abandoned. Although the commune structure was retained, ownership and management were returned to the collective level. Mao was severely criticized by some of his more pragmatic colleagues.

27-3c The Great Proletarian Cultural Revolution

But Mao was not yet ready to abandon either his power or his dream of a totally egalitarian society. In 1966, he returned to the attack, mobilizing discontented youth and disgruntled party members into revolutionary units soon to be known as Red Guards, who were urged to take to the streets to cleanse Chinese society—from local schools and factories around the country to government ministries in Beijing—of impure elements who (in Mao's mind, at least) were guilty of "taking the capitalist road." Supported by his wife, Jiang Qing (jahng CHING), and other radical party figures, Mao launched China on a new forced march toward communism.

The so-called **Great Proletarian Cultural Revolution** lasted for ten years, from 1966 to 1976. Some Western observers interpreted it as a simple power struggle between Mao Zedong and some of his key rivals such as Liu Shaoqi [lyoo show-CHEE ("ow" as in "how")], Mao's designated successor, and Deng Xiaoping [DUHNG show-PING ("ow" as in "how")], the party's general secretary. Both were removed from their positions, and Liu later died in a Chinese prison allegedly from torture. But real policy disagreements were involved. Mao and his supporters feared that capitalist values and the remnants of "feudalist" Confucian ideas would undermine ideological fervor and betray the revolutionary cause. He was convinced that only an atmosphere of "**uninterrupted revolution**" could enable the Chinese to overcome the lethargy of the past and achieve the final stage of utopian communism.

Mao's opponents argued for a more pragmatic strategy that gave priority to nation building over the ultimate Communist goal of spiritual transformation. (Deng Xiaoping reportedly once remarked, "Black cat, white cat, what does it matter so long as it catches the mice?") But with Mao's supporters now in power, the party carried out reforms that virtually eliminated any remaining profit incentives, established a new school system that emphasized "Mao Zedong thought," and stressed practical education at the elementary level at the expense of specialized training in science and the humanities in the universities. School learning was discouraged as a legacy of capitalism, and Mao's famous Little Red Book (officially, *Quotations of Chairman Mao Zedong*, a slim volume of aphorisms to encourage good behavior and revolutionary zeal) was hailed as the most important source of knowledge in all areas.

The radicals' efforts to destroy all vestiges of traditional society were reminiscent of the Reign of Terror in revolutionary France, when the Jacobins sought to destroy organized religion and even created a new revolutionary calendar. Red Guards rampaged through the country, torturing and killing thousands of alleged "capitalist roaders" in an effort to eradicate the "four olds" (old thought, old culture, old customs, and old habits). They destroyed temples and religious sculptures; they tore down street signs and replaced them with new ones carrying revolutionary names. At one point, the city of Shanghai even ordered that the significance of colors in stoplights be changed so that red (the revolutionary color) would indicate that traffic could move.

But a mood of revolutionary ferment and enthusiasm is difficult to sustain. Key groups—including bureaucrats, urban professionals, and many military officers—did not share Mao's belief in the benefits of "uninterrupted revolution" and constant turmoil. Personal accounts by young Chinese who took part in the movement show that their own initial enthusiasm often turned to disillusionment—especially when the victims were friends or members of their own families. Inevitably, the sense of anarchy and uncertainty caused popular support for the movement to erode, and when the end came in 1976 the vast majority of the population may well have welcomed its demise.

AP Images

27.5 Punishing China's Enemies During the Cultural Revolution. The Cultural Revolution, which began in 1966, was a massive effort by Mao Zedong and his radical supporters to eliminate rival elements within the Chinese Communist Party and the government. Accused of being "capitalist roaders," such individuals were subjected to public criticism and removed from their positions. Some were imprisoned or executed. Here Red Guards parade a victim wearing a dunce cap through the streets of Beijing.

27-3d From Mao to Deng

Mao Zedong died in September 1976 at age eighty-three. After a short but bitter succession struggle, the pragmatists led by Deng Xiaoping (1904–1997) seized power from the radicals and formally brought the Cultural Revolution to an end. The egalitarian policies of the previous decade were reversed, and a new program emphasizing economic modernization was introduced.

Under the leadership of Deng Xiaoping, who placed his supporters in key positions throughout the party and the government, attention focused on what were called the **Four Modernizations**: industry, agriculture, technology, and national defense. Many of the restrictions against private activities and profit incentives were eliminated, and people were encouraged to work hard to benefit themselves and Chinese society. The familiar slogan "Serve the people" was replaced by a new one repugnant to the tenets of Mao Zedong thought: "Create wealth for the people."

By adopting this pragmatic approach, China made great strides in ending its chronic problems of poverty and underdevelopment. Per capita income roughly doubled during the 1980s; housing, education, and sanitation improved; and both agricultural and industrial output skyrocketed. Some critics, both Chinese and foreign, complained that Deng's program had failed to address a "fifth modernization": democracy. In the late 1970s, ordinary citizens pasted "big character posters" criticizing the abuses of the past on the so-called Democracy Wall near Tiananmen (tee-AHN-ahn-muhn) Square in downtown Beijing. But it soon became clear that the new leaders would not tolerate any direct criticism of the Communist Party or of Marxist–Leninist ideology. Dissidents were suppressed, and some were sentenced to long prison terms.

27-3e Incident at Tiananmen Square

As long as economic conditions for the majority of Chinese were improving, the government was able to isolate dissidents from other elements in society. But in the late 1980s, an overheated economy led to rising inflation and growing discontent among salaried workers, especially in the cities. At the same time, corruption, nepotism, and favored treatment for senior officials and party members were provoking increasing criticism. In May 1989, student protesters carried placards demanding "Science and Democracy," an end to official corruption, and the resignation of China's aging party leadership. These demands received widespread support from the urban population (although notably less in rural areas) and led to massive demonstrations in Tiananmen Square.

The demonstrations divided the Chinese leaders. Reformist elements around party general secretary Zhao Ziyang (JOW dzee-YAHNG) were sympathetic to the protesters, but veteran leaders such as Deng Xiaoping saw the student demands for more democracy as a disguised call for an end to Chinese Communist Party (CCP) rule (see Opposing Viewpoints, "Students Appeal for Democracy," p. 697). After some hesitation, the government sent tanks and troops into Tiananmen Square to crush the demonstrators. Dissidents were arrested, an unknown number were killed, and the regime once again began to stress ideological purity and socialist values. Although the crackdown came under widespread criticism abroad, Chinese leaders insisted that economic reforms could take place only in conditions of party leadership and political stability.

In taking firm action against the demonstrators, Deng and other aging party leaders were undoubtedly counting on the fact that many Chinese, particularly in rural areas, feared a recurrence of the disorder of the Cultural Revolution and craved economic prosperity more than political reform. In the months after the crackdown, the regime issued new regulations requiring courses on Marxist–Leninist ideology in the schools, suppressed dissidents within the intellectual community, and made it clear that the CCP would not be allowed to lose its monopoly on power and that economic reforms would continue. Harsh punishments were imposed on those accused of undermining the Communist system and supporting its enemies abroad.

27-3f Riding the Tiger

After Tiananmen, party leaders began to realize the complexity of maintaining control and stability in a rapidly changing society. "When you ride the tiger," goes an ancient Chinese proverb, "it's hard to dismount." Accordingly, in the 1990s the government sought to nurture urban support by reducing the rate of inflation and guaranteeing the availability of consumer goods in demand among the rising middle class. Under Deng's successor, Jiang Zemin (JAHNG zuh-MIN) (b. 1926), the government promoted

rapid economic growth while cracking down harshly on political dissent. Massive construction projects, including a nationwide rail network, modern airports, and dams to provide hydroelectric power, were initiated throughout the country. As industrial production continued to rise, living standards, at least in urban areas, soon followed, and outside observers began to predict that China would become one of the economic superpowers of the twenty-first century.

But now a new challenge arose as lagging farm income, official corruption, and increasing environmental problems began to spark resentment in the countryside. Highly sensitive to the historic record that suggested that peasant revolt was often the harbinger of dynastic collapse, party leaders sought to contain the issues with a combination of the carrot and the stick. The problem was complicated, however, by the fact that with the rise of cell phones and the Internet, the Chinese people were becoming much more aware of events taking place around them. As the public exchange of ideas rapidly increased in the new electronic age, dissidents found a forum to voice their views, while countless ordinary people were newly enabled to exchange information on incidents and issues that official sources wished to suppress. Although the regime scrambled to arrest or intimidate key dissidents and limit public access to events taking place in China and around the world, it was facing an uphill battle.

New leaders installed in 2002 appeared aware of the magnitude of the problem. Hu Jintao [HOO jin-TOW ("ow" as in "how")] (b. 1943), the new party general secretary and head of state, called for further reforms to open up Chinese society, reduce the level of corruption, and bridge the yawning gap between rich and poor. But the new policies did not entirely fulfill expectations. Although the economy continued to grow rapidly during the first decade of the new millennium, many of the key issues of public concern remained unresolved. As party elders gathered in fall 2012 to select a new slate of leaders for the next decade, it was clear that rapid economic growth by itself was not a panacea for China's ills.

In the fall of 2010, Xi Jinping (SHEE jin-ping) (b. 1953), the son of one of Mao Zedong's closest comrades, was elected president of the People's Republic of China. As a young man, Xi had spent time in the United States and he was generally viewed as a pragmatist, but it soon became clear that he was determined to adopt an ambitious agenda to attack the country's problems and bring to fruition what he described as "the Chinese dream," a slogan that appeared to reflect above all the traditional imperial goal of wealth and power. Although one of his most highly publicized goals was to target the rampant corruption within the senior ranks of the party, he undercut his message by

Students Appeal for Democracy

Politics & Government

IN THE SPRING OF 1989, thousands of students gathered in Tiananmen Square in downtown Beijing. They were there to provide moral support to their many compatriots who had gone on a hunger strike trying to compel the Chinese government to reduce the level of official corruption and enact democratic reforms and open the political process to the Chinese people. The first selection is from an editorial published on April 26 by the official newspaper *People's Daily*. Fearing that the student demonstrations would get out of hand, as had happened during the Cultural Revolution, the editorial condemned the protests for being contrary to the CCP. The second selection is from a statement by Zhao Ziyang, the party general secretary, who argued that many of the students' demands were justified. On May 17, student leaders distributed flyers explaining the goals of the movement to participants and passersby, including the author of this chapter. The third selection is from one of these flyers.

People's Daily Editorial, April 26, 1989

This is a well-planned plot . . . to confuse the people and throw the country into turmoil. . . . Its real aim is to reject the Chinese Communist Party and the socialist system at the most fundamental level. . . . This is a most serious political struggle that concerns the whole Party and nation.

Statement by Party General Secretary Zhao Ziyang Before Party Colleagues, May 4, 1989

Let me tell you how I see all this. I think the student movement has two important characteristics. First, the students' slogans call for things like supporting the Constitution, promoting democracy, and fighting corruption. These demands all echo positions of the Party and the government. Second, a great many people from all parts of society are out there joining the demonstrations and backing the students. . . . This has grown into a nationwide protest. I think the best way to bring the thing to a quick end is to focus on the mainstream views of the majority.

"Why Do We Have to Undergo a Hunger Strike?"

By 2:00 P.M. today, the hunger strike carried out by the petition group in Tiananmen Square has been under way for 96 hours. By this morning, more than 600 participants have fainted. When these democracy fighters were lifted into the ambulances, no one who was present was not moved to tears.

Our petition group now undergoing the hunger strike demands that at a minimum the government agree to the following two points:

1. To engage on a sincere and equal basis in a dialogue with the "higher education dialogue group." In addition, to broadcast the actual dialogue in its entirety. We absolutely refuse to agree to a partial broadcast, to empty gestures, or to fabrications that dupe the people.

2. To evaluate in a fair and realistic way the patriotic democratic movement. Discard the label of

William J. Duiker

27.6 Student Demonstrations in Beijing

(continued)

"troublemaking" and redress the reputation of the patriotic democratic movement.

It is our view that the request for a dialogue between the people's government and the people is not an unreasonable one. Our party always follows the principle of seeking truths from actual facts. It is therefore only natural that the evaluation of this patriotic democratic movement should be done in accordance with the principle of seeking truths from actual facts.

Our classmates who are going through the hunger strike are the good sons and daughters of the people! One by one, they have fallen. In the meantime, our "public servants" are completely unmoved. Please, let us ask where your conscience is.

Q *What were the key demands of the protesters in Tiananmen Square? Why were they rejected by the Chinese government?*

Sources: From *People's Daily* editorial, April 26, 1989. Statement by party chairman Zhao Ziyang before party colleagues, May 4, 1989. Original flyer in possession of author.

---

simultaneously taking steps to strengthen the state-owned enterprises, a sector of the economy that was not only marked by inefficiency but also the source of much of the wealth in the hands of many leading government and party officials.

Xi was also quick to attack potential adversaries at home and abroad. Internally, he cracked down on critics who sought—in his words—"to negate the legitimacy of the long-term rule of the CCP." Externally he adopted an aggressive posture against perceived threats to national security from hostile Western forces and ideas. As he began his second term in office, President Xi continued to consolidate his power while seeking to "ride the tiger" of China's long-term growth into a major world power.

27-3g Back to Confucius?

Through this period of trial and error, senior leaders have remained steadfast in their belief that the Communist Party must remain the sole political force in charge of carrying out the revolution. Ever fearful of chaos, they are convinced that only a firm hand at the tiller can keep the ship of state from crashing onto the rocks. At the same time, they have tacitly come to recognize that Marxist exhortations are no longer an effective means of enforcing social discipline. Accordingly, they have increasingly turned to the time-honored nostrum of Confucianism as a tool to influence political and social attitudes. Ceremonies celebrating the birth of Confucius now receive official sanction, and hallowed social virtues such as righteousness, propriety, and filial piety are widely cited as an antidote to the tide of antisocial behavior.

In a striking departure from the precepts of Marxist internationalism, official sources in Beijing have also turned to Chinese history to defend their assertion that China is unique and will not follow the path of "peaceful evolution" (to use their term) toward a future democratic capitalist society. In words that turn the teachings of Mao Zedong on their head, President Xi has quoted the ideas of some of China's ancient Legalist thinkers while declaring that the party is "the loyal inheritor and promoter of China's traditional culture." The virtues of ancient State Confucianism are extolled, while the United States is publicly ridiculed for the allegedly dysfunctional character of its own democratic system of government.

The regime has also begun to rely on another familiar tactic to retain control—stoking the fires of nationalism. Although Chinese leaders have never been shy in defending what are now labeled their "core interests" within the eastern Pacific Rim, they have tended to adopt cautious policies in practice. Recently, however, China has begun to play an increasingly assertive role in the region. It has not been shy in seeking to counter U.S. influence in East and Southeast Asia, and it has aroused concern by claiming sole ownership over the Spratly (sprat-LEE) Islands in the South China Sea and over the Diaoyu (DYOW-you) Islands (also claimed by Japan, which calls them the Senkakus) near Taiwan (see Map 27.2). To strengthen their presence in the area, the PRC has recently built artificial islands not far from the coast of the Philippines and has made no secret of its determination to create a deepwater navy that can compete with potential rivals over influence within the region. In the meantime, relations with the United States over the island of Taiwan always a matter of considerable sensitivity on both sides, have become increasingly tense (see Chapter 30).

To some of its neighbors, China's new posture raises suspicions that Beijing is once again preparing to flex its muscle as it did periodically in the imperial era. Chinese leaders, however, view such actions as legitimate efforts to resume China's rightful role in the affairs of the region. After a century of humiliation at the hands of Western powers and neighboring Japan, the nation—in Mao's famous words at the Gate of Heavenly Peace in 1949—"has stood up," and no one will be permitted to humiliate it again.

Map 27.2 The People's Republic of China. This map shows China's current boundaries. Major regions are indicated in capital letters.

Which regions have movements against Chinese rule?

Most Chinese appear to approve of their government's assertive role in world affairs. In recent years, a fervent patriotism seems to be on the rise in China, one actively promoted by the party as a means of holding the country together. The decision by the International Olympic Committee to award the 2008 Summer Olympic Games to Beijing led to widespread celebration throughout the country. The event symbolized China's emergence as a major national power on the world stage. A large majority also support China's insistence that the island of Taiwan should be returned to the control of the motherland (see Chapter 30).

Pumping up the spirit of patriotism, however, is not the solution to all problems. Unrest is growing among China's national minorities: in Xinjiang (SHIN-jyahng), where restless Muslim peoples are observing with curiosity the emergence of independent Islamic states in Central Asia, and in Tibet, where the official policy of

CHRONOLOGY	China Under Communist Rule
New Democracy	1949–1955
Era of collectivization	1955–1958
Great Leap Forward	1958–1960
Great Proletarian Cultural Revolution	1966–1976
Death of Mao Zedong	1976
Era of Deng Xiaoping	1978–1997
Tiananmen Square incident	1989
Presidency of Jiang Zemin	1993–2002
Olympic Games held in Beijing	2008
Xi Jinping becomes president	2012

quelling separatist sentiment has led to the violent suppression of Tibetan culture and an influx of thousands of ethnic Chinese immigrants. In the meantime, the rise

27.7 The Potala Palace in Tibet. Tibet was a distant and reluctant appendage of the Chinese empire during the Qing Dynasty. Since the Communist Party's rise to power in 1949, the regime in Beijing has consistently sought to integrate Tibet into the People's Republic of China. Resistance to Chinese rule, however, has been widespread. In recent years, the Dalai Lama, the leading religious figure in Tibetan Buddhism, has attempted without success to persuade Chinese leaders to allow a measure of autonomy for the Tibetan people. In 2008, massive riots by frustrated Tibetans took place in the capital city of Lhasa (LAH-suh) just before the opening of the Olympic Games in Beijing. The Potala Palace, symbol of Tibetan identity, was constructed in the seventeenth century in Lhasa and serves today as the foremost symbol of the national and cultural aspirations of the Tibetan people.

of evangelical sects like the Falun Gong (FAH-loon GONG) religious movement (which the regime had attempted to eliminate as a potentially serious threat to its authority), is an additional indication that with the disintegration of the old Maoist utopia, the Chinese people will need more than a pallid version of Marxism–Leninism or a revived Confucianism to fill the gap.

27-4 "SERVE THE PEOPLE": CHINESE SOCIETY UNDER COMMUNISM

Q Focus Question: What significant political, economic, and social changes have taken place in China since the death of Mao Zedong?

When the Communist Party came to power in 1949, Chinese leaders made it clear that their policies would differ from the Soviet model in one key respect. While the Bolsheviks had relied almost exclusively on the use of force to achieve their objectives, the CCP carried out reforms aimed at winning support from the mass of the population. Although the land-reform program adopted in the early 1950s was marked by a violent struggle against "class enemies" in the countryside, the party's "mass line"

policy, as it was called, worked fairly well until the late 1950s, when Mao and his radical allies adopted policies such as the Great Leap Forward that began to alienate much of the population. Ideological purity was valued over expertise in building an advanced and prosperous society.

27-4a Economics in Command

When he came to power in the late 1970s, Deng Xiaoping recognized the need to restore credibility to a system on the verge of breakdown, and he hoped that rapid economic growth would satisfy the Chinese people and prevent them from demanding political reforms. Accordingly, the post-Mao leaders clearly emphasized economic performance over ideological purity. To stimulate the stagnant industrial sector, they reduced bureaucratic controls over state industries and allowed local managers to have more say over prices, salaries, and quality control. Productivity was encouraged by permitting bonuses for extra effort, a policy that had been discouraged during the Cultural Revolution. The regime also tolerated the emergence of a small private sector. The unemployed were encouraged to set up restaurants or small shops on their own initiative.

Finally, the regime opened up the country to foreign investment and technology. Special economic zones were established in urban centers near the coast (ironically, many were located in the old nineteenth-century treaty ports), where lucrative concessions were offered to encourage foreign firms to build factories. The tourist industry was encouraged, and students were sent abroad to study.

The new leaders stressed educational reform. The system adopted during the Cultural Revolution—emphasizing practical education and ideology at the expense of higher education and modern science—was rapidly abandoned (Mao's Little Red Book was even withdrawn from circulation), and a new system based generally on the Western model was instituted. Admission to higher education was based on success in merit examinations, and courses in science and mathematics received high priority.

Agricultural Reform   No economic reform program could succeed unless it included the countryside. Three decades of socialism had done little to increase food production or to lay the basis for a modern agricultural sector. China, with a population numbering 1 billion, could still barely feed itself. Peasants had little incentive to work and few opportunities to increase production through mechanization, the use of fertilizer, or better irrigation.

Under Deng, agricultural policy made a rapid about-face. Under the new **rural responsibility system**, collectives leased land to peasant families, who paid rent to the collective. Anything produced on the land above that payment could be sold on the private market or consumed. To soak up excess labor in the villages, the government encouraged the formation of so-called sideline industries, a modern equivalent of the traditional cottage industries in premodern China. Peasants raised fish, made consumer goods, and even assembled furniture and appliances for sale to their newly affluent compatriots. Some even opened small outdoor food stalls in the cities to sell snacks to passersby (see Comparative Illustration, "Sideline Industries: Creeping Capitalism in a Socialist Paradise," p. 691).

The reform program had a striking effect on rural production. Grain production increased rapidly, and farm income doubled during the 1980s. Yet reform also created problems. Income at the village level became more unequal as some enterprising farmers (known colloquially at the time as "ten-thousand-dollar households") earned profits several times those realized by their less fortunate or less industrious neighbors. When some farmers discovered that they could earn more by growing cash crops, they devoted less land to rice and other grain crops, thereby threatening the supply of China's most crucial staple. Finally, the agricultural policy threatened to undermine the government's population control program, which party leaders viewed as crucial to the success of the Four Modernizations.

Ever since a misguided period in the mid-1950s when Mao Zedong had argued that more labor would result in higher productivity, China had been attempting to limit its population growth. By 1970, the government had launched a stringent family planning program—including education, incentives, and penalties for noncompliance—to persuade the Chinese people to limit themselves to one child per family. The program had some initial success, and population growth was reduced drastically in the early 1980s. The rural responsibility system, however, undermined the program because it encouraged farm families to pay the penalties for having additional children in the belief that their labor would increase family income and provide the parents with a form of social security for their old age. Today, China's population has surpassed 1.4 billion.

China: The New Industrial Powerhouse

Still, the overall effects of the modernization program were impressive.

The standard of living improved for the majority of the population. Although a decade earlier the average Chinese had struggled to earn enough to buy a bicycle, by the late 1980s many were beginning to purchase refrigerators and color televisions. Yet the rapid growth of the economy created its own problems: inflationary pressures, increased corruption, and—most dangerous of all for the regime—rising expectations. Young people in particular resented restrictions on employment (many were still required to accept the jobs offered to them by the government or school officials) and opportunities to study abroad. Disillusionment ran high, especially in the cities, where lavish living by officials and rising prices for goods aroused widespread alienation and cynicism. Such conditions undoubtedly contributed to the unrest that erupted during the spring of 1989.

Since the 1990s, industrial growth rates have continued to be high as Chinese exports have increased dramatically and domestic capital has become increasingly available. The government finally recognized the need to close down some of the more inefficient state enterprises, and the private sector accounted for more than 10 percent of the gross domestic product by the beginning of the new century. A stock market opened, and with the country's entrance into the World Trade Organization (WTO) in 2001, China's prowess in the international marketplace improved dramatically. Today, China has the second-largest economy in the world and is the largest exporter of goods. Even the global economic crisis that struck the world in fall 2008 did not derail the Chinese juggernaut, which quickly recovered from the drop in demand for Chinese goods in countries suffering from the economic downturn.

As a result of these developments, China now possesses a large and increasingly affluent middle class and a burgeoning domestic market for consumer goods. The vast majority of urban Chinese now own a color television set, a refrigerator, and a washing machine. For the more affluent, a private automobile is increasingly a possibility, and in 2010, for the first time more vehicles were sold in China than in the United States.

As Chinese leaders have discovered, however, rapid economic change never comes without a cost. Closing state-run factories led to millions of dismissed workers each year, and the private sector initially struggled to absorb them even though it was growing at more than 20 percent annually. Poor working conditions and low salaries in Chinese factories have resulted in periodic outbreaks of labor unrest. Demographic conditions, however, are changing. The reduction in birth rates since the 1980s has creating a labor shortage, thus putting upward pressure on workers' salaries. As a result, China is facing inflation in the marketplace and increased competition from exports produced by factories located in lower-wage countries in South and Southeast Asia. In 2015, the government enacted a new "two child" policy in the hope of alleviating the problem in the future.

Discontent has also been increasing in the countryside, where farmers earn only about half as much as their urban counterparts. China's entry into the WTO was greeted with great optimism but has been of little benefit to farmers facing the challenges of cheap foreign imports. Taxes and local corruption add to their complaints. In desperation, millions of rural Chinese have left for the big cities, where many of them are unable to find steady employment and live in squalid conditions in crowded tenements or in the sprawling suburbs. Millions of others remain on their farms and attempt to augment their income by producing for the market or by increasing the size of their families despite the risk of stringent penalties. A land reform law passed in 2008 authorizes farmers to lease or transfer land-use rights, although in principle all land in rural areas belongs to the local government.

An Environmental Time Bomb   Another factor hindering China's economic advance is the impact of rapid industrialization on the environment. With the rising population, fertile land is in increasingly short supply (China's population has doubled since 1950, but only two-thirds as much irrigable land is available). Soil erosion is a major problem, especially in the north, where the desert is encroaching on farmlands. Water is also a problem. An ambitious plan to transport water by canals from the Yangzi River to the more arid northern provinces has run into several roadblocks. Another massive project to construct dams on the Yangzi River has sparked protests from environmentalists and local peoples forced to migrate from the area. Air pollution is ten times the level in the United States. To add to the challenge, more than 700,000 new cars and trucks appear on the country's roads each year. To reduce congestion on roadways, China is constructing a network for high-speed bullet trains that will connect all major regions in the country.

27-4b Chinese Society in Flux

At the root of Marxist–Leninist ideology is the idea of building a new citizen free from the prejudices, ignorance, and superstition of the "feudal" era and the capitalist desire for self-gratification. This new citizen would be characterized not only by a sense of racial and sexual equality but also by the selfless desire to contribute his or her utmost for the good of all.

Out with the Old: In with the New   The first order of business was to bring an end to the Confucian legacy in the new China. Like the progressive intellectuals of the New Culture movement, Mao and his colleagues viewed old values, old attitudes, and old customs as the foremost obstacles to their ambitious political objectives. At the root of the problem, in their view, was the time-honored Confucian emphasis on the primacy of the family—headed by the patriarch—as the key component in Chinese society. In 1950, a new marriage law guaranteed women equal rights with men and permitted wives for the first time to initiate divorce proceedings against their husbands. Women were granted the right to vote and encouraged to become active in the political process. At the local level, an increasing number of women became active in the CCP and collective organizations.

At first, the new government moved carefully on family issues to avoid unnecessarily alienating its supporters in the countryside. When collective farms were established in the mid-1950s, payment in the form of ration coupons for hours worked was made not to the individual but to the family head, thus maintaining the traditionally dominant position of the patriarch. When people's communes were established in the late 1950s, however, payments went to the individual, and children were encouraged to report any critical comments by their parents to the authorities. Such practices continued during the Cultural Revolution when children were expected to tell on their parents, students on their teachers, and employees on their superiors. By encouraging the more vulnerable elements in society—the young, the female, and the poor—to voice their bitterness, Mao was hoping to break the long tradition of dependency that marked Chinese civilization. Such denunciations had been issued against landlords during the land reform tribunals of the late 1940s and early 1950s. Later, during the Cultural Revolution, they were applied to other authority figures.

The post-Mao era brought a decisive shift away from revolutionary utopianism and toward a more pragmatic approach to social engineering. With some exceptions, family relationships became once more a private affair. But it soon became clear that old habits are hard to break. Although in large cities attitudes toward women, marriage, and the family have evolved in line with trends in Western countries, in rural areas the old norms of filial piety and the five relationships sometimes still hold sway. Arranged marriages, nepotism, and the mistreatment of females have returned (although such behavior most likely existed under the cloak of revolutionary piety for a generation). Expensive weddings are now increasingly common, along with payment of a dowry to the family of the groom. Prostitution and sex crimes against women appear also to be on the rise.

Other costs are also involved in privatization. Under the Maoist system, the elderly and the sick were provided with retirement benefits and health care by the state or by the collective organizations. Under current conditions, with the latter no longer playing such a social role and more workers operating in the private sector, the safety net has been removed (see Comparative Essay, "Family and Society in an Era of Change," p. 705). The government recently attempted to fill the gap by enacting a social security law, but eligibility is limited primarily to individuals in the urban sector of the economy because of a lack of funds. Those living in the countryside are essentially unprotected, prompting legislation in 2010 to provide modest pensions and medical insurance to the poorest members of Chinese society. Yet much more needs to be done. As the population ages, the lack of a retirement system represents a potential time bomb. The regime attempted to ease the problem recently when it promulgated a new law requiring adult children (often living in the cities) to provide occasional visits and necessary care to their aging parents in the countryside. Confucius would be pleased.

Lifestyle Changes: From Mao to Mod   The post-Mao era brought a decisive shift away from the puritanical ethic and embraced the ideal of material consumption. Taking advantage of slogans in the 1980s trumpeting such values as "create wealth for the people" and "to get rich is glorious," enterprising Chinese began to concentrate on improving their standard of living. For the first time, millions saw the prospect of a house or an urban apartment with a washing machine, television set, and indoor plumbing. Young people whose parents had given them patriotic names such as Build the Country, Protect Mao Zedong, and Assist Korea began to choose more elegant and cosmopolitan names for their own children. Some names—such as Surplus Grain or Bring a Younger Brother—expressed hope for the future.

The new attitudes were also reflected in physical appearance. For a generation after the civil war, clothing had been restricted to the traditional baggy "Mao suit" in olive drab or dark blue, but by the 1980s young people craved such fashionable Western items as designer jeans and trendy sneakers. Cosmetic surgery to create a more buxom figure or a more Western facial look became increasingly common among affluent young women in the cities. Many had the epicanthic fold over their eyelids removed or their noses enlarged—a curious decision in view of the tradition of referring derogatorily to foreigners as "big noses."

The growing emphasis on material accumulation in contemporary Chinese society has predictably led to an increased focus on the needs and wants of the individual as opposed to those of the group. On one hand, the regime's decision to follow what Mao Zedong would have termed the "capitalist road" has tended to produce citizens possess with greater creativity and independence of spirit. On the other hand, it can also lead to hedonistic behavior and a reluctance to endure sacrifices in the interests of the larger community. Many older Chinese blame the latter tendency on the regime's long-standing one-child policy. With most families limited to a single offspring, many parents over-indulged their children, who were sometimes derided by critics as "little emperors." The father in Image 27.8 seems delighted with his own "little emperor," who seems to love the attention.

The shift from Marxism toward the worship of consumerism is having another predictable effect by giving rise to a growing sense of rootlessness in Chinese society, especially among the young, who did not live through the difficult years before Mao Zedong died. The growing popularity of organized religion in China is undoubtedly one consequence. As the government has become somewhat more tolerant of religious belief, some Chinese have begun to return to the traditional Buddhist faith or to folk religions, and Buddhist and Taoist temples are crowded with worshipers. Despite official efforts to suppress its more evangelical forms, Christianity has become popular as well; like the "rice Christians" (persons who supposedly converted for economic reasons) of the past, many now view it as a symbol of success and cosmopolitanism.

27-4c China's Changing Culture

During the first half of the twentieth century, Chinese culture was strongly influenced by currents from the West (see Chapter 24). The rise to power of the Communists in 1949 added a new dimension to the debate over the future of culture in China. The new leaders rejected the Western attitude of "art for art's sake" and, like their Soviet counterparts, viewed culture as an important instrument of indoctrination. The standard would no longer be aesthetic quality or the personal preference of the artist but "art for life's sake," whereby culture would serve the interests of socialism.

Culture in a Revolutionary Era   At first, the new emphasis on socialist realism did not entirely extinguish traditional culture. Mao and his colleagues tolerated—and even encouraged—efforts by artists to synthesize traditional ideas with socialist concepts. During the Cultural Revolution, however, all forms of traditional culture came to be viewed as reactionary. Socialist realism became the only acceptable standard. All forms of traditional expression were forbidden, and the deification

Family and Society in an Era of Change

Family & Society One paradox of the modern world is that even in a time of political stability and economic prosperity for many people in the advanced capitalist societies, public cynicism about the system is increasingly widespread. Alienation and drug use are at dangerously high levels, and the rate of criminal activities in most areas remains much higher than in the years immediately after World War II. In recent years, public dissatisfaction with political leaders has reached new heights, even in prosperous countries in Europe and the United States.

Although various reasons have been advanced to explain this paradox, many observers contend that the decline of the traditional family system is responsible for many contemporary social problems. There has been a steady rise in the percentage of illegitimate births and single-parent families in countries throughout the Western world. In the United States, approximately half of all marriages end in divorce. Even in two-parent families, more and more

27.8 China's Little Emperors. Chinese leaders have launched a massive family planning program to curtail population growth. Urban families are restricted to a single child. In conformity with tradition, sons are especially prized, and some Chinese complain that many parents overindulge their children, turning them into spoiled "little emperors."

parents work full-time, leaving the children to fend for themselves on their return from school. In many countries in Europe, the birth rate has dropped to alarming levels, leading to a severe labor shortage that is attracting a rising number of immigrants from other parts of the world.

Observers point to several factors to explain these conditions: the growing emphasis on an individualistic lifestyle devoted to instant gratification, a phenomenon promoted vigorously by the advertising media; the rise of the feminist movement, which has freed women from the servitude imposed on their predecessors but at the expense of removing them from full-time responsibility for the care of the next generation; and the increasing mobility of contemporary life, which disrupts traditional family ties and creates a sense of rootlessness and impersonality in the individual's relationship to the surrounding environment.

These trends are not unique to Western civilization. The traditional nuclear family is also under attack in many societies around the world. Even in East Asia, where the Confucian tradition of family solidarity has been endlessly touted as a major factor in the region's economic success, the incidence of divorce and illegitimate births is on the rise, as is the percentage of women in the workforce. Older citizens frequently complain that the Asian youth of today are too materialistic, faddish, and steeped in the individualistic values of the West. Such criticisms are now voiced in mainland China as well as in the capitalist societies around its perimeter (see Chapter 30).

In societies less exposed to the corrosive effects of Western culture such as India, Africa, and the Middle East, traditional attitudes about the family continue to hold sway, and the tenacity of the family system should not be ignored, as Mao Zedong discovered to his dismay during the Great Leap Forward. Still, the trend toward a more individualistic lifestyle seems to be a worldwide phenomenon as the situation in China and many of its neighbors demonstrates. As young people move into the growing cities to pursue their careers, their elderly parents living in the countryside are often left to fend for themselves, sometimes in desperate straits. No wonder Chinese leaders are resurrecting Confucius as a zealous guardian of traditional virtues.

Q *To what degree and in what ways are young people in China becoming more like their counterparts in the West?*

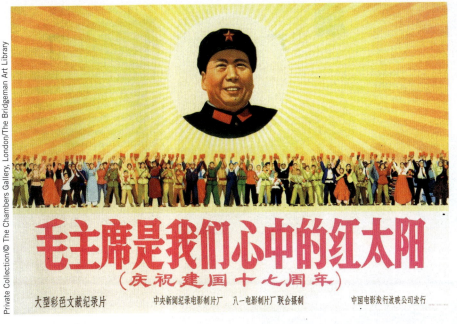

毛主席是我们心中的红太阳

（庆祝建国十七周年）

大型彩色文献纪录片　　　中央新闻纪录电影制片厂　　八一电影制片厂 联合摄制　　　中国电影发行放映公司发行

27.9 The Red Sun in Our Hearts.
During the Great Proletarian Cultural Revolution, Chinese art was restricted to topics that promoted revolution and the thoughts of Chairman Mao Zedong. All the knowledge that the true revolutionary required was to be found in Mao's Little Red Book, a collection of his sayings on proper revolutionary behavior. In this painting, Chairman Mao's portrait hovers above a crowd of his admirers, who wave copies of the book as a symbol of their total devotion to him and his vision of a future China.

of Mao and his central role in building a Communist paradise became virtually the only acceptable form of artistic expression.

The experience of author Ding Ling (DING LING) is characteristic of the shifting cultural climate in China. Born in 1904 and educated in a school for women set up by leftist intellectuals during the hectic years after the May Fourth Movement, she became involved in party activities in the early 1930s and settled in Yan'an, where she wrote her most famous novel, *The Sun Shines over the Sangan River*, which described the CCP's land reform program in favorable terms. It was awarded the Stalin Prize three years later.

During the early 1950s, Ding Ling was one of the most prominent literary lights of the new China, but in the more ideological climate at the end of the decade she was attacked for her individualism and her previous criticism of the party. Sentenced to hard labor on a commune during the Cultural Revolution, she was not released until the late 1970s after the death of Mao. Crippled and in poor health, she died in 1981.

Art and Architecture

After Mao's death, Chinese culture was finally released from the shackles of socialist realism. In painting, where the only acceptable standard for excellence for a decade was praise for the party and its policies, the new permissiveness led to a revival of interest in both traditional and Western forms. Although some painters continued to blend Eastern and Western styles, others imitated trends from abroad, experimenting with a wide range of previously prohibited art styles, including cubism and abstract painting. Since the 1990s, some Chinese artists, such as the world-famous Ai Weiwei (I WAY-WAY) (b. 1957), have aggressively challenged the government's authority despite persecution by the government.

Perhaps the most visible indication of China's determination to place its cultural achievements in the glare of global awareness has been in the field of architecture, where the regime has invested heavily in an explosive building boom that has been highlighted by projects connected with the 2008 Olympic Games in Beijing and has spread outward to China's many megacities. At a dizzying pace, renowned architects, both Chinese and foreign, are executing some of the new century's most original and experimental architectural designs. The gleaming vertiginous forest of skyscrapers currently rising in Shanghai's Pudong district is the quintessential example.

Literature

The limits of freedom of expression were most apparent in literature. During the early 1980s, party leaders encouraged Chinese writers to express their views on the mistakes of the past, and a new "literature of the wounded" began to describe the brutal and arbitrary character of the Cultural Revolution.

Such efforts quickly drew the ire of the authorities, however, who continue to insist that only the positive aspects of contemporary Chinese society be presented. Still, a few writers brave the displeasure of party leaders by portraying the shortcomings of the socialist system. Today, Chinese culture has been dramatically transformed by the nation's adoption of a market economy

27.10 The World City of Shanghai. Shanghai, China's largest city, has been an economic and cultural powerhouse in Asia for more than a century, and its venerable European-style buildings on the Bund have long been a symbol of its pursuit of wealth and power. In recent years, China's leaders have sought to expand the city's architectural achievements by building an ultramodern new city in Pudong (east of the river), once an industrial suburb. Although its futuristic skyscrapers along the east bank of the Huangpu River dwarf their European counterparts along the Bund and express the burgeoning ambition of China's leaders in the twenty-first century, the ever-present blanket of smog is a vivid reminder of the costs of rapid industrialization.

William J. Duiker

and the spread of the Internet. A new mass literature explores the aspirations and frustrations of a generation obsessed with material consumption and the right of individual expression. Lost in the din are the voices of China's rural poor.

27-4d Confucius and Marx: The Tenacity of Tradition

Why has communism survived in China, albeit in a substantially altered form, when it failed in Eastern Europe and the Soviet Union? One primary factor is probably cultural. Although the doctrine of Marxism–Leninism originated in Europe, many of its main precepts—such as the primacy of the community over the individual and the denial of the concept of private property—run counter to trends in Western civilization. This inherent conflict is especially evident in the societies of central Europe, which were strongly influenced by Enlightenment philosophy and the Industrial Revolution. These forces were weaker farther to the east, although they had begun to penetrate tsarist Russia by the end of the nineteenth century.

In contrast, Marxism–Leninism found a more receptive climate in China and other countries in the region influenced by Confucian tradition. In its political culture, the Communist system exhibits many of the same characteristics as traditional Confucianism—a single truth, an elite governing class, and an emphasis on obedience to the community and its governing representatives. Although a

significant and influential minority of the Chinese population—primarily urban and educated—finds the idea of personal freedom against the power of the state appealing, such concepts have little meaning in rural villages, where the interests of the community have always been emphasized over the desires of the individual. It is no accident that Chinese leaders now seek to reintroduce the precepts of State Confucianism to bolster a fading belief in the existence of a future Communist paradise.

Party leaders today are banking on the hope that China can be governed as it has always been—by an elite class of highly trained professionals dedicated to pursuing a predefined objective. In fact, however, real changes are taking place in China today. Although the youthful protesters in Tiananmen Square were comparable in some respects to the reformist elements of the early republic, the China of today is fundamentally different from that of the early twentieth century. Literacy rates and the standard of living are far higher, the pressures of outside powers are less threatening, and China has entered its own industrial and technological revolution. Many Chinese depend more on independent talk radio and the Internet for news and views than on the official media. While Sun Yat-sen, Chiang Kai-shek, and even Mao Zedong broke their lances on the rocks of centuries of tradition, poverty, and ignorance, the current leaders rule a country much more aware of the world and China's place in it. Although the shift in popular expectations may be gradual, China today is embarked on a journey to a future for which the past no longer provides a roadmap.

CHAPTER SUMMARY

For four decades after the end of World War II, the two major Communist powers appeared to have become permanent features on the international landscape. Suddenly, though, in the late 1980s, the Soviet Union entered a period of internal crisis that shook the foundations of Soviet society. In 1991, the system collapsed, to be replaced by a series of independent states based primarily on ethnic and cultural differences that had existed long before the Bolshevik Revolution. China went through an even longer era of instability beginning with the Cultural Revolution in 1966, but it managed to survive under a hybrid system that combines features of a Leninist command economy with capitalist practices adapted from the modern West.

Why were the outcomes so different? Although the cultural differences we have described were undoubtedly an important factor, the role of human action should not be ignored. While Mikhail Gorbachev introduced the idea of glasnost to permit the emergence of a more pluralistic political system in the Soviet Union, Chinese leaders crushed the protest movement in the spring of 1989 and reasserted the authority of the Communist Party. Deng Xiaoping's gamble paid off, and today the party stands at the height of its power.

REFLECTION QUESTIONS

Q How have six decades of Communist rule affected the concept of the family in China? How does the current state of the family in China compare with the family in other parts of the world?

Q What strategies were used by the leaders of the Soviet Union and the People's Republic of China as they sought to build Communist societies in their countries?

In what ways were the strategies different, and in what ways were they similar? To what degree were they successful?

Q How has the current generation of leadership in China made use of traditional values to solidify Communist control over the country? To what degree has this approach contradicted the theories of Karl Marx?

CHAPTER TIMELINE

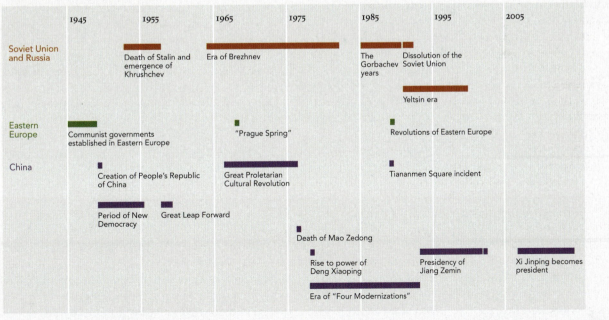

CHAPTER NOTES

1. Quoted in V. Zubok and C. Pleshakov, *Inside the Kremlin's Cold War: From Stalin to Khrushchev* (Cambridge, Mass., 1996), p. 166.

2. Quoted in H. Smith, *The New Russians* (New York, 1990), p. 74.

3. "Report on an Investigation of the Peasant Movement in Hunan (March 1927)," in *Quotations from Mao Tse-tung* (Beijing, 1976), p. 12.

4. Quoted in S. Karnow, *Mao and China: Inside China's Cultural Revolution* (New York, 1972), p. 95.

MindTap® is a fully online, highly personalized learning experience built upon Cengage Learning content. MindTap combines student learning tools—readings, multimedia, activities, and assessments—into a singular Learning Path that guides students through the course and helps students develop the critical thinking, analysis, and communication skills that are essential to academic and professional success.

Chapter Outline and Focus Questions

28-1 *Recovery and Renewal in Europe*

Q What problems have the nations of Western Europe faced since 1945, and what steps have they taken to try to solve these problems? What problems have Eastern European nations faced since 1989?

28-2 *Emergence of the Superpower: The United States*

Q What political, social, and economic changes has the United States experienced since 1945?

28-3 *The Development of Canada*

Q What political, social, and economic developments has Canada experienced since 1945?

28-4 *Latin America Since 1945*

Q What problems have the nations of Latin America faced since 1945, and what role has Marxist ideology played in their efforts to solve these problems?

28-5 *Society and Culture in the Western World*

Q What major social, cultural, and intellectual developments have occurred in Western Europe and North America since 1945?

Critical Thinking

Q *What were the similarities and differences between the major political, economic, and social developments in the first half of the twentieth century and those in the second half of the century?*

Connections to Today

Q *Since 1945, the nations of Europe and the Western Hemisphere have experienced many changes and challenges. What changes and challenges will these nations face over the next fifty years?*

Experience an interactive version of this period in ⁂ MINDTAP

© SZ Photo/SV-Bilderdienst/The Bridgeman Art Library

28.1 **Survivors in the Ruins of Berlin, Germany, at the End of World War II**

THE END OF WORLD WAR II IN EUROPE had been met with great joy. A visitor in Moscow reported, "I looked out of the window [at 2 A.M.], almost everywhere there were lights in the windows—people were staying awake. Everyone embraced everyone else, someone sobbed aloud." But after the celebrations, Europeans awoke to a devastating realization: their civilization was in ruins. Almost 40 million people (soldiers and civilians) had been killed over the last six years. Air raids and artillery bombardments had reduced many of the cities of Europe to heaps of rubble. The Polish capital of Warsaw had been almost completely obliterated. An American general described Berlin: "Wherever we looked, we saw desolation. It was like a city of the dead. Suffering and shock were visible in every face. Dead bodies still remained in canals and lakes and were being dug out from under bomb debris." Millions of Europeans faced starvation as grain harvests were only half their 1939 levels. Millions were also homeless.

Yet, by 1970, Western Europe had not only recovered from the effects of World War II but also experienced an economic resurgence that seemed nothing less than miraculous. Economic growth continued so long that the first postwar recession came as a shock in 1973. It was short-lived, however, and economic growth resumed. With this economic expansion came the creation of the welfare state—a prominent social development in postwar Europe. After the collapse of Communist governments in the revolutions of 1989, several Eastern European states sought to create market economies and join the military and economic unions first formed by Western European states.

The most significant factor after 1945 was the emergence of the United States as the world's richest and most powerful nation. American prosperity reached new heights in the first two decades after World War II, but the nation has nevertheless faced a series of social and economic problems—including racial division and staggering budget deficits—in the postwar era.

South of the United States, Latin America had its own unique heritage. Although some Latin Americans in the nineteenth century looked to the United States as a model for their own development, many strongly criticized U.S. military and economic domination of Central and South America in the twentieth century. At the same time, many Latin American countries struggled with economic and political instability.

Toward the end of the century, as the West adjusted from Cold War to post–Cold War realities, other changes were also shaping the Western outlook. The demographic face of European countries changed as massive numbers of immigrants created more ethnically diverse populations. New artistic and intellectual currents, the continued advance of science and technology, the effort to come to grips with environmental problems, and the women's liberation movement—all spoke of a vibrant, ever-changing world. At the same time, a devastating terrorist attack in the United States in 2001 made the Western world vividly aware of its vulnerability to international terrorism. Moreover, a financial collapse in 2008 threatened the economic security of the Western world as well as the entire global economy. But most important of all, Western nations, like all nations on the planet, had become acutely aware of the political and economic interdependence of the world's nations and the global nature of the challenges of the twenty-first century.

28-1 RECOVERY AND RENEWAL IN EUROPE

Q Focus Questions: What problems have the nations of Western Europe faced since 1945, and what steps have they taken to try to solve these problems? What problems have Eastern European nations faced since 1989?

All European nations faced similar problems at the end of World War II. First and foremost, they needed to rebuild their shattered economies. Remarkably, within a few years, an incredible economic revival brought renewed growth to Western Europe.

28-1a Western Europe: The Triumph of Democracy

With the economic aid of the Marshall Plan, the countries of Western Europe recovered relatively rapidly from the devastation of World War II. Between the early 1950s and late 1970s, industrial production surpassed all previous records, and Western Europe experienced virtually full employment.

France: From de Gaulle to New Uncertainties One man— Charles de Gaulle (SHAHRL duh GOHL) (1890–1970)— dominated the history of France for nearly a quarter century after the war. Initially, he had withdrawn from politics, but in 1958, frightened by the bitter divisions caused by the Algerian crisis (see Chapter 29), the leaders of the Fourth Republic offered to let de Gaulle take over the government and revise the constitution.

De Gaulle's constitution for the Fifth Republic greatly enhanced the office of the president, who now had the power to choose the prime minister, dissolve parliament, and supervise defense and foreign policy. Under de Gaulle, France became a major industrial producer and exporter, particularly in automobiles and armaments. But the nationalization (government ownership) of traditional industries such as coal, steel, and railroads led to large government deficits. The cost of living also increased faster than in the rest of Europe. Growing dissatisfaction led to a series of student protests in May 1968 that were followed by a general strike by labor unions. Although he restored order, de Gaulle resigned from office in April 1969 and died the next year.

The worsening of France's economic situation in the 1970s brought a shift to the left politically. By 1981, the Socialists had become the dominant party in the National

Assembly, and the Socialist leader, François Mitterrand (frahnh-SWAH MEE-tayr-rahnh) (1916–1995), was elected president. Mitterrand passed several measures to aid workers: an increased minimum wage, expanded social benefits, a fifth week of paid vacation, and a thirty-nine-hour workweek. The Socialists also enacted some more radical reforms, nationalizing major banks, the space and electronics industries, and important insurance firms.

The Socialist policies largely failed, however, and within three years, the Mitterrand government returned some of the economy to private enterprise. But France's economic decline continued, and a coalition of conservative parties won 80 percent of the seats in 1993. The move to the right was strengthened when the conservative mayor of Paris, Jacques Chirac (ZHAHK shee-RAK) (b. 1932), was elected president in May 1995 and was reelected in 2002.

Since the 1990s, French presidents have all faced the same difficult tasks, appeasing growing anti-immigrant sentiment and improving the French economy. Economic inequality has been fueled by an elite educational system and tight labor market, and growing immigration has led to social unrest. The majority of France's young immigrants, many of whom are Muslim, live in the suburbs of Paris. After years of high unemployment and a perceived lack of opportunities, frustrations erupted into riots in 2005.

Nicolas Sarkozy (nee-kohl-AH sar-koh-ZEE) (b. 1955), who was elected president in 2007, had campaigned on a promise to end the social turmoil. Instead of resolving the burgeoning social issues, Sarkozy chose to alter the thirty-five-hour workweek, lower taxes for the wealthy, and increase the retirement age for state workers. His unpopular measures and the global economic crises in 2008 led to his electoral defeat by Socialist Party leader François Hollande (frahn-SWAH oh-LAHN) (b. 1954), who became president in 2012.

Hollande promised to revoke his predecessor's tax breaks for the wealthy, return the retirement age to sixty-five, and raise taxes on corporations and banks. After much difficulty, Hollande successfully increased taxes on households making more than 1 million euros per year. Holland also reformed France's tight labor regulations that had made it difficult to lay off workers. However, his reforms were met with a low approval rating of 12 percent by 2014. Hollande was successful in navigating the country through the 2015 terrorist attacks in Paris, the worst terrorist attack since 2001 in New York City. Hollande did not run for reelection in 2017. In 2016, Emmanuel Macron (b. 1977) formed a new centrist political party, En March! ("Forward" or "Onward" in English). Macron's pro-European message appealed to French voters, who elected him as the youngest president in the history of France in 2017.

From West Germany to One Germany As noted in Chapter 26, the three western zones of Germany were unified as the Federal Republic of Germany in 1949. Konrad Adenauer (AD-uh-now-ur) (1876–1967), the leader of the Christian Democratic Union, served as chancellor from 1949 to 1963 and became the Federal Republic's "founding hero."

Adenauer's chancellorship is largely associated with the West German economy's remarkable resurrection. Although West Germany had only 52 percent of the territory of prewar Germany, by 1955 its gross domestic product exceeded that of prewar Germany. Unemployment fell from 8 percent in 1950 to 0.4 percent in 1965.

After the Adenauer era, German voters moved politically from the center-right of the Christian Democrats to the center-left; in 1969, the Social Democrats became the leading party. The first Social Democratic chancellor was Willy Brandt (VIL-ee BRAHNT) (1913–1992). In 1971, Brandt negotiated a treaty with East Germany that led to greater cultural, personal, and economic contacts between West and East Germany. In 1972, he received the Nobel Peace Prize for this "opening toward the east," which was known as *Ostpolitik* (OHST-poh-lee-teek).

In 1982, Christian Democrat Helmut Kohl (HEL-moot KOHL) (b. 1930) formed a new center-right government. Kohl benefited from an economic boom in the mid-1980s and the 1989 revolution in East Germany, which led in 1990 to the reunification of the two Germanies, making the new restored Germany and its 79 million people the leading power in Europe. Soon, however, the realization set in that the revitalization of eastern Germany would cost far more than anticipated, and Kohl's government faced the politically unpopular prospect of raising taxes substantially. Moreover, the virtual collapse of the economy in eastern Germany led to extremely high unemployment. In 1998, voters responded by returning the Social Democrats to power with the election of Gerhard Schröder (GAYR-hahrt SHRUR-dur) (b. 1944). But Schröder failed to cure Germany's economic woes. As a result of elections in 2005, Angela Merkel (AHNG-uh-luh MERK-uhl) (b. 1954), leader of the Christian Democrats, became Germany's first female chancellor.

Merkel pursued health-care reform and new energy policies at home while taking a leading role in the affairs of the European Union (EU). Merkel has overseen the expansion of Germany's economy, leading Germany to become the largest national economy in Europe. With that economy, Germany led the movement for reforms during the 2008 EU economic crises. Merkel has faced increasing criticism for her acceptance of thousands of Syrian refugees. The rise of immigrants in Germany has increased anti-immigrant tensions and led to the resurgence of populist political movements (see section 28-5e, "Guest Workers and Immigrants," p. 727).

The Decline of Great Britain The end of World War II left Britain with massive economic problems. In elections held immediately after the war, the Labour Party overwhelmingly defeated Winston Churchill's Conservatives. Labour's promise of far-reaching social welfare measures was quite appealing in a country with a tremendous shortage of consumer goods and housing. The new Labour government under Clement Attlee (1883–1967) proceeded to turn Britain into a modern **welfare state**.

The process began with the nationalization of the Bank of England, the coal and steel industries, public transportation, and public utilities such as electricity and gas. In 1946, the new government established a comprehensive social security program and nationalized medical insurance. A health act established a system of socialized medicine that forced doctors and dentists to work with state hospitals, although private practice could be maintained. The British welfare state became the model for most European nations.

Continuing economic problems, however, brought the Conservatives back into power from 1951 to 1964. Although they favored private enterprise, the Conservatives accepted the welfare state. By now the British economy had recovered from the war, but its slow growth reflected a long-term economic decline. At the same time, Britain's ability to play the role of a world power had declined substantially. Between 1964 and 1979, Conservatives and Labour alternated in power, but neither party was able to deal with the ailing economy.

In 1979, the Conservatives returned to power under Margaret Thatcher (1925–2013), who became the first woman prime minister in British history (see Film & History, *The Iron Lady*). The "Iron Lady," as she was called, broke the power of the labor unions, but she was not able to eliminate the basic components of the welfare state. Her economic policy, which was termed "Thatcherism," improved the economic situation—but at a price. The south of England, for example, prospered, but the old industrial areas of the Midlands and north declined and were beset by high unemployment, poverty, and sporadic violence.

Thatcher dominated British politics in the 1980s. But in 1990, Labour's fortunes revived when Thatcher's government attempted to replace local property taxes with a flat-rate tax payable by every adult. Critics argued that this was effectively a poll tax that would allow the rich to pay the same rate as the poor. In 1990, Thatcher resigned. Later, in new elections in 1997, the Labour Party won a landslide victory. The new prime minister, Tony Blair (b. 1953), was

28.2 Margaret Thatcher. Great Britain's first female prime minister, Margaret Thatcher was a strong leader who dominated British politics in the 1980s. This picture of Thatcher was taken during a meeting with French President François Mitterrand in 1986.

Peter Turnley/CORBIS

⊡ FILM & HISTORY

The Iron Lady

Watch *The Iron Lady* (2011), a film based on the life of Margaret Thatcher, played brilliantly by American actress Meryl Streep. In power from 1979 to 1990, Thatcher was a divisive figure in British politics; she was loved and hated in equal measure for her policies and actions. Unfortunately, the film touches only briefly on some of the most important events in her career as prime minister: her fight for the leadership of the Conservative Party, reform of the labor unions, privatization of state-owned industries, military intervention in the Falkland Islands, and reduction in social welfare benefits.

Everett Collection, Inc.

Q *What impression of Margaret Thatcher does the film provide? How accurate is that impression?*

MINDTAP See full-length Film & History feature in MindTap.
From Cengage

a moderate whose youthful energy instilled new vigor on the political scene. Blair was one of the leaders in forming an international coalition against terrorism after the terrorist attack on the United States on September 11, 2001. Four years later, however, his support of the U.S. war in Iraq, when a majority of Britons opposed it, caused his popularity to plummet. In summer 2007, he stepped down and allowed the new Labour Party leader, Gordon Brown (b. 1951), to become prime minister.

In 2010, in the wake of climbing unemployment and a global financial crisis, the Labour Party's thirteen-year rule ended when Conservative Party candidate David Cameron (b. 1966) became prime minister on the basis of a coalition with the Liberal Democrats. Cameron promised to decrease government debt by reducing government waste and cutting Britain's established welfare state. His austerity measures led to a sharp increase in unemployment in the public sector, while private sector jobs maintained steady growth. Despite government cuts, government deficits have almost doubled since 2007.

Cameron was reelected in 2015, but he resigned in 2016 following the exit of Britain from the EU. ("Brexit" was a portmanteau. a combination of the words *British* and *exit*.) Cameron had vowed to put forth a referendum on British membership in the EU in an effort to quell the growing dissatisfaction from conservatives who opposed EU trade restrictions and immigration policies. Cameron's negotiations with the EU parliament in Brussels, Belgium, failed to produce the desired result. Although Britain gained more rights over immigration, it was still required to seek approval for immigration changes from the European Commission and European Council. Cameron expected Britons to remain in the EU. However, he and the rest of the world awoke on June 25 to the news that voters had approved Brexit. A new chapter now began in the history of the European Union. Cameron immediately resigned and was replaced by Theresa Mary May (b. 1946) in July 2016.

28-1b Eastern Europe After Communism

The fall of Communist governments in Eastern Europe during the revolutions of 1989 brought an end to a postwar European order that had been imposed on unwilling peoples by the victorious forces of the Soviet Union (see Chapter 26). In 1989 and 1990, new governments throughout Eastern Europe worked diligently to scrap the old system and introduce the democratic procedures and market systems they believed would revitalize their scarred lands. But this process proved to be neither simple nor easy. The revival of the post–Cold War Eastern European states is evident in their desire to join both the North Atlantic Treaty Organization (NATO) and the European Union, the two major Cold War institutions of Western European unity (see section 28-1d, "The Unification of Europe," p. 716). In 1997, Poland, the Czech Republic, and Hungary became full members of NATO. In 2004, ten nations—including Hungary, Poland, the Czech Republic, Slovenia, Estonia, Latvia, and Lithuania—joined the EU. By 2013, the EU had expanded to include Bulgaria, Romania, and Croatia.

In some states, the shift to non-Communist rule was complicated by old problems, especially ethnic issues. Although Czechs and Slovaks agreed to a peaceful division of Czechoslovakia into the Czech Republic and Slovakia, the situation was quite different in Yugoslavia.

The Disintegration of Yugoslavia From its creation in 1919, Yugoslavia had been an artificial entity. Strong leaders—especially the dictatorial Marshal Tito after World War II—had managed to hold together six disparate republics and two autonomous provinces that made up the country. After Tito's death in 1980, no strong leader emerged, and eventually Yugoslavia was caught up in the reform movements sweeping through Eastern Europe.

After negotiations among the six republics failed, Slovenia and Croatia declared their independence in June 1991. Slobodan Milošević (sluh-BOH-dahn mih-LOH-suh-vich) (1941–2006), the leader of Serbia, rejected these efforts and asserted that these republics could be independent only if new border arrangements were made to accommodate their Serb minorities who did not want to live outside the boundaries of Serbia. Serbian forces attacked both new states and, although unsuccessful against Slovenia, captured one-third of Croatia's territory.

International recognition of independent Slovenia and Croatia in 1992 and of Macedonia and Bosnia and Herzegovina soon thereafter did not deter the Serbs, who now turned on Bosnia. By mid-1993, Serbian forces had acquired 70 percent of Bosnian territory. The Serbian policy of **ethnic cleansing**—killing or forcibly removing Bosnian Muslims from their lands—revived memories of Nazi atrocities in World War II. In the town of Srebrenica (sreb-bruh-NEET-suh), almost 8,000 men and boys were killed in a Serbian massacre. This account by a Muslim survivor from the town is eerily reminiscent of the activities of the Nazi Einsatzgruppen (see Chapter 25):

> When the truck stopped, they told us to get off in groups of five. We immediately heard shooting next to the trucks. . . . About ten Serbs with automatic rifles told us to lie down on the ground face first. As we were getting down, they started to shoot, and I fell into a pile of corpses. I felt hot liquid running down my face. I realized that I was only grazed. As they continued to shoot more groups, I kept on squeezing myself in between dead bodies.[1]

28.3 The War in Bosnia and Herzegovina. By mid-1993, irregular Serb forces had overrun much of Bosnia and Herzegovina amid scenes of untold suffering. This photograph shows a woman running past the bodies of victims of a mortar attack on Sarajevo on August 21, 1992. Three mortar rounds landed, killing at least three people.

By 1995, some 250,000 Bosnians (mostly civilians) had been killed, and 2 million others were homeless (see Historical Voices, "A Child's Account of the Shelling of Sarajevo," p. 715). As the fighting spread, European nations and the United States began to intervene to stop the bloodshed, and in 1995, a fragile cease-fire agreement was reached. An international peacekeeping force was stationed in the area to prevent further hostilities.

Peace in Bosnia and Herzegovina, however, did not bring peace to Yugoslavia. A new war erupted in 1999 over Kosovo (KAWSS-suh-voh), an autonomous province within the Serbian republic. Kosovo's inhabitants were mainly ethnic Albanians, but the province was also home to a Serbian minority. In 1994, groups of ethnic Albanians had founded the Kosovo Liberation Army (KLA) and begun a campaign against Serbian rule in Kosovo. When Serb forces began to massacre ethnic Albanians in an effort to crush the KLA, the United States and its NATO allies mounted a bombing campaign that forced Milošević to stop. In the elections of 2000, Milošević himself was ousted from power, and he was later put on trial by an international tribunal for war crimes against humanity for his ethnic cleansing policies. He died in a prison cell in The Hague in 2006 before his trial could be completed.

In 2004, Yugoslavia itself ceased to exist when the new national government officially renamed the truncated country Serbia and Montenegro. Two years later,

CHRONOLOGY	Western Europe
Welfare state emerges in Great Britain	1946
Konrad Adenauer becomes chancellor of West Germany	1949
Charles de Gaulle reassumes power in France	1958
Student protests in France	1968
Willy Brandt becomes chancellor of West Germany	1969
Margaret Thatcher becomes prime minister of Great Britain	1979
François Mitterrand becomes president of France	1981
Helmut Kohl becomes chancellor of West Germany	1982
Reunification of Germany	1990
Election of Jacques Chirac in France	1995
Labour Party victory in Great Britain	1997
Social Democratic victory in Germany	1998
Angela Merkel becomes chancellor of Germany	2005
Nicolas Sarkozy becomes president of France	2007
Election of David Cameron in Britain	2010
Election of François Hollande in France	2012
Resignation of David Cameron in Britain	2016
Theresa May appointed prime minister of Britain	2016
Election of Emmanuel Macron in France	2017

A Child's Account of the Shelling of Sarajevo

Politics & Government

WHEN BOSNIA-HERZEGOVINA DECLARED ITS INDEPENDENCE in March 1992, Serbian army units and groups of Bosnian Serbs went on the offensive and began to shell the capital city of Sarajevo. One of its residents was Zlata Filipovic, the ten-year-old daughter of a middle-class lawyer. Zlata was a fan of MTV and pizza, but when the Serbs began to shell Sarajevo from the hills above the city, her life changed dramatically, as is apparent in this excerpt from her diary.

Zlata Filipovic, *Zlata's Diary: A Child's Life in Sarajevo*

April 3, 1992: Daddy came back . . . all upset. He says there are terrible crowds at the train and bus stations. People are leaving Sarajevo.

April 4, 1992: There aren't many people in the streets. I guess it's fear of the stories about Sarajevo being bombed. But there's no bombing. . . .

April 5, 1992: I'm trying hard to concentrate so I can do my homework (reading), but I simply can't. Something is going on in town. You can hear gunfire from the hills.

April 6, 1992: Now they're shooting from the Holiday Inn, killing people in front of the parliament. . . . Maybe we'll go to the cellar. . . .

April 9, 1992: I'm not going to school. All the schools in Sarajevo are closed. . . .

April 14, 1992: People are leaving Sarajevo. The airport, train and bus stations are packed. . . .

April 18, 1992: There's shooting, shells are falling. This really is WAR. Mommy and Daddy are worried, they sit up late at night, talking. They're wondering what to do, but it's hard to know. . . . Mommy can't make up her mind—she's constantly in tears.

April 21, 1992: It's horrible in Sarajevo today. Shells falling, people and children getting killed, shooting. We will probably spend the night in the cellar.

April 26, 1992: We spent Thursday night with the Bobars again. The next day we had no electricity. We had no bread, so for the first time in her life Mommy baked some.

April 28, 1992: SNIFFLE! Everybody has gone. I'm left with no friends.

April 29, 1992: I'd write to you much more about the war if only I could. But I simply don't want to remember all these horrible things.

Q *How do you think Zlata Filipovic was able to deal with the new conditions in her life?*

Source: From Zlata Filipović, *Zlata's Diary, A Child's Life in Sarajevo* © 1994 by Fixot et editions Robert Laffont.

Montenegrins voted in favor of independence. Thus, by 2006, all six republics cobbled together to form Yugoslavia in 1918 were once again independent nations. In 2008, Kosovo unilaterally proclaimed its independence from Serbia and was recognized by most other nations as the seventh sovereign state to emerge from the former Yugoslavia.

28-1c The New Russia

Soon after the Soviet Union disintegrated in 1991, a new era began in Russia with the presidency of Boris Yeltsin. A new constitution created a two-chamber parliament and established a strong presidency. During the mid-1990s, Yeltsin was able to maintain a precarious grip on power while seeking to implement reforms that would lead to a pluralistic political system and a market economy. But the new post-Communist Russia remained as fragile as ever. Burgeoning economic inequality and rampant corruption shook the confidence of the Russian people in the superiority of the capitalist system over the Communist one. A nagging war in the Caucasus—where the people of Chechnya (CHECH-nee-uh) sought national independence from Russia—drained the government budget and exposed the decrepit state of the once-vaunted Red Army. Yeltsin was reelected in 1996, but his precarious health raised serious questions about his ability to govern.

The Putin Era At the end of 1999, Yeltsin suddenly resigned and was replaced by Vladimir Putin (VLAD-ihmeer POO-tin) (b. 1952), a former member of the KGB, the Soviet intelligence agency. Putin vowed to bring an end to the rampant corruption and to strengthen the role of the central government. He also vowed to bring the breakaway state of Chechnya back under Russian authority and to assume a more assertive role in international affairs. The new president took advantage of growing public anger at Western plans to expand the NATO alliance into Eastern Europe to restore Russia's position as an influential force in the world.

Putin attempted to deal with Russia's chronic problems by centralizing his control over the system and by silencing critics—notably in the Russian media. Although these moves were criticized in the West, many Russians sympathized with Putin's attempts to restore a sense of pride and discipline. Putin's popularity among the Russian people was also strengthened by Russia's growing prosperity in the first years of the century. Putin made significant economic reforms, and rising oil prices boosted the Russian economy, which grew dramatically until the 2008–2009 global economic crisis.

In 2008, Dmitry Medvedev (di-MEE-tree mehd-VYEH-dehf) (b. 1965) became president of Russia when Putin could not run for reelection under Russia's constitution. Instead, Putin became prime minister, and the two men shared power.

In 2012, despite public protests, Putin was again elected president to a six-year term. Putin has continued to crack down on any dissidents, including prominent politicians and journalists. An uprising in neighboring Ukraine in 2014 led to the annexation of Crimea and the city of Sevastopol by Russian forces. In response, the United States and the European Union issued sanctions against Russia. By 2015, Russia's economy faced an uncertain future as low oil prices and the unresolved Ukrainian crises destabilized the Russian economy. Russia was also accused of interfering on behalf of Republican candidate Donald Trump in the 2016 American presidential elections. Putin was reelected in 2018 to another term, although both Russian political opponents and international observers believe the election was neither free nor fair.

28-1d The Unification of Europe

As we saw in Chapter 26, the divisions created by the Cold War led the nations of Western Europe to seek military security by forming NATO in 1949. The destructiveness of two world wars, however, caused many thoughtful Europeans to look for some additional form of unity.

In 1957, France, West Germany, the Benelux countries (Belgium, the Netherlands, and Luxembourg), and Italy signed the Treaty of Rome, which created the European Economic Community (EEC). The EEC eliminated customs barriers for the six member nations and created a large free-trade area protected by a common external tariff. All the member nations benefited economically. In 1973, Great Britain, Ireland, and Denmark joined what now was called the European Community (EC). Greece joined in 1981, followed by Spain and Portugal in 1986. In 1995, Austria, Finland, and Sweden also became members.

The European Union   In the 1980s and 1990s, the EC moved toward even greater economic integration. The Treaty on European Union, which went into effect on January 1, 1994, turned the European Community into the European Union, a true economic and monetary union. By 2000, it contained 370 million people and constituted the world's largest single trading entity, transacting one-fourth of the world's commerce. One of its goals was achieved in 1999 with the introduction of a common currency, the euro. On January 1, 2002, the euro officially replaced twelve national currencies. By 2012, the euro had been adopted by seventeen countries and was serving approximately 327 million people.

A major crisis for the euro began in 2010, however, when Greece's burgeoning public debt threatened to cause the bankruptcy of that country as well as create financial difficulties for many European banks. Led by Germany, other EU members put together a financial rescue plan, but subsequently other nations—including Ireland, Portugal, and Spain—also faced serious financial problems.

In another step toward integration, the EU has established a common agricultural policy that provides subsidies to farmers to enable them to compete on the world market. In 1985, the Schengen Agreement proposed the elimination of border checks for members, and the subsequent Schengen Convention in 1990 created a common visa policy. The adoption of a common passport system has given millions of Europeans greater flexibility to travel. The EU has been less successful in setting common foreign policy goals, primarily because individual nations still see foreign policy as a national prerogative and are reluctant to relinquish their sovereignty to an intergovernmental institution. In 2009, the EU ratified the Lisbon Treaty, strengthening the bureaucratic power of the EU by creating a full-time presidential post and a new voting system that reflects the size of each country's population. It also provided more power for the European Parliament to promote the EU's foreign policy goals.

Toward a United Europe   At the beginning of the twenty-first century, the EU established a new goal: to incorporate into the union the states of Eastern and Southeastern Europe, including the nations that had recently emerged from Communist rule. Many of these states were considerably poorer than the current members, which raised the possibility that adding these nations might weaken the EU itself. To lessen that danger, the EU required applicants to demonstrate their commitment to both market capitalism and democracy, including respect for minorities and human rights. In 2004, the EU took the plunge and added ten new members: Cyprus, the Czech Republic, Estonia, Hungary, Latvia, Lithuania, Malta, Poland, Slovakia, and

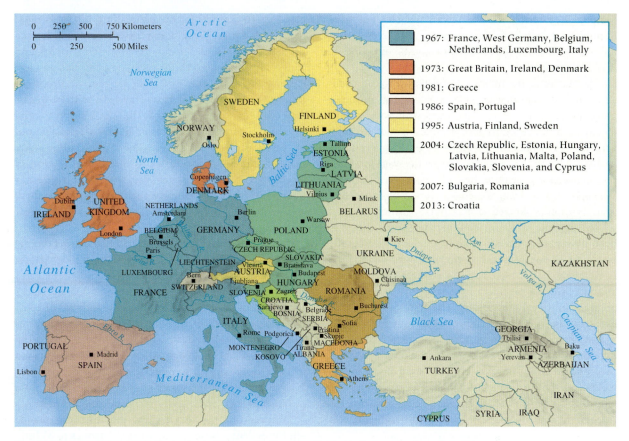

Map 28.1 European Union, 2013. Beginning in 1967 as the European Economic Community, the union of European states seeking to integrate their economies has gradually grown from six members to twenty-eight in 2013. By 2002, the European Union had achieved two major goals—the creation of a single internal market and a common currency—although it has been less successful at working toward common political and foreign policy goals.

Q *What additional nations do you think will eventually join the European Union?*

Slovenia, thereby enlarging the population of the EU to 455 million people. In 2007, the EU expanded again as Bulgaria and Romania joined the union. Croatia joined the EU in 2013 (see Map 28.1).

28-2 EMERGENCE OF THE SUPERPOWER: THE UNITED STATES

Q **Focus Question:** What political, social, and economic changes has the United States experienced since 1945?

At the end of World War II, the United States emerged as one of the world's two superpowers. As its Cold War confrontation with the Soviet Union intensified, the United States directed much of its energy toward combating the spread of communism. With the collapse of the Soviet Union at the beginning of the 1990s, the United States became the world's foremost military power.

28-2a American Politics and Society Through the Vietnam Era

Franklin Roosevelt's New Deal of the 1930s initiated a basic transformation of American society that included a dramatic increase in the role and power of the federal government, the rise of organized labor as a significant force in the economy and politics, a commitment to the welfare state, a grudging acceptance of ethnic minorities, and a willingness to experiment with deficit spending as a means of stimulating the economy. These trends were bolstered by the election of three Democratic presidents—Harry S. Truman in 1948, John F. Kennedy in 1960, and

Lyndon B. Johnson in 1964. Even the election of a Republican, Dwight D. Eisenhower, in 1952 and 1956 did not significantly alter the fundamental direction of American politics.

The economic boom after World War II fueled confidence in the American way of life. A shortage of consumer goods during the war left Americans with both surplus income and the desire to purchase these goods after the war. Then, too, the growing influence of organized labor enabled more and more workers to get the wage increases that spurred the growth of the domestic market. Between 1945 and 1973, real wages grew an average of 3 percent a year, the most prolonged advance in U.S. history.

Starting in the 1960s, however, problems that had been glossed over earlier came to the fore. The decade began on a youthful and optimistic note when John F. Kennedy (1917–1963), age forty-three, became the youngest elected president in U.S. history and the first born in the twentieth century. His administration, cut short by an assassin's bullet on November 22, 1963, focused primarily on foreign affairs. Kennedy's successor, Lyndon B. Johnson (1908–1973), who won a new term as president in a landslide in 1964, used his mandate to expand the welfare state that had begun under the New Deal. Johnson's programs included health care for the elderly and the War on Poverty, to be fought with food stamps and the Job Corps.

Johnson's other domestic passion was achieving equal rights for black Americans. In August 1963, the eloquent Reverend Martin Luther King Jr. (1929–1968) led the March on Washington for Jobs and Freedom to dramatize blacks' desire for freedom. This march and King's impassioned plea for racial equality had an electrifying effect on the American people. At President Johnson's initiative, Congress enacted the Civil Rights Act of 1964, which created the machinery to end segregation and discrimination in the workplace and all public accommodations. The Voting Rights Act of 1965 eliminated obstacles to black participation in elections in Southern states. But laws alone could not guarantee the Great Society that Johnson envisioned, and soon the administration faced bitter social unrest (see Image 28.4).

In the North and the West, blacks had enjoyed voting rights for many years, but local patterns of segregation resulted in considerably higher unemployment rates for blacks (and Hispanics) than for whites and left blacks segregated in huge urban ghettos. In the summer of 1965, race riots erupted in the Watts district of Los Angeles that led to thirty-four deaths and the destruction of more than a thousand buildings. After King was assassinated in 1968, riots erupted in more than 100 cities, including Washington, D.C., the nation's capital. The riots led to a "white backlash" and a severe racial division of America.

Antiwar protests also divided the American people after President Johnson committed U.S. troops to a costly war in Vietnam (see Chapter 26). The killing of four student protesters at Kent State University in 1970 by

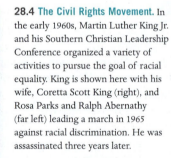

28.4 The Civil Rights Movement. In the early 1960s, Martin Luther King Jr. and his Southern Christian Leadership Conference organized a variety of activities to pursue the goal of racial equality. King is shown here with his wife, Coretta Scott King (right), and Rosa Parks and Ralph Abernathy (far left) leading a march in 1965 against racial discrimination. He was assassinated three years later.

Bob Adelman/Historical Premium/Corbis

the Ohio National Guard shocked both activists and ordinary Americans, and thereafter the antiwar movement began to subside. But the combination of antiwar demonstrations and riots in the cities caused many people to call for "law and order," an appeal used by Richard Nixon (1913–1994), the Republican presidential candidate in 1968. Nixon's election started a shift to the right in American politics.

28-2b The Shift Rightward After 1973

Nixon eventually ended American involvement in Vietnam by gradually withdrawing U.S. troops. Politically, he pursued a "Southern strategy" in which he calculated that "law and order" issues would appeal to Southern whites. The Republican strategy, however, also won support among white Democrats in northern cities, where court-mandated busing to achieve racial integration had provoked a white backlash.

As president, Nixon was paranoid about conspiracies and resorted to subversive methods of gaining political intelligence on his opponents. Nixon's zeal led to the Watergate scandal—the attempted bugging of Democratic National Headquarters, located in the Watergate apartment and hotel complex in Washington, D.C. Although Nixon repeatedly denied involvement in the affair, secret tapes he made of his own conversations in the White House revealed that he directed a coverup of crimes. On August 9, 1974, Nixon resigned the presidency rather than face possible impeachment and then trial by the U.S. Congress.

After Watergate, American politics focused on economic issues. Gerald Ford (1913–2006) became president when Nixon resigned, only to lose in the 1976 election to Jimmy Carter (b. 1924). Carter lost to Ronald Reagan (1911–2004), the chief exponent of right-wing Republican policies, following a period of economic decline in average earnings caused by high inflation as well as by a hostage crisis in Iran (see Chapter 29). The Reagan Revolution, as it has been called, sent U.S. policy in new directions. Reagan cut back on the welfare state by decreasing spending on food stamps, school lunch programs, and job programs. At the same time, he fostered the largest peacetime military buildup in American history. Total federal spending rose from $631 billion in 1981 to more than $1 trillion by 1986. The administration's spending policies produced record government deficits that loomed as an obstacle to long-term growth. In the 1970s, the total national debt was $420 billion; under Reagan it reached three times that level.

The inability of Reagan's successor, George H. W. Bush (b. 1924), to deal with the deficit problem, coupled with an economic downturn, led to the election of a Democrat, Bill Clinton (b. 1946), in 1992. A lengthy economic revival considerably aided Clinton's political fortunes, and a steady reduction in the government's budget deficit strengthened confidence in the national economy. Much of Clinton's second term, however, was overshadowed by charges of misconduct stemming from the president's affair with a White House intern. After a bitter partisan struggle, the U.S. Senate acquitted the president on two articles of impeachment brought by the Republican-controlled House of Representatives. Clinton's problems, however, helped Republican candidate George W Bush (b. 1946) win the presidential election in 2000.

The first four years of Bush's administration were largely occupied with the war on terrorism and the U.S.-led war on Iraq (see Chapter 29). The Department of Homeland Security was established after the 2001 terrorist assaults to help protect the country from future terrorist acts. At the same time, Bush pushed tax cuts through Congress that favored the wealthy, with the richest 1 percent of taxpayers receiving 40 percent of the tax cuts. The tax cuts helped produce record deficits reminiscent of the Reagan years. Environmentalists were disturbed by the administration's efforts to weaken environmental laws and regulations to benefit American corporations. During his second term, Bush's popularity plummeted as discontent grew over the Iraq War, financial corruption in the Republican Party, and the administration's poor handling of relief efforts after Hurricane Katrina devastated New Orleans in 2005.

The many controversies of the Bush administration led to the lowest approval ratings for a modern president and opened the door for a dramatic change in American politics. The new and often inspiring voice of Barack Obama (b. 1961), who called for "change we can believe in" and for ending the war in Iraq, led to an overwhelming Democratic victory in the 2008 elections and his reelection in 2012.

Once in office in 2009, Obama acted quickly to handle the worst economic recession since the Great Depression. The recession, which began in 2008, had caused unemployment to spike to 10 percent, while the economy witnessed the loss of more than 8.7 million jobs in a matter of months. Congress passed a $787 billion stimulus bill to bail out the American automobile industry and fuel economic growth. By 2017, the unemployment rate stood at 4.7 percent; under the Obama administration, the economy had added 15.8 million new jobs. In 2009, Obama persuaded Congress to pass a sweeping health care bill, the Affordable Care Act, providing most Americans with heath care coverage.

President Obama began his second term in 2012 facing a difficult crisis in American history. Following a massacre of twenty elementary students and six adults in Connecticut, Obama pushed for Congress to pass legislation strengthening background checks for gun purchases. The bill failed to pass the Republican-led Congress. Obama's other domestic initiatives included new legislation for equal pay for women and marriage equality for same-sex couples. Obama's foreign policy initiatives included opening diplomatic relations with Cuba, securing an Iran nuclear deal that reduced the Iranian nuclear weapons program, and the passage of the largest global climate change initiative, the Paris Agreement. Obama finished his tenure as president by campaigning on behalf of Democratic presidential candidate Hillary Rodham Clinton (b. 1947). In a surprising upset, despite winning the popular vote by almost 3 million people, she lost the electoral vote to Donald J. Trump (b. 1946), a reality television star and billionaire real estate developer with no prior political experience.

Trump's lack of political experience became evident in his first year of office. Despite Republican control of Congress and the White House, no significant legislation was passed until the end of 2017, when a tax bill was approved. Although touted as providing middle-class tax relief, the biggest benefits of the bill went to corporations and the wealthy. Trump's first year in office was overshadowed by the formal investigation of the president for obstruction of justice and possible collusion with Russia to interfere in the American presidential election.

28-3 THE DEVELOPMENT OF CANADA

Focus Question: What political, social, and economic developments has Canada experienced since 1945?

For twenty-five years after World War II, Canada experienced extraordinary economic prosperity as it set out on a new path of development, including the electronic, aircraft, nuclear, and chemical-engineering industries. Much of the Canadian growth, however, was financed by capital from the United States, which resulted in American ownership of many Canadian businesses.

After 1945, the Liberal Party continued to dominate Canadian politics. Under Lester Pearson (1897–1972), the Liberals created Canada's welfare state by enacting a national social security system (the Canada Pension Plan) and a national health-insurance program. The most prominent Liberal government, however, was that of Pierre Trudeau (PYAYR troo-DOH) (1919–2000), who came to power in 1968.

Economic recession in the early 1980s brought Brian Mulroney (b. 1939), leader of the Progressive Conservative Party, to power in 1984. Mulroney's government sought to privatize many of Canada's state-run corporations and negotiated a free-trade agreement with the United States. Bitterly resented by many Canadians, the agreement cost Mulroney's government much of its popularity. In 1993, the Conservatives were overwhelmingly defeated, and Liberal leader Jean Chrétien (ZHAHNH kray-TEN) (b. 1934) became prime minister. Chrétien's conservative fiscal policies, combined with strong economic growth, enabled his government to have a budgetary surplus by the late 1990s and led to another Liberal victory in the elections of 1997. Charges of widespread financial corruption in the government, however, led to a Conservative victory early in 2006, and Stephen Harper (b. 1959) became the new prime minister; he was reelected twice. Although Harper's conservative policies and tax cuts left Canada with an increased deficit, it was his unwillingness to communicate with the news media that led to a resounding victory of the Liberal Party in 2015 led by Justin Trudeau (b. 1971), the son of former prime minister Pierre Trudeau.

28-4 LATIN AMERICA SINCE 1945

Focus Question: What problems have the nations of Latin America faced since 1945, and what role has Marxist ideology played in their efforts to solve these problems?

The Great Depression of the 1930s had led to political instability in many Latin American countries that resulted in military coups and militaristic regimes (see Chapter 24). But the depression transformed Latin America from a traditional to a modern economic structure. Since the nineteenth century, Latin Americans had exported raw materials, especially minerals and foodstuffs, while buying the manufactured goods from the United States and industrialized countries in Europe. As a result of the depression, however, exports were cut in half, and the revenues available to buy manufactured goods declined, encouraging many Latin American countries to develop industries to produce goods that were formerly imported. Governments invested in the new industries, leading to government-run steel industries in Chile and Brazil and oil industries in Argentina and Mexico.

By the 1960s, however, Latin American countries were still dependent on the United States, Europe, and now Japan for the advanced technology needed for modern industries. High poverty rates meant small domestic markets, and many countries failed to find markets abroad for their products. These failures led to instability and a new reliance on military regimes, especially to curb the power of the new industrial middle class and working classes that had emerged as a result of industrialization. In the 1960s, repressive military regimes in Chile, Brazil, and Argentina abolished political parties and often returned to export–import economies financed by foreigners. However, debt to foreigners, mostly U.S. and European banks, increased in the 1970s from $27 billion to $315.3 billion. By

Map 28.2 South America

1982, several governments announced that they could no longer pay interest on their debts, and their economies began to crumble.

The debt crisis of the 1980s was accompanied by a move toward democracy. Many people realized that military power without popular consent was incapable of providing a strong state. By the 1980s and early 1990s, democratic regimes were in place everywhere except Cuba, some of the Central American states, Chile, and Paraguay. At the end of the twentieth century and beginning of the twenty-first, a noticeable political trend in Latin America has been the election of left-wing governments, evident in the election of Hugo Chávez (OOgoh CHAH-vez) (1954–2013) in Venezuela in 1998 and the election of his vice president, Nicolás Maduro Moros, in 2013; Luiz Inácio Lula de Silva (LWEES ee-NAHsyoh LOO-luh duh SEEL-vuh) (b. 1945) in Brazil in 2002, followed by Dilma Rousseff (DIL-muh ROO-seff) (b. 1947) in 2010; Michelle Bachelet (mih-SHELL BAHSH-uh-let) (b. 1951) in Chile in 2006 and again in 2013; and Daniel Ortega (dah-NYEL awr-TAY-guh) (b. 1945) in Nicaragua in 2007.

The United States has played an important role in Latin America since 1945. Since the 1920s, the United States had been the continent's foremost investor. As a result, American companies had gained control of large segments of important Latin American industries, including the copper and oil industries. This control by American investors reinforced a growing nationalist sentiment in Latin America against the United States as a neoimperialist power.

But the United States also tried to pursue a new relationship with Latin America. In 1948, the nations of the Western Hemisphere formed the Organization of American States, which was intended to eliminate unilateral interference by one state in the internal or external affairs of any other state. But as the Cold War intensified, American policy makers grew anxious about the possibility of Communist regimes arising in Central America and the Caribbean. They returned to a policy of unilateral action when they believed Soviet agents were attempting to establish Communist governments. Especially after the success of Castro in Cuba (see the next section), the desire of the United States to prevent "another Cuba" largely determined American policy toward Latin America. Until the end of the Cold War in the early 1990s, the United States provided massive military aid to anti-Communist regimes, regardless of their nature.

28-4a The Threat of Marxist Revolutions: The Example of Cuba

A dictatorship headed by Fulgencio Batista (1901–1973) and closely tied economically to American investors had ruled Cuba since 1934. In the 1950s, Batista's government came under attack by a strong opposition movement led by Fidel Castro among others. Castro maintained that only armed force could overthrow Batista, but when initial assaults on Batista's regime met with little success, Castro's forces turned to guerrilla warfare. Batista's regime responded with such brutality that he alienated his own supporters. The dictator fled in December 1958, and Castro's revolutionaries seized Havana on January 1, 1959.

Relations between Cuba and the United States quickly deteriorated early in 1960 when the Soviet Union agreed to buy Cuban sugar and provide $100 million in credits. In October 1960, the United States imposed a trade embargo on Cuba, which drove Castro closer to the Soviet Union. On January 3, 1961, the United States broke diplomatic relations with Cuba. New American president John F. Kennedy supported a coup attempt against Castro's government, but the landing of 1,400 Cuban exiles with

28.5 Fidel Castro. On January 1, 1959, a band of revolutionaries led by Fidel Castrol overthrew the authoritarian government of Fulgencio Batista. Castro (second from right) is shown here surrounded by some of his followers at a secret base near the Cuban coast in 1957.

door to U.S. and Cuban negotiations. In 2014, President Obama announced that the United States and Cuba would begin normalizing their relations by lifting the travel ban, opening Cuba to financial investment, and establishing a U.S. embassy in Cuba.

28-4b Nationalism and the Military: The Example of Argentina

The military became the power brokers of many twentieth-century Latin American nations. Fearful of the forces unleashed by industrialization, the military intervened in Argentinian politics in 1930 and propped up the cattle and wheat oligarchy that held the reins of power since the beginning of the century. In June 1943, a group of restless army officers overthrew the civilian oligarchy. One member of the new regime, Juan Perón (WAHN puh-ROHN) (1895–1974), used his position as labor secretary to curry favor with the workers, and in 1946 Perón was elected president.

To please his chief supporters—labor and the urban middle class—Perón pursued a policy of increased industrialization. At the same time, he sought to free Argentina from foreign investors. The government bought the railways; took over the banking, insurance, shipping, and communications industries; and regulated imports and exports. But Perón's regime was also authoritarian. His wife, Eva Perón, founded women's organizations to support the government while Perón organized fascist gangs modeled after Hitler's Brown Shirts that used violence to intimidate his opponents. Growing corruption in Perón's government and the alienation of more and more people by the regime's excesses encouraged the military to overthrow him in September 1955. Perón went into exile in Spain.

Overwhelmed by problems, however, the military leaders allowed Perón to return from exile. Reelected president in September 1973, Perón died one year later. In 1976, the military installed a new regime and used the occasion to kill more than 6,000 leftists. But economic problems persisted, and the regime tried to divert people's attention by invading the Falkland Islands in April 1982. Great Britain, which had controlled the islands since the nineteenth century, decisively defeated the Argentine forces. The loss discredited the military and opened the door to civilian rule and a democratic transfer of power in the 1980s and 1990s. Despite problems of foreign debt and inflation, Argentina has witnessed economic growth since 2003, first under the government of President Nestor Kirchner (NAY-stor KEERCH-nehr) (b. 1950) and then under his wife, Cristina Fernández de Kirchner (kris-TEE-nuh fehr-NAHN-des day KEERCH-nehr) (b. 1953), who in 2007

assistance from the Central Intelligence Agency at the Bay of Pigs on Cuba's southern coast on April 17, 1961, was a total military disaster. The Soviets now made an even greater commitment to Cuban independence by installing nuclear missiles in the country, an act that led to a showdown with the United States (see Chapter 26). As its part of the bargain to defuse the missile crisis, the United States agreed not to invade Cuba.

In Cuba, Castro's socialist revolution proceeded with mixed results. The Cuban people obtained some social gains, especially in health care and education. The regime provided free medical services for all citizens, and the population's health improved noticeably. Developing new schools and establishing teacher-training institutes tripled the number of teachers and wiped out illiteracy within ten years.

Eschewing rapid industrialization, Castro encouraged agricultural diversification. But the Cuban economy continued to rely on the production of sugar. Economic problems forced the regime to depend on Soviet subsidies and the purchase of Cuban sugar by Soviet bloc countries. After the collapse of these Communist regimes in 1989, Cuba lost their support. Although economic conditions continued to decline, Fidel Castro remained in power until illness forced him to resign the presidency in 2008. His brother, Raul Castro (b. 1931), succeeded him. Raul Castro's ascension to the presidency opened the became the first elected female president of Argentina. She was reelected in 2011. In 2015, former Buenos Aires mayor Mauricio Macri (b. 1959) was elected president as the leader of a coalition of center-right political parties.

28-4c The Mexican Way

During the 1950s and 1960s, Mexico's ruling party—the Institutional Revolutionary Party, or PRI—focused on a balanced program of industrial policy. Fifteen years of steady economic growth combined with low inflation and real gains in wages made those years seem a golden age in Mexico's economic development. But at the end of the 1960s, students began to protest the one-party system. On October 2, 1968, police opened fire on a demonstration of university students in Mexico City, killing hundreds of the students. Leaders of the PRI became concerned about the need to change the system.

During the 1970s, the next two presidents, Luis Echeverría (loo-EES eh-cheh-vahr-REE-uh) (b. 1922) and José López Portillo (hoh-SAY LOH-pehz pohr-TEE-yoh) (1920–2004), introduced reforms. Rules for registering political parties were eased, making their growth more likely, and greater freedom of debate in the press and at universities was allowed. But economic problems continued. In the late 1970s, vast new reserves of oil were discovered, making the government even more dependent on oil revenues. When world oil prices dropped in the mid-1980s, Mexico was no longer able to make payments on its $80 billion of foreign debt. The debt crisis and rising unemployment increased dissatisfaction with the government, as was evident in the 1988 election, when the PRI's candidate, Carlos Salinas (KAHR-lohs sah-LEE-nahs) (b. 1948), won by only a 50.3 percent majority instead of the expected landslide. Growing dissatisfaction with the government's economic policies finally led to the unthinkable: in 2000, Vicente Fox (vee-SEN-tay FOKS) (b. 1942) defeated the PRI candidate for the presidency. Despite high hopes, Fox's administration failed to deal with police corruption and bureaucratic inefficiency in the government. His successor, Felipe Calderón (feh-LEE-pay kahl-duh-ROHN) (b. 1963), made immigration reform a priority, with little success. In 2012, the PRI returned to power when its candidate, Enrique Peña Nieto (en-REE-kay PAYN-yah nee-EH-toh) (b. 1966), was elected to the presidency. Pena began his tenure as president with a 50 percent approval rating; by 2017 his approval rating had fallen to 17 percent following a gasoline crisis, the poor handling of the abduction and murder of forty-three students, intensifying drug war violence, and a decline in value of the Mexican peso.

28-5 SOCIETY AND CULTURE IN THE WESTERN WORLD

Focus Question: What major social, cultural, and intellectual developments have occurred in Western Europe and North America since 1945?

Socially, culturally, and intellectually, the Western world since 1945 has been marked by much diversity.

28-5a The Emergence of a New Society

During the postwar era, such products of new technologies as computers, television, jet planes, contraceptive devices, and new surgical techniques dramatically altered the nature of human life. Scientific advances and economic growth fueled the rapid changes in postwar society. Called a *technocratic society* by some observers and the **consumer society** by others, postwar Western society was marked by a fluid social structure and new movements for change.

Especially noticeable in European society after 1945 were the changes in the middle class. Such traditional middle-class groups as businesspeople and professionals in law and medicine were greatly augmented by increasing numbers of white-collar supervisory and administrative personnel employed by large companies and government agencies.

Changes also occurred among the traditional lower classes. Many people moved from rural to urban areas, and the number of people in agriculture declined drastically. But the size of the industrial working class did not expand. In West Germany, industrial workers made up 48 percent of the labor force throughout the 1950s and 1960s. Thereafter, the number of industrial workers began to dwindle as the number of white-collar service employees increased. At the same time, a substantial increase in real wages enabled the working classes to aspire to the consumption patterns of the middle class. Buying on installment plans became widespread in the 1950s and enabled workers to purchase televisions, home appliances, and automobiles.

Rising incomes and shorter working hours also increased the market for mass leisure activities. Between 1900 and 1980, the workweek fell from sixty hours to around forty hours, and the number of paid holidays increased. All aspects of popular culture—music, sports, media—became commercialized and offered opportunities for leisure activities.

Social change was also evident in educational patterns. Before World War II, higher education had largely remained the preserve of the wealthier classes. After the war, European states began to foster greater equality of opportunity in higher education by eliminating fees, and universities experienced an influx of students from the middle and lower classes.

But there were problems. Overcrowded classrooms, professors who paid little attention to students, administrators who acted in an authoritarian fashion, and an education that many deemed irrelevant to the modern age led to an outburst of student revolts in the late 1960s. In part, these were an extension of the anti–Vietnam War protests in American universities in the mid-1960s. There were several reasons for the student radicalism. Some students were genuinely motivated by the desire to reform the university. Others were protesting the Vietnam War, which they viewed as a product of Western imperialism. They also attacked the materialism of Western society and expressed concern about becoming cogs in a large, impersonal bureaucratic machine. For many students, the calls for democratic decision making in the universities reflected their deeper concerns about the direction of Western society.

28-5b The Permissive Society

Some critics referred to the new society of postwar Europe as the **permissive society**. Sweden took the lead in the so-called sexual revolution of the 1960s, and the rest of Europe and the United States soon followed. Sex education in the schools and the decriminalization of homosexuality were but two aspects of Sweden's liberal approach. The introduction of the birth control pill, which was widely available by the mid-1960s, gave people more freedom. Meanwhile, sexually explicit movies, plays, and books broke new ground in the treatment of once-hidden subjects.

The new standards were evident in the breakdown of the traditional family. Divorce rates increased dramatically, especially in the 1960s, and premarital and extramarital sexual experiences also rose substantially. A survey in the Netherlands in 1968 revealed that 78 percent of men and 86 percent of women had engaged in extramarital sex.

The 1960s also saw the emergence of the drug culture. Marijuana, although illegal, was widely used by university students. For young people more interested in higher levels of consciousness, Timothy Leary, who had done research at Harvard on the psychedelic (perception-altering) effects of LSD (lysergic acid diethylamide), became the high priest of hallucinogenic experiences.

New attitudes toward sex and the use of drugs were only two manifestations of a growing youth movement that questioned authority and fostered rebellion against the older generation. Spurred on by opposition to the Vietnam War and a growing political consciousness, the youth rebellion became a youth protest movement by the second half of the 1960s (see Historical Voices, "'The Times They Are A-Changin': The Music of Youthful Protest," p. 725).

28.6 The "Love-in." In the 1960s, outdoor public festivals for young people combined music, drugs, and sex. Flamboyant dress, face painting, free-form dancing, and drugs were vital ingredients in creating an atmosphere dedicated to "love and peace." Shown here are "hippies" dancing around a decorated bus at a so-called love-in during 1967's Summer of Love.

Henry Diltz/Documentary/CORBIS

"The Times They Are A-Changin'": The Music of Youthful Protest

Art & Ideas

IN THE 1960S, the lyrics of rock music reflected the rebellious mood of many young people. Bob Dylan (b. 1941), a vastly influential performer and recording artist, expressed the feelings of the younger generation. His song "The Times They Are a-Changin," released in 1964, has been called an "anthem for the protest movement."

Bob Dylan, "The Times They Are A-Changin'"

Come gather 'round people
Wherever you roam
And admit that the waters
Around you have grown
And accept it that soon
You'll be drenched to the bone
If your time to you
Is worth savin'
Then you better start swimming'
Or you'll sink like a stone
For the times they are a-changin' . . .
Come senators, congressmen
Please heed the call
Don't stand in the doorway
Don't block up the hall
For he that gets hurt
Will be he who has stalled
There's a battle outside
And it is ragin'
It'll soon shake your windows

And rattle your walls
For the times they are a-changin'
Come mothers and fathers
Throughout the land
And don't criticize
What you can't understand
Your sons and your daughters
Are beyond your command
Your old road
Is rapidly agin'
Please get out of the new one
If you can't lend your hand
For the times they are a-changin'
The line it is drawn
The curse it is cast
The slow one now
Will later be fast
As the present now
Will later be past
The order is
Rapidly fadin'
And the first one now
Will later be last
For the times they are a-changin'

 What caused the student campus revolts of the 1960s? What and whom does Dylan identify as the problem in this song?

28-5c Women in the Postwar World

Despite their enormous contributions to the war effort, women were removed from the workforce at the end of World War II so that soldiers returning home would have jobs. After the horrors of war, people seemed willing for awhile to return to traditional family practices. Female participation in the workforce declined, and birthrates rose, creating a "baby boom." This increase in the birthrate did not last, however, and the size of families began to decline by the mid-1960s. Largely responsible for this decline was the widespread practice of birth control. The condom, invented in the nineteenth century, was already in wide use, but the development of birth control pills in the 1960s provided a convenient and reliable means of birth control that quickly spread to all Western countries.

The trend toward smaller families contributed to changes in women's employment in both Europe and the United States, primarily because women now needed to devote far fewer years to rearing children. That led to a large increase in the number of married women in the workforce. At the beginning of the twentieth century, even working-class wives tended to stay at home if they could afford to do so. In the postwar period, this was no longer the case. In the United States, for example, in 1900, married women made up around 15 percent of the female labor force; by 1970, their number had increased to 62 percent.

But the increased number of women in the workforce did not change some old patterns. Working-class women in particular still earned less than men for equal work. In the 1960s, women earned only 60 percent of men's wages in Britain, 50 percent in France, and 63 percent in West Germany. In addition, women still tended to enter traditionally female jobs. Many women also still faced the double burden of earning income on the one hand and raising a family and maintaining the household on the other. Such inequalities led increasing numbers of women to rebel.

The Feminist Movement: the Quest for Liberation

The participation of women in World Wars I and II helped them achieve one of the major aims of the nineteenth-century feminist movement—the right to vote. After World War I, many governments acknowledged the contributions of women to the war effort by granting them suffrage. Sweden, Great Britain, Germany, Poland, Hungary, Austria, and Czechoslovakia did so in 1918, followed by the United States in 1920. Women in France and Italy did not obtain the right to vote until 1945. After World War II, little was heard of feminist concerns, but women began to assert their rights again and speak as feminists in the early 1960s. Along with the student upheavals of the late 1960s came renewed interest in feminism, or the **women's liberation movement**, as it was now called.

Of great importance to the emergence of the women's liberation movement was the work of Simone de Beauvoir (see-MUHN duh boh-VWAR) (1908–1986), who supported herself as a teacher and later as a writer. De Beauvoir believed that she lived a "liberated" life for a twentieth-century European woman, but she still came to perceive that as a woman she faced limits that men did not. In her highly influential work *The Second Sex* (1949), she argued that as a result of male-dominated societies, women had been defined by their differences from men and consequently received second-class status: "What particularly signalizes the situation of woman is that she—a free autonomous being like all human creatures—nevertheless finds herself in a world where men compel her to assume the status of the Other."[2]

Transformation in Women's Lives

To ensure natural replacement of a country's population, women need to produce an average of 2.1 children each. Many European countries fall far short of this mark; their populations stopped growing in the 1960s, and the trend has continued ever since. By the 1990s, the average number of children per mother was 1.4 in the nations of the European Union. At 1.31 in 2009, Spain's rate was among the lowest in the world.

At the same time, the number of women in the workforce has continued to rise. In Britain, for example, women accounted for 32 percent of the labor force in 1970 but 44 percent in 1990. Moreover, women have entered new employment areas. Greater access to universities and professional schools has enabled women to take jobs in law, medicine, government, business, and education. In the Soviet Union, for example, around 70 percent of doctors and teachers were women by 1990. Nevertheless, women are often paid less than men for comparable work and receive fewer promotions to management positions.

Feminists in the women's liberation movement came to believe that women themselves must transform the fundamental conditions of their lives. In the 1960s and 1970s, hundreds of thousands of European women gained a measure of control over their own bodies by working to repeal laws that outlawed contraception and abortion. Even in Catholic countries, where the church opposed abortion, legislation allowing contraception and abortion was passed in the 1970s and 1980s. Ireland did not allow abortion until 2018, when the Irish voted overwhelmingly to overturn the abortion ban.

Women in the West have also reached out to work with women from the rest of the world in changing the conditions of their lives. Between 1975 and 1995, the United Nations held a series of conferences on women's issues. These meetings made clear the differences between women from Western and non-Western countries. While women from Western countries spoke about political, economic, cultural, and sexual rights, women from developing countries in Latin America, Africa, and Asia focused on bringing an end to the violence, hunger, and disease that haunt their lives.

By 2017, the women's movement had taken on renewed momentum and activism following the campaign of presidential candidate Donald J. Trump. During Trump's campaign, he harshly criticized women and made sexually derogatory remarks; subsequent outrage led to large protest marches. The Women's March of January 21, 2017, was the largest single-day protest in U.S. history with more than 5 million people, and the march on Washington, D.C., was the second largest protest ever held in the capital.

28-5d The Growth of Terrorism

Acts of terror by individuals and groups opposed to governments have become a frightening aspect of modern Western society. During the late 1970s and early 1980s, small bands of terrorists used assassination, indiscriminate killing of civilians, hostage taking, and airplane hijacking to draw attention to their demands or to destabilize governments in the hope of achieving their political goals.

Motivations for terrorist acts varied considerably. Left- and right-wing terrorist groups flourished in the late 1970s and early 1980s, but terrorist acts also stemmed from militant nationalists who wished to create separatist states. Most prominent was the Irish Republican Army, which resorted to vicious attacks against the ruling government and innocent civilians in Northern Ireland. Although left- and right-wing terrorist activities declined in Europe in the 1980s, international terrorism continued.

The West and Islam   One of the major sources of terrorist activity against the West, especially in the United States, has come from some parts of the Muslim world. The ongoing Israeli–Palestinian conflict in which the United States has steadfastly supported Israel undoubtedly has helped give rise to anti-Western and especially anti-U.S. feeling among many Muslims. In 1979, a revolution in Iran that led to the overthrow of the shah and the creation of a new Islamic government led by Ayatollah Khomeini also fed anti-Western sentiment. In the eyes of the Ayatollah and his followers, the United States was the "great Satan," the powerful protector of Israel, and the enemy of Muslim peoples everywhere.

Palestinian terrorists mounted attacks on both Europeans and American tourists in Europe, including attacks on vacationers at airports in Rome and Vienna in 1985. State-sponsored terrorism was often an integral part of international terrorism. Militant governments—especially in Iran, Libya, and Syria—assisted terrorist organizations that carried out attacks on Europeans and Americans.

The involvement of the United States in the liberation of Kuwait in the Persian Gulf War in 1991 also had unexpected consequences in the relationship of Islam and the West. During that war, U.S. forces were stationed in Saudi Arabia, the location of many sacred Islamic sites. The presence of Americans was considered an affront to Islam by anti-Western Islamic groups especially that of Osama bin Laden and his followers. These anti-Western attitudes came to be shared by many radical Islamic groups, as has been evident in the 2003 bombing in Madrid, the 2005 bombing on subway trains in London, and the 2015 attacks in Paris at the headquarters of *Charlie Hebdo*, a French satirical magazine, and, on one Friday night alone, a soccer stadium, several cafes, and a music venue known as the Bataclan (see Historical Voices, "The West and Islam," p. 728).

In early 2014, a Muslim jihadist rebel group, the Islamic State of Iraq and Levant (ISIL; and also known as ISIS), captured significant territory in western Iraq and northern and central Syria. ISIL's use of extreme violence, ethnic cleansing, and Internet videos of beheadings of their captives has led to worldwide repudiation of the group and commitment from more than sixty countries to directly confront ISIL.

Terrorist Attack on the United States   One of the most destructive acts of terrorism occurred on September 11, 2001, in the United States. Terrorists hijacked four commercial jet airplanes and flew two of the airplanes into the towers of the World Trade Center in New York City, causing these buildings, as well as several surrounding buildings, to collapse. A third hijacked plane slammed into the Pentagon near Washington, D.C. The fourth plane, apparently headed for Washington, crashed in an isolated area of Pennsylvania. In total, more than three thousand people were killed.

These coordinated acts of terror were carried out by hijackers connected to the international terrorist organization known as al-Qaeda, once run by Osama bin Laden (1957–2011). A native of Saudi Arabia of Yemeni extraction, bin Laden used an inherited fortune to set up terrorist training camps in Afghanistan under the protection of that nation's militant fundamentalist Islamic rulers known as the Taliban. Under the direction of President Obama, special American forces killed Osama bin Laden in May 2011 at his compound in Pakistan.

U.S. president George W. Bush vowed to wage a war on terrorism and worked to create a coalition of nations to assist in ridding the world of al-Qaeda and other terrorist groups. Within weeks of the attack on United States, U.S. and NATO air forces began bombing Taliban-controlled command centers and al-Qaeda hiding places in Afghanistan. On the ground, Afghan forces, assisted by U.S. special forces, pushed the Taliban out and gained control of the country by the end of 2001. A democratic multiethnic government was installed but continues to face problems from revived Taliban activity (see Chapter 29).

28-5e Guest Workers and Immigrants

As the economies of the Western European countries revived in the 1950s and 1960s, a severe labor shortage forced them to rely on foreign workers. Thousands of Turks and eastern and southern Europeans relocated to Germany, North Africans to France, and people from the Caribbean, India, and Pakistan to Great Britain. Overall, there were probably 15 million **guest workers** in Europe in the 1980s.

Although these workers were recruited for economic reasons, their presence has created social and political problems for their host countries. The influx of foreigners has strained the social services of European countries, and

The West and Islam

Religion & Philosophy THE RISE OF LARGE SCALE TERRORIST ACTS, such as the attack in New York on September 11, 2001, or the Paris attack of November 13, 2015, are indicative of a larger issue—the growth of religious extremism in the Muslim world. Religious extremism has long been a part of religious history. In this selection, Abbas Amanat, historian of Middle Eastern history, analyzes the roots of Islamic radicalism, focusing on the resentment many Muslims have against the West.

Abbas Amanat, "Empowered Through Violence: The Reinvention of Islamic Extremism"

The emergence of the construct we call Islamic extremism, with its penchant for . . . violence, has its roots in the history of the Muslim sense of decline and its unhappy encounter with the dominant West. It is sobering to remind ourselves how frequently the Middle East, as one part of the Muslim world, has been visited by waves of violence in its recent history. Since the end of the Second World War, the area extending from Egypt and Turkey in the west to Afghanistan in the northwest and Yemen in the south has suffered at least ten major wars. . . .Casualties have run into millions. Populations have been uprooted, societies torn up by their roots, political structures demolished—all on a massive scale. . . .

In the minds of many, Western powers shared the blame, both directly and indirectly. Whether based on historical reality or faulty perception, holding the Western powers responsible made special sense against the backdrop of a powerful West and a powerless Middle East. From the days of the European colonial powers in the 19th century to the more recent interventions of the superpowers, there has been a pattern of diplomatic, military and economic presence tying the fate of the Middle East and its resources to the West. . . .

Mistrust toward the West deepened as a result of the problematic way the Middle East improvised its own version of modernity. . . . It is grappling endlessly with failed centralized planning, high birthrates, lopsided distribution of wealth, high unemployment, widespread corruption, inefficient bureaucracies, and environmental and health problems. The frustration endemic among the young urban classes . . . is a response to these conundrums. . . .

In dealing with these restive multitudes, the governments of the Middle East and their associated ruling elites have little to offer. They are themselves part of the problem as they contribute to the public perception of powerlessness. In the period right after World War II, nationalist ideologies were highly effective in mobilizing the public against the European colonial presence. The army officers who came to power in Egypt, Syria, Iraq, and elsewhere . . . invested heavily in anti-Western rhetoric. Yet facing the erosion of their own legitimacy, they learned to pay a lip service to their rising Islamic sentiments in their societies, exploiting them as a cushion between the elite and the masses and to suppress individual freedoms. . . .

The decisive shift came not inside the Arab world but with the 1979 revolution in Iran. The establishment of an Islamic republic under the leadership of the uncompromising Ayatollah Khomeini evoked throughout the Muslim world the long-cherished desire for creating a genuine Islamic regime. . . .

The Iraq–Iran War of 1980–1988 further established the appeal of the paradigm of martyrdom that had long been deeply rooted in Shi'a Islam. That conflict was portrayed as an apocalyptic jihad between the forces of truth and falsehood. . . . and the celebration of martyrdom found resonance far and wide. The . . . young Palestinians who eagerly volunteered for suicide bombing on behalf of the Hamas and Islamic Jihad, saw martyrdom as a way of empowerment.

Q *How do Middle Easterners perceive Westerners? Why have their perceptions changed?*

Source: Abbas Amanat, "Empowered Through Violence: The Reinvention of Islamic Extremism," from Strobe Talbott, *The Age of Terror* (New York, 2002).

high concentrations of guest workers, many of them nonwhite, in certain areas have led to tensions with the local native populations who oppose making their countries ethnically diverse. By 1998, English was not the first language of one-third of inner-city children in London. Foreign workers constitute almost one-fifth of the population in the German cities of Frankfurt, Munich, and Stuttgart. Antiforeign sentiment has increased with growing unemployment. In France, the growing number of Muslims has also led to restrictions on the display of Islamic symbols.

In 2004, France enacted a law prohibiting female students from wearing a headscarf (hijib) to school, whereas small religious symbols such as small crosses or medallions were not included. Critics argue that this law will exacerbate ethnic and religious tensions in France, but supporters maintain that it upholds the French tradition of secularism and equality for women.

In 2015, a sharp increase in migrants streamed into Europe. Conflicts in the Middle East, particularly in Syria, where civil war has decimated the country, led to an exodus of refugees from Syria, Iraq and Afghanistan. Europe accepted more than 1.2 million refugees in 2005, with Germany taking more than 800,000 of those refugees. German Prime Minister Angela Merkel has called for a universal quota system in the European Union. Many countries have rejected such a proposal, especially Eastern European countries such as Hungary and Poland, which are fairly homogenous after decades of ethnic cleansing.

The arrival of so many foreigners strained not only the social services of European countries but also the patience of many native residents who opposed the sudden ethnic diversification of their countries. Antiforeign sentiment increased, especially as domestic unemployment grew, and it was stoked by right-wing political parties that catered to people's complaints. Following the migration crises in 2015, anti-immigrant parties reemerged at the fore of European politics. In Hungary, the Jobbik party—an anti-immigration, populist, and economic protectionist party—is now Hungary's third largest political party. In France, the National Front party, founded by Nazi collaborators, is the most popular party for 18–34 year olds. In Germany the Alternative for Germany party, founded in 2013, today retains 25 percent of the votes in state elections.

28-5f The Environment and the Green Movements

Environmentalism first became an important item on the European political agenda in the 1970s. By that time, serious ecological problems had become all too apparent. Air pollution created by emissions from road vehicles, power plants, and industrial factories was causing respiratory illnesses and having corrosive effects on buildings and monuments. Many rivers, lakes, and seas had become so polluted that they posed serious health risks. In 1986, a disastrous accident at the Soviet nuclear power plant at Chernobyl, Ukraine, made Europeans even more aware of potential environmental hazards. The opening of Eastern Europe after the revolutions of 1989 revealed the environmental destruction caused by unfettered industrial pollution in that region.

Growing ecological awareness gave rise to Green movements and Green parties throughout Europe beginning in the 1970s. Most visible was the Green Party in Germany, which was officially organized in 1979 and had elected forty-two delegates to the West German parliament by 1987. Although the Green movements and parties have played an important role in making people aware of ecological problems, they have not supplanted the traditional political parties because traditional political parties have co-opted the environmental issues of the Greens. By the 1990s, European governments were taking steps to safeguard the environment and clean up the worse sources of pollution.

By the early twenty-first century, European cities began to recognize the need for urban sustainability. In 2015, world leaders met in Paris to sign the Paris Accord, a landmark climate agreement committing 195 nations to lower its carbon dioxide emissions. In 2014, American president Barack Obama and Chinese president Xi Jinping announced that they would jointly pursue plans to cut greenhouse gas emissions. Their commitment led the way for other countries to join. Although the agreement is probably not enough to stave off the worst effects of climate change, it is a fundamental shift in global policy and offers hope for the preservation of planet Earth. In 2017, U.S. President Trump, a denier of climate change, withdrew the United States from the Paris agreement even in the face of widespread opposition.

28-5g Western Culture Since 1945

Intellectually and culturally, the Western world since World War II has been notable for innovation as well as diversity. Especially since 1970, new directions have led some observers to speak of a "postmodern" cultural world.

Postwar Literature A significant trend in postwar literature was the theater of the absurd. Its most famous proponent was Irishman Samuel Beckett (1906–1990), who lived in France. In Beckett's *Waiting for Godot* (1952), the action on the stage is transparently unrealistic. Two men wait for someone, with whom they may or may not have an appointment. During the course of the play, nothing seems to be happening. The audience is never told if the action in front of them is real or imagined. Suspense is maintained not by having the audience wonder "What is going to happen next?" but simply "What is happening now?"

The theater of the absurd reflected its time. The postwar era was one of disillusionment with fixed ideological beliefs in politics and religion. The same disillusionment that underscored the bleak worldview of absurdist drama also inspired the **existentialism** of writers Albert Camus (ahl-BAYR ka-MOO) (1913–1960) and Jean-Paul Sartre (ZHAHNH-POHL SAR-truh) (1905–1980), who explored the world's meaninglessness. The beginning point of the existentialism of Sartre and Camus was the absence of God in the universe. Although the death of God was tragic, it also meant that humans had no preordained destiny and were utterly alone in the universe with no future and no hope. As Camus expressed it:

> A world that can be explained even with bad reasons is a familiar world. But, on the other hand, in a universe suddenly divested of illusions and lights, man feels an alien, a stranger. His exile is without remedy since he is deprived of the memory of a lost home or the hope of a promised land. This divorce between man and his life, the actor and his setting, is properly the feeling of absurdity.[3]

According to Camus, then, the world was absurd and without meaning; humans are also without meaning and purpose. Reduced to despair and depression, humans have but one source of hope—themselves.

Postmodernism   The term *postmodern* covers a variety of intellectual and artistic styles and ways of thinking that have been prominent since the 1970s. In the broadest sense, **postmodernism** rejects the modern Western belief in an objective truth and instead focuses on the relative nature of reality and knowledge.

Although existentialists wrestled with notions of meaning and existence, a group of French philosophers in the 1960s attempted to understand how meaning and knowledge operate through the study of language and signs. **Poststructuralism** or **deconstruction** as formulated by Jacques Derrida (ZHAHK DEH-ree-duh) (1930–2004), holds that culture is created and can therefore be analyzed in a variety of ways, according to the manner in which people create their own meaning. Hence, there is no fixed truth or universal meaning.

Michel Foucault (mih-SHELL foo-KOH) (1926–1984) drew on Derrida to explore relationships of power. Believing that "power is exercised, rather than possessed," Foucault argued that the diffusion of power and oppression marks all relationships. For example, any act of teaching entails components of assertion and submission as the student adopts the ideas of the person in power. Therefore, all norms are culturally produced and entail some degree of power struggle.

28-5h Trends in Art

After the war, the United States dominated the art world, much as it did the world of popular culture. New York City replaced Paris as the artistic center of the West.

The Guggenheim Museum, the Museum of Modern Art, and the Whitney Museum of Modern Art, together with New York's numerous art galleries, promoted modern art and helped determine artistic tastes throughout much of the world. One of the styles that became synonymous with the emergence of the New York art scene was **abstract expressionism**.

Dubbed "action painting" by one critic, abstract expressionism was energetic and spontaneous, qualities evident in the enormous canvases of Jackson Pollock (1912–1956). In such works as *Lavender Mist* (1950), paint seems to explode, enveloping the viewer with emotion and movement. Pollock's swirling forms and seemingly chaotic patterns broke all conventions of form and structure. Inspired by Native American sand painters, Pollock painted with the canvas on the floor. He explained, "On the floor I am more at ease. I feel nearer, more a part of

Hans Namuth/Science Source

28.7 Jackson Pollock at Work. After World War II, abstract expressionism moved to the center of the artistic mainstream. One of its best-known practitioners was Jackson Pollock, who achieved his ideal of total abstraction in his drip paintings. He is shown here at work at his Long Island studio. Pollock found it easier to cover his large canvases with exploding patterns of color when he put them on the floor.

the painting, since this way I can walk around it, work from four sides and be literally in the painting. When I am in the painting, I am not aware of what I am doing. There is pure harmony."

Postmodernism's eclectic commingling of past tradition with modernist innovation was especially evident in architecture. Robert Venturi argued that architects should look for inspiration as much to the Las Vegas Strip as to the historical styles of the past. The work of Charles Moore (1929–1993) provides an example. His Piazza d'Italia (1976–1980) in New Orleans is an outdoor plaza that combines classical Roman columns with stainless steel and neon lights. This blending of modern-day materials with historical references distinguished the postmodern architecture of the late 1970s and 1980s from the modernist glass box.

Throughout the 1980s and 1990s, the art and music industries increasingly adopted the techniques of marketing and advertising. With large sums of money invested in painters and musicians, pressure mounted to achieve critical and commercial success. Negotiating the distinction between art and popular culture was essential since many equated merit with sales or economic value.

Art in the Contemporary World Since the late 1980s, many artists in the art world have embraced technological and globalization challenges through new mediums and subject matter, often combining multiple media, including photography, film, sculpture, and installation to address the intersections of a new global identity. The tech boom of the 1990s brought a new generation of wealth to the art market, elevating artists and prices to rock star status. Advances in computer technology and the proliferation of handheld devices changed the ways in which art is produced and marketed. Negotiating the distinction between art and popular culture was essential as many people equated merit with sales or economic value rather than aesthetic considerations.

Artists also embraced the politics of identity, creating works that questioned gender, ethnicity, and sexual orientation. Shirin Neshat (SHIH-reen nay-SHAT) (b. 1957), an American artist who fled Iran during the Iranian Revolution, creates large-scale photographs painted with Farsi, or Persian calligraphy. Neshat's artworks question the violence and gendered norms projected onto the Middle Eastern body. Her work represents a growing body of artists exploring multiculturalism as a result of global migrations.

28-5i The World of Science and Technology

Many of the scientific and technological achievements since World War II have revolutionized people's lives.

28.8 Shirin Neshat, *Stripped* (1995). This photograph is part of Shirin Neshat's "Women of Allah" series, created after she returned to Iran following her sixteen years of living in America. She was surprised by the transformation of Iranian society following the Islamic Revolution and attempted to understand the place of women in this new state.

During World War II, university scientists were recruited to work for their governments and develop new weapons and practical instruments of war. British physicists played a crucial role in developing an improved radar system that helped defeat the German air force in the Battle of Britain in 1940. German scientists created self-propelled rockets as well as jet airplanes to keep Hitler's hopes alive for a miraculous turnaround in the war. The computer, too, was a wartime creation. British mathematician Alan Turing designed a primitive computer to assist British intelligence in breaking the secret codes of German ciphering machines. The most famous product of wartime scientific research was the atomic bomb, created by a team of American and European scientists under the guidance of the physicist J. Robert Oppenheimer. Although created for destructive purposes, many wartime developments such as computers and nuclear energy were soon adapted for peacetime uses.

The postwar alliance of science and technology led to an accelerated rate of change that became a fact of life in Western society (see Comparative Essay, "From the Industrial Age to the Technological Age," p. 732). One product of this alliance—the computer—may prove

From the Industrial Age to the Technological Age

Science & Technology As many observers have noted, the world economy is in transition to a "postindustrial age" that is both increasingly global and technology intensive. Since World War II, an array of technological changes— especially in transportation, communications, medicine, and agriculture—have transformed the world. These changes have also raised new questions and concerns. Some scientists worry that genetic engineering might accidentally result in new strains of deadly bacteria. Some doctors warn that the overuse of antibiotics has created

28.9 The Technological Age. A communication satellite is seen orbiting above Earth.

Adastra/Taxi/Getty Images

supergerms that are resistant to antibiotic treatment. Technological advances have also led to more deadly methods of destruction, including nuclear weapons.

The advent of the postindustrial world, which futurologist Alvin Toffler dubbed the "Third Wave" (the first two being the Agricultural and Industrial Revolutions), has led to difficulties for many people. They include blue-collar workers, whose jobs have disappeared as factories have moved abroad to use lower-cost labor; the poor and uneducated, who lack the technical skills to handle complex tasks; and even members of the middle class, who have lost their jobs as employers outsource jobs to compete in the global marketplace.

It is now increasingly clear that the Technological Revolution, like the Industrial Revolution that preceded it, will entail enormous consequences. The success of advanced capitalist states in the postwar era has been built on a consensus on the importance of two propositions: (1) the need for high levels of government investment in education, communications, and transportation; and (2) the desirability of maintaining open markets for the free exchange of goods.

Today, these assumptions are increasingly under attack as citizens refuse to vote for the tax increases required to support education and oppose the formation of trading alliances to promote the free movement of goods and labor across national borders. The breakdown of the public consensus raises serious questions about whether the coming challenges of the Third Wave can be successfully met without a rise in political and social tension.

Q *What is implied by the term "Third Wave," and what challenges does the Third Wave present to humanity?*

to be the most revolutionary of all the technological inventions of the twentieth century. Early computers were large, created enormous amounts of heat, and took up considerable space. The transistor and then the silicon chip revolutionized computer design. With the invention of the microprocessor in 1971, the road was open for the development of the personal computer. By the 1990s, the personal computer had become a fixture in businesses, schools, and homes. The Internet—the world's largest computer network, launched in the 1980s by the U.S. government—provides millions of people around the world with quick access to immense quantities of information, as well as rapid communication and commercial transactions. These new forms of communication have allowed for greater access to information and people in a short period.

Despite the marvels produced by science and technology, some people have come to question the assumption that scientific knowledge that allows us to manipulate the environment is always beneficial. They maintain that some technological advances have far-reaching side effects that are damaging to the environment. Chemical fertilizers, for example, were once touted for their ability to help farmers produce larger crops, but they have wreaked havoc with the ecological balance of streams, rivers, and woodlands.

28-5j The Explosion of Popular Culture

Since 1900, and especially since World War II, popular culture has played an important role in helping Western people define themselves. It also reflects the economic system that supports it because this system manufactures, distributes, and sells the images that people consume as popular culture. Thus, modern popular culture is inextricably tied to the mass consumer society in which it has emerged.

The United States has been the most influential force in shaping popular culture in the West and, to a lesser degree, the entire world. Through movies, music, advertising, and television, the United States has spread its particular form of consumerism and the American dream to millions around the world. In 1923, the *New York Morning Post* noted that "the film is to America what the flag was once to Britain. By its means Uncle Sam may hope some day . . . to Americanize the world."[4] That day has already come.

Motion pictures were the primary vehicle for the diffusion of American popular culture in the years immediately following World War I and continued to find ever wider markets as the century rolled on. Television, which was first developed in the 1930s, did not become readily available until the late 1940s, but there were 32 million sets in the United States by 1954 as television became the centerpiece of middle-class life. In the 1960s, as television spread around the world, American networks unloaded their products on Europe and the Third World at extraordinarily low prices.

The United States has also dominated popular music since the end of World War II. Jazz, blues, rhythm and blues, rap, and rock and roll have been by far the most popular music forms in the Western world—and much of the non-Western world—during this time. All of them originated in the United States, and all are rooted in African American musical innovations. These forms later spread to the rest of the world, inspiring local artists, who then transformed the music in their own ways.

In the postwar years, sports have become a major product of both popular culture and the leisure industry. Satellite television and various electronic breakthroughs have helped make sports a global phenomenon. Olympic Games can now be broadcast around the globe from anywhere in the world. In 2014, approximately 1 billion people watched the World Cup championship match. Sports have become a cheap form of entertainment, as fans do not have to leave their homes to enjoy athletic competitions. Many sports now receive the bulk of their yearly revenue from television contracts.

CHAPTER SUMMARY

Western Europe reinvented itself in the 1950s and 1960s as a remarkable economic recovery fostered a new optimism. Western European states embraced political democracy, and with the development of the European Community, many of them began to move toward economic unity.

A new European society also emerged after World War II. White-collar workers increased in number, and buying on installment plans helped create a consumer society. The welfare state provided both pensions and health care. Birth control led to smaller families, and more women joined the workforce.

Although many people were optimistic about a "new world order" after the collapse of communism, uncertainties still prevailed. Germany was successfully reunited, and the European Union adopted a common currency in the euro. Yugoslavia, however, disintegrated into warring states that eventually all became independent, and ethnic groups that had once been forced to live under distinct national banners began rebelling to form autonomous states. Although some were successful, others were brutally repressed.

In the Western Hemisphere, the United States and Canada built prosperous economies and relatively stable communities in the 1950s, but new problems there—including ethnic, racial, and linguistic differences, along with economic difficulties—dampened the optimism of earlier decades. Although some Latin

American nations shared in the economic growth of the 1950s and 1960s, growth was not accompanied by political stability. Not until the 1980s did democratic governments begin with consistency to replace oppressive military regimes.

While the "new world order" was fitfully developing, other challenges emerged. The arrival of many foreigners, especially in Western Europe, not only strained the social services of European countries but also led to anti-foreign sentiment. Environmental abuses led to growing threats not only to Europeans but also to all humans. Terrorism, especially that perpetrated by some parts of the Muslim world, emerged as a threat to many Western states. Since the end of World War II, terrorism seems to have replaced communism as the primary enemy of the West. At the beginning of the twenty-first century, a major realization has been the recognition that the problems afflicting the Western world have become global problems.

REFLECTION QUESTIONS

Q What were the major successes and failures of the Western European democracies between 1945 and 2017?

Q What directions did Eastern European nations take after they became free from Soviet control? Why did they react as they did?

Q What role did popular culture play in the Western world after 1945, and to what extent has it become globalized?

CHAPTER TIMELINE

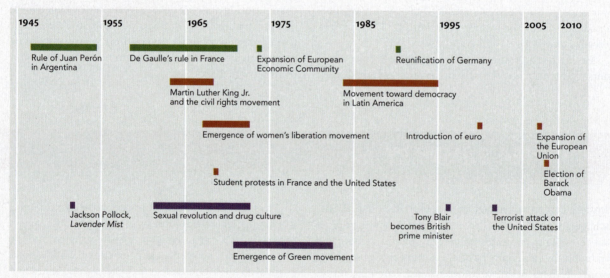

CHAPTER NOTES

1. Quoted in W. I. Hitchcock, *The Struggle for Europe: The Turbulent History of a Divided Continent, 1945–2002* (New York, 2003), pp. 399–400.

2. S. de Beauvoir, *The Second Sex,* trans. H. M. Parshley (New York, 1961), p. xxviii.

3. Quoted in H. Grosshans, *The Search for Modern Europe* (Boston, 1970), p. 421.

4. Quoted in R. Maltby, ed., *Passing Parade: A History of Popular Culture in the Twentieth Century* (New York, 1989), p. 11.

MINDTAP
From Cengage

MindTap® is a fully online, highly personalized learning experience built upon Cengage Learning content. MindTap combines student learning tools—readings, multimedia, activities, and assessments—into a singular Learning Path that guides students through the course and helps students develop the critical thinking, analysis, and communication skills that are essential to academic and professional success.

CHAPTER 29

CHALLENGES OF NATION BUILDING IN AFRICA AND THE MIDDLE EAST

Chapter Outline and Focus Questions

AHMED OUOBA/AFP/Getty Images

29.1 The Face of Islamic Extremism in Central Africa

Critical Thinking

Q *What factors can be advanced to explain the chronic instability and internal conflict that have characterized conditions in Africa and the Middle East since World War II?*

Connections to Today

Q *What possible strategies do you feel the peoples of Africa and the Middle East might adopt to assist them in establishing stable societies throughout both regions today?*

ON TAKING OVER THE CITY, they began to terrorize the inhabitants—cutting off the hands of suspected thieves, stoning adulterous couples to death, forbidding the playing of any kind of musical instrument, and desecrating the famous library and the shrines of local Sufi mystics. The invaders were fanatical tribal warriors who sought to impose their strict version of Islam on the population throughout the region.

The city was Timbuktu, once a fabled caravan stop on a major trade route snaking through the Sahara and more recently a sleepy river port in the western African country of Mali. The time was January 2013.

Timbuktu lies in the Sahel, a grassy region just south of the Sahara that stretches from the western tip of the African continent to the Nile River Valley in the east. Historically a geographic fault line between the arid desert and the rich tropical forest lands along the Atlantic coast to the south, in recent times the Sahel has become a political and ideological battleground as well, as Muslim pastoralists compete with Christian and animist farmers for scarce fertile land and access to precious water reserves. The struggle has been going on for centuries, but it has intensified in recent years as a result of the increasing desiccation of the region and the current tensions between Muslims and Christians throughout the world today. Dealing with this issue is only one challenge that many nations in Africa face today as they struggle to create stable and prosperous societies.

29-1 UHURU: THE STRUGGLE FOR INDEPENDENCE IN AFRICA

Q **Focus Question:** What role did nationalist movements play in the transition to independence in Africa, and how did such movements differ from their counterparts elsewhere?

In the three decades following the end of World War II, the peoples of Africa were gradually liberated from the formal trappings of European colonialism.

29-1a The Colonial Legacy

As in Asia, colonial rule had a mixed impact on the societies and peoples of Africa (see Chapter 21). The Western presence brought many short- and long-term benefits to Africa, including improved transportation and communication facilities, and in a few areas it laid the foundation for a modern industrial and commercial sector. Improved sanitation and medical care increased life expectancy. Yet the benefits of colonialism were distributed unequally, and the vast majority of Africans found their lives little improved if at all. Most Africans continued to be subsistence farmers growing food for their own consumption. Only South Africa and French-held Algeria developed modern industrial sectors, extensive

railroad networks, and modern communications systems. In both countries, European settlers were numerous, most investment capital for industrial ventures was European, and whites constituted almost the entire professional and managerial class. Members of the indigenous population were generally restricted to unskilled or semiskilled jobs at wages less than one-fifth those enjoyed by Europeans.

29-1b The Rise of Nationalism

Political organizations founded to promote African rights did not arise until after World War I, and then only in a few areas such as British-ruled Kenya and the Gold Coast. After World War II, following the example of independence movements elsewhere, groups organized political parties with independence as their objective. In the Gold Coast, Kwame Nkrumah (KWAH-may en-KROO-muh) (1909–1972) led the Convention People's Party, the first formal political party in black Africa. In the late 1940s, Jomo Kenyatta (JOH-moh ken-YAHT-uh) (1894–1978) founded the Kenya African National Union, which focused on economic issues but also had an implied political agenda.

For the most part, these political activities were basically nonviolent and were led by Western-educated African intellectuals. Their constituents were primarily urban professionals, merchants, and members of labor unions. But the demand for independence was not entirely restricted to the cities. In Kenya, for example, the widely publicized Mau Mau [MOW MOW ("ow" as in "how")] movement among the Kikuyu (ki-KOO-yoo) people used guerrilla and terror tactics as an essential element of its program to achieve *uhuru* (oo-HOO-roo) (Swahili for "freedom") from the British. Although most of the violence was directed against other Africans, the specter of a nationwide revolt alarmed the European population and convinced the British government in 1959 to promise eventual independence.

In South Africa, where the political system was dominated by European settlers, the transition to independence was equally complicated. Political activity by local Africans began with the formation of the African National Congress (ANC) in 1912. Initially, the ANC was dominated by Western-oriented intellectuals and had limited mass support. Its goal was to achieve economic and political reforms, including full equality for educated Africans, within the framework of the existing system. But the ANC's efforts met with little success, and conservative white parties managed to stiffen segregation laws and impose a policy of full legal segregation called **apartheid** (uh-PAHRT-hyt) in 1948. In response, the ANC became increasingly radicalized, and the prospects for a violent confrontation were growing by the 1950s.

Most black African nations achieved their independence in the late 1950s and 1960s, beginning with the Gold Coast, now renamed Ghana, in 1957 (see Map 29.1). It was soon followed by Nigeria; the Belgian Congo, which was renamed Zaire (zah-EER) and then the Democratic Republic of the Congo; Kenya; Tanganyika (tan-gan-YEE-kuh), which later joined with Zanzibar (ZAN-zi-bar) and was renamed Tanzania (tan-zuh-NEE-uh); and several other countries. Most French colonies agreed to accept independence within the framework of Charles de Gaulle's French Community, although the process was marked by violence in Algeria, where bitter resistance to French efforts to incorporate the colony into metropolitan France led to a protracted conflict that lasted until independence was granted in 1962. By the late 1960s, only parts of southern Africa and the Portuguese possessions of Mozambique and Angola remained under European rule.

29-2 THE ERA OF INDEPENDENCE

Q **Focus Question:** How have dreams clashed with realities in the independent nations of Africa, and how have African governments sought to meet these challenges?

The newly independent African states faced intimidating challenges. Although Western political institutions, values, and technology had been introduced, at least in the cities, the exposure to European civilization had been superficial at best for most Africans and tragic for many. At the outset of independence, most African societies were still primarily agrarian and traditional, and their modern sectors depended mainly on imports from the West.

29-2a The Destiny of Africa: Unity or Diversity?

Like their counterparts in South and Southeast Asia, most African leaders came from the urban middle class. They had studied in either Europe or the United States and spoke and read European languages. Although most were profoundly critical of colonial policies, they were initially inclined to accept the relevance of the Western model of governance to Africa and gave lip service to Western democratic values.

Their views on economics were somewhat more diverse. Some, like Jomo Kenyatta of Kenya and General Mobutu Sese Seko (moh-BOO-too SES-ay SEK-oh) (1930–1997) of Zaire, were advocates of Western-style capitalism. Others, like Julius Nyerere (ny-REHR-ee) (1922–1999) of Tanzania, Kwame Nkrumah of Ghana, and Sekou Touré (say-KOO too-RAY) (1922–1984) of Guinea, preferred an "African form of socialism" that bore slight resemblance to the Marxist–Leninist socialism practiced in the Soviet Union. According to its advocates, it was descended from traditional communal practices in precolonial Africa.

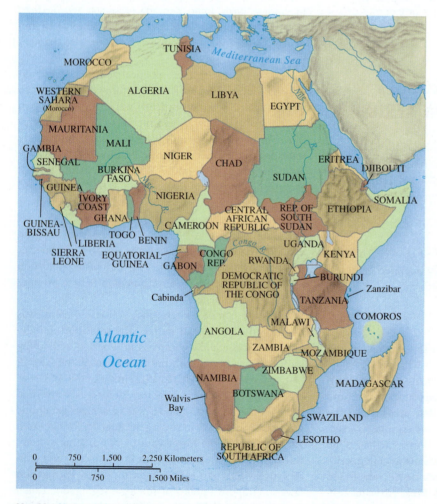

Map 29.1 Modern Africa. This map shows the independent states in Africa today.

Q *Why was unity so difficult to achieve in African regions?*

Toward African Unity

Interaction & Exchange — **IN MAY 1963,** the leaders of thirty-two African states met in Addis Ababa, the capital of Ethiopia, to discuss the creation of an organization that would represent the interests of all newly independent African countries. The result was the Organization of African Unity. An excerpt from its charter is presented here. Although the organization did not realize all of its founders' aspirations, it provided a useful forum for the discussion and resolution of common problems. In 2001, it was replaced by the African Union, which was designed to bring about increased cooperation among the states on the continent; unlike the OAU, the African Union has recognized the need on occasion to intervene in the internal affairs of member nations.

Charter of the Organization of African Unity

We, the Heads of African States and Governments assembled in the City of Addis Ababa, Ethiopia;

CONVINCED that it is the inalienable right of all people to control their own destiny;

CONSCIOUS of the fact that freedom, equality, justice, and dignity are essential objectives for the achievement of the legitimate aspirations of the African peoples;

CONSCIOUS of our responsibility to harness the natural and human resources of our continent for the total advancement of our peoples in spheres of human endeavor;

INSPIRED by a common determination to promote understanding among our peoples and cooperation among our States in response to the aspirations of our peoples for brotherhood and solidarity, in a larger unity transcending ethnic and national differences;

CONVINCED that, in order to translate this determination into a dynamic force in the cause of human progress, conditions for peace and security must be established and maintained;

DETERMINED to safeguard and consolidate the hard-won independence as well as the sovereignty and territorial integrity of our States, and to fight against neocolonialism in all its forms;

DEDICATED to the general progress of Africa; . . .

DESIROUS that all African States should henceforth unite so that the welfare and well-being of their peoples can be assured;

RESOLVED to reinforce the links between our states by establishing and strengthening common institutions;

HAVE agreed to the present Charter.

Q *What are the key objectives expressed in this charter? To what degree have they been achieved?*

Source: J. Woronoff, *Organizing African Unity* (Scarecrow Press, 1980), pp. 642–649.

At first, most of the new African leaders accepted the national boundaries established during the colonial era. But as we have seen, these boundaries were artificial creations of the colonial powers. Virtually every new state included widely diverse ethnic, linguistic, and territorial groups. Zaire (today the Democratic Republic of the Congo), for example, was composed of more than 200 territorial groups speaking 75 different languages. Such conditions posed a severe challenge to the task of forming cohesive nation-states.

Moreover, several leaders—including Nkrumah of Ghana, Touré of Guinea, and Nyerere of Tanganyika— were enticed by **Pan-Africanism**, the concept of a continental unity that transcended national boundaries. Some were motivated by the belief that traditional African civilization—symbolized by its countless villages embodying the humanistic and spiritual qualities of the African people—could serve as antidotes to the relentless European drive for political hegemony

and economic profit. Only Africa, they felt, could save the world from the plague that threatened ultimately to destroy human civilization.

Nkrumah of Ghana in particular hoped that a Pan-African union could be established that would unite all of the new countries of the continent in a broader community. His dream was not widely shared by other African political figures, however, who eventually settled on a more innocuous concept of regional cooperation on key issues. The concrete manifestation of this idea was the Organization of African Unity (OAU), founded in Addis Ababa (AH-diss AH-bah-buh) in 1963 (see Historical Voices, "Toward African Unity").

29-2b Dream and Reality: Political and Economic Conditions in Independent Africa

The OAU's program called for an Africa based on freedom, equality, justice, and dignity and on the unity, solidarity, prosperity, and territorial integrity of African states. It did not take long for reality to set in. Vast disparities in education and wealth made it hard to establish material prosperity in much of Africa. Expectations that independence would lead to stable political structures based on "one person, one vote" were soon disappointed as the initial phase of pluralistic governments gave way to a series of military regimes and one-party states. Between 1957 and 1982, more than seventy leaders of African countries were overthrown by violence, and the pace has not abated in recent years.

The Problem of Neocolonialism Part of the problem could be (and was) ascribed to the lingering effects of colonialism. Most new countries in Africa were dependent on the export of a single crop or natural resource. When prices fluctuated or dropped, these countries were at the mercy of the vagaries of international markets. In several cases, the resources were still controlled by foreigners, leading to the charge that colonialism had been succeeded by **neocolonialism**, in which Western domination was maintained primarily by economic rather than by political or military means. To make matters worse, most African states had to import technology and manufactured goods from the West, and the prices of those goods rose more rapidly than those of the export products.

The new states contributed to their own problems. Scarce national resources were squandered on military equipment or expensive consumer goods rather than used to create the infrastructure needed to provide the foundation for an industrial economy. Corruption, a painful reality throughout the modern world, became almost a way of life in Africa as bribery became necessary to obtain even the most basic services.

Many of the problems encountered by the new nations of Africa were also ascribed to the fact that independence did not bring an end to Western interference in Africa's political affairs. During the Cold War, both superpowers routinely interfered in the internal affairs of African states, notably when the United States engineered the overthrow of leftist leader Patrice Lumumba (put-TREES loo-MOOM-buh) (1925–1961) in the Congo and the Soviet Union similarly interfered in Ethiopia and Angola.

The Population Bomb Finally, rapid population growth crippled efforts to create modern economies. By the 1980s, annual population growth averaged nearly 3 percent throughout Africa, the highest rate of any continent. Unfortunately, spreading drought conditions and the inexorable spread of the Sahara (usually known as *desertification*, caused partly by overcultivation of the land) led to widespread hunger and starvation, first in West African countries such as Niger and Mali and then in Ethiopia, Somalia, and Sudan.

Predictions are that the population of Africa will increase by more than 1 billion by the year 2050, although that estimate does not take into account the prevalence of acquired immunodeficiency syndrome (AIDS), which has reached epidemic proportions in Africa. According to a United Nations study, at least 5 percent of the entire population of sub-Saharan Africa is infected with the virus, including a high percentage of the urban middle class. More than 65 percent of the AIDS cases reported around the world are on the continent of Africa.

Although economic growth has quickened in recent years, poverty is still widespread in Africa, particularly among the three-quarters of the population still living off the land. Urban areas have grown tremendously; as in much of Asia, however, most are surrounded by massive squatter settlements of rural peoples who have fled to the cities in search of a better life. The expansion of the cities has overwhelmed fragile transportation and sanitation systems and led to rising pollution and perpetual traffic jams, and millions are forced to live without running water and electricity. Meanwhile, the fortunate few (all too often government officials on the take) live the high life and emulate the consumerism of the West (in a particularly expressive phrase, the rich in many East African countries are known as *wabenzi*, or "Mercedes-Benz people").

29-2c The Search for Solutions

Although the problems of nation building described here have afflicted all of the emerging states of Africa to one degree or another, each has sought to deal with the challenge in its own way, sometimes with strikingly different consequences. Some African countries have made dramatic improvements in the past two decades, but others have encountered increasing difficulties. Despite all its shared problems, Africa today remains one of the most diverse regions of the globe. A brief account of several cases will illustrate the complexity of the problem.

Tanzania: An African Route to Socialism Concern over the dangers of economic inequality inspired several African leaders to restrict foreign investment and nationalize the major industries and utilities while promoting democratic ideals and values. Julius Nyerere of Tanzania was the most consistent, promoting the ideals of socialism and self-reliance through his Arusha (uh-ROO-shuh) Declaration of 1967, which set forth the principles for building a socialist society in Africa. Nyerere did not seek to establish a Leninist-style dictatorship of the proletariat in Tanzania, but neither was he a proponent of a multiparty democracy, which in his view would be divisive under the conditions prevailing in Africa. Importing the Western parliamentary system into Africa, he argued, could lead to violence because the opposition parties would be viewed as traitors by the majority of the population.

Taking advantage of his powerful political influence, Nyerere placed limitations on income and established village collectives to avoid the corrosive effects of economic inequality and government corruption. Sympathetic foreign countries provided considerable economic aid to assist the experiment, and many observers noted that levels of corruption, political instability, and ethnic strife were lower in Tanzania than in many other African countries. Nyerere's vision was not shared by all of his compatriots, however. Political elements on the island of Zanzibar, citing the stagnation brought by two decades of socialism, agitated for autonomy or even total separation from the mainland. Tanzania also has poor soil, inadequate rainfall, and limited resources, all of which have contributed to its slow growth and continuing rural and urban poverty.

In 1985, Nyerere voluntarily retired from the presidency. In his farewell speech, he confessed that he had failed to achieve many of his ambitious goals to create a socialist society in Africa. But Nyerere insisted that many of his policies had succeeded in improving social and economic conditions, and he argued that the only real solution was to consolidate the multitude of small countries in the region into a larger East African federation. Today, a quarter of a century later, Nyerere's Party of the Revolution continues to rule the country.

Kenya: The Perils of Capitalism

The countries that opted for capitalism faced their own dilemmas. Neighboring Kenya, blessed with better soil in the highlands, a local tradition of aggressive commerce, and a residue of European settlers, welcomed foreign investment and profit incentives. The results have been mixed. Kenya has a strong current of indigenous African capitalism and a substantial middle class that is mostly based in the capital of Nairobi (ny-ROH-bee). But landlessness, unemployment, and income inequities are high, even by African standards. The rate of population growth—around 2.5 percent annually—is one of the highest in the world. Almost 80 percent of the population remains rural, and 50 percent of the people live below the poverty line.

Kenya's problems have been exacerbated by chronic disputes between disparate ethnic groups and simmering tensions between farmers and pastoralists. For many years, the country maintained a fragile political stability under the dictatorial rule of President Daniel arap Moi (uh-RHAP moh-YEE) (b. 1924), one of the most authoritarian of African leaders. Plagued by charges of corruption, Moi

finally agreed to retire in 2002, but the problem continues to fester under the rule of the current president, Uhuru Kenyatta (b. 1961), the son of the nation's popular first president, whose party has been plagued with charges of corruption, ethnic favoritism, and election irregularities.

South Africa: An End to Apartheid

Until recently, Africa's greatest success story was South Africa. Under strong international pressure, the white government—which had long maintained a policy of racial segregation (apartheid) and restricted black sovereignty to a series of small "Bantustans" in relatively infertile areas of the country—finally accepted the inevitability of African involvement in the political process and the national economy. In 1990, the government of President Frederik W. de Klerk (b. 1936) released African National Congress leader Nelson Mandela (man-DELL-uh) (1918–2013) from prison, where he had been held since 1964. In 1993, the two leaders agreed to hold democratic national elections the following spring. In the meantime, ANC representatives agreed to take part in a transitional coalition government with de Klerk's National Party. Those elections resulted in a substantial majority for the ANC, and Mandela became president. In May 1996, a new constitution was approved that called for a multiracial state.

In 1999, a major step toward political stability was taken when Mandela stepped down from the presidency and was followed by his long-time disciple Thabo Mbeki (TAH-boh uhm-BAY-kee) (b. 1942). Mbeki's conservative economic policies earned the support of some white voters and the country's new black elite but were criticized by labor unions, which contended that the benefits of the new black leadership were not seeping down to the poor. In 2008, disgruntled ANC members forced Mbeki out of office. A year later, his one-time vice president and rival Jacob Zuma (ZOO-muh) (b. 1942) was elected president. Zuma won reelection six years later, but high unemployment and charges of government corruption have tarnished the image of the ANC and Zuma was forced to resign. Still, South Africa remains the wealthiest nation in Africa and the best hope that a multiracial society can succeed on the continent.

Nigeria: A Nation Divided

If the situation in South Africa provides grounds for modest optimism, the situation in Nigeria provides reason for serious concern. Africa's largest country in terms of population and one of its wealthiest because of substantial oil reserves, Nigeria was for many years in the grip of military strongmen. During his rule, General Sani Abacha (SAH-nee ah-BAH-chuh) (1943–1998) ruthlessly suppressed all opposition and was charged with selling out national interests to foreign oil companies. When Abacha died in 1998 under mysterious

29.2 An End to Apartheid. In 1994, Nelson Mandela, the long-time head of the African National Congress (ANC), was elected president of the Republic of South Africa and the policy of apartheid officially came to an end. Shown here in an iconic photograph, Mandela stands between his predecessor F. W. de Klerk and his chief lieutenant and eventual successor as chief of state, Thabo Mbeki. The ANC remains in power today, twenty years later.

circumstances, national elections led to the creation of a civilian government under Olusegun Obasanjo (ohl-OOseh-goon oh-buh-SAHN-joh) (b. 1937).

Civilian leadership has not been a panacea for Nigeria's problems, however. Although Obasanjo promised reforms to bring an end to the corruption and favoritism that had long plagued Nigerian politics, the results were disappointing (the state power company—known as NEPA—was so inefficient that Nigerians joked that the initials stood for "never expect power again"). Equally serious has been the challenge of resolving the country's territorial and religious disputes. Unified in 1914 into a single colony by the British for their own convenience, since independence Nigeria has been faced with the uneasy reality of a Muslim north and a Christian south. In early 2000, religious tensions between Christians and Muslims began to escalate when riots broke out in several northern cities as a result of the decision by Muslim provincial officials to apply shari'a throughout their jurisdictions. The election of Goodluck Jonathan (b. 1951), a Christian, as president in 2013 led to new protests among Muslims in the northern part of the country. Churches and mosques were burned, and massacres took place on both sides of the religious divide. The unrest has been fueled in part by the terrorist activities of Boko Haram (BOH-ko har-AHM), an al-Qaeda affiliate active in the region. Efforts by the government to quell the uprising have been hindered by reports of widespread brutality committed by Nigerian military units against civilians. The replacement of Goodluck Jonathan by the one-time military strongman Muhammadu Buhari (Moo-HAHM-ah-doo Boo-HAR-ee) in 2015 aroused hopes that a new administration could calm tensions and restore some semblance of order to the country, but so far passions have not diminished even as the nation's economy slumps because of unstable oil prices.

Tensions in the Desert The religious tensions that erupted in Nigeria have spilled over into neighboring states on the border of the Sahara. In Mali, a radical Islamic group seized power in the northern part of the country, applying strict punishments on local residents for alleged infractions against shari'a law and destroying Muslim shrines in the historic city of Timbuktu. French military units were dispatched to the region in early 2013 and drove the rebels out of major population centers, but the threat of Islamic radicalism has not subsided (see Comparative Essay, "Religion and Society," p. 753).

A similar rift has been at the root of the lengthy civil war that has been raging far to the east in Sudan. Conflict between Muslim pastoralists—supported by the central government in Khartoum—and predominantly Christian black farmers in the southern part of the country raged for years until the government finally agreed to permit a plebiscite in the south under the sponsorship of the United Nations to determine whether the southern population wished to secede from the country. In elections held in early 2011, voters overwhelmingly supported independence as the new nation of the Republic of South Sudan, but tribal disputes and tensions along the common border have led to chronic unrest in the new country.

The dispute between Muslims and Christians throughout the southern Sahara is a contemporary African variant of the traditional tensions that have existed between farmers and pastoralists throughout recorded history. Muslim cattle herders migrating southward to escape the increasing desiccation of the grasslands south of the Sahara compete for precious land with primarily Christian farmers. As a result of the religious revival now under way throughout the continent, the confrontation often leads to outbreaks of violence with strong religious and ethnic overtones and threatens the integrity of several of the states in the region.

CHRONOLOGY	Modern Africa	
Ghana gains independence from Great Britain		1957
Algeria gains independence from France		1962
Formation of the Organization of African Unity		1963
Biafra revolt in Nigeria		1966–1970
Arusha Declaration in Tanzania		1967
Nelson Mandela elected president of South Africa		1994
Genocide in Central Africa		1996–2000
Creation of the African Union		2001
Civil war breaks out in Darfur province in Sudan		2004
Ethnic riots in Kenya		2008
Jacob Zuma becomes president of South Africa		2009
Independence for the Republic of South Sudan		2011
Radical terrorists take over the city of Timbuktu		2013

Central Africa: Cauldron of Conflict But perhaps the most tragic situation was in Central Africa, where a chronic conflict between the minority Tutsis and the Hutu majority in Ruanda and Burundi led in the 1990s to a bitter civil war. Thousands of refugees fled to neighboring Zaire, where General Mobutu Sese Seko had long ruled with an iron hand. In 1997, military forces led by Mobutu's long-time opponent Laurent-Désiré Kabila (loh-RAHN-DAY-zeeray kah-BEE-luh) (1939–2001) managed to topple the general's corrupt government. Once in power, Kabila renamed the country the Democratic Republic of the Congo and promised a return to democratic practices, but Kabila was assassinated in 2001. He was succeeded by his son, Joseph Kabila (b. 1971). Peace talks to end the conflict began that fall, but continued fighting has led to horrific casualties among civilians.

29-2d Africa: A Continent in Flux

The brief survey of events in some of the more important African countries provided here illustrates the enormous difficulty that historians of Africa face in drawing any general conclusions about the pace and scope of change that has taken place in the continent in recent decades. Progress in some areas has been countered by growing problems elsewhere, and signs of hope in one region contrast with feelings of despair in another.

The shifting fortunes experienced throughout the continent are most prominently illustrated in the political arena. Over the past two decades, the collapse of one-party regimes has led to the emergence of fragile democracies in several countries. In other instances, however, democratic governments have erupted in civil war or been replaced by authoritarian rulers. Although many African leaders voice their support for the principles of democracy and human rights, such concepts clearly have not yet struck deep roots in the soil of the continent.

Similarly, the economic picture in Africa has also been mixed. Most African states are still poor and their populations illiterate. Moreover, African concerns continue to carry little weight in the international community. A recent agreement by the World Trade Organization (WTO) on the need to reduce agricultural subsidies in the advanced nations has been widely ignored. Some observers argue that external assistance cannot succeed unless the nations of Africa adopt measures to bring about good government and sound economic policies.

Despite the African continent's chronic economic problems, however, there are signs of hope. The overall rate of economic growth for the region as a whole is twice what it was during the 1980s and 1990s. African countries were also less affected by the recent economic downturn than was much of the rest of the world. Although poverty, AIDS, and a lack of education and infrastructure are still major impediments in much of the region, rising commodity prices are enabling many countries to make additional investments and reduce their national debts.

The African Union: A Glimmer of Hope A significant part of the problem is that Africans must find better ways to cooperate with one another and protect and promote their own interests. A first step in that direction was taken in 1991 when the OAU agreed to establish the African Economic Community. In 2001, the OAU was replaced by the **African Union**, which is intended to provide greater political and economic integration throughout the continent on the pattern of the European Union (see Chapter 28). The new organization has already sought to mediate several of the conflicts in the region. In 2015, talks got under way to create an African free trade zone to promote trade among the countries within the continent, creating an internal market consisting of 54 nations and more than 1 billion people. As Africa evolves, it is useful to remember that economic and political change is often an agonizingly slow and painful process. Introduced to industrialization and concepts of Western democracy only a century ago, African societies are still groping for ways to graft Western political institutions and economic practices onto a structure still significantly influenced by traditional values and attitudes.

29-3 CONTINUITY AND CHANGE IN MODERN AFRICAN SOCIETIES

Q **Focus Questions:** How did the rise of independent states affect the lives and the role of women in African societies? How does that role compare with the role played by women in other parts of the contemporary world?

In general, the impact of the West has been greater on urban and educated Africans and less on their rural and illiterate compatriots. After all, the colonial presence was first and most firmly established in the cities. Many cities are direct products of the colonial experience, including Dakar, Lagos, Johannesburg, Cape Town, Brazzaville, and Nairobi. Most African cities today look like their counterparts elsewhere in the world. They have high-rise buildings, blocks of residential apartments, wide boulevards, neon lights, movie theaters, and traffic jams.

29-3a Education

Europeans introduced modern Western education into Africa in the nineteenth century. At first, the schools concentrated on vocational training, with some instruction in European languages and Western civilization. Eventually, pressure from Africans led to the introduction of professional training, and the first institutes of higher learning were established in the early twentieth century.

With independence, African countries established their own state-run schools. The emphasis was on the primary level, but high schools and universities were established in major cities. The basic objectives have been to introduce vocational training and improve literacy rates. Unfortunately, both funding and trained teachers are scarce in most countries and few rural areas have schools, so religious organizations often are the only source of education in rural villages. In Image 29.3, students in the Muslim country of Niger are being instructed in the Arabic language so that they can read the Qur'an. In general, illiteracy in Africa remains high, estimated at around 70 percent of the population across the continent. There has been a perceptible shift toward education in the vernacular languages. In West Africa, only one in four adults or so is conversant in a Western language.

29-3b Urban and Rural Life

The cities are where the African elites live and work. Like their contemporaries in other developing countries, affluent Africans have been strongly attracted to the glittering material aspects of Western culture. They live in Western-style homes or apartments and eat Western foods stored in Western refrigerators, and those who can afford it drive Western cars. It has been said, not wholly in praise, that there are more Mercedes-Benz automobiles in Nigeria than in Germany, where they are manufactured.

Outside the major cities, where some three-quarters of the continent's inhabitants live, Western influence has had less impact. Millions of people throughout Africa live much as their ancestors did—in thatch huts without modern plumbing and electricity; they farm or hunt by traditional methods, practice time-honored family rituals, and believe in the traditional deities. Even here, however, change is taking place. Slavery has been eliminated, for the most part, although there have been persistent reports of raids by slave traders on defenseless villages in the southern Sudan. Economic need, though, has brought about massive migrations as some people leave to work on plantations, others move to the cities, and still others

29.3 Learning the ABCs in Niger. Educating the young is one of the most crucial problems for many African societies today. Few governments are able to allocate the funds necessary to meet the challenge, so religious organizations—Muslim or Christian—often take up the slack. In this photo, students at a madrasa—a Muslim school designed to teach the Qur'an—are learning how to read Arabic, the language of Islam's holy scripture. Madrasas are one of the most prominent forms of schooling in Muslim societies in West Africa today.

After marriage, African women appear to occupy a more equal position than their counterparts in most Asian countries. Each marriage partner tends to maintain a separate income, and women often have the right to possess property separate from their husbands. Although many wives still defer to their husbands in the traditional manner, others are like the woman in Abioseh Nicol's story "A Truly Married Woman," who, after years of living as a common-law wife with her husband, is finally able to provide the price and finalize the marriage. After the wedding, she declares, "For twelve years I have got up every morning at five to make tea for you and breakfast. Now I am a truly married woman [and] you must treat me with a little more respect. You are now my husband and not a lover. Get up and make yourself a cup of tea."[1]

Women in Rural Areas In rural areas, where traditional attitudes continue to exert a strong influence, individuals may still be subordinated to communalism. In some societies, female genital mutilation, the traditional rite of passage for a young girl's transit to womanhood, is still widely practiced. Polygamy is also not uncommon, and arranged marriages are still the rule rather than the exception. The dichotomy between rural and urban values can lead to acute tensions. Many African villagers regard the cities as the fount of evil, decadence, and corruption. Women in particular have suffered from the tension between the pull of the city and the village. As men are drawn to the cities in search of employment and excitement, their wives and girlfriends are left behind, both literally and figuratively, in the village.

flee abroad or to refugee camps to escape starvation. Migration itself is a wrenching experience, disrupting familiar family and village ties and enforcing new social relationships.

29-3c African Women

Independence has had a significant impact on gender roles in African society. Almost without exception, the new governments established the principle of sexual equality and permitted women to vote and run for political office. Yet, as elsewhere, women continue to operate at a disability in a world dominated by males. Politics remains a male preserve, and although a few professions such as teaching, child care, and clerical work are dominated by women, most African women are employed in menial positions such as agricultural laborer, factory worker, and retail trade worker or as domestics. Education is open to all at the elementary level, but women make up less than 20 percent of students at the upper levels in most African societies today.

Urban Women Not surprisingly, women have made the greatest strides in the cities. Like men, most urban women now marry on the basis of personal choice, although a significant minority is still willing to accept parents' selection.

29-3d African Culture

Inevitably, the tension between traditional and modern, indigenous and foreign, and individual and communal that has permeated contemporary African society has spilled over into culture. In general, in the visual arts and music, utility and ritual have given way to pleasure and decoration. In the process, Africans have been affected to a certain extent by foreign influences but have retained their distinctive characteristics. Wood carving, metalwork,

Experience an interactive version of this period in ✷ MINDTAP   *29-3 Continuity and Change in Modern African Societies* ■ **745**

29.4 Salt of the Earth. During the precolonial era, many West African societies were forced to import salt from Mediterranean countries in exchange for tropical products and gold. Today, the people of Senegal satisfy their domestic needs by mining salt deposits in lakes like this one in the interior of the country. These lakes are the remnants of vast seas that covered the region of the Sahara in prehistoric times. Note that women are doing much of the heavy labor while men hold the managerial positions.

painting, and sculpture, for example, have preserved their traditional forms but are now increasingly adapted to serve the tourist industry and the export market.

Literature Since independence, no area of African culture has been so strongly affected by political and social events as literature. Angry at the negative portrayal of Africa in Western literature, African authors initially wrote primarily for a European audience as a means of establishing black dignity and purpose. Many glorified the emotional and communal aspects of the traditional African experience (see Opposing Viewpoints, "Africa: Dark Continent or Radiant Land?" p. 747). The Nigerian novelist Chinua Achebe (CHIN-wah ah-CHAY-bay) (b. 1930) sought in his writings to interpret African history from an African perspective in order to forge a new sense of African identity.

More recently, the African novel has turned its attention to the shortcomings of the continent's indigenous leaders. Two prominent writers in this genre are Kenyan Ngugi Wa Thiong'o (GOO-gee wah tee-AHNG-goh) (b. 1938) and Wole Soyinka (woh-LAY soh-YEENK-kuh) (b. 1934) of Nigeria. In their writings, both have been harshly critical of the corruption and hypocrisy of many contemporary African governments.

29-3e What Is the Future of Africa?

Nowhere in the developing world is the dilemma of continuity and change more agonizing than in Africa. Mesmerized by the spectacle of Western affluence yet repulsed by the bloody trail from slavery to World War II and the atomic age, African intellectuals have been torn between the dual images of Western materialism and African uniqueness. Historians of the continent disagree whether the root of the problem is to be found in the neoimperialist attitudes practiced by wealthy industrial countries abroad or in the misguided policies adopted by African leaders themselves. For the average African, of course, such intellectual dilemmas pale before the daily challenge of survival. But the fundamental gap between traditional and modern is wide in Africa and will be difficult to bridge.

What is the future of Africa? It seems almost foolhardy to try answering such a question given the degree of ethnic, linguistic, and cultural diversity that exists throughout the vast continent. It is not surprising that visions of the future are equally diverse. Some Africans still yearn for the dreams embodied in the program of the OAU. In his novel titled *The Open Sore of a Continent*, Wole Soyinka placed the primary responsibility for

Africa: Dark Continent or Radiant Land?

 Interaction & Exchange

COLONIALISM CAMOUFLAGED ITS ECONOMIC OBJECTIVES under the cloak of a "civilizing mission," which in Africa was aimed at illuminating the so-called Dark Continent with Europe's brilliant civilization. In 1899, Polish-born author Joseph Conrad (1857–1924) of England fictionalized his harrowing journey up the Congo River in the novella *Heart of Darkness*. Conrad's protagonist, Marlow, travels upriver to locate a Belgian trader who has mysteriously disappeared. The novella describes Marlow's gradual recognition of the egregious excesses of colonial rule, as well as his realization that such evil lurks in everyone's heart. The story concludes with a cry: "The horror! The horror!" Voicing views that reflected his Victorian perspective, Conrad described an Africa that was incomprehensible, sensual, and primitive.

Over the years, Conrad's work has provoked much debate. Author Chinua Achebe, for one, lambasted *Heart of Darkness* as a radical diatribe. Since independence, many African writers have been prompted to counter Conrad's portrayal by reaffirming the dignity and purpose of the African people. One of the first to do so was Guinean author Camara Laye (1928–1980), who in 1954 composed a brilliant novel, *The Radiance of the King*, that can be viewed as the mirror image of Conrad's *Heart of Darkness*. In Laye's work, Clarence, another European protagonist, undertakes a journey into the impenetrable heart of Africa. This time, however, he is enlightened by the process, thereby obtaining self-knowledge and ultimately salvation.

Joseph Conrad, *Heart of Darkness*

We penetrated deeper and deeper into the heart of darkness. It was very quiet there. At night sometimes the roll of drums behind the curtain of trees would run up the river and remain sustained faintly, as if hovering in the air high over our heads, till the first break of day. Whether it meant war, peace, or prayer we could not tell. . . . But suddenly, as we struggled round a bend, there would be a glimpse of rush walls, of peaked grass-roofs, a burst of yells, a whirl of black limbs, a mass of hands clapping, of feet stamping, of bodies swaying, of eyes rolling, under the droop of heavy and motionless foliage. The steamer toiled along slowly on the edge of a black and incomprehensible frenzy. The prehistoric man was cursing us, praying to us, welcoming us—who could tell? We were cut off from the comprehension of our surroundings; we glided past like phantoms, wondering and secretly appalled, as sane men would be before an enthusiastic outbreak in a madhouse.

Camara Laye, *The Radiance of the King*

At that very moment the king turned his head, turned it imperceptibly, and his glance fell upon Clarence. . . .

"Yes, no one is as base as I, as naked as I," he thought. "And you, lord, you are willing to rest your eyes upon me!" Or was it because of his very nakedness? . . . "Because of your very nakedness!" the look seemed to say. "That terrifying void that is within you and which opens to receive me; your hunger which calls to my hunger; your very baseness which did not exist until I gave it leave; and the great shame you feel. . . ."

When he had come before the king, when he stood in the great radiance of the king, still ravaged by the tongue of fire, but alive still, and living only through the touch of that fire, Clarence fell upon his knees, for it seemed to him that he was finally at the end of his seeking, and at the end of all seekings.

Q *Compare the depictions of the continent of Africa in these two passages. Is Laye making a response to Conrad? If so, what is it?*

Source: From *Heart of Darkness* by Joseph Conrad. Penguin Books, 1991. From *The Radiance of the King* by Camara Laye, translated from the French by James Kirkup. New York: Vintage, 1989.

Africa's problems on the very concept of the modern nation-state, which was introduced to Africa arbitrarily by Europeans. Novelist Ngugi Wa Thiong-o has called for "an internationalization of all the democratic and social struggles for human equality, justice, peace, and progress."[2] Others have discarded the democratic ideal and turned their attention to systems based on the subordination of the individual to the community as the guiding principle of national development. Like all peoples, Africans must ultimately find their own solutions within the context of their own traditions, not by imitating the example of others.

29-4 CRESCENT OF CONFLICT

Q **Focus Questions:** Why does the Middle East appear to be one of the most unstable and conflict-ridden regions in the world today? What historical factors might help explain this phenomenon?

"We Muslims are of one family even though we live under different governments and in various regions."[3] So said Ayatollah Ruholla Khomeini (ah-yah-TUL-uh roo-HUL-uh khoh-MAY-nee), the Islamic religious figure and leader of the 1979 revolution that overthrew the shah in Iran. The ayatollah's remark was dismissed by some as just a pious wish by a religious mystic. In fact, however, it illustrates a crucial aspect of the political dynamics in the region: if the concept of cultural uniqueness represents an alternative to the system of nation-states in Africa, then the desire for Muslim unity has played a similar role in the Middle East. In both regions, a yearning for a sense of community beyond national borders tugs at the emotions and intellect of their inhabitants.

A dramatic example of the powerful force of pan-Islamic sentiment took place on September 11, 2001, when Muslim militants hijacked four U.S. airliners and turned them into missiles aimed at the center of world capitalism. The headquarters of the terrorist network that carried out the attack—known as al-Qaeda and led by Osama bin Laden (see Chapter 28)—was located in Afghanistan, but the militants themselves came from several different Muslim states. Although moderate Muslims throughout the world condemned the attack, it was clear that bin Laden and his cohorts had tapped into a wellspring of hostility and resentment directed at much of the Western world.

What were the sources of Muslim anger? In a speech released on videotape shortly after the attack, bin Laden declared that the attacks were a response to the "humiliation and disgrace" that have afflicted the Islamic world for more than eighty years, a period dating back to the end of World War I when the remnants of the Ottoman Empire in Asia were divided among the colonial powers (see Historical Voices, "The Arab Case for Palestine," p. 747). For the Middle East, the period between the two world wars was an era of transition. With the fall of the Ottoman and Persian Empires, new modernizing regimes emerged in Turkey and Iran, and a more traditionalist but fiercely independent government was established in Saudi Arabia. Elsewhere, however, European influence was on the ascendant; the British and French had mandates in Syria, Lebanon, Jordan, and Palestine, and British influence persisted in Iraq, in southern Arabia, and throughout the Nile Valley. Then, during World War II, the region became the cockpit of European rivalries once again because of the Suez Canal and the growing importance of oil.

29-4a The Question of Palestine

The restoration of peace led to the emergence of several independent states in the Middle East. Jordan, Lebanon, and Syria—all European mandates before the war—became independent. Although still under a degree of Western influence, Egypt, Iran, and Iraq became increasingly autonomous. Sympathy for the idea of Arab unity led to the formation of the Arab League in 1945, but different points of view among its members prevented it from achieving anything of substance.

Palestine was the one question on which all Muslim states in the area could agree. As tensions between Jews and Arabs in that mandate intensified during the 1930s, the British attempted to limit Jewish immigration into the area and firmly rejected proposals for independence, despite the promise made in the 1917 Balfour Declaration that Palestine should become a national home for the Jewish people (see Chapter 24).

After World War II ended, the situation drifted rapidly toward crisis as thousands of Jewish refugees, many of them from displaced persons camps in Europe, sought to migrate to Palestine despite Arab complaints and British efforts to prevent their arrival (see Historical Voices, "The Arab Case for Palestine," p. 747). As violence between Muslims and Jews intensified in the fall of 1947, the issue was taken up in the United Nations General Assembly. After an intense debate, the assembly voted to approve the partition of Palestine into two separate states, one for the Jews and one for the Arabs. The city of Jerusalem was to be placed under international control. A UN commission was established to iron out the details and determine the future boundaries.

During the next several months, growing hostility between Jewish and Arab forces—the latter increasingly supported by neighboring Muslim states—caused the British to announce their withdrawal of peacekeeping forces by May 15, 1948. Shortly after the stroke of midnight, as the British mandate formally came to a close, Zionist leader David Ben-Gurion (ben-GOOR-ee-uhn) (1886–1973) announced the independence of the state of Israel and established its temporary capital at Tel Aviv. Later that same day, the new state was formally recognized by the United States even as military forces from several neighboring Muslim states—all of which had vigorously opposed the formation of a Jewish state in the

The Arab Case for Palestine

Politics & Government

AS MORE AND MORE JEWS IMMIGRATED to Palestine after World War II, the world powers began to discuss how to handle the growing tensions in the area. In 1946, the Arab Office in Jerusalem issued a statement outlining its case against the Zionist proposal to transform Palestine into a Jewish state. The statement declared that any solution to the Palestinian problem "must recognize the right of the indigenous inhabitants of Palestine to continue in occupation of the country and to preserve its traditional character." Further, it stated, any representative government in Palestine "should be based upon the principle of absolute equality of all citizens irrespective of race and religion." The following selection is an excerpt from this document.

The Problem of Palestine

1. The whole Arab People is unalterably opposed to the attempt to impose Jewish immigration and settlement upon it, and ultimately to establish a Jewish State in Palestine. Its opposition is based primarily upon right. The Arabs of Palestine are descendants of the indigenous inhabitants of the country, who have been in occupation of it since the beginning of history; they cannot agree that it is right to subject an indigenous population against its will to alien immigrants, whose claim is based upon a historical connection which ceased effectively many centuries ago. Moreover they form the majority of the population; as such they cannot submit to a policy of immigration which if pursued for long will turn them from a majority into a minority in an alien state; and they claim the democratic right of a majority to make its own decisions in matters of urgent national concern. . . .

2. In addition to the question of right, the Arabs oppose the claims of political Zionism because of the effects which Zionist settlement has already had upon their situation and is likely to have to an even greater extent in the future. Negatively, it has diverted the whole course of their national development. Geographically Palestine is part of Syria; its indigenous inhabitants belong to the Syrian branch of the Arab family of nations; all their culture and tradition link them to the other Arab peoples; and until 1917 Palestine formed part of the Ottoman Empire which included also several of the other Arab countries. The presence and claims of the Zionists, and the support given them by certain Western Powers have resulted in Palestine being cut off from the other Arab countries and subjected to a regime, administrative, legal, fiscal, and educational, different from that of the sister-countries. Quite apart from the inconvenience to individuals and the dislocation of trade which this separation has caused, it has prevented Palestine [from] participating fully in the general development of the Arab world.

Q *How did the authors of this document justify their opposition to the establishment of an independent Jewish state in Israel? What counterarguments were presented by spokespersons for the Zionist movement as presented in the document in Chapter 24 (see "The Zionist Case for Palestine," p. 608)?*

Source: From Akram Khater, *Sources in the History of the Modern Middle East*, 2d ed. (Cengage, 2011), pp. 179–190.

region—entered Israeli-held territory but were beaten back. Thousands of Arab residents of the new state fled into neighboring areas, while Israeli forces seized control of the western sections of Jerusalem, which many Jewish leaders wished to become the capital of the new state. Internal dissonance among the Arabs, combined with the strength of Jewish resistance groups, contributed to the failure of the invasion, but the bitterness between the two sides did not subside. The Muslim states refused to recognize the new state of Israel, which became a member of the United Nations, legitimizing it in the eyes of the rest of the world. The stage for future conflict was set.

The exodus of thousands of Palestinian refugees into neighboring Muslim states had repercussions that are still felt today. Jordan, which had become an independent kingdom under its Hashemite (HASH-uh-myt) ruler, was flooded by the arrival of 1 million urban Palestinians, overwhelming its own half million people, most of whom were Bedouins. To the north, the state of Lebanon had been created to provide the local Christian community with a country of their own, but the arrival of the Palestinian refugees upset the delicate balance between Christians and Muslims. Moreover, the creation of Lebanon had angered the Syrians, who had lost that land as well as other territories to Turkey as a result of European decisions before and after World War II.

29-4b Nasser and Pan-Arabism

The dispute over Palestine placed Egypt in an uncomfortable position. Technically, Egypt was not an Arab state. King Farouk (fuh-ROOK) (1920–1965), who had acceded to power in 1936, had frequently declared support for the Arab cause, but the Egyptian people shared little of the culture of the peoples across the Red Sea. In 1952, Farouk, whose corrupt habits had severely eroded his early popularity, was overthrown by a military coup engineered by young military officers who abolished the monarchy and established a republic.

In 1954, one of those officers, Colonel Gamal Abdul Nasser (guh-MAHL AB-dool NAH-sur) (1918–1970), seized power in his own right and immediately adopted a policy of neutrality in foreign affairs while expressing sympathy for the Arab cause. Two years later, Nasser suddenly nationalized the Suez Canal Company, which had been under British and French administration. Seeing a threat to their route to the Indian Ocean, the British and the French launched a joint attack on Egypt to protect their investment. They were joined by Israel, whose leaders had grown exasperated at sporadic Arab commando raids on Israeli territory and now decided to strike back. But the Eisenhower administration in the United States, concerned that the attack smacked of a revival of colonialism, supported Nasser and brought about the withdrawal of foreign forces from Egypt and of Israeli troops from the Sinai Peninsula.

The United Arab Republic Nasser now turned to **Pan-Arabism**. In 1958, Egypt united with Syria to form the United Arab Republic (UAR). The union had been proposed by the Ba'ath (BAHTH) Party, which advocated the unity of all Arab states in a new socialist society. Nasser was named president of the new state.

Egypt and Syria hoped that the union would eventually include all Arab states, but other Arab leaders, including young King Hussein (1935–1999) of Jordan and the kings of Iraq and Saudi Arabia, were suspicious. The latter two in particular feared Pan-Arabism on the reasonable assumption that they would be asked to share their vast oil revenues with the poorer states of the Middle East.

In the end, Nasser's plans brought an end to the UAR. When the government announced the nationalization of a large number of industries and utilities in 1961, a military coup overthrew the Ba'ath leaders in Damascus, and the new authorities declared that Syria would end its relationship with Egypt.

Nasser, however, was not ready to abandon the dream of Pan-Arabism. In 1964, the Palestine Liberation Organization (PLO) was set up under Egyptian sponsorship to represent the interests of the Palestinians. According to its charter, only the Palestinian people (and thus not Jewish immigrants from abroad) had the right to form a state in the old British mandate. A guerrilla movement called al-Fatah (al-FAH-tuh), which was led by the dissident PLO figure Yasir Arafat (yah-SEER ah-ruh-FAHT) (1929–2004), began to launch terrorist attacks on Israeli territory.

29-4c The Arab–Israeli Dispute

Growing Arab hostility was a constant threat to the security of Israel, whose leaders dedicated themselves to creating a Jewish homeland. The government attempted to build a democratic and modern state that would be a magnet for Jews throughout the world and a symbol of Jewish achievement. But ensuring the survival of the tiny state surrounded by antagonistic Arab neighbors was a considerable challenge that was made even more difficult by divisions within the Israeli population. Immigrants from Europe tended to be secular and even socialist in their views, whereas those from the Middle East were often politically and religiously conservative. The state was also home to Christians as well as Muslim Palestinians who had not fled to other countries. To balance these diverse interests, Israel established a parliament called the Knesset (kuh-NESS-it) that was modeled on European legislatures, with proportional representation based on the number of votes each party received in the general election. The parties were so numerous that none ever received a majority of votes, and all governments had to be formed from coalitions of several parties.

The Six-Day War In the spring of 1967, Nasser attempted to improve his standing in the Arab world by imposing a blockade against Israeli commerce through the Gulf of Aqaba. Concerned that it might be isolated, Israel suddenly launched air strikes against Egypt and several of its Arab neighbors in June 1967. Israeli armies then broke the blockade at the head of the Gulf of Aqaba and occupied the Sinai Peninsula. Other Israeli forces seized Jordanian territory on the West Bank of the Jordan River (Jordan's King Hussein had recently signed an alliance with Egypt and placed his army under Egyptian command), occupied the remainder of the city of Jerusalem, and seized Syrian military positions in the Golan Heights, along the Israeli–Syrian border (see Map 29.2). Israel's brief, six-day war had tripled the size of its territory; 1 million Palestinians were

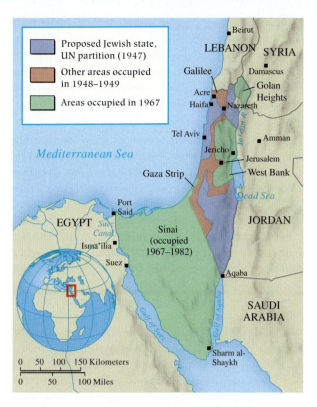

Map 29.2 Israel and its Neighbors. This map shows the evolution of the state of Israel since its founding in 1948. Areas occupied by Israel after the Six-Day War in 1967 are indicated in green.

Legend:
- Proposed Jewish state, UN partition (1947)
- Other areas occupied in 1948–1949
- Areas occupied in 1967

Map labels: LEBANON, SYRIA, Beirut, Damascus, Galilee, Golan Heights, Acre, Haifa, Nazareth, Tel Aviv, Amman, Jericho, Jerusalem, West Bank, Gaza Strip, Dead Sea, Mediterranean Sea, Port Said, JORDAN, EGYPT, Suez Canal, Isma'ilia, Sinai (occupied 1967–1982), Suez, Aqaba, SAUDI ARABIA, Gulf of Suez, Gulf of Aqaba, Sharm al-Shaykh

Scale: 0 50 100 150 Kilometers / 0 50 100 Miles

added inside its borders, most of them located on the West Bank of the Jordan River.

During the next few years, the focus of the Arab–Israeli dispute shifted as Arab states demanded the return of the territories lost in the 1967 war. Nasser died in 1970 and was succeeded by his vice president, ex-general Anwar al-Sadat (ahn-WAHR al-sah-DAHT) (1918–1981). Sadat attempted to renew Arab unity through a new confrontation with Israel. In 1973, on Yom Kippur (the Jewish Day of Atonement), an Israeli national holiday, Egyptian forces suddenly launched an air and artillery attack on Israeli positions in the Sinai just east of the Suez Canal, while Syrian armies attacked Israeli positions in the Golan Heights. After early Arab successes, the Israelis managed to recoup some of their losses on both fronts.

The Camp David Agreement   After his election as U.S. president in 1976, Jimmy Carter began to press for a compromise peace based on Israel's return of territories occupied during the 1967 war and Arab recognition of the state of Israel. In September 1978, Sadat and Israeli prime minister Menachem Begin (muh-NAH-kuhm BAY-gin) (1913–1992) met with Carter at Camp David, the presidential retreat in Maryland. In the first treaty signed with a Muslim state, Israel agreed to withdraw from the Sinai but not from other occupied territories unless other Muslim countries recognized Israel. The promise of the Camp David agreement however, was not fulfilled. One reason was the assassination of Sadat by Islamic militants in October 1981. But there were deeper causes, including the continued unwillingness of many Arab governments to recognize Israel and the Israeli government's continued encouragement of Jewish settlements in the occupied West Bank.

The PLO and the Intifada   During the 1980s, the militancy of the Palestinians increased, leading to rising unrest and

29.5 The Camp David Accords. Prime Minister Menachem Begin of Israel and President Anwar al-Sadat hold a joint press conference after the signing of the Camp David Accords in September 1978. Tragically, Sadat paid a high price for his courage in signing the agreement: he was assassinated in Cairo by a Muslim terrorist two years later.

David Hume Kennerly/Getty Images

what was popularly labeled the *intifada* (in-tuh-FAH-duh) (uprising) among PLO supporters living inside Israel. Angered by terrorist attacks that resulted in heavy casualties, many Israeli citizens lost confidence that their security needs were being adequately protected. National elections held in 1996 led to the formation of a new government under Benjamin Netanyahu (net-ahn-YAH-hoo) (b. 1949), whose new government quickly adopted a tougher stance on negotiations with the Palestinians, leading to a virtual stalemate in the peace process.

The death of PLO leader Yasir Arafat in 2004 and his replacement by Mahmoud Abbas (mah-MOOD ah-BAHS) (b. 1935), a Palestinian moderate, raised modest hopes for progress in peace talks, but the victory of Hamas (HAH-mahs)—a militant organization dedicated to the destruction of the state of Israel—in Palestinian elections held in 2005 hardened attitudes on both sides. As prospects for a two-state solution to the problem seem to dim by the day, the prospect of a negotiated peace now appears as distant as ever.

29-4d Revolution in Iran

In the late 1970s, another trouble spot arose in Iran, one of the key oil-exporting countries in the region. Under the leadership of Shah Mohammad Reza Pahlavi (ree-ZAH PAH-luh-vee) (1919–1980), who had taken over from his father in 1941, Iran had become one of the richest countries in the Middle East. During the 1950s and 1960s, Iran became a prime ally of the United States, which hoped that Iran could become a force for stability in the Persian Gulf. With U.S. support, the shah attempted to carry through a series of social and economic reforms to transform the country into the most advanced in the region.

Under the surface, however, trouble was brewing. Despite an ambitious land reform program, many peasants were still landless, unemployment among intellectuals was dangerously high, and the urban middle class was squeezed by high inflation. Some of the unrest took the form of religious discontent as millions of devout Muslims looked with distaste at a new Iranian civilization based on greed, sexual license, and material accumulation.

The Fall of the Shah   Leading the opposition was Ayatollah Ruholla Khomeini (1900–1989), an austere Shi'ite cleric who had been exiled to Iraq and then to France because of his outspoken opposition to the shah's regime. From Paris, Khomeini continued his attacks in print, on television, and in radio broadcasts. By the late 1970s, large numbers of Iranians began to respond to Khomeini's diatribes against the "satanic regime," and demonstrations by his supporters were repressed with ferocity by the police. But workers' strikes grew in intensity. In 1979, the government collapsed when the shah was in the United States for medical treatment and was replaced by a hastily formed Islamic republic. The new government, dominated by Shi'ite clergy under the guidance of Ayatollah Khomeini, immediately began to introduce traditional Islamic law (see Comparative Essay, "Religion and Society," p. 753). A new reign of terror ensued as supporters of the shah were rounded up and executed.

Though much of the outside world focused on the U.S. embassy in Tehran, where militants held a few dozen foreign hostages, the Iranian Revolution involved much more. In the eyes of the Ayatollah and his followers, the United States was "the great Satan," the powerful protector of Israel, and the enemy of Muslim peoples everywhere. Furthermore, it was responsible for the corruption of Iranian society under the shah. With economic conditions in Iran rapidly deteriorating, the Islamic revolutionary government finally agreed to free the hostages in return for the release of Iranian assets in the United States.

During the late 1990s, the intensity of the Iranian Revolution moderated slightly as a new president, moderate cleric Mohammad Khatami (KHAH-tah-mee) (b. 1941), displayed a modest tolerance for loosening clerical control over freedom of expression and social activities. But rising public criticism of rampant official corruption and a high rate of inflation sparked a new wave of government repression. Under Khatami's successor, Mahmoud Ahmadinejad (mah-MOOD ah-mah-dee-nee ZHAHD) (b. 1956), newspapers were censored, universities were purged of disloyal or "un-Islamic" elements, and religious militants raided private homes in search of blasphemous activities. Ahmadinejad also called publicly for the destruction of the state of Israel and aroused global unease by promoting the country's nuclear energy program, which was designed ostensibly for peaceful purposes. Several major nations joined

Religion and Society

The nineteenth and twentieth centuries witnessed a steady trend toward the secularization of society as many people increasingly turned from religion to science for explanations of natural phenomena and answers to the challenges of everyday life.

In recent years, however, the trend has reversed as religious faith in all its guises appears to be reviving in much of the world. Although the percentage of people attending religious services on a regular basis or professing firm religious convictions has been dropping steadily in many countries, the intensity of religious belief appears to be growing among the faithful. This phenomenon has been widely publicized in the United States, where the evangelical movement has become a significant force in politics and an influential factor in defining many social issues. But it has also occurred in Latin America, where a drop in membership in the Roman Catholic Church has been offset by significant increases in the popularity of evangelical Protestant sects. In the Muslim world, the influence of traditional Islam has been steadily on the rise, not only in the Middle East but also in non-Arab countries such as Malaysia and Indonesia (see Chapter 30). In Africa, as we

observe in this chapter, the appeal of both Christianity and Islam appears to be on the rise. Even in Russia and China, where half a century of communist rule sought to eradicate faith in a supreme being as the "opiate of the people," the popularity of religion is growing.

One major reason for the increasing intensity of religious belief in contemporary life is the desire in many communities to counter the widespread sense of malaise brought on by the absence of any sense of meaning and purpose in life—a purpose that religious faith provides for some people. For many evangelical Christians in the United States, for example, the adoption of a Christian lifestyle is seen as a necessary prerequisite for resolving problems of crime, drugs, and social alienation. The trend toward a strict interpretation of the Qur'an similarly reflects the conviction among many Muslims throughout the world that only adherence to traditional teachings can counter the corruption, materialism, and hedonism that they observe in their societies today.

Religious faith also provides a sense of community at a time when village and family ties are declining in many countries. In areas like the Middle East, it serves as a wall of defense against the threatening "other," whether represented by a dictatorial regime from within or a rapacious imperialism from without. In parts of West Africa, it marks a sharp dividing line between the steppe and the sown, the pastoralist and the farmer. Historical evidence suggests, then, that although religious fervor may enhance the sense of community and commitment among believers, it can have a highly divisive impact on society as a whole and break down the fragile bonds that knit various peoples together into the modern nation-state. In today's world, religious tensions are more often the source of conflict than ideological differences. If religion divides as well as unites, it will be a continuing challenge for religious leaders of all faiths to promote tolerance for peoples of other persuasions.

William J. Duiker

29.6 Muslims at Prayer in the Blue Mosque in Istanbul. Even in contemporary Turkey, where founding president Mustafa Kemal Atatürk brought an end to the caliphate and introduced secular reforms throughout the country after World War I, the influence of traditional Islamic practices is growing today, as sponsored by the country's current president, Recep Erdoğan.

Q *What are some of the reasons for the growing intensity of religious faith in many parts of the world today?*

the United States in declaring a trade embargo on trade with Iran.

In 2013, growing discontent within the younger generation—where the rate of unemployment was as much as 40 percent—helped elect a moderate candidate, Hassan Rouhani (hah-SAHN roh-HAH-nee) (b. 1948), to the presidency. His election produced a sliver of hope that the era of confrontation with Western nations might be brought to a close. In 2015, a breakthrough multipower agreement ended the trade embargo in return for a halt in Iran's nuclear program. Still, despite the outbreak of widespread popular protests over deteriorating economic conditions in Iran, the determination of the country's conservative leadership to spread its influence throughout the region appears undiminished. In retaliation, in 2018 the U.S. administration of President Donald Trump reinstated its sanctions against Iran.

29-4e Crisis in the Persian Gulf

Although much of the Iranians' anger was directed against the United States during the early phases of the revolution, Iran had equally hated enemies closer to home. To the north, the Soviet Union, driven by atheistic communism, was viewed as the latest incarnation of the Russian threat of previous centuries. To the west was a militant and hostile Iraq, now under the leadership of the ambitious Saddam Hussein (suh-DAHM hoo-SAYN) (1937–2006). Iraq had just passed through a turbulent period. The monarchy had been overthrown by a military coup in 1958, but conflicts within the ruling military junta led to chronic instability. In 1979, Colonel Saddam Hussein, a prominent member of the local Ba'athist Party, seized power on his own.

The Vision of Saddam Hussein Saddam Hussein was a fervent believer in the Ba'athist vision of a single Arab state in the Middle East and soon began to persecute non-Arab elements in Iraq, including Persians and Kurds. He then turned his sights to the east.

Iraq and Iran had long had an uneasy relationship that was fueled by religious differences—Iranian Islam is predominantly Shi'ite, while the ruling caste in Iraq was Sunni—and a perennial dispute over borderlands adjacent to the Persian Gulf, the vital waterway for the export of oil from both countries. In 1980, charging Iran for having violated a territorial agreement, Saddam Hussein suddenly launched an attack on his neighbor. The war was a bloody one and lasted for nearly ten years. Poison gas was used against civilians, and children were employed to clear minefields. Finally, with both sides virtually exhausted, a cease-fire was arranged in the fall of 1988. But the bitter conflict with Iran had not slaked Saddam Hussein's

appetite for territorial expansion. In early August 1990, Iraqi military forces suddenly moved across the border and occupied the small neighboring country of Kuwait at the head of the Gulf. Although the immediate pretext was the claim that Kuwait was pumping oil from fields inside Iraqi territory, the underlying reason was Iraq's contention that Kuwait was legally a part of Iraq. Kuwait had been part of the Ottoman Empire until the beginning of the twentieth century, when the local prince had agreed to place his patrimony under British protection. When Iraq became independent in 1932, it claimed the area on the grounds that the state of Kuwait had been created by British imperialism, but opposition from major Western powers and other countries in the region, which feared the consequences of a "greater Iraq," prevented an Iraqi takeover.

The Persian Gulf War The Iraqi invasion of Kuwait in 1990 sparked an international outcry, and the United States assembled a multinational coalition that, under the name Operation Desert Storm, liberated the country and destroyed a substantial part of Iraq's armed forces. But the allied forces did not occupy Baghdad out of concern that doing so would cause a breakup of the country, an eventuality that would operate to the benefit of Iran. The allies hoped instead that Saddam's regime would be ousted by an internal revolt. In the meantime, harsh economic sanctions were imposed on the Iraqi government as the condition for peace. The anticipated overthrow of Saddam Hussein did not materialize, however, and his tireless efforts to evade the conditions of the cease-fire continued to bedevil U.S. president Bill Clinton and his successor, George W. Bush.

29-4f Turmoil in the Middle East

The terrorist attacks launched against U.S. targets in September 2001 added a new dimension to the Middle Eastern equation. The operation had been orchestrated by an organization called al-Qaeda that, under the leadership of Osama bin Laden, had begun to recruit followers from all over the Muslim world with the objective of waging terrorist attacks against prominent targets in Europe and the United States. Al-Qaeda's objective was to destabilize those governments that—in the eyes of Osama and his associates—were propping up dictators in the Middle East and weakening the forces of the true faith of Islam (see Historical Voices, "I Accuse!" p. 755).

Conflicts in Afghanistan and Iraq After the failure of the Soviet Union to quell the rebellion in that mountainous country during the 1980s, a fundamentalist Muslim group known as the Taliban, which had been

I Accuse!

Politics & Government — **IN 1998, OSAMA BIN LADEN** was virtually unknown outside the Middle East. But this scion of a wealthy industrialist from Saudi Arabia was on a mission—to avenge the hostile acts perpetrated on his fellow Muslims by the United States and its allies. Having taken part in the successful guerrilla war against Soviet occupation troops in Afghanistan during the 1980s, Osama now turned his ire on the tyrannical regimes in the Middle East and their great protector, the United States. In the following excerpts from a 1998 interview, he defends the use of terror against those he deems enemies of Islam. Three years later, his followers launched the surprise attacks that led to more than 3,000 deaths on September 11, 2001.

Interview with Osama bin Laden by His Followers (1998)

What is the meaning of your call for Muslims to take up arms against America in particular, and what is the message that you wish to send to the West in general?

The call to wage war against America was made because America has spearheaded the crusade against the Islamic nation, sending tens of thousands of its troops to the land of the two Holy Mosques [Saudi Arabia], over and above its meddling in its affairs and its politics and its support of the oppressive, corrupt, and tyrannical regime that is in control. These are the reasons behind the singling out of America as a target. And not exempt from responsibility are those Western regimes whose presence in the region offers support to the American troops there. We know at least one reason behind the symbolic participation of the Western forces and that is to support the Jewish and Zionist plans for expansion of what is called the Great Israel. Surely, their presence is not out of concern over their interests in the region. . . . Their presence has no meaning save one and that is to offer support to the Jews in Palestine who are in need of their Christian brothers to achieve full control over the Arab Peninsula which they intend to make an important part of the so called Greater Israel.

Many of the Arabic as well as the Western mass media accuse you of terrorism and of supporting terrorism. What do you have to say to that?

Every state and every civilization and culture has to resort to terrorism under certain circumstances for the purpose of abolishing tyranny and corruption. Every country in the world has its own security system and its own security forces, its own police, and its own army. They are all designed to terrorize whoever even contemplates an attack on that country or its citizens. The terrorism we practice is of the commendable kind for it is directed at the tyrants and the aggressors and the enemies of Allah, the tyrants, the traitors who commit acts of treason against their own countries and their own faith and their own prophet and their own nation. Terrorizing those and punishing them are necessary measures to straighten things and to make them right. Tyrants and oppressors who subject the Arab nation to aggression ought to be punished. . . . America heads the list of aggressors against Muslims. The recurrence of aggression against Muslims everywhere is proof enough. For over half a century, Muslims in Palestine have been slaughtered and assaulted and robbed of their honor and of their property. Their houses have been blasted, their crops destroyed. And the strange thing is that any act by them to avenge themselves or to lift the injustice befalling them causes great agitation in the United Nations, which hastens to call for an emergency meeting only to convict the victim and to censure the wronged and the tyrannized whose children have been killed and whose crops have been destroyed and whose farms have been pulverized. . . .

In today's wars, there are no morals, and it is clear that mankind has descended to the lowest degrees of decadence and oppression. They rip us of our wealth and of our resources and of our oil. Our religion is under attack. They kill and murder our brothers. They compromise our honor and our dignity and if we dare to utter a single word of protest against the injustice, we are called terrorists. This is compounded injustice. And the United Nations insistence to convict the victims and support the aggressors constitutes a serious precedent that shows the extent of injustice that has been allowed to take root in this land.

Q *What reasons does Osama bin Laden present to justify the terrorist attacks carried out by his followers around the world? How would you respond to his charges?*

Source: From Akram Khater, *Sources in the History of the Modern Middle East*, 2e. © 2011 Cengage Learning, pp. 294–295.

Emboldened by its initial success in evicting the Taliban from its dominant position in Afghanistan, the Bush administration broadened its regional objectives. Charging that Iraqi dictator Saddam Hussein had not only provided support to bin Laden's terrorist organization but also stockpiled weapons of mass destruction for use against his enemies, the White House ordered U.S.-led forces to occupy Iraq and topple the Saddam regime in March 2003. In the months that followed, occupation forces sought to restore stability to the country while setting out plans for building a democratic society. Although Saddam Hussein was captured by U.S. troops and later executed, however, the new Iraqi government soon descended into turmoil as sectarian clashes took place between Sunni and Shi'ite elements, and armed resistance by militant Muslim elements broke out throughout the country.

On coming into office in 2009, U.S. President Barack Obama gradually replaced U.S. occupation forces with U.S.-trained Iraqi troops, but the situation was slow to stabilize as Sunni militants, some of them infiltrated from neighboring Syria, unleashed attacks that threatened the undermine the fragile stability of the Shi'ite-dominated Iraqi state (see Map 29.4).

False Dawn: The Arab Spring As the wave of unrest threatened to engulf the entire region, popular protests broke out in several countries in the Middle East in the early months of 2011. Beginning in Tunisia, they spread rapidly to Egypt—where they brought about

supported covertly by the United States during the war, seized power in Kabul and ruled the country with a fanaticism reminiscent of the Cultural Revolution in China. Backed by conservative religious forces in Pakistan, the Taliban provided a base of operations for Osama bin Laden's al-Qaeda terrorist network, which had already established its operational headquarters in the country. After the attacks of September 11, however, a coalition of forces led by the United States overthrew the Taliban and attempted to build a new and moderate government in Afghanistan. But the country's history of bitter internecine warfare among tribal groups presented a severe challenge to those efforts, and although al-Qaeda was dealt a major blow when Osama bin Laden was killed by U.S. special operations forces in northern Pakistan in May 2011, Taliban forces have managed to regroup in Afghanistan and continue to operate in mountainous regions throughout the country (see Map 29.3).

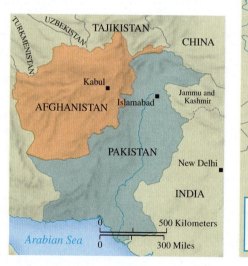

Map 29.3 Afghanistan and Pakistan

Map 29.4 Iraq

GEORGE OURFALIAN/Getty Images

29.7 The Destruction of Aleppo.
One of the most disastrous consequences of the civil war in Syria has been its effect on the people living in that war-torn country. With hundreds of thousands of casualties and countless other people fleeing for safety abroad, those remaining in ancient cities like Aleppo are caught in the crossfire of tenacious opposing forces, as this photograph graphically demonstrates.

the resignation of longtime President Hosni Mubarak (HAHS-nee moo-BAHrahk) (b. 1929), despite his efforts to quell the unrest, often by violent means. The uprisings (dubbed by pundits as "the Arab Spring") aroused hopes around the world that the seeds of democracy had been planted in a region long dominated by autocratic governments.

It soon became clear, however, that such optimism was drastically misplaced because unstable conditions led rapidly to the outbreak of civil unrest in several other countries throughout the region. In Egypt itself, a newly elected government under Prime Minister Mohamed Morsi (b. 1951) (a member of the one-time radical Muslim Brotherhood) antagonized moderates by its strict interpretation of Islamic law and was soon replaced by a new military junta. In Libya, the dictatorial regime of Muammar Qaddafi was toppled by a popular revolt that soon descended into civil war. Bitter fighting between Sunni and Shi'ite elements in Yemen led to a proxy war between bitter rivals Saudi Arabia and Iran.

But the consequences of spreading violence were most ominous in Syria, where a variety of ethnic groups rose up in opposition to the minority Shi'ite government led by President Bashir al-Assad (bah-SHAHR al-ah-SAHD) (b. 1965). Although some resistance forces sought to form a more pluralistic society or, like the Kurds, were struggling to realize their dream of creating an independent Kurdistan, other resistance groups allied with militants operating in neighboring Iraq to form a new terrorist organization, popularly called the Islamic State of Iraq and Syria (ISIS). The goal of ISIS leaders was to create a caliphate that would rule the entire region according to the tenets of fundamentalist Islam. As ISIS began to seek recruits among restive Muslims elsewhere, terrorist attacks carried out by its supporters spread rapidly throughout the world. Meanwhile, casualties resulting from the civil war within Syria numbered in the hundreds of thousands, unleashing a mass migration of frightened refugees into continental Europe.

29-5 SOCIETY AND CULTURE IN THE CONTEMPORARY MIDDLE EAST

Focus Question: How have religious issues affected political, economic, and social conditions in the Middle East in recent decades?

In the Middle East today, all aspects of society and culture—from political and economic issues to literature, art, and the role of the family—are intertwined with questions of religious faith.

29-5a Varieties of Government: The Politics of Islam

When U.S. forces invaded Iraq in 2003, Bush administration officials argued that the overthrow of Saddam Hussein's regime would open the door to the establishment of democratic values throughout the region. To many seasoned observers, however, ambitious schemes drafted by outsiders to remake the Middle East in the Western image appear unrealistic because democratic values are not deeply rooted in the culture of the region. Although the popular uprisings that have taken place in many countries in recent years are a clear sign that the feudal ways of the past are no longer adequate, few countries in the Middle East have managed to make the transition to broad-based pluralistic societies based on the concept of equal rights and a peaceful transfer of power. A few Arab nations—such as Jordan and the Persian Gulf ministates of Bahrain, Kuwait, and the United Arab Emirates (UAE)—have engaged in limited forms of democratic experimentation, but they too continue to repress dissident activities. Similar conditions prevail in the North African nations of Tunisia and Morocco. In general, however, Muslim leaders insist that only authoritarian rule can prevent the spread of civil disorder and Islamic radicalism throughout the region. The recent rise of ISIS, whose leaders openly declare their intention to establish a new caliphate to impose strict Islamic principles throughout the region, appears to justify their fears.

The only exception to the rule appeared to be Turkey, where free elections and power sharing have become more prevalent in recent years. For decades, the military played the dominant role in Turkish politics while enforcing Kamal Ataturk's policy of secularism and ethnic tolerance, but in 2007 a Muslim-based political party won peaceful elections and took power in Ankara. The new government of Prime Minister Recep Erdoğan (b. 1954) earned popular support by adopting a moderate stance on religious issues and by carrying out numerous economic reforms. In recent years, however, official corruption, a perceived favoritism to Islam, and the silencing of dissenting voices (an attempted coup in 2016 was suppressed with brutal efficiency) have severely tested the government's popularity. Erdoğan, who has now assumed the presidency, appears unfazed by such criticism and openly promotes the past glories of the Ottoman Empire. With the population bitterly divided and a destructive civil war in Syria being waged at Turkey's doorstep, it remains an open question whether the country's recent experiment with political pluralism will succeed.

Are the critics correct that the Islamic faith is not fertile ground for the establishment of democratic institutions? For many years, many Western governments accepted the logic of such contentions, provoking some critics to charge that they coddled Middle Eastern dictatorships as a means of preserving access to the vast oil reserves in the region. The recent wave of popular unrest initially aroused hopes that a new order was waiting in the wings, but as sectarian

conflicts have spread rapidly throughout the region, the current signs suggest that this wave of political and social instability is likely to continue for the indefinite future. As we await the consequences, the fate of the region hangs in the balance.

29-5b The Economics of the Middle East: Oil and Sand

Few areas exhibit a greater disparity of individual and national wealth than the Middle East. While millions live in abject poverty, a fortunate few rank among the wealthiest people in the world. The primary reason for this disparity is oil. Unfortunately for most of the region's peoples, oil reserves are distributed unevenly and often located in areas where the population density is low. Egypt and Turkey, with more than 75 million inhabitants apiece, have almost no oil reserves. The combined population of oil-rich Kuwait, the UAE, and Saudi Arabia is some 35 million people. This disparity in wealth inspired Nasser's quest for Arab unity but has also posed a major obstacle to that unity (see the Comparative Illustration "From Rags to Riches in the Middle East" on p. 759).

Economics and Islam The Qur'an provides little guidance to Muslims searching for economic policies appropriate to their faith, although it is clear in its concern for the overall welfare of the community. Thus, it is no surprise that the states of the Middle East have adopted diverse approaches to the challenge of developing strong and stable economies. Some, like Nasser in Egypt, were attracted to a form of socialism with a high degree of government intervention in the economy. Others have turned to the capitalist model to achieve their goals. Regardless of the strategy employed, many Middle Eastern states have been plagued with problems of rapid population growth, widespread corruption, and a lack of adequate educational and technological skills, all of which have acted as a drag on economic growth.

One key problem is rural poverty. Arable land is in short supply throughout the region and is often concentrated in the hands of wealthy landowners. Some countriessuch as Egypt and Iran have adopted ambitious land reform programs, although with mixed success. In any case, there are many structural obstacles to rural prosperity, including rapid population growth, low agricultural productivity, and a lack of water resources. Much of the Arabian Peninsula is desert, and those who inhabit the area—like the lonely shepherd from Yemen shown in Image 29.8—are barely able to scratch out a livelihood. Emigration to the cities has not been a panacea, because few Middle

COMPARATIVE ILLUSTRATION

From Rags to Riches in the Middle East

Politics & Government | **FEW PARTS OF THE WORLD** exhibit such a glaring contrast between conditions of wealth and poverty as the contemporary Middle East. Although much of the population in the region still lives in impoverished conditions barely above the means of subsistence, a fortunate few possess among the highest standards of living in the entire world. Image 29.8a shows

a shepherd with his donkey and two camels in the Arabian desert scratching out a living near the coast of Yemen. Image 29.8b shows the skyline of the modern city of Abu Dhabi in the United Arab Emirates.

 Which are the wealthiest states in the region? Which are the poorest?

Yvonne V. Duiker

29.8a

William J. Duiker

29.8b

Eastern leaders have managed to adopt policies calculated to place their country on a path of sustained economic growth.

Some poor states have encouraged emigration to oil-rich states with small populations such as Saudi Arabia and the United Arab Emirates. In times of political turmoil and economic recession, as is occurring today with the rapid decline in the price of oil, the UAE have taken measures to evict foreigners and reduce their migrant population. Even in the absence of such a threat, migrant workers—many of them living in substandard housing—are a volatile force in the politics of the region.

29-5c The Islamic Revival

In recent years, developments in the Middle East have often been described in terms of a resurgence of traditional values and customs in response to Western influence. Indeed, some conservative religious forces have consciously attempted to eliminate foreign influence by returning to allegedly "pure" Islamic forms of belief and

behavior, and such views have undoubtedly been a major factor in the recent popularity of terrorist movements such as al-Qaeda and ISIS.

Modernist Islam In the early twentieth century, many Muslim intellectuals responded to growing Western influence by trying to create a "modernized" Islam that would not clash with the demands of the new century. This process was officially espoused in countries such as Turkey, Egypt, and Iran. Mustafa Kemal Atatürk embraced the strategy when he attempted to secularize the Islamic religion in the new Turkish republic. The Turkish model was imitated by Shah Reza Khan and his son Mohammad Reza Pahlavi in Iran and then by Nasser in postwar Egypt, all of whom attempted to honor Islamic values while asserting the primacy of other issues such as political and economic development. Religion, in effect, had become the handmaiden of political power, national identity, and economic prosperity.

These secularizing trends were especially prevalent among the political, intellectual, and economic elites in urban areas but had less influence in the countryside, among the poor, and among devout elements within the clergy. Many clerics believed that Western influence in the cities had given birth to political and economic corruption, sexual promiscuity, hedonism, individualism, and the prevalence of alcohol, pornography, and drugs. Although such practices had long existed in the Middle East, they were now far more visible and socially acceptable.

Return to Tradition   Reaction among Muslim conservatives against the modernist movement within the Middle East gradually built up after World War II and reached its zenith in the late 1970s with the return of Ayatollah Khomeini to Iran. It is not surprising that Iran took the lead in light of its long tradition of ideological purity within the Shi'ite sect, as well as the uncompromisingly secular character of the shah's reforms in the postwar era. Almost forty years later, key elements within the Iranian political and religious leadership continue to enforce traditional Islamic customs and beliefs despite a growing counterreaction from within the younger generation, many of whom are increasingly attracted to the glittering Western lifestyle they see on social media (see Film & History, *Persepolis*).

The cultural and social impact of the Iranian Revolution soon began to spread throughout the Middle East, where discontent with political and social conditions had already intensified in several countries. It has even reached Southeast Asia, where conservative Islamic groups in such once-moderate Muslim countries as Malaysia and Indonesia have become more forceful in demanding the imposition of shari'a law in their multicultural and multiethnic societies. The trend was also notable in Egypt, where militant groups such as the Muslim Brotherhood, formed in 1928 as a means of promoting personal piety, began to engage in terrorism, including the assassination of President Anwar al-Sadat and attacks on foreign tourists, who are considered carriers of corrupt Western influence. In recent years, the Brotherhood has adopted a more moderate public stance and received broad support in elections held after the overthrow of the Mubarak regime, although, as we have seen above, its behavior when in power aroused concerns among critics and led to its eventual downfall.

Even in Turkey, generally considered the most secular of Islamic societies, the victory of Islamic parties in recent elections has led to efforts on their part to guarantee the rights of devout Muslims to display their faith publicly. Such policies have opened a growing divide between secular elements among the urban middle class and more traditionalist forces in the countryside that represent the base of President Erdogan's political influence.

29-5d Women in the Middle East

Nowhere have the fault lines between tradition and modernity in Muslim societies in the Middle East been as sharp as in the ongoing debate over the role of women. At the beginning of the twentieth century, women's place in Middle Eastern society had changed little since the death of the Prophet Muhammad. Women were secluded in their homes and had few legal, political, or social rights.

During the first decades of the twentieth century, advocates of modernist views began to contend that Islamic doctrine was not inherently opposed to women's rights. To modernists, Islamic traditions such as female seclusion, wearing the veil, and polygamy were actually pre-Islamic folk traditions that had been tolerated in the early Islamic era and continued to be practiced in later centuries. As we have seen, such views had considerable impact on many Middle Eastern societies, including Turkey and Iran. In Egypt, a vocal feminist movement arose in educated women's circles in Cairo as early as the 1920s.

After the Iranian Revolution of 1979, a more traditional view of women's role began to prevail in many Middle Eastern countries. In once-tolerant societies such as Turkey and Egypt, women began to dress more conservatively and to cover their hair in public. The practice gradually

---

⊕ FILM & HISTORY

Persepolis

The film *Persepolis* (2007) is an animated movie written and directed by Iranian writer Marjane Satrapi. Based on her autobiographical novel, it traces her reaction to growing up in a repressive theocratic regime in Tehran and then to her disillusionment while living in a hedonistic and morally challenged Europe. The film has been criticized by some in the Middle East for its portrayal of modern Islam.

Q   *Why might a devout Muslim find some aspects of life in a modern Western society morally unacceptable today?*

MINDTAP See full-length Film & History feature in MindTap.
From Cengage

spread to Muslim-majority countries in Southeast Asia like Malaysia and Indonesia.

But the most conservative attitudes by far prevailed in Saudi Arabia where, following Wahhabi religious tradition, women not only were segregated and expected to wear the veil in public but also were severely limited in their economic and educational opportunities. They were even forbidden to drive automobiles or attend sporting events with their male counterparts. Madrasas—religious schools—established with Saudi financing promoted such policies elsewhere within the Islamic community of nations.

Women's rights have been extended, however, in some countries in the region. In 1999, women obtained the right to vote in Kuwait, and in freewheeling Qatar, the rambunctious rival of the UAE in the Persian Gulf, women play open and active roles in society. Women have been granted equal rights with their husbands to seek divorce in Egypt. In Iran, women continue to have many freedoms that they lacked before the twentieth century; for example, they can receive military training, vote, practice birth control, and publish fiction. Most important, today nearly 60 percent of university entrants in Iran are women.

Even in Saudi Arabia, there have been tantalizing signs that change is in the air. In recent years, there has been some loosening of the laws restricting women's right to work in commercial establishments, and women were given formal permission to drive vehicles as well as attend soccer matches in public in 2017. That dramatic change in policy seems to reflect the determination of the kingdom's new ruler, Crown Prince Mohammed bin Salman (b. 1985), to bring his country into the modern world. As if in response, Iran—Saudi Arabia's chief rival for leadership over the Islamic world—quickly announced that the religious police, who enforce conservative clothing styles on women appearing in public, have been instructed to be more tolerant in seeking to enforce the country's strict dress code.

29-5e Literature and Art

As in other areas of Asia and Africa, the encounter with the West in the nineteenth and twentieth centuries stimulated a cultural renaissance in the Middle East. Muslim authors translated Western works into Arabic and Persian and began to experiment with new literary forms.

Literature Iran has produced one of the most prominent national literatures in the contemporary Middle East. Since World War II, Iranian literature has been hampered somewhat by political considerations because it has been expected to serve whoever was in charge—first the Pahlavi monarchy, then the Islamic republic. Nevertheless, Iranian writers are among the most prolific in the region and often write in prose, which has finally been accepted as the equal of poetry.

Despite the male-oriented character of Iranian society, many of the new writers have been women. Since the revolution, the veil and the *chador* (CHUH-der or CHAH-der), an all-enveloping cloak, have become the central metaphor in Iranian women's writing. Those who favor the veil and chador praise them as the last bastion of defense against Western cultural imperialism. Behind the veil, the Islamic woman can breathe freely, unpolluted by foreign exploitation and moral corruption. Other Iranian women, however, consider the chador a "mobile prison" or an oppressive anachronism from the Dark Ages. Whether or not they accept the veil and chador, women writers are a vital part of contemporary Iranian literature and are addressing all aspects of social issues.

Like Iran, Egypt in the twentieth century experienced a flowering of literature accelerated by the establishment of the Egyptian republic in the early 1950s. The most illustrious contemporary Egyptian writer was Naguib Mahfouz (nah-GEEB mah-FOOZ) (1911–2006), who won the Nobel Prize for Literature in 1988. His *Cairo Trilogy* (1952) chronicles three generations of a merchant family in Cairo during the tumultuous years between the world wars. Mahfouz was particularly adept at blending panoramic historical events with the intimate lives of ordinary human beings. Unlike many other modern writers, he was essentially optimistic and hoped that religion and science could work together for the overall betterment of humankind.

Music and Politics Like literature, music in the contemporary Middle East has been strongly influenced by that of the modern West. In Israel, many contemporary young rock stars voice lyrics as irreverent toward the tradition of their elders as their contemporaries in Europe and the United States. The rock music popular among Palestinians, on the other hand, makes greater use of Arab musical motifs and is closely tied to a political message. One recording, "The Song of the Engineer," lauds Yahya Khan (1966–1996), a Palestinian accused of manufacturing many of the explosive devices used in terrorist attacks on Israeli citizens. As the Arab Spring spread from Tunisia and Egypt throughout the region, many performers were inspired to use their music for openly political purposes. The song "Come On, Bashar, Leave" became popular as a rallying cry against the current president of Syria for dissidents in that country.

The Middle East is one of the most unstable regions in the world today. This turbulence results partly from the continued interference of outsiders attracted by the massive oil reserves in the vicinity of the Persian Gulf. This outside involvement has underlined the humiliating weakness of Muslim nations in their relationship with the West and also identified Western policies with unpopular dictators.

But internal factors are equally if not more important in provoking the chronic turmoil within the region. One divisive issue is the tug-of-war between the sense of ethnic identity in the form of nationalism and the intense longing to be part of a broader Islamic community, a dream that dates back to the time of the Prophet Muhammad. Although the motives for seeking Arab unity are sometimes self-serving—two such examples are Nasser and Saddam Hussein—there is no doubt that the sentiment is widespread within the population and has fueled the recent rise of support for the ISIS, whose stated objective is to produce a caliphate that will erase national boundaries throughout the region.

Another reason for the current unrest in the Middle East is the intense debate over the role of religion in civil society. Muslims, of course, are not alone in believing that a purer form of religious faith is the best antidote for such social evils as hedonism, sexual license, and political corruption. But it is hard to deny that the issue has been pursued with more anger and passion in the Middle East than in almost any other part of the world. In fact, many Muslim societies in the region have yet to come to terms with a world characterized by dramatic social and technological change. The result is stagnant economies, and the emergence of a deep-seated sense of anger and frustration, especially among the young, that is surging through much of the Islamic world today, a sense of resentment that is directed as much at the region's internal leadership as at allegedly hostile forces in the West. Today, the world is reaping the harvest of that bitterness, and the consequences cannot yet be foreseen.

REFLECTION QUESTIONS

Q What are some of the key reasons advanced to explain why democratic institutions have been slow to take root in the Middle East?

Q Why do tensions between farmers and pastoral peoples appear to be on the rise in Africa today? In what parts of the continent is the problem most serious?

Q Why do you think religious or ethnic issues play such a significant role in provoking conflict in Africa and the Middle East today? How do such issues contribute to the popularity of radical terrorist organizations in the region?

CHAPTER TIMELINE

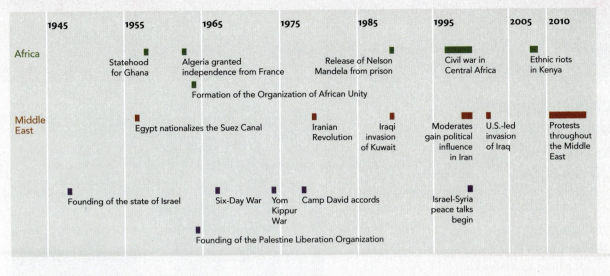

	1945	1955	1965	1975	1985	1995	2005	2010

Africa

Statehood for Ghana

Algeria granted independence from France

Release of Nelson Mandela from prison

Civil war in Central Africa

Ethnic riots in Kenya

Formation of the Organization of African Unity

Middle East

Egypt nationalizes the Suez Canal

Iranian Revolution

Iraqi invasion of Kuwait

Moderates gain political influence in Iran

U.S.-led invasion of Iraq

Protests throughout the Middle East

Founding of the state of Israel

Six-Day War

Yom Kippur War

Camp David accords

Israel-Syria peace talks begin

Founding of the Palestine Liberation Organization

CHAPTER NOTES

1. A. Nicol, *A Truly Married Woman and Other Stories* (London, 1965), p. 12.
2. Ngugi Wa Thiong'o, *Decolonizing the Mind: The Politics of Language in African Literature* (Portsmouth, N.H., 1986), p. 103.
3. Quoted in R. R. Andersen, R. F. Seibert, and J. G. Wagner, *Politics and Change in the Middle East: Sources of Conflict and Accommodation,* 4th ed. (Englewood Cliffs, N.J., 1982), p. 51.

MINDTAP
From Cengage

MindTap® is a fully online, highly personalized learning experience built upon Cengage Learning content. MindTap combines student learning tools—readings, multimedia, activities, and assessments—into a singular Learning Path that guides students through the course and helps students develop the critical thinking, analysis, and communication skills that are essential to academic and professional success.

Chapter Outline and Focus Questions

30-1 *South Asia*

Q How did Mahatma Gandhi's and Jawaharlal Nehru's goals for India differ, and what role did each leader's views play in shaping modern India?

30-2 *Southeast Asia*

Q What kinds of problems have the nations of Southeast Asia faced since 1945, and how did they attempt to solve them?

30-3 *Japan: Asian Giant*

Q How did the Allied occupation after World War II change Japan's political and economic institutions, and what remained unchanged? How would you compare what Japan has achieved since the end of World War II with what has occurred in mainland China during the same time period?

30-4 *The Little Tigers*

Q What factors have contributed to the economic success achieved by the Little Tigers in the years following the end of World War II?

Critical Thinking

Q *How would you compare the performances of the nations of South, Southeast, and East Asia since World War II with those experienced by their counterparts in Africa and Middle East during the same time period? What do you think accounts for the differences?*

Connections to Today

Q *What lessons do you think the so-called Little Tigers can provide for other nations seeking a path toward economic development and prosperity? Can such lessons be followed in other parts of the world?*

Buena Vista Images/The Image Bank/Getty Images

30.1 **The Petronas Towers in Kuala Lumpur, Malaysia**

AT THE DAWN OF THE NEW MILLENNIUM, first-time visitors to the Malaysian capital of Kuala Lumpur (KWAH-luh loom-POOR) were astonished to observe a pair of twin towers thrusting above the surrounding buildings and into the clouds. The Petronas Towers rise 1,483 feet from ground level; they were the world's tallest buildings at the time of their completion in 1998. (They have since been surpassed by Taipei 101 in Taiwan, the Shanghai World Financial Center, and the Burj Khalifa in Dubai.)

Beyond their status as an architectural achievement, the Petronas Towers announced the emergence of Southeast Asia—and of the rest of eastern Asia as well—as a major player on the international scene. It is no accident that the foundations of the building were laid on the site of the Selangor Cricket Club, a symbol of British colonial hegemony in Southeast Asia. "These towers," commented one local official, "will do wonders for Asia's self-esteem and confidence, which I think is very important, and which I think at this moment are at the point of takeoff."[1]

That the nations of the Pacific Rim would become a driving force in global development was all but unimaginable in the decades immediately following the end of World War II when bitter conflicts in Korea and Vietnam and unstable conditions elsewhere in the region were visible manifestations of a region in turmoil. Yet today, many of the countries in eastern Asia have become models of successful nation building characterized by economic prosperity and political stability. Several cities in the region, including Hong Kong, Singapore, Tokyo, and Shanghai, have become major capitals of finance and monuments of economic prowess, rivaling the traditional centers of New York, London, Berlin, and Paris. They have heralded the opening of what has been called the "Pacific Century."

30-1 SOUTH ASIA

> **Focus Question:** How did Mahatma Gandhi's and Jawaharlal Nehru's goals for India differ, and what role did each leader's views play in shaping modern India?

In 1947, nearly two centuries of British colonial rule came to an end when two new independent nations, India and Pakistan, came into being.

30-1a The End of the British Raj

During the 1930s, the nationalist movement in India was severely shaken by factional disagreements between Hindus and Muslims. The outbreak of World War II temporarily subdued these sectarian clashes, but they erupted again after the war ended in 1945. Battles between Hindus and Muslims broke out in several cities, and Muhammad Ali Jinnah (muh-HAM-ad ah-LEE JIN-uh) (1876–1948), leader of the Muslim League, demanded the creation of a separate state for each. Meanwhile, the Labour Party, which had long been critical of the British colonial legacy on both moral and economic grounds, had come to power in Britain, and the new prime minister, Clement Attlee, announced that power would be transferred to "responsible Indian hands" by June 1948.

But the imminence of independence did not dampen communal strife. As riots escalated, the British reluctantly accepted the inevitability of partition and declared that on August 15, 1947, two independent nations—Hindu India and Muslim Pakistan—would be established. Pakistan would be divided between the main area of Muslim habitation in the Indus River Valley in the west and a separate territory in east Bengal 2,000 miles to the east. Although Mahatma Gandhi warned that partition would provoke "an orgy of blood,"[2] he was increasingly regarded as a figure of the past, and his views were ignored.

The British instructed the rulers in the princely states to choose which state they would join by August 15, but problems arose in predominantly Hindu Hyderabad (HY-der-uh-bahd), where the nawab (viceroy) was a Muslim, and mountainous Kashmir (KAZH-meer), where a Hindu prince ruled over a Muslim population. After independence was declared, the flight of millions of Hindus and Muslims across the borders led to violence and the deaths of more than 1 million people. One of the casualties was Gandhi, who was assassinated on January 30, 1948, as he was going to morning prayer (see Film & History, *Gandhi*). The assassin, a Hindu militant, was apparently motivated by Gandhi's opposition to a Hindu India.

30-1b Independent India

With independence, the Indian National Congress, now renamed the Congress Party, assumed governing responsibility under Jawaharlal Nehru (juh-WAH-hur-lahl NAY-roo), the new prime minister. The prospect must have been intimidating. The vast majority of India's 400 million

☑ FILM & HISTORY

Gandhi

The epic movie *Gandhi* (1982), directed by British filmmaker Richard Attenborough, quickly became a blockbuster film. In the title role, actor Ben Kingsley presents a faithful rendition of its subject, the one-time Indian lawyer who led the resistance of his countrymen in the long struggle for independence against British colonial rule.

 Why do you think Mahatma Gandhi became such a widely admired—if controversial—figure in his lifetime?

Columbia Pictures/Everett Collection

⚡ **MINDTAP** See full-length Film & History feature in MindTap.
From Cengage

people were poor and illiterate. The new nation encompassed a significant number of ethnic groups and fourteen major languages. Although Congress Party leaders spoke bravely of building a new nation, Indian society still bore the scars of past wars and divisions.

The government's first problem was to resolve disputes left over from the transition period. The rulers of Hyderabad and Kashmir had both followed their own preferences rather than the wishes of their subject populations. Nehru was determined to include both states within India. In 1948, Indian troops invaded Hyderabad and annexed the area. India was also able to seize most of Kashmir but at the cost of creating an intractable problem that has poisoned relations with Pakistan to the present day.

An Experiment in Democratic Socialism

Under Nehru's leadership, India adopted a political system on the British model, with a figurehead president and a parliamentary form of government. Several political parties operated legally, but the Congress Party was dominant at both the central and the local levels because of its enormous prestige and charismatic leadership.

Nehru had been influenced by British socialism and patterned his economic policy roughly after the program of the British Labour Party. The state took over ownership of the major industries and resources, transportation, and utilities, although private enterprise was permitted at the local and retail levels. Farmland remained in private hands, but rural cooperatives were officially encouraged.

In other respects, Nehru was a devotee of Western materialism. He was convinced that India must industrialize to succeed. In advocating industrialization, Nehru departed sharply from Gandhi, who believed that materialism was morally corrupting and that only simplicity and nonviolence (as represented by the traditional Indian village and the symbolic spinning wheel) could save India and the world itself from self-destruction (see Opposing Viewpoints, "Two Visions for India," p. 767).

The primary themes of Nehru's foreign policy were anticolonialism and antiracism. Under his guidance, India took a neutral stance in the Cold War and sought to provide leadership to all newly independent nations in Asia, Africa, and Latin America. India's neutrality put it at odds with the United States, which during the 1950s was trying to mobilize all nations against what it viewed as the menace of international communism.

India's relations with Pakistan continued to be troubled. India refused to consider Pakistan's claim to Kashmir, even though the majority of the population there were Muslims. Tension between the two countries persisted,

erupting into war in 1965. In 1971, when riots against the Pakistani government broke out in East Pakistan, India intervened on the side of East Pakistan, which declared its independence as the new nation of Bangladesh (see Map 30.1).

The Post-Nehru Era

Nehru's death in 1964 aroused concern that Indian democracy was dependent on the Nehru mystique. When his successor, a Congress Party veteran, died in 1966, party leaders selected Nehru's daughter, Indira Gandhi (in-DEER-uh GAHN-dee) (no relation to Mahatma Gandhi), as the new prime minister. Gandhi (1917–1984) was inexperienced in politics, but she quickly showed the steely determination of her father.

Like Nehru, Indira Gandhi embraced democratic socialism and a policy of neutrality in foreign affairs, but she was more activist in promoting her objectives than her father. To combat rural poverty, she nationalized banks, provided loans to peasants on easy terms, built low-cost housing, distributed land to the landless, and introduced electoral reforms to enfranchise the poor.

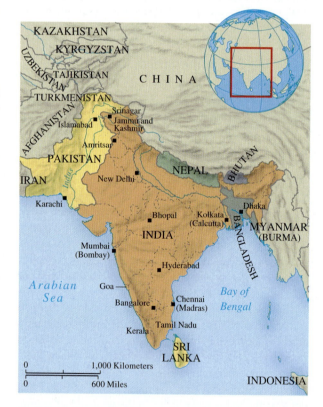

Map 30.1 Modern South Asia. This map shows the boundaries of all the states in contemporary South Asia.

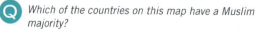 *Which of the countries on this map have a Muslim majority?*

Two Visions for India

Politics & Government ALTHOUGH JAWAHARLAL NEHRU AND MOHANDAS GANDHI agreed on their desire for an independent India, their visions of the future of their homeland were dramatically different. Nehru favored industrialization to build material prosperity, whereas Gandhi praised the simple virtues of manual labor. The first excerpt is from a speech by Nehru; the second is from a letter written by Gandhi to Nehru.

Nehru's Socialist Creed

I am convinced that the only key to the solution of the world's problems and of India's problems lies in socialism, and when I use this word I do so not in a vague humanitarian way but in the scientific economic sense. . . . I see no way of ending the poverty, the vast unemployment, the degradation and the subjection of the Indian people except through socialism. That involves vast and revolutionary changes in our political and social structure, the ending of vested interests in land and industry, as well as the feudal and autocratic Indian states system. That means the ending of private property, except in a restricted sense, and the replacement of the present profit system by a higher ideal of cooperative service. . . . In short, it means a new civilization, radically different from the present capitalist order. Some glimpse we can have of this new civilization in the territories of the U.S.S.R. Much has happened there which has pained me greatly and with which I disagree, but I look upon that great and fascinating unfolding of a new order and a new civilization as the most promising feature of our dismal age.

Mohandas Gandhi, A Letter to Jawaharlal Nehru

I believe that if India, and through India the world, is to achieve real freedom, then sooner or later we shall have to go and live in the villages—in huts, not in palaces. Millions of people can never live in cities and palaces in comfort and peace. Nor can they do so by killing one another, that is, by resorting to violence and untruth. . . . We can have the vision of . . . truth and nonviolence only in the simplicity of the villages. That simplicity resides in the spinning wheel and what is implied by the spinning wheel. . . .

You will not be able to understand me if you think that I am talking about the villages of today. My ideal village still exists only in my imagination. . . . In this village of my dreams the villager will not be dull— he will be all awareness. He will not live like an animal in filth and darkness. Men and women will live in freedom, prepared to face the whole world. There will be no plague, no cholera, and no smallpox. Nobody will be allowed to be idle or to wallow in luxury. Everyone will have to do body labor. Granting all this, I can still envisage a number of things that will have to be organized on a large scale. Perhaps there will even be railways and also post and telegraph offices. I do not know what things there will be or will not be. Nor am I bothered about it. If I can make sure of the essential thing, other things will follow in due course. But if I give up the essential thing, I give up everything.

Q *What are the key differences between these two views on the future of India? Why do you think Nehru's proposals triumphed over Gandhi's?*

Sources: From *Sources of Indian Tradition*, Vol. 2, 2e by Stephen Hay, pp. 317–319. Copyright © 1988 by Columbia University Press, New York. From Gandhi "Letter to Jawaharlal Nehru" pp. 328–331 from *Gandhi in India: In His Own Words*, Martin Green, ed. Copyright © 1987 by Navajivan Trust. Lebanon, NH: University Press of New England.

Gandhi was especially worried by India's growing population, so she adopted a policy of forced sterilization in an effort to curb the growth rate. This policy proved unpopular, however, and—along with growing official corruption and Gandhi's authoritarian tactics—led to her defeat in the general election of 1975, the first time the Congress Party had failed to win a majority at the national level.

A minority government of procapitalist parties was formed, but Gandhi was back in power within two years.

She now faced a new challenge, however, in the rise of religious strife. The most dangerous situation was in the Punjab (pun-JAHB), where militant Sikhs (SEEKS or SEE-ikhz) were demanding autonomy or even independence from India. Gandhi did not shrink from a confrontation and attacked Sikh rebels hiding in their Golden Temple in the city of Amritsar (uhm-RIT-ser). The incident aroused widespread anger within the Sikh community, and Sikh members of Gandhi's personal bodyguard assassinated her in 1984.

By now, Congress Party politicians were convinced that the party could not remain in power without a member of the Nehru family at the helm. Gandhi's son Rajiv Gandhi (rah-JEEV GAHN-dee) (1944–1991), a commercial airline pilot with little interest in politics, was persuaded to replace his mother as prime minister. Rajiv lacked the strong ideological and political convictions of his mother and grandfather and allowed a greater role for private enterprise. But his government was criticized for cronyism, inefficiency, and corruption.

Rajiv Gandhi also sought to play a role in regional affairs, mediating a dispute between the government in Sri Lanka and Tamil rebels (known as the Elam Tigers) who were ethnically related to the majority population in southern India. The decision cost him his life: while campaigning for reelection in 1991, he was assassinated by a member of the Tiger organization. India faced the future without a member of the Nehru family as prime minister.

During the early 1990s, the Congress Party remained the leading party, but the powerful hold it once had on the Indian electorate had evaporated. New parties such as the militantly Hindu Bharatiya Janata (BAR-ruh-tee-uh JAHnuh-tuh) Party (BJP), actively vied with the Congress Party for control of the central and state governments. Growing political instability at the center was accompanied by rising tensions between Hindus and Muslims.

When a coalition government formed under Congress leadership collapsed, the BJP under Prime Minister A. B. Vajpayee (VAHJ-py-ee) (b. 1924) ascended to power and played on Hindu sensibilities to build its political base. The new government based its success on an aggressive program of privatization in the industrial and commercial sectors and made a major effort to promote the nation's small but growing technological base. But BJP leaders had underestimated the discontent of India's poorer citizens, and in 2004 the Congress Party was returned to power on a program dedicated to carrying out reforms in rural areas, including public works projects and hot lunch programs for all primary school children. Pervasive corruption and sectarian strife between Muslims and Hindus continued to bedevil the Congress government, and the BJP stormed back into power under Prime Minister Narendra Modi in 2014. The Modi government has attempted with limited success to curtail the endemic levels of corruption within Indian society while promoting rapid economic growth.

30-1c The Land of the Pure: Pakistan Since Independence

When Pakistan achieved independence in August 1947, unlike its neighbor India it was in all respects a new nation based on religious conviction rather than historical or ethnic tradition. The unique state consisted of two separate territories 2,000 miles apart. West Pakistan, including the Indus River basin and the West Punjab, was perennially short of water and populated by dry crop farmers and peoples of the steppe. East Pakistan was made up of the marshy deltas of the Ganges and Brahmaputra Rivers. Densely populated with mainly Muslim rice farmers, it was the home of the artistic and intellectual Bengalis (ben-GAH-leez).

The peoples of West Pakistan were especially diverse and included, among others, Pushtuns, Baluchis (buh-LOO-cheez), and Punjabis (pun-JAHB-eez). The Pushtuns are organized on a tribal basis and have kinship ties with the majority population in neighboring Afghanistan. Many are nomadic and cross the border on a regular basis with their flocks. The Baluchis straddle the border with Iran, and the Punjab was divided between Pakistan and India at the moment of independence.

Even though the new state was an essentially Muslim society, its first years were marked by intense internal conflicts over religious, linguistic, and regional issues. Muhammad Ali Jinnah's vision of a democratic state that would ensure freedom of religion and equal treatment for all was opposed by those who advocated a state based on Islamic principles, and eventually Islamic law became the basis for the legal and social system. Ethnic and territorial

CHRONOLOGY	South Asia Since 1945	
India and Pakistan become independent	1947
Assassination of Mahatma Gandhi	1948
Death of Jawaharlal Nehru	1964
Indo–Pakistani War	1965
Indira Gandhi elected prime minister	1966
Bangladesh declares its independence	1971
Assassination of Indira Gandhi	1984
Assassination of Rajiv Gandhi	1991
Military coup overthrows civilian government in Pakistan	1999
U.S.-led forces oust Taliban in Afghanistan	2001
Congress Party returns to power in India	2004
Assassination of Benazir Bhutto in Pakistan	2007
Massive floods in the Indus River Valley	2010
Osama bin Laden killed in Pakistan	2011
Election of Narendra Modi as prime minister of India	2014

differences also plagued the new nation. Many residents of East Pakistan felt that the government, which was based in the west, ignored their needs. In 1971, East Pakistanis unilaterally declared the creation of the independent state of Bangladesh. West Pakistani troops tried to restore order, but rebel forces eventually prevailed with Indian support.

The breakup of divided Pakistan undermined the authority of the military regime that had ruled since 1958, and the country experienced a period of civilian rule, but charges of official corruption brought the army back into power in 1979. By now, however, problems began to escalate on the domestic front. The influence of radical Islam had been growing, even within the ranks of the military, and in recent years it has peaked because of the war in Afghanistan. Half of the population lives in poverty, and illiteracy is widespread. Plagued by the dispute over Kashmir, relations with India remain fragile, and chronic conflicts among the various ethnic groups undermine the search for stability.

30-1d Poverty and Pluralism in South Asia

The leaders of the new states that emerged in South Asia after World War II faced many problems. The peoples of South Asia were still overwhelmingly poor and illiterate, and the sectarian, ethnic, and cultural divisions that had plagued Indian society for centuries had not dissipated.

The Politics of Communalism

Perhaps the most sincere effort to create democratic institutions was in India, where the new constitution called for social justice, liberty, equality of status and opportunity, and fraternity. All citizens were guaranteed protection from discrimination based on religious belief, race, caste, gender, or place of birth.

In actuality, several distinctive characteristics made the political system in India less than fully democratic in the Western sense but may have enabled it to survive. In essence, India became a one-party state for years. As the leading force in the independence movement, the Congress Party earned massive public support that enabled it to retain its preeminent position in Indian politics for three decades. Only after Nehru's death in 1964 did problems emerge that had been disguised by his adept maneuvering. As a party too long in power, Congress became complacent and all too easily fell prey to the temptations of corruption and pork-barrel politics. Today the party's aura has faded, and it is viewed by most Indians as merely one among several competing groups in the political arena.

One primary challenge for the establishment of democratic values throughout South Asia was **communalism**. Beneath the surface unity of the new republic lay age-old ethnic, linguistic, and religious divisions. Because of India's

vast size and complex history, no national language had ever emerged. Hindi—which is spoken mainly in northern India—was the most prevalent, but it was the native language of less than one-third of the population. During the colonial period, English had served as the official language of government, but it was spoken only by the educated elite and represented an affront to national pride. After its declaration of independence, India recognized fourteen official tongues, making the parliament sometimes sound like the Tower of Babel, but non-English and non-Hindi speakers remained at a distinct disadvantage in the political arena.

Jawaharlal Nehru had managed to finesse the issue by relying on his prestige as the founder of the republic, but problems began to surface after his death. During the 1980s, religious tensions began to increase as relations between Hindus and Muslims deteriorated in many parts of the country. The rise of the BJP added fuel to the fire, as militant Hindu groups began to demand a state that would cater to the Hindu majority, now numbering more than 700 million people. Sectarian violence between Hindus and Muslims has escalated in recent years, provoking Congress Party leader Manmohan Singh (MUHN-moh-hahn SING) (b. 1932) to lament in 2004 what he called an assault on India's "composite culture." The bloody attack by Islamic radicals in the city of Mumbai (MUM-bye) four years later was a graphic indication that the pluralistic tradition of India remains under siege.[3]

The Economy

Socialism was Nehru's answer to the social and economic inequality that had long afflicted the subcontinent. His series of five-year plans led to the creation of a relatively large state-run industrial sector primarily concerned with steel, vehicles, and textiles. Industrial production almost tripled between 1950 and 1965, and per capita income rose by 50 percent between 1950 and 1980, although it was still less than $300 (in U.S. dollars). By the 1970s, however, industrial growth had slowed. The lack of modern infrastructure was a problem, as was the rising price of oil, most of which had to be imported.

India's major economic weakness, however, was in agriculture. At independence, mechanization was almost unknown, fertilizer was rarely used, and most farms were small and uneconomical because of the Hindu tradition of dividing the land equally among all male children. As a result, the vast majority of the Indian people lived in conditions of abject poverty. Landless laborers outnumbered landowners by almost two to one. The government attempted to relieve the problem by redistributing land to the poor, limiting the size of landholdings, and encouraging farmers to form voluntary cooperatives. But all three programs ran into widespread opposition.

Another problem was rapid population growth. Even before independence, the country had difficulty supporting its people. In the 1950s and 1960s, the population grew by more than 2 percent annually, twice the nineteenth-century rate. Beginning in the 1960s, the Indian government sought to curb population growth through Indira Gandhi's program combining monetary rewards and compulsory sterilization. But popular resistance undermined the program, and the goals were scaled back in the 1970s. Although the trend today is toward smaller families, India is still on target to become the world's most populous nation, surpassing China by the year 2025.

After Indira Gandhi's death in 1984, her son Rajiv proved more receptive to foreign investment and a greater role for the private sector in the economy. India began to export more manufactured goods, including computer software. The pace of change has accelerated under Rajiv Gandhi's successors, who have continued to transfer state-run industries to private hands. These policies have stimulated the growth of a prosperous new middle class, which is now estimated at more than 100 million. Consumerism has soared, and sales of television sets, DVD players, cell phones, and even automobiles have increased dramatically. Equally important, Western imports are being replaced by new products manufactured in India with Indian brand names, and large multinational corporations such as the retail giant Walmart have had trouble breaking into the Indian market.

One consequence of India's entrance into the industrial age has been the emergence of a small but vibrant technological sector that provides many important services to the world's advanced nations. The city of Bangalore (BEHNG-uh-lohr) in south India has become an important technological center, benefiting from low wages and the presence of skilled labor that is proficient in English.

As in the industrialized countries of the West, economic growth in India has been accompanied by environmental damage. Water and air pollution has led to illness and death for many people, and an environmental movement has emerged. Some critics who reflect the traditional anti-imperialist attitude of Indian intellectuals blame Western capitalist corporations for the problem—as in, for example, the highly publicized case of leakage from a foreign-owned chemical plant at Bhopal (boh-PAHL). Much of the problem, however, comes from state-owned factories erected with Soviet aid. And not all the environmental damage can be ascribed to industrialization. The Ganges River is so polluted by human overuse that it is risky for Hindu believers to bathe in it, and air and water pollution is so extensive that it constitutes a severe health problem in urban areas throughout the subcontinent (see Comparative Essay, "One World, One Environment," p. 778).

Moreover, many Indians have not benefited from the new prosperity. Nearly one-third of the population lives below the national poverty line. Millions continue to live in urban slums such as the famous "City of Joy" in Kolkata (Calcutta), and most farm families remain desperately poor. In India's countless villages, millions of rural people rely—like the women in this photo from a village near Aurangabad—on local wells for their access to a clean water supply (see Comparative Illustration, "Two Indias," p. 771). Despite the socialist rhetoric of India's leaders, the inequality of wealth in India is as pronounced as it is in capitalist nations in the West. Indeed, India has been described as two nations: an educated urban India of 100 million people surrounded by more than nine times that many impoverished peasants in the countryside.

Such problems are even more serious in neighboring Pakistan and Bangladesh. The overwhelming majority of Pakistan's citizens are poor, and at least half are illiterate. Recent flooding along the Indus River has had a devastating effect on people living in the region and was described by a United Nations official as the worst humanitarian crisis in the organization's sixty-five-year history; typhoons are frequent in the Bay of Bengal and often cause severe damage in low-lying areas of Bangladesh. Prospects for the future are not bright because both countries have high birthrates and lack a modern technological sector to serve as a magnet for an emerging educated middle class.

Caste, Class, and Gender The Indian constitution of 1950 guaranteed equal treatment and opportunity for all, regardless of caste, and it prohibited discrimination based on untouchability. In recent years, the government has enacted many laws guaranteeing access to education and employment to all Indians, regardless of caste affiliation, and many individuals of low caste have attained high positions in Indian society. Nevertheless, prejudice is hard to eliminate, and the problem persists, particularly in rural villages, where *harijans* (HAR-ihjans), now called **dalits** (DAH-lits), still perform menial tasks and are often denied fundamental rights.

Gender equality has also been difficult to establish. After independence, India's leaders sought to equalize treatment of the sexes, and the constitution expressly forbade discrimination based on gender and called for equal pay for equal work. Laws were passed that prohibited child marriage, sati, and the payment of a dowry by the bride's family. Women were encouraged to attend school and enter the labor market.

Such laws, along with the dynamics of economic and social change, have had major effects on the lives of many

Two Indias

Earth & Environment

CONTEMPORARY INDIA is a study in contrasts. In Image 30.2a, middle-class students learn to use a computer, a symbol of their country's recent drive to join the global technological marketplace. Yet India today remains primarily a nation of villages. In Image 30.2b, women in colorful saris fill their pails with water at the village well. As in many developing countries, the scarcity of water is one of India's most crucial problems.

 In what other regions of the world is lack of water a serious problem?

30.2a

30.2b

Indian women. Middle-class women in urban areas are much more likely to seek employment outside the home, and many hold managerial and professional positions, although many couples still consult with their parents or an astrologer before deciding whether to go through with a marriage. Like other aspects of life, the role of women has changed much less in rural areas. Female children are still far less likely to receive an education. The overall literacy rate in India today is around 60 percent, but it is less than 50 percent among women. Laws relating to dowry, child marriage, and inheritance are routinely ignored in the countryside. The young bride shown in Image 30.3 (p. 772) may have had little role in the selection of her future husband, and her face seems to suggest that she can barely comprehend what her future life has to offer. There have been a few highly publicized cases of sati, although undoubtedly more women die of mistreatment at the hands of their husbands or of other members of their families.

30-1e South Asian Literature Since Independence

Recent decades have witnessed a prodigious outpouring of literature in India. Because of the vast quantity of works published (India is currently the third-largest publisher of English-language books in the world), only a few of the most prominent fiction writers can be mentioned here. Anita Desai (dess-SY) (b. 1937) is one of the first prominent female writers to emerge from contemporary India. Her writing focuses on the struggle of Indian women to achieve a degree of independence. In her first novel, *Cry, the Peacock*, the heroine finally seeks liberation by murdering her husband, preferring freedom at any cost to remaining a captive of traditional society.

The most controversial writer from India today is Salman Rushdie (b. 1947). In *Midnight's Children* (1980), he linked his protagonist—who was born on the night of independence—to the history of modern India, its achievements, and its frustrations. Rushdie's later novels

30.3 **Young Hindu Bride in Gold Bangles.** Awaiting the marriage ceremony, a young bride sits with her female relatives at the Meenakshi Hindu temple, one of the largest in southern India. Although child marriage is illegal, many Indian girls are still married at a young age. With the marital union arranged by the parents, this young bride may never have met her future husband. Bedecked in gold jewelry and rich silks—part of her dowry—she nervously awaits the priest's blessing before she moves to her husband's home. There she will begin a life of servitude to her in-laws.

One disadvantage of the eclectic approach, which seeks to blend the old and the new rather than force a choice of one over the other, is that sometimes contrasting traditions cannot be reconciled. In his book *India: A Wounded Civilization*, V. S. Naipaul (NY-pahl) (b. 1932), a well-known Trinidadian author of Indian descent, charged that Mahatma Gandhi's glorification of poverty and the simple Indian village was an obstacle to efforts to overcome the poverty, ignorance, and degradation of India's past and build a prosperous modern society. Gandhi's vision of a spiritual India, Naipaul complained, was a balm for defeatism and an excuse for failure.

Yet the appeal of Gandhi's philosophy remains a major part of the country's heritage. As historian Martha Nussbaum points out in *The Clash Within: Democracy, Religious Violence, and India's Future*, much of India's rural population continues to hold traditional beliefs—such as the concept of karma and inherent caste distinctions—that are incompatible with the capitalist work ethic and the democratic belief in equality before the law. Yet these beliefs provide a measure of identity and solace often lacking in other societies where such traditional spiritual underpinnings have eroded.

India also faces other serious challenges. As a democratic and pluralistic society, it is unable to launch major programs without popular consent and thus cannot move as quickly or often as effectively as an authoritarian system like China's. On the other hand, India's institutions provide a mechanism to prevent the emergence of a despotic government interested only in its own survival. Rich in tradition and experience, India must seek its own path to the future.

have tackled such problems as religious intolerance, political tyranny, social injustice, and greed and corruption. His attack on Islamic fundamentalism in *The Satanic Verses* (1988) won plaudits from literary critics but provoked widespread criticism among Muslims, including a death sentence by Iran's Ayatollah Khomeini.

 HISTORIANS DEBATE 30-1f **What Is the Future of India?**

Indian society looks increasingly Western in form, if not in content, and the distinction between traditional and modern, or indigenous and cosmopolitan, sometimes seems to be a simple dichotomy between rural and urban. The major cities appear modern and westernized, but the villages have changed little since precolonial days.

Yet traditional practices appear to be more resilient in India than in many other societies, and the result is often a synthesis rather than a clash between conflicting institutions and values. Clothing styles in the streets (where the sari and the dhoti continue to be popular), religious practices in the temples, and social relationships in the home all testify to the importance of tradition in India.

30-2 SOUTHEAST ASIA

Q **Focus Question:** What kinds of problems have the nations of Southeast Asia faced since 1945, and how did they attempt to solve them?

Japanese wartime occupation greatly affected the attitudes of Southeast Asians. It demonstrated the vulnerability of colonial rule in the region and showed that an Asian power could defeat Europeans. The Allied governments themselves also contributed— sometimes unwittingly— to rising aspirations for independence by promising self-determination for all peoples at the end of the war.

Some followed through on their promise. In July 1946, the United States granted total independence to the Philippines, although U.S. citizens retained economic and commercial interests in the new country. The British, too, were willing to bring an end to a century of imperialism in the region. In 1948, the Union of Burma received its independence. Malaya's turn came in 1957 after a Communist guerrilla movement had been suppressed.

The French and the Dutch, however, regarded their colonies in the region as economic necessities as well as symbols of national grandeur and therefore refused to turn them over to nationalist movements at the end of the war. The Dutch attempted to suppress a rebellion in the East Indies led by the fiery nationalist Sukarno (soo-KAHR-noh) (1901–1970). Under pressure from the United States, which feared a Communist victory there, the Dutch finally agreed in 1950 to recognize the new Republic of Indonesia. As we have seen, the situation was even more complicated in Vietnam, where the French refused to recognize Ho Chi Minh's new government in the fall of 1945—a product of what was known as the August Revolution—and sought to reimpose colonial rule. Only in 1954 would Vietnam—temporarily divided into two zones—receive its independence under the Geneva Accords (see Chapter 26).

30-2a In the Shadow of the Cold War

Unfortunately, the new nations of Southeast Asia faced the challenges of independence during intense global turmoil because of the rise of the Cold War. Although some anticolonialist leaders within the region admired Western political institutions and hoped to adapt them to their own countries, others were influenced by the Marxist critique of world capitalism and sought to bring about revolutionary changes on the model of the Soviet Union or the new China. Within a few years after the end of World War II, the Cold War was raging in Southeast Asia (see Map 30.2).

The Search for a New Political Culture   In the immediate aftermath of independence, most new nations in the region adopted constitutions patterned on Western democratic models, and multiparty political systems quickly sprang into operation. By the 1960s, however, most of these budding experiments in democracy had been abandoned or were under serious threat. Some had been replaced by military or one-party autocratic regimes. In Burma, a government based on the British parliamentary system and dedicated to nonviolent Buddhism and moderate Marxism had given way to a military dictatorship. In Thailand,

too, the military now ruled. In the Philippines, President Ferdinand Marcos (MAHR-kohs) (1917–1989) discarded democratic restraints and established his own centralized control. In South Vietnam, pressure from Communist-led insurgents forced Ngo Dinh Diem to rule by authoritarian means even as he paid lip service to the Western democratic model. Under the rule of Ho Chi Minh and his colleagues, North Vietnam made no pretense of following the Western model and became a Communist dictatorship.

One key reason why democratic institutions failed to take root in postwar Southeast Asia was that independence had not brought material prosperity or ended economic inequality and the domination of the local economies by foreign interests. Most economies in the region were still characterized by tiny industrial sectors; they lacked technology, educational resources, and capital investment. Disillusionment that the bright promise of independence was not being fulfilled was quick to spread.

The presence of widespread ethnic, linguistic, cultural, and economic differences also made the transition to Western-style democracy difficult. In Malaya, for example, the majority Malays—most of whom were farmers—feared economic and political domination by the local Chinese minority, who were much more experienced in industry and commerce. In 1961, the Federation of Malaya, whose ruling party was dominated by Malays, integrated former British possessions on the island of Borneo into the new Union of Malaysia to increase the non-Chinese proportion of the country's population. An affirmative action program was adopted to enhance the economic and cultural dominance of the indigenous Malay population within the broader society.

The most prominent example of a failed experiment in democracy was Indonesia. In 1950, the nation's new leaders drew up a constitution creating a parliamentary system under a titular presidency. One core principle of the new constitution called for the creation of a secular state that would reflect the diversity of religious beliefs throughout the islands. Sukarno was elected the first president. A spellbinding orator, Sukarno had played a major role in creating a sense of national identity among the disparate peoples of the Indonesian Archipelago.

But Sukarno soon grew exasperated at the incessant maneuvering among Muslims, Communists, and the army, and in the late 1950s he dissolved the constitution and attempted to rule on his own through what he called "**guided democracy**." As he described it, guided democracy was closer to Indonesian traditions and superior to the Western variety (see Historical Voices, "The Golden Throat of President Sukarno," p. 775). Highly suspicious of the West, Sukarno nationalized foreign-owned enterprises and sought economic aid from China and the

Map 30.2 Modern Southeast Asia. Shown here are the countries that make up contemporary Southeast Asia. The names of major islands are indicated in *italic* type.

Q *Which Southeast Asian countries have democratic governments?*

Soviet Union while relying for domestic support on the Indonesian Communist Party.

Many leading members of the army and the Muslim community resented Sukarno's increasing reliance on the Communists. In 1965, military officers launched a coup d'état in confusing conditions that provoked a mass popular uprising that resulted in the slaughter of several hundred thousand suspected Communists; many of the victims were overseas Chinese, who had been long distrusted by the Muslim majority. In 1967, a military government under General Suharto (soo-HAHR-toh) (1921–2008) was installed.

The new government made no pretense of reverting to democratic rule, but it did restore good relations with the West and sought foreign investment to repair the country's

ravaged economy. It also adopted measures to placate demands from Muslims, some of whom demanded the creation of a state based on Islamic law, something contrary to the secular principle enshrined in the 1950 constitution.

30-2b Southeast Asia in the New Millennium

With the end of the Vietnam War and the gradual rapprochement between China and the United States in the late 1970s, the ferment and uncertainty that had marked the early postwar period in Southeast Asia gradually gave way to an era of greater political stability and material prosperity. In the Philippines, the dictatorial Marcos regime was overthrown by a massive public uprising in 1986 and replaced by a democratically elected government

The Golden Throat of President Sukarno

Politics & Government

INDONESIAN NATIONALIST SUKARNO was a spellbinding speaker and charismatic leader of his nation's struggle for independence. After rising to the presidency after Indonesian independence was achieved in 1950, he chafed for years under a constitution that limited the powers of the presidency, and he concentrated authority in his own hands under a new constitution that promulgated a new system known as "guided democracy" in 1959. Under this system, central leadership would be vested in the hands of a *sesepuh*—an elder—who would lead the Indonesian people under a benevolent dictatorship. In the passage cited here, he describes the new system and how—in his view—it accords with the character of the Indonesian people. The sesepuh, of course, would be himself.

"The Political Manifesto"

With our return to the 1945 Constitution, we have already "rediscovered the Revolution . . ." We now feel ourselves to be a wanderer who after ten years of roving around all over the world to find a place to live outside of his country, at last has returned to the home of his birth—has come home to his own houses, as the buffalo comes home to his pen. . . .

The devil of liberalism, the devil of federalism, the devil of individualism, the devil of suku-ism [familism].. the devil of corruption . . . , the devil of the multiparty system—all kinds of devils have jumped on us in the realm of the Inferno, and now we are undergoing purgatory in all fields. Re-orientation, re-ordering, re-tooling, re-shaping, re-making—all of that is necessary, so that we will be able to continue our journey on the rails of the Revolution. . . .

Let the imperialists abroad be in an uproar! They accuse us that the 1945 Constitution is "Japanese-made." They also impute that the authority of the President within the framework of the present 1945 Constitution starts from the base of military dictatorship.

Once again, let them be in an uproar! . . . The 1945 Constitution is the genuine reflection of the identity of the Indonesia nation, who since ancient times based their system of Government of *musjawarah* [deliberation] and *mufakat* [consensus] with the leadership of one central authority in the hands of a "sesepu"—an elder—who did not dictate, but led, and protected. Indonesian democracy since ancient times has been Guided Democracy, and this is characteristic of all original democracies in Asia.

Yes, indeed, without concealing anything we have made a complete divorce from western democracy, which is free-fight liberalism, but on the other hand since ancient times we have flatly rejected dictatorships. Guided Democracy is the democracy of the family system, without the anarchy of liberalism, without the autocracy of a dictatorship. . . .

Source: H. J. Benda and J. Larkin, *The World of Southeast Asia: Selected Historical Readings* (New York, 1967), pp. 248–250.

---

under President Corazon Aquino (KOR-uh-zahn ah-KEE-noh) (1933–2009), the widow of a popular politician who had been assassinated a few years earlier. Aquino and her successors have still had to compete for popular election, although they have been unable to resolve many of the country's chronic economic and social challenges. The current president, Rodrigo Duterte (b. 1945), is an outspoken populist who has vigorously pursued drug pushers and other criminal elements in the country. A long-running dispute rages on the southern island of Mindanao (min-duh-NAH-oh), where dissident Muslim groups continue to agitate—sometimes by violent means—for autonomy or independence.

Similar trends are at work elsewhere in the region. Malaysia is a practicing democracy, although the ruling coalition of various ethnic groups has had chronic difficulties in satisfying demands of militant Muslims who seek to create an Islamic state. In 2018, the ruling government was voted out of office for the first time on charges of chronic corruption. In neighboring Thailand, a fragile democracy, has long sought to function under the watch of the military, which declared martial law over the country in 2014 in a period of massive antigovernment protests. In Burma (renamed Myanmar in 1989), the forces of greater popular participation were long silenced by a repressive military regime known as SLORC. Recently, however, the military junta agreed to a gradual transition to civilian leadership under the National League for Democracy, led by Aung San Suu Kyi (AWNG SAHN SOO CHEE), the admired daughter of a World War II nationalist leader. The new government faces intimidating challenges, however, from anemic economic growth and a bitter conflict between the

30.4 A Prayer to Lord Buddha. Myanmar (also known as Burma) is one of the most devout Buddhist countries in the world. For the country's majority Theravada Buddhist community, religion is a constant presence in their lives, and their children are often sent for training in the local temple as young as five years of age. The most sacred site in Myanmar is the Shwedagon Temple, allegedly established by disciples of Siddhartha Gautama in the city of Yangon in the fifth century BCE. Even today the temple receives constant visitors, who worship at its many chapels surrounding its massive golden stupa.

country's Buddhist majority and a Muslim minority group known as the Rohingya (row-HING-ya) Government efforts to expel the Rohingya have resulted in widespread criticism from abroad.

Financial Crisis and Recovery The trend toward more representative systems of government in the region has been partly the result of increasing prosperity and the growth of an affluent and educated middle class. Although some countries such as Myanmar and the Philippines are still relatively poor and predominantly agrarian, most of the remaining states in the region have been undergoing rapid economic development. The process has not taken place, however, without periodic setbacks. In 1997, a financial crisis—triggered by growing budget deficits and irresponsible investment practices—swept through the region. A few years later, a massive tsunami struck the Malay Peninsula and the Indonesian islands, causing thousands of casualties as well as substantial economic damage. Eventually, however, the economies in the region managed to weather such crises. Blessed with abundant natural resources, including oil reserves, precious metals, and tropical products, the nations of Southeast Asia enjoy an annual growth rate greater than most parts of the world. One serious challenge, however, is posed by the danger of growing environmental pollution. The problem is caused partly by the widespread practice of cutting down rain forests to clear land for the cultivation of important tropical products such as rubber, coffee, and palm oil. Meanwhile, the draining of underground aquifers and the rise in sea levels throughout the region has caused flooding in major cities such as Bangkok and Jakarta (see Comparative Essay, "One World, One Environment," p. 778).

Indonesia After Suharto

For years, a major exception to the trend toward political pluralism in Southeast Asia was Indonesia, where Suharto ruled without restraint. But in 1997, protests against widespread official corruption, coupled with Muslim demands for a larger role for Islam in Indonesian society, led to violent street riots and calls for Suharto's resignation. Forced to step down in the spring of 1998, Suharto was replaced by his deputy, B. J. Habibie (hab-BEEBee) (b. 1936), who called for the establishment of a national assembly to select a new government based on popular aspirations.

In 2004, General Susilo Yudhyono (soo-SEE-loh yood-heh-YOH-noh) (b. 1949) was elected president of Indonesia. The new chief executive inaugurated a new era of economic reform and political stability, and power was transferred peacefully ten years later to his successor, Jakarta mayor Joko Widodo. Although pressure from some Muslim groups to abandon the country's secular tradition—punctuated by a bloody attack by local terrorists on tourist sites on the island of Bali—lies just beneath the surface, the level of religious and ethnic tension between Islamic groups and various national minorities has declined somewhat, and the fact that democratic elections can take place holds promise for the future.

Vietnam: The God that Failed

As always, Vietnam has been a special case. After achieving victory over South Vietnam in spring 1975 (see Chapter 26), Communist leaders in Hanoi, heady with their success, pursued the rapid reunification of the two zones under Communist Party rule while laying out plans to carry out a socialist transformation throughout the country (now renamed the Socialist Republic of Vietnam). The result was an economic and social disaster as the economy virtually collapsed and more than 1 million people fled to neighboring countries. In 1986, party leaders decided to follow the Soviet example by introducing their own version of perestroika in Vietnam (see Chapter 27). Today the country possesses a mixed capitalist–socialist economy along Chinese lines and has become increasingly integrated into the global marketplace. As in China, however, the government remains suspicious of Western-style democracy and represses any opposition to the Communist Party's guiding role over the state.

CHRONOLOGY	Southeast Asia Since 1945
August Revolution in Vietnam	1945
Philippines becomes independent	1946
Burma becomes independent	1948
Republic of Indonesia becomes independent	1950
Malaya becomes independent	1957
Beginning of Sukarno's guided democracy in Indonesia	1959
Military seizes power in Indonesia	1965
Association of Southeast Asian Nations (ASEAN) founded	1967
Fall of Saigon to North Vietnamese forces	1975
Vietnamese invade Cambodia	1978
Corazon Aquino elected president of the Philippines	1986
Vietnamese withdraw from Cambodia	1991
Suharto steps down as president of Indonesia	1998
Tsunami causes widespread death and destruction throughout region	2004
Election of President Joko Widodo in Indonesia	2014

30-2c Regional Conflict and Cooperation: The Rise of ASEAN

Southeast Asian states have periodically been hampered by serious tensions among themselves. Some of these tensions were a consequence of historical rivalries and territorial disputes that had been submerged during the long era of colonial rule. Cambodia, for example, has bickered with both of its neighbors, Thailand and Vietnam, over mutual frontiers drawn up originally by the French for their own convenience.

After the fall of Saigon and the reunification of Vietnam under Communist rule in 1975, the lingering border dispute between Cambodia and Vietnam erupted again. In April 1975, a revolutionary regime under the leadership of the Khmer Rouge (KMAIR ROOZH) dictator Pol Pot (POHL PAHT) (c. 1928–1998) came to power in Cambodia and brutally massacred more than 1 million Cambodians. Then, claiming that vast territories in the Mekong River Delta had been seized by the Vietnamese in previous centuries, the Khmer Rouge regime launched attacks across the common border. In response, Vietnamese forces

One World, One Environment

Earth & Environment A crucial factor affecting the evolution of society and the global economy in the early twenty-first century is the growing concern over the impact of industrialization on the environment. Humans have always caused some harm to their natural surroundings, but never has the ecological damage been as significant and extensive as during the past century. Chemicals and other pollutants introduced into the atmosphere or into rivers, lakes, and oceans have increasingly threatened the health and well-being of all living species.

For many years, environmental concern was focused on the developed countries of the West, where industrial effluents, automobile exhausts, and the use of artificial fertilizers and insecticides led to urban smog, extensive damage to crops and wildlife, and a major reduction of the ozone layer in the upper atmosphere. In recent years, the problem has spread elsewhere. China's headlong rush to industrialization has resulted in major ecological damage in that country. Industrial smog has created almost unlivable conditions in many cities in Asia, while hillsides denuded of their forests have led to severe erosion and loss of farmlands. Rain forest destruction is a growing problem in many parts of the world, notably in Brazil and Indonesia. With the forest cover across the earth rapidly disappearing, there is less plant life to perform the crucial process of reducing carbon dioxide levels in the atmosphere.

One positive note is that environmental concerns have begun to take on a global character. As it has become increasingly clear that the release of carbon dioxide and other gases into the atmosphere as a result of industrialization plays a significant part in producing global warming, the issue has become a source of widespread international concern. If, as many scientists predict, worldwide temperatures continue to increase, the rise in sea levels could pose a major threat to low-lying islands and coastal areas throughout the world, while climatic change could lead to severe droughts or excessive rainfall in cultivated areas.

It is one thing to recognize a problem, however, and another to solve it. Cooperative efforts among nations to alleviate environmental problems have all too often been hindered by economic forces or by political, ethnic, and religious disputes. A 1997 conference on global warming held in Kyoto, Japan, for example, was marked by bitter disagreement over the degree to which developing countries should share the burden of cleaning up the environment. In 2001, U.S. President George W. Bush refused to sign the Kyoto Agreement on the grounds that it discriminated against advanced Western countries. The fact is that few nations have been willing to take unilateral action that might pose an obstacle to economic development plans or lead to a rise in unemployment. An international agreement held in Paris and organized under the auspices of the United Nations was signed by almost 200 nations in December 2015. Whether the stated goal to reduce substantially the emission of greenhouse gases in order to bring about a reduction in the rate of global warming will be achieved, however, is still uncertain.

William J. Duiker

30.5 A Forest Fire on the Island of Sumatra. Man-made forest fires are one of the most prevalent forms of environmental pollution in Southeast Asia today as precious rain forests are clear-cut to make room for valuable export crops such as rubber, coffee, and palm oil. Shown here, a forest fire on the Indonesian island of Sumatra casts a pall of acrid smoke over neighboring communities.

Q *What kinds of environmental problems have recently taken place in the region of South Asia? Have they all been the result of human action?*

invaded Cambodia in December 1978 and installed a pro-Hanoi regime in Phnom Penh (puh-NAHM PEN). Fearful of Vietnam's increasing power in the region, China launched a brief attack on Vietnam to demonstrate its displeasure.

The outbreak of war among the erstwhile Communist allies aroused the concern of other countries in the neighborhood. In 1967, several non-Communist countries had established the Association of Southeast Asian Nations, or **ASEAN**. Composed of Indonesia, Malaysia, Thailand, Singapore, and the Philippines, ASEAN at first concentrated on cooperative social and economic endeavors, but after the Vietnam War ended, it cooperated with other states in an effort to force the Vietnamese to withdraw from Cambodia. In 1991, the Vietnamese finally withdrew, and a new government was formed in Phnom Penh. The ruling party continues to follow the example of its neighbor Vietnam, however, in suppressing any threats to its monopoly of power.

The growth of ASEAN from a weak collection of diverse states into a stronger organization whose members cooperate militarily and politically has helped provide the nations of Southeast Asia with a more cohesive voice to represent their interests on the world stage. The admission of Myanmar and the Indochinese states into the organization has extended its reach and provided it with greater leverage in dealing with China, whose claims of ownership over islands in the South China Sea have aroused widespread concern in the region.

30-2d Daily Life: Town and Country in Contemporary Southeast Asia

The urban–rural dichotomy observed in India also is found in Southeast Asia, where the cities resemble those in the West while the countryside often appears little changed from precolonial days. In cities such as Bangkok, Manila, and Jakarta, broad boulevards lined with skyscrapers and clogged with heavy traffic alternate with muddy lanes passing through neighborhoods packed with wooden shacks topped by thatch or rusty tin roofs. Nevertheless, in recent decades, millions of Southeast Asians have fled to these urban slums. Although most available jobs are menial, the pay is better than in the villages.

Traditional Customs, Modern Values   The urban migrants change not only their physical surroundings but also their attitudes and values. Sometimes the move leads to a decline in traditional beliefs. Nevertheless, Buddhist, Muslim, and Confucian beliefs remain strong, even in cosmopolitan cities such as Bangkok, Jakarta, and Singapore. This preference for the traditional also shows up in lifestyle. Native dress—or an eclectic blend of Asian and Western dress—is still common. Traditional music, art, theater, and dance remain popular, although rock music has become fashionable among the young, and Western films continue to dominate the market. In Thailand, many traditionalists lament the decline of Buddhist beliefs and practices, while thoughtful Indonesians are concerned at the impact of mass tourism in Bali, where the island's unique Hindu culture sometimes appears overwhelmed (see Image 30.6).

Changing Roles for Women   One of the most significant changes in Southeast Asia in recent decades has been in the role of women in society. In general, women in the region have historically faced fewer restrictions on their activities and enjoyed a higher status than women elsewhere in Asia. Nevertheless, they have not been the equal of men in every respect. With independence, Southeast Asian women gained new rights. Virtually every constitution adopted by the newly independent states granted women full legal and political rights, including the right to work. Today, women have increased opportunities for education and have entered careers previously reserved for men.

Yet women are not truly equal to men in any country in Southeast Asia. In Vietnam, until recently no women had served in the Communist Party's ruling politburo. Throughout the region, women rarely hold senior positions in government service or in the boardrooms of major corporations, although some have served as head of state. In Islamic countries such as Malaysia and Indonesia, women are expected to dress modestly and wear traditional Muslim headdress.

30-2e A Region in Flux

Today, the Western image of a Southeast Asia mired in the Vietnam conflict and the tensions of the Cold War has become a distant memory. In ASEAN, the states in the region have created the framework for a regional organization that can serve their common political, economic, technological, and security interests. A few members of ASEAN are already on the road to advanced development.

To be sure, there are challenges to overcome. The financial crisis that erupted in fall 2008 continues to test the resilience of local economies that depend on robust foreign markets for their exports. Myanmar is only beginning to emerge from a long period of isolation. The Indochinese countries remain potentially unstable and have not been fully integrated into the region as a whole. Finally, terrorist groups inspired by al-Qaeda continue to operate, especially in Indonesia. All things considered, however, the situation is more promising today than would have seemed possible a generation ago. Unlike the situation in Africa and the Middle East, the nations of Southeast Asia have put aside

William J. Duiker

30.6 Tourism and Tradition in Bali. The influence of modern Western culture has had a corrosive effect on contemporary societies throughout Southeast Asia. Traditional forms of art and architecture, music, and film have been replaced by their modern Western equivalents. The small island of Bali in eastern Indonesia has managed to preserve much of its traditional way of life by presenting it to visitors as a tourist experience. Although the tourist district in the capital of Denpasar is overrun with modern hotels, bars, and tourist shops, residents of the island still seek to preserve elements of their heritage as an outpost of Hindu culture in a country with 90 percent Muslim citizens. This photo shows Balinese actors at a theatrical performance on a familiar theme from the classical Indian repertoire. In an ironic twist, tourism in Bali helps preserve traditional culture even as it undermines its relevance in the daily lives of the islanders.

the bitter legacy of the colonial era and the Cold War to embrace the wave of globalization that has been sweeping the world in recent years.

30-3 JAPAN: ASIAN GIANT

Q **Focus Questions:** How did the Allied occupation after World War II change Japan's political and economic institutions, and what remained unchanged? How would you compare what Japan has achieved since the end of World War II with what has occurred in mainland China during the same time period?

In August 1945, Japan was in ruins, its cities destroyed, its vast Asian Empire in ashes, its land occupied by a foreign army. Half a century later, Japan had emerged as the second-greatest industrial power in the world, democratic in form and content and a source of stability throughout the region. Its success led to a popular belief that the world was about to enter a Pacific Century.

30-3a Occupation Reforms: The Transformation of Modern Japan

For five years after the end of the war in the Pacific, Japan was governed by an Allied administration under the command of U.S. General Douglas MacArthur. As commander of the occupation administration, MacArthur was responsible for demilitarizing Japanese society, destroying the Japanese war machine, trying Japanese civilian and military officials charged with war crimes, and laying the foundations of postwar Japanese society.

Administrators of the Allied occupation started with the conviction that Japanese expansionism was directly linked to the institutional and ideological foundation of the Meiji Constitution. Accordingly, they set out to change Japanese politics into something closer to the pluralistic model used in most Western societies. A constitution reflecting such individualistic values was presented to the Japanese, who were compelled to accept the document even although they had provided little input. To undercut the mystique of the state represented by the Meiji concept of kokutai, Allied officials also sought to remodel the educational system along American lines so that it would turn out independent individuals rather than automatons subject to manipulation by the central government. Wartime textbooks were cleansed of their propagandistic content or completely scrapped, and the 1890 imperial rescript on education emphasizing the concept of loyalty to the state was repealed. Cultural items as familiar to Americans as Coca Cola, chewing gum, and baseball were strongly encouraged.

Allied Occupation officials also believed it was essential to bring about major changes in the Japanese economy to reduce the ability of the central government to harness its production to the interests of the state. One sturdy pillar of Japanese militarism had been the giant business cartels known as *zaibatsu* (see Chapter 24). Allied policy was designed to break up the zaibatsu into smaller units in the belief that corporate concentration not only hindered competition but also was inherently undemocratic and conducive to political authoritarianism. Occupation planners also intended to promote the formation of independent labor unions to lessen the power of the state over the economy and provide a mouthpiece for downtrodden Japanese workers. Finally, economic inequality in rural areas was to be reduced by a comprehensive land reform program that would turn the land over to those who farmed it. In 1945, half of the population of Japan still lived on farms, and half of all farmers were still tenants. Under the land reform program, all lands owned by absentee landlords and all cultivated landholdings over an established maximum were sold on easy credit terms to the tenants.

Dream and Reality   The Allied program was an ambitious and even audacious plan to remake Japanese society and has been praised for its clear-sighted vision and altruistic motives. Parts of the program—the constitution, the land reforms, and the educational system—succeeded brilliantly. But as other concerns began to intervene, changes were made that were not always successful. In particular, with the advent of the Cold War in the late 1940s, the goal of decentralizing the Japanese economy gave way to the desire to make Japan a key partner in the effort to defend East Asia against international communism. Convinced of the need to promote economic recovery in Japan, U.S. policy makers began to show more tolerance for the zaibatsu. Concerned about growing radicalism within the new labor movement, U.S. occupation authorities placed less emphasis on the independence of the labor unions.

The Cold War also affected U.S. foreign relations with Japan. On September 8, 1951, the United States and other former belligerent nations signed a peace treaty restoring Japanese independence. In turn, Japan renounced any claim to such former colonies or territories as Taiwan, Korea, and southern Sakhalin and the Kurile Islands (see Map 30.3). On the same day, Japan and the United States signed a defensive alliance and agreed that the latter could maintain military bases on the Japanese islands. Japan was now formally independent but in a new dependency relationship with the United States. A provision in the new constitution renounced war as an instrument of national policy and prohibited the raising of an army (see Historical Voices, "Japan Renounces War," p. 782).

Map 30.3 Modern Japan. Shown here are the four main islands that make up the contemporary state of Japan.

Q *Which island is the largest?*

Japan Renounces War

Politics & Government ON MAY 3, 1947, a new Japanese constitution went into effect to replace the Meiji Constitution of 1890. The process of drafting the document had taken place under the watchful guidance of General Douglas MacArthur, the supreme commander of the Allied Powers, who was determined to guarantee that the militaristic tendencies of the prewar Japanese government would not be resurrected in the postwar era. This point of view was explicitly included in the new constitution. According to Article 9 of the new charter, Japan renounced war as an instrument of national policy and eventually decided to maintain only a limited number of so-called self-defense forces to protect itself against external attack. From that time on, Japan relied on the United States for its protection and security.

Excerpts from the Japanese Constitution of 1947

We, the Japanese people, acting through our duly elected representatives in the National Diet, determined that we shall secure for ourselves and our posterity the fruits of peaceful cooperation with all nations and the blessings of liberty throughout this land, and resolved that never again shall we be visited with the horrors of war through the action of government, do proclaim that sovereign power resides with the people and do firmly establish this Constitution. Government is a sacred trust of the people, the authority for which is derived from the people, the powers of which are exercised by the representatives of the people, and the benefits of which are enjoyed by the people. This is a universal principle of mankind upon which this Constitution is founded. We reject and revoke all constitutions, laws, ordinances, and rescripts in conflict herewith.

We, the Japanese people, desire peace for all time and are deeply conscious of the high ideals controlling human relationship, and we have determined to preserve our security and existence, trusting in the justice and faith of the peace-loving peoples of the world. We desire to occupy an honored place in an international society striving for the preservation of peace, and the banishment of tyranny and slavery, oppression and intolerance for all time from the earth. We recognize that all peoples of the world have the right to live in peace, free from fear and want.

We believe that no nation is responsible to itself alone, but that laws of political morality are universal; and that obedience to such laws is incumbent upon all nations who would sustain their own sovereignty and justify their sovereign relationship with other nations.

We, the Japanese people, pledge our national honor to accomplish these high ideals and purposes with all our resources.

Chapter I. The Emperor

Article 1. The Emperor shall be the symbol of the State and of the unity of the people, deriving his position from the will of the people with whom resides sovereign power. . . .

Chapter II. Renunciation of War

Article 9. (1) Aspiring sincerely to an international peace based on justice and order, the Japanese people forever renounce war as a sovereign right of the nation and the threat or use of force as a mean of settling international disputes.

(2) In order to accomplish the aim of the preceding paragraph, land, sea, and air forces, as well as other war potential, will never be maintained. The right of belligerency of the state will not be recognized.

Q *What is the current status of Article 9 of the Japanese Constitution? Why are some observers demanding that this provision be changed?*

Source: From the Japanese Constitution of 1947. Accessed at: http://history.hanover.edu/texts/1947con.html.

30-3b Politics and Government

As we saw previously, the Allied occupation administrators were determined to dismantle the institutional and ideological underpinnings of the Meiji political system and introduce democratic values in postwar Japan. In reality, several characteristics of the postwar Japanese political system reflected the tenacity of the traditional political culture. Although Japan now had a multiparty system with two major parties, the Liberal Democrats (LDP) and the Socialists, in practice there was a "government party" and a permanent opposition—the Liberal Democrats were not voted out of office for thirty years. The most important maneuvering in the postwar era was often not between the LDP and its rival political parties, but among competing factions within the LDP itself. That tradition changed suddenly in 1993 when the ruling Liberal Democrats, shaken by a sluggish economy and chronic reports of corruption and cronyism between politicians and business interests, failed to win a majority of seats in parliamentary elections. The new coalition government of minority parties, however, quickly split into feuding factions, and the LDP returned to power in 1995. Bureaucratic resistance to reform, chronic factionalism, and charges of corruption have continued to plague the political process, however, and the inept response to the massive offshore tsunamis that hit the island of Honshu in 2011 has seriously eroded public confidence in the political system. In 2012, veteran Liberal Democratic politician Shinzo Abe (SHIN-dzoh AH-bay) (b. 1954) was elected prime minister on a promise to revive the lagging Japanese economy by stimulating competition and adopting tough new fiscal policies. Abe has managed to stabilize the economy, but his foreign policy has aroused unease throughout Asia because of his often-voiced desire to revise the Japanese constitution so that the country can play a more active military role in the region.

30-3c The Economy

Nowhere are the changes taking place in postwar Japan so visible as in the economic sector, where Japan developed into a major industrial and technological power in the space of a few decades, surpassing such advanced Western societies as Germany, France, and Great Britain. Although this "Japanese miracle" has often been described as a direct product of the policies adopted during the occupation period, note that Japanese economic growth began with the Meiji reforms in the late nineteenth century. These helped transform Japan from a primarily agricultural society based on semifeudal institutions to an advanced industrial and commercial powerhouse.

A key factor in postwar Japanese economic policy was the product of the decision by Allied occupation officials to scale back the policy of breaking up the zaibatsu. Looser ties between companies were still allowed, and a new type of informal relationship, sometimes called the *keiretsu* (key-RET-soo), or "interlocking arrangement," began to take shape. Through such arrangements among suppliers, wholesalers, retailers, and financial institutions, the zaibatsu system was reconstituted under a new name. Another factor was the success of the postwar land reform program, which created a strong class of yeoman farmers; tenants declined to around 10 percent of the rural population. Prosperous farmers soon became a prime source of support for the LDP in Japanese politics.

The "Japanese Miracle"? During the fifty years following the end of World War II, Japan repeated the stunning results of the Meiji era. In 1950, the Japanese gross domestic product was only around one-third that of Great Britain or France. Thirty years later, it was larger than both put together and far more than half that of the United States. Japan became one of the greatest exporting nations in the world, and its per capita income matched or surpassed that of most advanced Western states.

Much of the credit for the country's stunning emergence as a global economic powerhouse was assigned to the fact that the central government continued to play an active role in various aspects of the economy, mediating management–labor disputes, establishing price and wage policies, and subsiding vital industries and enterprises producing goods for export. This tradition of government intervention in the economy has often been cited as a key reason for the efficiency of Japanese industry and the emergence of the country as an industrial giant.

A Miracle Tarnished? In recent years, however, the Japanese economy has run into serious difficulties, raising the question of whether the Japanese model is as appealing as many observers earlier declared. A steady rise in the value of the yen increased the price of Japanese goods abroad and burst the bubble of investment by Japanese banks that had taken place under the umbrella of government protection. At the same time, exports—long the driving force behind the emergence of Japan into the world's second largest economy—faced increasing competition from hungry and aggressive rivals such as South Korea and Taiwan. Lacking a domestic market equivalent in size to the United States, the Japanese economy slipped into a recession during the 1990s that has not yet entirely abated almost three decades later.

These economic difficulties have placed heavy pressure on some of the vaunted features of the Japanese economy. Japanese consumers have become increasingly critical of the quality of some domestic products. The tradition of lifetime employment created a bloated white-collar workforce and has made downsizing difficult. Today, job security is on the decline as increasing numbers of workers are being laid off. Around 16 percent of the population lives in poverty, a figure only slightly lower than the United States. A disproportionate burden has fallen on women, who lack seniority and continue to suffer from various forms of discrimination in the workplace.

Some observers ascribe the country's recent economic difficulties to political factors. The practice of providing the central government with an influential role in managing the economy has recently come under fire, as Japanese corporations that once sought government protection from imports have now begun to argue that deregulation is needed to enable Japanese firms to innovate in order to keep up with international competition. Such reforms, however, have been resisted by powerful government ministries in Tokyo, which are accustomed to playing an active role in national affairs.

30-3d A Society in Transition

During the occupation, Allied planners set out to change social characteristics that they believed had contributed to Japanese aggressiveness before and during World War II. The new educational system removed all references to filial piety, patriotism, and loyalty to the emperor while emphasizing the individualistic values of Western civilization. The new constitution and a revised civil code eliminated remaining legal restrictions on women's rights to obtain a divorce, hold a job, or change their domicile. Women were guaranteed the right to vote and were encouraged to enter politics.

Such efforts to remake Japanese behavior through legislation have had mixed success. During the past sixty years, Japan has unquestionably become a more individualistic and egalitarian society. At the same time, many of the distinctive characteristics of traditional Japanese society have persisted to the present day, although in somewhat altered form. The emphasis on loyalty to the group and community relationships, for example, is reflected in the strength of corporate loyalties in postwar Japan, although the attitude has eroded in recent years. Such qualities, of course, can also have negative consequences. Minorities such as the eta, now known as the *Burakumin* (BOOR-uh-koo-min), and Korean residents in Japan continue to be subjected to legal and social discrimination. Treatment of the latter is especially controversial because thousands of ethnic Korean women have charged that they were conscripted to serve as prostitutes (euphemistically called "comfort women") for Japanese soldiers during the war. Negotiations on the issue have been dragging on for several years.

Emphasis on the work ethic also remains strong. The tradition of hard work is taught at a young age. The Japanese school year runs for 240 days a year, compared with 180 days in the United States, and work assignments outside class tend to be more extensive. The results are impressive: Japanese schoolchildren consistently earn higher scores on achievement tests than children in other advanced countries. At the same time, this devotion to success has often been accompanied by bullying by teachers and an emphasis on conformity (see Comparative Illustration, "From Conformity to Counterculture," p. 785).

By all accounts, however, independent thinking is on the increase in Japan. In some cases, it leads to antisocial behavior such as crime or membership in a teenage gang. Usually, it is expressed in more indirect ways, such as the recent fashion among young people of dyeing their hair brown (known in Japanese as "tea hair"). Because the practice is banned in many schools and generally frowned on by the older generation (one police chief dumped a pitcher of beer on a student with brown hair whom he noticed in a bar), many young Japanese dye their hair as a gesture of independence. When seeking employment or getting married, however, they often return their hair to its natural color.

Women in Japanese Society   One of the most tenacious legacies of the past in Japanese society is sexual inequality. Although women are now legally protected against discrimination in employment, few have reached senior levels in business, education, or politics. Women now make up nearly 50 percent of the workforce, but most are in retail or service occupations. Less than 10 percent of managerial workers in Japan are women, compared with nearly half in the United States. There is a feminist movement in Japan, but it has none of the vigor and mass support of its counterpart in the United States.

The Demographic Crisis   Many of Japan's current dilemmas stem from its growing demographic problems. The country now has the highest proportion of people older than sixty-five of any industrialized country—almost 23 percent of the country's total population. By 2024, an estimated one-third of the Japanese population will be over age sixty-five, and the median age will be fifty, ten years older than that of the United States. This demographic profile is the result of both declining fertility and a low level of immigration. Immigrants make up only 1 percent of the total population of Japan. Together, the aging population and the absence of immigrants are creating the prospect of a dramatic labor shortage in coming years. Nevertheless, prejudice against foreigners persists in Japan, and the government remains reluctant to ease restrictions against immigrants from other countries in the region.

Japan's aging population has many implications for the future. Traditionally, it was the responsibility of the eldest child in a Japanese family to care for aging parents, but that system is beginning to break down because of limited housing space and the growing tendency of working-age women to seek jobs in the marketplace. The proportion of Japanese older than sixty-five who live with their children has dropped from 80 percent in 1970 to around 50 percent today. At the same time, public and private pension plans are under increasing financial pressure, partly because of the low birthrate and the graying population.

Religion and Culture   As in the West, increasing urbanization has led to a decline in the practice of organized religion in Japan, although evangelical sects have proliferated in recent years. The largest and best-known sect is

From Conformity to Counterculture

William J. Duiker

30.7a

Family & Society

TRADITIONALLY, SCHOOLCHILDREN IN JAPAN have worn uniforms to promote conformity with the country's communitarian social mores. Image 30.7a, young students dressed in identical uniforms are on a field trip to Kyoto's Nijo Castle, which was built in 1603 by Tokugawa Ieyasu. Recently, however, a youth counterculture has emerged in Japan. In Image 30.7b, fashion-conscious teenagers with "tea hair"—heirs of Japan's long era of affluence—revel in their expensive hip-hop outfits, platform shoes, and layered dresses. Such fashion choices symbolize the growing revolt against conformity in contemporary Japan.

Q *How would you compare the social requirements and privileges of Japanese children with those of other cultures that we have encountered in this text?*

Barry Cronin/Newsmakers/Getty Images

30.7b

Soka Gakkai (SOH-kuh GAK-ky), a lay Buddhist organization that has attracted millions of followers and formed its own political party, the Komeito (koh-MAYtoh). Zen Buddhism retains its popularity, and some business people seek to use Zen techniques to learn how to focus their willpower to outwit competitors. Many Japanese also follow Shinto, which is no longer identified for its reverence of the emperor and the state.

Western literature, art, and music have also had a major impact on Japanese society. After World War II, many writers who had been active before the war resurfaced, but now their writing reflected demoralization. Many were attracted to existentialism, and some turned to hedonism and nihilism. For these disillusioned authors, defeat was compounded by fear of the Americanization of postwar Japan. One of the best examples of this attitude was novelist Yukio Mishima (yoo-KEEoh mi-SHEE-muh) (1925–1970), who led a crusade to stem the tide of what he described as America's "universal and uniform 'Coca-Colonization'" of the world in general and Japan in particular.[4] Mishima's

Experience an interactive version of this period in ⚡ MINDTAP ritual suicide in 1970 was the subject of widespread speculation and transformed him into a cult figure.

One of Japan's most serious-minded contemporary authors is Kenzaburo Oe (ken-zuh-BOO-roh OH-ay) (b. 1935). His work, rewarded with a Nobel Prize for Literature in 1994, focuses on Japan's ongoing quest for modern identity and purpose. His characters reflect the spiritual anguish precipitated by the collapse of the imperial Japanese tradition and the subsequent adoption of Western culture—a trend that Oe contends has culminated in unabashed materialism, cultural decline, and a moral void. Yet unlike Mishima, Oe does not wish to reinstill the imperial traditions of the past but rather seeks to regain spiritual meaning by retrieving the sense of communality and innocence found in rural Japan.

Since the 1970s, increasing affluence and a high literacy rate have contributed to a massive quantity of publications, ranging from popular potboilers to first-rate fiction. Much of this new literature deals with the common concerns of all affluent industrialized nations, including the effects of urbanization, advanced technology, and mass consumption. A wildly popular genre is the "art-manga," or graphic novel. Some members of the youth counterculture have used manga to rebel against Japan's rigid educational and conformist pressures.

30-3e The Japanese Difference

What is the reason for Japan's continuing uniqueness in the world today? Explanations tend to fall into two major categories. Some analysts point to cultural factors: the Japanese are naturally group oriented and find it easy to cooperate with one another. Traditionally hard-working and frugal, they are more inclined to save than to consume, a trait that boosts the savings rate and labor productivity. Like all Confucian societies, the Japanese value education, so the labor force is highly skilled.

Other observers provide more practical reasons for Japan's striking success in the postwar era. Paradoxically, Japan benefited from the total destruction of its industrial base during World War and did not have to contend with antiquated plants that held back industrial development in the United States. Secure under U.S. protection, Japan's defense spending is also much lower than that of the United States. In addition, the Japanese government has actively sought to promote the nation's business interests through

the Ministry of International Trade and Industry, thus gaining advantages in competition with more laissez-faire economies.

Whatever the case, the Japanese "economic miracle" has recently been shaken by the long recession, and there are indications of a growing tendency toward hedonism and individualism among Japanese youth. Older Japanese frequently complain that the younger generation lacks their sense of community and willingness to sacrifice. There are also signs that the concept of loyalty to one's employer may be beginning to erode among Japanese youth. Some observers have predicted that with increasing affluence Japan will become more like the industrialized societies in the West. Although Japan is unlikely to evolve into a photocopy of the United States or Western Europe, the vaunted image of millions of dedicated "salarymen" heading off to work with their briefcases and their pinstriped suits may no longer be an accurate portrayal of reality in contemporary Japan.

30-4 THE LITTLE TIGERS

Q **Focus Question:** What factors have contributed to the economic success achieved by the Little Tigers in the years following the end of World War II?

The success of postwar Japan in meeting the challenge from the capitalist West soon caught the eye of other Asian nations. By the 1980s, several smaller states in the region—known collectively as the "Little Tigers"—had successively followed the Japanese example.

30-4a Korea: A Peninsula Divided

In 1953, the Korean people were exhausted from three years of bitter fraternal war, a conflict that devastated the economy of the peninsula and took the lives of an estimated 4 million Koreans on both sides of the 38th parallel. North of the truce line was the People's Republic of Korea (PRK), a police state under the dictatorial rule of the Communist leader Kim Il-Sung (KIM ILL SOONG) (1912–1994). To the south was the Republic of Korea (ROK), under the equally autocratic President Syngman Rhee (SING-muhn REE) (1875–1965), a fierce anti-Communist who had led the resistance to the

Map 30.4 The Korean Peninsula since 1953

northern invasion. Dramatic changes have taken place in the past half century, however, and today the ROK is a predominantly democratic society with an advanced industrial economy generally viewed as one of the most competitive in the world. The PRK, however, has been stuck in a time warp, and under its current ruler, Kim Il-Sung's grandson Kim Jong Un (b. 1984), remains one of the most closed societies on Earth.

What had happened to transform an impoverished country into a second "economic miracle" comparable to Japan? In part, the country benefited from a strong government dedicated to achieving rapid economic growth based on the export of consumer goods and electronics. As in Japan, large government-supported corporations known as *chaebol* (jay-BOHL) were the bedrock of economic growth. Another key to success was the country's reliance on Confucian principles of hard work, thrift, and respect for education.

South Korea's rapid transformation has been accompanied by several social problems as traditional and modern values come into conflict. Moreover, like many other countries in the region, the ROK was slow to develop stable democratic institutions. But after three decades of sometimes oppressive military rule, a vigorous multiparty system has gradually emerged, and in 2012 the country elected its first woman president. Relations with the communist regime in the North, however, remain tense, as the communist leadership in that impoverished country continues to view the outside world with suspicion. A program run by the North Korean regime to develop an intercontinental ballistic missile system with nuclear warheads, have led to increased tensions in the region and in June 2018 a bilateral meeting between Kim and U.S. president Donald Trump was held in Singapore in a bid to defuse the issue.

30-4b Taiwan: The Other China

Although it had been defeated in the civil war with the Communists, the Republic of China (ROC), now on Taiwan, contended that it remained the legitimate representative of the Chinese people and would eventually return in triumph to the mainland. Bolstered by a 1954 security treaty with the United States, it now sought to place its main focus on nation building. Manufacturing

Map 30.5 Modern Taiwan

Map 30.6 The Republic of Singapore

and commerce were encouraged, and a land reform program brought an end to rural poverty. In contrast to its mainland rival, respect for Chinese tradition was actively preserved. Within a generation, the standard of living had increased substantially and, especially after the death of Chiang Kai-shek in 1975, a more pluralistic form of government began to emerge. (See Map 30.5.)

But political liberalization had its dangers. For example, when the Democratic Progressive Party (DPP), an organization based primarily on support from indigenous Taiwanese, won national elections in 2000, the new government threatened to declare an independent Republic of Taiwan. The possibility of such a development angered the government in Beijing, which continues to affirm its intention to reunite the island with the mainland. The return to power of the Guomindang Party in 2008 eased relations with the PRC, but when the DPP returned to office under Tsai Ing-wen, the country's first woman president, tensions increased once again. Although economic and cultural relations between Taiwan and the mainland have been steadily increasing in recent years, reunification seems as distant as ever.

30-4c Singapore and Hong Kong: The Littlest Tigers

The smallest but by no means the least successful of the Little Tigers are Singapore and Hong Kong. Both contain large populations densely packed into small territories. Singapore, once a British colony and briefly a part of the state of Malaysia, is now an independent nation (see Map 30.6). Hong Kong was a British colony until it was returned to PRC control in 1997 (see Map 30.7). In recent years, both have emerged as industrial powerhouses, with standards of living well above those of their neighbors.

The success of Singapore must be ascribed in good measure to the will and energy of its political leaders. Under the first prime minister, Lee Kuan-yew (LEE kwahn-YOO) (1923–2015), the government cultivated an attractive business climate while engaging in public works projects to feed, house, and educate its 2 million citizens. Making good use of its strategic position in the area, the city-state has relied on shipbuilding, oil refineries, tourism, electronics, and finance to become the economic hub of the entire region.

As in the other Little Tigers, an authoritarian political system initially provided a stable environment for economic growth. Until his retirement in 1990, Lee Kuan-yew and his People's Action Party dominated Singapore politics, and opposition elements were intimidated into silence or arrested. The prime minister openly declared that the Western model of pluralist democracy was not appropriate for Singapore. Confucian values of thrift, hard work, and obedience to authority were promoted as the ideology of the state. (See Image 30.8.)

But economic success has begun to undermine the authoritarian foundations of the system, as today a more

Map 30.7 Hong Kong

sophisticated citizenry voices aspirations for more political freedoms and an end to government paternalism. In 2004, Lee Hsienluong (lee she-ENN-lahng) (b. 1952), the son of Lee Kuan-yew, became prime minister. Under his leadership, the government has relaxed its restrictions on freedom of speech and assembly, and elections held in 2011 resulted in growing support for members of opposition parties.

The future of Hong Kong is not so clear-cut. As in Singapore, sensible government policies and the hard work of its people have enabled Hong Kong to thrive. At first, the prosperity of the colony depended on a plentiful supply of cheap labor. Inundated with refugees from the mainland during the 1950s and 1960s, the population of Hong Kong burgeoned to more than 6 million. More recently, Hong Kong has benefited from increased tourism, manufacturing, and the growing economic prosperity

Source: Photograph by William J. Duiker.

30.8 Singapore: Asia's City of the Future. Since achieving its independence in 1965, the city-state of Singapore has emerged as one of the modern and efficiently run cities in Southeast Asia, if not the world. A recent symbol of this achievement is located on recently reclaimed land in the harbor, where eighteen so-called supertrees have been constructed in a public park adjacent to downtown skyscrapers. Built of concrete and steel, with wire rods for branches, these artificial trees rise up as much as 50 meters in height and are festooned with more than 160,000 tropical plants divided among 200 species. Fed by numerous solar panels and rainwater catches, these hanging gardens offer a look at the future as human communities seek to find ever more innovative ways to feed their growing populations.

CHRONOLOGY	Japan and the Little Tigers Since World War II	
End of World War II in the Pacific	1945	
Chiang Kai-shek retreats to Taiwan	1949	
End of U.S. occupation of Japan	1951	
Korean War	1950–1953	
U.S.–ROC security treaty	1954	
Syngman Rhee overthrown in South Korea	1960	
Rise to power of Park Chung-hee in South Korea	1961	
Independence of Singapore	1965	
Death of Chiang Kai-shek	1975	
Park Chung-hee assassinated	1979	
Student riots in South Korea	1987	
Lee Kuan-yew era ends in Singapore	1990	
First free general elections on Taiwan	1992	
Return of Hong Kong to Chinese control	1997	
Financial crisis hits region	1997	
Chen Shuibian elected president of Taiwan	2000	
Junichiro Koizumi prime minister of Japan	2001–2006	
Nationalist Party returns to power in Taiwan	2007	
Earthquake and tsunami in Japan	2011	
Tsai In-wen becomes first woman president of Taiwan	2016	
Impeachment of Prime Minister Park Guen-hye in Korea	2016	

of neighboring Guangdong Province, the most prosperous region of the PRC. Unlike the other societies discussed in this chapter, Hong Kong has relied on an unbridled free-market system rather than active state intervention in the economy. At the same time, by allocating substantial funds for transportation, sanitation, education, and public housing, the government has created favorable conditions for economic development.

When Britain's ninety-nine-year lease on the New Territories, the food basket of the colony, expired on July 1, 1997, Hong Kong returned to mainland authority (see Historical Voices, "Return to the Motherland," p. 790).

Although the Chinese promised the British that the people of Hong Kong would live under a capitalist system and be essentially self-governing for fifty years, recent actions and statements by Chinese leaders have raised questions among local residents about the degree of autonomy Hong Kong will continue to have under Chinese rule. Popular protests launched against threats to local autonomy have placed Beijing in an awkward situation as it proclaims the concept of "one government, two systems" as a solution to the dispute with the government on Taiwan.

HISTORIANS DEBATE 30-4d **The East Asian Miracle: Fact or Myth?**

What explains the striking ability of Japan and the four Little Tigers to transform themselves into export-oriented societies capable of competing with the advanced nations of Europe and the Western Hemisphere? Some analysts point to the traditional character traits of Confucian societies such as thrift, a work ethic, respect for education, and obedience to authority. In a recent poll of Asian executives, more than 80 percent expressed the belief that Asian values differ from those of the West, and most felt that such values have contributed significantly to the region's recent success. Other observers place more emphasis on deliberate steps taken by government and economic leaders to meet the political, economic, and social challenges their societies face.

There seems no reason to doubt that cultural factors connected to East Asian social traditions have contributed to the economic success of these societies. Certainly, habits such as frugality, industriousness, and subordination of individual desires have all played a role in their governments' ability to concentrate on the collective interest. As this and preceding chapters have shown, however, without active encouragement by political elites, such traditions cannot be effectively harnessed for the good of society as a whole. The creative talents of the Chinese people, for example, were not efficiently used under Mao Zedong during the frenetic years of the Cultural Revolution. Only when pragmatists like Deng Xiaoping took charge and began to place a high priority on economic development were the stunning advances of recent decades achieved. By the same token, political elites elsewhere in East Asia were aware of traditional values and were willing to use them for national purposes. In effect, the rapid rise of East Asia in the postwar era was no miracle, but a fortuitous combination of favorable cultural factors and deliberate human action.

HISTORICAL VOICES

Return to the Motherland

Politics & Government

AFTER LENGTHY NEGOTIATIONS, in 1984 China and Great Britain agreed that Hong Kong would return to Chinese sovereignty on July 1, 1997. Key sections of the agreement are included here. In succeeding years, authorities of the two countries held further negotiations. Some of the discussions raised questions in the minds of Hong Kong residents as to whether their individual liberties would indeed be respected after the colony's return to China.

The Joint Declaration on Hong Kong

The Hong Kong Special Administrative Region will be directly under the authority of the Central People's Government of the People's Republic of China. The Hong Kong Special Administrative Region will enjoy a high degree of autonomy, except in foreign and defense affairs, which are the responsibility of the Central People's Government.

The Hong Kong Special Administrative Region will be vested with executive, legislative, and independent judicial power, including that of final adjudication. The laws currently in force in Hong Kong will remain basically unchanged.

Source: From Kevin Rafferty, *City on the Rocks* (New York: Penguin, 1991).

The Government of the Hong Kong Special Administrative Region will be composed of local inhabitants. The chief executive will be appointed by the Central People's Government on the basis of the results of elections or consultations by the chief executive of the Hong Kong Special Administrative Region for appointment by the Central People's Government. . . .

The current social and economic systems in Hong Kong will remain unchanged, and so will the lifestyle. Rights and freedoms, including those of the person, of speech, of the press, of assembly, of association, of travel, of movement, of correspondence, of strike, of choice of occupation, of academic research, and of religious belief will be ensured by law. . . . Private property, ownership of enterprises, legitimate right of inheritance, and foreign investment will be protected by law.

Q *To what degree are the people of Hong Kong self-governing under these regulations? How do the regulations infringe on the freedom of the population?*

CHAPTER SUMMARY

In the years following the end of World War II, the peoples of Asia emerged from a century of imperial rule to face the challenge of building stable and prosperous independent states. Initially, progress was slow as new political leaders were forced to deal with the legacy of colonialism, external interference, and internal disagreements over their visions for the future. By the end of the century, however, most nations in the area were beginning to lay the foundations for the creation of advanced industrial societies. Today, major Asian states such as China, Japan, and India have become serious competitors of the advanced Western nations in the international marketplace.

To some observers, these economic achievements have sometimes come at a high price in the form of political authoritarianism and a lack of attention to human rights. Rapid economic development has also exacted an environmental cost. Industrial pollution in China and India and the destruction of forest cover in Southeast Asia increasingly threaten the fragile ecosystem and create friction among

nations in the region. Unless these countries cooperate effectively to deal with these environmental challenges in future years, these problems will ultimately undermine the dramatic economic and social progress that has taken place.

Still, a look at the historical record suggests that, for the most part, the nations of southern and eastern Asia have made dramatic progress in coping with the multiple challenges of independence. Political pluralism is often a by-product of economic growth, while a rising standard of living should enable the peoples of the region to meet the social and environmental challenges that lie ahead.

REFLECTION QUESTIONS

Q What kinds of environmental problems are currently being faced by the nations of southern and eastern Asia? How have the region's political leaders sought to deal with the problems?

Q How has independence affected the role of women in southern and eastern Asia? How does the position of women in the region compare with that of their counterparts elsewhere?

Q How have the nations in the region dealt with the challenge of integrating their ethnic and religious minorities into their political systems?

CHAPTER TIMELINE

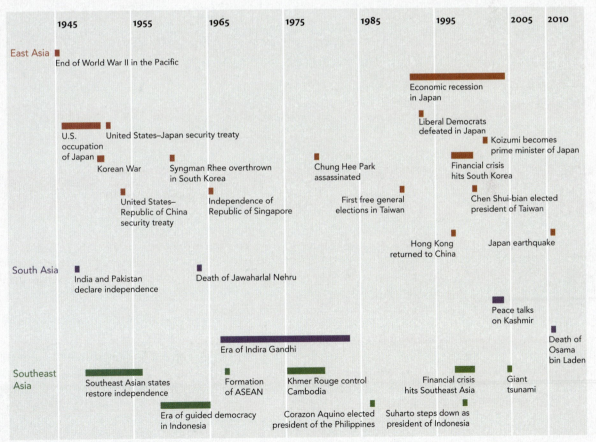

CHAPTER NOTES

1. *New York Times*, May 2, 1996.
2. Quoted in L. Collins and D. Lapierre, *Freedom at Midnight* (New York, 1975), p. 252.
3. Quoted in S. Sengupta, "In World's Largest Democracy, Tolerance Is a Weak Pillar," *New York Times*, October 29, 2008.
4. Y. Mishima and G. Bownas, eds., *New Writing in Japan* (Harmondsworth, England, 1972), p. 16.

MINDTAP
From Cengage

MindTap® is a fully online, highly personalized learning experience built upon Cengage Learning content. MindTap combines student learning tools—readings, multimedia, activities, and assessments—into a singular Learning Path that guides students through the course and helps students develop the critical thinking, analysis, and communication skills that are essential to academic and professional success.

ON A VISIT TO NUREMBERG, Germany, with his family in 2000, Jackson Spielvogel, one of the authors of this textbook, was startled to find that the main railroad station where he had once arrived as a Fulbright student was now adorned with McDonald's Golden Arches. McDonald's was the brainstorm of two brothers who opened a cheap burger restaurant in California in 1940. When they expanded their operations to Arizona, they began to use two yellow arches to make their building visible from blocks away. After Ray Kroc, an enterprising businessman, bought the burgeoning business, McDonald's arches rapidly spread all over the United States. And they didn't stop there. The fast-food industry, which now relied on computers for the automated processing of its food, found an international market. McDonald's spread to Japan in 1971 and to Russia and China in 1990; by 1995, more than half of all McDonald's restaurants were located outside the United States. By 2000, McDonald's was serving 50 million people a day.

E.1 Starbucks in China. Starbucks is an American coffee company founded in Seattle, Washington, in 1971. Starbucks now operates over 24,000 locations in over 72 countries worldwide. The highest number of Starbucks locations—more than 13,000—are found in the United States, and the second highest number—more than 3,000—are found in China. The image above shows two Starbucks patrons drinking coffee outside a Starbucks coffee shop in Tianjin, China.

McDonald's is but one of numerous U.S. companies that use the latest technology and actively seek global markets. Indeed, sociologists have coined the term *McDonaldization* to refer to "the process whereby the principles of the fast-food restaurant are coming to dominate more and more sectors of American society as well as the rest of the world."[1] Multinational corporations like McDonald's have brought about a worldwide homogenization of societies and made us aware of the political, economic, and social interdependence of the world's nations and the global nature of our contemporary problems. An important part of this global awareness is the technological dimension. New technology has made possible levels of world communication that simply did not exist before. At the same time that Osama bin Laden and al-Qaeda were denouncing the forces of modernization, they were spreading their message through the use of recently developed telecommunication systems. The Technological Revolution has tied peoples and nations closely together and contributed to **globalization,** the term that is frequently used to describe the process by which peoples and nations have become more interdependent.

Of course, as we have seen in world history, globalization is a process that is centuries old. Ever since *Homo sapiens sapiens* moved out of Africa and gradually populated the world, globalization has been occurring. During the Middle Ages, the Mongol conquests inaugurated what one scholar has called the "idea of the unified conceptualization of the globe," creating a "basic information circuit" that spread commodities, ideas, and inventions from one end of the Eurasian supercontinent to the other. Between 1500 and 1815, a maritime trade network extended throughout the entire populated world. And after 1815, the spread of Western imperialism to most parts of the world led to the domination of subject peoples, but it also tied the peoples of the world together in new ways. Aided by the technological advances of the twentieth and twenty-first centuries, globalization is now proceeding at an accelerated pace.

793

E-1 THE GLOBAL ECONOMY

Especially since the 1970s, the world has developed a **global economy** in which the production, distribution, and sale of goods are accomplished on a worldwide scale. Several international institutions have contributed to the rise of the global economy. Soon after the end of World War II, the United States and other nations established the World Bank and the International Monetary Fund (IMF) as a means of expanding global markets and avoiding economic crises such as the Great Depression of the 1930s. The World Bank comprises five international organizations, largely controlled by developed countries, which provide grants, loans, and advice for economic development to developing countries. The IMF oversees the global financial system by supervising exchange rates and offering financial and technical assistance to developing nations. Today, 189 countries are members of the IMF. Critics have argued, however, that both the World Bank and the IMF sometimes push non-Western nations to adopt inappropriate Western economic practices that only aggravate the poverty and debt of developing nations.

Another reflection of the new global economic order is the **multinational** or **transnational corporation** (a company that has divisions in more than two countries). Prominent examples of multinational corporations include General Electric, Apple, ExxonMobil, Samsung, and Sony. These companies are among the two hundred largest multinational corporations, which are responsible for more than half of the world's industrial production. In 2000, some 71 percent of these corporations were headquartered in just three countries—the United States, Japan, and Germany. Changes in telecommunications and distribution have made it easier for corporations to be multinational. In addition, the electronics products so much in demand today, such as iPads, digital cameras, and computers, are much lighter and easier to transport than the steel, coal, and other heavy goods in earlier centuries. These supercorporations have come to dominate much of the world's investment capital, technology, and markets. A recent comparison of corporate sales and national gross domestic product revealed that only forty-nine of the world's hundred largest economic entities are nations; the remaining fifty-one are corporations. For this reason, some observers believe that economic globalization is more appropriately labeled "corporate globalization."

Another important component of economic globalization is free trade. In 1947, talks led to the creation of the General Agreement on Tariffs and Trade (GATT), a global trade organization that was replaced in 1995 by the World Trade Organization (WTO). Made up of 164 member nations, the WTO arranges trade agreements and settles trade disputes. The WTO's goal is to open up world markets and maximize global production, but many critics charge that the WTO has ignored environmental and health concerns, enabling multinational corporations to enter countries with minimal human rights or environmental standards. Free-market practices have harmed small and developing countries, and created an ever-growing gap between rich and poor nations.

The relaxation of trade barriers created a boom in international trade in the last quarter of the twentieth century. In 1973, international trade was valued at $1.7 trillion; by 2015, it had increased to $16 trillion. At the same time, international financial transactions involving such instruments as bonds and equities were becoming an increasingly important component of the global economy. The value of transactions involving financial instruments rose to fifty times the value of world trade in goods. The global economy had entered a new era of finance, in which profits from financial transactions outpaced profits from manufactured goods, leading to catastrophic consequences in 2008.

E-1a The End of Excess

Since the 1970s, the production, distribution, and sale of goods has been happening on a global scale. At the same time, international financial transactions involving financial instruments such as bonds and equities were becoming an increasingly important component of the globalized economy. Many consumers in Europe and the United States took part in the growing financialization of the economy—relaxation of mortgage lending led to a rapid housing boom in the early 2000s. Since 1945, housing prices had kept pace with the overall rate of inflation. In 1997, however, home prices began a sharp increase, and by 2007 home prices had increased by more than 45 percent after adjusting for inflation. At its peak in 2006, the wealth created by the housing bubble generated more than $1 trillion in annual demand. Investment banks capitalized on the housing boom by selling collateralized debt obligations (CDOs), financial investments based on bundles of mortgages. Banks in New York sold these CDOs to banks in Europe and elsewhere, spreading the wealth and risk of investment. Many of the mortgages used as investments had been subprime—issued to borrowers with low credit ratings and a high likelihood of default. Beginning in 2006, as the low introductory rates on these subprime mortgages expired, default rates increased.

The global economy experienced worldwide financial troubles beginning in 2007, following the collapse of the U.S. housing market. By September 2008, a number of large financial institutions, including insurance and mortgage companies, investment firms, and banks, were approaching or had fallen into bankruptcy. The rapid collapse of financial investments and falling housing prices caused a precipitous decline in the U.S. stock market as stocks lost almost $8 trillion in value from mid-September to November 2008.

Ultimately, the crash of the U.S. housing market led to a worldwide recession. As the American economy slowed, trade decreased worldwide. Production in Asia also decreased, and prices of commodities fell, including the price of oil, which had an impact on Middle Eastern countries and on Russia. The collapse of the global economy exposed the weak balance sheets of Europe's smaller countries—Greece, Ireland, and Portugal faced International Monetary Fund (IMF) bailouts—while larger nations struggled to recapitalize by cutting social services. In the United States, a stimulus and successful passage of health care reform led to a recovery of the U.S. economy, with unemployment at 4.7 percent by 2016. Despite the economic recovery, stagnant wages, high health care expenses, and higher education costs have contributed to growing economic inequality.

E-2 GLOBAL CULTURE AND THE DIGITAL AGE

Since the invention of the microprocessor in 1971, the capabilities of computers have expanded by leaps and bounds, resulting in today's digital age. Beginning in the 1980s, companies like Apple and Microsoft competed to create more powerful computers and software. By the 1990s, the booming technology industry had made Microsoft founder Bill Gates the richest man in the world. Much of this success was due to several innovations that made computers indispensable for communication, information, and entertainment.

E-2a Global Communication

The advent of electronic mail, or e-mail, transformed communication in the mid-1990s. At the same time, the Internet, especially its World Wide Web, was becoming an information exchange for people around the world. As web capabilities have increased, new forms of communication have emerged. These include Twitter, a communications platform that allows people to send instant updates from their cellphones to their friends; Facebook and Snapchat, social networking sites; and YouTube, an Internet site now used for international news broadcasts.

Advances in telecommunications led first to cellular or mobile phones and later to smartphones. Though cellular phones existed in the 1970s and 1980s, it was not until the 1990s, when their digital components were reduced in size,

that these devices became truly portable. The ubiquity of cellphones and their ability to transfer data electronically have made text messaging a global form of communication. Text and instant messaging have revolutionized written language, as shorthand script has replaced complete sentences for relaying brief messages. Worldwide, the number of people with access to a mobile phone increased from 12.4 million in 1990 to almost 6 billion in 2013.

A number of the innovations that have enhanced consumers' ability to share music, watch movies, and search the web were introduced by Apple, Inc., and later imitated by other companies. The iPod, a portable digital music player, has revolutionized the music industry, as downloading music electronically from the Internet has largely replaced the purchasing of physical recordings. The iPhone enables users to connect to the Internet from their phone, allowing information to be instantly updated for various telecommunication sites, such as Twitter and Facebook. The iPad, a handheld tablet computer, is challenging computer sales worldwide, as almost 7.5 million iPads were sold in the first six months.

These developments in communications are also affecting current events. The ubiquitous nature of smartphones allows people to utilize social networking sites for mass protests, as demonstrated in Egypt in 2011 and in the United States in 2017.

E-2b Reality in the Digital Age

Advances in communication and information during the digital age have led many people to suggest that world cultures are becoming increasingly interdependent and homogenized. Many contemporary artists have questioned the effects of the computer age on identity and material reality. According to some, the era of virtual reality has displaced cultural uniqueness and bodily presence.

The Body and Identity in Contemporary Art   By focusing on bodily experience and cultural norms, contemporary artists have attempted to restore what has been lost in the digital age. Kiki Smith (b. 1954), an American artist born in Germany, creates sculptures of the human body that often focus on anatomical processes. These works, commonly made of wax or plaster, question the politics surrounding the body, including AIDS and domestic abuse, while reconnecting to bodily experiences.

Contemporary artists also continue to explore the interaction between the Western and non-Western world, particularly the **multiculturalism** generated by global migrations. For example, the art of Yinka Shonibare (YEEN-kuh SHOH-nih-bar-eh) (b. 1962), who was born in London, raised in Nigeria, and now resides in England, investigates the notion of hybrid identity as he creates clothing and life-size figures that fuse European designs with African traditions.

E-3 GLOBALIZATION AND THE ENVIRONMENTAL CRISIS

As many people take a global perspective in the twenty-first century, they are realizing that everywhere on the planet, human beings are interdependent in terms of the air they breathe, the water they drink, the food they consume, and the climate that affects their lives. At the same time, however, human activities are creating environmental challenges that threaten the very foundation of human existence on earth.

One problem is population growth. As of April 2017, the world population was estimated at more than 7.5 billion people. At its current rate of growth, one birth every eight seconds, the world population could reach 12.8 billion by 2050, according to the United Nations' long-range population projections. The result has been an increased demand for food and other resources that has put great pressure on the earth's ecosystems. At the same time, the failure to grow enough food for more and more people, a problem exacerbated by drought conditions developing on several continents, has created a severe problem, as an estimated 1 billion people worldwide today suffer from hunger. Every year, more than 8 million people die of hunger, many of them young children.

Another problem is the pattern of consumption as the wealthy nations of the Northern Hemisphere consume vast quantities of the planet's natural resources. The United States, for example, which has 6 percent of the world's people, consumes 30 to 40 percent of its resources. The spread of these consumption patterns to other parts of the world raises serious questions about the ability of the planet to sustain itself and its population. As a result of the growing Chinese economy, for example, more automobiles are now sold annually in China than in the United States.

Yet another threat to the environment is **global climate change**, which has the potential to create a worldwide crisis. Virtually all of the world's scientists agree that the **greenhouse effect**, the warming of the earth because of the buildup of carbon dioxide in the atmosphere, is contributing to devastating droughts and storms, the melting of the polar ice caps, and rising sea levels that could inundate coastal regions in the second half of the twenty-first century. Most of the warming of the planet has occurred in the past 35 years, with 16 of the 17 warmest years on record occurring since 2001. 2016 was the hottest year on record

since modern recordkeeping began in 1880. Also alarming is the potential loss of biodiversity. Seven out of ten biologists believe the planet is now experiencing alarming extinction rates among both plant and animal species.

E-3a The Social Challenges of Globalization

Since 1945, tens of millions of people have migrated from one part of the world to another. These migrations have occurred for many reasons. Persecution for political reasons caused many people from Pakistan, Bangladesh, Sri Lanka, and eastern Europe to seek refuge in western European countries, while brutal civil wars in Asia, Africa, the Middle East, and Europe led millions of refugees to seek safety in neighboring countries. Most people who have migrated, however, have done so to find jobs. Latin Americans seeking a better life have migrated to the United States, while guest workers from Turkey, southern and eastern Europe, North Africa, India, and Pakistan have migrated to more prosperous western European countries. In 2013, nearly 230 million people, about 3.2 percent of the world's population, lived outside the country where they were born.

The migration of millions of people has also provoked a social backlash in many countries. Foreign workers often become scapegoats when countries face economic problems. Political parties in France and Norway, for example, have called for the removal of blacks, Muslims, and Arabs in order to protect the ethnic or cultural purity of their nations, while in Asian countries, there is animosity against other Asian ethnic groups. The problem of foreigners has also led to a more general attack on globalization itself as being responsible for a host of social ills that are undermining national sovereignty.

Another challenge of globalization is the wide gap between rich and poor nations. The rich nations, or **developed nations,** are located mainly in the Northern Hemisphere. They include the United States, Canada, Germany, and Japan, which have well-organized industrial and agricultural systems, advanced technologies, and effective educational systems. The poor nations, or **developing nations,** include many nations in Africa, Asia, and Latin America, which often have primarily agricultural economies with little technology. A serious problem in many developing nations is explosive population growth, which has led to severe food shortages often caused by poor soil but also by economic factors. Growing crops for export to developed countries, for example, may lead to enormous profits for large landowners but leaves many small farmers with little land on which to grow food.

Civil wars have also created food shortages. Not only does war disrupt normal farming operations, but warring groups try to limit access to food to weaken or kill their enemies. In Sudan, 1.3 million people starved when combatants of a civil war in the 1980s prevented food from reaching them. As unrest continued during the early 2000s in Sudan's Darfur region, families were forced to leave their farms. As a result, an estimated seventy thousand people had starved by mid-2004. In 2006, Syria faced its worst drought in over 900 years; millions moved into the cities in search of food and work. The cities were already overcrowded with Iraqi refugees who had fled the American-led invasion in 2003. The civil unrest that ensued has led to mass casualties, generated over 5 million refugees, and displaced more than 7 million others in search of food and safety.

E-3b Global Movements and New Hopes

As people have become aware that the problems humans face are not just national or regional but global in scope, they have responded to this challenge in different ways. One approach has been to develop grassroots social movements, including ones devoted to environmental concerns, women's and men's liberation, human potential, appropriate technology, and nonviolence. "Think globally, act locally" is frequently the slogan of these grassroots groups. Related to the emergence of these social movements is the growth of **nongovernmental organizations (NGOs).** According to one analyst, NGOs are an important instrument in the cultivation of global perspectives: "Since NGOs by definition are identified with interests that transcend national boundaries, we expect all NGOs to define problems in global terms, to take account of human interests and needs as they are found in all parts of the planet."[2] NGOs are often represented at the United Nations and include professional, business, and cooperative organizations; foundations; religious, peace, and disarmament groups; youth and women's organizations; environmental and human rights groups; and research institutes. The number of international NGOs increased from 176 in 1910 to 1 million in 2017.

And yet hopes for global approaches to global problems have also been hindered by political, ethnic, and religious differences. Pollution of the Rhine River by factories along its banks provokes angry disputes among European nations, and the United States and Canada have argued about the effects of acid rain on Canadian forests. While droughts in Russia and China wreak havoc on the world's grain supply, floods in Pakistan challenge the stability of Asia. The collapse of the Soviet Union and its satellite system seemed to offer hope for more international cooperation on global issues, but it has had almost the opposite effect. The bloody conflict in the former Yugoslavia indicates the dangers inherent in the rise of nationalist sentiment among various ethnic and religious groups in eastern Europe. At the same time, religious conflict continues to plague the Middle East, threatening to destabilize the entire region. The widening gap between wealthy nations and poor, developing nations threatens global economic stability. Many conflicts begin with regional issues and then develop into international concerns. International terrorist groups seek to wreak havoc around the world.

Thus, even as the world becomes more global in culture and interdependent in its mutual relations, centrifugal forces are still at work attempting to redefine the political, cultural, and ethnic ways in which the world is divided. Such efforts are often disruptive and can sometimes work against measures to enhance our human destiny. But they also represent an integral part of human character and human history and cannot be suppressed in the relentless drive to create a world society.

There are already initial signs that as the common dangers posed by environmental damage, overpopulation, and scarcity of resources become even more apparent, societies around the world might find ample reason to turn their attention from cultural differences to the demands of global interdependence. The greatest challenge of the twenty-first century may be to reconcile the drive for individual and group identity with the common needs of the human community.

CHAPTER NOTES

1. Quoted in J. N. Pieterse, *Globalization and Culture* (Lanham, Md., 2004), p. 49.
2. E. Boulding, *Women in the Twentieth Century World* (New York, 1977), pp. 187–188.

MINDTAP From Cengage

MindTap® is a fully online, highly personalized learning experience built upon Cengage Learning content. MindTap combines student learning tools—readings, multimedia, activities, and assessments—into a singular Learning Path that guides students through the course and helps students develop the critical thinking, analysis, and communication skills that are essential to academic and professional success.

GLOSSARY

abbess the head of a convent or monastery for women.

abbot the head of a monastery.

absolutism a form of government where the sovereign power or ultimate authority rested in the hands of a monarch who claimed to rule by divine right and was therefore responsible only to God.

Abstract Expressionism a post–World War II artistic movement that broke with all conventions of form and structure in favor of total abstraction.

abstract painting an artistic movement that developed early in the twentieth century in which artists focused on color to avoid any references to visual reality.

African Union the organization that replaced the Organization of African Unity in 2001; designed to bring about increased political and economic integration of African states.

Amerindians earliest inhabitants of North and South America. Original theories suggested migration from Siberia across the Bering Land Bridge; more recent evidence suggests migration also occurred by sea from regions of the South Pacific to South America.

apartheid the system of racial segregation practiced in the Republic of South Africa until the 1990s, which involved political, legal, and economic discrimination against nonwhites.

aristocracy a class of hereditary nobility in medieval Europe; a warrior class who shared a distinctive lifestyle based on the institution of knighthood, although there were social divisions within the group based on extremes of wealth.

ASEAN the Association of Southeast Asian Nations, formed in 1967 to promote the prosperity and political stability of its member nations. Currently, Brunei, Cambodia, Indonesia, Laos, Malaysia, Myanmar, the Philippines, Singapore, Thailand, and Vietnam are members. Other countries in the region participate as "observer" members.

assimilation the concept, originating in France, that the colonial peoples should be assimilated into the parent French culture.

association the concept developed by French colonial officials that colonial peoples should be permitted to retain their precolonial cultural traditions.

Atman in Brahmanism, the individual soul.

Ausgleich the "Compromise" of 1867 that created the dual monarchy of Austria-Hungary. Austria and Hungary each had its own capital, constitution, and legislative assembly, but were united under one monarch.

bakufu the centralized government set up in Japan in the twelfth century. *See also* shogunate system.

banners originally established in 1639 by the Qing Dynasty, the eight banners were administrative divisions into which all Manchu families were placed. Banners quickly evolved into the basis of Manchu military organization, with each required to raise and support a prescribed number of troops.

bard in Africa, a professional storyteller.

Baroque a style that dominated Western painting, sculpture, architecture, and music from about 1580 to 1730, generally characterized by elaborate ornamentation and dramatic effects. Important practitioners included Bernini, Rubens, Handel, and Bach.

Bedouins nomadic tribes originally from northern Arabia, who became important traders after the domestication of the camel during the first millennium B.C.E. Early converts to Islam, their values and practices deeply affected the religion of Islam.

Berbers an ethnic group indigenous to western North Africa.

bey a provincial governor in the Ottoman Empire.

bhakti in Hinduism, devotion as a means of religious observance open to all persons regardless of class.

Black Death the outbreak of plague (mostly bubonic) in the mid-fourteenth century that killed from 25 to 50 percent of Europe's population.

blitzkrieg "lightning war." A war conducted with great speed and force, as in Germany's advance at the beginning of World War II.

bodhi wisdom in India. Sometimes described as complete awareness of the true nature of the universe.

bodhisattvas in some schools of Buddhism, individuals who have achieved enlightenment but, because of their great compassion, have chosen to renounce Nirvana and to remain on earth in spirit form to help all human beings achieve release from reincarnation.

Boers the Afrikaans-speaking descendants of Dutch settlers in southern Africa who left the Cape Colony in the nineteenth century to settle in the Orange Free State and Transvaal; defeated by the British in the Boer War (1899–1902) and ultimately incorporated into the Union of South Africa.

bonsai the cultivation of stunted trees and shrubs to create exquisite nature scenes in miniature; originated in China in the first millenium B.C.E. and imported to Japan between 700 and 900 C.E.

Brahman the Hindu word roughly equivalent to God; the Divine basis of all being; regarded as the source and sum of the cosmos.

Brahmanism the early religious beliefs of the Aryan people in India, which eventually gave rise to Hinduism.

brahmin a member of the Hindu priestly caste or class; literally "one who has realized or attempts to realize Brahman." Traditionally, duties of a *brahmin* include studying Hindu religious scriptures and transmitting them to others orally. The priests of Hindu temples are *brahmin*.

Brezhnev Doctrine the doctrine, enunciated by Leonid Brezhnev, that the Soviet Union had a right to intervene if socialism was threatened in another socialist state; used to justify the use of Soviet troops in Czechoslovakia in 1968.

Buddhism a religion and philosophy based on the teachings of Siddhartha Gautama in about 500 B.C.E. Principally practiced in China, India, and other parts of Asia, Buddhism has 360 million followers and is considered a major world religion.

Burakumin a Japanese minority similar to *dalits* (untouchables) in Indian culture. Past and current discrimination has resulted in lower educational attainment and socioeconomic status for members of this group. Movements with objectives ranging from "liberation" to integration have tried over the years to change this situation.

Bushido the code of conduct observed by samurai warriors; comparable to the European concept of chivalry.

caliph the secular leader of the Islamic community.

calpulli in Aztec society, a kinship group, often of a thousand or more, which served as an intermediary with the central government, providing taxes and conscript labor to the state.

capitalism beginning in the Middle Ages, an economic system in which people invested in trade and goods in order to make profits.

caravels mobile sailing ships with both lateen and square sails that began to be constructed in Europe in the sixteenth century.

caste system a system of rigid social hierarchy in which all members of that society are assigned by birth to specific "ranks" and inherit specific roles and privileges.

Catholic Reformation a movement for the reform of the Catholic Church in the sixteenth century.

caudillos strong leaders in nineteenth-century Latin America who were usually supported by the landed elites and ruled chiefly by military force, though some were popular; they included both modernizers and destructive dictators.

centuriate assembly the chief popular assembly of the Roman republic. It passed laws and elected the chief magistrates.

chaebol a South Korean business structure similar to the Japanese *keiretsu*.

Chan a Chinese sect (Zen in Japanese) influenced by Daoist ideas that called for mind training and a strict regimen as a means of seeking enlightenment.

chinampas in Mesoamerica, artificial islands crisscrossed by canals that provided water for crops and easy transportation to local markets.

chonmin in Korea, the lowest class in society consisting of slaves and workers in certain undesirable occupations such as butchers; literally, "base people."

Christian (northern Renaissance) humanism an intellectual movement in northern Europe in the late fifteenth and early sixteenth centuries that combined the interest in the classics of the Italian Renaissance with an interest in the sources of early Christianity, including the New Testament and the writings of the church fathers.

chu nom an adaptation of Chinese written characters to provide a writing system for spoken Vietnamese; in use by the ninth century C.E.

civil disobedience the tactic of using illegal but nonviolent means of protest; designed by the Indian nationalist leader Mohandas Gandhi to resist British colonial rule.

civilization a complex culture in which large numbers of humans share a variety of common elements, including cities; religion; political, military, and social structures; material complexity; writing; and significant artistic and intellectual activity.

civil service examination an elaborate Chinese system of selecting bureaucrats on merit, first introduced in 165 C.E., developed by the Tang Dynasty in the seventh century C.E. and refined under the Song Dynasty; later adopted in Vietnam and with less success in Japan and Korea. It contributed to efficient government, upward mobility, and cultural uniformity.

class struggle the basis of the Marxist analysis of history, which says that the owners of the means of production have always oppressed the workers and predicts an inevitable revolution. See *also* Marxism.

Cold War the ideological conflict between the Soviet Union and the United States after World War II.

Columbian Exchange the exchange of animals, plants, and culture, but also communicable diseases and human populations including slaves, between the Western and Eastern Hemispheres that occurred after Columbus's voyages to the Americas.

common law law common to the entire kingdom of England; imposed by the king's courts beginning in the twelfth century to replace the customary law used in county and feudal courts, which varied from place to place.

communalism in South Asia, the tendency of people to band together in mutually antagonistic social subgroups; elsewhere used to describe unifying trends in the larger community.

Communist International (Comintern) a worldwide organization of Communist parties, founded by Lenin in 1919, dedicated to the advancement of world revolution; also known as the Third International.

Confucianism a system of thought based on the teachings of Confucius (551–479 B.C.E.) that developed into the ruling ideology of the Chinese state. See *also* Neo-Confucianism.

conquistadors "conquerors." Leaders in the Spanish conquests in the Americas, especially Mexico and Peru, in the sixteenth century.

conscription a military draft.

conservatism an ideology based on tradition and social stability that favored the maintenance of established institutions, organized religion, and obedience to authority and resisted change, especially abrupt change.

consuls the chief executive officers of the Roman republic. Two were chosen annually to administer the government and lead the army in battle.

consumer society a term applied to Western society after World War II as the working classes adopted the consumption patterns of the middle class and installment plans, credit cards, and easy credit made consumer goods such as appliances and automobiles widely available.

containment a policy adopted by the United States in the Cold War. It called for the use of any means, but hopefully short of all-out war, to limit Soviet expansion.

Continental system Napoleon's effort to bar British goods from the continent of Europe in the hope of weakening Britain's economy and destroying its capacity to wage war.

Contras in Nicaragua in the 1980s, an anti-Sandinista guerrilla movement supported by the U.S. Reagan administration.

Coptic a form of Christianity, originally Egyptian, that has thrived in Ethiopia since the fourth century C.E.

cottage industry a system of textile manufacturing in which spinners and weavers worked at home in their cottages using raw materials supplied to them by capitalist entrepreneurs.

council of the plebs in the Roman republic, a council only for the plebeians. After 287 B.C.E., its resolutions were binding on all Romans.

creoles in Latin America, American-born descendants of Europeans.

crusade in the Middle Ages, a military campaign in defense of Christendom.

Cubism an artistic style developed at the beginning of the twentieth century, especially by Pablo Picasso, that used geometric designs to re-create reality in the viewer's mind.

cuneiform "wedge-shaped." A system of writing developed by the Sumerians that consisted of wedge-shaped impressions made by a reed stylus on clay tablets.

Dadaism an artistic movement in the 1920s and 1930s by artists who were revolted by the senseless slaughter of World War I and used their "anti-art" to express contempt for the Western tradition.

daimyo prominent Japanese families who provided allegiance to the local shogun in exchange for protection; similar to vassals in Europe.

dalits commonly referred to as untouchables; the lowest level of Indian society, technically outside the caste system and considered less than human; named *harijans* ("children of God") by Gandhi, they remain the object of discrimination despite affirmative action programs.

Dao a Chinese philosophical concept, literally "the Way," central to both Confucianism and Daoism, that describes the behavior proper to each member of society; somewhat similar to the Indian concept of *dharma*.

Daoism a Chinese philosophy traditionally ascribed to the perhaps legendary Lao Tzu, which holds that acceptance and spontaneity are the keys to harmonious interaction with the universal order; an alternative to Confucianism.

decolonization the process of becoming free of colonial status and achieving statehood; occurred in most of the world's colonies between 1947 and 1962.

deficit spending the concept, developed by John Maynard Keynes in the 1930s, that in times of economic depression governments should stimulate demand by hiring people to do public works, such as building highways, even if this increases the public debt.

deism belief in God as the creator of the universe who, after setting it in motion, ceased to have any direct involvement in it and allowed it to run according to its own natural laws.

demesne the part of a manor retained under the direct control of the lord and worked by the serfs as part of their labor services.

denazification after World War II, the Allied policy of rooting out any traces of Nazism in German society by bringing prominent Nazis to trial for war crimes and purging any known Nazis from political office.

de-Stalinization the policy of denouncing and undoing the most repressive aspects of Stalin's regime; begun by Nikita Khrushchev in 1956.

détente the relaxation of tension between the Soviet Union and the United States that occurred in the 1970s.

developed nations a term used to refer to rich nations, primarily in the Northern Hemisphere, that have well-organized industrial and agricultural systems, advanced technologies, and effective educational systems.

developing nations a term used to refer to poor nations, mainly in the Southern Hemisphere, that have primarily agricultural economies with little technology and serious over-population problems.

devshirme in the Ottoman Empire, a system (literally, "collection") of training talented children to be administrators or members of the sultan's harem; originally meritocratic, by the seventeenth century, it degenerated into a hereditary caste.

dharma in Hinduism and Buddhism, the law that governs the universe, and specifically human behavior.

dictator in the Roman republic, an official granted unlimited power to run the state for a short period of time, usually six months, during an emergency.

diffusion hypothesis the hypothesis that the Yellow River Valley was the ancient heartland of Chinese civilization and that technological and cultural achievements radiated from there to other parts of East Asia. Recent discoveries of other early agricultural communities in China have led to some modification of the hypothesis to allow for other centers of civilization.

diocese the area under the jurisdiction of a Christian bishop; based originally on Roman administrative districts.

direct rule a concept devised by European colonial governments to rule their colonial subjects without the participation of local authorities. It was most often applied in colonial societies in Africa.

divine-right monarchy a monarchy based on the belief that monarchs receive their power directly from God and are responsible to no one except God.

dyarchy during the Qing Dynasty in China, a system in which all important national and provincial administrative positions were shared equally by Chinese and Manchus, which helped to consolidate both Manchu rule and their assimilation.

Einsatzgruppen in Nazi Germany, special strike forces in the SS that played an important role in rounding up and killing Jews.

El Niño periodic changes in water temperature at the surface of the Pacific Ocean, which can lead to major environmental changes and may have led to the collapse of the Moche civilization in what is now Peru.

emir "commander" in Arabic; a title used by Muslim rulers in southern Spain and elsewhere.

encomienda a grant from the Spanish monarch to colonial conquistadors.

encomienda system the system by which Spain first governed its American colonies. Holders of an *encomienda* were supposed to protect the Indians while using them as laborers and collecting tribute, but in practice they exploited them.

enlightened absolutism an absolute monarchy where the ruler follows the principles of the Enlightenment by introducing reforms for the improvement of society, allowing freedom of speech and the press, permitting religious toleration, expanding education, and ruling in accordance with the laws.

Enlightenment an eighteenth-century intellectual movement, led by the philosophes, that stressed the application of reason and the scientific method to all aspects of life.

Epicureanism a philosophy founded by Epicurus in the fourth century B.C.E. that taught that happiness (freedom from emotional turmoil) could be achieved through the pursuit of pleasure (intellectual rather than sensual pleasure).

eta in feudal Japan, a class of hereditary slaves who were responsible for what were considered degrading occupations, such as curing leather and burying the dead.

ethnic cleansing the policy of killing or forcibly removing people of another ethnic group; used by the Serbs against Bosnian Muslims in the 1990s.

eunuch a man whose testicles have been removed; a standard feature of the Chinese imperial system, the Ottoman Empire, and the Mughal Dynasty, among others.

existentialism a philosophical movement that arose after World War II that emphasized the meaninglessness of life, born of the desperation caused by two world wars.

fascism an ideology or movement that exalts the nation above the individual and calls for a centralized government with a dictatorial leader, economic and social regimentation, and forcible suppression of opposition; in particular, the ideology of Mussolini's Fascist regime in Italy.

feminism   the belief in the social, political, and economic equality of the sexes; also, organized activity to advance women's rights.

fief   a landed estate granted to a vassal in exchange for military services.

filial piety   in traditional China, in particular, a hierarchical system in which every family member has his or her place, subordinate to a patriarch who has in turn reciprocal responsibilities.

Final Solution   the physical extermination of the Jewish people by the Nazis during World War II.

Five Pillars of Islam   the core requirements of the Muslim faith: belief in Allah and his Prophet Muhammad; prescribed prayers; observation of Ramadan; pilgrimage to Mecca; and giving alms to the poor.

five relationships   in traditional China, the hierarchical interpersonal associations considered crucial to social order, within the family, between friends, and with the king.

foot binding   an extremely painful process, common in China throughout the second millenium C.E., that compressed girls' feet to half their natural size, representing submissiveness and self-discipline, which were considered necessary attributes for an ideal wife.

Four Modernizations   the slogan for radical reforms of Chinese industry, agriculture, technology, and national defense, instituted by Deng Xiaoping after his accession to power in the late 1970s.

genin   landless laborers in feudal Japan, who were effectively slaves.

genro   the ruling clique of aristocrats in Meiji Japan.

geocentric theory   the idea that the earth is at the center of the universe and that the sun and other celestial objects revolve around the earth.

glasnost   "openness." Mikhail Gorbachev's policy of encouraging Soviet citizens to openly discuss the strengths and weaknesses of the Soviet Union.

global climate change   the changes in climate, including an increase in the temperature of the earth's atmosphere, caused by the greenhouse effect.

global economy   an interdependent economy in which the production, distribution, and sale of goods are accomplished on a worldwide scale.

globalization   a term referring to the trend by which peoples and nations have become more interdependent; often used to refer to the development of a global economy and culture.

good emperors   the five emperors who ruled from 96 to 180 (Nerva, Trajan, Hadrian, Antoninus Pius, and Marcus Aurelius), a period of peace and prosperity for the Roman Empire.

Good Neighbor policy   a policy adopted by the administration of President Franklin D. Roosevelt to practice restraint in U.S. relations with Latin American nations.

Gothic   a term used to describe the art and especially the architecture of Europe in the twelfth, thirteenth, and fourteenth centuries.

Gothic literature   a form of literature used by Romantics to emphasize the bizarre and unusual, especially evident in horror stories.

Grand Council   the top of the government hierarchy in the Song Dynasty in China.

grand vizier   the chief executive in the Ottoman Empire, under the sultan.

Great Leap Forward   a short-lived, radical experiment in China, started in 1958, that created vast rural communes and attempted to replace the family as the fundamental social unit.

Great Proletarian Cultural Revolution   an attempt to destroy all vestiges of tradition in China in order to create a totally egalitar-

ian society. Launched by Mao Zedong in 1966, it devolved into virtual anarchy and lasted only until Mao's death in 1976.

greenhouse effect   the warming of the earth caused by the buildup of carbon dioxide in the atmosphere as a result of human activity.

guest workers   foreign workers working temporarily in European countries.

guided democracy   the name given by President Sukarno of Indonesia in the late 1950s to his style of government, which theoretically operated by consensus.

guild   an association of people with common interests and concerns, especially people working in the same craft. In medieval Europe, guilds came to control much of the production process and to restrict entry into various trades.

guru   teacher, especially in the Hindu, Buddhist and Sikh religious traditions, where it is an important honorific.

Hadith   a collection of the sayings of the Prophet Muhammad, used to supplement the revelations contained in the Qur'an.

harem   the private domain of a ruler such as the sultan in the Ottoman Empire or the caliph of Baghdad, generally large and mostly inhabited by the extended family.

Hegira   the flight of Muhammad from Mecca to Medina in 622, which marks the first date on the official calendar of Islam.

heliocentric theory   the idea that the sun (not the earth) is at the center of the universe.

helots   serfs in ancient Sparta, who were permanently bound to the land that they worked for their Spartan masters.

heresy   the holding of religious doctrines different from the official teachings of the church.

hieroglyphics   a highly pictorial system of writing most often associated with ancient Egypt. Also used (with different "pictographs") by other ancient peoples such as the Maya.

high colonialism   the more formal phase of European colonial policy in Africa after World War I when the colonial administrative network was extended to outlying areas and more emphasis was placed on improving social services and fostering economic development, especially the exploitation of natural resources, to enable the colonies to achieve self-sufficiency.

high culture   the literary and artistic culture of the educated and wealthy ruling classes.

Hinayana   the scornful name for Theravada Buddhism ("lesser vehicle") used by devotees of Mahayana Buddhism.

Hinduism   the main religion in India. It emphasizes reincarnation, based on the results of the previous life, and the desirability of escaping this cycle. Its various forms feature both asceticism and the pleasures of ordinary life, and encompass a multitude of gods as different manifestations of one ultimate reality.

hominids   the earliest humanlike creatures. They flourished in East and South Africa as long as 3 to 4 million years ago.

Hopewell culture   a Native American society that flourished from about 200 B.C.E. to 400 C.E., noted for large burial mounds and extensive manufacturing. Largely based in Ohio, its traders ranged as far as the Gulf of Mexico.

hoplites   heavily armed infantry soldiers used in ancient Greece in a phalanx formation.

hydraulic society   a society organized around a large irrigation system to control the allocation of water.

iconoclasm   an eighth-century Byzantine movement against the use of icons (pictures of sacred figures), which was condemned as idolatry.

iconoclast a member of an eighth-century Byzantine movement against the use of icons (pictures of sacred figures), which it condemned as idolatry.

imam an Islamic religious leader. Some traditions say there is only one per generation; others use the term more broadly.

Impressionism an artistic movement that originated in France in the 1870s. Impressionists sought to capture their impressions of the changing effects of light on objects in nature.

indirect rule a colonial policy of foreign rule in cooperation with local political elites. Though implemented in much of India and Malaya and in parts of Africa, it was not feasible where resistance was strong.

indulgence the remission of part or all of the temporal punishment in purgatory due to sin; granted for charitable contributions and other good deeds. Indulgences became a regular practice of the Christian church in the High Middle Ages, and their abuse was instrumental in sparking Luther's reform movement in the sixteenth century.

informal empire the growing presence of Europeans in Africa during the first decades of the nineteenth century. During this period, most African states were nonetheless still able to maintain their independence.

interdict in the Catholic Church, a censure by which a region or country is deprived of receiving the sacraments.

intervention, principle of the idea, after the Congress of Vienna, that the Great Powers of Europe had the right to send armies into countries experiencing revolution to restore legitimate monarchs to their thrones.

intifada the "uprising" of Palestinians living under Israeli control, especially in the 1980s and 1990s.

Jainism an Indian religion, founded in the fifth century B.C.E., that stresses extreme simplicity.

Janissaries an elite core of eight thousand troops personally loyal to the sultan of the Ottoman Empire.

jati a kinship group, the basic social organization of traditional Indian society, to some extent specialized by occupation.

jihad in Islam, "striving in the way of the Lord." The term is ambiguous and has been subject to varying interpretations, from the practice of conducting raids against local neighbors to the conduct of "holy war" against unbelievers.

justification by faith the primary doctrine of the Protestant Reformation; taught that humans are saved not through good works, but by the grace of God, bestowed freely through the sacrifice of Jesus.

kami spirits worshiped in early Japan that resided in trees, rivers, and streams. *See also* Shinto.

karma a fundamental concept in Hindu (and later Buddhist, Jain, and Sikh) philosophy, that rebirth in a future life is determined by actions in this or other lives. The word refers to the entire process, to the individual's actions, and also to the cumulative result of those actions, for instance, a store of good or bad *karma*.

keiretsu a type of powerful industrial or financial conglomerate that emerged in post–World War II Japan following the abolition of the *zaibatsu*.

khanates Mongol kingdoms, in particular the subdivisions of Genghis Khan's empire ruled by his heirs.

kokutai the core ideology of the Japanese state, particularly during the Meiji Restoration, stressing the uniqueness of the Japanese system and the supreme authority of the emperor.

kowtow the ritual of prostration and touching the forehead to the ground, demanded of all foreign ambassadors to the Chinese court as a symbol of submission.

kshatriya originally, the warrior class of Aryan society in India; ranked below (sometimes equal to) *brahmins;* in modern times, often government workers or soldiers.

laissez-faire "to let alone." An economic doctrine that holds that an economy is best served when the government does not interfere but allows the economy to self-regulate according to the forces of supply and demand.

latifundia large landed estates in the Roman Empire (singular: *latifundium*).

lay investiture the practice in which a layperson chose a bishop and invested him with the symbols of both his temporal office and his spiritual office; led to the Investiture Controversy, which was ended by compromise in the Concordat of Worms in 1122.

Legalism a Chinese philosophy that argued that human beings were by nature evil and would follow the correct path only if coerced by harsh laws and stiff punishments. Adopted as official ideology by the Qin Dynasty, it was later rejected but remained influential.

legitimacy, principle of the idea that after the Napoleonic wars peace could best be reestablished in Europe by restoring legitimate monarchs who would preserve traditional institutions; guided Metternich at the Congress of Vienna.

liberal arts the seven areas of study that formed the basis of education in medieval and early modern Europe. Following Boethius and other late Roman authors, they consisted of grammar, rhetoric, and dialectic or logic (the *trivium)* and arithmetic, geometry, astronomy, and music (the *quadrivium).*

liberalism an ideology based on the belief that people should be as free from restraint as possible. Economic liberalism is the idea that the government should not interfere in the workings of the economy. Political liberalism is the idea that there should be restraints on the exercise of power so that people can enjoy basic civil rights in a constitutional state with a representative assembly.

limited (constitutional) monarchy a system of government in which the monarch is limited by a representative assembly and by the duty to rule in accordance with the laws of the land.

lineage group the descendants of a common ancestor; relatives, often as opposed to immediate family.

Longshan a Neolithic society from near the Yellow River in China, sometimes identified by its black pottery.

maharaja originally, a king in the Aryan society of early India (a great raja); later used more generally to denote an important ruler.

Mahayana a school of Buddhism that promotes the idea of universal salvation through the intercession of bodhisattvas; predominant in north Asia.

majlis a council of elders among the Bedouins of the Roman era.

Malayo-Polynesian a family of languages whose speakers originated on Taiwan or in southeastern China and spread from there to the Malay Peninsula, the Indonesian Archipelago, and many islands of the South Pacific.

Mandate of Heaven the justification for the rule of the Zhou Dynasty in China. The king was charged to maintain order as a representative of Heaven, which was viewed as an impersonal law of nature.

mandates a system established after World War I whereby a nation officially administered a territory (mandate) on behalf of the League of Nations. Thus, France administered Lebanon and Syria as mandates, and Britain administered Iraq and Palestine.

manor an agricultural estate operated by a lord and worked by peasants who performed labor services and paid various rents and fees to the lord in exchange for protection and sustenance.

mansa in the West African state of Mali, a chieftain who served as both religious and administrative leader and was responsible for forwarding tax revenues from the village to higher levels of government.

Marshall Plan the European Recovery Program, under which the United States provided financial aid to European countries to help them rebuild after World War II.

Marxism the political, economic, and social theories of Karl Marx, which included the idea that history is the story of class struggle and that ultimately the proletariat will overthrow the bourgeoisie and establish a dictatorship en route to a classless society.

mass education a state-run educational system, usually free and compulsory, that aims to ensure that all children in society have at least a basic education.

mass leisure forms of leisure that appeal to large numbers of people in a society, including the working classes; emerged at the end of the nineteenth century to provide workers with amusements after work and on weekends; used during the twentieth century by totalitarian states to control their populations.

mass politics a political order characterized by mass political parties and universal male and (eventually) female suffrage.

mass society a society in which the concerns of the majority— the lower classes—play a prominent role; characterized by extension of voting rights, an improved standard of living for the lower classes, and mass education.

matrilinear passing through the female line, for example, from a father to his sister's son rather than his own, as practiced in some African societies; not necessarily, or even usually, combined with matriarchy, in which women rule.

megaliths large stones, widely used in Europe from around 4000 to 1500 B.C.E. to create monuments, including sophisticated astronomical observatories.

Meiji Restoration the period during the late nineteenth and early twentieth centuries in which fundamental economic and cultural changes occurred in Japan, tranforming it from a feudal and agrarian society to an industrial and technological society.

mercantilism an economic theory that held that a nation's prosperity depended on its supply of gold and silver and that the total volume of trade is unchangeable; therefore, advocated that the government play an active role in the economy by encouraging exports and discouraging imports, especially through the use of tariffs.

Mesoamerica the region stretching roughly from modern central Mexico to Honduras, in which the Olmec, Maya, Aztec, and other civilizations developed.

Middle Passage the journey of slaves from Africa to the Americas as the middle leg of the triangular trade.

Middle Path a central concept of Buddhism, which advocates avoiding extremes of both materialism and asceticism; also known as the Eightfold Way.

mihrab the niche in a mosque's wall that indicates the direction of Mecca, usually containing an ornately decorated panel representing Allah.

militarism a policy of aggressive military preparedness; in particular, the large armies based on mass conscription and complex, inflexible plans for mobilization that most European nations had before World War I.

millet an administrative unit in the Ottoman Empire used to organize religious groups.

Modernism the new artistic and literary styles that emerged in the decades before 1914 as artists rebelled against traditional efforts to portray reality as accurately as possible (leading to Impressionism and Cubism) and writers explored new forms.

monasticism a movement that began in early Christianity whose purpose was to create communities of men or women who practiced a communal life dedicated to God as a moral example to the world around them.

monk a man who chooses to live a communal life divorced from the world in order to dedicate himself totally to the will of God.

monotheistic/monotheism having only one god; the doctrine or belief that there is only one god.

Multiculturalism a term referring to the connection of several cultural or ethnic groups within a society.

multinational corporation a company with divisions in more than two countries.

nationalism a sense of national consciousness based on awareness of being part of a community—a "nation"—that has common institutions, traditions, language, and customs and that becomes the focus of the individual's primary political loyalty.

nation-state a form of political organization in which a relatively homogeneous people inhabits a sovereign state, as opposed to a state containing people of several nationalities.

natural law a body of laws or specific principles held to be derived from nature and binding upon all human society even in the absence of positive laws.

natural rights certain inalienable rights to which all people are entitled; include the right to life, liberty, and property, freedom of speech and religion, and equality before the law.

natural selection Darwin's idea that organisms that are most adaptable to their environment survive and pass on the variations that enabled them to survive, while other, less adaptable organisms become extinct; "survival of the fittest."

neocolonialism the use of economic rather than political or military means to maintain Western domination of developing nations.

Neo-Confucianism the dominant ideology of China during the second millennium C.E. It combined the metaphysical speculations of Buddhism and Daoism with the pragmatic Confucian approach to society, maintaining that the world is real, not illusory, and that fulfillment comes from participation, not withdrawal. It encouraged an intellectual environment that valued continuity over change and tradition over innovation.

Neolithic Revolution the shift from gathering plants and hunting animals for sustenance to producing food by systematic agriculture that occurred gradually between 10,000 and 4000 B.C.E. (the Neolithic or "New Stone" Age).

New Culture Movement a protest launched at Peking University after the failure of the 1911 revolution, aimed at abolishing the remnants of the old system and introducing Western values and institutions into China.

New Democracy the initial program of the Chinese Communist government, from 1949 to 1955, focusing on honest government, land reform, social justice, and peace rather than on the utopian goal of a classless society.

New Economic Policy   a modified version of the old capitalist system introduced in the Soviet Union by Lenin in 1921 to revive the economy after the ravages of the civil war and war communism.

new imperialism   the revival of imperialism after 1880 in which European nations established colonies throughout much of Asia and Africa.

new monarchies   the governments of France, England, and Spain at the end of the fifteenth century, where the rulers were successful in reestablishing or extending centralized royal authority, suppressing the nobility, controlling the church, and insisting upon the loyalty of all peoples living in their territories.

Nirvana   in Buddhist thought, enlightenment, the ultimate transcendence from the illusion of the material world; release from the wheel of life.

Nok culture   in northern Nigeria, one of the most active early ironworking societies in Africa, artifacts from which date back as far as 500 B.C.E.

Nonaligned Movement   an organization of neutralist nations established in the 1950s to provide a counterpoise between the socialist bloc, headed by the Soviet Union, and the capitalist nations led by the United States. Chief sponsors of the movement were Jawaharlal Nehru of India, Gamal Abdul Nasser of Egypt, and Sukarno of Indonesia.

noncentralized societies   societies characterized by autonomous villages organized by clans and ruled by a local chieftain or clan head; typical of the southern half of the African continent before the eleventh century C.E.

nongovernmental organizations (NGOs)   organizations that have no government ties and work to address world problems.

nun   a woman who withdraws from the world and joins a religious community; the female equivalent of a monk.

old regime/old order   the political and social system of France in the eighteenth century before the Revolution.

oligarchy   rule by a few.

Open Door Notes   a series of letters sent in 1899 by U.S. Secretary of State John Hay to Great Britain, France, Germany, Italy, Japan, and Russia, calling for equal economic access to the China market for all states and for the maintenance of the territorial and administrative integrity of the Chinese Empire.

organic evolution   Darwin's principle that all plants and animals have evolved over a long period of time from earlier and simpler forms of life.

Paleolithic Age   the period of human history when humans used simple stone tools (ca. 2,500,000–10,000 B.C.E.).

Pan-Africanism   the concept of African continental unity and solidarity in which the common interests of African countries transcend national boundaries.

Pan-Arabism   a movement promoted by Egyptian president Gamal Abdul Nasser and other Middle Eastern leaders to unify all Arab peoples in a single supra-national organization. After Nasser's death in 1971, the movement languished.

pantheism   a doctrine that equates God with the universe and all that is in it.

pariahs   members of the lowest level of traditional Indian society, technically outside the class system itself; also known as untouchables.

pasha   an administrative official of the Ottoman Empire, responsible for collecting taxes and maintaining order in the provinces; later, some became hereditary rulers.

paterfamilias   the dominant male in a Roman family whose powers over his wife and children were theoretically unlimited, though they were sometimes circumvented in practice.

patriarchal/patriarchy   a society in which the father is supreme in the clan or family; more generally, a society dominated by men.

patricians   great landowners who became the ruling class in the Roman republic.

patrilinear   passing through the male line, from father to son; often combined with patriarchy.

pax Romana   "Roman peace." A term used to refer to the stability and prosperity that Roman rule brought to the Mediterranean world and much of western Europe during the first and second centuries C.E.

peaceful coexistence   the policy adopted by the Soviet Union under Khrushchev in 1955, and continued by his successors, that called for economic and ideological rivalry with the West rather than nuclear war.

perestroika   "restructuring." A term applied to Mikhail Gorbachev's economic, political, and social reforms in the Soviet Union.

permissive society   a term applied to Western society after World War II to reflect the new sexual freedom and the emergence of a drug culture.

phalanx   a rectangular formation of tightly massed infantry soldiers.

pharaoh   the most common title used for ancient Egyptian kings. Pharaohs possessed absolute power and were seen as divine.

philosophes   intellectuals of the eighteenth-century Enlightenment who believed in applying a spirit of rational criticism to all things, including religion and politics, and who focused on improving and enjoying this world, rather than on the afterlife.

plebeians   the class of Roman citizens who included nonpatrician landowners, craftspeople, merchants, and small farmers in the Roman republic. Their struggle for equal rights with the patricians dominated much of the republic's history.

pogroms   organized massacres of Jews.

polis   an ancient Greek city-state encompassing both an urban area and its surrounding countryside; a small but autonomous political unit where all major political and social activities were carried out in a central location.

polygyny   the practice of having more than one wife at a time.

polytheistic/polytheism   having many gods; belief in or the worship of more than one god.

popular culture   as opposed to high culture, the unofficial, written and unwritten culture of the masses, much of which was passed down orally; centers on public and group activities such as festivals. In the twentieth and twenty-first centuries, the entertainment, recreation, and pleasures that people purchase as part of mass consumer society.

portolani   charts of landmasses and coastlines made by navigators and mathematicians in the thirteenth and fourteenth centuries.

Post-Impressionism   an artistic movement that began in France in the 1880s. Post-Impressionists sought to use color and line in their art to express inner feelings and produce a personal statement of reality.

Postmodernism   a term used to cover a variety of artistic and intellectual styles and ways of thinking prominent since the 1970s.

poststructuralism (deconstruction) a theory formulated by Jacques Derrida in the 1960s, holding that there is no fixed, universal truth because culture is created and can therefore be analyzed in various ways.

praetorian guard the military unit that served as the personal bodyguard of the Roman emperors.

praetors the two senior Roman judges, who had executive authority when the consuls were away from the city and could also lead armies.

Prakrit an ancient Indian language, a simplified form of Sanskrit.

predestination the belief, associated with Calvinism, that God, as a consequence of his foreknowledge of all events, has predetermined those who will be saved (the elect) and those who will be damned.

proletariat the industrial working class; in Marxism, the class that will ultimately overthrow the bourgeoisie.

Protestant Reformation the western European religious reform movement in the sixteenth century that divided Christianity into Catholic and Protestant groups.

psychoanalysis a method developed by Sigmund Freud to resolve a patient's psychic conflict.

pueblo a three-story adobe communal house with a timbered roof. Pueblos were constructed by the Ancient Pueblo people in what is now the southwestern United States starting around the ninth century C.E.

Pueblo Bonito a large settlement built by the Ancient Pueblo people in what is now New Mexico in the ninth century C.E. It contained several hundred compounds housing several thousand residents.

puja in India, a popular tradition focused on personal worship that began to replace the Brahmanical emphasis on court sacrifice and asceticism during the early centuries of the first millennium C.E.; an aspect of the transition from Brahmanism to Hinduism.

purdah the Indian term for the practice among Muslims and some Hindus of isolating women and preventing them from associating with men outside the home.

Pure Land a Buddhist sect, originally Chinese but later popular in Japan, which taught that devotion alone could lead to enlightenment and release.

quipu an Inka record-keeping system that used knotted strings rather than writing.

raj the British colonial regime in India.

raja originally, a chieftain in the Aryan society of early India, a representative of the gods; later used more generally to denote a ruler.

Ramadan the holy month of Islam, during which believers fast from dawn to sunset. Since the Islamic calendar is lunar, Ramadan migrates through the seasons.

Realism in the nineteenth century, a school of painting that emphasized the everyday life of ordinary people, depicted with photographic realism.

Realpolitik "politics of reality." Politics based on practical concerns rather than theory or ethics.

reincarnation the idea that the individual soul is reborn in a different form after death. In Hindu and Buddhist thought, release from this cycle is the objective of all living souls.

relativity theory Einstein's theory that holds, among other things, that (1) space and time are not absolute but are relative to the observer and interwoven into a four-dimensional space-time continuum and (2) matter is a form of energy (E = mc^2).

relics the bones of Christian saints or objects intimately associated with saints that were considered worthy of veneration.

Renaissance the "rebirth" of classical culture that occurred in Italy between ca. 1350 and ca. 1550; also, the earlier revivals of Classical culture that occurred under Charlemagne and in the twelfth century.

Renaissance humanism an intellectual movement in Renaissance Italy based on the study of the Greek and Roman classics.

rentier a person who lives on income from property and is not personally involved in its operation.

revisionism a socialist doctrine that rejected Marx's emphasis on class struggle and revolution and argued instead that workers should work through political parties to bring about gradual change.

revolutionary socialism the socialist doctrine that violent action was the only way to achieve the goals of socialism.

rococo a style, especially of decoration and architecture, that developed from the Baroque and spread throughout Europe by the 1730s. While still elaborate, it emphasized curves, lightness, and charm in the pursuit of pleasure, happiness, and love.

Romanticism a nineteenth-century intellectual and artistic movement that rejected the Enlightenment's emphasis on reason. Instead, Romantics stressed the importance of intuition, feeling, emotion, and imagination as sources of knowing.

ronin Japanese warriors made unemployed by developments in the early modern era, since samurai were forbidden by tradition to engage in commerce.

rural responsibility system post-Maoist land reform in China, under which collectives leased land to peasant families, who could consume or sell their surplus production and keep the profits.

sacraments rites considered imperative for a Christian's salvation. By the thirteenth century consisted of the Eucharist or Lord's Supper, baptism, marriage, penance, extreme unction, holy orders, and confirmation of children; Protestant reformers of the sixteenth century generally recognized only two—baptism and communion (the Lord's Supper).

sakoku during the Tokugawa Shogunate in Japan, the policy of closing the country to trade with Europe and encouraging domestic production of goods that had previously been imported.

samurai literally "retainers"; similar to European knights. Usually in service to a particular shogun, these Japanese warriors lived by a strict code of ethics and duty.

Sanskrit an early Indo-European language, in which the Vedas were composed, beginning in the second millenium B.C.E. It survived as the language of literature and the bureaucracy in India for centuries after its decline as a spoken tongue.

sati the Hindu ritual requiring a wife to throw herself upon her deceased husband's funeral pyre.

satori enlightenment, in the Japanese, especially Zen, Buddhist tradition.

satrap/satrapy a governor with both civil and military duties in the ancient Persian Empire, which was divided into satrapies, or provinces, each administered by a satrap.

satyagraha the Hindi term for the practice of nonviolent resistance, as advocated by Mohandas Gandhi; literally, "hold fast to the truth."

scholar-gentry in Song Dynasty China, candidates who passed the civil service examinations and whose families were nonaristocratic landowners; eventually, a majority of the bureaucracy.

Scholasticism   the philosophical and theological system of the medieval schools, which emphasized rigorous analysis of contradictory authorities; often used to try to reconcile faith and reason.

School of Mind   a philosophy espoused by Wang Yangming during the mid-Ming era of China, which argued that mind and the universe were a single unit and knowledge was therefore obtained through internal self-searching rather than through investigation of the outside world; for a while, a significant but unofficial rival to Neo-Confucianism.

scientific method   a method of seeking knowledge through inductive principles; uses experiments and observations to develop generalizations.

Scientific Revolution   the transition from the medieval world-view to a largely secular, rational, and materialistic perspective; began in the seventeenth century and was popularized in the eighteenth.

secularization   the process of becoming more concerned with material, worldly, temporal things and less with spiritual and religious things.

self-strengthening   a late-nineteenth-century Chinese policy by which Western technology would be adopted while Confucian principles and institutions were maintained intact.

senate/senators   the leading council of the Roman republic; composed of about three hundred men (senators) who served for life and dominated much of the political life of the republic.

separation of powers   a doctrine enunciated by Montesquieu in the eighteenth century that separate executive, legislative, and judicial powers serve to limit and control each other.

sepoys   native troops hired by the East India Company to protect British interests in South Asia; formed the basis of the British Indian Army.

serf   a peasant who is bound to the land and obliged to provide labor services and pay various rents and fees to the lord; considered unfree but not a slave because serfs could not be bought and sold.

shari'a   a law code, originally drawn up by Muslim scholars shortly after the death of Muhammad, that provides believers with a set of prescriptions to regulate their daily lives.

sheikh   originally, the ruler of a Bedouin tribe; later, also used as a more general honorific.

Shi'ite   the second largest tradition of Islam, which split from the majority Sunni soon after the death of Muhammad, in a disagreement over the succession; especially significant in Iran and Iraq.

Shinto   a kind of state religion in Japan, derived from beliefs in nature spirits and until recently linked with belief in the divinity of the emperor and the sacredness of the Japanese nation.

shogun   a powerful Japanese leader, originally military, who ruled under the titular authority of the emperor.

shogunate system   the system of government in Japan in which the emperor exercised only titular authority while the shogun (regional military dictators) exercised actual political power.

Sikhism   a religion, founded in the early sixteenth century in the Punjab that began as an attempt to reconcile the Hindu and Muslim traditions and developed into a significant alternative to both.

sipahis   in the Ottoman Empire, local cavalry elites, who held fiefdoms and collected taxes.

Social Darwinism   the application of Darwin's principle of organic evolution to the social order; led to the belief that progress comes from the struggle for survival as the fittest advance and the weak decline.

Socratic method   a form of teaching that uses a question-and-answer format to enable students to reach conclusions by using their own reasoning.

soviets   councils of workers' and soldiers' deputies formed throughout Russia in 1917; played an important role in the Bolshevik Revolution.

sphere of influence   a territory or region over which an outside nation exercises political or economic influence.

Star Wars   nickname of the Strategic Defense Initiative, proposed by President Reagan, which was intended to provide a shield that would destroy any incoming missiles; named after a popular science-fiction movie.

State Confucianism   the integration of Confucian doctrine with Legalist practice under the Han Dynasty in China, which became the basis of Chinese political thought until the modern era.

Stoicism   a philosophy founded by Zeno in the fourth century B.C.E. that taught that one could obtain happiness by accepting one's lot and living in harmony with the will of God, thereby achieving inner peace.

stupa   originally a stone tower holding relics of the Buddha; more generally a place for devotion, often architecturally impressive and surmounted with a spire.

Sublime Porte   the office of the grand vizier in the Ottoman Empire.

sudras   the classes that represented the great bulk of the Indian population from ancient times, mostly peasants, artisans or manual laborers; ranked below *brahmins, kshatriyas,* and *vaisyas,* but above the pariahs.

suffragists   those who advocate the extension of the right to vote (suffrage), especially to women.

Sufism   a mystical school of Islam, noted for its music, dance, and poetry, which became prominent in about the thirteenth century.

sultan   "holder of power," a title commonly used by Muslim rulers in the Ottoman Empire, Egypt, and elsewhere; still in use in parts of Asia, sometimes for regional authorities.

Sunni   the largest tradition of Islam, from which the Shi'ites split soon after the death of Muhammad, in a disagreement over the succession.

Supreme Ultimate   according to Neo-Confucianists, a transcendent world, distinct from the material world in which humans live, but to which humans may aspire; a set of abstract principles, roughly equivalent to the Dao.

Surrealism   an artistic movement that arose between World War I and World War II. Surrealists portrayed recognizable objects in unrecognizable relationships in order to reveal the world of the unconscious.

Swahili   a mixed African-Arabian culture that developed by the twelfth century along the east coast of Africa; also, the national language of Kenya and Tanzania.

Taika reforms   the seventh-century "great change" reforms that established the centralized Japanese state.

taille   a French tax on land or property, developed by King Louis XI in the fifteenth century as the financial basis of the monarchy. It was largely paid by the peasantry; the nobility and the clergy were exempt.

Taisho democracy   the era of the 1920s in Japan when universal (male) suffrage was instituted, political parties expanded, and other democratic institutions appeared to flourish. The process of democratization proved fragile, however, and failed to continue into the 1930s.

Tantrism   a mystical Buddhist sect that emphasized the importance of magical symbols and ritual in seeking a path to enlightenment.

Theravada   a school of Buddhism that stresses personal behavior and the quest for understanding as a means of release from the wheel of life, rather than the intercession of bodhisattvas; predominant in Sri Lanka and Southeast Asia.

three obediences   the traditional duties of Japanese women, in permanent subservience: child to father, wife to husband, and widow to son.

three people's principles   the three principles on which the program of Sun Yat-sen's Revolutionary Alliance (Tongmenghui) was based: nationalism (meaning primarily the elimination of Manchu rule over China), democracy, and people's livelihood.

totalitarian state   a state characterized by government control over all aspects of economic, social, political, cultural, and intellectual life; the subordination of the individual to the state; and insistence that the masses be actively involved in the regime's goals.

total war   warfare in which all of a nation's resources, including civilians at home as well as soldiers in the field, are mobilized for the war effort.

transnational corporation   another term for a "multinational corporation," or a company with divisions in more than two countries.

trench warfare   warfare in which the opposing forces attack and counterattack from a relatively permanent system of trenches protected by barbed wire; characteristic of World War I.

Triangular Trade   a term used to describe a form of international trade taking place between three countries or regions of the world.

tribunes of the plebs   beginning in 494 B.C.E., Roman officials who were given the power to protect plebeians against arrest by patrician magistrates.

Truman Doctrine   the doctrine enunciated by Harry Truman in 1947 that the United States would provide economic aid to countries that were threatened by Communist expansion.

twice-born   the males of the higher castes in traditional Indian society, who underwent an initiation ceremony at puberty.

tyrant/tyranny   in an ancient Greek *polis* (or an Italian city-state during the Renaissance), a ruler who came to power in an unconstitutional way and ruled without being subject to the law.

uhuru   "freedom" in Swahili; a key slogan in the African independence movements, especially in Kenya.

uji   a clan in early Japanese tribal society.

ulama   a convocation of leading Muslim scholars, the earliest of which shortly after the death of Muhammad drew up a law code, called the *shari'a,* based largely on the Qur'an and the sayings of the Prophet, to provide believers with a set of prescriptions to regulate their daily lives.

umma   the Muslim community, as a whole.

uninterrupted revolution   the goal of the Great Proletarian Cultural Revolution launched by Mao Zedong in 1966.

vaisya   the third-ranked class in traditional Indian society, usually merchants.

varna   Indian classes, or castes.

vassal   a person granted a fief, or landed estate, in exchange for providing military services to the lord and fulfilling certain other obligations, such as appearing at the lord's court when summoned and making a payment on the knighting of the lord's eldest son.

veneration of ancestors   the extension of filial piety to include care for the deceased, for instance, by burning replicas of useful objects to accompany them on their journey to the next world.

viceroy   the administrative head of the provinces of New Spain and Peru in the Americas.

Viet Cong   the popular name applied to the resistance forces led by the National Front for the Liberation of South Vietnam (NLF) in South Vietnam. Literally, "Viet Communists."

Vietnam syndrome   the presumption, from the 1970s on, that the U.S. public would object to a protracted military entanglement abroad, such as another Vietnam-type conflict.

vizier   the prime minister in the Abbasid caliphate and elsewhere, a chief executive.

war communism   Lenin's policy of nationalizing industrial and other facilities and requisitioning the peasants' produce during the civil war in Russia.

welfare state   a social/political system in which the government assumes the primary responsibility for the social welfare of its citizens by providing such things as social security, unemployment benefits, and health care.

well-field system   the theoretical pattern of land ownership in early China, named for the appearance of the Chinese character for "well," in which farmland was divided into nine segments and a peasant family would cultivate one for their own use and cooperate with seven others to cultivate the ninth for the landlord.

White Lotus   a Chinese Buddhist sect, founded in 1133 C.E., that sought political reform; in 1796–1804, a Chinese peasant revolt.

women's liberation movement   the struggle for equal rights for women, which has deep roots in history but achieved new prominence under this name in the 1960s, building on the work of, among others, Simone de Beauvoir and Betty Friedan.

world-machine   Newton's conception of the universe as one huge, regulated, and uniform machine that operated according to natural laws in absolute time, space, and motion.

yangban   the aristocratic class in Korea. During the Choson Dynasty, entry into the bureaucracy was limited to members of this class.

Yangshao   a Neolithic society from near the Yellow River in China, sometimes identified by its painted pottery.

yoga   "union"; the practice of body training that evolved from the early asceticism and remains an important element of Hindu religious practice.

Young Turks   a successful Turkish reformist group in the late nineteenth and early twentieth centuries.

zaibatsu   powerful business cartels formed in Japan during the Meiji era and outlawed following World War II.

zamindars   Indian tax collectors, who were assigned land, from which they kept part of the revenue. The British revived the system in a misguided attempt to create a landed gentry.

Zen Buddhism (in Chinese, Chan or Ch'an) a school of Buddhism particularly important in Japan, some of whose adherents stress that enlightenment (*satori*) can be achieved suddenly, though others emphasize lengthy meditation.

ziggurat a massive stepped tower upon which a temple dedicated to the chief god or goddess of a Sumerian city was built.

Zionism an international movement that called for the establishment of a Jewish state or a refuge for Jews in Palestine.

Zoroastrianism a religion founded by the Persian Zoroaster in the seventh century B.C.E.; characterized by worship of a supreme god Ahuramazda who represents the good against the evil spirit, identified as Ahriman.

INDEX

annexation by Nazi Germany, 633
annexation of the Serbs, 494
anti-Semitism in, 518–19
assassination of Franz Ferdinand, 577–78
in Concert of Europe, 483
constitution of, 591
declares war on Serbia, 578
in Dual Monarchy, 491
enlightened absolutism in, 454–55
European unification and, 488–89
France and, 484
German annexation of, 633
German unification and, 489
Habsburgs in, 382, 386
joins the EEC, 716
military of. *See* World War I (1914–1918)
Napoleon and, 466
and Paris Peace Conference, 589–592
revolution of 1848, 486
Seven Years' War and, 456–57
Turks and, 385
Versailles Treaty and, 632
women in, 725
in World War I. *See* World War I
   (1914–1918)
in World War II. *See* World War II (1939–1945)
Austria-Hungary
  capital cities in, 491
  outbreak of war, summer 1914, 577
  Triple Alliance (1882), 495
Austrian Empire, revolutions in 1848, 485–86
Austrian Empire (Habsburgs)
  Joseph II's reforms in, 454
  Ottoman Empire and, 385
  Thirty Years' War, 382
Authors. *See names of specific authors and works*
Avignon, 456
Axis Powers, 638–641
Ayacucho, battle at, 501
Ayatollah. *See* Khomeini, Ruhollah (Ayatollah)
Ayuthaya, Thailand, 364
Azerbaijan, 402, 656
Aztec civilization
  and Spanish conquests, 351
Azuela, Mariano, 623

B

Ba Jin, 619
Ba'athi Party, 750, 754
Babington, Thomas, 487–88
Babur, 406
Bachelet, Michelle, 720
Bahrain, 758
Bakufu (tent government), 434, 563–64
Balance of Truth (Chelebi), 401
Balboa, Vasco Núñez de, 355
Balearic Islands, 382, 395, 456, 466, 481, 485, 493, 576, 592, 636, 660
Balfour, Lord Arthur, 609–10
Balfour Declaration, 610–11
Bali, 774, 777, 779–780
Balkans, crisis in 19th century, 495
Baltic region, 588, 640, 642
Baluchi people, 768
"banana republics," 621
Bananas, 503, 614, 621
Bandar Abbas, 405
Bangalore, 770
Bangkok, religion in, 778

Bangladesh, 766
  economy in, 770
Bank of England, 458, 712
Banners (military units), 422
Bantu-speaking peoples, 539
  gold trade and, 358
  and Portuguese gold mines, 357
Bantustans, 741
Barbary Coast, 396
Baroque art, 387–89, 448–49
Baroque style, 351, 387–89, 409, 448–49
Bartolo, Domenico di, 376
Barton, Clara, 511
Basho, 436
Basilicas, 389
Bastille, 442–43
Basutoland (Lesotho), 540, 738
Batavia, 535
Batista, Fulgencio, 671, 721
Battle of Britan, 731
Battle of Chacabuco, 501
Battle of Midway Island, 638
Battle of the Coral Sea, 638
Battles
  of Adowa, 544–45
  Borodino, 467
  Britain, 647, 731
  Buxar, 411
  Chacabuco, 501
  Coral Sea, 638
  First Battle of the Marne, 580
  Kursk, 640
  Leyte Gulf, 641
  Masurian Lakes, 580
  Midway Island, 638
  Plassey, 411, 457
  Somme River, 575
  Stalingrad, 638–640
  Tannenberg, 580
Bay of Bengal, 410
Bay of Pigs, Cuba, 671, 721–22
Bayazid I, 393
Beauvoir, Simone de, 726
Bechuanaland (Botswana), 540
Beckett, Samuel, 729
Bedouins, 749
Beer Hall Putsch, 628
Begin, Menachem, 751
Beijing, China, student protests in, 695
Belarus, announces demise of Soviet
   Union, 691
Belgian Congo, 539. *See also* Democratic
   Republic of the Congo; Zaire
Belgium, 489–490, 494
  colonization in Congo, 539–540
  imperialism by, 529, 539–542
  Industrial Revolution in, 467, 476–77,
   480–81
  NATO in, 658
  neutrality and Germany, 578–581
Belize, 451
Bell, Alexander Graham, 480
Belloc, Hilaire, 544
Benelux countries, 716
Bengal, 407, 411, 413, 423, 451, 457, 531,
   765
Bengali people, 410, 530, 768
Ben-Gurion, David, 748
Benin, 362, 451, 738

Berlin, 659. *See also* East Berlin; West Berlin
  after World War II. *See* Berlin Wall
  crisis over, 669–670
Berlin Academy, 448
Berlin Airlift, 658
Berlin blockade, 658
Berlin Conference, 542
Berlin Wall, 677, 679
Bernini, Gian Lorenzo, 389
Beveridge, Albert, 533, 547
Beys (governors), 393
Bharain, 758
Bharatiya Janata Party (BJP), 768–69
Bhopal, 770
Bible, 370–71, 404. *See also* Hebrew Bible;
   New Testament
Bicycles, 480
Big Three of the Grand Alliance, Allied war
   conferences, 648–49
Bill of Rights
  in England, 387
  in United States, 453
Bin Laden, Osama, 727, 748, 754–56,
   768, 793
Biology, discoveries in, 515
Birth control, 510, 596, 603, 724–25, 761
Birthrate
  in Africa, 740
  baby boom, 725
  in Europe, 589
  in India, 769
  in Japan, 783
  post WWI, 589
  in South Asia, 768
  in West Africa, 360
Bishops, 370, 374–75, 383, 459
Bismarck, Count Otto von, 489, 493–95, 540
BJP (Bharatiya Janata Party), 768–69
Black Hand, 577–78
Black Hole of Calcutta, 411
The Black Man's Burden (Morel), 529
Black Sea region, 358, 454, 691
Blair, Tony, 712–13
"Blank check," 577–78
Blank mind (*tabula rasa*), 445
Blitz, 645
Blitzkrieg (lightning war), 635
Block printing, 436, 446
Blockade of Berlin, 658
Body and identity, 795–96
Boer Republics, 541–42
Boer War, 541
Boers, 538
  occupation by Hitler, 632
Boleyn, Anne, 374, 378
Bolívar, Simón, 498–501
Bolivia, 354, 501, 621, 720
Bolshevik Revolution, 584, 587, 679
Bolsheviks, 587, 611, 628
Bombay (Mumbai), India, 602
Bombing of cities, 645–47
Bombing raids, in World War II, 627, 634, 637,
   644–47
Bonaparte. *See* Napoleon I Bonaparte
Bonaparte, Charles Louis Napoleon. *See*
   Napoleon III
Boroughs, 388
Bosnia, 713–14
  placed under Austrian protection, 495